"A vivid, warts-and-all portrait of the man behind *WrestleMania*—and much of the worst of contemporary politics."

—*Kirkus Reviews*

"To understand what's at the heart of carny culture is to understand what's at the heart of a huge swathe of the American experience. As Abraham Riesman demonstrates in this highly readable, sharp and compelling book, professional wrestling embodies this idea both on screen and off, in the arenas and in the conference rooms. This is a serious work about the legacy of confidence games, abandonment, abuse, and power. Whether or not you are a lifelong wrestling mark like me, *Ringmaster* is essential reading."

—Brian Koppelman, cocreator of *Billions*
and cowriter of *Rounders*

"No faking! *Ringmaster* is one of the best biographies I've read in years—smart, entertaining, impressively reported, and beautifully written. Wrestling fans will devour it, but everyone who wants to better understand this crazy country and one of its truly original characters ought to read it."

—Jonathan Eig, author of *Ali: A Life*

"Abraham Riesman has given us a fascinating, rigorously researched account of the life and times of the ultimate ringmaster, Vince McMahon. This is the story of how the world of professional wrestling has become our world. The rules of the game are now so gamed in American politics and daily life that the real, if ever there was a real, has gone up in a puff of hyperbolic smoke-and-mirrors. *Ringmaster* helps us to see how we got to this point. How we get ourselves out of it remains an open question."

—Sharon Mazer, author of *Professional Wrestling:
Sport and Spectacle*

"Though it's hard to pinpoint the date, one morning wrestling fans like myself woke up and realized the pastime that had largely defined our youths and imaginations had jumped the firewall and, somehow, some way, began infecting the rest of the world. What Abraham Riesman has done here is invite readers to see that fundamental and disturbing truth, to wrestle with just how we've come to live in this bizarre un-reality, and possibly begin sorting through the wreckage. An absolute triumph. As must-read as must-read can get."

—Jared Yates Sexton, author of *The Midnight Kingdom: A History of Power, Paranoia, and the Coming Crisis*

RINGMASTER

VINCE McMAHON
AND THE UNMAKING
OF AMERICA

ABRAHAM JOSEPHINE RIESMAN

ATRIA PAPERBACK
New York   London   Toronto   Sydney   New Delhi

ATRIA
PAPERBACK

An Imprint of Simon & Schuster, LLC
1230 Avenue of the Americas
New York, NY 10020

First Atria Paperback edition April 2024

ATRIA PAPERBACK and colophon are trademarks of Simon & Schuster, LLC

Simon & Schuster: Celebrating 100 Years of Publishing in 2024

For information about special discounts for bulk purchases, please contact Simon & Schuster Special Sales at 1-866-506-1949 or business@simonandschuster.com.

The Simon & Schuster Speakers Bureau can bring authors to your live event. For more information or to book an event, contact the Simon & Schuster Speakers Bureau at 1-866-248-3049 or visit our website at www.simonspeakers.com.

Manufactured in the United States of America

1   3   5   7   9   10   8   6   4   2

Library of Congress Control Number: 2022943649

ISBN 978-1-9821-6944-2
ISBN 978-1-9821-6945-9 (pbk)
ISBN 978-1-9821-6946-6 (ebook)

For my mother,
who custom-stitched me a tearaway T-shirt
after I first saw Hulk Hogan on TV when I was six

"It's still *real* to me, damn it!"

DAVID WILLS

CONTENTS

OVERTURE

SHOOT

We begin at the end of the world.

It's April 14, 2020. The COVID-19 pandemic has killed roughly thirty thousand Americans. The unpredictable US president has done nothing of substance to contain the virus and is, per usual, issuing bizarre and contradictory statements via Twitter. The ruling Republican Party is working overtime to attack the idea that public health should even be a function of government. People are cowering in their homes, terrified and angry, eager for distraction, guidance, or both. Only essential businesses are open. All sports seasons have been canceled. All filming of movies and shows has been called off. All of which means the nation is facing an unprecedented, world-historical threat: there's nothing good on TV.

"People have been starved for content," says Florida's arch-Republican governor, Ron DeSantis, at a news conference that day. "I mean, if you think about it, we've never had a period like this in modern American history, where you've had such little new content, particularly in the sporting realm. I mean, people are watching—y'know, we're watching, like, reruns from the early 2000s."

But there is nothing to fear. The governor has a solution: wrestling will save us.

Five days prior, without announcing anything to the public, DeSantis had amended his state's COVID work restrictions, authorizing in-person work for "employees at a professional sports and media production with a national audience," if such a company meets certain criteria. As it turns out, there's only one athletic entity that fits, according to DeSantis's office: World Wrestling Entertainment, the multibillion-dollar firm that has dominated pro wrestling for decades.

If you only had a passing familiarity with WWE, you might be baffled.

How on earth could this spectacle—not quite sports, not quite theater, and not quite palatable for the highbrow snobs of the world—be in the same category as hospitals and groceries? But if you talked to an astute political analyst or any wrestling fan, they'd tell you that it all made perfect sense. This was just Vince McMahon, WWE's then-CEO, in action.

It helps, for example, to know that Vince's wife, Linda McMahon, was an influential Republican donor and former cabinet member whose super PAC, America First Action, had just announced it would spend $18.5 million on Republican ads in Florida.

It also didn't hurt that Vince's longtime friend Donald Trump was the first—and very possibly not the last—member of the WWE Hall of Fame to occupy the Oval Office.

Whatever the reasoning, the message was simple. No matter how bad things got, no matter how many people perished, no matter how great the threat to the American experiment, the nation could rest assured of one thing: we would be entertained.

There is no art form more intrinsically and blatantly American—in its casual violence, its bombastic braggadocio, its virulent jingoism, its populist defiance of respectability, and its intermittently awe-inspiring beauty—than professional wrestling. This lucrative enterprise is not a legitimate competition, but it is indisputably an expression of creativity. Its practitioners have a time-worn saying: "This ain't ballet." But it's not *that* far from ballet: a kinetic method of storytelling, one that requires tremendous skill (and physical pain) to perform.

Although a wrestling match is infinitely customizable, the typical setup is as familiar as apple pie. Two wrestlers enter a raised square platform—the ring. Its floor is hard, but there's foam padding and a canvas cover that acts as a kind of weak trampoline. At each corner are metal ring posts, with thick stretchable cords wrapped around them. The wrestlers tussle inside the ring, grabbing each other for semi-choreographed, semi-improvised attacks, flips, and falls ("bumps") that require cooperation and mutual expertise to execute. If the match isn't scripted as a draw for one reason or another, one of the wrestlers "wins" by either pressing their opponent's shoulders to the canvas until a referee counts to three (a "pin"), or by putting their opponent in enough fictional—or at least exaggerated—pain that they give up (a "submission").

There are, broadly speaking, two roles wrestlers can play in the ring: that of the *face* and that of the *heel*. "Face" is short for "babyface": the innocent, unblemished hero. The etymology of "heel" is more complicated, but one theory holds that the term has its roots in the Hebrew Bible, where Jacob grabbed his brother Esau's heel during their birth in an attempt to come out first and steal his twin's birthright.

Traditionally, fans are supposed to root for the face. But in wrestling—as is the case in much of the best fiction—the good guy isn't necessarily the protagonist. Just as important, and sometimes more so, is the heel, the one who seeks to get ahead through malice, who feeds off the hatred of the crowd, and who often gains the upper hand at the match's end, breaking the hearts of all who want to see justice done.

In the initial phases of his career, as a hidden-hand executive, Vince McMahon created and deployed many heels in the standard fashion. But then he did something remarkable: he made himself into one. He wrote himself into his company's own show as a crude, sadistic exaggeration of himself, becoming the saga's supreme supervillain. He thrived on the fact that he made countless millions of fans love to despise him, even as they shoveled money into his pockets.

He was the head of the operation in real life, but also in the realm of what is known as *kayfabe*.

Kayfabe (rhymes with "Hey, babe") is a term of unclear linguistic origin. It emerged from the world of carnivals in the 1800s and, in its original definition, simply denoted the public-facing fictions of professional wrestling.

If two wrestlers are billed as brothers despite not actually being related, that would make them kayfabe brothers.

As a verb, to observe the forms is "to stay in kayfabe" or simply "to kayfabe."

As a noun, it referred to the business's central conceit: that it *was* a legitimate, unscripted athletic competition.

For nearly a century, this illusion was maintained at all costs, in a kind of industry omertà. A heel and a face who were sworn kayfabe enemies couldn't be seen drinking together in their off-hours; a wrestler billed as Iranian couldn't be known to be Italian.

Even wrestlers themselves sometimes had trouble keeping track of what was kayfabe and what was not, so they developed two more terms:

a *work* was anything that was kayfabe, and anything that was real was a *shoot*.

These days, if you're a wrestling fan, you understand that wrestling is fiction. You know that the wrestler who is crowned champion got that title not because he "won" it in an unscripted competition, but because he has the talent as a performer to carry the role. But then again, he might also be there solely because of political maneuvering behind the scenes. That ambiguity is where the fun begins.

Maybe you heard that another guy should have been champ, but was snubbed because of a personality conflict with the boss. But then you *also* heard that the so-called personality conflict is just what they *want* you to think is the truth, to build drama for the show. But wait, maybe it *is* real—they could be passing it off as a work, but maybe, actually, those guys really *do* hate each other . . .

This new status quo is what we might call *neokayfabe*. It says that pro wrestling, with all its spectacle, is a lie—but that the lie encodes a deeper truth, discernible to those few who know how to look beyond what's in front of them. To those fans adept in reading the signs, another narrative emerges, and another beyond that. Suddenly, the pleasure of watching a match has less to do with who wins than with the excitement of decoding it.

Maybe a heel gets caught in a sex scandal, or is accused of beating his girlfriend; no matter, just have him own it as part of his gimmick. The fans may be offended by his continued presence on their screens, but their offense can only make him more successful—and there will always be those who respect him, even like him, for his "honesty" about his vices.

Neokayfabe exists in the tension not just between fantasy and reality, but also between revulsion and attraction, honor and hedonism, irony and earnestness.

Call pro wrestling low art, if you must, but it is art, nonetheless. And if wrestling is an art, one man is both its Michelangelo and its Medici.

Vince McMahon's forty-plus-year reign as the central figure of American wrestling has largely been defined by his consolidation of mainstream pro wrestling into a single entertainment. When he began his rise in the early 1980s, wrestling was a parochial industry, divided into dozens of local fiefdoms across the country; Vince demolished or absorbed all of them and created the first truly national operation. When challengers appeared, Vince annihilated them—and often assimilated and co-opted the survivors, no matter how loudly they had once cursed his name. For many years, in his industry, Vince achieved something every tycoon dreams of, but few achieve: he made himself the only game in town.

Nearly all the living household names of American wrestling were molded into global icons under his guidance and at his whim: Dwayne "The Rock" Johnson, "Stone Cold" Steve Austin, John Cena, Dave Bautista, Bret "The Hitman" Hart, and Hulk Hogan, among many others. There's a longer list of people whose names he ground into dust. He has reinvented and saved his industry over and over again, never apologizing for the pain his ambition has caused.

Scandals and accusations have accumulated around him over the decades. He is alleged to have raped his company's first female referee, Rita Chatterton, and to have sexually assaulted a tanning salon employee. There is credible evidence that he helped cover up a homicide. He employed two men who were accused of making sexual advances on underage children, only firing them after a media furor. He has been accused of pushing the steroid use and allowing the head trauma that ravaged the bodies and minds of his performers; meanwhile, he fought tooth and nail to keep those same performers from organizing against him. That's not to mention the open bigotry of the characters and story lines he has crafted and pushed, and the impact they had on the countless young fans who grew up watching them.

The allegations against Vince reached a crescendo in the summer of 2022, when reports emerged of well over $12 million in alleged hush-money payments he'd made to former female employees with whom he'd had sexual relations. When those payments were reported, regulators launched investigations and Vince, after about a month of trying to wait it out, abruptly resigned. For a moment, his time at the top seemed to be over. But he clawed his way back to the boardroom and, as of this writing, is the company's executive chairman.

Even in the coverage of these chilling revelations, the wrestling industry was still regarded by many as a joke, something so silly that it's beneath analysis or investigation. But Vince and wrestling are hardly sideshows. Major public figures have had their careers launched or significantly boosted thanks to Vince. Artists, athletes, and industrialists have been inspired by his programming and ethos. Officeholders have won elections with the help of his largesse. And, lest we forget, there's the Trump factor.

Vince is likely the closest thing to a friend that Donald Trump has. So intimate are the former WWE CEO and the forty-fifth president that Vince is said to be one of the only people whose calls Trump takes in private, forcing his retinue to leave the room so the two old chums can chat in confidence. There are profound differences between them, to be sure, but they've each been heirs to difficult fathers and share both a disregard for respectable morality and an uncanny habit of bouncing back from defeat. For more than three decades, Trump has watched and admired Vince's product. He has been both host and performer at many of Vince's wrestling extravaganzas, honing his abilities as a rabble-rouser. Through Trump, Vince's wrestling-infused mentality has reached the highest levels of the American system.

This is a story about how a country built a man, and how that man reshaped his country.

This is a story about evil and its uses, and what you can get away with when you sledgehammer down the walls between fact and fiction.

This is a story about a heel.

FACES

"McMahon Junior is the modern-day Hitler of
professional wrestling, and if you told him that to his face,
he'd take you out and buy you the biggest steak you could eat."

"NATURE BOY" BUDDY ROGERS

1

FALL
(1945–1957)

Vince McMahon, like many of his wrestlers, didn't grow up with the name he now uses. His father ran a successful wrestling promotion that stretched throughout the Northeast, but Vince was born and raised far away from that empire. He wasn't even a wrestling fan as a child. WWE has often highlighted the boss's adoration for the man everyone now calls "Vince Senior." But until young Vince was an adolescent, he'd never met the man. He was Vinnie Lupton, and he didn't know if he loved his dad or not.

In his formative years, Vinnie was the son of two people of whom he rarely speaks: Vicki Hanner and Leo Lupton Jr.—his mother and stepfather.

Which is to say, he was a son of North Carolina, however much he may obscure that fact. The sizable Hanner and Lupton clans had been in the state for generations. The Hanners arrived in the colony before it became a founding component of the United States, and by the time of the Civil War, they had settled in as farmers—some of them slaveholders. For example, the most renowned member of Vince's maternal family prior to him was John Henry Hanner, who, when he died in 1850, held ten people in captivity, making his 614-acre farm (located in what is now Greensboro) one of the area's larger forced-work camps.

But by the time Victoria Elizabeth Hanner was born in 1920, the family had been in a decades-long decline. Her mother was a farmer's daughter; her father an itinerant mechanic who rambled back and forth between North and South Carolina, barely making a living while working on automobiles.

Vicki appears to have been born in Florence, South Carolina, and raised in Sanford, North Carolina. She then did a jaunt at Bob Jones College in faraway Cleveland, Tennessee. However, a North Carolina birth

index of 1939 informs us that Victoria Hanner—who would have been
either eighteen or nineteen at the time—gave birth to a child many miles
from both home and school, in Charlotte. In the column for the father's
name, there is only a series of dashes. The baby—Vince's oldest sibling—
was named Gloria Faye Hanner, and there is no record of what became
of her.

On December 6, 1941, just a few hours before the surprise attack on
Pearl Harbor, Vicki married an Ohio-born soldier named Louis Patacca,
who was stationed at a nearby military base. That marriage, her first of
four, was doomed. Patacca was shipped up to New York City, and Vicki
found someone else to occupy her time.

We don't know how she met Vince's father, but they may have had their
first tryst around June 30, 1942, while New York–based Vincent James
McMahon was doing his own military service in Wilmington, North
Carolina—a local newspaper item mentions that a visiting "Victoria Patacca" had lost a diamond ring. As of January 1943, Vicki was pregnant
with her lover's child.

Patacca filed a vitriolic divorce petition on August 18, 1943, claiming
his estranged wife had withheld the fact of Gloria's birth from him and
had cheated on him with other soldiers. Vicki didn't respond; the divorce
wasn't resolved as of at least four years later, if it ever was. The military
moved Vincent James McMahon back to New York, where his and Vicki's
first child, a boy dubbed Roderick James "Rod" McMahon, was born out
of wedlock on October 12.

We do not know what happened between these two young parents for
the next eleven months. But we know they got married on September 4,
1944, in South Carolina's Horry County, where authorities didn't seem to
note that Vicki's divorce was still pending in the next state over. By the end
of November, she was pregnant again.

On August 18, 1945, three days after Japan laid down its arms, Vincent J. McMahon was discharged from the New York base that had been
his final station. Vicki was about to give birth in North Carolina.

The couple's second son entered the world at 7:14 a.m. on August 24,
in Pinehurst, North Carolina's Moore County Hospital. Vicki named
the child after its father: Vincent Kennedy McMahon. Kennedy was her
mother's maiden name.

On September 16, the infant Vince was baptized in a Moore County

Catholic church. The Hanners were Presbyterians, but the McMahons were Catholics, so this was probably the last influence the father would have on his son's life for years.

By the time young Vince was old enough to remember anything, the man was gone.

"You know, I'm not big on excuses," Vince told an interviewer from *Playboy* in the latter half of 2000. "When I hear people from the projects, or anywhere else, blame their actions on the way they grew up, I think it's a crock of shit. You can rise above it."

The topic of conversation was Vince's own upbringing. He was talking about being sexually abused as a child.

The reporter pointed out how terrible it must have been for him. Vince bristled. "This country gives you opportunity if you want to take it, so don't blame your environment," Vince replied. "I look down on people who use their environment as a crutch."

The reporter brought up Vince losing his virginity. Vince paused. "That was at a very young age," he said. "I remember, probably in the first grade, being invited to a matinee film with my stepbrother and his girl-friends, and I remember them playing with me. Playing with my penis, and giggling. I thought that was pretty cool. That was my initiation into sex. At that age you don't necessarily achieve an erection, but it was cool."

He also recalled incidents involving a local whom he described as "a girl my age who was, in essence, my cousin": "I remember the two of us being so curious about each other's bodies, but not knowing what the hell to do," Vince said. "We would go into the woods and get naked together. It felt good. And, for some reason, I wanted to put crushed leaves into her." He told the interviewer he didn't actually remember when he putatively lost his virginity.

"Your growing-up was pretty accelerated," the reporter said.

"God, yes," said Vince.

The interviewer brought up Vince's childhood family unit. Vince said he lived with his mother "and my real asshole of a stepfather, a man who enjoyed kicking people around."

"Your stepfather beat you?" the interviewer asked.

Vince's reply: "Leo Lupton. It's unfortunate that he died before I could kill him. I would have enjoyed that."

★ ★ ★

Leo Hubert Lupton Jr. was born in New Bern, North Carolina, in 1917 and dropped out of high school after his freshman year. He trained as an electrician and married a girl named Peggy Lane in 1939. Their marriage was troubled, to say the least. In May of 1940, Peggy gave birth to their first child, Richard. But scarcely a year later, Leo had been convicted of abandoning his family and was sentenced to "two years on the roads," according to a brief, cryptic newspaper item. However, a later newspaper item implies he and Peggy were back together three months later, when their daughter, Ernestine—better known as "Teenie"—was born in September of 1941.

Leo's troubles were compounded upon enlisting in the Navy for service in the Pacific in August of 1944. Although he held the honor of being on a boat that was present in Tokyo Bay when the Japanese instrument of surrender was signed, his wife had a stillbirth while he was at sea. Upon returning to North Carolina, he and Peggy separated, and he held on to the kids. He appears to have moved with them into his parents' house in the South Carolina town of Mount Pleasant. Vicki's parents were also living in Mount Pleasant at the time, making it likely that a parental connection was how the couple met.

Vicki filed for divorce from young Vinnie's father on grounds of desertion, but in a curious way: she filed in faraway Leon County, Florida, the region in the Panhandle that contains Tallahassee, and her listed residence was in Lakeland, Florida—roughly 250 miles even farther south. Divorces were easy to obtain in Florida back then, so it seems likely that she somehow feigned to move there in order to obtain residency, then sought the legal separation, all while actually living in the Carolinas.

Whatever the details, the divorce was granted on March 18, 1947, and, on April 5, Vicki walked the aisle for the third time in less than six years, marrying Leo at her parents' house. Suddenly, Vinnie, not yet two years old, had two new siblings and, more consequentially, his first father figure.

"He hit you with his tools, didn't he?" the *Playboy* interviewer asked, referring to Leo.

"Sure," was Vince's reply.

"He hit your brother, too?" came the follow-up.

"No," Vince said. "I was the only one of the kids who would speak up, and that's what provoked the attacks. You would think that after being on the receiving end of numerous attacks I would wise up, but I couldn't. I refused to. I felt I should say something, even though I knew what the result would be."

Some of that speaking up, according to Vince, was advocating on behalf of his mother after Leo would hit her. "That's an awful way to learn how a man behaves," the interviewer said.

"I learned how *not* to be," Vince mused. "One thing I loathe is a man who will strike a woman. There's never an excuse for that." That said, the woman in question was not without blame, in Vince's eyes.

"Was the abuse all physical, or was there sexual abuse, too?" the interviewer asked.

"That's not anything I would like to embellish," Vince said. "Just because it was weird."

"Did it come from the same man?"

"No," Vince said. "It wasn't . . ."—a pause—". . . it wasn't from the male."

"It's well known that you're estranged from your mother," the reporter pointed out. "Have we found the reason?"

Vince paused. He nodded. All he could bring himself to say was, "Without saying that, I'd say that's pretty close."

Not long after the *Playboy* interview was published, Vince appeared on *The Howard Stern Show* to talk up a pay-per-view event, *WrestleMania X-Seven*, and promote his failing proprietary football league, the XFL. But Stern, as is his wont, wanted to talk about sex. The shock jock led off the interview by saying he'd read that Vince was molested by his mother.

"I didn't say that," Vince countered in a tone that suggested a rising shield. "That was the *inference*."

Stern's cohost, Robin Quivers, asked, "What did she do?"

Vince didn't answer.

Stern posited, "I don't know, but, whatever it was, it was *not good*."

Vince blurted out an obviously forced laugh.

"Vince, you get all choked up when you talk about it, right?" Stern asked.

"I'd rather not talk about that stuff," Vince replied.

Quivers: "Your mother is around and you don't talk to her?"

Vince: "Uh, not a lot."

Stern: "Boy, did she blow it. Because man, you're a billionaire!"

"Does she get any money from the WWF?" Quivers asked, referring to WWE by its then-current name.

Stern interrupted the question to add, "I just realized, when I said, 'Did she *blow it*'—that's the question!" Everyone in the studio yelled out a mock-disapproving "*Ohhh!*" at the host's dick joke.

Well, everyone other than Vince.

"Vince, I apologize," Stern said. "That would be traumatic."

"That would be traumatic," Vince said. "Right."

I once tracked down Terry Lupton, Leo's grandson through Richard, and spoke to him on the phone. He didn't remember much about Leo, but what he did wasn't flattering.

"The only time that I met him was when I was a little, little, little guy," Terry said. "And I just remember vividly how it was around Leo, and how my dad was around Leo. Even as a grown man with kids and a wife, my dad was still completely scared of Leo."

The occasion was a fishing trip. "I remember, vividly, my dad talking to us," Terry recalls, "and saying, 'Don't say a word [to Leo]. Nothing.' Kind of warning us." Terry did as he was told. "We went fishing with him and, sitting around, eating the fish we caught for the day, I didn't say a word."

In the *Playboy* interview, after Vince had gone on his tangent about not using trauma as a crutch, the reporter offered up a thought: "Surely it must shape a person."

"No doubt," came Vince's reply. "I don't think we escape our experiences. Things you may think you've pushed to the recesses of your mind, they'll surface at the most inopportune time, when you least expect it. We *can* use those things, turn them into positives—change for the better. But they do tend to resurface."

Shortly after they got married, Vicki and Leo were in North Carolina's Moore County, where Vinnie had been born, building a life for their blended nuclear family, all of whom were now known as Luptons. Indeed, a childhood friend of Rod's recalls Rod and Vinnie not even knowing how to say their Irish birth surname: according to him, they pronounced it "Mack-Mahone."

Vince would later say he didn't know why his parents were separated or what the terms of the separation were. He admitted to occasional fantasies that somehow his mom and his "real dad" would get back together. "Bizarre," he added. "Obviously, they didn't."

Vinnie Lupton first came up in Southern Pines, a poor township with a population of roughly four thousand, snuggled next to the better-known Pinehurst, an affluent golf resort city. Like most southern towns of the time, Southern Pines was segregated: there was a Black side of town and a white side. West Southern Pines had briefly been an independent township entirely comprised of the descendants of enslaved people, from 1923 to 1931, making it one of the first Black-run cities to be incorporated in the state. Southern Pines proper, on the other hand, had long been a "sundown town"—a place where Black people were barred from living or owning businesses.

Vinnie's first house was right on the dividing line. It "was what we would call a 'sketchy area' now," says Sarah Mathews, a white resident of Vinnie's generation. She recalls babysitting just a block or two away from the home where Vinnie first lived: "I mean, there were just some trees separating where I was babysitting from the Black community," she says. "I sat on the floor next to the table with the telephone on it because I was so frightened, so that I could call my parents if I heard any noise. I never babysat there again."

Vicki volunteered with the town's Boy Scout troop, played tennis in local tournaments, and even participated in community theater: in August of 1953, she was in *On Stage America*, which the local paper described as "an old-fashioned musical minstrel [show] with a modern patriotic twist." She performed as a member of the so-called Pickininny Chorus, presumably in blackface.

In 1956, around when Vinnie was ten, the Lupton unit packed up and moved to distant Weeksville, North Carolina. Located just outside of Elizabeth City, up on the northeast coast, Weeksville was largely farmland, though it seems probable that Leo was hired to do electrical work for a nearby Coast Guard base. There was slightly more contact between the Black and white populations there than in Moore, but it was largely restricted to Black farmers doing underpaid labor for white farmers. The schools were still totally segregated, and Vinnie attended the white one, in a sixth-grade class of just thirty-two kids. It is here that we get our earliest independent glimpse of Vinnie's personality.

The mythological youth of Vince McMahon is that of a rough-and-tumble hoodlum who barely got out alive. "I was totally unruly," he told the *Playboy* interviewer. "Would not go to school. Did things that were unlawful, but I never got caught." Or, as he put it on another occasion, "It's frustrating for a child to know that you're different and you don't fit in. Maybe you're not quite as bright and you're made fun of, and kids will do that. I guess, maybe, I always resorted back to the one common denominator when I was terribly frustrated like that. And that, of course, would be physicality."

However, the picture that emerges from those who knew him is, surprisingly, of a kind child who made friends with ease. "He was, from what I can remember, fairly popular, and he was liked by the girls as well as the boys," recalls classmate Shell Davis, who became the boy's best friend in town. "Most everyone knew him, liked him, that sort of thing."

Vinnie was not a loud or abrasive child: Rod's best friend from the period, James Fletcher, says that, despite encountering Vinnie at some length, the younger kid didn't make a big impression. That said, as Davis puts it, Vinnie "was more extroverted than introverted"; not a show-off, but "very sociable, very friendly, very outgoing to his peers."

Indeed, despite his claims to the contrary, it appears Vinnie was more of a lover than a fighter until well after he'd entered the world of professional adults. Whatever trauma he endured, it had not made him cruel. Not yet.

After just about a year, Leo moved his family once again, this time to Craven County, where he'd been born. Within just a few months, a belated reunion would, in its way, tilt the axis of history.

For millennia, people around the world have engaged in *legitimate* wrestling, where people grapple with one another, unaided by weaponry, until one of them is the victor. It has often been called our species' oldest sport, and it may well be. *The Epic of Gilgamesh*, the Sumerian epic written more than four thousand years ago, prominently features wrestling. The biblical Jacob (or *Ya'akov*—"God's heel") gained the name "Israel" after a wrestling match. One possible translation of *Isra'el* is "wrestles with God."

The Greeks and Romans famously prized the sport. Wrestlers have been heroes in West Africa since time immemorial. Settlers wrestled in America's colonial days; so did enslaved people. George Washington wrestled, as did Abraham Lincoln, who fought in roughly three hundred matches—indeed, a famous one in New Salem, Illinois, in 1831 made Honest Abe a local celebrity and was a key factor in putting him on the path to politics. Perhaps wrestling, however uncivilized it may seem, is inextricable from civilization.

Irish immigrants of the 1830s and '40s popularized a native form of Irish wrestling called "collar-and-elbow" in the American Northeast. It was a popular way to defend your Irish region's honor, in addition to being a hell of a lot of fun to watch. The Civil War and its attendant conscription brought Irish Americans and their customs into contact with countless other men from around the Union. Soon, people from all backgrounds were fascinated by collar-and-elbow. Just two years after the peace at Appomattox, the first American wrestling champion, James Hiram McLaughlin of New York, was crowned.

That's all well and good, but the real fun was just starting to percolate. English immigrants brought another new style from Europe, called "catch-as-catch-can," and its holds became the foundation of what we think of as pro wrestling. Yet another style, this one from France but erroneously referred to as "Greco-Roman wrestling," arrived soon afterward. In all these forms, one would extract a win through a submission or a pin—a "fall," in the parlance of the trade.

Excitement about wrestling was high and the time was ripe for innovation. However, there is no one person who came up with the idea of *staging* matches with predetermined outcomes. Rather, it seems to have been an organic convergence of two institutions: athletics and the traveling circus.

Wandering entertainment caravans were another long-standing human creation, and the post–Civil War growth of interest in organized sports opened the door for entrepreneurs and showmen to combine those models and create journeying athletic troupes. In order to guarantee a good time for the spectators, people in charge of the troupes started to covertly stage what were then known as "hippodrome" bouts: matches for which the ending was, unbeknownst to onlookers, mapped out in advance. However, this was *never* to be divulged to the general populace.

This was when the term *kayfabe* emerged. Possibly a garbled version of Pig Latin for "fake," it became a secret code word and one of the core tenets of the trade. Hippodroming was not confined to wrestling—it was, in fact, a general problem in the early days of organized sports in the

US—but kayfabe eventually belonged to wrestling alone. While artifice withered away in other sports industries, what became known as "professional" wrestling only got more and more fake.

An oligarchy of promoters started to emerge in the 1910s and early '20s, when wrestlers like Evan "Strangler" Lewis, Joe "Toots" Mondt, and Robert H. Friedrich (who, confusingly enough, *also* went by the name "Strangler Lewis") were national superstars. Soon, *characters* were the order of the day. Promoters, having abandoned athletic legitimacy behind the scenes, instead made their wrestlers work the crowd into a froth through archetypes. The matches—still billed as legitimate contests—now had clearly differentiated good guys (clean, fit, American) and bad guys (dirty, ugly, often foreign).

It was a genius idea. The nascent motion picture industry capitalized on the soaring popularity of wrestling by regularly putting wrestlers in movies—a tradition that continues to this day, often to great success for all parties involved. Wrestling was a chaotic industry: there was no central governing body, which led to territorial disputes and multiple brawlers claiming to be the national champion. But it was *lucrative* chaos.

So it's little wonder that, come 1931, an Irish American named Jess McMahon was interested in getting a piece of the action.

Roderick James "Jess" McMahon—Vince's grandfather—was born in New York City in 1882 to a pair of Irish immigrants. His father, Roderick, died when Jess was only six; his mother, Eliza Dowling McMahon, never remarried and raised the entire family of six children from there on out as a single mom. But Eliza was the heiress to a wealthy real estate developer, and her late husband had also made a small fortune as a landlord. Their lives were softened by their money and by America's expanding definitions of whiteness.

As a young man, Jess started promoting sports at an athletic club in his home neighborhood of West Harlem and gained a college degree. He married a woman named Rose McGinn. By July 6, 1914, when their second son, Vincent James, was born, Jess was rising to become one of the most successful promoters in New York boxing. He soon put up fights featuring legends such as Jack Johnson and Jess Willard and became matchmaker at the legendary Madison Square Garden in 1925. The venue would become a center of McMahon power.

As of 1929, Jess, Rose, and their kids were living in Rockaway Beach,

Queens, and teenage Vincent was studying at the pricey La Salle Military Academy on Long Island. A news item about Jess in the *New York Evening Post* quoted a letter allegedly written by Vincent to his older brother from a summer camp in Massachusetts, where he wrote that he had "learned how to follow up a left-jab with a right cross knockout punch" and made his brother swear not to tell their father, "for I want to surprise him one of these days." Fighting was now a family business.

And the business was diversifying: in 1931, Jess, lured by a colleague, made the historically consequential decision to promote his first professional wrestling match. Over the next decade and a half, he would continue working in the world of boxing, but also built out a wrestling fiefdom. He began by setting up pro wrestling matches on Long Island; by decade's end, he was booking them throughout Kings County, too, becoming one of the leading promoters in the New York City area. In the mid-1940s, he expanded his operations to Washington, DC. In 1946, he sent his son Vincent to live in the nation's capital and be his man on the ground.

It was good timing for Vincent. He was a year out of the army, unencumbered by the ex-wife and two children he'd left behind in the South. His twenties, before the war, had been spent aimlessly, but now he took to the family business with a fervor. In less than three years, he was hired as the general manager of DC's Turner's Arena, the heart of wrestling in the city, where he'd stage matches, as well as basketball games, concerts, and dances. He did well enough that in 1952, he subleased the arena for himself, and secured exclusive rights to promote wrestling in the city. He got married again, to a petite, glamorous local woman named Juanita Wynne.

On November 21, 1954, at age seventy-two, Jess died. He'd had a cerebral hemorrhage at a wrestling match in Wilkes-Barre, Pennsylvania, a few days earlier. The business he'd built was firmly in his son's hands.

Vince Senior was a tall man with pudgy cheeks, a dimpled smile, and voluminous hair. When he was dealing with wrestlers and fellow promoters, he was all smooth edges and easy charm. "He was always in a suit and tie, always dressed impeccably," recalls one old-school wrestler who worked extensively with Vince Senior. "He was someone who was basically revered by everybody in the industry, just from the way he treated everybody."

"You could be angry at [Vince Senior] for a payoff; you'd walk in, you'd voice your complaint, you'd walk out, you'd feel great—and yet, you got no more money," another of his wrestlers would later say. "When he was sticking it to you, he always made you feel good while he was doing it."

The mid-1950s brought with it the advent of mass television ownership, and wrestling shows—cheap to produce, delightful to watch— became some of the most popular programming of the day. Vince Senior renamed Turner's Arena as the Capitol Arena and started broadcasting his shows through the DuMont network in 1956. *Heavyweight Wrestling from Washington* was a smash, airing every Wednesday night in markets across the country.

There were promoters who thought TV would kill live wrestling because people could just watch it remotely without buying a ticket. Vince Senior saw things differently: "We are getting reservation orders from as far north as Chambersburg, Pennsylvania, and as far south as Staunton, Virginia," he told the *Washington Post and Times Herald* in March of 1956. "If this is the way television kills promoters, I'm going to die a rich man."

Within two years, three events changed professional wrestling forever.

One came in August of 1957, when Vince Senior and business partners Toots Mondt and Johnny Doyle founded Capitol Wrestling Corporation— a business entity that would one day be known as WWE.

Another was the release, that same year, of French literary theorist Roland Barthes's book *Mythologies*, which included an essay called "The World of Wrestling." It was a forceful, lyrical meditation on the artifice and glory of the pseudo-sport, and the first great justification of wrestling as art.

"The virtue of all-in wrestling is that it is the spectacle of excess," Barthes began. "Here we find a grandiloquence which must have been that of ancient theatres."

He ironically described legitimate, nonstaged combat as "false wrestling"; it was only by faking it that the event could become transcendently *real*.

"There is no more a problem of truth in wrestling than in the theater," Barthes declared. "In both, what is expected is the intelligible representation of moral situations which are usually private." It was now safer for everyone, high or low, to take wrestling seriously.

The third event came with no fanfare and no documentation. Yet, in the long run, it was one of the pivotal events in wrestling history.

Vinnie Lupton met his real father.

2

JUICE
(1957–1970)

Vinnie was twelve. He and the rest of his Lupton family unit were now ensconced in Craven County, North Carolina, where Vicki's parents had also settled. Possibly to stay away from Leo, Vinnie was living on and off at his grandparents' house—as Vince would later put it, Vicki's mom, Victoria Kennedy Hanner, "helped rear me" and "always had a home for me whenever I needed it."

Meanwhile, in DC, Vince Senior was living a life young Vinnie could barely have imagined.

His second wife, Juanita Wynne McMahon, never bore children. But the couple were not precisely childless. Only a few years after vanishing from his own sons' lives, Vince Senior stepped in to become paterfamilias—emotionally and financially—to a different abandoned family: that of his wife's niece, Hazel Miedzinski, whose husband had left her alone with three children. Carolyn Miedzinski and her brother and sister were about the same age as Rod and Vinnie—indeed, Carolyn was born just a few months after Vince.

To the Miedzinski children, Vince Senior was a reliable, affectionate parent.

He was "there almost daily," Carolyn, now in her mid-seventies and known as Carolyn Reardon, remembers. "Uncle Vince is the only father I ever knew."

Vince Senior lived near the Miedzinskis in DC most of the year, and in the summers the family—Vince, Juanita, Hazel, and the kids—would take off to the seashore. First, they would stay at a rented house in Atlantic City; later, Vince Senior purchased one in Rehoboth Beach, Delaware. The two-floor Rehoboth residence, painted gray with yellow window shutters, was a vacationer's paradise, worlds away from the hovels of Vince's simultaneous childhood.

"When you walked off the deck, you walked directly into the sand," Carolyn says. "You'd go over to a little dune, which was a couple hundred feet away, and you were on the ocean."

These summers together were celebrations of familial affection. They'd swim, they'd laugh, they'd play cards in the sweltering night. "We used to go around the house and just say, 'I love you! I love you!'—kind of announcing to everybody that you loved them," Carolyn says.

Tall, calm Vince Senior presided over it all. "Uncle Vince was the most loving person you'd ever want to know," she says. "He was very genuine. He'd sit and listen to whatever you had to say, no matter what. Extremely a family man. Family, family, family."

What happened in 1957 that made Vince Senior decide it was time to finally reunite with his biological sons? It's hard to say. Vince Senior's mother, Rose, was sixty-six that year and would die in February of 1958; perhaps she wanted to meet her only grandchildren before she passed.

Vince has sometimes told a version of his first meeting with his father in which Vince Senior and Rose were the first to arrive in North Carolina for what could only have been an awkward visit with the Lupton clan. But in a previously unpublished interview, Vince laid out a version of events in which it was *Juanita*, not Vince Senior, who made the pilgrimage with Rose.

"She was very interested in the two children he had fathered," he told a reporter in 2002. "She came down to North Carolina with my grandmother Rose, and I was living with my grandmother on my mom's side at the time. She met myself and my brother Rod, and then subsequently everybody went to New York. My dad was living in Washington, DC, but we went to New York first. My dad came up [from DC]."

What was it like for the boy who had always been Vinnie Lupton to step into the picture-book world of the McMahon-Miedzinskis? To reunite with a biological father who, for all the years Vinnie was struggling under Leo and Vicki Lupton, had lavished affection on three children who were unrelated to him by blood?

Vince has always told this part the same way, in terms that verge on the romantic, even the erotic:

"When I met my dad," he put it once, "I fell in love with him."

"I fell in love with him the moment I met him," he said another time.

On another occasion: "There was just an instant attraction that my dad felt and that I felt. He was just a wonderful, caring, bright man."

"I must have behaved myself, because I got invited up to be with him," Vince told the *Playboy* reporter.

"You must have been aching for him all that time," the reporter said.

"Didn't know it, though," Vince said. "It's funny how you don't know what you're missing if you never had it. . . .

"There's a tendency to try to play catch-up, but you can't," he continued. "You missed those years. There would always be something missing between us, but there was no reason to discuss it. I was grateful for the chance to spend time with him. . . .

"We got very, very close," Vince said. "But we both knew we could never go back."

Vince McMahon's resentments have powered him to success just as much as his passions, if not more so. Take, for example, one of the most entertaining and popular story lines in the history of American pro wrestling, that of the rivalry between two WWF characters, "Stone Cold" Steve Austin and "Mr. McMahon." The former was played by a wrestler born with the name Steven Anderson, and the latter by Vince himself.

At the turn of the millennium, Stone Cold and Mr. McMahon had a long-running feud in which Austin was the archetypal disgruntled employee, a shit-talking Texan in perpetual on-screen rebellion against the boss.

Mr. McMahon, the antagonist in this scenario, was a narcissistic, hyper-macho sadist/billionaire who longed to crush Austin, body and spirit. Vince, like his father, is a tall man—six-foot-two, according to an official WWE encyclopedia—but, unlike Vince Senior, he worked out in the gym. Quite a lot, in fact.

By the time he was playing Mr. McMahon, his pectoral muscles looked as though they had been crafted by a Roman sculptor. So, too, did his gorgeous salt-and-pepper helmet of hair. His rubber face could explode into any emotion he chose. Even when he wore a suit and tie, you could sense how badly he wanted to tear them off and start brawling.

At the time, the WWF was one of the most popular entertainment brands in the country, with well over five million viewers tuning in for its flagship shows every week. This iteration of Vince—crimson-faced, inferno-eyed, unsettlingly buff for a man in his fifties, shouting "*You're fired!*" at people with such force that you always wondered whether you were finally watching his vocal cords snap—seared itself into the brains of a significant percentage of American millennials, especially those who were boys. This is the Vince they assume they know and are sometimes ashamed to say they have loved.

Yet Vince, who oversaw and approved nearly every creative aspect of his shows while he was in power, has always maintained that his life was the inspiration for *both* figures, not just the one he played.

"I'm Stone Cold Steve Austin's character; that's really who I am on the inside," Vince would later say while describing the creation of the feud. "I understand the common man because that's really who I am."

He isn't, he explained, what he appears to be. "You never change who you really are. You put a suit on, and all that kind of stuff, and have some money in the bank," he said. "I guess some people do change with money in the bank . . . I'm still the same guy."

The creative engine of the feud, for Vince, was his attempt to work out his own childhood grudges. "When someone would, as a kid, even growing up, pretend that they were better than me—Oh my god, *wow*, that made me angry," he said. "The old thing of, like, they've got, quote, 'money,' or, 'So and so's got money!' Ugh, *man* . . .

"I understood because of my childhood," he continued. "It's just really, really screwed up, but I learned from it. It's what it was, and that's part of who I am today. . . .

"Understanding is psychology," he said. "So it was pretty easy for me to do the reversal: *Okay, then, I'm going to be the guy that I despised when I was growing up.*"

Vince Senior was never quite able to comfortably blend his two families— the children he'd left, and the ones he'd taken in.

As of the summer of 1959, Vinnie became a teenage interloper in the life his father had built for himself. And he was the only one, it seems: Carolyn says she was aware of Rod, and was in cordial contact with him as an adult, but she doesn't recall Vince Senior's eldest son ever visiting during their childhood, for reasons unknown. It was Vinnie alone who would show up, occasionally, for a weekend here and there. He was an awkward fit.

"I think Uncle Vince was a very warm, loving person," Carolyn reiterates. "I never saw any warmth in young Vincent."

She continues: "I got the impression that young Vincent got in the family and was like, *Who are these other people?* Were we interference? Were we freeloaders? I don't know what young Vincent ever thought. I think he tolerated us. I never got close to young Vincent. I think he was definitely not as warm and fuzzy as we are."

For his part, Vince says he never heard the words "I love you" from his biological father when he was growing up. "He never said it," Vince recalled. "Maybe he would say something complimentary about me to somebody else, but not to my face."

If Vinnie couldn't connect with his father in family settings, he tried to find him through his work.

Vince has never mentioned watching wrestling prior to meeting his father. There was plenty of wrestling on North Carolina TV when he was coming up, but if he ever watched it, it wasn't a major factor in his life. His love of his father is what led to his love of wrestling.

"I loved it from the day I saw it," Vince later said. "The characters!"

There was one particular character that he flipped for: Dr. Jerry Graham, the flashy in-ring persona of aging grappler Jerry Matthews. Graham was a bad guy, a heel, doing evil as a matter of course—but he always looked like he was having a hell of a time doing it.

"Oh, boy. It's 1959 and I'm looking up at Jerry Graham and he's lighting cigars with $100 bills," Vince recalled in an interview. "My dad wouldn't let me spend an enormous amount of time with him, but I'd sneak away when I could and go riding with the good doctor." Vince went into a reverie about Graham:

He spent more money than anybody I know. . . . He wore red pants and a riverboat-gambler shirt. The shirt was either white or red: If it was red, it had white ruffles; if it was white, it had red ruffles. He wore red shoes and rode around Washington in a blood-red 1959 Cadillac, smoking a cigar. He'd run red lights, blowing the horn, and people would scatter. If they didn't get out of the way, he'd . . . yell. Go off on someone verbally.

Later, Vince said he learned that Graham could be a "mean drunk," and he started to see through the wrestler's charisma. But for a time, Vince recalled, "I thought Jerry Graham walked on water."

★ ★ ★

Whether or not Vince picked up on it at the time, Jerry Graham was a living example of wrestling's three-word code, which Vince would learn well:

Protect the Business.

The dominant force in the industry at the time was an organization known as the National Wrestling Alliance (NWA). Formed in 1948, it was no more and no less than a wrestling cartel. Rather than letting the open markets of labor and capital decide where wrestling would go, this tiny handful of leading promoters from across the US and Canada would deal with one another behind closed doors to quietly settle disputes and manipulate the ecosystem as they saw fit.

Vince Senior's Capitol had an on-again, off-again affiliate relationship with the NWA—it was not a full member, but certainly not an enemy. In 1959, a man named Bill Olivas, who'd once wrestled under the moniker "The Elephant Boy," tested the NWA by setting up wrestling shows in Virginia—right at Vince Senior's doorstep. According to Olivas, the NWA helped Capitol out by executing an intimidation campaign; he claimed a promoter's underling even pulled a knife on him and told him to knock it off.

Olivas complained to the Virginia State Athletic Commission, which, in turn, asked for the FBI's help in investigating NWA collusion. Vince Senior was accused of participating in the intimidation, and thus became a government target. His main problem was that the loose-lipped Graham knew too much.

The state of Virginia held hearings on the Olivas matter, and they summoned Vince Senior and Graham, among many others, to testify. According to an FBI memo sent to Director J. Edgar Hoover, Graham had been interviewed by an agent and was planning to verify Olivas's claims, but when he testified, he "denied knowledge of any of the facts charged by Olivas."

Vince Senior, having done his duty—and, more importantly, having shown impressive ticket-sales numbers—was embraced by the NWA and upgraded to full member in 1960.

The feds were pretty sure they knew why things had gone cockeyed. They had put a hidden microphone in the waiting room for the hearings and picked up Vince Senior telling a fellow NWA promoter that he'd put the fear of God into Graham.

On the tape (which Hoover doesn't seem to have ever followed up on), Vince Senior said he'd told Graham not to speak out of turn, "because if you do, you're hanging yourself. You know where your bread is buttered." He then summed up his philosophy about how a wrestler should think, one his son would later adopt:

"Self-preservation? Fuck it."

Other than his brief glimpses of another life in his father's house by the ocean, Vince was stuck in Craven County with the Luptons. They lived at one point in a trailer park in the middle of nowhere, and, at another, near Havelock's recently constructed Cherry Point Marine Corps Air Station, where it seems likely that Leo was working. The cluster of cheaply built military housing where the family lived was known locally as "Splinterville."

Havelock High School was moderately sized, with graduating classes that hovered around ninety, yet none of Vince's fellow students that I could track down remember much about him. Go through the archives of the local paper, *The Havelock Progress*, and you'll see no mention of him throughout the entirety of his time in the area. This is especially notable because his siblings—Richard, Teenie, and Rod—were all staples of the news outlet, popping up in reports about Teenie's presence at youth parties or the boys' high-scoring performances in basketball games. Sports were huge at Havelock High. Vince participated in none of them.

Vince's description of his days in Havelock is that of contemporaneous America's chief bogeyman: a juvenile delinquent. "By the time I was 14 . . . I was pretty much a man then," Vince once said. As an example, he described running moonshine and getting caught by the cops.

Vince has said that rumbles with the Marines stationed at Cherry Point were also on the menu. "They'd pull up and there we were, me and my group of guys, going at it with the Marines," he said. The interviewer asked him to elaborate. "Most of them were in great condition," Vince said,

> but they didn't know how to pick a fight. I'm not saying they were easy pickings. They got their testosterone going and they were all liquored up. Some of them were real tough. But me and my guys were street fighters. I mean, maybe you've been through basic training and you

know how to operate a bayonet. That's different from sticking your finger in somebody's eye or hitting a guy in the throat, which comes naturally to a street fighter. And they can't believe you're not "fighting fair." Suddenly they can't breathe and/or see, and they realize: *Oh my god, am I in for an ass-kicking.*

Sitting around a table at a Bojangles fast-food franchise in Havelock, some old-timers who remembered Vinnie and the Luptons tell me there were, indeed, occasional scuffles between locals and the Marines—but Vinnie wasn't in them.

"At the time, the town had some rough people in it," says William McClees, who overlapped with Vince at Havelock High School. "We were a group of kids that . . ."—he pauses to choose his words—". . . enjoyed the Marines' company."

"We liked to antagonize them and engage them in activity," chimes in Doug Franks with a grin.

Vinnie may have wanted that kind of action, but Franks says he didn't get it. "He was too young for that," Franks says. "Vince was not a part of it. But he grouped up with a bunch of wannabes and we just considered him a little punk at the time. That's the best way I know to describe him."

I ask if Vince and his wannabes ever got into any fights, or if they just hung around. "They were hanging around in their own group, trying to be tough guys," Franks recalls. "The only time I ever knew he got into anything was when he broke his hand or his wrist in a fight with a boy named Harvey Helms." Neither Franks nor McClees recalls what the fight was over, just that it was a very isolated incident.

Vinnie "walked around with a cast on his hand and his wrist for three or four months," Franks says. "It was his claim to fame."

"I kinda had a crush on him," says classmate Sandy Clark. "He just seemed to be older and more mature than the rest of the people at the high school." Donna Dees, another classmate, used to see him at weekly dances in the local "teen club" and says he never caused trouble; however, "He sure could dance!"

The one person Vince truly connected with in Craven was the woman who would become his wife.

Although Vinnie was not a churchgoer, Vicki sang in a local church choir and he attended one day.

He walked in, sat down, and, as he once told the story, saw a girl in the choir: he "immediately saw these beautiful blue eyes, and it was like, *Wow!*"

It was a local named Linda Marie Edwards. Her eyes weren't the only thing he noticed. "I saw this statuesque, relatively *buxom* young lady, and I said, 'Yeah, okay! We've got some promise here!'" Vince was sixteen years old at the time. Linda was thirteen.

The McMahons don't talk about what happened next between the two teens, preferring to skip to their marriage almost five years later, after both of them had reached the age of consent. But, in Vince's recounting, as much as he might have admired young Linda's body, he may have been even more enamored of her parents, both employees at Cherry Point and both apparently quite loving toward their only child.

Despite everything he'd already seen of the affectionate McMahon-Miedzinski family, Vince claims the Edwardses were his first encounter with a loving and functional home. "I had no idea what a family was until I met Linda, and saw how they lived," Vince once said. "It was an *Ozzie and Harriet* life. There wasn't screaming and beating. *You see*, I thought, *there's something else*. I wanted some of that stability and love. And then I wanted more of it."

As he tumbled through adolescence, Vinnie fell in love with his father, his father's business, his father's top heel, and his wife-to-be, all in quick succession. Eventually, there would be no boundary between all these elements in Vince's life. For him, family is business, business is violence, and violence is, in its way, love.

Vinnie's fortunes took a whiplash-inducing turn for the better in the early 1960s. The first change was one of scenery. He had done eighth, ninth, and tenth grade at Havelock High, living through a turbulent period when the school became one of the first in the state to integrate Blacks and whites. He says he hated it at the school and was so incorrigible that he was going to be kicked out. "I could go to a state-supported institution," he later said, "or I could go to military school."

Vince Senior shelled out the cash for Vince to escape North Carolina. He enrolled at the Fishburne Military School in Waynesboro, Virginia, in the autumn of 1962.

"I had no reputation, so it was a new beginning," Vince later recalled, "a great chance to start over and create a *new* reputation."

One of the first orders of business was throwing his childhood name into the dustbin of history: there was no Vinnie Lupton in Fishburne's eleventh-grade class—but there *was* a Vince McMahon. That shift was partly due to his new surroundings offering an opportunity, but it also wouldn't have been accurate to call him a Lupton anymore. Things had fallen apart for Vicki and Leo, and she sued him for divorce; on June 3, 1963, it was finalized. Vicki became romantically involved with one Harold Askew of Ebensburg, Pennsylvania, and they married about seven months after the divorce.

For his part, Leo absconded to Palm Beach, Florida, and in October of 1966 he married a woman twenty-eight years his junior—almost exactly Vince's age, in fact. She was Vince's "cousin," with whom Vince had sexually played amidst the pines of Moore County as a child. The next year, she and Leo had a child, Kevin. The couple stayed together until Leo died, twenty-two years later.

As Kevin tells it, Leo never spoke about his past in his lifetime, so Kevin only learned about the Vince connection when he was an adult. Until then, "I never knew he was married to that lady," he told me, referring to Vicki. "I never knew Vince was his stepkid."

According to Kevin, Leo was "an average dad" who regularly took him hunting and fishing. "I wouldn't say he was mean," Kevin said, referring to Leo. "But he believed that if you fucked up, you got punished." He declined to elaborate.

When I asked if he'd heard any of Vince's abuse claims, Kevin demurred: "I've heard a few things through the grapevine, but I never took them to heart," he said. "If Vince says they didn't get along, maybe Vince wasn't that good of a person, either."

Just before we hung up, Kevin said there's one thing he'd like me to ask Vince, if I talk to him: "I'd like to know why he hasn't tried to contact me at all."

Two new wrestling promotions emerged circa 1963, each of them massively significant. One is well known to all in the trade. The other has gone almost entirely unreported until now.

Each was run by a McMahon.

Vince Senior's first tenure in the NWA ended up being a poor fit. He fell behind on dues payments and even threatened to resign just a year after he was admitted. Late 1962 brought a dispute with the rest of the cartel over who should hold their national championship: Vince Senior wanted to keep the belt on his swaggering, blue-chip heel, "Nature Boy" Buddy Rogers (Herman Rohde), but the others wanted to give it to someone else. Some say the NWA feared Capitol might break away from the organization and take the belt with it, which would have represented a supreme crisis of legitimacy in the age of old kayfabe. Others say it was a mutually agreed-upon divorce.

Either way, a title match was held in Toronto on January 24, at which Rogers agreed to perform the role of the loser and let semiretired legend Lou Thesz become NWA champ. Vince Senior and veteran promoter Toots Mondt decided to strike out on their own and in January 1963 launched their own wrestling federation under the Capitol auspices. In it, Buddy Rogers was billed as the incumbent champion; their kayfabe didn't accept the NWA's kayfabe.

They called it the World Wide Wrestling Federation, or WWWF.

While Vince Senior had been navigating those choppy waters, his son was making a mediocre run at legitimate sports.

Vinnie had become a big guy, broad-chested and solid. He used his size to become a not-bad defensive tackle on the football team ("He liked to hit," says one classmate) and a so-so member of the (legitimate) wrestling team.

"Vince was a good guy," says Gary Grier, one of Vince's roommates, "but he never played any sports before he came to Fishburne. He didn't know a whole lot about football or anything else, really, other than wrestling. And the wrestling he knew was the wrestling his dad was involved with, not collegiate or high school wrestling."

So Vince set out to recreate his father's type of wrestling at Fishburne.

He's never talked about the first, makeshift pro wrestling shows he staged there. No WWE special has ever mentioned it. But it was at Fishburne that Vince McMahon, wrestling promoter, made his debut.

The shows happened in the gym after school hours, apparently with the administration's approval, complete with costumes and gimmicks. "He would put on little wrestling matches like you see on TV today, the same stuff," Grier says. "Everybody had a stage name and he had 'em all figured out."

Vince wrestled under the moniker "Ape Man" McMahon.

"He was marketing wrestling back when we were in high school," classmate Jeff Lawyer says. "He was just into dress-up, putting on masks or something, and he would wrestle. Just to have fun. Sometimes people would participate, sometimes they'd just come watch. . . . Vince was Vince: he loved to wrestle."

Classmate Roland Broeman singles out a specific trait Vince was starting to exhibit at these shows, one that would eventually be immortalized in countless animated GIFs: "He had a walk about him," Broeman says. "A strut. Like Baby Huey"—an anthropomorphic duck from a popular cartoon. "I used to tease him about it."

Vince also, surprisingly, dabbled in another kind of all-American spectacle: the medicine show.

"We would go over to Fairfax Hall, the girls' school across town, and he would put on a healing show over there," Grier remembers. "He had a fella named 'Dutch' Lindsay, Charles Lindsay—Dutch was a kinda short, stocky guy—and he'd grab Dutch by his head and do this healing routine, and Dutch would fall to the ground and Vince would 'heal' him."

For the participants, these shows were just about their only chance to interact with members of the other sex. Rules against male-female hangouts were strictly enforced at the girls school: "It was hard to get someone outta Fairfax Hall" is how Grier puts it. "I mean, they were all as willing as anybody, but it was just tough."

Vince had a girl back home, of course. "I never met Linda," says Grier. "As far as I know, she never came to Fishburne. But he talked about her a lot." In general, Grier says, sex was distant from Vince's actions and conversations. "He didn't date a lot," the roommate concludes. "He was into wrestling."

On the rare occasions when Vince has talked about his time at Fishburne, he's described himself, per usual, as a reckless iconoclast who couldn't be bound by the school's strict norms. He's said the full extent of his crimes there will never be known.

"I wasn't caught for some stuff that would have meant immediate dismissal, like stealing the commandant's car," Vince said. "He also had a dog he was nuts about. I love animals, but one day I couldn't resist giving that dog a laxative. I put the laxative in some hamburger and the dog did his business all over the commandant's apartment, which thrilled me greatly."

In Vince's version of events, such transgressions eventually earned him

Fishburne's first-ever student court-martial. In one interview, he vaguely said the fracas was over "insubordination"; in another, he said it was because there were rumors he was going to sabotage finals week. In one version of the story, young Vince was cleared because of a popular uprising from students and teachers.

"The morning of graduation," Vince once said, "I walked up to this old colonel we had and said, 'You thought I was going to fuck up finals. But now, wait and see what I'm going to do.' He recoiled, and then I said, 'Just kidding.'"

However, no one from Fishburne that I was able to speak to has any memory of Vince being court-martialed. Fishburne, itself, couldn't provide any confirmation of such an event. Indeed, Vince's friends say he wasn't even that much of a problem student, on the whole.

"He was a fair student, but he didn't work real hard, not at the academic thing," Grier recalls. "He got good grades, but he never worked too hard at it. I had to wake Vince up to go to his college boards. He'd fallen asleep."

"He was a character, but I don't remember him getting into any trouble," says Lawyer.

Broeman agrees: "I don't recall him getting into fights or anything like that, no."

"Everybody bragged a lot and talked a lot, but I can't remember him being any worse than anyone else," says Grier. "We all stretch the truth."

Vince graduated from Fishburne in the spring of 1964 and, that fall, began his college studies in the business administration program of East Carolina University, situated just an hour's drive north of Craven County, in Greenville. He and Linda were wed in New Bern on August 13, 1966, just after Linda graduated from New Bern High School. She joined her husband as a student at ECU and entered the French program on an accelerated track so the two of them could graduate together, which they did on June 1, 1969. By then, she was pregnant.

Vince "hated economics" and "wasn't wild about statistics, either," and it took him five years to get his diploma. He claims he convinced multiple professors to change his grades in order to get him to the 2.001 GPA required for graduation, pleading about his need to support his nascent family.

"Now, they figure this kid has either made up a hell of a story, or maybe it's true; either way, it didn't hurt them to change the grade," Vince would later say, anticipating much about his future artistic strategy. "I delivered it with lots of conviction, because it was true. Not that I couldn't have delivered it with conviction had it *not* been true."

His son, Shane Brandon McMahon, came into the world on January 15, 1970. In time, the boy would become Vince's heir apparent, then disappear from the wrestling scene in a cloud of shame. But, as the Me Decade dawned, perhaps the most notable thing about Shane was the fact that he was born in Maryland.

The burgeoning McMahon family unit was now based in Gaithersburg, about two dozen miles northwest of Vince Senior's DC headquarters. Vince had, after twenty-four intermittently excruciating years, finally and irrevocably escaped North Carolina. Although he would return to the urban centers of the Tar Heel State for wrestling shows later in life, he never lived there again. No one among the dozens upon dozens of residents of Moore, Weeksville, or Craven to whom I spoke has any recollection of him even visiting.

Over a decade and a half after he fled the state, an interviewer would point out that Vince had "a little southern accent."

"Traces," was Vince's response. "I went to school in Waynesboro, Virginia—military school—and grew up, to an extent, around Washington, DC, which, at that time, was very southern."

And that was it. No mention of North Carolina. Vinnie Lupton and his whole world had been excised from Vince's biography.

The family unit in which Vince was raised was scattered by then. Rod, Vicki, and Harold had moved to a trailer park in Millington, Tennessee, by 1967; the latter two then moved to Pembroke Pines, Florida, in 1969, while Rod married and wound up in Texas. Teenie went to Virginia. Richard became a Mormon and moved to Utah. None of them returned.

On the last day of my trip to North Carolina, I get up early to meet Shell Davis, Vinnie Lupton's sixth-grade best friend.

He'd appeared on a 1957 yearbook page from Vinnie's elementary school in Weeksville, and a local woman to whom I'd shown it had said he was still around. She called Davis and told him I was writing about Vinnie Lupton, the boy who had grown up to become Vince McMahon.

That last bit was news to Davis.

"I know of Vince McMahon, and I have seen him on TV, and I know that he's the CEO of WWE," he told me over the phone in advance of our meeting. "But I had no idea that they were one and the same."

We meet just after dawn on a country road that cuts through wide, flat, freshly plowed fields. There isn't a single other person to be seen. Davis chose the spot because it's where the Luptons lived. The clan dwelled in a cheap house, surrounded by farmland. They only stuck around for a year.

All that year, Vinnie and little Shell would sit together on the bus, go to each other's houses, and do the things kids do: "Sports. Riding bikes. Hide-and-seek. You'd go outside and you'd stay all day."

But Davis, a lifelong farmer, never got to say goodbye to Vinnie. "I didn't realize that he left," he says, "until school started in seventh grade and he didn't show back up."

A few months later, Vinnie would meet Vince Senior. Davis was the last friend the boy had before he started becoming a McMahon.

Throughout North Carolina, nearly all the buildings in which Vince grew up have been torn down. The sites where they were are now paved over, or, as is the case in Weeksville, overgrown.

"You see the tree up there?" Davis asks.

I say yes.

"The house was right there, by the tree."

Where he points, there is now only emptiness.

Even if Vince wanted to go home, there would be none left for him to find.

3

PLAY-BY-PLAY

(1970–1982)

In order to know what Vince accomplished, we must know what he destroyed.

By the time of Vince's college graduation in 1969, the National Wrestling Alliance's regime had solidified into an amoral but seemingly stable syndicate. It was an oligopoly, with a small cohort of men controlling the whole market, and the keystone of the peace was the so-called territory system. The US and Canada were divided into geographical "territories," with one promotion allotted to each of more than two dozen of them.

They were their own little universes, no two of them alike. One territory might be known for accomplished technical execution; another might be known for its gimmick matches and rampant bloodletting. One promoter might have a reputation as a hard-ass who'd swindle you as soon as look at you; the promoter in the next territory over might be a real swell guy (right up to the moment he cut you from the roster). The system was weighted against the wrestlers—"workers" in industry lingo—in countless ways, but at least there were enough active companies that, if things didn't work out at one firm, you might try your luck elsewhere. The territory system had its flaws, but it had far more variety than what would follow it.

There was an intimacy between fan and promotion: these were regional organizations, and, if you liked wrestling, your local promoter's approach would shape your entire viewpoint about what wrestling was and could be. You might be aware from wrestling magazines that other promotions existed, and wrestlers from other territories would stop by from time to time. But you went to show after show with the same rotating cast, participating in the comfort of catharsis, often in venues small enough that you could get within trash-throwing distance of your local heel.

Wrestling was its own strange bubble, cut off from mainstream respect or attention. Americans generally knew what wrestling was, and children almost certainly watched at least a little of it at live shows or on weekend TV broadcasts. But that was about it, as far as places to find the artform. There was very little crossover between it and forms of media that were deemed hip by the public. Wrestling was a thrill, a hoot, or a curiosity. But it wasn't cool.

Most of the promotions were NWA members, including Vince Senior's WWWF, which was welcomed back into the fold in 1971. Promoters were like Old Hollywood studio bosses, claiming wrestlers for themselves and loaning them out to peers as they saw fit. There was still a major non-NWA promotion based out of Minneapolis called the American Wrestling Association (AWA) that had limited presence in other promoters' regions, but, for the most part, it was a time of centrally coordinated Pax Americana.

Innovation threatened the balance. After American wrestling's initial period of TV mega-popularity in the 1950s, there had been a glut and subsequent collapse on the small screen. Shows like Vince Senior's old program on the DuMont network stopped being syndicated nationally. That suited the NWA fine, because each territory could claim hegemony for its respective TV markets, keeping conflict to a minimum. If you lived on the periphery near another territory, your antenna might pick up its shows, but you were generally stuck with whatever local promotion happened to have a deal with your local TV station, often broadcasting on Saturday mornings.

The play-by-play commentary for viewers of the WWWF's televised programming was provided by a man named Ray Morgan. Morgan was an ace at the job, but he also happened to be a member of the national broadcasters' union, AFTRA. And McMahons hate unions.

Vince has often said he happened to be backstage in the cloak room with his father at a wrestling show in Hamburg, Pennsylvania, when an altercation took place.

"Ray wanted a raise," Vince recalled in a typical version of the anecdote. "We're about to go on the air, and Ray says to my dad, 'I'm not going out there unless you give me what I want.'"

Vince Senior was unfazed. He had a habit, often remarked upon, of carrying loose change in his pockets and jingling the coins in his palm when he was thinking. "My dad had his quarters—he used to have a bunch of quarters in his hands; he'd play with the quarters," Vince said. "He looked at Ray. He didn't say anything. And he finally said, 'I'm not going to give you the raise.' Ray got up and walked out."

Vince, in his own telling, was astounded, but not in any way sympathetic to the man who had just been axed. "I'm sitting in this cloak room and I'm saying to myself, *Wow, that was awesome!*" he said. "I was just proud to be there and listen to all that, and proud of my dad, proud of the fact he told this guy to take off."

But, of course, the firing posed an immediate problem, as Vince recounted: "About two minutes later, I said, 'Dad, what are you going to do now?' He looked at me and he said, 'You're going to be the announcer.'" Vince says he did as he was told and took over the microphone that night.

Vince claimed he "had no experience whatsoever, none, zip." He'd been doing odd jobs since graduation; Linda had a paralegal position at a law firm. They were doing okay. But this was his chance to break into his elusive father's business. By January 31, 1972, in a miraculous leap of nepotism, Vince was announcing at Madison Square Garden.

It appears that Vince's oft-told tale about his path to the announcer's table may have been a conflation of a few events, though the counterevidence hardly changes the harsh tenor of the firing. According to arbitration documents from an unconnected legal case involving Capitol, Morgan had negotiated with Vince Senior and AFTRA to get a pay raise. Vince Senior, it seems, agreed to the raise, then promptly fired Morgan and gave Vince the position—but *at the rate Morgan had been promised.*

In other words, Vince Senior didn't even save any money by hiring his son instead of giving Ray Morgan what he wanted. What he saved was his reputation as someone who was not to be screwed with. This was, perhaps, the first time Vince had seen such a merciless exercise in raw financial power and spite.

It was not lost on him.

The typical portrayal of the two Vinces McMahon depicts their relationship as healthy and almost blissful: the ambitious, respectful son and the kind, magnanimous father. But, while Vince describes his father glowingly, the stories he tells actually tend to depict his father as a cold man, perpetually dissatisfied with his once-estranged son's biggest ideas. And while they worked together for a dozen years, Vince has never offered much reflective insight into anything that happened behind closed doors with his dad, be it personal or professional. That said, there are plenty of dots to connect.

There is a story that is illuminating, one passed down by J. J. Dillon (James Morrison), an ex-wrestler who worked for Vince Senior (and, later, Vince). He says Vince Senior was beloved by the Boys, the term of art for a wrestling roster. "The old-timers had such adoration for the father," Dillon says. "I could even go so far as to say it was almost an impossibility for his son to come along and ever completely fill his father's shoes and have that same level of respect."

Sometime later, Vince the younger told Dillon about a conversation he'd had with Vince Senior. The father's wisdom, as imparted to the son, was: "Wrestlers are like seagulls: all they do is eat, shit, and squawk all day."

Dillon was taken aback, and never forgot it—he even went so far as to name his memoir *Wrestlers Are Like Seagulls: From McMahon to McMahon.* "That gave an insight there into how his father truly felt, deep inside," Dillon says, "though he never spoke openly that way." Whatever Vince's relationship with Vince Senior was like, it included tutelage in the cynical art of being an employer.

Vince also started acting as Vince Senior's emissary in some of the northernmost points of the WWWF imperium, up around Maine and New Hampshire, where—or so Vince claims—the previous guy to hold the job had been skimming off the top. Vince typically raises the stakes on the story by saying he'd been begging his dad for a shot at making it big in wrestling, and that he got it under one condition from Vince Senior: "If you don't make it, don't ever ask me again."

"His father, I believe, was a tough guy," says John Aldi, a friend of Vince's from the period. "He was not easy, I don't think." Nevertheless, Vince wouldn't complain. "He'd definitely toe the line with his father," Aldi says. "When his father called, he certainly did whatever he wanted him to do."

The gig largely consisted of wooing and wining local vendors and venue owners, then collecting cash from them after the shows—unglamorous work, to be sure. "The money came in a garbage bag," Aldi recalls.

So, while living with Linda in their new home of West Hartford, Connecticut—he drove as far north as Maine and as far south as Virginia to get to WWWF shows—Vince sought to increase his fortune. Vince and

four people who shared his accountant, including Aldi, formed an investment group. "It was visions of sugarplums," Vince would later say of the
venture. "It was, 'Look how successful I am! I guess I really am somebody.'"

In September 1973, they acquired a Connecticut cement plant from a
World War I veteran and a fifty-acre horse farm from a married couple.
The ventures rapidly fell apart before the group could finish making the
payments on them. The McMahons were not obligated to reimburse the
veteran or the couple, so they opted not to do so until their nonpayment
was caught, more than thirty-five years later.

It was Vince's first of many experiences of abject failure in the non-
wrestling world. However, he hadn't invested much emotional energy in
this particular endeavor. He had bigger fish to fry, says Aldi: "Vince liked
the action and the promotion of the wrestling business."

Aldi also spent time with Linda, though not as much. He, like most
people who describe her, makes her sound like a gentle enigma. "She's a
very nice person, very smart," he recalls. "Kept a good house. She was a
housewife, at the time, but then she helped Vince with the wrestling promotions."

Vince began having at least one affair, which upset Aldi: "When that
happened, I told him that the grass is not greener on the other side. 'You've
got a good woman. You should stay by her. You've got a good family.'" The
fling was brief, according to Aldi. But it would not be the last.

Another new chunk of income was supposed to come from a live spectacle, but, surprisingly, not one in the realm of wrestling. Instead, it was
going to be a rocket-ship blastoff lasting half a minute—though it was also
supposed to be much more than that.

Bob Arum, then and now one of the most successful promoters in
boxing, had been doing business with Vince Senior for some time, thanks
to the emerging technology of closed-circuit broadcasting. If you couldn't
make it to the place where an event was occurring, you could attend a
screening—typically at a movie theater or sports venue—where a live feed
would be shown on a screen.

Boxing promoters, long tied to the wrestling industry, used to call upon
wrestling promoters to help get turnout up at the screenings. As such, on
a few occasions, Arum had collaborated with Vince Senior, whom Arum
describes as "a tremendously charismatic guy; very, very honest; a pleasure to do business with." Then came a fateful phone conversation.

"Sometime in 1974, I think it was, I got a call from Senior," Arum recalls, "who said to me, 'My son wants to go into the promotion business, and it might be good if he hung around you guys in the boxing thing so he could learn something.' And I said, 'Fine, that's great.' He didn't ask for a salary or anything." Vince would take up a residency in the offices of Arum's company, Top Rank, and soak up the lessons of the industry that had initially made the McMahon name great.

Or, at least, that was the plan. As Arum puts it, Vince "wasn't on the scene for a week when he came to me and he said, 'I got this great idea: I know this guy who's been jumping over trucks with a motorcycle, Evel Knievel, and now he wants to, with a space rocket, jump over the Snake River Canyon'"—a gorgeous natural vista near Twin Falls, Idaho.

The Montana-born Knievel was by then a national icon for his televised motorcycle stunts, in which he'd leap over rows of large objects, usually vehicles. There were Evel Knievel toys, clothes, even a theatrical biopic starring George Hamilton. For years, Knievel had been threatening in interviews to outdo himself with a jump across Snake River. Now, Vince wanted to make that threat a reality.

Vince says he was the one who initially approached Knievel after seeing the latter perform on ABC's *Wide World of Sports*. According to Knievel's biographer, twenty-eight-year-old Vince made a single phone call to Knievel and was convincing enough that he was granted an audience with the real-life superhero at his Montana home.

Much like Dr. Jerry Graham, Knievel knew how to live the high life at all costs, and picked Vince up from the airport in a customized white Cadillac with wheels so big, they couldn't easily make turns; they had to take a long, roundabout path to the stunt artist's home. "You knew he was a different kind of cat right there," Vince would later recall. "A showman."

Although their shared love of flashy extravaganzas allowed the two men to hit it off, Vince said something about the visit took him aback. "The only thing that surprised me was the way Knievel treated his family," he remembered. "I'd never seen anything like it. He was pretty dogmatic with his wife, ordering her around, and he wasn't all that kind to his kids. I kept wondering if this was a show he was putting on for the guy from New York or what it was. He was particularly rude to his wife." Perhaps familial alarm bells started ringing for him.

Vince's instincts were on the money: Knievel was, by all accounts, an abusive and narcissistic bigot. But if Vince detected any of that, it wasn't enough to deter him, and by the time he spoke to Arum, he had Knievel on board for an event whose very appeal lay in the fact that countless people might end up watching a man die hideously, live over the airwaves.

"I said, 'Are you fuckin' crazy?'" Arum recalls. "It was ridiculous. So I refused." But all was not lost: Vince and Knievel were simultaneously speaking to ABC about the idea of broadcasting a replay a week later, and Arum soon got a call from the network. "They thought it was a great idea," he says, "and that, if we agreed to do it, they would, in effect, make additional dates available for our boxing shows." He still thought it was lunacy, but televised boxing slots were hard to come by, so Arum acquiesced, and on the weekend of May 25, 1974, he and Vince flew to Ohio to meet up with the touring Knievel.

Arum says it didn't take long for the conversation to get awkward. "There are three kinds of people I can't stand," the daredevil allegedly said. "New Yorkers, lawyers, and Jews." Arum happened to be all three, but he and Vince were in too deep to back out now—or so Arum thought.

"It took Vince one week to realize what a scumbag nutcase Knievel was," Arum says. "And that was the last we heard from Vince. He left me with the package, and he decamped."

To be fair, Vince didn't financially divest from the event, although his father apparently would have liked him to. Vince Senior wasn't pleased with the situation and what it would mean for the McMahon reputation.

"He hated the canyon jump," Vince would later say of his dad. "I had a chance to sell our interest [in the jump] later on, and my father was yelling at me to make a deal. He said I should take any price, sell it all for a couple of dollars, give it away, just get out. I never did."

Meanwhile, Arum spent the summer touring the United States with Knievel to build up excitement for the jump. It was set to be accompanied by a massive fair on-site and, presumably, long periods of announcers speculating about the jump, then analyzing what had just happened. But the rocket prototype wasn't working, the money was running out, and Knievel, himself, was a complete nightmare to be around.

To wit: "We were staying at a motel near an army base," Arum says. "Off-duty soldiers, with their girlfriends, were swimming in the pool. Knievel got out on the balcony and yelled, 'Shut the fuck up!' Of course, they didn't, and he got a gun and fired it into the pool. He was totally out of his fuckin' mind. But I got stuck with him."

By the day of the jump, September 8, 1974, the whole thing was already a disaster, with meager closed-circuit ticket sales and minimal crowds in Idaho. The rocket was just barely functional by then, but the jump didn't even work—Knievel's parachute deployed early and he and his bike drifted down to the canyon floor below without making it anywhere near the other side (or, for that matter, dying). Vince and Linda are estimated to have personally lost $250,000 on the stunt. It was not the last time that Vince's shame would be broadcast live around the country.

And yet, despite all that, Arum became the first in a long line of jilted professional partners to find themselves working with Vince again. As is often the case, it was the once-estranged partner who reversed course and came back to Vince, in this case about a year and a half later.

Arum was promoting Muhammad Ali in a boxing match at the time, but Ali's manager abruptly asked if they could cancel it. "He said, 'The Japanese people have come to us with a lot of money for Ali to fight this wrestler, Inoki, in Japan,'" Arum recalls. Kanji "Antonio" Inoki was, Arum learned, the biggest pro wrestler in the country, and the fight was supposed to take place at Tokyo's famous Budokan arena. Japan had its own, domesticated form of pro wrestling they called *puroresu*, with the same basic premise and a thousand little variations. The Japanese public took wrestling seriously as both industry and artform. But Arum was an American.

"I said, 'What the fuck? How does a boxer fight a wrestler?'" Arum was intrigued—it was Ali, after all—but needed guidance on such an unusual pairing. "So I got ahold of Vince Jr. and I said, 'How do I do this?'" Arum says. "And Vince, of course, had brilliance when it came to wrestling, and gave me the scenario." He recounts Vince's plan, which involved a well-worn wrestling practice known as "blading," in which a wrestler will covertly cut their own skin to make it look as though they've endured enormous damage:

The scenario was—and I'll never forget it—that Ali, after two or three rounds, was going to be ostensibly pounding the hell out of Inoki for fake, but make it *look* real. And Inoki was the kind of wrestler that had a razor, like you shave with, in his mouth, and he would take the razor out, and slit his [own] eyebrows. And, as Ali was punishing him, the blood would be falling down, and Ali would turn to the referee: "Please, stop the fight!" The referee wouldn't. Then Ali turns around and says, "You gotta stop the fight!" Inoki would jump on his back, pin him—one, two, three count. Inoki would win the fight, everybody'd be happy, Ali would leave with a big paycheck.

Arum loved it, and both Vince and Vince Senior hopped on board to help promote the event. The trouble was, Ali had no interest in being a loser, however unfair the fight. Indeed, there wasn't even agreement on whether the fight would be staged (à la Inoki—though this was still the age of kayfabe, when no one would publicly admit such fiction) or genuine (as Ali was, of course, used to, though he had long admired ostentatious midcentury pro wrestler "Gorgeous" George Wagner).

Vince, Vince Senior, Ali's trainer, and a Los Angeles wrestling promoter named Mike LeBell released a set of ostensible rules to an eager press on May 28, 1976. They suggested that this would be a legitimate contest, featuring a mishmash of wrestling and boxing maneuvers. LeBell linked Ali up with an infamous, trash-talking wrestling heel named "Classy" Freddie Blassie for a series of much observed public appearances, including on WWWF television. Budokan sold out, and Vince Senior came close to doing the same at Shea Stadium for a closed-circuit telecast event (tickets were an astounding $10 a pop). You could even catch it on big screens in the United Kingdom. Although confusion reigned about what, exactly, would happen, excitement was high.

Mere days before the Ali-Inoki fight took place, nearly everyone was on the same page: the fight *should* be fixed and Ali should *not* emerge as the winner on Inoki's home turf. Everyone, that is, except Ali, who still refused to take the fall. Vince says he was sent to Tokyo as Vince Senior's emissary to ensure that things went as planned, i.e., with an inconclusive finish that allowed everyone to save face to one extent or another.

In Vince's telling, he went to Ali's room and discussed the matter with him. Ali refused to play ball. So Vince lunged forward and grabbed Ali in a wrestling hold by surprise, then took him down to the floor, just to demonstrate that Inoki might do the same.

Or so Vince says. "I certainly remember Vince being there and spending time around Ali," recalled Bob Goodman, a publicist who was regularly around Ali at the time. "But wrestling Ali to the ground would have been a little strange to me."

Vince later said he had updated his plan for the fight to make it Ali-proof: LeBell's brother, Gene, was going to be the referee, and would sneak the razor blade in. Then, at some point, Gene would use it to cut up Ali's forehead . . . but without warning the champ.

"Even Ali wouldn't know what the fuck was happening," Vince later recounted. "Ali wouldn't get hurt, but he would bleed profusely because Gene would do a damn good job, and Gene would have to stop the fight because of the blood. Thus, the fans would want to see a return match or some damn thing."

If the story is true, Vince was proposing a surprise assault with a potentially deadly weapon—something that was, of course, incredibly illegal, both in the rules of sport and the rules of the law. "I don't know how my dad found out about this—wind, telegraph, telephone—but he knew I was up to no good over there," Vince continued. "He said, 'Goddammit, you're dealing with Muhammad Ali, and you're going to get into trouble legally in Japan. Get your ass back here now.'"

For what it's worth, Mike LeBell maintained that Vince didn't even come to Japan. Mike had just formed a joint company with Vince Senior, called the Atlantic and Pacific Wrestling Corporation, and the two were close. But, as LeBell later put it, "Vince McMahon, *Junior* didn't mean much to me at the time." Someday, not too far in the future, he would.

Whether Vince went to Japan or not, he wasn't present at Budokan on June 26, the day of the match. Perhaps that was lucky, as the whole thing was a debacle. Right to the very end, no one knew if it was going to be fixed or not. "It ends up with, we have no rules, we have no nothing," Arum recalls. "And the fight, itself, is a complete dud." Before the opening bell even finished ringing, Inoki dashed toward Ali and launched himself, feetfirst, at the champ. Ali sidestepped it and Inoki took another chance at a kick, missed, and landed on his back. Then he just lay there.

Inoki refused to stand. "Ali is running around: '*You yellow motherfucker! Get up and fight!*'" Arum recalls. "I mean, it was horrible." Inoki did get up and started a mix of play-fighting and actual attacks. At one point, Ali threw a punch and obviously missed Inoki, but Inoki went against the ropes as if he'd been hit, anyway. This sort of nonsense went on for fifteen rounds before Inoki, who had spikes in his shoes, kicked Ali's leg, causing it to gash and bleed. Gene LeBell mercifully called the fight a draw before the infuriated Japanese crowd could burn the place down.

Vince, far away at Shea Stadium, had, once again, failed. And, once again, it had been a failure that threatened his father's reputation and relationships. But all was not lost.

The marketing push had been great until the actual match—maybe, if you had actual high-quality content for a closed-circuit event, you could hit the jackpot. Arum suspects Vince was thinking along those lines: "I think that really introduced him to the fact that he could roll up the wrestling business and present it where you could get a tremendous amount of fans on a national basis."

On April 19, 1976, just two months before the Ali-Inoki match was set to occur, Vince and Linda declared bankruptcy, saying that they were around $1 million in debt.

In better news, they welcomed a daughter, Stephanie Marie McMahon, on September 24, a few months after the fight. She would grow up to become one of the stars of her father's programming, bathing in the hatred of crowds who would mercilessly chant "*Slut! Slut! Slut!*" at her. Undeterred by such treatment, she would go on to become a major WWE executive and ended up succeeding Vince as CEO. There would be no more children for Vince, as far as we know.

When Aldi, Vince's coinvestor and friend, looks back on Vince in the period of their friendship, he sees a "nice person, a no-bullcrap kinda guy." He expresses a sentiment that's common among most who reminisce about Vince, no matter how much trouble he may have gotten them into: "He was always driven."

But this was not yet the outlandishly boorish Vince of later fame and infamy. How else could he keep getting back up from the mat at this stage of his rise to power, if he weren't a charmer? "He was always a gentleman, Vince," Aldi says. "He could be tough, but he was always a gentleman."

Bob Arum agrees, in spite of all the grief young Vince caused him. "I have only the greatest respect for him, both as a showman and as a principled guy," Arum says. "You might not like what he says, but you can always trust in his honesty."

December 17, 1976, brought an ominous development: an up-and-coming media tycoon from Georgia by the name of Robert Edward "Ted" Turner III made his Atlanta-based TV station WTCG nationally available via a new force called satellite television. TBS (short for Turner Broadcasting System) was, as Turner dubbed it, a "superstation," and it beamed into living rooms of early adopters across America. When it arrived, it bore, among other things, a healthy helping of good old-fashioned "rasslin'," as the massive southern fan base often referred to the artform.

A cardinal rule of the industry had been quietly shattered beyond repair. Turner, in one fell swoop, had violated every televised territorial boundary. He had already been locally airing shows made by Jim Barnett's Georgia Championship Wrestling (GCW), and, now, wrestling fans anywhere around North America had that most sacred and dangerous of things: consumer choice.

Broadcasts that came through satellite TV or another developing technology, cable TV, were a growing concern for the NWA members. Vince Senior had already tested the waters: he'd started running monthly WWWF shows on regional—not national—cable in 1973 through a brand-new channel called Home Box Office (HBO), then through the newly founded Madison Square Garden Network. So he was ready when, in 1977, the latter channel spun off the Madison Square Garden Sports Network, eventually rebranded as the USA Network, which would be distributed nationally via cable. For the first time in two decades, the whole of America could, if they ponied up the cash for an installation, enjoy Vince Senior's offerings.

GCW and the WWWF had been grudgingly allowed by the NWA to move forward with their distribution leaps. It was a matter of kicking the can down the road: as of 1977, a small fraction of households actually had access to cable or satellite, making the question a lower priority than it would inevitably later become. But with every promoter now facing the prospect of Barnett's and Vince Senior's reach increasing, tensions were suddenly ramping up to levels not seen since the 1940s.

None of that seems to have bothered Vince much. The thirtysomething was still one of the main announcers for his father's company, and he was finding his voice—or, at least, *a* voice, as he would go on to have more than one of them. With a nasal, theatrical, nonregional baritone largely lifted from Howard Cosell of *Wide World of Sports*, Vince fulfilled his three jobs, which were to (1) keep the energy of the match flowing for the home audience, (2) do ringside or backstage "interviews" with the wrestlers to push story lines, and (3) reinforce kayfabe by describing the in-ring action with total (faked) sincerity.

If you listened very closely when he got excited, you could hear the faintest trace of a Tar Heel accent.

While doing play-by-play commentary, Vince wasn't uniquely electrifying, but he was more than competent, acting as a familiar narrator to countless viewers during a period when the WWWF was flush with talent and verve.

"Bobo, with a hard right hand!" he cried at a televised MSG match between wrestlers Bobo Brazil (Houston Harris) and Jerry "Crusher" Blackwell. "And Blackwell, still standing on his feet. Rocked back again, has Crusher Blackwell. Bobo, winding up, giving him another shot—down he'll go!" As the men tussled, Vince advanced the story with tepid analysis: "Before the match tonight in the Garden, Bobo claims that he really has it all together, probably more so than at any other time in his wrestling career," he said. "And, from what we're seeing at the moment, that's probably true."

More notable were the interview segments. They weren't exactly dialogues, per se. The questions in a kayfabe pro wrestling interview are mainly just a chance for the wrestlers to preen and shout, delivering monologued threats to their foes in order to promote future matches—"cutting a promo," in the argot of the trade. If the wrestler wasn't so articulate, or even if he was, then some shit-talking would often be performed by a non-combatant "manager," typically an ex-wrestler or an industry hanger-on. Vince would offer a prompt ("Do you have anything to say to your opponent?" or the like) and then react to whatever was said.

He wasn't stellar at it. "In a TV show that was filled with really strange people, he was one of the strangest," recalls journalist Ray Tennenbaum, who grew up watching Vince throughout the 1970s. "He didn't seem that great at his job, and he didn't seem very comfortable holding the mic; he seemed a little bit embarrassed about it."

Vince's look was a key part of the strangeness: "He was basically as tall as the wrestlers, and he always looked like a bodybuilder wearing a suit," Tennenbaum recalls. "The suits, I couldn't really tell if they were designed to emphasize his shoulders or if he bought them off the rack and the fabric just kind of draped off him."

While interviewing heels—one of the biggest was Gorilla Monsoon

(Robert Marella)—Vince would telegraph disdain for their vanity and cruelty. "He'd adopt this indignation and disgust," as Tennenbaum puts it. "It was hilarious. When he had to interview a heel, he could just spit out the wrestler's name: *Gorilla Monsewwwwn*."

Tennenbaum says the faux-outrage meant Vince was hogging the spotlight and throwing off the natural energy of a promo. He contrasts Vince with AWA announcer "Mean" Gene Okerlund: "That's one of the reasons why Okerlund was a better announcer: because Okerlund played it like a journalist," Tennenbaum says. "Whereas Vince was, like, the arbiter of righteousness."

It's important to remember that, as of the late 1970s, Vince still held no real power in the wrestling industry. He was feared by no one. Some reports say he was the one behind the shortening of the WWWF's initials by one "W," making it the World Wrestling Federation, or WWF, in 1979. But there is no available proof of his influence on that matter. However, that doesn't mean he wasn't paying attention, nor that he was without ambition elsewhere.

He was still doing local promoting for his dad in New England and, around the same time as the corporate name change, he booked a show at the Cape Cod Coliseum of South Yarmouth, Massachusetts. In doing so, he spoke with the venue's owner and eventually landed on an idea: What if he and Linda bought the place outright? The couple scrounged up the cash to do it and were in control by the summer of 1979. A little later, they bought the local hockey team, the Cape Cod Buccaneers. They ran both entities under the aegis of a new company they formed. They called it Titan Sports.

Vince and Linda decamped to South Yarmouth with their kids. Among their first achievements was bringing the Boston Bruins hockey team to the Coliseum for their first-ever appearance in Cape Cod. Historically, the Coliseum had only hosted events during the summer, when the Cape fills up with people, but Vince and Linda changed course and started booking year-round. They hired the venue's first marketing director in an effort to drum up excitement. Most controversially, Vince and Linda brought rock concerts back to the Coliseum for the first time after a too-wild Ted Nugent show held by the previous owner had led to an informal ban.

There was resistance from citizens and businesses who said out-of-control audiences were wreaking havoc in their revelry. Vince was unsympathetic to calls for reinstating the ban. "There's not anything to say I can't do anything," he told a local paper, "as long as it's in good taste."

Shane and Stephanie were catching early glimpses of their father's line of work. Shane has said he started working on the cleanup crew after concerts when he was eleven, then graduated to manual labor at the WWF. In that same period, Stephanie had her first encounter with a wrestler: Vince had taken his three-year-old girl backstage at a wrestling show, and the hirsute and feral George "The Animal" Steele (Jim Myers) grunted in her direction, terrifying her.

"I ran straight for my father's arms—the safest place I knew—and he just laughed out loud," Stephanie would later recall. "He thought it was the funniest thing."

However, Vince himself has indicated that his relationship with his kids wasn't always a breeze. "I'm a disciplinarian," he told a reporter in 2005. "I'm real big on respect. I was on the road a lot. And I'm sure when I was at home, the kids wanted me back on the road." He didn't elaborate further.

The key moment of Vince and Linda's time on the Cape came in early 1981. Their various changes had worked local officials and politicians into an angry froth, and there had been attempts to rein them in via a modification of their licenses. The biggest proposed change was going to severely limit sales of alcohol—a move that the McMahons thought would be disastrous. So, for the first time in their lives, Vince and Linda got into politics.

On January 27, they hit the town legislators—they're called selectmen there—with a stunning show of force at the final hearing on the licensing matter. "The hearing brought out the largest crowd of spectators to a Yarmouth's selectmen's meeting in recent history," a local news item declared. "Over 150 supporters of the Cape Cod Coliseum filled the town hall hearing room . . . and lined the basement steps to hear the board's decision. . . .

"Four hours later," the paper continued, "when the smoke had cleared and the selectmen had voted on five motions concerning the Coliseum licenses, owners Vince and Linda McMahon left the hearing with fewer formal restrictions on their operations than had been in effect at the beginning of the meeting."

Whether or not their tactic of collective intimidation was what swayed the selectmen, the result was a stunning victory for the McMahons. The town fully ceded decision making on an array of matters—most importantly, which events should or shouldn't be alcohol-free—to Vince and Linda. The couple had achieved the businessman's dream of self-regulation, and not for the last time.

These Cape Cod years were a turning point for Vince. They were his first taste of life as an honest-to-God business owner.

The businessman Vince admired most, Vince Senior, had troubles of his own. The peace between the promotions was cracking.

Turner's TBS was a hit. By early 1981, Jim Barnett leveraged GCW's national visibility into shows in Ohio, Michigan, and West Virginia—all defunct or dying territories that were ripe for the plucking. The expansion fell apart due to financial mismanagement, but a precedent had been set, and the NWA had been unable to stop it. The year 1981 also saw the AWA invade the San Francisco Bay Area, Salt Lake City, and Las Vegas. Adding to the chaos was the retirement of the aging, long-standing, beloved president of the NWA, Sam Muchnick. The threads that held the system together were being torn asunder, one by one.

Paradoxically, wrestling was also more popular than it had been in decades. Memphis wrestling titan Jerry Lawler had a much publicized, reality-bending feud with popular mainstream actor/comedian Andy Kaufman, bringing a great deal of attention and outré hipness to the artform. The blockbuster film *Rocky III* prominently featured the titular boxer in an Ali-Inoki-style mixed-rules match against a blindingly blond wrestler, played by an up-and-comer who went by the name Hulk Hogan. Wrestling was a rumbling volcano, as hot as it was volatile.

But Vince Senior, nearing age sixty-eight, was tired. After nearly forty years in the wrestling industry, he was thinking of calling it quits. In Vince's telling, the WWF "was making more money than it had ever made, and so my dad was thinking, *It just can't get any better than this*. And he was looking to get out."

But that didn't mean he was planning to leave the company to his son. Remarkably, Vince Senior had never designated Vince as his corporate successor. It was up to Vince to come to his father and propose that he be the next owner of the WWF. Vince Senior was reluctant. He eventually told Vince he'd allow the sale, but, in typical fashion, he wasn't overly kind to his child. Vince would have to pay $1 million ($822,132 of it to

Vince Senior, himself) in a series of four payments to Vince Senior and the WWF's three minority shareholders over the course of the year—and, if he couldn't make all of them, the existing ownership would keep both the company *and* whatever money Vince had already paid.

Vince has been vague about how, exactly, he raised the cash to make these payments. He would later tell a reporter that he obtained the sums "by using mirrors" with the help of a "guru" and a "real sharp guy." However it happened, Vince seems to have pulled the money together and, in a meeting that was kept surreptitious so as not to rattle the industry, went to New York to get to brass tacks with Vince Senior and the shareholders.

On June 5, 1982, they signed the documents, the first payment was made, and Vince became the lord-in-waiting of the empire that his forebears had built throughout the previous century. He had been raised with nothing. Now, he stood to gain everything.

Vince was about to smash up the smoke-filled room of honorable thieves and back-channel cooperation that Vince Senior had respected and thrived in.

"I knew my dad wouldn't have really sold me the business," Vince would later say, "had he known what I was going to do."

4

GET OVER, ACT I
(1982–1984)

O kay, get out your notebooks," the essay began. "This here is lecture time. Wrestling Goes Mainstream. An outcome that is vile, it's loath-some, it may even cause cancer—don't laugh, this is *serious*."

The writer was Richard Meltzer, one of the first critics to probe rock music in a literary mode, a musician who cowrote more than a dozen songs for Blue Öyster Cult, and a former wrestling diehard (no relation to wrestling journalist Dave Meltzer, who we'll get to later).

It was 1985, three years into Vince's reign as owner of the WWF, and Meltzer had a slate of grievances to bring against contemporary wrestling, which he listed in the manner of the authors of the Declaration of Inde-pendence laying charges against King George:

"I HOLD THESE TRUTHS TO BE SELF-EVIDENT . . ."

He bemoaned the increasingly chiseled bodies of the performers: "What we're faced with is Slob Disenfranchisement of the most nefarious ilk."

He bristled at the promotion's newly tacky visual aesthetic: "seamless, sanitized, canned-featured, digitally animated, color-commentated, slo-mo'ed and SLICK."

He sneered at the fact that the industry's "current sense of market is defined wholly and simply by that lowest of common Denoms: children, hipsters, and morons," and that such folks were "principally Caucasian."

These hated alterations were the direct result of young Vince Mc-Mahon's ascent: "With the WWF running, basically, the whole entire show, and the NWA, AWA, etc. reduced *collectively* to less than a sliver of the pie, wrestling's once mighty Pluralism—its infrastructural one-up on all-American athleto-monistic hooey—has been sent the way of the horse, the buggy, the Bill of Rights."

Though the complaints were wide-ranging, they all flowed from Meltzer's primary point: "Wrestling has gone from being something *uniquely* fake, *archetypally* fake, paradigmatically *fake for real*, to something non-ironically fake per se, standardly fake like Everything is fake: movies, TV, 'real' sports, fashion trends, heart transplants, national elections."

These were not Barthes's operatic wrestling epiphanies. Something was rotten in the state of kayfabe.

"The Last Wrestling Piece," published in *The San Diego Reader*, is a revealing document of its time. Today, the WWF of the 1980s is regularly remembered by fans—and official WWE narratives—as a kind of Golden Age, a period when wrestling was huge, the wrestlers even huger, and the content comparatively wholesome. But, at the time, Meltzer's point of view was common: the WWF was regarded by wide swaths of wrestling's existing audience as a disruptive and destructive force—the beginning of the end for the Business.

So, too, was it regarded by the industry's ruling class. Other promoters did their level best to halt the rocket-boosted steamroller that was the younger Vince McMahon, a man they'd previously thought of in generally the same way the schoolkids in North Carolina had regarded him: as a barely noticed nonentity. He'd been a mere commentator, only there by the grace of his admired father. But, within a decade, Vince had toppled or assimilated all but one of the major promotions. Within two decades, there were no competitors left.

Vince was not the only person changing the face of wrestling in the 1980s. In the official WWE story, he is always held up as the singular force revolutionizing the industry in that period, but, like most conquistadors, he benefited from certain events beyond his control. And other promoters, too, exploited new technology, came up with dynamic new ideas, and trained charismatic performers. Their achievements were not enough to stop Vince.

Indeed, he tended to simply incorporate others' concepts and talent into his own strategy, exploit them more effectively than their inventors had, and take the lion's share of the credit after victory. He eroded institutions. He deceived and dissembled. He played upon resentments and divisions among his rivals. He eagerly sold the golden calves of glitz, glamour, and Reaganite hyper-patriotism. He befriended Donald Trump. In other words, it was in the 1980s that Vince found out he could win at life by becoming an archetypal rich yuppie.

As Richard Meltzer put it in his essay, "All that's going on is Vince Jr. performing insidious thus-&-such with [wrestling's] legitimate mass popularity at its base, structurally redistributing the remaining world's access to its variables & whatnot 'til he gets to have it All and Then Some—conspicuously." It was morning in America.

But we're getting ahead of ourselves.

Back on June 5, 1982, not long after signing the paperwork to take over the WWF, Vince slid into the announcer's chair at Madison Square Garden.

The show that night would be shot for a live airing of *Madison Square Garden Presents*, meaning Vince's voice would be heard live around the country via cable and satellite. He was flying solo that night, by himself in the booth, talking to the viewers at home. The wrestling nuts of the Northeast, by now long familiar with Vince's awkward cadences, would hear a voice that betrayed no more excitement than usual.

But what did he feel as he narrated the action? Only about half a dozen people on Planet Earth knew about the deal he'd just made, and only he knew what he truly wanted to do in its wake. For the first time in his life, Vince alone saw the full picture; everyone else was playing catch-up.

Did he put thoughts of ownership aside so he could more effectively call the matches? Or was he consciously thinking of it as a survey of the kingdom he now had on lease? The show featured a representative sample of the company's top talent—he may have been sizing up people he now saw as subordinate to him.

On the microphone, Vince described what he saw, which was a wide-ranging showcase of grapplers, many of them legends or legends-to-be, who had just become both his boons and his burdens. The show was, indeed, a perfect snapshot of the state of the company: its cast and its aesthetic; its politics, its poetics, its perils.

As had long been true in wrestling, especially Vince's dad's brand of it, there were heaping helpings of ethnic pageantry, designed to rile the crowd up at either end of the cheer-boo spectrum. A grappler named Ivan Putski (born Józef Bednarski in Kraków) drew huge cheers with his rallying slogan of "Polish Power"; his opponent was a stereotypically sinister and enigmatic Japanese heel named Masanori Saito, who just went by "Mr. Saito" in the ring.

Native American hero Chief Jay Strongbow fought in a tag team alongside his brother, Jules, though, in reality, they were neither Native nor related—their birth names were Luke Scarpa and Francis Huntington.

Most beloved of all the racial caricatures was Jimmy "Superfly" Snuka, a high-flying daredevil from the nation of Fiji (really) who had just joined in January. His thick, curly hair draped down the sides of his head, framing his stoic face. He was muscular and graceful, but was marketed as a kind of real-life Tarzan, complete with a leopard-print loincloth.

These were archetypes that Vince and his audience could understand and embrace.

That night, Snuka went up against WWF champion Bob Backlund, and the crowd had lucratively mixed feelings about the wild man from the South Pacific. They loved to boo him because he was great at playing the heel, but as soon as he began his ascent of one of the ring posts, the crowd couldn't help but lose their minds with cheers, knowing he was about to execute one of his patented, death-defying leaps onto his opponent.

"Mr. Snuka, at the top rope," Vince called as Snuka stood up straight atop the post and raised his hands. Snuka jumped, flipped a somersault in midair, and just barely missed a prostrated Backlund, who had rolled out of the way. "Wow, *unbelievable!*" Vince shouted, overloading the microphone.

In another match, the Strongbows played the faces against heel team Adrian Adonis (Keith Franke) and Jesse "The Body" Ventura. Ventura was an eccentric and imposing military vet (he never saw combat, but would later tell a reporter, "Until you have hunted man, you haven't hunted yet") with a strange Midwestern drawl that accented every vowel to within an inch of its life. Constantly admiring his own male form and clad in colorful scarves and tops that would look right at home in a contemporary gay bar, but ostensibly heterosexual, Ventura was a perfect example of wrestling's long-standing and uneasy détente between machismo and camp. Less than two decades later, he would become governor of Minnesota.

Speaking of tag teams, gender roles, and power: there was only one women's match that night. So-called ladies' wrestling had a long and intermittently glorious history in North America, but it had been languishing for decades. The most commonly identified culprit for holding it back was a combatant that night: fifty-eight-year-old Lillian Ellison, better known as "The Fabulous Moolah."

A stout, scowling arch-heel, she had for about thirty years been the de facto dictator of women's wrestling, and had left deep scars on the younger women she both trained and undermined. She would eventually partner with Vince to execute a scheme that effectively marked the end of women's wrestling as a serious form until well after her death.

"Boy," Vince observed as she gained the upper hand in the MSG match, "that Moolah is *crafty!*"

And, both literally and figuratively towering above them all, there was André. The greatest attraction that the WWF had access to as of that night was André Roussimoff, a seven-foot-plus child of Bulgarian and Polish immigrants to France who had been plucked from rural obscurity by a French wrestling promoter in 1964, then had moved to the US to work for Vince Senior in 1973. It was Vince Senior who first started billing the quarter-ton Roussimoff as "André the Giant."

Like some kind of antediluvian titan, André would wander the ring, gravity preventing him from doing much in the way of acrobatics. An insurmountable accent kept him from making much sense on the microphone during interviews. There are stories of him consuming three to five bottles of wine a day, or however much it took to get drunk in defiance of his size and tolerance. Wrestlers still tell of watching him drink upward of a hundred beers in a single sitting. He was a few months younger than Vince, but André the Giant always seemed like an ancient myth—and, indeed, his nickname was "The Eighth Wonder of the World." His pure-hearted persona and inconceivable size made him a sensation, arguably the most famous wrestler on earth.

That night, André battled Blackjack Mulligan (Robert Windham), who looked diminutive in comparison at just six-foot-nine. For the first nine minutes, they traded chops, throws, and holds, with André eventually "juicing" (that is, covertly and purposefully bloodying) his own forehead, turning himself into a plasma-faced mess. After a referee disqualified both combatants, they continued to brawl outside the ring.

"André, coming right after him, my *goodness!*" Vince bellowed into the mic as the crowd screamed with delight. André then turned to some classic wrestling props: the trusty steel folding chairs stacked at ringside. "André *throws* in a chair!" Vince screamed. "Another one! André is *angry!* He's throwing things *all* around! André has gone *berserk! André has gone berserk!*"

These were the pieces on Vince's board; the army with which he would build his empire.

But he would not be building that empire alone—at least not yet.

For the next year, Vince would *not* be the sole person in charge of the WWF. Vince Senior was still the top dog, not a lame duck. Until Vince was in full control, whatever the younger man wanted to do, he had to do with Vince Senior's approval.

Over the following months, the two men would repeatedly clash behind the scenes over Vince's expansionism. But at the outset, their philosophies were more in sync than one might believe. Vince Senior, in fact, had already made a stab in the direction of territorial expansion.

Back in March of 1982, when Vince Senior was still unambiguously in charge, he had purchased a TV slot in the Buffalo market. The small promotion that had been operating there had gone under. Other companies tried to take up a presence, but they'd failed. Vince Senior's purchase of the TV slot was his attempt to plant a flag in upstate New York—and, through the magic of terrestrial broadcast television, viewers in Toronto could get a sampling of his product, too.

A few months later, the WWF made its move. On August 9, the company triumphantly returned to Buffalo with a live show featuring, among others, Putski, Saito, and—quite literally flying above them all—Snuka. Other than André, no one was a bigger draw. Vince had dreams for that man.

The WWF had made its first expansion since Vince had cut the deal with his father, and it had been a total success. Vince Senior had no reason to be displeased.

Vince's next advance, too, was gentle, and perfectly in line with Vince Senior's dealings. Mike LeBell, the Los Angeles promoter who had helped out on the Ali-Inoki disaster, was generally regarded as a supremely unpleasant and dishonest man, even by the standards of his profession. As Freddie Blassie put it in his memoir, "Even during the best of times, I was always waiting for [LeBell] to put a hatchet in my back. I feel pretty confident saying that every wrestler in the territory felt the same way. Because of all the publicity we got in L.A., you'd wind up with the press clippings while he wound up with the money."

Despite, or maybe because of, LeBell's rapaciousness, Vince Senior had been close with him. Their jointly owned Atlantic and Pacific Wrestling Corporation had been built in 1976 so they could share talent, data, and money, and the two men reportedly spoke multiple times every week.

However, LeBell was cash-strapped by the time Vince called him in 1982 with a proposal. They met for coffee at O'Hare International Airport in Chicago, midway between their two bases of operations, and talked business. By meeting's end, LeBell had reluctantly agreed to let Vince buy the Southern California territory outright.

The McMahon wrestling outfit, which had always been a Northeastern operation, was now bicoastal. NWA members were concerned about what this meant for the balance of power, of course. But they had other worries to distract them.

At the syndicate's annual meeting, held that year in Puerto Rico, the hottest topic was cable and satellite superstations. Ted Turner's TBS was still the biggest of them, bringing Georgia Championship Wrestling to the nation. In August 1982, their show even got a flashy new name: *World Championship Wrestling*.

Unbeknownst to viewers, GCW was racked by internal division between co-owner Jim Barnett and Ole Anderson, who was his "booker"— the guy given the weighty task of mapping out story lines and deciding who was going to beat whom. They each represented much about the questionable morals of the NWA.

Barnett was a bespectacled nonwrestler from Oklahoma City with a business degree and a somewhat openly gay lifestyle. He had been among the most powerful promoters of the preceding decade. He developed a reputation as a colorful, beloved personality, a friend of celebrities, and a pathbreaker for gay men in the athletics industry.

Anderson (born Alan Robert Rogowski), by contrast, was a deeply disliked ex-wrestler—"Ole was a true curmudgeon; he very much liked to bully people," is how one former colleague put it to me.

That said, the beloved Barnett had also been accused of running an informal brothel during the early 1960s, in which he induced college football players to have sex with himself and others—including actor Rock Hudson. It's hard to find a blameless man in wrestling.

At the 1982 Puerto Rico NWA meetup, Barnett told the members that the decision to take GCW national had been undertaken by Turner, not him, and that he wasn't as sanguine about superstations. Whether or not that claim was true, and whether or not it had been a good decision on Turner's part, Barnett now offered to use this new exposure to boost wrestlers from other promotions who wanted to do guest slots. Anderson, meanwhile, was on board with Turner's expansion and quietly seethed at his business partner.

Chaos was growing. The promoters of the weakened West Texas territory attempted their own risky expansion elsewhere in California, but poor management doomed the effort, and the company went under, leaving the area up for grabs. WWF, GCW, Southern Championship Wrestling, World Class Championship Wrestling, and Global Wrestling were all reported to be eyeing those areas hungrily.

The wrestling-TV landscape was racked with earthquakes. Southwest Championship Wrestling scored a show that debuted on cable's USA Network. New Year's Day 1983 brought the debut of the WWF on local Southern California TV. A week later, it was announced that the WWF had secured a slot on an Akron station, thus opening the door for an invasion of Ohio. It was going to be a bumpy year.

Barnett became an unlikely ally, helping the WWF stage its first Ohio show in February. Though he still co-owned the WWF's chief rival, he had halfway defected to aid Vince, all in an effort to undermine Turner and Anderson, both of whom he loathed and distrusted. Vince benefited from corporate treason.

Vince's assertion of power was on full display March 5, when his WWF made its Southern California live debut with a show in San Diego. André was the scripted victor in a seventeen-man "battle royal," a type of match where a crowd of wrestlers all duke it out at once, throwing each other out of the ring until only one man remains. The next day brought a show in L.A. where André beat *eighteen* men. The SoCal coup de grâce came when they returned to the region for a show at the L.A. Sports Arena on April 23, at which Vince's stable of fighters—especially Snuka—electrified a crowd of 5,500 people.

Vince must have been elated about that L.A. show. He's said time and again that the main thing he loves about his business is the incomparable rush that comes from satisfying consumers in the most spectacular way possible. "The biggest thrill in the world is entertaining the public; there is no bigger thrill than that," Vince once told a wrestling magazine. That quotation, with full attribution to Vince, would one day be tweeted out by Donald Trump.

★ ★ ★

On the all-too-common occasions when wrestlers die of wrestling-related causes—painkiller overdose, steroid-related organ failure, traumatic brain injury, in-ring snafu, and the like—the wrestling community has a tendency to write the deaths off as the cost of the lifestyle. Amid the grief, there's a voice in the backs of fans' and colleagues' minds, telling them that the deceased knew what they were getting into when they sold their bodies to the Business. *C'est la vie, c'est la guerre*, the voice says.

But only a true sadist would assert that wrestlers' dead wives and girlfriends had it coming.

Nancy Argentino was born and raised in Brooklyn. Her parents, working-class Catholics, adored her. "My younger sister and I always say that Nancy was the favorite because she never gave my mother a hard time," her older sister, Lorraine Salome, has said. Nancy was "a very intelligent girl" and "she always had a job," Salome added, but also pointed out that she "was very innocent. Even though we lived in a big city, she lived a sheltered life."

Argentino had been working as a dental assistant when a friend of hers started dating a WWF wrestler named Johnny Rodz (John Rodriguez). Though Nancy had never had any interest in wrestling, she started attending shows with her pal at MSG, and Rodz introduced them to the Boys backstage. Argentino was a classically beautiful woman, and the handsome Snuka—who was, unbeknownst to her, married—quickly took an interest in her.

In short order, the pair started dating and she became his driver and chaperone. Still fresh on the WWF roster, Snuka was already a mess: his previous handler, Buddy Rogers, later told a reporter that Snuka was hooked on cocaine and other drugs, making him difficult to control. And now, he was her mess.

Their romance was, as one might expect, turbulent. On January 18, 1983, just over a week after the WWF had announced its expansion into the Ohio market, officers responded to reports of a loud, physical fight between two guests at a motel in Salina, New York. Upon arriving, the cops and their attack dogs had a hell of a time trying to subdue Snuka, who was six feet tall and weighed more than 225 pounds.

As local paper *The Morning Call* reported in a 2013 reinvestigation of the case, an officer said Snuka grabbed Argentino by the hair when she ran out of the room and dragged her face against the drywall. Her officially listed injuries included a contusion in her neck, possible fractured ribs, and an injury to her lower back. Snuka was charged with assault and resisting arrest.

Although Vince wasn't morally bothered enough by the charges to fire his cash cow, the grappler was nonetheless putting his boss in a tight spot. According to another reinvestigation of the incident, one by wrestling journalist David Bixenspan, Argentino had been planning to pursue charges against Snuka. However, she abruptly opted to sign an affidavit claiming she was "in no way seeking prosecution" against him.

Why? Part of the answer may lie in a police report about Argentino that Bixenspan uncovered. It states, "Vince McMahon tried to talk her out of making the complaint against Snuka."

In April, the wrestler took a deal in which he pleaded guilty to harassment in exchange for all the other charges being dropped. Snuka donated $1,500 to Ronald McDonald House Charities and walked away a free man.

On Sunday, May 8, Argentino called her mom to wish her a happy Mother's Day and say she'd swing by the family home sometime soon. She never did.

What happened next is a matter of dispute. The WWF used to tape several weeks' worth of episodes of their flagship TV show at once, on one marathon day, every third week. For efficiency's sake, the tapings happened at fixed venues, and, at this point in WWF history, most were done in the small Pennsylvania city of Allentown. What we know for sure is that there was a taping on May 10; that Snuka and Argentino were staying at the George Washington Motor Lodge in Whitehall, just outside of Allentown; and that paramedics responded to a call from Snuka about an injured woman there just before midnight. They found Argentino unconscious and near death, her sculpted boyfriend at her side.

Initially, Snuka said they had been in some kind of physical scuffle. "I had to basically drag things out of him," recalled paramedic Shirley Reeve, "and he just said that they must have wrestled a little bit too much the night before, when he pushed her over and she had hit her head." He claimed she had seemed fine until about twenty-four hours later, when he came back from his matches and saw she was having difficulty breathing, at which point, he said, he had called for an ambulance.

He told this version of the story to three employees at the emergency room of Lehigh Valley Hospital. Finally, he told it to the hospital chaplain; Argentino had died at 1:50 a.m.

The coroner recommended a police interview. Some cops took Snuka back to the hotel room for questioning around 9 a.m. Snuka's in-ring rival and real-life compatriot, Don Muraco, who had been staying at the same motel, allegedly called Vince and found the boss two steps ahead. "Vince says, 'Have you heard anything about Snuka and his girlfriend?'" Muraco later recalled. "I said, 'As a matter of fact, here I am with Lt. So-and-So,' and I put him on the phone to Vince."

The potential for scandal—dead girl, live wrestler, previous incident, blind eye turned—was enormous. Vince was less than a month away from securing ownership of his father's company, and now it was all in jeopardy.

To make matters worse, Snuka changed his story in that morning confab. This time, he told the police that he had been driving with Argentino in the early hours of the previous morning, that she'd needed to relieve herself in some roadside bushes, and that she'd slipped and hit her head on the pavement while coming back to the car.

A wrestler who was trying to defend Snuka would, decades later, inadvertently undermine this story when he told a documentary crew that he was in the car with them that early morning and had no recollection of the roadside incident.

But that was the story Snuka held on to for the rest of his life, and he never offered a satisfying answer as to why he'd said anything different beforehand.

Vince had no interest in antagonizing the cops. At that point in his career, he had severely proscribed clout within wrestling, and virtually none outside of it. So the WWF cooperated, as police records and later interviews demonstrated. But significant questions remain about what happened between Vince and the authorities.

Whatever Vince said over the phone to the police that morning must have been persuasive, as Snuka was released without charges. A few weeks later, while the Argentinos mourned and raged, Snuka returned to TV. He and Muraco were in the middle of a feud in the story line of the WWF, and no one at the company stopped the money train. Muraco later said he was worried about a potential murder investigation "just out of my own selfish motivation, you know? I didn't wanna lose my golden goose, because there was a lot of money down the road to be made."

Argentino's younger sister, Louise Argentino, would later recall that Vince or one of his proxies (she didn't remember the name and just called him Snuka's "promoter") called Argentino's mother not long after her daughter was buried. "Mrs. Argentino, I'm so sorry for your loss," the sister remembered him saying. "Do you think $25,000 would help you?" The mother hung up on him.

The evidence against Snuka was enormous: in addition to all of the above factors, an autopsy had resulted in the medical examiner concluding, "I believe that the case should be investigated as a homicide until proven otherwise." So Vince and Snuka walked into a meeting with the district attorney, the assistant district attorney, the medical examiner, and various police officers on the case on June 1. It was the very day he was set to make his final payment on the WWF purchase.

The rest of the case proceedings were detailed extensively in police records, but, notably, the official record of what happened in that fateful meeting contains no information about what Vince said. The then–assistant district attorney, Robert Steinberg, later recalled that Vince "did all the talking": "I remember Vince McMahon being what Vince McMahon has always been—very effusive," he told a newspaper reporter during a later reinvestigation. "A showman."

More crucially, we have Snuka's account of what happened.

Snuka was a good soldier. "Jimmy talked to me a lot about Vince—he called him 'Brother Vinnie,'" Snuka's third wife would later say. "And Jimmy felt very close to Vince, and he trusted him one hundred percent." Illiterate in English, he would endorse anything Vince put in front of him. As the wife put it, "He would sign papers and he had no idea what they said."

Once again, Snuka ceded the legal thinking to Vince. The wrestler had a brief account of the June 1 meeting in his 2012 memoir, and this handful of sentences has fascinated wrestling conspiracy theorists ever since:

At one point, I went with Vince McMahon Jr. to either a court or law office, I don't remember which because I was still in shock. All I remember is he had a briefcase with him. I don't know what happened. I think Vince Jr. picked me up from the hotel and took me there. He didn't say anything to me.

Much speculation has been made about the briefcase that Snuka recalls Vince bringing to the table. Vince has never been known as a carrier of briefcases (at least when he's not using them to beat someone up on television), so, if he had one that day, it certainly raises the question of what was in it. Whatever it was, it was helpful: no charges were filed and Snuka never served a day of prison time for the rest of his life.

Though there is, perhaps, a perverse thrill in imagining that Vince paid off a police department and district attorney to cover up a murder, one shouldn't underestimate petty misogyny's ability to scuttle a domestic violence investigation.

I called up Fred Conjour, who was Whitehall's chief of police during the investigation. He wasn't at the meeting with Vince and the DA, so he balked on discussing it, and he added that "nobody really knows, exactly, what happened when [Argentino] got injured."

He went on: "I don't wanna sound unsympathetic," he told me, but Argentino "had been running around with Snuka for a number of years and had had problems with him, but continued to stay with him. That's not a news story, I guess, but it certainly doesn't paint her as an innocent victim."

The death of Nancy Argentino isn't new information in wrestling. Wrestlers are inveterate gossips; everyone knew she'd died under suspicious circumstances and that she'd been with Snuka when the sirens started wailing.

But kayfabe applies outside of the ring, too, and you can always pretend—to yourself and others—that you don't see what's in front of you.

When Snuka put out his memoir, it was filled to the brim with praise from wrestling personalities: a foreword by "Rowdy" Roddy Piper, an introduction by Mick Foley, and declarations of praise from Gene Okerlund, Kurt Angle, Jeff Hardy, Tommy Dreamer, and other boldfaced names from WWE.

Only after a reinvestigation of Argentino's death led to new murder and involuntary manslaughter charges in 2015 did WWE quietly remove him from their Hall of Fame. The case ended when Snuka, mentally and physically decayed after his decades in the ring, was found unfit to stand trial.

When Snuka died at age seventy-three in 2017, WWE aired a tender tribute to him, set to a melancholy song about saying goodbye to a loved one. Dozens of WWE wrestlers past and present—including Dwayne "The Rock" Johnson, Roman Reigns, and Snuka's own daughter, Tamina, who had been put on the WWE roster a few years prior—tweeted out their adoration and grief.

"#RIPSuperfly one of the greatest icons in the history of our business," read a tweet from Stephanie McMahon's account. "Sending our love and prayers to the entire family."

Vince, nearly thirty-eight, made that final payment on June 1, 1983. He was officially the owner of the WWF—though you wouldn't know it from the company's televised shows, where he was still in kayfabe as the mere ringside announcer.

Vince Senior was still a member of the NWA board of directors, so he wasn't quite retired, but the familial torch had been sold to his second-born son.

Vince and Linda still owned the Cape Cod Coliseum, but in 1983, they moved to Greenwich, Connecticut.

The next year, Cape Cod's *Barnstable Patriot* reported that Vince and Linda had, without public warning, agreed to sell the Coliseum to Christmas Tree Shops, a retail chain.

"The 7,000-seat rink and concert hall will become warehousing and office space," the reporter wrote. The area would have no more hockey games, rock shows, or the like. It would not be the last time a McMahon concern was sold for parts.

Nevertheless, Linda told the paper, "I think the Coliseum has very definitely succeeded." Just three years after they had scored a bully's victory over the government of South Yarmouth to support their arena business there, the endeavor was an afterthought.

Greenwich was not a place the McMahons would lose interest in; as of this writing, they are still living there. Shane and Stephanie would live out the rest of their youth there, luxury having returned to the McMahon child-rearing process after skipping Vince and Rod's generation. Shane—who would later satirize himself on TV for thinking the "mean streets of Greenwich" made him fearsome—was evolving into a wannabe tough guy. At age thirteen, he graduated from the inside crew to working in the WWF's warehouse, but started working for a brick mason after he and his father reached an impasse: "I wanted to get a raise—but my dad said no," Shane later said. "And I was just like, 'OK.'"

We know less about young Stephanie, who has rarely discussed her childhood—she takes after her mother in her commitment to privacy about her personal life. However, early in her on-screen career, she spoke to the in-house WWF magazine and said, "When I was younger, I was a little bit of a ham, and I used to dance. I took ballet, jazz, tap, point—everything. That was extra-curricular, as well as playing sports in school." But, she hastened to add, "My first love, first and foremost, has always been the World Wrestling Federation."

Though Vince was, in many contexts, the corporate face of the re-vamped WWF, one should not discount the degree to which the megaloma-nia was a collaboration. Vince and Linda's dealmaking and administration were like the songwriting of John Lennon and Paul McCartney: you can never really know who was responsible for what.

"There's no question about who runs the business," said a CEO with whom Linda dealt in this period. "She was the primary negotiator and dealmaker. We had one conceptual meeting with Vince up in Stamford. The rest were with Linda. She takes strong positions on things she really knows about, but she has a wonderful temperament. She's quite at odds with what every man feels happens at the WWF."

It may well be that Linda was the genius who found the cash for all the expensive endeavors that the WWF had undertaken. Her role was not exactly hidden, but its details were obscure.

That said, by all accounts, it seems that Vince was, indeed, the driving *creative* force at the time, as he had no staff of writers at his disposal. At this point, he was the sole booker. Vince Senior felt that his son needed assistance, so, from his home in Florida, the elder McMahon called up a Canadian ex-wrestler and booker named George Scott and asked him to help Vince out. But, at the outset, Vince just sent Scott down to Atlanta to manage a scheme he was plotting in Georgia.

Vince was the first booker for his version of the WWF, and he re-mained the last word on all booking until his brief resignation four de-cades later. The details of Vince's interactions with his father in this period are hidden from view, but the fact that the father fixed his son up with Scott, and that the son then shuffled Scott away, implies that their visions were already clashing.

Wrestlers, too, had deep trepidations about Vince becoming the boss. "At first, when he took over, some of the talent was going nuts," wrote Vince confidant Pat Patterson in his memoir. "*The kid is going to kill the business. The kid doesn't know what he's doing.* I heard it more than a few times."

There was reason to fear the instability Vince was creating. After all, the workers were already toiling in one of the most precarious professions in the American workforce.

Informed government regulation of wrestling has never existed in America. There has never been a union for wrestlers. Wrestlers are not staffers; everything is freelance. There is no off-season. There is no employer-provided health insurance. The travel is relentless. In lieu of serious medical care, this physically grueling ecosystem has historically been a free-for-all of drink and drugs to ease the pain and bulk the body—all of it permitted by promoters. And the pay, as one might expect, is terrible in comparison to every other athletic industry of its size.

So, why bother? Here lies one of the grand, tragic ironies of wrestling: much like with ballet, in order to achieve success as a wrestler, you have to want it to a degree that is both inspiring and objectively unhealthy. You have to love it more than you love your own body and mind. Your love has to overcome your instincts for self-preservation, let alone self-interest. That love, once it burns, is hard to snuff out. It's the love that comes from athletic achievement and the gratitude of the audience, yes, but it's more than that.

"See, what a lot of people don't understand is, once you step in that ring, you're addicted," is how a former WWF grappler named Princess Victoria (Vickie Otis) once put it. Those words could be comfortably placed in the mouth of any wrestler. There's a particular chemistry, perhaps even a magic, in acting out a thrill-packed, physically exhausting pantomime of the human experience to thunderous cheers and boos. People talk about wrestling characters as successors to the flamboyant, archetypal gods of ancient myth. Imagine a job that lets you feel like Zeus.

Vince, like countless other wrestling promoters before him, knew how to exploit that dangerous love. He shared it, himself, of course—even though his earliest years hadn't included trips to the wrestling arena, and even though he has long sought fame outside of wrestling, he is no fake fan. His love of wrestling, like (and tied up in) his feelings about his father, is passionate. But there's a crucial difference between him and the wrestlers he employs: outside the ring, the talent have neither power nor protection. The most dedicated performers keep coming back to the ring for their fix, no matter how much he hurts them.

Which is not to say Vince has always been cruel to the Boys; far from it. In the early years of his regime, he devised a winning management strategy: throw money at them. He began to snatch up wrestlers from rival promotions by offering them larger paydays than they'd ever seen. Suddenly, they had the impression that their best years were ahead of them, or at least that a bigger check was on its way next week. Vince could be fun and kind to his talent, and many who worked for him in his early years have fond memories of him. But other actions suggest a belief that it's better to be feared than loved.

For example, in August of 1983, the NWA gathered at a Las Vegas hotel for their annual meeting, and it almost immediately fell into tumult and anger over Vince. Jim Barnett resigned as the organization's secretary and treasurer due to clashes with Ole Anderson over both TV strategies and Barnett's informal alliance with Vince. NWA president Bob Geigel denounced Vince's expansionism, saying it would kill the industry. The board of directors was overhauled, with only two out of seven previous members returning—and with Anderson in one of the seats.

At a climactic meeting, Anderson yelled, "If you want war, McMahon, I'll give you war!"

In response, Vince simply walked out of the room.

Further ticking off rival promoters, that very weekend saw the publication of a three-page feature on the WWF in the massively circulated *Parade* magazine. The story was all fluff and praise, with lush descriptions of wrestlers like Strongbow, André, Backlund, and, of course, Snuka. It all winked at wrestling's fakeness—the headline was "Where the Good Guys (Almost) Always Win"—while never outright identifying it as such. Though the piece focused on the wrestlers and didn't mention their new boss, the profile was a huge coup for Vince, whose company aspired to become the most visible brand in American wrestling during a time of growing consumer demand.

Within a week, WWF shows debuted in two new TV slots. One was on a Cincinnati station, further entrenching the company's beachhead in Ohio. The other was a new, patriotism-themed program called *All-American Wrestling*, which debuted on the USA cable network, appropriately enough. USA had been airing Texas-based Southwest Championship Wrestling in that slot, and the change was unannounced. Viewers just turned on the set at the appointed time and saw Vince's product, enraging both fans and promoters. It would not be the last time he pulled something like that.

As Vince Senior was, confusingly enough, still a dues-paying member of the NWA board, there was a familial conflict of interest that Anderson had been quick to point out at the Las Vegas meeting. No one outside the WWF—or, for the most part, inside of it—was quite sure how the new power structure at the WWF even worked.

"My dad would get a phone call just about every other week from one of his cronies that he had been doing business with for years," Vince later said. "And it's like, 'God, that damn kid—what the hell's he doing? He's coming to Kansas City? That sonuvabitch is gonna wind up in the bottom of a river!'"

According to Vince, his father wasn't pleased with what he'd been doing, but the elder man didn't have much leverage anymore, given that he wasn't the owner. As Vince later put it in an unpublished interview, "My dad was on the outside now."

On August 31, Vince Senior sent a letter to Geigel stating that both he and the WWF were withdrawing from the NWA, effective immediately. Within a month, the now rogue WWF invaded Northern California with a show in San Jose.

No doubt, fatigue was a factor in Vince Senior's acquiescence. "He just kind of lost his zest," said Vince. That's hardly surprising, as Vince Senior had developed cancer.

"From day one, Uncle Vincent was a sun worshipper," says niece Carolyn. "When he was in Rehoboth, that's all he did: sit outside in the sun." Vince Senior didn't wear sunscreen, and, she says, he developed skin cancer multiple times, having the growths successfully removed each time. But he started having urinary problems and saw a doctor; in November of 1983, he was informed that he had a malignant melanoma in his prostate.

"By the time they actually discovered it," the son said, "he was really sick."

Every great artist needs a muse, and Vince found his at the bottom of a bottle of hair bleach.

Terry Bollea was born about eight years after Vince, in Augusta, Georgia, in 1953, and grew up in the impoverished Tampa, Florida, neighborhood of Port Tampa.

"The perception is that's where all the poor people in Tampa live," Bollea wrote in his second memoir, "that it's full of football players and wrestlers and all kinds of redneck tough guys. That's not a negative thing. If you're from Port Tampa, there's a certain mystique about it. So people always assumed that I was a whole lot tougher than I really was."

Bollea loved wrestling from a young age, falling in love with icons like Bob Orton Sr., Dusty Rhodes (Virgil Runnels), and "Superstar" Billy Graham (Eldridge Coleman)—especially the latter. Graham was the massive, prickish, smooth-talking kayfabe younger brother of Vince's beloved Dr. Jerry Graham. While Vince had loved Jerry's sinister glee, Bollea was more interested in Billy's supernatural physique.

"I can remember the first time I saw him on TV," Bollea wrote of Superstar, "climbing up to the second turnbuckle and facing the crowd with his arms up, and those massive twenty-two-inch biceps. He looked inhuman. I remember thinking, *I want to be just like* that *guy someday!* He looked like this golden god, you know?"

Bollea, initially a flabby kid, started working out in his teen years at the suggestion of a friend and, in his early twenties, became a longshoreman. "I was the first white guy ever to get into the longshoremen's union in Tampa, believe it or not," he proudly noted in the memoir.

(Decades later, Bollea would be caught on tape making a paranoid rant about his daughter possibly dating a Black man. "I'm a racist to a point," he said to a friend in the recording. "Fucking niggers . . . If we're gonna fuck with niggers, let's get a rich one!" If he held such sentiments earlier in his professional life, he kept them quieter.)

Along with longshoremanning, Bollea worked as a musician; he played the bass. As of 1976, he was playing in a local rock group called Ruckus, and during their gigs as a bar band, he'd occasionally see wrestlers drinking in the crowd—Superstar among them. Bollea has said he cornered Graham for conversations, in which he realized that wrestlers were just normal humans like him. Perhaps he could be one of them.

Not long afterward, Bollea went to a wrestling show and noticed a wrestler mouthing instructions to his opponent, leading young Terry to realize that wrestling is fixed, "a revelation that would change my life forever."

"After all this time, nobody'd ever smartened me up to the notion that wrestling was fake, let alone that the ending of the match was predetermined," Bollea wrote. "Even as kids, we all had moments where we wondered about it. It seemed like common sense that if I'm beating some guy up and I throw him against the ropes, I'm not gonna just stand there and let him bounce off the ropes and come back and knock me over, right? Why did they do stuff like that?" Now, understanding came to him as if in a vision.

"I can see it's not a one-off thing," Hogan wrote. He realized the wrestler he was watching was "creating this tension in the ring where it looks like he's about to get beat, so that he can suddenly turn it around and make a comeback. And he does. And the crowd goes nuts! My whole world changed. Right in that moment I thought to myself, *I can do this. I can do this!*"

He reached out to a local wrestling manager and started training in the ring arts. Thus began one of the most important careers in the history of pro wrestling and American pop culture.

In his second memoir, Bollea recounted an anecdote about the inception of his wrestling saga. It's not often remarked upon, but it's crucial for understanding the abusive culture of wrestling, as well as later allegations against one of Vince's top advisers.

It was August 10, 1977, and Bollea was slated to have his in-ring debut in Fort Myers. He was getting a ride to the venue from two established grapplers then working in Florida, Buddy Colt (Ron Read) and, more importantly, Quebecois import Pat Patterson (Pierre Clermont), who would later go to the WWF and become a key staffer. Patterson was openly gay, and has often been held up as a trailblazer for queer representation in the industry, especially since his 2020 death.

However, he was also an alleged sexual harasser.

"We got you in the car 'cause we've been chosen to initiate you tonight," Patterson allegedly told Bollea.

The younger man was confused.

"Well," came Patterson's clarification, "we've got about a hundred and fifty miles to go, and before you get to the arena, you have to give one of us a blow job."

The twenty-three-year-old Bollea protested: he wasn't gay and had no desire to do anything like that. He hoped for a punch line, but the older Patterson and Colt looked and sounded deadly serious.

"I can't do this," Bollea told them. "This is fucked up."

As is common for sexual harassment victims, he recalled feeling shame and terror: "I just wanted to wrestle, and they took advantage of how serious and focused I was," he wrote. "They tortured me. It was the longest car ride of my life. On top of worrying about the match, how I'd do, if I'd look like a fool in front of a stadium full of people, they put this fear into me that they wouldn't let me wrestle at all if I didn't do this horrible thing."

The car got to the parking lot. "Okay," said one of the older men (Bollea didn't specify which). "Since you didn't give one of us a blow job before your match, we're gonna have to tell all the other guys that you failed your initiation. So after your match, in the shower in the locker room, everybody's gonna grab you and fuck you in the ass."

Bollea laced up his boots and overcame his dread to execute his twenty-minute match against B. Brian Blair (Brian Leslie Blair), "and instead of basking in the moment of finishing my first match in this arena full of people, I'm only thinking about one thing: *Now I've gotta go back in the dressing room and fight for my fucking life*," he wrote. "I was shaking, practically bawling, thinking, *I don't want to be a wrestler anymore*."

As Bollea nervously opened the locker room door, he found all the wrestlers waiting with beers in their hands, shouting their congratulations at him for becoming one of them. It had all been a prank—a "rib," in the parlance of the Boys, and not even a particularly extreme one, on the scale of how these men can treat each other. After this hazing ritual, "the other wrestlers stopped treating me like some dumb-ass kid. For a moment at least, they treated me like one of their own."

But the trauma lingers: "I didn't understand why they would do something like that," Bollea wrote. "It's still so weird to think about. Even now, it still upsets me."

So, around three months later, when Bollea's trainers told him—not ribbing—that they were going to transfer him to Kansas City, it's hardly a surprise that he just quit. He started managing a bar in Cocoa Beach, then opened up his own gym alongside a partner. It was in this period that he started doing steroids.

★ ★ ★

Steroids were new to the American public (European athletes had been using them for decades) and not yet illegal as of the late 1970s, so muscle-conscious men like Bollea went nuts for them. As he put it, "There was no indication that this stuff could hurt you—or kill you—and anyone who used the stuff was the best spokesperson possible because they all looked great!"

Of course, the world would later learn these chemicals were horrible for one's body in the long run. "But I was young and invincible, you know?" Bollea wrote. "I took pills every day and shot up about every third day. The results were incredible, so I just kept going. In just a couple of months I was seeing that sort of Greek-god swell I envisioned."

The now larger, unnaturally blond Bollea couldn't long escape the gravitational pull of the ring.

He called up Billy Graham and asked for a piece of the action. Soon, he was wrestling for the promoter who ran Alabama and the Florida Panhandle, as well as being loaned out across the South.

Bollea started wrestling as Terry Boulder. Then, allegedly after promoter Jerry Jarrett pointed out how big Bollea looked next to *The Incredible Hulk* TV star Lou Ferrigno when they were coincidentally booked on the same Memphis TV show, Bollea gained a new ring name: Terry "The Hulk" Boulder.

Beneath his cartoonishly expressive eyes and fast-talking mouth, fans saw a uniquely memorable body. It had been common to see rotund wrestlers, and it had been common to see ripped ones, but Hogan was a curious mix. His limbs were jacked; his midsection, not so much.

"I was eating everything in sight," Bollea wrote. "I decided that the perfect wrestler should have big arms and a big belly. I just thought that's the way you should look—that a bodybuilder's six-pack wasn't the way to go. It was too unrelatable to the crowd."

Bollea was making roughly $25 per match—an unforgivably common sum for journeyman wrestlers of that era—and, after a while, decided to quit again in 1979. But, according to Bollea, just before he could hang up the tights, a wrestler introduced him to Vince Senior.

The elder McMahon had been tracking Bollea from afar, it seems, and saw potential, or at least astounding size. He made an appealing offer: Bollea would earn more money, have someone to drive him on the long trips to matches, and get an apartment in Connecticut. More importantly, he promised to make Bollea a star.

One catch: Vince Senior liked to pander to ethnic groups and wanted a fellow Irishman in his stable, so he ordered Bollea to change his ring name. From now on, Bollea would still be a Hulk, but he'd have a surname that translated, appropriately enough, to "young warrior" in the tongue of Vince Senior's ancestral homeland: Hogan.

Bollea, despite having barely a drop of Irish blood in his body, acquiesced (though he refused to dye his hair red), and the character known as Hulk Hogan made his debut on November 13, 1979, at a TV taping in Allentown.

"As for McMahon's promise to make me a star? He didn't follow through quite the way I expected," was Bollea's recollection. It turned out he had been hired less as a protagonist than as a foil. The six-foot-seven, 320-odd-pound Bollea was an imposing figure, and Vince Senior did what he did with all his biggest guys: he had him regularly fight André as a heel, drawing furious boos as he attacked the somewhat gentle giant.

Neither man could actually wrestle all that well, on a technical level: Bollea was stiff and ungraceful in his movements, and André was too big to do much refined motor control, so they both relied on their superhuman size, theatrical delivery, and bestial enthusiasm on the mic to electrify the crowd. It worked.

For a time, at least. American wrestling promoters have long had deals with Japanese promotions in which each side will loan out some of their talent to make overseas visits, and Vince Senior saw fit to send Bollea to the Land of the Rising Sun in 1980. When he returned, Bollea received an urgent message from Sylvester Stallone, the actor and filmmaker behind the *Rocky* boxing movie franchise. He wanted Bollea to play a wrestler named Thunderlips, who fights the title character in *Rocky III*. However, Vince Senior wouldn't approve a leave of absence to shoot it. As Bollea put it, "Stallone wanted me more than Vince McMahon Sr., so I went to LA and shot his film."

Prior to its release, Bollea went to work for Verne Gagne's AWA as a heel, but, after the movie was released, his raw charisma and star power led Gagne to start billing him as a babyface. The audiences couldn't get enough of the balding, soft-tummied, overtanned man and his ability to interact with the teeming masses in the arenas.

The movie proved to be a turning point in Bollea's life. In addition to granting him renown, it gave him something that was rare for wrestlers back then: entrance music.

After *Rocky III* premiered on May 28, 1982, Bollea started coming to the ring while the soundtrack's hit single, Survivor's piston-pumping "Eye of the Tiger," blared from the speakers. Finally, Bollea was making a real name for himself. He was, as wrestlers put it, "getting over."

Rocky III came out just days before Vince and his dad shook on the corporate handoff plan for the WWF, so Vince had plenty of concerns to occupy him for the next year. But, at some point in the latter half of 1983, when he wasn't juggling regional takeovers and possible cover-ups, he called Bollea.

Bollea knew of Vince and had met him in passing, but they had no real relationship, and he felt he'd been burned by the guy's dad, so Bollea was tentative.

"Hey, I know my dad fired you," Vince said, according to Bollea's memoir, "but my dad's gonna retire, and I'm takin' over the business. We've been watchin' how great you're doin' in Minnesota. We want to bring you in and make you our champion."

Vince insisted on an in-person meeting, so he flew to Minneapolis. In Bollea's telling, they went to the townhouse the wrestler shared with his fiancée and they all "sat around drinking wine and eating pizza, talking about his vision."

If it happened the way Bollea tells it, this was the first time we know of that Vince had detailed his plan to someone other than perhaps his wife. It was a plan for empire.

"The idea," Bollea wrote, "was to take the WWF to venues all across the country and around the world, with Hulk Hogan leading the charge, and to go national with big TV events."

Bollea was taken aback, but impressed. "With all the fly-by-night promoters and even the great promoters I'd worked with in this business, I had never encountered a vision as big as Vince's," he wrote. "It lined up with all I had in my head about how big this thing could become—the monstrous vision I had when I first realized that wrestling was as much a performance as it was a sporting event, when I knew that I could be great at it. Vince's passion got me so fired up, there was no way I could say no to the guy."

Around 4 a.m., they shook on a deal.

All of this was completely unbeknownst to Gagne. Indeed, it's possible the reason Vince had insisted on an in-person meeting with Hogan was because he was going to be in town anyway to negotiate with the AWA chief. At some point in 1982 or '83, Vince contacted Gagne to see if he might be interested in selling the AWA to him. Gagne said he was open to the notion, if the right price could be found.

They convened in Minneapolis a few weeks later (perhaps on the same trip where Vince explained his grand plan to Bollea) and Verne and his son, Greg, laid out a proposal for the sale. Vince seemed intrigued, though noncommittal, as the Gagnes drove him back to the airport.

"And I'll never forget," Greg would later recall, "as he got out of the car and was walking down the turnwell, he turned to my dad and I and said, 'I don't negotiate!' And we didn't know what the hell that meant."

As it turned out, it meant Vince may have been lightly interested in the prospect of buying the AWA, but that was merely a backup plan. The real action was happening behind their backs. For one thing, Vince had opened a back channel to KPLR, the station that carried the AWA's show in St. Louis—a major wrestling market, as well as the heart of the NWA—and was negotiating a takeover of their slot.

When it came to televised innovation, Gagne had been Vince before Vince was Vince—in the 1960s, he'd pioneered a strategy in which he would send free reels of wrestling footage to any TV station that would air them. The catch was, he'd make sure to incorporate teases for his live shows in the station's broadcast area, thus boosting ticket sales, which were the main metric of success for a wrestling promotion. He was still doing that as of 1983, and he made a reel highlighting his hottest young star, the Hulkster himself, who was set to tour various markets in just a few weeks.

It was shipped out in mid-December.

On December 15, Gagne got a telegram from Bollea.

"I'm not coming back" was its one-line message.

At the time, the WWF champion was still the volatile and aging Bob Backlund, who had held the title for nearly six years. Though he had a manic energy in the ring and had been a favorite of Vince Senior's, his character was far blander than the colorful new crop of young figures like Hogan. Vince, now ensconced in power, had little use for Backlund.

So the WWF stunned the world on December 26, 1983, when Vince had the all-American Backlund drop his belt to none other than the Iron Sheik (Hossein Khosrow Ali Vaziri), an ostensibly pro-Ayatollah Iranian heel, at MSG.

Vincent James McMahon had lived to see his era ignominiously end.

The very next night, the WWF followed up on its successful closing of the deal with KPLR by staging a live show in St. Louis—effectively a march on the decaying NWA imperium's capital.

To add insult to injury, it was at that show that Bollea made his triumphant return to the employ of the McMahons, beating Bill Dixon to great applause.

Vince Senior was furious about his son's latest encroachments on the AWA and NWA, according to Vince.

"After St. Louis and Minneapolis, [he said], 'Oh, my god, Vinnie! Jesus Christ!'" the younger McMahon later recalled. "Yada yada: 'How could you *do* that?'"

The elder man suggested that Vince invite his rival promoters to New York and "open the door" for peace. Vince refused.

According to Vince, Vince Senior threatened to publicly sever ties with the WWF in protest on multiple occasions, only backing down after being calmed by his son.

On December 30, 1983, the WWF invaded Detroit. On New Year's Eve, Vince did a segment on a WWF TV broadcast where, ostensibly still just a mere announcer, he prophesied war.

There could soon be a "virtual flood of wrestling talent into the World Wrestling Federation the likes of which we've never seen before," he declared. "I see 1984 as being perhaps the most turbulent year in professional wrestling."

The announcer's microphone was now comfortable in Vince's hands, but he wanted to pass it to someone else. Around this time, it seems he was able to place a call to none other than his vocal model, *Wide World of Sports* legend Howard Cosell.

"I had never heard of him," Cosell recalled in his memoir, "but after a quick and precise introduction, he promptly got down to business. He wanted me to be the primary announcer on his wrestling telecasts."

The rest of Cosell's reconstructed dialogue from his phone call with Vince is worth reading in full:

"You can't be serious," I said, laughing.

"I'm dead serious," he said.

"Come on. Boxing was bad enough, and now you want me to end my career calling phony wrestling matches. Good Lord, you must be crazy."

"I'm not crazy," McMahon said, and I could hear anger creeping into his voice. "You really should think about it."

"I don't have to think about it, Vince. I don't want any part of it."

"Well, fuck you, Howard!" he said. "Wrestling's going to be the biggest sport in this country and I don't need you anyway!"

I couldn't believe my ears. Just like that, the guy turned on me. "Wrestling will be king," he said. "You're making the biggest mistake of your life."

"That may be, Vince, but I'm not going to do it."

Cosell was stunned. "After I hung up, I thought McMahon was a real kook," he wrote. "I still do. But he's an incredibly successful one."

In fact, part of Vince's success can be found right there in his announcing.

Calling matches was a perfect way to semi-subliminally influence viewers. They were never fully paying attention to the commentary, since the gladiatorial fun is what they came there for, but Vince could talk up wrestlers he was trying to get over, undermine ones he was trying to needle, and generally control the way his product was being sold. He was that voice in the back of your head, gently shaping your world with his words.

On January 23, 1984, only a year and a half after he made his first payment and surveyed his workers at Madison Square Garden, Vince brought his beefy ruffians and flashy superheroes back to that venue for a fateful night.

The arena had sold out its twenty-thousand-odd seats, so a simulcast via closed circuit was done for more than four thousand people at the nearby Felt Forum.

The lineup was solid: the Masked Superstar pinned Chief Jay Strongbow; the Haiti Kid and Tiger Jackson defeated Dana Carpenter and Pancho Boy; Snuka beat Rene Goulet with a flying crossbody from the top rope; and André teamed with Rocky Johnson and Tony Atlas to go up against Afa, Sika, and Samula.

But that's not what people were there for. They'd come to see America reclaim its rightful place in the world.

They'd come to see Hogan fight the Sheik.

The planning of that night may have featured the final attempt Vince Senior ever made to put out the wildfire his son had set.

Vince's proposal, of course, had been for Bollea to win the championship by beating the Sheik. But Backlund had a long history with Vince Senior, and, according to Bollea, Backlund said he thought a newbie like Bollea shouldn't have the belt.

The elder McMahon's cancer was still a secret, but he was living on borrowed time, and he had his legacy to consider.

According to Bollea, Vince Senior called a meeting in Allentown during a TV taping day, January 3, 1984, just twenty days before the MSG match. The attendees were Vince Senior, Vince, Bollea, and Backlund.

"You know, Terry, maybe Bob's got a point," Vince Senior told Bollea. "Maybe we should wait and see how everything works out, and think about putting the belt on you six months from now."

Bollea told Vince Senior he would walk if they didn't give him the belt as planned, and got up to leave.

"But Vince Jr. stopped me," Bollea wrote.

"Look," Vince said, "my dad's just a little worried. I have to talk to him."

If what happened next really happened, it was a watershed moment for Vince, the boy who had fallen in love with his father a quarter century before. At the very least, it's notable that Vince allowed Bollea to tell the anecdote in a WWE-approved memoir.

"He pulled his dad aside for a long conversation," Bollea wrote. "I don't know what he said, but he eventually came back to me and said, 'We're goin' with things as planned.'"

What could have happened in that man-to-man discussion? How did this rare moment of visible disunity in the family ranks get resolved in favor of the son? In an unpublished interview, Vince once told a reporter about the final argument he had with his father over the future of the company, and the timing makes it likely that he was referring to this conversation about Backlund's complaints.

As Vince recounted it, Vince Senior was mad, but he was also tired. They had been arguing for months, their already bittersweet relationship only growing more sour.

"I can't be in business with you, if you're threatening to quit all the time," Vince had been telling his dad. "It's not the right thing to do."

The dying man would have to choose between his son and the rest of the industry.

He weighed Vince against the den of thieving promoters and aberrant wrestlers who had made him rich.

Finally, Vince Senior declared his verdict.

"You know what?" the father said to the son. "You're right. *Fuck those guys.*"

The McMahons decided to ignore Backlund and move forward with the plan.

After a match on that January night that lasted less than six minutes, Bollea did his patented finishing maneuver—a simple leg drop accompanied by wild gesticulation—and went for the pin.

One, two, three, the referee counted with slaps of the canvas.

The match was over.

The crowd exploded.

Hulk Hogan had won. *Vince* had won. His father, and more importantly his father's ethos, had lost.

Speaking of fathers: in the locker room, announcer Gene Okerlund (another new addition swiped from the AWA) and a camera crew descended upon Bollea's parents, Pete and Ruth (identified as Pete and Ruth *Hogan*, of course—they, too, were now part of kayfabe) for an interview alongside their ecstatic son.

"Well, we're very proud of him," the smiling Pete said in a flat, nervous voice. "He's very dedicated. A real professional."

Okerlund tried to get the energy back up, yelling a prompt: "You gotta be proud of him, Mom and Dad!"

But Hogan, the golden belt over his golden shoulder, rammed his head toward the mic and bellowed a characteristically over-the-top interruption, his voice hoarse and his eyes wider than dinner plates: "You know somethin', Mean Gene? Pete and Ruth are the people that trained me from the day I could toddle, man! And they're the ones that sent me and made these twenty-four-inch pythons!"—his term for his biceps. "This is Pete's belt and Ruth's belt, and we're gonna stand behind it all the way, daddy! It's USA and Hulkamania, *runnin' wild!*"

Indeed. Within the next four months, WWF TV shows invaded regional markets in an avalanche, putting Vince in direct conflict with no fewer than five rival promotions. "We can bring in new talent, more sophisticated marketing techniques and a new approach," he boasted to the *St. Louis Post-Dispatch*. Never mind that the talent had been developed elsewhere and that the marketing techniques were often copied—the approach, to be sure, was new. For better and for worse.

"The consumer isn't going to suffer," Vince told the reporter from the *Post-Dispatch*. "The consumer is going to be the winner."

As Richard Meltzer put it, "In the cultural chain of late-century being, if wrestling is in crisis, what isn't?"

5

GET OVER, ACT II

(1984)

For the better part of a century, wrestling promoters divided fans into two categories: *marks* and *smarts*.

As with "kayfabe," "mark" is a term with roots in old carny slang. Like players of fixed carnival games, marks were those who believed wrestling was, on some level, a legitimate athletic competition. Smarts were the fans who knew wrestling was a fiction, yet still found it fascinating as an industry and an artform.

Though it was impossible to determine the exact ratio of smarts to marks among wrestling fans, it was always an article of faith in the industry that the vast majority of fans were marks, and that it was vital to keep them that way. If too many fans smartened up—if the true nature of wrestling became widely known—the Business would collapse under the weight of reality. The entire point of the elaborate rituals of kayfabe was to maintain what wrestlers assumed was an audience composed almost exclusively of naïve believers.

It's not clear at all, however, that this audience ever existed.

As early as 1905, news outlets were running stories about how nearly all wrestling matches were predetermined, and they kept doing so at regular intervals for decades. In the early 1930s, promoter Jack Pfefer infamously told a reporter that wrestling was fixed. And anyone who has ever tried to replicate wrestling moves in their backyard or living room will quickly surmise that they require a cooperative partner to pull off. Yet these revelations never had much long-term effect on the industry.

When you start to think about it, the existence of marks in great numbers starts to seem unlikely. It's possible that the majority of wrestling fans have *always* been smarts.

It's possible that the illusion at the heart of wrestling was not that fans believed wrestling was real, but that *wrestlers believed that fans believed it*.

"A lot of wrestlers got off on the idea that they were con men, fooling the public," says veteran wrestling journalist Dave Meltzer.

"If you talk to wrestlers from that era, and go, 'What percentage of the fans in the building thought it was real?' they'll say, 'One hundred percent,'" Meltzer says. Promoters "drummed into [wrestlers'] heads" that not only did the audience believe, but that any breach in that belief "would kill the industry," Meltzer says. "That's what they were taught and that's what they learned: if people thought that it wasn't real, the industry would die. So you have to protect it at all costs."

Meanwhile, the fans maintained the pose of belief so as not to be rude to their heroes. "We all acted like it was real the minute we paid for our ticket and crossed into the lobby," Meltzer says, recalling his childhood in the days of old kayfabe. "When [wrestlers] talked to the fans, the fans never treated them like they thought it was fake, because that's disrespectful."

Same goes for the groupies the wrestlers slept with, Meltzer adds: "Every one of them knew it wasn't real, and every one of them pretended around the wrestlers that they thought it was."

Meltzer (again, no relation to Richard) became a smart at age nine, around 1969, just after he'd moved with his family to San Jose. He recalls going to his first wrestling show and believing it was real. But at his second show, he observed more closely.

"And that was that," Meltzer adds. "I never thought of it as real again, as far as a real sport. I thought of it as real *entertainment* for the rest of my life."

He was smart, but he was also smitten. Soon, the precocious Meltzer was voraciously reading wrestling magazines and attending shows. More importantly, he was reading photocopied newsletters about the industry—and making his own. At ten, he briefly published *The California Wrestling Report*, with an estimated circulation of one hundred. By fourteen he'd started over with *The International Wrestling Gazette*, which ended up with about 150. He became a fixture at the local promotion's main arena, a spot just south of San Francisco called the Cow Palace, carrying a tape recorder to take notes.

Dave had chaperones to these shows. Usually, it would be two older girls he knew, both around sixteen, who were happy to accompany him for their own reasons: after the shows, "they would go out and they would have sex with various wrestlers," Meltzer recalls. "They'd go with the guys, I'd stay in the VIP parking lot for two hours and I would transcribe my notes, and around 2 or 2:30 [a.m.], we'd go home." The age of consent in California as of that time, the mid-1970s, was eighteen.

Back then, the entertainment industry, in general, was rife with what we recognize today as statutory rape. Rock gods and movie stars were routinely having sex with underage fans, and the wrestling world was no different.

"Every territory had that," Meltzer says of this groupie tradition. "You ever heard the term 'payment in pussy'? In wrestling, in the small territories, where guys didn't make any money, the big thing was, 'If you come in, you'll have nothing but women.' Because they were big on television, so women flocked to them. You wouldn't make money, but you'd get lots of sex." Wrestlers called their groupies "ring rats"—or, more commonly, just "rats."

Meltzer recalls those days with a sort of resigned frankness: "That was the business back then. Every single one of those guys has a skeleton from thirty years ago. And Vince probably has a million of them."

Today, Meltzer is known as the most prolific American wrestling journalist of all time. His first two newsletters only lasted a few years, but his third, the *Wrestling Observer Newsletter*, began in 1982 and is still in weekly publication, in print and online, as of this writing. It started as a side project while Meltzer worked as a newspaper sportswriter, but eventually became his full-time job. He is the sole editor and usually sole author of all the *Observer*'s issues, many of which run to twenty-five thousand words or more. His confrontational style and scoops of mysterious provenance have made him one of the most divisive figures in wrestling, right up there with Vince. Indeed, since the early 1980s, the two men's destinies have been intertwined.

By the time Hogan was awarded the WWF championship in January of 1984, Meltzer had roughly five hundred subscribers. Except for the *Observer*, there was virtually no serious journalism in or about wrestling. Mainstream media coverage was, generally speaking, condescending and ignorant. There were industry magazines and newsletters, sure, but they tended to either be woefully underinformed or deferential to kayfabe. Not so with the *Observer*, which always operated from the assumption that Santa Claus wasn't real, however virile he may look. As a result, Meltzer says, he was constantly on the phone with people in the industry who wanted to blow the whistle, push an agenda, misdirect him, or just vent. And there was much to vent about.

The February 1984 issue went out too early to include coverage of Hogan's championship "win," but Meltzer had seen it was coming, and he didn't like it. The issue's opening column, headlined "NO PRISONERS," was full of passionate intensity: "The wrestling war has begun," Meltzer declared at the top. "What started out a few years back with many people speculating on what the long term effect of cable TV [would be] has wound up with its most inevitable result—the consolidation of the major pro wrestling promotions into a few select and very powerful hands."

Meltzer outlined the shocks of the previous year, then predicted a grim future, one in which the championship would pass to Hogan and duped fans would believe he deserved it. In those days, a dedicated smart admired a wrestler for his skill—it takes considerable athleticism and technique to pull off the moves and make them look natural—and newsletters were obsessed with who "won" or "lost" a match, not because readers assumed the match had been legit, but because they assumed a victory rewarded the artistry of the performers they loved to watch.

The idea that Hogan could be handed such an honor despite exhibiting such a poor grasp of wrestling basics infuriated smarts like Meltzer. They preferred the NWA's talented then-champ, Ric Flair (Richard Fliehr). They feared the warping of the artform.

"The average fan, seeing Hogan as champion, will perceive him as the 'real' champion," Meltzer wrote. "Even a superior wrestler like Flair, because he has neither the size or physique, nor as great an aura of invincibility surrounding him, would [not] be able to draw as champion against Hogan."

Whatever the details of the future would be, Meltzer knew Vince was hardly done with his expansion, and was certain that more blood would be shed. "Once McMahon has the stars, and what fans perceive to be the real champion, plus exposure, which he's made great strides in obtaining during the past year, then few can stand up against him," Meltzer wrote. "I know that most fans who have a real love for wrestling have dreaded this inevitable attack for a long time. I don't really know what the final result will be. The actions of the past month, however, leave me with a very pessimistic view."

Looking back now, Meltzer says that, if anything, his younger self wasn't being hyperbolic enough.

"Maybe the most important year in wrestling history would be 1984, when I think about it," he tells me. "In 1984, there were the machinations every single week. That was the year that changed everything." The territory system didn't disappear that year, "but the seeds were sown in '84," he says. "When [Vince] went out, it was obvious to me that the Kansas Cities and the Portlands—those types of territories were doomed, and there would be a few that survived. But you know what, I was even wrong on those."

The readers of the *Observer* could sense the earth moving beneath them, and knew exactly who was responsible. In the next issue, readers responded to Meltzer's declarations, and they concurred with the scribe's tone of alarm. Mick Karch of St. Louis Park, Minnesota, was speaking for many smarts when he called Vince "a real threat to the stability of pro wrestling, which obviously was doing quite well until he decided to overrun the sport like Hannibal."

Some diehards looked at Vince's glitzy, talent-poaching ways and declared that the fundamentals of his promotion were actually quite weak. "Granted, they have several excellent heels," wrote Norm Dooley of New Albany, Indiana, "but they have the worst line-up of good guys to ever step into a wrestling ring. Even a Greg Valentine, a Roddy Piper, and a Sgt. Slaughter"—all recent acquisitions—"can't do anything with Ivan Putski, Jay Strongbow, Sal Bellomo, Tony Garea, Tony Atlas, etc."

Not all of the letter writers saw Vince as evil, per se, but all acknowledged how much dread his name was beginning to instill. Vince was "the prototype that Orwell foresaw when he wrote his novel," wrote one Rich Dorf of Wilkes-Barre, Pennsylvania. "Are his actions going to turn into a Hitler-type Blitzkrieg and result in a 'scorched earth' policy, or will he turn [out] in the long run beneficial to the business?"

Whether Vince would be bad for the Business, as a whole, was an open question; it was already clear he'd be bad for individual businesses. The acts of aggression came in a rising wave through early 1984: a broadcast deal in Chicago; the acquisition of the sizzling heel "Dr. D" David Shults; a television-slot takeover in San Francisco; an invasion in Baltimore; a spot on Sacramento TV. And an even bigger shock was on its way.

In April, Vince caught wind that two major stockholders in Georgia Championship Wrestling were looking to get out of the industry and sell their shares. Intrigued, Vince and Linda arranged a meeting with them and a few other GCW investors. The odd man out was Ole Anderson, who hated the McMahons and was tending to his sick mother in Wisconsin. Nevertheless, the assembled stockholders sold a collective 67.5 percent of GCW to Vince and Linda on April 19, 1984. Vince now had a foot in the door at Ted Turner's empire.

Anderson was horrified. Not long afterward (some accounts say the next day, though Anderson says it was a couple of weeks), Vince and Linda made a triumphant visit to Turner's offices and ran into Anderson.

"He said, 'Ole, I'd like you to meet my wife, Linda,'" Anderson would recall, years later. "I said, 'Fuck her, and fuck you!'"

Vince spoke with Ted Turner, and the two reached an agreement: Vince would take over GCW's slot on TBS, but only under the condition that Vince use high-quality, first-run material and work out of Turner's studios. There was to be no dumping of lesser matches or things already seen on other WWF programming. Vince gave his assurances to Turner.

Meanwhile, Vince's first cable show, *All-American Wrestling*, had become the first big ratings smash on USA Network, and founder/CEO Kay Koplovitz craved more. There was a hole in the channel's Tuesday night schedule, and Koplovitz reached out to Vince to see if he had any ideas about filling it. Vince, who was already producing four ongoing wrestling TV shows, had no ideas. But soon after, he was dining with a friend, an aspiring director named Nelson Sweglar, and mentioned the problem. Sweglar proposed a talk show. Vince was into it. Koplovitz was into it. Bingo.

The result was *Tuesday Night Titans* (later just *TNT*), an entertainment product unlike anything previously conceived in wrestling, and perhaps the most useful and representative artifact we have of Vince's creative approach in the mid-1980s. Largely forgotten today, the show's strange, shambolic energy and mix of hilarity and cringe is all pure Vince. Indeed, it was Vince's first-ever starring role.

He was the host, sitting behind an unattractive desk on a dime-store set in Baltimore. Cheap cutouts of skyscrapers were matted behind him.

On a couch to his right was the Ed McMahon to his Johnny Carson: an English ex-wrestler with a slightly awkward, High Victorian English accent named Lord Alfred Hayes (in reality, he was just a nonaristocrat from London named Al Hayes). The show consisted of interviews with wrestlers and other WWF personalities—entirely in kayfabe, of course— interspersed with archival footage from matches both recent and ancient, as well as skits and teases of future competitions.

The most fascinating thing about watching old episodes of *TNT* is just how *awkward* Vince was. He had been doing WWF TV in one form or another for twelve years, and had become reasonably adept at calling a match, yet still had no great ease with the camera.

Take, for example, his first words on the first episode: "Hello, everyone; welcome to *Tuesday Night Titans*," he intoned at the top, then emitted a string of tortured sentences: "Indeed, this is a most unusual treatment of the World Wrestling Federation. This show, perhaps possessing potential greatness from a number of standpoints, which we will speak of momentarily. But right now, we would like to introduce you to one of the potential moments of greatness, perhaps. It's Britain's answer to Idi Amin"—the murderous former dictator of Uganda—"my co-host, indeed, Lord Alfred Hayes!"

Hayes contorted his face a little and responded, "I don't know whether I like that answer or not." The Brit stopped for half a second to think, then asked, "What *has* happened to Idi Amin?"

Vince's face took on a smile of barely hidden panic at this setup for a witty rejoinder. He paused. "Well, I'm not quite certain what's happened to Idi Amin, obviously," Vince said, fumbling the ball. "However, perhaps, one of his protégés, maybe two of them, here with us: Afa and Sika, the Wild Samoans"—a tag team of Samoan wrestlers (Afa Anoa'i and Sika Anoa'i, respectively) who had nothing to do with Amin, other than that people tended to depict all three individuals as mentally opaque savages.

"Ha, absolutely wild men," Hayes said with glee. "Absolutely wild. I wonder what they have in mind for us?"

Vince and Hayes first talked up a recent match between "Mr. Wonderful" Paul Orndorff and B. Brian Blair and showed a clip, speaking of the way Orndorff had (in kayfabe) cheated to win. The discussion was all about the psychology of intimidation: Hayes stumblingly asked, "Did you see the way that Mr. Wonderful, the pose that he adopted as he entered the ring? He said, 'This ring is *mine*. This young man opposite me is *mine*. Everybody is *mine*.' "

Far more gripping was a pretaped spot with the aforementioned David Shults (whose last name has often been styled, inaccurately, as Schultz). This section of the show was, in a word, terrifying. Born and raised in poverty in a small Tennessee town, "Dr. D" was a consummate heel who took the role with the utmost seriousness, so committed to the bit that he'd refuse to sign autographs.

Towering above the interviewer, his thick shag carpet of curly blond hair hanging over a cutoff T-shirt with the word "PRIMO" emblazoned on it, Shults stared directly at the viewer and launched into a monologue that's almost the Platonic ideal of a heel promo in the age of old kayfabe:

Now, I got one thing to say: I'm still looking for a fight. I'm still look-ing for a *man*. I don't care how big you are, how tall you are, how small you are, how weak you are. I don't care what kinda language you speak! I don't care where you come from! I don't care what color your skin is. All I want is somebody to come in and fight the Doctor and gimme a decent fight. Give me some pain! Give me some competition! Give me somebody that might stand up to me!

At that point, Shults's eyes narrowed, and his volume rose even higher.

You know, all through life, baby, I'm the guy that went to school with you people out there, when you was growin' up, *and took your lunch money from ya!* If my momma stood here and talked to me bad, I'd slap her. But she knows better. . . . If my wife stood here and talked to me, *I'd knock her head off!*

Matters somehow got more intense from there. In a skit filmed in what looked like a rural cabin, billed as Shults's home, he introduced his osten-sible wife and two young sons (in reality, all Vince-chosen actors). The point of the skit was to portray domestic abuse.

In a scene that perhaps could have been plucked from the Lupton household, Shults spent the segment getting gradually angrier with his kayfabe family, eventually screaming at his wife (whom he only addressed as "woman") over her choice to serve pizza for dinner. "You think you married a fool?" he bellowed. "You're makin' a fool outta me, is what you're doin'! On national TV!" He ordered her to cook something else, then threatened to beat one of his sons for smiling.

There followed some dull wrestling clips, a recap of babyface wrestler Tito Santana (Merced Solis) having dinner with a child fan who won a contest, a letter-bag segment (the first missive, allegedly from someone in San Francisco: "Dear Vince, were you ever a wrestler? You seem to know so much about it!"), and a racist segment in which the Wild Samoans muttered in their "native language" while "cooking" a "traditional" Samoan meal comprised of the boiled heads and guts of fish.

Then "Captain" Lou Albano showed up.

Albano was a bombastic ex-wrestler who had become even more famous as a heel manager, talking up and aiding various baddies of the ring. The size of his midsection was rivaled by the size of his mangy salt-and-pepper beard, which he'd adorn and contort with rubber bands—one of his idiosyncratic trademarks, along with his piercings, Hawaiian shirts, and flip-flops. He talked fast and well, and his main job on *TNT* that night was chatting up a story line that would prove to be massively consequential for the WWF: his feud with pop star Cyndi Lauper.

Lauper and her boyfriend/manager, David Wolff, had been trying to figure out who should play Lauper's disapproving father in the music video for her anticipated mega-hit "Girls Just Want to Have Fun." Wolff, a longtime wrestling fan, had suggested Albano. In Wolff's recollection, Lauper perked up and shouted, "I know Captain Lou!"—by chance, the two had met on a flight from Puerto Rico before Lauper was famous, got along great, and had exchanged numbers. He got the part in the video, which went into massive rotation at the hot new cable channel known as MTV. Vince saw an opportunity.

Kayfabe eats everything. If something happens to a wrestling figure in real life, it becomes fair game to add to the story line, albeit in a warped form. In this case, Vince, Albano, Lauper, and Wolff concocted a story where Albano would tout his role in the video and claim that he was responsible for all of Lauper's success. He'd then talk shit about women, which would prompt Lauper to declare war. The *Tuesday Night Titans* premiere demonstrated Vince's and Albano's ability to goad people with a raw-nerve issue like feminism. "Remember: *I, Captain Lou Albano, made this woman!*" the man shouted from the interview couch.

"And I stress the fact, 'woman,' because what woman on her own has ever made it?"

Albano then launched into a promo that a modern viewer cannot help but compare to the thoughts and cadences of the forty-fifth president of the United States: "I've got a very high IQ: a hundred and fifty-seven," he said. "And I can sit back and relate my mental strategies by sitting, by talking, by stressing. In the medulla of my brain lies the brain of a genius!" He spoke of psychiatrists examining him: "They said, 'Captain, you've got it all together!' Said, 'Captain Lou, you can do it all! You can make champions in wrestling or in rock and roll!' Because I'm able to *converse*. You got that word? 'Converse.'"

"Communication," Vince said.

Albano concurred: "Communication."

That debut episode of *Tuesday Night Titans* aired on May 29, 1984.

Vince Senior had died two days earlier.

"I went to the hospital and I kissed him," Vince would later recall of his final visit with his father. "I've always been demonstrative. If I don't like you, I'll tell you. If I love you, male or female, I'll hug you and say I love you. But my dad was old Irish. The old Irish, for some reason I don't understand, they don't show affection."

The cancer, only discovered about six months prior, had progressed devastatingly.

"He was always so proud of his hair," Vince later told a reporter. "It was like mine. He had a hell of a 'head of hair,' he called it. He gave me those genes."

And no one would have mistaken Vince Senior for a bodybuilder, but, according to Vince, "he was a swimmer, so he had big legs."

Then came chemo.

"His hair fell out, and all that," Vince said.

"He was a skeleton," Carolyn Reardon, Vince Senior's ward, recalls.

Throughout their relationship, and even through the old man's illness, Vince claimed his father remained reserved. "It's certainly not the way that my kids, Shane and Stephanie, were brought up—I don't know how many times a day I tell them I love them," Vince has said. "But not my dad."

That changed, perhaps, in Vince Senior's last days. "That time in the hospital, I kissed him and said I loved him," Vince recalled. "He didn't like to be kissed, but I took advantage of him. Then I started to go. I hadn't quite gotten through the door when I heard him: '*I love you, Vinnie!*' He didn't just say it, he yelled it."

It was the first and last time he'd ever hear his father say those words.

At the very end, Vince Senior, whom so many wrestlers and promoters had looked up to and respected, had few visitors at the hospital. The funeral, when it came, was small and closed to the public, says Carolyn, and the burial was even more exclusive.

"What I saw on the tail end was my uncle wanting to be private," Carolyn says.

But some think there was another reason for the lack of colleagues and subordinates paying their respects.

"There was a very small wrestling contingent," Jim Barnett would later recall, "because all of Vince Senior's friends from the business were mad at Vinnie."

At least that part squares with Carolyn's memory. "People who loved Uncle Vincent," she says, "did not love Junior."

6

GET OVER, ACT III
(1984–1985)

In the beginning, Wendi Richter was a girl who loved horses. Growing up in Bossier City, Louisiana, she dreamed of being a horse trainer, even going so far as to work in a stable when she was a kid. But when she was seventeen, she found something she loved more.

One day in the late 1970s, she attended a local wrestling show with a friend. As it happened, there was a match that night for the Women's World Championship, a title that had originated with the NWA, but had long since drifted away from any single institution or promotion. Only one person got to choose who held the belt—and she had chosen herself as its bearer since before Richter was born. She was Lillian Ellison, known to all as "The Fabulous Moolah."

Moolah had been brought up in the business in the late 1940s by a sleazy promoter of women's wrestling matches named Billy Wolfe, who was notorious for coercing his wrestlers into sex with himself and others. Moolah survived the training, was granted the championship in 1956, and had held on to it ever since. By the time Richter saw her in Louisiana, Moolah had settled into playing the part of the aging queen heel who will stop at nothing to stay on top. Like all the best wrestler gimmicks, it was deeply rooted in reality.

Moolah was essentially unbeatable. As is so often true in the Business, her invincibility was not due to physicality, artistry, or popularity—she was now in her mid-fifties and had never been that technically adept—but rather due to politics. First with her husband, and then alone after they divorced, Moolah had maneuvered her way into a monopoly: every promoter understood that Moolah was in charge of women's wrestling and that it was up to her to decide which ladies got over and which got left behind. In her way, she predated Vince as the first wrestling boss to operate across every state in the union.

Richter, of course, knew none of that as she watched Moolah defeat a young woman known as Vivian St. John (Suzanne Miller) in order to retain the belt. "I thought to myself, *I could beat that woman. I could beat Moolah,*" Richter said. "And I did, four years later."

They were wild years. Right after the match, Richter walked up to the referee, an eccentric ex-wrestler named Sputnik Monroe (Roscoe Merrick), and said she wanted to wrestle. Monroe got Richter in touch with Moolah, and Moolah laid out the deal: Richter would move to Moolah's training camp in South Carolina, she would pay Moolah a flat $500 fee, she would pay Moolah around $100 as monthly rent for a room, and she would pay Moolah 25 percent of everything she earned after that, in perpetuity. Take it or leave it.

The teenage Richter didn't hesitate to say yes.

But when she got to South Carolina, she found that Moolah wouldn't exactly hold up her end of the deal: "Moolah never trained me, she just took the money and made the girls living there do it for nothing," she said later.

In a barn with no heating or air-conditioning, she learned how to "take a bump"—that is, how to fall down forcefully (while it may look like they're getting knocked down by their opponents, wrestlers almost always hit the mat under their own power). "You just practice throwing yourself down on the mat, over and over, forward, backwards, flipping," she recalled. "It was hard. The mat's not soft; it's like [a] table. There was a little foam pad and boards underneath it. It was painful."

Richter was also learning how to improvise and communicate with another wrestler constructively in the ring. Like a pair of swing dancers, wrestlers have to anticipate and meet each other's improvised moves in a collaborative and (relatively) safe way, in between the moments in the match that are mapped out in advance. Eye contact, body language, and experience are all required, and ideally, two wrestlers working a match protect each other from real injury.

"You've always got to think about what they're thinking," Richter said, "what they're going to do, what you could do to counter that, do you want to go with it. For your own safety." A miscommunication in the ring can be deadly.

According to people who trained and worked with her, Moolah kept up the tradition of forced prostitution in women's wrestling. To pick just one example, wrestler Princess Victoria remembered Moolah telling her to go out with a man from the industry and informing her, "Y'know, hon, the nicer you are to him, the bigger your payday'll be. And you could really use a payday." When Victoria refused, Moolah confiscated her wrestling equipment, kicked her out of the South Carolina compound, and terminated her bookings. Victoria never wrestled professionally again.

If Richter was put in such a situation, she has kept quiet about it. Indeed, she was taught to keep quiet about a lot of things.

"I love wrestling," Richter said. "To protect this business, to me, is like protecting the country."

Under Moolah's watchful eye, Richter wrestled for various promotions. She occasionally wrestled in matches with Moolah herself, where she found all those lessons about mutual communication in the ring were useless. Moolah wrestled "stiff"—that is, she made sure to actually hurt her opponent.

"She'd kick me in the chest, in the nose, in the mouth," Richter said. "You're not supposed to hit someone in their chest—a woman anyway—or their private areas. That's just not right. But she did."

Whatever Moolah's personal grudges against Richter may or may not have been, the younger woman was a moneymaker, and it wasn't long before she came to the attention of Vince.

Cyndi Lauper was good on the mic, but there was no way Vince was going to get the diminutive pop star to actually train and wrestle. He needed proxies to compete on behalf of the two sides in this war of the sexes.

For Albano, he chose Moolah. For Lauper, he chose Richter.

The Lauper-Albano feud story line was a key component of Vince's success. Lauper was huge on MTV, and she and Wolff brought Vince into conversations with the channel. Soon, the two companies worked out a deal to collaborate. It was this partnership that would launch the WWF to unseen heights.

The first steps were taken in June of 1984, with a pair of delightful WWF cameos from Lauper—her technicolor aesthetic, her bravado, and her high Queens whine all fit perfectly in a wrestling setting. She was so good at getting mad at Albano for his chauvinism that TV's *Entertainment Tonight* and other outlets had reported on the feud as though it were both on the level and worthy of mainstream attention.

That suited Vince fine. He was making a play for the zeitgeist.

He bought a station slot in enemy territory in Sacramento. He bought another in the Twin Cities, the capital of Verne Gagne's AWA. He had also poached announcer Gene Okerlund, who had been a beloved part of Gagne's show. In an interview, Okerlund said Vince "doesn't want to drive [the AWA] out of business" and that Verne Gagne was "still going to be able to exist." (These claims would, of course, not be borne out.)

Six days later, WWF TV debuted in Portland, Oregon. Three days after that, the WWF did a show in Oakland for around 10,200 spectators. And so on.

Vince oversaw more invasions, takeovers, and hires as the summer continued, prompting an emergency meeting of the NWA and AWA in Chicago, at which Gagne, Jim Crockett, Ole Anderson, and a few other promoters vowed to cooperate against Vince. They agreed to a new project, eventually dubbed Pro Wrestling USA, which would be a kind of promotional mixing bowl where top talent could wrestle before the cameras of a nationally syndicated TV show.

They had few other options. All that was keeping Vince from taking over GCW—and, with it, its coveted TBS slot—was a temporary court order requested by Anderson in the wake of the surreptitious vote to sell. Average fans didn't know any of these behind-the-scenes negotiations were occurring, but the fates of their viewing schedules were being determined. Vince's top competitor was on the verge of crumbling. Anything could happen.

July 14, 1984, was a Saturday, and every Saturday night, at 6:05 p.m. Eastern, GCW's *World Championship Wrestling* aired on TBS from the network's Atlanta studio. That week, the broadcast started in standard fashion: there was an opening animation of wrestling clips overlaid on top of a spinning globe, followed by the show logo and a star-wipe to dependable cohost/commentator Freddie Miller.

"Hello, everybody, and welcome to *World Championship Wrestling*," he intoned, smiling. "On behalf of WTBS, it's a pleasure to welcome the World Wrestling Federation."

What?

"Exciting new matches; great competitors from all over the world," Miller continued. "And here's the man to tell ya all about it. Here's Vince McMahon. Vince?" He turned to his right and into the frame walked none other than the man who would be king, clad in a checkered tan suit and light blue button-down.

"Thank you very much, Freddie," Vince said, shaking the man's hand.

"Welcome aboard," said Miller.

It was, to put it mildly, one of the most shocking moments in the history of an industry built on shock. The GCW takeover had finally gone through on July 11, and this was how the world was finding out. It was the wrestling equivalent of turning on the State of the Union speech and seeing the Speaker of the House cheerfully announce that the president of the United States had been replaced by the Soviet premier. Fans of southern-style wrestling, who derided the WWF as silly and destructive, were abruptly finding out that there was no real national competition anymore. There was no alternative. They called it Black Saturday.

The rest of the broadcast was almost confrontationally crappy. The matches were low-grade filler from inessential WWF shows. There was an ad for the WWF's newly launched glossy magazine, which old-school fans already despised for its shallowness and corporate self-worship. An on-screen graphic made sure to remind you, around the half-hour mark, that you were listening to the "Voice of: Vince McMahon." At the end, they cut back to the studio, where Vince and Miller grinned and talked about the future.

"Vince, I wanna say this: I think the wrestling fans got a sample today," said Miller, "and they're in for a treat."

It's hard to overstate just how stunning this development was, and how bizarre it was to learn of it through such theatrical surprise.

"It was at that point I realized: Holy shit, this is a tectonic shift in this little-followed, little-known, goofy little fringe form of junk entertainment that's in my blood but that nobody took seriously," recalls journalist Irv Muchnick (nephew of former NWA chief Sam Muchnick), who covered the industry and was watching live that fateful night. "Suddenly, I realized that Vince, this sort of underestimated guy called 'Junior,' was his own power broker."

★ ★ ★

A few days later, on July 23, MTV and Madison Square Garden Network both aired a special called *The Brawl to End It All*. Both broadcasts reached their climax when Wendi Richter stepped into the ring with Moolah and, as per the plan, was allowed to pin the diva and get the belt. But, depending on which channel you watched, you got one of two very different television products.

On MSG Network, you could see a full evening of wrestling, announced by Gorilla Monsoon and Gene Okerlund in the usual fashion. But if you tuned in to MTV, you saw something else altogether. Flanked by video screens, first-generation MTV video jockey Alan Hunter introduced clips from WWF programming that explained the story so far. This was crucial: countless MTV fans who had never seen wrestling before were tuning in and needed to have their wheels greased. Eventually, Hunter tossed to the Richter-Moolah match. It was a slightly strange one, with a confusing set of narrative choices near the end, but that was hardly the point. The point was: Richter won. As her arm was raised in victory, the crowd's enthusiasm won out over its confusion.

The MTV broadcast showed the festivities in the locker room after Richter's victory, with male wrestlers rushing in to congratulate her while Gene Okerlund held a microphone. Even Hulk Hogan popped by, shirtless and in jeans, to hug Richter and declare, "This is the Marilyn Monroe of the professional wrestling world!"

"It's such a change to have everyone on my side!" Richter yelled into the microphone.

In an interview decades later, Richter was asked about doing the story line. "It was wonderful," she said.

The interviewer asked if she had been thinking about what getting the belt might mean for her future. Richter's response was blunt and unromantic.

"I knew that I had to make as much money as I could because at any time you could get injured and when you get injured nobody wants you, they don't know you anymore," Richter said. "I had to get what I could while I could, because women don't make what men do. As far as women in sports, the career span isn't as long either. No one wants to see an old woman in the ring, but they'll pay to watch an old, beer-bellied man out there."

Moolah wasn't happy about giving up the championship, and convincing her to play the loser hadn't been easy. Nor was she happy that Vince, at Richter's request, told her to stop taking that 25 percent cut of Richter's earnings. But Vince made sure the elder woman was well compensated for both of these concessions.

"Moolah had been very jealous and guarded of that championship for a long time, but Vince was able to write the appropriate amount of money on a check, and that changed Moolah's mind," longtime promoter/historian/manager Jim Cornette once said. "And also, by doing that, Moolah got Vince McMahon, Jr.'s loyalty for life."

As it turned out, *The Brawl to End It All* was a success when it aired on July 23. It reportedly garnered the biggest viewership MTV had ever had for any kind of programming as of then. Vince's tale of sexism thwarted was evidence, in his mind and those of others, that he could truly break wrestling into the mainstream, make it current, make it hip, in a way no promoter ever had before.

(Hot off the heels of that broadcast, no doubt in an effort to capitalize on the WWF's ostensible women's-lib bona fides, Vince made history again: the summer of 1984 saw the hiring of the WWF's first female referee. She was a woman named Rita Chatterton, though she was billed simply as "Rita Marie." Her hiring didn't make the news the way the Lauper feud had. Her firing one day would.)

Meanwhile, Vince's biggest problem was growing in Georgia. Upon losing GCW to Vince, Ole Anderson formed a new company, creatively dubbed Championship Wrestling from Georgia (CWG), and reached out to Ted Turner. The latter was displeased with Vince, who had violated Turner's edicts about the content of *World Championship Wrestling*. So Turner decided to give Anderson and CWG a TBS slot on Saturday mornings. The NWA members were elated. Gagne and Charlotte-based promoter Jim Crockett Jr. told Anderson they'd provide help. The anti-Vince coalition was back on the boards.

Indeed, despite his lightning victories, Vince was in a difficult financial position. Well, really, it was *because* of those victories: all those TV slots, wrestlers, and promotions were expensive. His and Linda's tax liens from the 1970s were finally lifted, luckily for them, but they were bleeding money on the expansion. And yet, Vince was thinking even bigger.

It was around this time that Vince and Linda went on a fateful vacation. "They were on a trip, a vacation for a week in Martinique, maybe it was St. Maarten," Jim Barnett later recalled. "They came back and said they'd like to do this big show in Madison Square Garden" with famous people "to ring the bell, referee; all kinds of celebrities." A Super Bowl of wrestling—except only one team, the WWF, would be playing.

They were also lifting the concept from a competitor. Crockett had concocted a so-called supercard—a wrestling term denoting a special-occasion show—called Starrcade. It had debuted in November of 1983, and had been broadcast around the South at closed-circuit screenings—the technology Vince had failed to fully capitalize on with Evel Knievel and Muhammad Ali years before. Though Vince is often given credit for originating the idea of a wrestling extravaganza that people watched remotely for a price, he merely borrowed and improved upon it, albeit to greater consequence.

But what to call this extravaganza? Vince held a brainstorming session in which someone suggested the name "Mania." George Scott, who had recently been put back on co-booking duties, immediately countered with "WrestleMania." Or was it ring announcer Howard Finkel who proposed that term, as Finkel himself has claimed? Or perhaps it was a short-lived new hire from a dying promotion named Rex Jones, as Dave Meltzer has reported. Whatever the case, Vince had his heart set on a different name, one that could easily have become the winner: "The Colossal Tussle." Scott lobbied hard to reverse course and go with WrestleMania. He must have been convincing.

Journalist Ray Tennenbaum was reporting out a long feature on wrestling, which was set to run in *The New Yorker*, though it was eventually killed for unclear reasons. For the piece, he spoke to a wide array of wrestling personalities, who in those days were still easily available to reporters. One such personality was Buddy Rogers, the legendary "Nature Boy" of pro wrestling and Vince Senior's first champion in the WWWF, who was now in his early sixties. He was pessimistic.

"See, Crockett won't let Gagne get any bigger than Crockett is, and Gagne won't let Crockett get any bigger than Gagne is," Rogers observed. "They both want to devour McMahon, but instead of uniting—saying, 'Hey man, the hell with this personality struggle, let's eat that son of a bitch up,' which they're very capable of doing—well, daddy, you take it from me: Gagne and Crockett will be at each other's throats the moment one gets bigger than the other."

He went on: "McMahon Junior is the modern-day Hitler of professional wrestling, and if you told him that to his face, he'd take you out and buy you the biggest steak you could eat," Rogers told Tennenbaum. "He thrives on the people around him hating his guts. He loves it."

Most of all, Rogers was wary of where Vince was taking the profession. "Wouldn't you have to be pretty stupid to inhale what he's putting across—and have a love for wrestling?" he rhetorically asked. "How long do you think what he's doing is going to resemble wrestling?"

"I don't watch myself on TV," Roderick Toombs said as the cameras rolled, his boyish eyes dim but still smoldering behind a worn-out face. "I hate that guy. 'Cause I know what that guy's thinking. I know what that guy's capable of doing. I know what he's thought of. And there's nothing nice about that guy at all."

"That guy being you?" the interviewer asked.

"That guy being *Roddy Piper*," Toombs replied—which was, in its way, both a "yes" and a "no."

It was 2003, and Toombs was speaking to an interviewer from HBO's *Real Sports with Bryant Gumbel* for a segment on untimely deaths in pro wrestling. He wasn't dead yet, but he felt it was coming, and he wasn't ready. He was Canadian, so he had it better than most wrestlers, in that he had a government pension coming his way. Theoretically.

"What would you have me do at forty-nine, when my pension plan, I can't take out until I'm sixty-five?" he asked the interviewer. "I'm not gonna make sixty-five. Let's just face facts, guys." As it turned out, he was right.

For decades, Toombs wrestled as the kilt-wearing "Rowdy" Roddy Piper, first in the territories, then for Vince and the WWF. Broad-chested, mop-haired, and possessing a nasal Winnipeg accent, he could play at both ends of the moral spectrum. But he was best known as the frenetic heel supreme of the 1980s, howling out bigotry and chauvinism for the growing national wrestling audience to rail against—or, if they were so inclined, agree with. Either would do just fine. This was wrestling, after all.

Vince snatched Toombs from Jim Crockett Productions in 1984 as part of his national conquest. Toombs started as a manager while he recovered from some real-life injuries, then debuted as an in-ring performer. But he excelled most as a raconteur. Toombs got a regular segment at WWF events, called "Piper's Pit": like a sweatier version of Vince on *Tuesday Night Titans*, he'd play at being a kind of chat-show host, doing interviews with wrestling figures as a vehicle for advancing various story lines.

Watching "Piper's Pit" segments today is often an endurance test even for those long inured to wrestling's baseline levels of racism and misogyny. Piper went out of his way to talk to Black wrestlers about soul food; he leered at his female guests; he hit Jimmy Snuka on the head with a coconut; and so on. Toombs was a generally pleasant guy, so it was no easy task for him to keep up Piper's unbridled prejudice, especially when a promoter might have him doing up to ninety days of hard-traveling work in a row.

He needed help. Speaking to the HBO reporter years later, Toombs rattled off just a handful of the pills he, and everyone around him, was taking: uppers, downers, muscle-builders . . . "You get this goin', and then you start drinking alcohol," he said. "Deadly combination."

He continued, describing a common chemical itinerary for wrestlers of that generation:

> You bring cocaine into the picture. Somebody gives [a wrestler] an eight-ball of coke. Well, he goes, *I'm up. I'm eating. Okay, here's my buddies. I'll have some drinks. Holy hell, it's four o'clock?* "What time's your plane?" "Seven!" "When do you need to get up?" "Five-thirty!" "Ah!" Does a line, gets on the plane. It's time to fight: *Psssh*, no downers there. No, let's *go*. But it'd be nice to have a little painkiller in ya as you go in. Or a lot. And *whooom*.

Of course, by then, "it's 10:30 and you're"—Toombs broke into his banshee Piper voice—" 'Hi, how are ya!' Y'know? 'Now whaddaya wanna do?!' *Fwooosh*. Just do the cycle again."

Elsewhere in that HBO segment, Vince appeared. The reporter asked him why so many of his ex-wrestlers die premature deaths.

"Why don't you ask yourself that question?" Vince snapped back. "I mean, are you indicating that's my responsibility? These people are dead because—"

"I'm asking you if it, in any way, shape, or form, falls on your shoulders," the reporter interjected.

"I would accept no responsibility, whatsoever, for their untimely deaths,"

Vince said. "None, whatsoever. As far as . . . And you've got that look on your face, like, 'Jeez, Vince, how can you possibly say that?'"

"Well, but 'none whatsoever'?" the reporter countered. "I mean, they wrestled for you. They were part of your organization. They worked a couple hundred nights a year for you!"

Vince paused.

Then he puffed out his lips and widened his eyes until he resembled an aggressive chimpanzee. He mocked the reporter's speaking style by babbling out whiny nonsense noises. He reached over and tried to slap the reporter's papers out of his hand. This weird, abrupt aggression toward the startled journalist is terrifying to watch, far more so than watching old Roddy Piper heel promos.

"Oh my god, you can't believe—" Vince said, cutting himself off. "Can you see that look? 'Oh, how can you possibly say that, Vince? How can you look that way?' And you give me the old 'sympathetic' stuff?"

"No, no, I'm honestly curious!" the reporter countered.

"Because I told ya: these individuals worked for our organization at one time; they also worked for other organizations," Vince said. "I'm not responsible for the way the business was then, wasn't responsible for how they grew up in the business, and whatever personal bad habits they developed. Why am I responsible for that? I gave them the opportunity."

"Well," said the reporter, "you ran it."

"I ran one organization at that time."

"You controlled the biggest organization."

"I don't think we were the biggest at that time, quite frankly," Vince said. "Okay? We're the sole surviving organization now. But, as far as looking back on all of this: these individuals developed a lot of bad habits. That's not my responsibility."

Regardless of whose responsibility it was, Toombs was having a lot less fun in the 1980s than it looked like. "Many hotel rooms, I have just sat there, and I call it the silent scream," he told the HBO reporter. "You just sit there and tears'll just come down and you'll just sit there, and . . . Fuckin' hours, man. *Hours.* Because there's no answer. There's . . ." He paused and shook his head, searching for the words. "There's no place to turn. And when you do turn, who cares? You're just a dumb professional wrestler."

It was a dangerous thing, being a heel. The most robust jeers only came when you really came across as a bone-deep asshole. If you did your job right, people genuinely hated you.

"It followed you everywhere," said Toombs's son, Colt. "Three times, they actually stabbed him, to the point where he had a leather jacket that was Kevlar-lined and it was stab-proof." But Toombs was a man so addicted to the ring that even this wouldn't make him kick the habit.

Vince could work with that.

Vince made Toombs a key player in the next story arc. WrestleMania had been locked in to occur in the spring, and Vince needed to drum up sufficient interest to sell out the roughly two hundred theaters they had booked for the live closed-circuit broadcast. He landed on an idea: the WWF would hold an award ceremony for Cyndi Lauper and Roddy Piper would disrupt the otherwise earnest event. It was booked to happen during a wrestling show at MSG—a hometown crowd for Lauper—and all would flow from that. A date for the stunt was set: December 28.

It was to be an evening of significance twice over. The ABC news program *20/20* wanted to do a segment on wrestling, and Vince had also agreed to allow their correspondent John Stossel to film some interviews backstage that night. Stossel had already been in touch with a disgruntled (non-WWF) wrestler who wanted to discuss labor abuses in the industry. That wasn't the angle Stossel and *20/20* were interested in, though. Stossel just wanted to prove that wrestling was fake.

As the winter afternoon waned into evening on the 28th, the wrestlers arrived in the familiar MSG locker room. Among them was David Shults, who was putting his boots on when Vince arrived. As Shults later recounted, Vince told him, "Listen, we got a guy out here making a joke out of the business. I want you to go out and interview with him. Blast him. Tear his ass up. Stay in character, Dr. D." Even if this dialogue never happened, it didn't really need to—Shults, pro that he was, already knew that kayfabe had to be upheld at all costs. *Protect the Business.*

So Shults went out to talk with Stossel.

"Why are you called 'Dr. D'?" Stossel asked Shults from behind the camera, the film crew's bright lights casting a shadow onto the blank concrete behind Shults's skull.

"Why not?" Shults replied, his eyes those of a killer. It went downhill from there.

Eventually, Stossel got to his point: "I think this is fake," he said.

Later, Shults would recall the moment clearly, since it was the one that essentially led to the end of his career.

"Now, I'm thinkin', *Vince wanted me to stay in character*," Shults would tell a reporter. "Dr. D would slap the hell out of somebody that said that."

And so, in character, Shults growled, "You think it's fake?" and slapped Stossel on his left ear so hard that he would successfully win money for hearing damage in a later lawsuit. Stossel dropped to the floor, gripping the side of his head.

"What's that?" Shults asked. "Is that fake? Huh? What the hell's wrong with ya?" Stossel rose to his feet. "That's an open-hand slap, huh?" Shults said. "You think it's fake, you son of a bitch?" He slapped Stossel on the right ear, knocking him down once again.

Stossel jumped back up, and he and his crew scrambled away down the hall. Shults went to the ring to wrestle.

By the time the match was over, Stossel was already talking about pressing charges. Vince told Shults he should get out of the building immediately. Shults did as he was told. He would never work at MSG again.

Not long after Shults left the venue in disgrace, Wendi Richter arrived at the ring alongside Lauper and Wolff. Legendary broadcaster Dick Clark presented Lauper with a special achievement award "for your contributions to the world of women's wrestling." Lauper took the mic and yelled out a grateful and gracious speech to the assembled thousands. Then she called out to the crowd, addressing none other than her old foe, Lou Albano, who was in the stands.

There had been a recent story line—silly, even by WWF standards—in which it was revealed that Albano's previous misogyny and misanthropy had been the result of a brain disease. Now he was cured, and together he and Lauper had raised four million non-kayfabe dollars for multiple sclerosis research. Albano made his way to the ring, Lauper presented him with a framed gold record, and the two erstwhile enemies embraced.

That's when a shirtless Roddy Piper climbed into the ring with them.

This was the part Vince had scripted for Toombs: Lauper's first appearance on WWF TV had been in a "Piper's Pit" segment, so now, the story line demanded that Piper take credit for Albano's and Lauper's achievements. Piper grabbed the award, took the microphone, and gloated.

"Even though it was me that set this up," he said, "and it was me that started it, I wanna present you with this . . ."—and then he bashed both frame and record over Albano's head.

The petite Lauper leapt to help the Captain, only to be kicked in the gut by Piper, who then grabbed Wolff and slammed him into the canvas. The crowd went nuts over this, predictably, but there was more in store for them.

"Look out!" announcer Gorilla Monsoon yelled. "The Hulkster's hitting the ring!" In ran the company's tanned top commodity. Piper turned tail and fled, escorted by a man dressed as a police officer.

Such was the beginning of the kayfabe clash of Hogan and Piper.

The event had been the first installment of a serial story that Vince would direct over the course of the next few months. It was told not just in his own programming, not just in wrestling magazines, but in mainstream headlines across the nation. He was attempting to carry out an arc of high-stakes live events that would push the limits of what wrestling—what kayfabe—could do.

It is here that we get our first glimpse of the WWF's financial situation. According to a lawsuit filed years later that forced the company to reveal some of its metrics, gross income for the year 1984 had been $29,596,974.

By the end of 1985, income would reach $63,125,159—an increase of more than 113 percent.

That explosion wouldn't have happened if not for the Hogan-Piper story. February 1985 brought its next chapter, which further interwove the WWF into broader American pop culture. The WWF universe of faces and heels was about to expand to include a man who was, at that brief, shining moment, one of the biggest television personalities in the world: the mohawked actor Laurence Tureaud, known by the moniker Mr. T.

With his extravagant chains and trademark phrase, "I pity the fool," ex-bodyguard Tureaud had been the baddie in *Rocky III* (outranking Hogan in the film) and was now one of the leads on the action TV series *The A-Team*, which was in its third hit season. What's more, his Saturday-morning cartoon show, simply titled *Mister T*, was heading into its third season, as well, and it was a smash with kids. T had somehow pulled off a balancing act between hulking adult muscle man and beloved children's mascot. Vince must have seen this as a model for what his own WWF superstars could do.

In fact, Hogan was already on his way to stardom with the under-ten demographic: he was set to attend the annual American International Toy Fair in New York to hawk the brand-new Hulk Hogan action figure. A wire report from the UPI noted that the item was part of a broader trend in American childhood: "The toy industry has decided that death, destruction, and other violent pursuits will dominate this year's selection of playthings for America's youngsters," the piece read.

This was just the trend Vince seemed to be banking on—so Mr. T was a natural fit.

T first made an appearance at a nonbroadcast show in Los Angeles—the same day as the Toy Fair, February 11. Shults was there that night, and he was mad. He'd been sent to Japan for a few weeks, and on his return, as he claimed later, Vince ordered him to sign a statement taking the blame for the whole Stossel incident. Shults refused.

When he saw Mr. T in the dressing room, his anger boiled over at seeing a nonwrestler joining the show.

"I didn't think Mr. T should be coming in to go in a wrestling match, when he's never wrestled or anything, and [have Vince] pay him more than he pays any of his wrestlers," Shults later said.

There is some dispute about what happened next. Some say Shults made a beeline to attack T, only for Vince to intervene. Shults says he wanted to attack T and didn't, but was fired for threatening him. The police were summoned and Shults was escorted out in handcuffs.

T's debut on WWF television was just as intense, but more scripted. It came in a segment aired on February 16, as part of a broadcast of the WWF's *Championship Wrestling*. Piper hosted an installment of "Piper's Pit" on the *A-Team* set, pretaped in Hollywood.

"They told me to come down here and talk to you because what you got here is this great, successful show," Piper told T, "and you guys are portraying these bad guys, and they wanted to know—since I *am* a bad guy, actual, in real life, and I do beat folks up for a living—they wanted to know: how does it feel to be portraying someone like myself?"

"You ain't *nothin'*, man," T responded. He said Piper shouldn't have insulted Cyndi Lauper, as "she happens to be my friend—we go out together sometimes, I like her singing." They shoved and shouted and were pulled apart.

At this point, the WWF was incorporating recognizable faces from both the rock world (Lauper) and Hollywood (T). This was revolutionary: actors and musicians had hardly ever ended up in a wrestling ring before, and rarely as key players in the drama. Further blurring the lines between wrestling and the other pillars of the entertainment industry, MTV and WWF started putting each other's talent in cameos on each other's shows, with Piper and various other heels declaring war on the very concept of rock 'n' roll (Piper preferred bagpipes).

The branded name for the endeavor was "The Rock and Wrestling Connection"—and thus, on February 18, Volvo-driving yuppies and hair-dyed rock fans alike flipped on MTV and found themselves, some for the first time, watching wrestling.

The War to Settle the Score—a sequel to *The Brawl to End It All*—is far less venerated now than the first WrestleMania. However, far more people watched the MTV broadcast when it aired, and the first WrestleMania could not have succeeded without it. What's more, it was, as art, a vastly superior finished product.

It was one of the only times a major WWF presentation has ever been written by someone from outside the organization. Journalist Charles M. Young, now dead, had garnered success and street cred for his coverage of the punk rock scene, and somehow—probably through MTV's influence—he'd been put in charge of scripting most of the show. Buffered by MTV from Vince's control, the enthusiastically leftist Young was able to freely interpret the outlines of Vince's story—perhaps even better than Vince himself could have.

The hosts were Okerlund and VJ Alan Hunter. Both Okerlund (bald-topped, aging, mustachioed, curvy) and Hunter (slender, youthful, angular, hair like an electric shock) were clad in tuxedos—complete with cummerbunds—and seated in director's chairs. Their dialogue, written by Young, was dripping with both serious reverence and sarcastic rebuke.

Together, they walked the audience through the story thus far: Lauper's feud with Albano, the choosing of champions, Richter's victory over Moolah, Albano's apology to Lauper—"I haven't been so shocked by a reconciliation," Okerlund intoned, "since *Hitler* made up with *Stalin*, back in 1939!"—and the wrestling sleight-of-hand that had transferred the story's tension to Piper vs. Hogan, the match that was to be the main course for the broadcast. Hogan's renown was on a rapid ascent, but if you didn't like him—and one gets the feeling Young wasn't all that impressed with the blond beast—you could at least enjoy Young's sly commentary on how amusing, how totalitarian the overpraise of Vince's golden boy sounded on normal WWF broadcasts.

"Certainly, one of our most admired champions in years," Okerlund said of Hogan, using Young's words. "He's been able to combine compassion, brute strength, intuition, and the *latest* in wrestling science."

Piper, on the other hand, was portrayed as nothing less than satanic. They tossed to a clip of him yelling at a female reporter from MTV about Lauper: "She's gonna sit there and lay down and grab my leg? A hundred and four pounds? Me, who's beat everybody in the world? And [she] expects me to sit there and do nothing about it? So I kick her twelve yards across the field!"

Back in the studio, Hunter was aghast. "Gene, I don't understand why men with such attitudes are even allowed to wrestle!" the VJ said. "I mean, all of the surveys have shown that the American public is sick of negativity! So why not emphasize the positive?"

"Good question," Okerlund replied. "Because the World Wrestling Federation, being based here in America, respects the First Amendment. Free speech has gotta apply to *everyone*. Even to those who would advocate kicking a defenseless woman twelve yards across a wrestling ring. Alan, the truth shall emerge from *free expostulation*."

Along those lines, they tossed to clips of sound bites in which celebrities made pronouncements about the match. They had been told to talk shit about Piper.

"Don't mess with the rock 'n' rollers, bro—we'll snuff you out," said Ted Nugent.

Dee Snider of Twisted Sister had fighting words, too: "Listen, Piper: rock 'n' roll's gonna getcha, man! And you are goin' *down!*"

Even Little Richard—an inspiration for many a flashy pro wrestler—wanted in on the action, it seemed: "Roddy! You better watch out! The Hulk is gonna be on you like ugly on a *ape!*"

More remarkably, they also rolled clips of taunts from none other than feminist icon Gloria Steinem and the recently defeated Democratic candidate for vice president, Representative Geraldine Ferraro.

"Listen, I'm here because I'm really angry at this guy," Steinem said from behind her tinted shades. "This Roddy Piper is a disgrace to rock and roll, he certainly is not fit to wear a skirt, and he's gonna pay for what he's done to Cyndi Lauper."

Ferraro was more brief: "Roddy Piper," she said to the camera, "why don't you come out and fight like a man?"

Of course, Steinem and Ferraro didn't go to wrestling shows, but they had both attended *Ms.* magazine's Women of the Year breakfast, where Lauper was an honoree. Lauper, along with an MTV camera crew, had interviewed both women. Most of the questions were standard political fare, but she also asked them to take a couple of seconds to say something about Piper, and that was all they used for the special.

(Ferraro would later say she had been told that the clip would be used "in good taste," adding, "Maybe I should have known better.")

The feminist bona fides of both the WWF and MTV thus bolstered, it was time to stake a claim on the cultural intelligentsia. The most fascinating bit of the night was a series of brief clips from a roundtable discussion, filmed on a crowded day at Kaplan's Deli on 47th Street, in which Young himself (billed in the on-screen text as "Charles M. Young: World's Foremost Rock Critic") and three other culture writers of the day yelled at each other about music and grappling.

"The contention between the connection of rock and wrestling is the dialectic between the two!" crowed Merle Ginsberg of *Rolling Stone.* "You've got, y'know, rock on the one hand: romantic, chaotic. You've got wrestling, which is Catholic, order, *male.*"

"The link goes back to the Greeks and the Romans, who invented wrestling," said Vic Garbarini of *Musician* magazine. "I mean, they used the word '*competitio*'—that meant 'to struggle together *with,*' not struggle *against.* And that's what a rock band does! You struggle *with* each other."

Young gave himself the most mysterious and provocative line of the show. "The fact is, in rock 'n' roll, the fan, the critic, is free to recontextualize meaning," he said, his mouth full and a crumb dangling from his beard. "No such freedom exists in professional wrestling."

There had actually been a full card of eleven matches at MSG that night, but the MTV audience only saw the main event. Unbeknownst to MTV viewers, who'd just seen a celebration of Richter's previous victory against Moolah, Richter's match that night featured her *losing* the belt to Moolah disciple Leilani Kai (Patty Seymour)—all to set her up for the big climax at WrestleMania. For Vince, everything was pointing toward WrestleMania.

Finally, the broadcast dissolved to the live match between Hogan and Piper. *The War to Settle the Score* is only available in pirated versions of old recordings, and that's for the best, because a pirate's lack of concern for music-licensing rights allows you to watch Hogan enter the main hall of MSG while "Eye of the Tiger" vibrates off every surface, as was intended. You can almost feel the elation that the crowd felt as they heard those anxious thrashes of the guitar while their mustachioed caricature made his way to the center of the action.

Both Hogan and Piper were always better on the mic than they were in the ring, but that was the point of Vince's aesthetic revolution: it was all about the sizzle; the steak was a secondary matter. After seven minutes and forty seconds of halfway-decent combat, the match ended in a deliberately unresolved fashion. There was interference from both combatants' allies; Mr. T, who had been shown in the audience, eventually ran into the ring to scare off Piper and his cohort. The match was ruled as a disqualification. Hogan retained the championship. The crowd was on fire with further anticipation. All went as planned.

Back in the locker room, there were interviews with competitors and visiting celebs. Hogan vowed at the top of his lungs that the "war isn't ended with one battle." Actor Joe Piscopo said the Hulkster got some sweat on him and added, "I thought it was pretty hot." Danny DeVito, who was working with Albano on Brian De Palma's *Wise Guys*, told Okerlund he'd never been to a wrestling match before, "but I'm coming again—it's incredible."

At that moment, a post-shower Piper walked in, dripping wet, clad only in a towel, and interrupted DeVito to issue threats to Hogan through the camera.

"If ya want this *geek*, Mr. T, to come in, I'll be glad to put an X where the T is! *I don't really give a damn, man!*" Piper howled. "If you wanna see me, next time, bring the goof. Bring the little *black* man into the ring!"

Some two million people had watched—a roughly 500 percent increase in viewership for that time slot. Wrestling hadn't had viewership numbers like that since the 1950s.

As the broadcast approached its conclusion, the unmistakable visage of Andy Warhol drifted into the frame. He'd come to the show with some friends and had accidentally wandered near the room, then became intrigued and entered. Clad in a beige trench coat over a black turtleneck, he looked equal parts baffled and amused as Okerlund called him over for a quick chat.

"Your impressions of what took place earlier on here?" Mean Gene asked.

"Oh, I'm speechless," came Warhol's monotone reply.

"Well, you've *gotta* be!" said Okerlund. "I mean, I saw jaws drop to the floor!"

"It's just so exciting. I just don't know what to say."

"Have you ever seen such total bedlam and pandemonium in your entire life?"

"Never," the artist said.

His face flickered into a tiny, involuntary half-smile.

"Your impressions of the Rock and Wrestling Connection? Don't you think that they got together tonight here and banded together and stood on firm ground?"

"It's the best I've ever seen in my whole life," Warhol intoned. "The most exciting thing."

It wasn't just that Vince's product had broken into the mainstream consciousness—wrestling had done that plenty of times before. It was that he had made wrestling, for the first time since the days of Vince's great-grandfather, *cool*. Of course, coolness is notoriously difficult to quantify, but the WWF was more than happy to try.

In the run-up to WrestleMania, the WWF's national TV ad-sales representative, Frank Tomeo, told a reporter that Vince had "87 percent coverage" of American homes with TVs and that attendance at live wrestling events "rose last year by 32 percent to 9.5 million, a percentage topped only by the National Football League." There's reason to doubt these numbers: Tomeo's source was sportswriter Bert Randolph Sugar, who wrote glossy and hagiographic picture books about wrestling. That said, Nielsen reported that four of the top ten most watched shows on cable were WWF programs. *Tuesday Night Titans* was, astoundingly, the number-one cable show in Manhattan.

"It scarcely matters that wrestling's reputed popularity with the quiche-and-Volvo crowd is largely the result of media manipulation," wrote *Sports Illustrated* reporter Bruce Newman in a cover story that came out later in the year. "The man doing most of the manipulating is McMahon, who has given wrestling the upscale demographics—or the illusion of same—it never had before."

He went on, marveling: "Somehow, McMahon and his WWF have convinced a good part of the press that the knuckle-draggers who traditionally made up wrestling crowds have been booted out of the bleachers and replaced by Wharton graduates."

Even the Paper of Record was weighing in now. "You may not like professional wrestling on television (for a while, only small children would admit they even watched it), but twist the dial and there it is, especially on cable, where wrestlers are now more ubiquitous than Gospel preachers," wrote *New York Times* television critic John Corry in a March 14 column. "CBS is preparing a Saturday morning cartoon series based on characters like Sergeant Slaughter and the Iron Sheik. Bloomingdale's beach towels cannot be far behind."

But Corry wasn't a snob: he made clear that his trepidation came from his appreciation for the art. "Does this mean wrestling will now lose something? Almost certainly it does," he wrote. "Shabby charm will quietly expire, and the circus will be done in by its own success."

Ted Turner didn't like where Vince was taking wrestling, either, but for his own reasons. He was fed up with his ostensible broadcast partner unloading all his worst material on TBS. In retaliation, Turner gave a TBS show to Bill Watts of Mid-South Wrestling, and reportedly went so far as to personally meet with Vince to tell him he wanted Vince off his channel. One way or the other, Vince could take a hint.

On Vince's behalf, Jim Barnett approached Jim Crockett Jr. with a proposition: Vince would sell Crockett the *World Championship Wrestling* time slot. Vince and Linda would then gradually dissolve GCW as an entity. It was a rare defeat for Vince, but he'd never invested much in the Georgian endeavor, anyway, so he sold it for a song. It would prove to be a regrettable move, though not just yet.

Vince's primary concern at the time was the public perception of him and his empire in the run-up to WrestleMania, his riskiest gamble. With the help of public relations firm Bozell & Jacobs, he executed a media blitz unlike anything before seen in wrestling. There were stories in newspapers around the country about this upcoming orgy of sweat and muscle. *NBC SportsWorld* ran an episode on the WWF and wrestling on March 17. In fact, Vince and NBC exec Dick Ebersol were becoming fast friends. Big things lay in their future.

Vince talked up WrestleMania on *TNT*, of course, but there were appearances on "real" talk shows, as well. Hogan and Mr. T were guests on Richard Belzer's *Hot Properties* on March 27 and, at Belzer's urging, Hogan put the host in a submission hold. However, Hogan held a little too tightly and Belzer passed out. After collapsing to the floor, he was revived and eventually sued the WWF for $5 million. But there really was no such thing as bad publicity, and the incident only generated more buzz for Vince's brand trinity: Hogan, the WWF, and WrestleMania.

The next night, Mr. T walked onto the soundstage of television's gap-toothed sentinel of hipness, David Letterman, to far less incident. Two nights later, a lucky break: Actor/comedian Steve Landesberg was supposed to host *Saturday Night Live* on March 30, the night before WrestleMania, but had to give up the gig at the last minute due to a family emergency, and Hogan and T stepped in to host. That meant roughly twenty-three million people, many of whom had no affinity for wrestling, got to see T and the Hulkster give their pitch for the next night's big show.

The WWF was getting good exposure, and advertisers and hipsters were warming up, but not quite sold. Vince had good reason to worry that not enough people would watch WrestleMania. These days, the stories about how heavily he was betting on the event are legion: the company's official chronicles proclaim that, had this expensive project obeyed the laws of gravity and not gotten over, all the achievements Vince had accumulated in the previous twenty-one months would have been for naught.

In a rarity, the legends are likely true—Vince's expansions were hurting his rivals, but they were also bleeding him dry. As one anonymous rival promoter put it to a reporter from *The Village Voice*, Vince "goes around telling everybody what a marketing genius he is, but believe me, it's not marketing—it's money. His method is just to buy everyone else out." The expansion couldn't go on forever without a massive cash infusion. He needed butts in seats.

The stakes were personal, too.

Vince and Linda moved their family to an exclusive gated community in Greenwich, Connecticut, called Conyers Farm in February of 1985—just a few weeks before WrestleMania. They reportedly outfitted the house with chandeliers, jeweled tchotchkes, and even a painting of Vince riding a Harley against a backdrop of violet clouds.

"The whole thing was done by a decorator," an anonymous family friend of the McMahons once told a reporter. "Not one single knickknack was theirs. Down the road, they'd feel entitled to their wealth . . . but, back then, it was new to them. Vince and Linda were just amazed by the things they had in their own home. Vince liked to say, 'It wasn't that long ago that I was pumping my own septic tank.'"

Shane and Stephanie embraced lifestyles of the young nouveau riche. The boy, by then in high school, seems to have aspired to juvenile delinquency much in the lackluster way his dad once had, back in North Carolina. Shane "had three or four friends that he hung around with," one of Vince's employees from this era later recalled. "They got caught by the police one night when they were cruising around town, smashing mailboxes with a baseball bat. I don't know what the outcome was, but Shane was just a typical teenager who always wanted to be a rebel like his father."

Grade-school Stephanie was less violent, on the whole; that same ex-employee remarked that she was "just a very pretty, polite young lady." But lest you think she was a pacifist: "One time, I did kick a boy in the shin for saying that wrestling was fake and making fun of my father," she said. "I've always been very protective of my family and our business."

It was all part of a lifestyle Vince couldn't afford at the time, and all of it was set to fall apart if WrestleMania didn't succeed.

You can't watch the first WrestleMania anymore; not really.

You can log into WWE's authorized streaming partner, Peacock, and watch something that purports to be the first WrestleMania, but it is an altered document. Media pirates have reconstructed a replica of what the show, today known as *WrestleMania I*, must have been like, but it's hard to come by. If WWE has an original copy, they have never allowed it to be seen after the initial live broadcast.

You cannot stream the show with the original rock and pop music that played when the wrestlers entered and left the ring: Queen's "Another One Bites the Dust" for Junkyard Dog (Sylvester Ritter), famed pop instrumental "Axel F" for the closing music, and so on. These may seem like small concerns, but they aren't.

WrestleMania I was the peak of the Rock and Wrestling Connection, and the music was enormously important to how the WWF was received in that axial period. This is Vince we're talking about: the hype-up is just as important as the execution, if not more so. Today, you can only get the wrestling, not the rock, so you'll never truly *feel* why it all succeeded.

Self-congratulation and bombast were the orders of the day. The first thing you saw if you were in one of the closed-circuit theaters screening the event was a vision of outer space, into which a photo of the World Trade Center flew. As Phil Collins and Philip Bailey's "Easy Lover" banged out and an animation of the New York City skyline rolled, Vince shouted, "From Madison Square Garden, the World Wrestling Federation presents: *WrestleMania!*"

"The World Wrestling Federation presents the wrestling extravaganza of all time [*sic*], WrestleMania!" Gorilla Monsoon declared to the viewer next to newly minted announcer Jesse Ventura, enormous headsets wrapped over their skulls. Monsoon tossed it to ring announcer Howard Finkel, who brought Gene Okerlund out to sing the national anthem, a cappella.

"I didn't believe Mean Gene Okerlund had it in him," Ventura declared, "but he rates right up there with Robert Goulet!"

"Unbelievable!" said Monsoon.

Vince scrounged up every celebrity he could talk or trick into being there. The sixty-six-year-old pianist and "guest timekeeper" Liberace was there, dancing a kick-line with a few Rockettes, and New York Yankees manager Billy Martin was invited to the ring as the guest announcer.

Richter arguably had the match of the night. She and Leilani Kai had their promised rematch, with a screeching Lauper in her corner and Moolah (clad in her trademark dollar-sign-embossed sunglasses) in Kai's. Richter and Kai had always gotten along, and they put on a convincing, gymnastic, and emotionally satisfying show.

After about six minutes, Kai executed a crossbody—a jump from one of the ring posts, throwing her diagonal torso into Richter. Once they were on the canvas, Richter flipped Kai over and pinned her. *One, two, three*—Richter had officially been granted the championship again. As "Girls Just Want to Have Fun" blared over the speakers, Richter pumped her fists in red-cheeked joy, holding Lauper aloft on her shoulder. She put the pop star down and they held hands, twirling in a circle like schoolkids. They turned toward Moolah and yelled inaudible taunts.

"Look at this ecstatic duo, as they are just *beside* themselves," Monsoon crowed to the viewers. "Look at the *smiles* on the faces!"

It was time for the main event. The biggest celebrity get of the night was none other than Muhammad Ali, who was acting as one of two guest referees for the tag-teamed match, in which Piper and Orndorff would attempt to tear down Hogan and Mr. T. The ref inside the ring was Pat Patterson, the man who had so traumatically faux-propositioned Hogan before his first career match, just eight years before, and who was now rising in Vince's organization. Meanwhile, Ali was ostensibly supposed to prevent shenanigans outside the ring.

The match took forever to get cooking: every time some action started up, it would be interrupted by tension-building stage business. T had trained in the basics of wrestling for a number of weeks, but no one would confuse him with a professional.

In fact, there had been disagreement behind the scenes about how the big match would go: Toombs—the man who wrestled as Roddy Piper—didn't want the inexperienced T to pin him, as Vince had proposed. It wasn't just a matter of personal pride.

"Roddy worried that if Mr. T pinned him—if a TV star could waltz into the ring and beat the WWF's top contender for the heavyweight title—then no gimmick or celebrity appearance could repair the damage that decision would do to the whole business of pro wrestling, never mind the WWF," wrote Toombs's children, Ariel and Colt, in their biography of him. "Mr. T would move on, that feather forever in his cap, and the wrestlers would be left looking like pushovers." Toombs was, in other words, trying to Protect the Business—in this case, from Vince's hunger for mainstream validation.

Toombs had a remarkably good bargaining position at the time, as he had resolutely refused to sign an exclusive contract with Vince. So Vince had no choice but to alter his plans and have the match end with Hogan pinning Orndorff. After Patterson slapped the canvas that third time and gave the victory to T and the Hulkster, the nearly twenty thousand people at MSG erupted and history was sealed. More than one million people had watched the closed-circuit broadcasts, making it the most watched full wrestling card in American history to that point. Vince's experiment had worked.

Dave Meltzer, in his write-up for the *Wrestling Observer*, concluded that, "for the most part, WrestleMania was an overwhelming success," but largely due to a reason both dull and crucial: "The important point of this is the effect all this recent hoopla has had on the people who make the real decisions in our lives—the TV advertisers."

It was Meltzer's theory that, although the WWF *was* doing well, it was vastly overstating how much it had captured the public's imagination, all in an effort to woo corporations that might want to advertise on Vince's programming.

"Even though readers of this publication are aware that 'skyrocketing' TV ratings for [WWF] wrestling is as much a myth as Hulk Hogan's actual wrestling ability, few realize that, and certainly almost nobody in the advertising business does," Meltzer concluded. "If everyone says enough times that [WWF] reaches the Yuppies . . . then enough advertisers will believe it and be willing to pay higher ad rates than the TV ratings indicate they should."

Meltzer, as one can glean, was not nearly so sanguine about what was happening as Vince was. Looking at all the pronouncements and programming that the WWF had put forth recently "has made it hard for me to enjoy even good promotions," Meltzer wrote. "This reaction, in and of itself, is an incorrect one, but, unfortunately, after watching Wrestle[M]ania, even the latest from Mid-South and Japan didn't excite me like it should have."

The other, elder Meltzer, Richard, had watched WrestleMania on a screen at the Los Angeles Memorial Sports Arena. He'd hated how the children in the crowd kept losing it over what he regarded as garbage. "You know how at baseball they think every fly ball is a home run and they scream and prance accordingly?" he asked in "The Last Wrestling Piece." "Well this is worse—and the triggers are endless."

He loathed the main event's ending, but saw an unintentional hidden message in the broadcast's final moments, when Piper abandoned the fictionally unconscious Orndorff in the ring "to let him regain 'consh' in the presence (sole) of his ENEMIES. What a rude, modern awakening! What a beyond-the-scope stripmine of the trans-WWF subconscious!"

Overall, Richard acknowledged that Vince made good TV. The problem was, television was all Vince had made:

At ALL times the *function* of televised wrestling—other, of course, than (ad-inducing) entertainment *now*—has been the setting up and telegraphing of grudges between designated combatants so's to spur live gates (here, there, everywhere) at shows featuring *un*televised contests between 'em; no other sport has sold itself so well by means of the airwaves, or rather so *exclusively* via same.

But now, Vince was sapping the sacred experience of being at a live wrestling show by betting everything on a televised product. And an undeserving one, at that.

"Snake bites tail—untelevised is televised—heavens gape wider than pussy as one-million-plus prepare to bear witness," he wrote. "The Absolute unfolds Itself. The gift of fire (it's a *drug*, y'dig?) to Man. Which'd probably be as exciting as hell if you gave half a fuck."

There has yet to be a year without a WrestleMania since the first one. WrestleMania has been observed as a national communal event more times than Martin Luther King Jr. Day, which only went into federal effect the next year. Each WrestleMania opens with the singing of a patriotic standard while kitschy montages cascade across the screen. Icons of the USA such as Gladys Knight, John Legend, and Ray Charles have belted out their devotion to the dream on Vince's stage. I was conceived in the same month as the broadcast of *WrestleMania I* and have thus never known a world in which Vince McMahon has not been a living metonym for American success.

I called up Richard Meltzer and asked him what he thought of Vince. "He wanted his story to be that he pulled himself up by the bootstraps, and here he was, another Great American Story," Meltzer told me. "And that's the worst, when wrestling became a Great American Story. That's terminal. Shoot it in the head."

7

GET OVER, FINALE

(1985)

Sometime in the mid-1980s, a gifted wrestling commentator in his early thirties named Jim Ross was at a gathering of territorial promoters. He later told a story about it that may well be apocryphal, yet is entirely plausible.

As Ross's story goes, he was occupying a bathroom stall at the conference when "famous wrestling promoters, hall-of-fame men, some of the most famous men in pro wrestling history" filed in. They started anxiously griping about what to do with the meddlesome promoter who had upended everything. One of these eminences offered a blunt solution.

"I could have the motherfucker killed for $700," he said. "Why don't we just do that?"

Vince's mansion on Hurlingham Drive featured an outdoor pool, and in the wake of the first WrestleMania, you could find Vince there, getting some much needed semi-relaxation. For two weeks after that show of shows, the company did something extremely unusual: it took a break. There were no live performances in that stretch. It gave Vince time to catch his breath and break in his new home—which he could now, retroactively, afford—without the usual disruption of travel. But Vince never really likes to rest. While his children splashed, he, Linda, and George Scott were mapping out what was to come. Poolside soon became a site for business.

Suddenly, everything was becoming—for lack of a better word—*corporate*. Wrestling had long been a rough-and-tumble industry of backroom cash and handshake deals, but Vince and Linda were shaping it into the kind of outfit that a mainstream reporter would take seriously as a business. For one thing, they'd started opening WWF shows with a little animated graphic of their blocky, metallic logo forming and glistening in outer space while a voice intoned a simple tagline: "The recognized symbol of excellence in *sports entertainment*."

Sports entertainment: there it was, the neologism that symbolized it all. Although it would be years before Vince made the term "wrestling" verboten on his programming, he was clearly already trying to reframe what the viewer was consuming. Previously, everyone in the industry would simply speak of wrestling (falsely) as a sport. Now, at Vince's behest, it was being coyly acknowledged for what it actually was.

The introduction of "sports entertainment" as a term was a first step toward ending kayfabe. For the remainder of the 1980s, Vince would execute a delicate and ironic maneuver: he would increasingly emphasize the *fakeness* of his business (and, by implication, the Business, in general) in a bid to be treated like a *real* business.

To achieve that end, Vince also had to get the company's legal affairs in order. He introduced a standard contract, one that kept wrestlers tied exclusively to the WWF for two years, then told everyone on the roster that they'd be let go if they didn't sign. Well, everyone except André the Giant, it seems.

In the *Observer*, Dave Meltzer had a scoop: "Although Andre and Vince Junior don't get along particularly well and Andre refused to sign a contract for Vince (which is supposed to mean automatic termination but in this case it didn't), he won't leave the fold out of loyalty to the family, particularly Vince, Sr.'s widow."

Vince, too, was still close with Juanita, or had at least continued to support her and Hazel ("Young Vincent, being very generous, would send them on cruises and trips all around the world," Hazel's daughter Carolyn recalls), and it may be that Juanita's influence was the link that kept the two men from breaking apart. André wouldn't leave, and Vince, for his part, wouldn't insist he sign the contract.

But Vince *would* insist on adding stipulations to his agreements with venues, forbidding them from hosting a rival wrestling promotion for ten days before and after a WWF event. Perhaps more unnerving was his choice to start trademarking his wrestlers' gimmick names, thus preventing them from taking their characters with them elsewhere. The notion of the wrestler as a free agent was becoming even more of a lie under Vince (not that they would ever gain the benefits and rights of normal employees).

And who was going to stop him? The hits kept coming. His friend-ship with NBC's Dick Ebersol led to the creation of *Saturday Night's Main Event*, an hour-and-a-half-long wrestling show that aired in *Saturday Night Live*'s hallowed slot on occasions when *SNL* wasn't running. The WWF aired *The Wrestling Classic*, its first offering in a new cable tech-nology people were calling "pay-per-view." Vince snatched up two up-and-coming sons of journeyman wrestler and outlaw Kentucky promoter Angelo Poffo named Lanny and Randall; Lanny wrestled under his own name, but his brother took the nom de guerre of "Macho Man" Randy Savage. Vince took control of young Dave Meltzer's old haunt, the Cow Palace. He ended the AWA's exclusivity deal with Chicagoland's massive Rosemont Horizon.

Meanwhile, Verne Gagne's former superstar was becoming a full-blown icon. When Bruce Newman's feature was published in late April of 1985, Hogan became the first pro wrestler to ever grace the cover of *Sports Illustrated*—a development that surely rankled more than a few sports purists. By that time, production was already well underway on *Hulk Hogan's Rock 'n' Wrestling*, a simplistic kids' cartoon for CBS in which the various heels and faces of the WWF got into wacky predicaments that typically had nothing to do with wrestling: Hogan tries to help an hon-est politician win an election against a devious baddie, Roddy Piper and Junkyard Dog have a car race, the Iron Sheik teaches his nephew's baseball team how to cheat, and so on. (I asked the creator of the show if he'd do an interview about it; he declined, saying, "I have no recollection of anything about the show other than the fact that I wrote the scripts.")

The launch of the cartoon was emblematic of Vince's wholesale com-modification of wrestling. Wrestlers had long been playing fake charac-ters, of course. But here, the characters had nothing to do with the magic that happens in a wrestling ring—indeed, the wrestlers didn't even actu-ally do the voice-overs for their supposed alter egos, as Mr. T had done in his cartoon. Although Jimmy Snuka was no longer wrestling for the WWF by September 1985 (likely because of a new civil lawsuit filed against him by the Argentino family), his animated self continued to leap into homes around the country every Saturday morning.

The humans who portrayed these characters, who sweated and bled for the WWF, were now reduced to intellectual property—neutered, por-table, and quite literally two-dimensional. Vince was building a world in which labor was entirely subservient not just to an individual boss, but to what Americans would come to call a "brand."

Wendi Richter had been working hard for the company, but she had never been happy with the way Vince treated her. Although she was grateful to him for the opportunity to reach the top of American women's wrestling, she couldn't abide the fact that she, the top woman, was being paid significantly less than the top men.

This had been true throughout Richter's interactions with Vince, going all the way back to her initial hire. "Before I ever started working exclusively with him, I asked him, 'How much am I going to make a year?' and he leaned back and said, 'A lot,'" Richter recalls to me. "And I thought, *Well, that's not helping me a whole lot.* A lot to someone may not be a lot to someone else. It wasn't descriptive enough." That said, "I didn't have very many choices—that was the best territory at that time. It was basically, 'Take it or leave it.'"

She, like every other WWF wrestler, got paid a portion of the gate for any given show she performed at, but these payouts were ranked based on various factors, and the individual amounts were up to the discretion of the promoter. As such, Richter said she would make between $500 and $1,000 a show, but that was it—and her male equivalent, Hulk Hogan, was surely making far more than that.

Richter says she didn't directly interact much with Vince, but when she did, "our conversations were mainly about reimbursement, what I'm getting paid. I always felt like women wrestlers should be making more than what they were. It was probably less than half [of what the men were making]." Emphasis on "probably," as Vince refused to disclose pay information: "He never would be specific."

Vince would field Richter's complaints with grace. "He would pacify me with what he could," Richter said. He would tell her attendance was down "or whatever, some excuse. He did say I had a legitimate gripe." Vince was more of a sweet-talker back then. He hadn't yet bloomed into the figure who terrified everyone who worked for him. But he was on the verge.

Richter was the WWF women's champion as of the brisk, dry Manhattan afternoon of November 25, 1985. That night, she was scheduled to go up against Penny Mitchell, who wrestled as the Spider (or the Spider

Lady; it was mutable), in a title bout at MSG. It was a match in which Richter, per usual, was scripted as the winner. She says she had her typical money chat with Vince beforehand: "I wasn't ugly, or yelled, or anything like that," she recalled. "I always told him, 'Vince, I need to make more. I'm not bringing home enough to justify being on the road like this.'"

Vince was noncommittal. Richter laced up her boots.

The ongoing story line at the time was that Moolah hated Richter for her beauty and success, and therefore managed female wrestlers who would go up against the champ, to no avail. The Spider was one of them. She wrestled in a full-body black costume, complete with a balaclava-like mask, and from the very start of the match, something seemed off. The figure in the mask was too stout to be Mitchell.

"I'd wrestled the Spider Lady before," Richter would later say, "and I didn't recall her being that size."

They started the match. Immediately, Richter saw that it was a shoot, not a work—the Spider was wrestling stiff, dealing real blows in ways that deliberately caused pain. That wasn't the match that had been planned.

Under the spotlights and before the gaze of thousands of spectators, Richter had a revelation: "I knew it was Moolah."

The crowd agreed with her assessment. They hadn't had any trouble sussing out who was under the mask, and were already chanting Moolah's name as a taunt.

After almost nine minutes of low blows and cheap shots, the masked opponent pinned Richter to the mat with a simple move known as a "small package"—"Something that you easily kick out of," Richter said. "And I did." She popped her shoulder up to end the pin.

"Whoa, was *that* close!" Gorilla Monsoon told the viewing audience. Then, as Richter started rising to her feet, the referee stretched his arm out to signal the end of the match; the bell rang.

"What was that?" Monsoon asked, sounding genuinely baffled. The Spider lifted her fists in victory while Richter wobbled in fury and confusion. Then she dashed toward the Spider and grabbed the back of her head. She tugged and tugged at the mask until it ripped off, revealing the dyed-henna tresses of the heel queen.

"And look at that," Monsoon declared. "It *is* Moolah!"

The crowd erupted in confused yelling. Moolah tried to get away, but Richter hit her in the back of the head, grabbed a fistful of hair, lifted her up, and dropped Moolah's body on her knee—a "backbreaker," in wrestling terms. It was clear she wasn't using her full strength, but she was definitely enraged. With Moolah prone, Richter pinned her and started screaming to the ref, "*Take it back! Take it back!*" However, as Monsoon put it, "I think this match is over."

After a little more hair-pulling and impotent screaming, Richter stormed off to a corner. The cameras were fixed on Moolah, who gazed out at the crowd with a face that did not suggest joy, only cruel confidence.

"That *is* Moolah," Monsoon said again. "There's no question about it."

Vince had carried off a rare maneuver, what wrestlers call a "screwjob": an instance in which a wrestler agrees to perform a particular match, only to have the promoter flip the script without informing them. As Richter has sometimes told it, she was scripted to win the match against the Spider Lady, and had no knowledge that Moolah, instead, would be cast as the victor.

However, she has, at other times, implied that she knew it was Moolah under the mask all along, which seems plausible: she'd worked with Moolah, wrestled her before. Moolah had a very distinctive silhouette and way of moving in the ring. The fans identified her instantly.

Whichever way Richter tells it, she says the ending of the match was a complete surprise to her.

Alone in the ring, Richter paced about in her neon-green leotard and glittering eyeshadow, her voluminous hair now a bird's nest. She stared in only one direction: directly at the camera, at the viewer, like Truth emerging from her well to shame fankind. She yelled something that the mic didn't pick up, but you can make out the first two words from reading her lips: "*I'll fuckin'* . . ."

She told it this way: "I was so angry that I just walked right out of the building, right in my wrestling suit, wrestling boots. I grabbed my wrestling bag, went out, and hailed a cab. It was cold, it was in November, and I went to the airport in my wrestling outfit, got my ticket, and then I went in the bathroom and put my clothes on in the airport." She never wrestled for Vince again.

Viewers—smarts and marks alike, in whatever proportion they existed—were left to sort out the narrative for themselves. To any true marks who were watching, it looked like Richter had been undermined; they wondered if the ref was corrupt. The smarts who knew wrestling was scripted assumed the undermining they'd seen was just another part of the story line. It wouldn't be until years later, after another, more famous screwjob, that smarts would look back and recognize what they'd seen.

But Wendi Richter wouldn't be the one to tell them. Only long after the death of traditional kayfabe would she talk publicly about what she'd experienced that night.

Richter was a good soldier of the Business. And Vince, to a certain extent, now *was* the Business. She wouldn't go to the press. She wouldn't tell the other wrestlers. Even someone as plugged in to wrestling rumors as Dave Meltzer didn't hear whispers that it had been a screwjob until more than a decade later. At the time, it was a personal message and a private humiliation.

Richter wrestled for other promotions for a bit, then enrolled in community college and got a master's degree in occupational therapy. "I make like three times in therapy than what I made from Vince McMahon," she said in 2005. "Can you believe that? I'm in my bed every night, have a husband, have animals. There's life after wrestling."

But is there?

Richter agreed to be inducted into the WWE Hall of Fame in 2010. There was no mention of her final match for the company at any point during the ceremony.

When I ask Richter what she thinks of Vince, she surprises me with how positive she is.

"I think he made a tremendous impact in the wrestling world," she says.

She adds that she wishes Vince hadn't destroyed the territory system, but when I ask if he ever acted in a way around her that she felt was sexist, she bristles.

"Never, no," she says, her tone heating up.

"He was a complete gentleman. And anyone that would say anything different, I would believe is a damn liar."

8

HIGH SPOT

(1985–1987)

Bret Hart grew up hearing the screams from the basement.

Sometimes, the screams were coming from grown men his father brought home from the ring or the gym. Sometimes, they were coming from Bret's own throat.

Bret's father was Stu Hart, and Stu was a shooter: that is, he was a wrestler who prided himself on his ability to inflict real, non-kayfabe pain. He'd founded Stampede Wrestling in Calgary, which became Western Canada's largest promotion, but he'd started out in legitimate wrestling and retained those skills. Anyone foolish enough to doubt the veracity of his technique would be led into his Calgary house's basement, nicknamed the Dungeon, and put through hell.

Bret loved and respected his father. He was also terrified of him. Stu's temper was quick and brutal, and often visited on Bret, whose sisters loved to "set him up."

"As soon as my dad walked in the room, they'd be on their knees, looking like I beat them to a pulp," Bret tells me. "He fell for it every time."

Bret remembers his father "mauling" him: cuffing him across the room, wrapping big hands over his nose and mouth so he couldn't breathe.

"I can remember thinking, *This is it—this is how it's gonna end*," he tells me. "*I'm gonna die on the rug and it's gonna be my dad apologizing to my mom about how sorry he is that he took it too far.*"

But it wasn't his dad's fault, Bret hastens to say. He had to keep order somehow in a family of twelve kids. "No matter what I went through, I thought my dad always did the best he could," Bret tells me. "I always forgave him and loved him, despite what happened."

Bret was his parents' eighth child, and at his birth in 1957 Stu immediately predicted great things: Bret, he announced, would be the biggest of his sons. As a teenager, having survived all those maulings, Bret would descend into the Dungeon to be initiated into the grappling arts. (He would've preferred to go to film school, but there was no arguing with his father.) He emerged well on his way to becoming the colossus Stu had envisioned: tall and broad-shouldered, with long curly brown hair and the hopeful face of a friendly Doberman. He was dedicated to the Business, trained from birth to endure at all costs.

Vince bought Stampede from Stu in the autumn of 1984. Bret was part of the package. He met Vince for the first time at his WWF debut, on August 29 in Ontario. Chief Jay Strongbow, now a WWF staff apparatchik, told Bret how his match would go, then waved over to Vince, whom Strongbow referred to as "The Emperor."

With his pompadour, padded red sports jacket, and white running shoes, the Emperor looked to Bret like no one so much as Big Boy, the grinning hamburger chain mascot. This was the man who now had ultimate power over his life.

Vince, for his part, seemed equally unimpressed with his new acquisition, Bret would recall: he looked Bret over and commented, "I like my wrestlers to spend a lot of time in the gym." Bret, of course, had spent plenty of time in gyms—both his father's dungeon and others. What Vince meant was that he didn't have the look, as Bret put it later, of a "human basketball."

"With Vince McMahon in the ascendant," Bret would write later in his memoir, "it was the dawn of the age of steroid freaks."

As Jake "The Snake" Roberts (Aurelian Smith Jr.), a gravel-voiced Texan who also started working at the WWF in this period, put it: wrestlers could easily obtain steroids. "Doesn't matter. Whatever the fuck you wanted. There might've been a handful of guys that didn't take it, but everybody else, they were either taking speed or downers—or both—and steroids. Whatever you wanted, you could get. You could get as much of it as you wanted."

A Pennsylvania-based urologist named George Zahorian was the company's go-to for steroids and certain other drugs.

It wasn't just the workers; the boss himself was allegedly happy to partake.

"Vince was coked out of his mind," wrestler Matt Borne would later say.

Vince's chauffeur, Jim Stuart, once told a reporter that Vince "would be doing drugs in the back of the limo." In one particular incident, the driver said, Vince was "back there with a couple of friends, and they're drinking and doing coke and laughing," telling Stuart to drive 100 miles per hour. "What if we get pulled over?" Stuart recalled asking. Vince's reply: "I'll handle that when it comes. I'll get out of it."

Though Vince has never spoken publicly about using cocaine, rumors about it are widespread: "I can snort as much of that stuff as anyone can put in front of me and never get hooked," is how he allegedly put it to someone close to him.

He has no such discretion about his personal use of steroids, which were still legal back then. "Steroids work," Vince would say in an *Esquire* interview, years later. "When I took steroids back in my forties, I could feel a tremendous difference."

Vince's gym-rat tendencies had only grown since his high school days at Fishburne. He worked out nearly every day, pushing himself far past the limits of mere good health. As he once put it, "I find the gym to be a socially acceptable way for me to rid myself of this superaggression that I have."

According to one account, Vince "even went so far as to hire an assistant whose primary job was to keep tabs on his high-protein diet and feed him huge quantities of tuna fish" and "new employees who walked by the kitchen attached to his office were usually taken aback by the strong smell."

It would be more than a decade before Vince actually stepped into the ring or did anything that involved public use of his musculature. Whatever his reasons for working out were, they were private, not professional.

On June 30, 1986, Vince appeared on a sports-oriented TV show hosted by broadcasting legend Larry King.

"Are you the Don King of wrestling?" the host asked, referring to the famed boxing promoter.

"No," Vince replied. "I am the Walt Disney of wrestling."

Not exactly.

The men of the WWF were addicted to many things—substances were only one.

"The road really screwed up my sex life," Jake the Snake once said. "You get some type of thing, or whatever. Then, all of a sudden, you can have it every day. But then, all of a sudden, you wanna get selective. And, all of a sudden, one a day's not enough. Then you do two a day.

Then three a day. Then two at a time. Then two at a time with toys. Then two at a time: 'I'll just watch.' And it just gets more bizarre and more bizarre."

Vince was having his own fun, too.

"When Linda and I got married, I promised her two things: that I'd always love her and that there would never be a boring moment," he would tell a reporter many years later. "I've lived up to both promises. I have always been . . ."—and here he paused—". . . loyal."

"And faithful?" the reporter asked.

"Not necessarily faithful," Vince confessed. "I probably lied to myself, thinking she knew who I was when we got married. The wild guy. But I never, ever threw anything in her face. I was discreet. And Linda never suffered from a lack of attention, physical or emotional. . . .

"It's not something I'm proud of," Vince added. "I just didn't realize the impact of messing with other people's lives. Notwithstanding the impact on my wife, I'm talking about the havoc you create in other lives, just from wanting to have a good time. . . . The sex was terrific, but from an emotional standpoint, I regret it."

Rita Chatterton got into the Business because of a vow.

Born Rita Filicoski and raised in the Albany area, she was the first female referee in the history of the WWF, hired during the faux-feminist heights of the Lauper-Albano feud. She hadn't grown up as a wrestling fan, though it was regularly on the family television. It was her little brother who was obsessed. "From the time he was a little boy, it's all he talked about," Chatterton tells me. He was killed in a car crash in 1979, at the age of eighteen.

"The day he was killed, I went into his room," Chatterton says. "He had a notepad there. He had all the wrestling schools listed: how much it was gonna cost, how he'd pay for it."

She was a divorced mother in her mid-twenties, working as a delivery driver for the company that made Wonder Bread. But, in that moment, she made a fateful decision: "I decided to go into wrestling for him."

However, she sustained an unrelated injury before she could start training. "My body just couldn't handle what the wrestlers were going through," she says. "So I decided, in the hospital, to become a referee."

Chatterton perused her brother's book of wrestling schools. She called up the only one on the East Coast: Passariello's Quest Athletic Facility, in Orange, New Jersey. She had to beg, but was eventually allowed to train.

Referees are just as much a part of the show as the grapplers. They count the *one-two-three* that ends matches, but there's much more to the role. They have to be ready to take bumps when the wrestlers pretend to get rough with them, to feign distraction or unconsciousness at key moments, or to otherwise advance the plot. What's more, in the days of old kayfabe, many states required wrestling refs to be officially approved by the local athletic commission, though such approval tended to be granted easily and with a wink.

Female referees were vanishingly rare, and there had never been one in the WWF. Chatterton aimed to change that.

A slight and graceful woman with a high, soft voice, she would put her long, sandy hair into a ponytail when she stepped into the ring for training. "It was really funny," says Passariello, "because she was tiny, so to push the big guys apart was cute."

The workouts could be grueling, but Chatterton had caught the wrestling bug.

She got certified, and, in mid-1984, the New York Athletic Commission assigned Chatterton to her first show: a WWF visit at the Orange County Fairgrounds, in Middletown, New York. She says that, when she arrived, Pat Patterson walked up to her.

"Who are you here with?" he asked her, thinking she was merely a romantic partner of one of the Boys.

"I'm by myself," she replied. "I'm your referee tonight."

Patterson thought it was a rib: "I've been in this business thirty years; you'll have to do better than that," he said.

Chatterton said she was serious. She showed him her license.

"He's looking at the license," Chatterton recalls, "looks back at me, looks at the license, does this three or four times, then throws it at me and says, 'Who in their right fucking mind would give a female a ref's license?'"

Chatterton says Patterson even offered to give her the money she would've been paid that night, so long as she didn't actually work the show. Nevertheless, after a tense argument in which Chatterton says she threatened to sue the WWF, she was allowed to work the show—but just a women's tag-team match, no more.

"The women were told to break my legs," Chatterton says, "and make sure I didn't wanna get in the ring again."

If that order was, indeed, given, the women didn't follow through on it. In fact, Chatterton had an amazing experience: "Once the match started, once the bell rings, it's like the outside doesn't even exist," she says. "The whole universe is in that squared circle."

The athletic commission assigned her to some more shows, and she soon decided she was going to join the WWF. She worked her connections and got in touch with George Scott, who told her he'd talk to Vince. The next day, her phone rang.

"Rita?" the voice on the other line said. "Vince McMahon here."

She paused for a long moment.

"Are you there?" he asked.

She said she was.

Vince said he'd heard good things about her. "I'd like you on television soon," the boss continued. "How about Saturday night? Can you make it to Madison Square Garden?"

That would be quite the step up, to say the least. "It was insane," she recalls. "I'm used to doing little three-, four-thousand-people venues. Nothing compared to MSG."

"I'll be there," she told Vince.

Vince also offered a warning: "Keep yourself clean," he said, in Chatterton's telling. "I don't wanna see you messing around with any of the wrestlers. You keep it professional." She said she would.

Chatterton made her TV debut in January of 1985 in a match at MSG. In-ring announcer Howard Finkel hyped her up to the assembled crowd: "For the first time in World Wrestling Federation history—and, for that matter, Madison Square Garden history—sanctioned by the New York State Athletic Commission, for this upcoming matchup, for the *first time ever*, a lady referee!"

In that match, combatants Moondog Spot (Larry Booker) and Blackjack Mulligan (Robert Windham) towered over the novice ref. She held an appropriately stern look on her face as she reprimanded Spot for attempting to use his trademark weapon, a large bone. "I am impressed," Gene Okerlund declared to the TV audience while watching her break up an illegal scuffle. "She quickly got Mulligan to back off."

Gorilla Monsoon offered his own praise, saying this unusual ref "certainly knows the rules."

"Just being in the ring, it was magic," Chatterton says of that match.

Part of it was the typical sorcery of participating in the artform, but there was also "me knowing that nobody else can ever be the first."

Soon, she was appearing regularly at WWF shows. She even made an appearance on the March 1, 1985, episode of *TNT*. At one point in the interview, Vince sized her up, a glazed smile on his face.

"I mean, you weigh approximately 120 to 130 pounds—not getting personal, somewhere in there," Vince said. "And for you to step into the ring with the *giants*—I mean, you realize what can *happen* to you, do you not?"

In Chatterton's telling, she traveled to Poughkeepsie's Mid-Hudson Civic Center, where the WWF regularly held tapings of its televised matches, in July of 1986. She wanted to get an audience with Vince and talk about her future with the company. She says she found him in a hallway, and he told her they should talk after the show, at a nearby diner. So she drove to the diner and found Vince there—along with about a dozen other people.

"We're sitting at this big, round table," Chatterton tells me. She brought up her career. "Vince McMahon put his finger to his mouth, in a *shhh* sign."

She got up and used the bathroom. "When I come out of the ladies' room, McMahon's standing there," she recalls, "and he says, 'I don't wanna talk to you about your career in front of all these people, because it's none of their business.'" She thought that sounded reasonable. He suggested they go to another diner down the street, just the two of them.

They left the building, Vince got into his limousine, and Chatterton was getting into her car, when he rolled down his window.

As Chatterton puts it, Vince said, "I'm tired, let's talk here," referring to his limo. "It'll only take ten minutes." Vince's chauffeur, Jim Stuart, left the limo and went into the diner. According to Chatterton, she and Vince were alone in the vehicle.

"He starts talking about a half-a-million-dollar-a-year contract," she would later tell a talk-show audience. "Next thing I know, Vince McMahon is unzipping his pants. . . ."

"Vince continued to, you know, 'If you want a half-a-million-dollar contract, you're going to have to satisfy me, and this is the way things have to go,'" she continued. "Vince grabbed my hand, kept trying to put my hand on him. I was scared. At the end, my wrist was all purple, black, and blue. Things just didn't . . . He just . . . God, he just didn't stop. This man just didn't stop."

According to Chatterton's account on the talk show, Vince said, "How's your daughter going to go to college? Of course, she doesn't *have* to go to college."

As Chatterton put it, "I was forced into oral sex with Vince McMahon. When I couldn't complete his desires, he got really angry, started ripping off my jeans, pulled me on top of him, and told me again that, if I wanted a half-a-million-dollar-a-year contract, that I had to satisfy him. He could make me or break me, and if I didn't satisfy him, I was blackballed, that was it, I was done."

"One of the things that sticks with me, and always will," she tells me, "was, after he got done doing his business, he looked at me and said, 'Remember when I told you not to mess with any of the wrestlers? Well, you just did.' "

As she told the talk-show audience, Vince "just sat back and had this big smile and this big grin and just started laughing at me."

Vince's lawyers have denied the claim that he raped Rita Chatterton.

It was becoming clear to Bret Hart that he had gone from being the biggest star in Stampede to being an overlooked, underbooked worker in the WWF.

Vince had stocked the company full of talent, but there were only so many hours of TV programming to go around. Not everyone would get a "push"—anointment from the front office as one of the promotion's featured characters.

"There was growing tension in the dressing room," Bret wrote in his acclaimed 2007 memoir, which was based on extensive audio diaries that he kept throughout his life. "It was like Vince and George [Scott] were walking by with that tray of big steaks again, and every dog in the kennel was snapping and jumping pretty high." Jump though he might, Bret couldn't quite sink his teeth in.

He'd been put to work in a heel tag team with his brother-in-law, Jim "The Anvil" Neidhart. Managed by a fast-talking Mississippian named Jimmy Hart (no relation), they called themselves the Hart Foundation. Bret adopted the nickname "The Hitman," and it was duly trademarked by the WWF.

Neidhart was another Stu Hart disciple, as were David "Davey Boy" Smith and Tom "Dynamite Kid" Billington, two Englishmen who wrestled as the British Bulldogs and had married into the Hart family. Bret and the three other former Calgary wrestlers remained a unit within the larger WWF ecosystem. All of them still felt loyal to Stu, even as they were eager to prove themselves to their new boss.

But although the former Stampede wrestlers didn't realize it at the time, they were, essentially, stolen goods.

When Vince had bought out Stampede in August of 1984, he had promised Stu $100,000 a year for ten years and 10 percent of the box office receipts at shows in Calgary and Edmonton. But by the fall of 1985, Vince still hadn't paid Stu a dime.

Bret only found out about this years later, doing research for his memoir. "I remember my mom told me, 'We didn't get a penny. We didn't get one cent,'" he tells me. "And I remember saying, 'Why didn't you tell me that you never got paid?' And she goes, 'We didn't want you to get fired. We thought if we protested or made any kind of a stink about it, we were fearful you would get fired.'"

Vince eventually told Stu that he could reopen Stampede, should he choose, and that, if the WWF *did* ever return to the region, Stu would get a percentage of the box office—*five* percent, to be exact.

And that was that. Stu couldn't afford to sue, and he couldn't afford to complain. His son's career was on the line.

Meanwhile, Bret had a big show to audition for.

Given the success of the first WrestleMania, a sequel was a foregone conclusion, but *WrestleMania 2* (the official styling of the numbers over the years would haphazardly change from Arabic to Roman) was going to be an order of magnitude more ambitious than its predecessor. The idea was to stage the event in not one, not two, but *three* different arenas across the country, simultaneously.

There would be action in Los Angeles, Chicagoland, and Long Island. The telecast would show a full match in one city, then toss to a match at another, then another, then back. There would be a different announcing team for each location, as well. On top of all that, one of the matches would be a twenty-man battle royal involving not just wrestlers, but also half a dozen barely trained current and former National Football League players.

Fed up with the industry, Jesse Ventura used the run-up to *Wrestle-Mania 2* as an opportunity to unionize. He'd managed to join the Screen Actors Guild after appearing in *Predator* and, as he would later recall, he "gave a speech to the Boys" without Vince's knowledge, urging them to band together for collective bargaining. People seemed enthusiastic. "The next night, I got a call from Vince, who basically threatened to fire me if I ever brought it up again and read me the riot act," Ventura said. (Ventura believed that Hogan ratted him out, but no evidence has emerged to support this.) "So when I came back to Vince, I told him point blank, 'Vince, I won't ever bring up a union again.' I said, 'If these guys are too stupid to fight for their rights, I have my union now.'"

WrestleMania 2, held on April 7, 1986, was an overextended disappointment, overloaded with celebrity guests of dubious levels of fame. Mr. T was brought back for a (fixed) boxing match with Roddy Piper that was mostly notable for the guest judges, all summoned by guest announcer Joan Rivers: Darryl "Chocolate Thunder" Dawkins of the New Jersey Nets, aging crooner Cab Calloway, and none other than convicted Watergate burglar G. Gordon Liddy (who, like the heel he'd always been, drew enormous boos). Even Ricky Schroder of TV's *Silver Spoons* was there, acting as guest timekeeper for the mediocre main-event match between Hogan and the enormous King Kong Bundy (Christopher Pallies).

Although it drew around 250,000 pay-per-view buys—an enormous number for the new technology—they didn't fill all the seats in all the venues. The people who did buy tickets grew surly over the course of the evening: the alternating between cities meant any given crowd had to sit through long periods when they were merely watching on giant screens as the action happened more than a thousand miles away.

WrestleMania 2 turned a profit, but not by much.

If there had still been real competition for audiences in the wrestling world, *WrestleMania 2* would have been a dangerous misstep. But the other promotions—those that hadn't already folded or sold out to Vince—were on their last legs. Crockett and Gagne, as Buddy Rogers had predicted, simply couldn't work out their differences. Gagne began back-channel negotiations with Vince for a possible sale and Crockett—by now the de facto leader of the rump NWA—had to move forward alone with an ambitious national tour called the Great American Bash. No one could make a serious dent in the public perception of the WWF as a juggernaut.

Crockett had filed a federal antitrust lawsuit against Vince and Titan Sports in December of 1985, claiming he'd been unlawfully strong-armed out of a venue and a TV station. Two weeks later, the WWF held a show in Charlotte, the heart of Crockett country, and only got away with it because it was ostensibly a benefit show for the family of a recently deceased WWF wrestler who had been born in the city. Mike LeBell had sued Vince for money he said he was owed, but he only had an oral agreement as evidence, so the matter was dismissed. Crockett's lawsuit eventually fizzled, too.

The AWA's home arena had long been the St. Paul Civic Center in the Twin Cities, but as the year wound down, the venue informed Verne Gagne that the WWF now had an exclusive contract. On top of that, Crockett had invaded Gagne's territory in Wisconsin and Minnesota, making the latter promoter an all-but-totally-defeated man.

"Vince McMahon, Jr. took our income, took our life away from us, took everything away from us," Verne's son Greg would later say. "He was bad."

That quote, surprisingly enough, was given to a WWE film crew for a hagiographic 2006 pseudo-documentary about Vince. In that same film, Vince had nothing nice to say about his defeated rivals.

"I don't have much sympathy for those individuals who, quote, 'lost their jobs,'" Vince said. "What we're talking about is: people who managed and owned these territories, they were protected. It wasn't the real world. It certainly wasn't our capitalistic society."

The good news rolled in every day for Vince. Starting with the fall 1986 TV season, WWF tapings would be liberated from their fixed locations in the Northeast. Now, WWF shows would film on a roving basis, moving freely from city to city, something completely unimaginable in the old status quo. *Saturday Night's Main Event* kept drawing eye-widening ratings, often bigger than *Saturday Night Live* got.

USA Network's *All-American Wrestling* was placing in the top fifteen in cable ratings across all genres. Indeed, Vince's pioneering experiments in cable TV were arguably the main product propping up the USA Network—and the entire cable medium, as it developed and expanded.

Riding high on all this victory, Vince even opened a steakhouse in Raleigh with a pal from his time at Fishburne. They called it Vinnie's.

Titan's VP of marketing, Basil DeVito Jr., spoke to a reporter around this time, and he used the language of American empire to describe his boss's mission.

"When Vince took over from his father, he saw the Manifest Destiny which the WWF is approaching today," DeVito mused. "It has been said that our best research is lodged firmly in Vince McMahon's gut."

In 1986, the WWF earned $77,413,379 in gross income—more than $14 million more than the previous year.

Vince's gut was leading the way on all creative decisions now. Vince had taken George Scott off booking duties, leaving himself as sole booker—he didn't like to share his toys, and Scott had become increasingly alienated from the promotion under Vince's leadership.

"It was terrible," Scott later told an interviewer. "Doing the booking, there'd be four to five guys that wouldn't show up for matches. It was all through drugs." After an argument with Hogan, the star stopped listening to Scott's orders. "Hogan wasn't mine," Scott recalled. "I had no control over him."

As George "The Animal" Steele would later put it, "Wrestling as it was went stage left after George Scott left."

Steroids and coke may have been the WWF's bread and butter, but André the Giant's intoxicant of choice remained alcohol.

So much had changed in just a few short years, but one thing was pretty consistent: André's drawing power. If Hulk Hogan was a superhero, André was more like a national monument: you didn't cheer him on so much as you paid homage in exchange for being in his presence. But monuments fall into disrepair, and André was ailing. He drank so much partly to dull the pain from his acromegaly—the pituitary gland disorder that had given him his prodigious size but also caused a host of ailments, from aching joints to spinal stenosis. The condition was debilitating on its own, but decades of abusing his body in the ring had made things exponentially worse.

Hollywood, then, was a lifeline for André, much as it would be for many other wrestlers to come. In late 1986, he got the chance to take a break and film a supporting role in the Rob Reiner–directed fantasy romance *The Princess Bride*. As the gentle strongman Fezzik, André played a sweeter, simpler, nonalcoholic version of himself—the person he might have been if he'd never left his rural French village. The movie filmed in England and Ireland, and the cast and crew all fell in love with André. He allegedly ran up a $40,000 bar tab while working on the film, but he was about as happy as he had ever been in his life.

Then he got a phone call from Vince about the plan for the third WrestleMania.

"They were turning him into a villain," *Princess Bride* actor Billy Crystal later recalled. "And he was very mad that they were changing his persona, that he was gonna become a bad guy in the wrestling world."

Sure enough, that was Vince's vision. André would do the unthinkable: he'd turn heel. Not only that, he'd turn heel on *Hogan*. Their rivalry would culminate in a championship match (André had never held the belt) at *WrestleMania III*, scheduled to be held in Michigan's cavernous Pontiac Silverdome. It was to be the Irresistible Force going up against the Immovable Object. There was no bigger possible main event within the WWF roster.

André did as he was told.

Over the course of a series of charged "Piper's Pit" installments filmed in January, André was made to utter cryptic threats to Hogan, hinting, in his halting English, that their friendship was on unsteady ground. In a climactic moment, it was revealed that André was in league with arch-heel manager Bobby "The Brain" Heenan.

"Wait, what's goin' on here?" Hogan said to André in a terrified tone when he saw the Giant lumber in alongside Heenan.

"It's not happenin'!" Hogan said in anxious denial, grabbing André by the shoulders.

"Take your hands off mine shoulders!" André grumbled, barely intelligible. "Look at me when I'm talking to you! I'm here for one reason: to challenge you for a world championship match in the WrestleMania!"

"André, please, no," Hogan said. "We're *friends*, André, *please!*"

"You can't believe it?" Heenan said. "Maybe you'll believe *this*, Hogan!"

André grabbed Hogan's crucifix chain and "Hulkamania" T-shirt, tore them off the champ's chest, then tossed the ruined accoutrements to the floor and stomped off with Heenan.

Hogan fell to his knees. His chest had a slight cut from either the cross or André's nails, and droplets of blood started to emerge from it. He spoke, his voice as shredded as the tank top and necklace that he now held impotently in his hands.

"André, what are you *doin'*, man?" he said, even though André was gone. "You can't *leave* like this, man! You *can't!*"

Piper knelt down to Hogan's eye level and gently grazed the wronged man's chest. "You're bleeding," Piper said, his voice quiet and unnervingly beautiful. He lifted Hogan up to his feet and they walked away as the camera cut to commercial.

It continued like this, as a story of trust betrayed and morals undone. In segments aired throughout the first months of 1987, the rivalry built. André inevitably challenged Hogan to a match for the belt, and Hogan had no choice but to growl-shout the word "*Yes!*" with a passionate reluctance. They both participated in a nonchampionship battle royal on the tenth installment of *Saturday Night's Main Event*, and André tossed Hogan out of the ring, causing Hogan to lose—what if, the viewer was supposed to wonder, this beast gone rabid were able to triumph over the hero when the belt was on the line?

By the time the story line was set to climax, at *Wrestlemania III* on March 29, 1987, André—per his doctors—absolutely should not have been wrestling.

"On that day, [André] had promised not to drink," WWF commentator Édouard Carpentier would later recall. "But he had bought his wine bottles. He was looking at Vince while drinking his wine, mocking him. I asked him why he was drinking, since it was a big match, and he told me it was none of my business. No one knew he was drunk in the ring that night."

The weight of André's enormous bones was destroying his legs, and he had to wear a back brace under his black, single-strapped caveman leotard. His face was pale, his teeth stained, his eyes half-dead. However, his dreadful appearance only added to the intended effect of making André look like he'd sold his soul.

After about eleven minutes of lackluster grappling, all of which was rewarded with enthusiasm by the crowd, Hogan managed to lift André's enormous body—at that point, about 550 pounds—just barely high enough that he could then invert the man and slam him into the mat. Hogan went for the pin. *One, two, three*—it was over. The masses exploded with joy.

It was a miraculous moment for Vince, that climax at the Pontiac Silverdome. He'd packed a massive venue and the PPV was seen live by an estimated 1 million to 1.5 million people. It was quite the feather in Vince's cap. People who had once taken him as a flash in the pan now had to acknowledge that he was here for good.

The two grapplers, prone on the canvas, struggled to breathe and longed for chemical relief. Both of them, as it turned out, were in horrible pain. Hogan has even claimed he sustained a nearly career-ending injury while executing the final body slam.

"I've got a big hole in my back muscle where it tore right in half that night," Hogan later wrote. "That was the price I paid to lift André the Giant."

André had, in wrestling terms, dutifully "done the job," i.e., lost the match. He so rarely lost matches in his career by then that it was an epochal event. One of André's key selling points under the terms of kayfabe had been his supposed invulnerability. Vince took that from him, and audiences never looked at him the same way again in his lifetime. André had "put Hogan over"—which is to say, lost in such a way as to make Hogan look formidable, and he did it at the order of a promoter he was coming to hate. The main event of *WrestleMania III* remains André's best-known match. But it was, in its way, a tragedy for the Giant.

André would later warn Bret Hart about their employer. "André told me with a sour look on his face, 'Vince is nothing like his father. When his father gave me his word, that was all I needed,'" Bret recalled. "André was like an old circus elephant, and I sensed that, if Vince had his way, this circus was moving on without him."

Over a year prior, the WWF had released a novelty LP called *The Wrestling Album*, in which wrestlers sang kitschy standards or character-specific original tunes. It had been musically abysmal, but peaked on the Billboard charts at the 84th-place slot—an impressive showing for a novelty record, and a sign of the WWF's growing cultural capital. In September of 1987, the WWF and Epic Records released a sequel album called *Piledriver: The Wrestling Album II.*

This time, Vince himself was one of the featured performers.

He sang a track called "Stand Back." The lyrics were at once straightforward and strange:

> When I was just a boy, everybody told me
> What I should do, and who I should be
> I got some advice; I finally have to say
> Stand back

It wasn't all that thrilling to listen to, with its chintzy instrumentation and Vince's lackluster vocal performance. If you put the record on and were out of the loop about Vince's true role—and most fans were—this song must have been baffling. Why would a lowly announcer sing a song about naked ambition?

> *They never understood the kinda man I am*
> *I do my own thinking; got a lotta big plans*

Few could appreciate how well the lyrics captured the frustrations and aspirations of the man who had once been Vinnie Lupton. Vince hadn't spoken about his childhood to the public yet, so the thematic perfection of the song was lost on most. And yet, to those who knew he ran the WWF, the song was a crystal-clear provocation against all who dared oppose him.

He sang that he was "a man runnin' wild, headed for the top"; that he would never slow down, was "never gonna stop." Then came a chilling couplet that predicted the future:

> *Along the way, you're gonna see a lotta men drop*
> *Baby, watch 'em drop*

This was Vince as insider troll, unable to resist a chance to play out his personal grievances in code. There he was, perhaps kidding and perhaps not, telling those who knew how to listen exactly who he was—or, at least, what he wanted them to think he was: a heel.

Jim Crockett was set to hold the *Starrcade '87* PPV on Thanksgiving; Vince responded by announcing that the WWF would hold a new event called the Survivor Series on PPV the same day. What's more, Vince added a stipulation: if a cable company presented Starrcade, they would be denied the next WrestleMania. In the end, out of two hundred cable companies that had planned to broadcast *Starrcade '87*, only five stuck with Crockett.

Vince's grand finale to the year 1987 was the second annual Slammy Awards, on December 16—a sequel to a spoof awards show Vince had staged the previous year to promote that low-rent first album. Technically, this follow-up was billed as "The 37th Annual Slammy Awards"— a cheeky joke about Vince's intentions to build an eternal institution. Indeed, the whole night was filled with cheeky jokes.

Vince was learning how to play for the people who were smart to the business, not just the marks and fair-weather ironists. It was a genius maneuver: just as WWF wrestling was getting so ostentatiously fake that many smarts couldn't get into the kayfabe story lines anymore, he was beginning to offer a kind of meta-story, a saga about what was happening behind the story lines.

He was introducing neokayfabe.

Vince performed "Stand Back" onstage at the Slammys, clad in a vest-and-slacks outfit that would have felt right at home on Sonny Bono over a decade earlier. Beautiful women in frilly dresses pranced around him, smiles glued on their faces. A row of his top wrestlers—including George Steele, rising star Randy Savage, even ornery Jake the Snake—pretended to play saxophones or trumpets for almost four minutes. Hogan, for his part, was forced to resume his old job as the rhythm section, pretending to play an electric bass.

Vince did simple choreography while approximating the notes of the boasts and angrily gurgling the threats, singing that if they "wanna bring me down," he had bad news for them: "I promise you'll lose."

The last number of the night was a song from *Piledriver* called "If You Only Knew." Virtually every wrestler on the roster was trotted out to sing as a group, shuffling back and forth and clapping on two and four.

Ostensibly, the lyrics came from the perspective of a wrestler doing a promo about how much he'd mess up his opponent. But Bret Hart had a theory about what was really going on.

"There we were," the wrestler wrote later, "actually singing about how our destiny belonged to Vince."

In just a handful of well-chosen, cheerfully sung phrases, the chorus perfectly captured a sentiment of total domination and threatened destruction:

> *If you only knew what I'm gonna do to you*
> *You'd be runnin' outta here as fast as your feet could carry you*
> *Your destiny belongs to me*

"To the best of my knowledge," Bret wrote, "no wrestler was ever paid one cent for anything having to do with the Slammys or the *Piledriver* album."

TURNS

"It's fun because some of it's true,
you know what I mean?"

VINCE McMAHON

9

PUSH

(1987–1990)

Even before he started accepting their campaign dollars, Rick Santorum owed a debt to the McMahon family. After all, he'd spent countless hours enjoying Vince Senior's programming when he was coming up.

"I freely admit, as a boy in Pittsburgh, I watched the 'Living Legend' Bruno Sammartino and George 'The Animal' Steele on Saturday morning wrestling," the archconservative Pennsylvania senator wrote in his 2005 book, *It Takes a Family: Conservatism and the Common Good*. He celebrated the fact that wrestling was "non-elite" and that, even when the bad guys won, "you always at least knew that they were bad, and were invited to boo."

In early 1987, Santorum was twenty-eight years old, and firmly committed to the conservative agenda. He had been chairman of his school's chapter of College Republicans, worked for a Republican lawmaker in the Pennsylvania state senate, gone to law school, and joined the Pittsburgh firm Kirkpatrick & Lockhart as a prelude to a political career. In Santorum's first year there, the firm acquired what would end up being a long-term client: Vince McMahon.

As tends to be the case with lawyers, Vince came to Kirkpatrick & Lockhart in a moment of panic. In January of 1987, Bret Hart's tag-team partner, Jim Neidhart, allegedly attacked a female flight attendant while traveling from Tampa to Pittsburgh. When the plane landed, Neidhart was arrested. The company's regular lawyer called Kirkpatrick & Lockhart lawyer Jerry McDevitt.

"I assume he probably regrets making the call, since I ended up stealing the client," McDevitt would later say. "But he asks me if I would represent Neidhart. I said I would, and that was the start of the whole relationship." As of this writing, that relationship has never been broken. McDevitt, a gimlet-eyed man who speaks in a slow monotone while he describes how he's destroyed people, would one day call himself the McMahons' "family consigliere."

McDevitt got Neidhart released on bail in time to perform at *Wrestle-Mania III*, and defended him when the case went to trial that April. When Neidhart was acquitted on all charges, Vince was pleased—and eager to further engage McDevitt's services in other matters. He and Linda needed legal help in Pennsylvania. They were trying to deregulate pro wrestling.

In the majority of the US, pro wrestling was still overseen by local athletic commissions, typically whichever ones also handled boxing. In those states, kayfabe was codified in law: just as they would monitor a legitimate sport, inspectors would inspect the ring for safety, check the health of the wrestlers, and watch the show to make sure nobody got hurt. Promoters, in turn, paid taxes that funded the system.

The state commissions were mostly lax and often corrupt. Blading was technically forbidden, but regularly happened without penalty. Pennsylvania's state-appointed doctor was none other than steroid pusher George Zahorian—himself an eager and longtime wrestling fan who occasionally made on-camera appearances to issue kayfabe medical pronouncements.

But even this level of supervision was too much for Vince and Linda. Their successful effort to escape South Yarmouth's rules for the Cape Cod Coliseum just a few years prior had technically been their first political act. But deregulation was their true induction into the world of conservative politics.

At some point around the run-up to the first WrestleMania, the WWF had started lobbying for deregulation in Connecticut. On May 15, 1985, Republican state representative Loren E. Dickinson had presented a bill that would remove most government oversight of wrestler health and safety. A WWF lawyer had appeared before the body to defend the effort with a remarkable admission: he said wrestling was fake.

"We consider ourselves in the same class or league as the circus and the Harlem Globetrotters," the lawyer had said, adding that while such performances featured "terrific athletes" and "tremendous entertainment," they nevertheless "do not have the regulation by the government." If something wasn't real, how dangerous could it be?

The legislature was convinced, and the bill quietly passed into law that May. From then on, wrestling in the state where Vince's business was headquartered would be something of a free-for-all, in terms of health and safety standards.

As of 1987, the McMahons had replicated their Connecticut victory in Delaware, were making progress in New Jersey, and had their sights set on another major market, one that was home turf for Kirkpatrick & Lockhart: Pennsylvania.

There, the state athletic commission was vulnerable; under a sunset provision, its existence was up for review by lawmakers. McDevitt's firm was happy to take the job of assisting the McMahons with their campaign to make sure the sun never rose again. The responsibility for the lobbying account fell to the new hire—Santorum.

It was a dream assignment for the young lawyer. Santorum loved wrestling as a kid, but he loved kneecapping the government even more. "Pennsylvania was the most pernicious of states when it came to regulation," he'd later tell a reporter. "They made you pay all this money to the boxing commission. They used to just rape these guys."

Santorum was aggressive in his efforts to sway legislators and officials to Vince and Linda's point of view. He'd regularly treat leading lawmakers and members of the governor's staff to free WWF tickets, plying them with "plenty of food, booze, and soft drinks," as the *Philadelphia Inquirer* put it.

After those shows were over, the *Inquirer* continued, the honored governmental guests would be hustled backstage so they could see beyond the veil. The idea of inviting people backstage, let alone *politicians*, to learn the secrets of the Business would have been wholly alien to Vince Senior's generation.

Santorum helped Linda prepare for her testimony in Pennsylvania's capitol before a session of the committee reviewing the athletic commission on June 11, 1987—one that went unreported on in the media.

She was preceded by two executives from the athletic commission, who pleaded with legislators to allow them to make sure the wrestlers were safe and healthy. The chairman of the state athletic commission, James J. Binns, argued that, if the state got rid of wrestling regulations, they would be replaced by "the 'good old boy' system of 'live and let live' and 'let's just see what we can do to get beyond this problem.'"

The committee members were less interested in worker safety than they were in trying to parse out the question of whether wrestling was real. After

Binns delivered his opening statement, the first question from a legislator was, "Do you believe honestly that wrestling is a competitive sport?"

"It is not, sir," Binns replied. "Wrestling is an exhibition."

That line was just what Linda and Santorum needed to hear. Indeed, Linda doubled down on it in her prepared statement.

"We provide quality, family entertainment for all age groups and for people from all walks of life," she told the group. "Unlike professional boxers, professional wrestlers are not competing in contests where points are scored, and the winner determined, by potentially injurious blows struck at an opponent. Instead, like the skilled athletes you see in the circus or the Harlem Globetrotters, our athletes are well-conditioned professionals who are the best at what they do. And what they do is entertain people."

She claimed a double standard was at work. "Does the Liquor Control Board assign an agent to every tavern? Does the Game Commission assign a game warden to every hunter?" she asked. "To such questions, the answer is obviously 'no,' and these are areas where real dangers exist to society. There is no such danger in wrestling."

It was a classic misdirection, but it also functioned as a cynical societal critique: *Real violence isn't regulated, so why should we innocent fakers have to suffer?*

Just eight days after his wife's testimony, Vince acted as the master of ceremonies for the opening night of the 1987 Connecticut Special Olympics. The *Hartford Courant* covered the speech in a brief news item and led with a daring sentence: "Vince McMahon, president of the World Wrestling Federation, admitted it—some professional wrestling matches are arranged."

Apparently, at some point in the evening, Vince had "agreed when it was suggested that the outcome of matches was arranged," then made the waters murky by adding that that wasn't *always* the case: "Sometimes, even we're surprised at the outcome," he said. He called the WWF a "hybrid of entertainment and sport."

(Someone asked Vince whether he ever wrestled professionally. No, Vince said: "I'm not mean enough.")

Even as the McMahons were busy assuring legislators—and Special Olympics volunteers and local reporters—that wrestling was fake, their workers faced dire consequences for letting the pretense of kayfabe slip even a little. The previous month, the Iron Sheik, a heel, and "Hacksaw" Jim

Duggan, a face, had been caught driving together with drugs and booze on the Garden State Parkway. Vince had been livid. He didn't care much about their safety or the law, but he did care about having control. Duggan and the Sheik were summarily fired.

Kayfabe could only be violated on Vince's terms.

If you hung around conservative lecture circuits in the mid-aughts, Rick Santorum would be a familiar figure. But so, too, would be the man who was by then legally known by the mononym "Warrior."

He'd always been a gripping and loquacious public speaker, especially in his heyday as a WWF wrestler. But he'd also always been his own worst enemy, and, by 2005, he was a wrestling pariah delivering hateful lectures to college students.

Take, for example, one he did in a lecture hall at the University of Connecticut that year. There, he railed against "moral relativity," which he characterized as the belief that "there are no absolutes, no right or wrong, no true or false, no good or evil, no objective judgements, no objective analyses." Under moral relativity, he said, "the bum is as legitimate as the businessman."

"That could very well be!" yelled a woman in the crowd.

Someone in the audience began a sentence: "The homosexuals . . ." and the woman said, "Oh, Jesus."

Warrior, a wrinkling husk of a formerly mighty man, sneered back, "Don't have an orgasm on me, honey." The crowd cheered.

"Let me come down off my politically correct horse," Warrior said, prompting laughter from the audience, then added another example of a "moral relativist" belief: "That queers are as legitimate as heterosexuals."

"How are they not?" asked someone in the crowd.

Warrior looked furious and howled back, "Because *queering doesn't make the world work!*"

A machismo-drunk orator with loathsome politics; a man despised by nearly all who got to know him; an outsider with little desire to learn the details of his hastily chosen career: the man's mother named him James Brian Hellwig. He had first risen to prominence in the world of 1980s bodybuilding, only to become the most famous wrestler who never really learned to wrestle.

But even if the ring arts eluded him, there was one thing Hellwig knew how to do better than just about anyone: sculpt his body. Indeed, his success in the WWF owes much to the success of bodybuilding. It still portrayed itself as a legitimate competition. But, in reality, it was like wrestling on even more steroids.

In some ways, bodybuilding dates back to the physical fitness men's magazines of the 1930s. But it also shares a common lineage with wrestling (and, for that matter, superhero comics): the circus strongman. Audiences have long desired to see men with abnormally impressive physiques who can perform incredible acts of strength. Sometimes, that involves fighting; other times, just flexing.

Competitions in which muscular men get rated by judges on their physical appearance had become an American staple. Men who had spent countless hours lifting weights, obeying obscure diets, and—by the 1980s—taking copious amounts of steroids would grunt and pose for judges who graded them on their various attributes. It was glorious for the age of channel-surfing—you couldn't help but be fascinated by the pure image of a man so inflated that he looked like an insect's carapace.

Actor and future California governor Arnold Schwarzenegger had first found fame through the world of competitive bodybuilding in the 1960s. By the late 1980s, Schwarzenegger was one of the biggest stars in the world; even if he wasn't competing in bodybuilding anymore, what man wouldn't want to look like *that*? Bodybuilding—or more accurately, the ideal physique bodybuilding promoted—became an obsession, putting pressure on men everywhere, including Vince and his wrestlers, to look "cut" and steroidal.

Bodybuilding was a world that perfectly suited Hellwig, a boy who'd been born and raised in poverty in small-town Indiana, abandoned by his father and bullied by his peers. He got into chiropractic and hoped to start his own business purveying it, making money through professional bodybuilding. By 1985, with the help of steroids, he was a stunning physical specimen: bulbous, veiny, and perpetually scowling beneath his tangled jungle of a hairdo.

There was backflow between the world of bodybuilding and that of wrestling. Like many other bodybuilders, Hellwig and a bodybuilding pal named Steve Borden started experimenting with the squared circle, forming a tag team called the Freedom Fighters and wrestling for Jerry Jarrett in Memphis.

There was only one problem: they stank.

Hellwig worked stiff and was terrible at a key wrestling art: depicting suffering. He never sold the pain or impact of their opponents' blows. But the duo were imposing to gaze upon and Hellwig's high-energy promos got the crowd riled up, which was a solid way to keep getting work.

Hellwig arrived at the WWF in June of 1987 as a rising star. He also arrived with a gimmick: he'd taken to wearing angular face paint on his eyes and cheeks and tying colorful, unexplained streamers to his biceps. He called himself the Dingo Warrior. There was no real logic behind the name. Vince gave it the axe after a few months.

"What kind of warrior is a Dingo Warrior?" Vince later said. "That didn't sound too menacing to me." It was the Dingo part that made the least sense, so Vince simply replaced it with a new word; a superlative, in fact.

"For all you WWF fans out there lookin' for some type of direction, you came to the right place, brother: 'cause *you're looking at the Ultimate Warrior!*" Hellwig bellowed in his next promo. "Look real deep in my eyes and jump on my back, because I'm gonna *take you through the wall!* And if you look at these veins, the only blood that runs through these veins is the *power of the Warrior!*"

Warrior would later speak about that promo as though he had witnessed the birth of another man, one who occupied his body but was beyond his control. "His energy, his mannerisms, his jargon began to come together there," Warrior said in an interview near the end of his life.

The other members of the company couldn't stand Warrior. Bobby Heenan perhaps summed up the consensus best when he said the following to a WWE documentary crew:

> To me, the man had no idea about wrestling. Didn't care about the history of this business, didn't care about anything. It was like the guy just came out of Gold's Gym and had a can of tuna, a raw egg and said, "Hey! I saw a [WWF] truck over there. I can call them and learn how to wrestle." He knew nothing! Nothing!

That's not an entirely inaccurate description of Warrior's approach: as he told the UConn crowd, when he got into the Business, "I said, *Yeah, people who are on TV make money.*" Even when he started to get over, his goal "wasn't to get into professional wrestling and continue to stay in professional wrestling."

And yet, Vince took an interest in him. Why? The boss's own explanations are always vague. "Warrior kind of captured this rebellious spirit, I think, of many people in the '80s, and sort of symbolized that, in a way," is how Vince once put it. "He has a natural charisma, and a presence about him. . . . He seemed to have a lot of heart, and he seemed to have a great deal of ambition."

Part of the reason, of course, is that the crowd loved Warrior. It wasn't just that his physique made Schwarzenegger seem positively reed-thin; his high-octane habits—running to the ring instead of sauntering over to it, screaming out cosmic word-jazz in his promos, matches in which he "won" so quickly that the crowd could pretend it was due to his world-historical strength—fit well with the go-go zeitgeist.

Vince also needed a backup, in case Hogan ever faltered—and Vince, like his father before him, simply can't resist booking unusually large men in places of prominence. Better to cultivate Warrior now, just in case.

But perhaps there was something Vince and Warrior shared in their worldview. Both of them longed to succeed outside of wrestling, and neither of them had a shred of nostalgia for the way the industry used to be. They believed in pulling yourself up by your bootstraps and looking down upon those who couldn't. They loved size, strength, and aggression. They were, in their particular way, men's men.

In that 2005 UConn speech, Warrior summed up his philosophy a little over halfway through.

"Liberals believe in a utopian society where everything is equal," he told the students. "Life doesn't work that way. It's a good-for-nothing *joke* that it can; and, worse, an oppressive, evil fraud to then pursue it as a goal."

As a kid growing up in Queens, Donald Trump loved wrestling.

He was called "Donny" back then. He and his friends were the target demographic for Jess McMahon and Vince Senior's wrestling product. They watched it on TV.

"He would get an idea in his head, and he'd be wrong," one of those friends, Donald Kass, later told a reporter, "and you would tell him he was wrong. And the next day, he would say the same thing. You could never convince him of anything. . . .

"There was this wrestler called Antonino Rocca," Kass said, referring to one of Vince Senior's top-drawing babyfaces, "and Donald referred to him as 'Rocky Antonino.'

"We'd say, 'No Donald, it's *Antonino Rocca*.' But the next day, it was still 'Rocky Antonino.'

"To Donald," Kass said, "it was always 'Rocky Antonino.'"

Donald Trump and Vince McMahon appear to have first met in an appropriate venue for two icons of the baby boomer generation: "We were his guests for a Rolling Stones concert," Linda would later recall. Trump had sent a message to Vince saying, as Linda put it, "he wanted to have a chance to be with the greatest promoter in the world." The show was in East Rutherford, New Jersey, the two couples hit it off, and a friendship was sparked. "It was great to be there with him and we enjoyed it very much," Linda would later say of meeting Trump.

But Vince and the future president might just as easily have met in any number of other venues. It was hard to avoid Trump if you were trying to be someone in the New York area at the time—and Vince was definitely trying to be someone. However it happened, it now seems inevitable.

The first business dealing between the two was, it seems, neither man's idea.

According to WWE's official history, that honor goes to Titan exec Basil DeVito Jr. and Trump associate Mark Grossinger Etess. The two were apparently on a panel discussion about sports and entertainment, held in Atlantic City, and struck up a conversation there. As DeVito put it years later, "He said to me, 'Gee, I'd really love to bring WrestleMania to Atlantic City.'" A brand partnership was born. *WrestleMania IV* would be held in Atlantic City, where Trump had a hotel and casino, and Trump would be its official sponsor.

Trump was, in his way, much like the wrestlers he'd be endorsing: a man pretending to be far richer than he was; an image-conscious neurotic constantly saying he couldn't care less about what people said of him. He could cut an impromptu promo for a gossip columnist or a TV camera and immediately get over in the arena of mass media. He was well on his way to being the Tri-State Area's most successful heel.

The company hyped up the Trump connection on their programming. Trump made his WWF debut, of sorts, in a little pretaped promo that is strange to watch now, given how subdued and gracious he sounds—maybe a consequence of his younger age, or maybe of his admiration for the artform and Vince.

"I will tell you, I have probably never had an event where more people are asking for more tickets than what they're doing with *WrestleMania IV*," Trump told the camera from his surprisingly small desk. "We're honored to have it, and we look forward to having a great time."

DeVito told Etess that he was worried about the audience: Would casual casino-goers really be the right fit for the elaborate narrative pageantry of a WWF PPV? As DeVito recalled, Etess said, "Well, why don't we create events together? Why don't we create a festival for a couple of days?"

And so it was that the weekend of March 26–27, 1988, was designated as a WrestleMania fan festival, drawing WWF enthusiasts and entertaining potential ticket-buyers on the Boardwalk with all kinds of silliness: a 5K race featuring both WWF talent and civilians, a concert at which various WWF figures performed, even a Sunday-morning WrestleMania brunch. "Everybody in the country wanted this event, and we were able to get it," Trump told the crowd at one of the events. "And that's a great honor for Trump and for Atlantic City."

When the main program finally began, the first thing viewers saw was an opening animation of a Trump Plaza–branded slot machine flying through a blue void. The camera cut to the arena, with text informing you the action was happening at the Trump Plaza Hotel and Casino.

But this was kayfabe. In reality, the event was taking place across the boardwalk at the Atlantic City Convention Center. This kind of casual deception was as natural to Vince as it was to Trump, who had already made a habit of blurring hype and truth if it furthered his interests.

Though you'd never know it from the way WWE talks about *WrestleMania IV* today, the show was something of a disaster. The casino crowd didn't understand the wrestling, the wrestling crowd didn't like the casino crowd, and the product, itself, was hardly top-shelf. "The Trump Plaza should have been called the Trump Mausoleum," was how Dave Meltzer recapped the show in the *Wrestling Observer*. "I saw it and I still don't believe it. Was it a dream? Was it a nightmare? All I know is, in every sense of the word, it was a bomb."

Attendance and PPV buy rates were down dramatically from the previous year's astronomical WrestleMania. But the success of *Wrestle-Mania IV* should not be measured in terms of the event, itself; rather, we must look to the relationship that was forged there. It was this coproduction of this event that first put them into close contact. That friendship would be greatly consequential for both men in the years to come.

Warrior didn't earn it. That's the narrative Vince, and his organization, would later tell about the Ultimate Warrior: he didn't earn the push he got from Vince, and the fact that he left the WWF in disgrace was no one's fault but his own. He wasn't skilled and didn't care to learn—that's indisputable to anyone who watches his old matches. He had an unpleasant demeanor and bloated ego; also demonstrably true, though in that regard, he was hardly alone in the industry. But Warrior's most damning trait, in the official narrative of the WWE, is that *he didn't love the Business enough*.

"He went strictly to showbusiness," Vince would later say of Warrior. "A shortcut route to fame and fortune, as opposed to practicing a craft and learning an art form that the better performers strive to do every single night. . . .

"Ultimate Warrior was supposed to lead the company and the brand into the next century," Vince said. "That didn't exactly happen."

But, for a time, it was the plan. Vince, seeing whatever he saw in Warrior, decided to push him hard. He booked the wrestler to have an incredibly long "winning" streak, in which wrestler after wrestler had to reluctantly do the job for Warrior.

The matches were often humiliatingly short, with Warrior hardly responding to his co-performer's attacks. He'd regularly get to his finishing move (lifting his opponent's body over his head, then dropping it unceremoniously to the canvas) in less than a minute. Frequently, he would nonchalantly place his boot on the man's chest while the referee counted to three, rather than the standard practice of pinning with one's whole body. Even the once-unstoppable André the Giant had to regularly roll over for the newbie. Fans ate it up.

Warrior cut a promo in the fall of 1988, not long after he was given his first title, the Intercontinental Championship. The belt was strapped around his oiled torso. The soliloquy began with him ululating a kind of chant-growl in a low voice, "*ya-ya-ya-ya*," which he seamlessly blended into a loud and characteristically surreal prose poem:

> *You can feel it, too!* You can feel it! The same *sweat* that flows outta *my body* right now is the same sweat that flows outta *yours!* The same *blood* that flows through *these veins* is the same blood that flows outta *yours!* . . . Jump on my back, grab a body part, and *hang on!* Because if we have to swim across the Atlantic, if we have to go clear across all the continents of the world, *we will survive!*

"He would go off in almost a trance and almost speak in tongues," is how Vince would later describe Warrior's promo style.

But if Warrior was lackluster in the ring, nonsensical on the mic, it didn't matter: Vince kept pushing him.

Historically, in order to make it in the Business, you had to pay your dues pretty extensively and get over with fans on your own before you'd get the big opportunities from the big promoters. Even Hogan, who Dave Meltzer had seen as an unrealistic and unworthy champion, had put in six years of work in the wrestling industry before he got to win a WWF belt. It took Warrior less than three.

Vince had changed the rules. Sure, Warrior looked and sounded unique, but he would have been nowhere with the crowds if Vince hadn't forced all his opponents to let themselves be squashed into comical irrelevance. Warrior's push was Vince bludgeoning the roster and the public with the two weapons he'd been wielding to such great and sudden success: narrative and hyperbole.

The death of old kayfabe came much in the way Hemingway described the onset of bankruptcy: gradually, then suddenly.

For years, Vince and Linda had been testing the public's suspension of disbelief and the press's willingness to go along with the gag. Sometimes, as in the Pennsylvania and Connecticut deregulation pushes, they discreetly claimed wrestling was fake to tear down regulations; other times, it was merely to save the company's skin in lawsuits.

Talk-show host Richard Belzer had sued Titan Sports and Hulk Hogan for the incident in which he'd been choked out on live television. Linda had said in sealed testimony that Hogan was just playing around, not act-ing with malicious intent. You see, wrestling promoted and advertised "scenes, scenarios, interplays, actions, feuds, grudges, friendships and as-sociations which further enhance the illusion that professional wrestlers are indeed the characters they play and perform." (The lawsuit was settled before it could go to trial.)

Similarly, in the spring of 1985, *20/20*'s John Stossel had sued the WWF for damage suffered by Dr. D's backstage slaps. Vince gave sealed testimony for that one, too; at one point, he said wrestling matches were prearranged. Neither that statement, nor Linda's, was initially picked up by the press.

Pennsylvania, where the commission that regulated wrestling had been at risk, had been a site of great success for the McMahons. "At a [WWF] show in Hershey," reported journalist Irv Muchnick in the June 1988 issue of *Washington Monthly*, "they handed out complimentary tickets, hors d'oeuvres, beer, and soda to the chairman of the state house Government Committee and more than twenty staff members of the Governor's Office of Legislative Affairs and the Department of State."

Sure enough: "Three months later, the vote flattened the commission." Muchnick quoted Dave Meltzer: "In other words, as usual, Vince McMahon got exactly what he wanted."

Muchnick's article didn't get much attention in mainstream discourse, but it did attract one notable reader.

"I got a call one day from a guy named Rick Santorum," Muchnick tells me. "It was one of the strangest conversations that I've ever had. [Santo-rum] said, 'I'm reading this article, and it's *hilarious!*'"

Santorum then started reading passages from the article. "He cackled," Muchnick recalls. "While the radio was blaring, at the same time, he was reading my article out loud. He was high on *something*. I think it was just politico adrenaline, I guess."

But the event that pulled the trigger and killed kayfabe as it had been known for a century ended up occurring in the state where Trump and Vince had staged their first event together: New Jersey.

There, in addition to all the ostensible health and safety regulations, the state charged a tax for TV sporting events filmed in the state, includ-ing $61,639 for *WrestleMania IV*. Just before that event, the WWF found a high-profile Republican lobbyist and lawyer named John P. Sheridan Jr., and contracted him to help them lobby for wrestling deregulation—

i.e., an end to the tax and an end to health-and-safety oversight—in the Garden State. Sheridan knew just the state senator to talk to: Francis J. McManimon.

The lawmaker was a Democrat, but that hardly mattered. As former McManimon legislative assistant Al Komjathy tells me, "Here in New Jersey, the only day there's 'Republicans' and 'Democrats' is on Election Day." The McMahons have been bipartisan when it's good for business.

More important than McManimon's party affiliation was Komjathy's intense enthusiasm for WWF wrestling, which began in his childhood and continues to this day: "Me and my best friends, we talk about Vince McMahon all the time," says Komjathy.

Vince and Linda pulled out the stops to charm McManimon. He and members of his staff, including Komjathy, were given tickets to *Wrestle-Mania IV*. "We sat at ringside," Komjathy remembers. "Donald Trump was sitting on the other side, and the Macho Man fell into our lap!"

Komjathy and his boss asked the WWF about the health and safety of the wrestlers—what would happen if the state doctors weren't there to check on them? As Komjathy recalls, "They told us, 'Look, we've got a lot of money invested in those people. It's in our best interest to make sure they're safe, y'know?'" He and McManimon were sufficiently convinced.

In the spring of 1988, the senator introduced a bill to deregulate wrestling. The language of the bill defined professional wrestling as "an activity in which participants struggle hand-in-hand primarily for the purpose of providing entertainment to spectators rather than conducting a bona fide athletic contest."

McManimon introduced the McMahons to the senate president, as well as its speaker. The lobbyist Sheridan kept the charm offensive on with more free trips to wrestling shows, in addition to the usual political horse-trading. Lawmakers debated and revised the bill.

Finally, on February 10, 1989, the time came for a vote.

The bill hadn't received much media attention, even in the New Jersey press. But when the New Jersey bureau chief for the *New York Times*, Peter Kerr, learned about the vote, he headed to the state capitol in Trenton. There, he witnessed the vote: 37 to 1 in favor of deregulation.

In legislative terms, the vote ended up being a bust; the bill died in the state assembly, and wrestling wouldn't be deregulated in New Jersey until 1997. And its language about "exhibitions" and "entertainment" was quite similar to the recent WWF-backed laws in Connecticut, Pennsylvania, and elsewhere. But the February 10 vote was different. This time, thanks to Kerr, the whole world was watching.

"Now It Can Be Told: Those Pro Wrestlers Are Just Having Fun," declared a front-page headline in the late edition of that day's *New York Times*.

Kerr began his article by writing, "The promoters of professional wrestling have disclosed that their terrifying towers in spandex tights, massive creatures like Bam Bam Bigelow, Hulk Hogan and André the Giant, are really no more dangerous to one another than Santa Claus, the Easter Bunny and the Tooth Fairy. But please don't repeat this. Millions of grown men and women just don't want to know."

Komjathy was quoted in the article, saying, "If this thing were real, there would be broken bones all over the place."

The next day, the *New York Post* ran its own story about wrestling. Its reporter had managed to uncover Vince's testimony in the Stossel suit, and Linda's testimony in the Belzer suit, further confirming that the WWF was admitting to staged bouts. Newspapers had previously revealed that truth in long-gone eras of wrestling, but this time felt like a true ending. Two of the most important newspapers in the English language—and, subsequently, TV news and other media outlets—had destroyed the idea that wrestling was a legitimate competition.

Everyone, whether they liked it or not, was a smart now.

Though Vince had articulated the argument that wrestling was fake in closed testimony and lobbying, the *Times* and *Post* stories caught him off guard. He wasn't quite ready for the arrival of the world he had created, and reportedly told his wrestlers to cancel all media appearances until he could arrange a PR offensive.

Roddy Piper appeared on ABC's *Good Morning America* on the 13th. "America, read my lips: *I'm no phony!*" he declared, aping the newly inaugurated President Bush. Piper continued with a classically vague defense of his profession: "If wrestling is entertainment, and beating up people is [fans'] way of deriving entertainment, I'm one of the greatest entertainers in the world."

WWF commentator Jesse Ventura did an ESPN interview in which he waxed libertarian, saying, "I think the press is missing the whole point. It's a little-known fact that, in many states, you have 14 [regulators] in suits sitting around the ring and doing absolutely nothing."

The WWF's rivals, suddenly naked without kayfabe, swore up and down that they were fully on the level. As Memphis's Jerry Lawler put it in his weekly TV show, "See, I *told* you that kind of stuff Vince McMahon's been doing up in New York wasn't wrestling!"

When Verne Gagne was asked by the *New York Times* for his reaction, he had a similar response. "They've got a cartoon going there," the bitter and defeated Minnesotan said. "It's a circus. And a lot of 'em don't even know how to wrestle. Some are just bodybuilders, and some puffed themselves up with steroids."

Gagne couldn't resist one last dig at his erstwhile meal ticket: "I once asked Hulk Hogan what his athletic background was," Gagne told the reporter. "He said, 'Oh, I played some Little League baseball, and I played the guitar in my high school band.' And he calls himself a wrestling champion!"

And, of course, Ted Turner was only too happy to capitalize on the chaos. His wrestling operation, the iron nub of the once mighty National Wrestling Alliance, introduced a new tagline: "This Is the NWA: *We Wrestle!*"

The WWF, too, kept up standard kayfabe on its programming, if for no other reason than inertia. But Vince and Linda plowed ahead on their campaign for deregulation, lobbying in state after state with the same general strategy.

Herein lay a dangerous irony. Vince had been pushing the Ultimate Warrior, but Warrior's success depended wholly on kayfabe. If you fully acknowledged that everything was made up, then there would be no reason to believe in Warrior's purported superstrength. You'd see that the guy could hardly even sell a punch.

If pro wrestling was going to survive this harsh new reality, kayfabe would have to evolve.

The timing of the New Jersey furor was inauspicious for Vince, as it was almost WrestleMania season once again. *WrestleMania V* was going to take place back at the Atlantic City Convention Hall, once again falsely branded as the Trump Plaza Hotel and Casino.

"The Trump organization had done such a great job with *WrestleMania IV* that it was hard to imagine a better host for the event," reads an official WWF history of the event co-written by exec Basil DeVito Jr. "They wanted us back, and we were willing to consider a return engagement. In listening to their pitch, and in recalling the previous year's success, we realized that Trump had a very clear understanding of our needs and the ways in which WrestleMania could be taken to a national audience."

The big story line in the lead-up was a saga involving Hogan and the then-champion, Randy Savage. The two men had joined forces since the last WrestleMania, becoming a duo known by the name "The Mega Powers." But, in the story line, Savage's longtime manager and real-life wife, "Miss" Elizabeth Hulette, had become a bone of contention between them: the fiercely jealous Savage was convinced that Hogan had lust in his heart for the woman—something Hogan strenuously denied.

They were slated to have a match at *WrestleMania V* that would be a matter of both the title belt and heterosexual honor. Although Miss Elizabeth was the catalyst for the whole thing, her role in the run-up consisted of theatrically debating which man she should side with, then announcing on an episode of *Saturday Night's Main Event* that she'd remain neutral.

This was the kind of thing that the top women in the WWF were doing as of then. You hardly ever saw a women's match anymore, not even ones with Moolah. Sherri Russell, a wrestler who made her bones in the AWA, showed up in the WWF in 1987, and soon after started going by "Sensational Sherri." But by the lead-up to the fifth WrestleMania, she was being rebranded as a sexy temptress whose purpose was to contrast with virtuous Elizabeth as the other half of the WWF's growing Madonna-whore complex. Any wrestling she did was now purely ornamental.

The sexism was everywhere at April 2, 1989's *WrestleMania V*, if you were looking for it. The show began with the putative WWF women's champion, Rockin' Robin (Robin Denise Smith), singing an off-key rendition of "America the Beautiful," and that was a wrap on her—she didn't have a match that night. No women did. But there was a surprise, non-combat cameo from none other than Jimmy Snuka (he had been fined $500,000 in the Argentino family's civil suit, but hadn't paid a cent of it). And, of course, there was Trump.

"Can you give us some idea what an event of this magnitude means, not only to Atlantic City, but to the Trump Organization?" WWF announcer Sean Mooney asked the future president while he was standing at ringside.

"It's been fantastic," Trump said. "It's been unbelievable. The traffic, the numbers of people—we're really honored to be here and honored that you folks joined us. It's a great honor." Whenever Trump talked about Wrestle-Mania, he always used that word, *honor*.

"Have the casinos been busy?"

"They are *packed*," Trump said, likely falsely—he was always exaggerating the crowds in his Atlantic City casinos. "The whole town is *packed*. It's been a real boon to the town. It's been just a great thing and an unbelievable event. Everybody's excited, we're all enjoying ourselves."

"Well, I know *I'm* going to leave a few dollars in Atlantic City," the announcer concluded with a smile.

"I hope so," said Trump.

The tagline for the whole evening was "The Mega Powers Explode," and the match lived up to the hyperbole, with both wild-eyed maniacs working the crowd in their signature ways and engaging in a fight now regarded as generally pretty solid. Poor, conflicted Elizabeth intervened on behalf of *both* men before being ejected by the referee, and Hogan won. It was his second time winning the top belt, and the first time at a WrestleMania.

Trump took those achievements very seriously. You could see him in his front-row seat throughout the match, completely rapt. As soon as Hogan won, he gave the champ a standing ovation. Long minutes later, while Monsoon absurdly called Hogan "the greatest professional athlete in the world," Trump was still there, beaming.

It was an adventure in Hollywood that would bring Vince and Hogan closer than they'd ever been, then drive them bitterly apart.

Hogan was still a massive presence in American culture. Kids around the world could rattle off the "Three Demandments" that, in his promos, he urged all his fans to obey: "Train, say your prayers, and eat your vitamins!"

Vince and Hogan traveled together and were in constant dialogue about their ambitions. "The thing about Vince is he could match me toe-to-toe in the obsession department," Hogan wrote. "With his aggressiveness and my focus, we were a match made in heaven. Even though we were totally different types of people, our work ethic was hardcore. I used to call him the Terminator."

Their curious synergy was the driving force behind their biggest play for mainstream fame yet, a would-be Hollywood blockbuster with Hogan in the starring role, returning to the Tinseltown exposure that had previously helped him so much with *Rocky III.*

The film's origins are murky. I tried to interview the credited writer, director, and producers for interviews; all turned me down or were nowhere to be found. In his first memoir, Hogan wrote that he had been approached about making a wrestling-oriented movie called *No Holds Barred*, but that "Vince and the company weren't involved. Then Vince stepped in and said, 'I'll produce this movie and I'll pay you the same amount of money that you would have gotten.'" Hogan did what he generally did: what Vince wanted.

"Originally, a writer had been hired to come up with the script for *No Holds Barred*," Hogan continued. "But when he turned it in, it sucked. Of course, he was going to get credit for it even if it got rewritten fifty times, because that's how the Writers Guild works. But Vince and I didn't care about who got credit for it." No, they just wanted a hit movie. And who knew action and delight better than them?

So, according to Hogan, he and Vince locked themselves in a hotel room near a beach outside St. Petersburg and, for either two or three days straight (depending on which of his memoirs you believe), they "wrote it from beginning to end without stopping, without sleeping."

Hogan would play wrestling champion Rip Thomas, who fights for a WWF-like promotion in a world where, apparently, pro wrestling is legitimate. He gets wined and dined by a rival operation, run by a greedy, Ted Turner–esque television magnate. Thomas turns them down, only to be thrown into an overly complicated plot that builds to a climactic match between Rip and a bare-knuckle street fighter known only as Zeus.

"We had to write the final fight scene between my character and Zeus, the guy we had set up as the villain," Hogan wrote. Frustrated, the wrestler went to use the bathroom.

"I was so tired that as soon as my ass hit the seat, my eyes closed and I started daydreaming," he continued. "And in my daydream, the whole fight scene was playing itself out, and you know what? It was great. All of a sudden I started yelling, 'I got it! I got it!'"

Hogan started babbling the whole thing out. "I told him to write as fast as he could," Hogan recalled. "We didn't have a tape recorder or anything, so Vince just scribbled down everything I said."

Eventually, production began in Georgia. "When we finished working

our eighteen-hour days and we were ready to drop, we would go train at
Lee Haney's Animal Kingdom in Atlanta," Hogan wrote. "And when we
were done training, usually at about three o'clock in the morning, we'd pop
the trunk of our car and drink a beer. Vince would call it our 'heart attack
beer.' We would drink it to calm our nerves. Then we would go to sleep for
three or four hours and be back on the set at 6 a.m."

No Holds Barred was released on June 2, 1989. It ended up being produced by a WWE subsidiary that Vince had named "Shane Productions"
(a nod to his teenage son), but was distributed by New Line. The film
opened at the number-two slot in the box office, but was a critical disaster.
Even the reviewers who appreciated wrestling were disgusted. As the Chicago Tribune's Gene Siskel put it, "The film is utterly lacking in the campy
quality of the World Wrestling Federation telecasts."

The film had a disappointing opening weekend take—less than $5
million—and ticket sales dropped off a cliff soon afterward. The micro-
budget production was a net loss for Vince. Between Hogan's poor acting
and Vince's undermining of the kayfabe ideal upon which the narrative
had been built, No Holds Barred was a laughingstock that only made
Hollywood success more unlikely for Vince and Hogan.

Like any couple that experiences a mutual tragedy, the pair's bond was
strained by the release of No Holds Barred. "It was the first time that Vince
paid Hogan a million dollars for anything," read the account of journalists Shaun Assael and Mike Mooneyham, "and after it was clear No Holds
Barred didn't have a prayer of earning his investment back, he was incensed that Hogan insisted on receiving the full fee."

"Signs of strain between Emperor Vince and The Hulkster, those
former soulmates, had begun to show," Bret recalled in his memoir. "It
looked like Hulk's incomparable star power was starting to drive Vince
crazy because it gave Hulk power over him. Vince, being Vince, prepared
a first-strike policy, though the war was still in the head-game stage and
Vince was fairly subtle about it."

All of this was good news for the Ultimate Warrior. If Vince had initially pushed the man because of his physique and crowd-pleasing intensity, he now pushed him even harder because he needed a replacement for
Hogan on deck. Vince placated Hogan with a greater degree of influence
over how often he worked, but the boss lavished attention on his new
favorite.

"Vince would send little zingers Hulk's way, joking that he was too old, too slow, always with a needle in it under the laughs," Bret recalled. "Since he had given Hulk control of his own schedule, it was hard for Hulk to complain."

Vince booked Hogan and Warrior to start a rivalry—a dangerous choice, given that both of them were babyfaces. At January's Royal Rumble, Hogan and Warrior had a brief standoff during the titular battle royal. They stared and circled like wary hawks, then lunged at the ropes to start running and gaining momentum for an attack. Each man kept expertly evading the other until, finally, they each reached out a single arm and smacked each other in the heads with a mutual *thwap*—a double "clothesline," as they call that move. Soon, the heels were upon them and conventional morals resumed, but the crowd had eaten up that perverse hero-versus-hero moment like candy. Vince was testing the emotional limits of the crowd and the talent.

A February 10, 1990, WWF TV broadcast brought an astounding announcement: Hogan and Warrior would fight in the main event at *WrestleMania VI*. But even then, Vince had not decided who would win. The wrestlers' agonized waiting ended around Valentine's Day, when Vince dropped a neutron bomb on Hogan: he wanted him to drop the championship belt to Warrior at the big PPV.

Hogan is diplomatic in his depiction of what followed. "I didn't agree with him," Hogan wrote in his first memoir. "I didn't think the guy could carry the load. Then again, maybe I didn't give Vince a choice in the matter. By that time, my mind wasn't focused on wrestling the way it should have been. Seven years of carrying the load as the main guy had taken its toll on me. I was tired and I was starting to get hurt a lot. I was beat." What's more, he was taking another stab at movie stardom, this time with the title role in an action comedy called *Suburban Commando*, and would need some time off. Still, doing the job for Warrior didn't sit right with him.

"Hogan agreed to do it, but showed up in the dressing room with a long face and a distrustful look in his eye, clearly afraid that this was a sign that he was on the way down," Bret recalled. "It was the first time I saw Hulk Hogan second-guess himself."

For the rest of the locker room, Hogan going up against Warrior was a real lesser-of-two-evils situation. Hogan "was still the WWF's biggest draw and worked whenever he felt like it," Bret wrote. "He still flew on a Learjet and had his own limo, and a manservant . . . who carried his bags. Basically he was in, out, and gone. Although Hogan was still deeply respected, to the boys, he had become a guy we used to know."

That said, Bret added, "most of us couldn't stand Warrior, who had blossomed into a grunting prima donna. He flew first class with a paid valet, traveled to the arenas by limo and had his own private I'm-the-star dressing room. He never sat with us in the locker room bullshitting or playing cards." Both Hogan and Warrior were full of hot air, but at least one of them halfway gave a shit about the Business. You can see any number of coming political elections prefigured. "In the war Vince was launching," Bret wrote, "we were still rooting for Hulk."

Deserving or not, Hogan was the final champion of the old version of kayfabe. He had first won the title under the century-old pretense that wrestling was real; he would now lose it in a world where wrestling had been labeled as a fraud. He had dutifully carried the golden belt across the threshold into whatever this strange new era was. His reward was public shame.

WrestleMania VI was held at SkyDome in Toronto on April 1, 1990, allegedly setting an attendance record for the massive venue at 67,678. Each attendee witnessed the end of wrestling as they knew it.

It was a stacked card of matches, but none of them generated the kind of excitement felt in the facility at the moment of apocalypse.

Hogan and Warrior had each cut stirring promos earlier in the evening, the weight of history clearly burdening both of them.

"Hulkamania is running wild like it's never ran before!" Hogan claimed. "Ultimate Warrior, you must realize that, when you step in the SkyDome, when you feel the energy that's gonna run wild throughout the arena, *those are my people! That's my energy, brother!*"

He continued, offering pitiful magnanimity: "And once I get you down on your knees, Ultimate Warrior, I'm gonna ask you one question, brother. I'm gonna ask you, '*Do you want to live forever?*'" he crowed. "And if your answer is 'Yes,' Ultimate Warrior, then *breathe* your last breath into my body! *I can save ya! My Hulkamaniacs can save ya! We can turn the darkness that you live in into the light!*"

Warrior's rebuttal, filmed in a separate locker room, was far more convincing: "Hulk Hogan, *I must ask you now*, as you asked me, *do you, Hulk Hogan*, want your ideas, your beliefs, to *live forever?*"—he whispered the last two words. "For, Hulk Hogan, in this normal world, physically, none of us can live forever! But the places you have taken the Hulkamaniacs, the *ideas* and *beliefs* you have given them, *can live through me, Hulk Hogan!*"

It would all come down to the moment when the torch would be irreversibly passed. "I will look at you," Warrior said, "and you will realize then that I have come *to do no one no harm!* But only, Hulk Hogan, to take what we both believe in *to places it shall never have been!*"

The big match, when it finally came, was actually quite wonderful; arguably the best either man ever had. They were more nimble and convincing than usual, each pushing their chemically manipulated bodies to their physical limits. There were towering throws, explosive punches, and vigorous holds. Soon, each man was doing his finishing move on the other, to great applause. Warrior jumped on top of Hogan, the referee slapped the canvas thrice, and that was it.

"*Unbelievable!*" Gorilla Monsoon yelped on his commentator's mic.

Hogan, looking every inch like a man whose era had ended, began to cry.

In 1990, the WWF took in the highest level of gross income it had in any year in its history: $138,336,119. In 1984, that figure had only been $29,596,974. Income had increased by more than 367 percent in just six years.

Richard Meltzer had been correct in his analysis and predictions in "The Last Wrestling Piece." Wrestling was no longer fake in a revelatory or liberatory way. There had been something magical about the tension between fantasy and reality in the artform, much as there had been for America at large. But those fantasies were gone now, and no one knew what to do with the new reality. Vince was entering a wasteland of his own making, one in which he would lose his way. He would eventually bring wrestling to a new kind of transcendent untruth. To get there, everyone would have to pay the cost.

German sociologist Max Weber once declared that the central challenge of modernity was *Entzauberung*—disenchantment. "It is the destiny of our age," he said, "given the rationalization and intellectualization of the times, and especially given the disenchantment of the world—its loss of magic—that the ultimate and most sublime values have retreated from public life."

Vince had proven to the wrestling world what Trump would one day prove to everyone else: nothing was true, and everything was permitted.

10

HEAT, ACT I
(1990–1991)

"I first met Saddam Hussein when I was a junior in high school," Adnan Alkaissy would recall. "He was very polite, very nice, wore nice clothes, and was really sort of shy."

Adnan and Saddam were both children of prominent and devoutly Muslim families, raised in Baghdad. The boys lived in Adhamiya, the neighborhood that has long acted as the intellectual hub of the city. Young Saddam "always had a book or newspaper with him wherever he went," Adnan wrote in his memoir. The two of them "used to hang out after school together at a little open-air coffee shop near the Tigris River in Baghdad. There, we played dominos, chess, cards, and would sit around and watch TV or listen to music with our friends."

Eventually, Saddam transferred to another school, and the friendship petered out. Adnan got serious about sports and earned the chance to study abroad at Oklahoma State University. Early on in his US journey, Adnan had met a Quebecois wrestler of the kayfabe variety and, desperate for cash, eventually decided to give pro wrestling a whirl. Of course, he fell in love.

"It was really exciting to see how you could manipulate the crowd to do just about anything," he added. "I mean, to have so many people right at your fingertips was very exciting."

By the time Adnan—now a bronzed bruiser with a kind smile—moved back to Baghdad in 1969, the bookish Saddam had grown up and done well for himself. Hussein was ostensibly the humble deputy of Iraq's president, but this was kayfabe: in reality, he was the guiding hand of his country's politics.

Adnan was summoned to an audience with his old school chum. They met at the latter's office. After catching up and exchanging compliments, Saddam got to the point.

"He said that he really enjoyed pro wrestling, but had never seen it in person, only on television," Adnan recalled. "He wanted me to bring it to Iraq as soon as possible so that everyone could enjoy it." In other words, Saddam "was going to give the people something much more interesting to focus on than the government and politics."

But Saddam's lack of familiarity with the artform had made him into a complete mark.

"Saddam thought this was all real," Adnan wrote.

Adnan started recruiting wrestlers from the West to "compete" with him in high-profile events at Baghdad's al-Shaab Stadium. Rolling in regime-supplied cash, he swiftly became Ba'athist Iraq's biggest celebrity. Saddam loved the matches, but told Adnan to up the ante.

So, in late 1970, Adnan approached the up-and-coming André Roussimoff—not yet dubbed André the Giant—for a dance in Babylon. The occasion was the fiftieth birthday of the Iraqi army, and "the stadium was filled with tens of thousands of Iraqi soldiers—all with their Kalashnikov rifles."

Saddam, too, was armed, and seated in the front row. Adnan went over to him and received a wish for good luck. Then, Saddam pulled Adnan close and whispered forcefully into the wrestler's ear.

"Be victorious, Adnan," he said. "We are all counting on you. Be victorious. This guy is big, but he is a pussy. I know that you can beat him. If he hurts you in any way, he is going to get *this*."

Saddam lifted up his coat to reveal a solid-gold pistol.

"I will put every bullet in there in his fat head," he said, "and send him back to France in a pine box."

Saddam "also told me that Iraq was counting on me to win and that I had better not let down the country or the people on such a special day," Adnan wrote. "He didn't actually threaten me, but the way he looked at me, I knew that, if I didn't win, I was going to be in big trouble."

This was a problem for Adnan. It was a best-of-three-falls match, and he and André had decided that, while Adnan was going to win overall by snagging falls one and three, André would get to pin Adnan for number two. "But," Adnan recalled, "I didn't know what Saddam might do if André beat me"—even just for one of the three falls.

The match was about to begin; it was too late to go backstage and re-group with André. So Adnan had to covertly alert his "opponent" in the ring. "It was tough to do, but when we got into a headlock position, I whispered it to him in his ear and he nodded OK," Adnan wrote. "I prayed that he heard me all right, because I did not want that big SOB pinning me out there and then getting shot to death right on top of me."

Luckily, André had gotten the message, and Adnan pinned the big man once, then a second time. The referee raised the Iraqi hero's arm in victory.

"The crowd went ballistic," Adnan wrote. "They all started shooting their guns up into the air to celebrate."

André, on the other hand, "was terrified and just lay down on the mat. He didn't know if they were shooting at him or not. He was nearly in tears, he was so scared."

After that, Saddam started paying Adnan to wrestle in countries throughout the Arab world. He would introduce his muscular champion to every visiting dignitary: Muammar Gaddafi, Yasser Arafat, Idi Amin—even a young Donald Rumsfeld.

"[Saddam] liked having me there because he could use me to keep the conversations light," Adnan wrote. "He loved to talk about wrestling, and if I could divert the attention away from politics, that was all right by him."

By mid-1990, America was at war.

Not with Saddam—not yet—but with an entity President George H. W. Bush publicly described as a dangerous and pernicious enemy: drugs. It had been about a decade since crack had first appeared on the streets of American cities, five years since the word "crack" had first appeared in the *New York Times*. In 1988, a sprinter was stripped of his gold medal for using steroids during that year's Olympic games, and the news was flooded with stories about rampant use of performance-enhancing drugs in sports. By 1989, after a bipartisan act of Congress established the Office of National Drug Control Policy, the nation was in the full grip of a moral panic over drugs, and steroids came to the forefront.

Some of the outrage was related to the delegitimization of the sacred myth of sporting meritocracy. Some of it was about the emerging scientific consensus that steroid abuse wreaked havoc on people's bodies. And some of it was swept up into the overall horror over an "epidemic" of substance abuse among the youth of the nation.

In 1990, the federal government published a study claiming that more than a quarter of a million adolescents had used steroids. "Because of the insidious, short-term appeal of these drugs," the secretary of health and human services said upon the report's release, "it is essential that our teachers, coaches and others in contact with young athletes make extra efforts to present the very real health hazards that steroids hold."

Federal lawmakers, too, were called upon to protect the kids. The Anabolic Steroids Control Act of 1990 made nonprescription steroids illegal, and established penalties for "physical trainers or advisers who endeavor to persuade or induce individuals to possess or use anabolic steroids." Steroids were now an active combatant in the ever-deepening War on Drugs.

Wrestling, of course, became a target: there was a perception that teens would try to emulate their bulky athletic heroes by taking steroids. At the same time it was being made clear to the public how central, and disastrous, steroid use had become in the industry.

In February 1990, an ailing Superstar Billy Graham, Hulk Hogan's hero and model, laid up in a hospital bed, came forward on television to say he'd used steroids and that they'd ruined his body. Around the same time, an athletic coach from the University of Virginia went to Dr. George Zahorian's office to buy steroids while wearing a wire for the FBI. Through a series of whispered connections, the McMahons learned of the federal investigation of Zahorian, and cut ties with him just before he was arrested.

It would seem reasonable for Vince to totally distance himself from steroids. But after jettisoning Zahorian, he actually did just the opposite.

Vince was leaning into the McMahon family's obsession with big men in a new way. At the very moment when performance-enhancing drugs were becoming the most radioactive topic in athletics, Vince branched out into an industry that celebrated uncanny male forms in its own toxic way: bodybuilding.

The bodybuilding industry was then dominated by a pair of self-glorifying monopolists named Joe and Ben Weider. The Weiders ran both the International Federation of Body Builders (IFBB) and the Mr. Olympia competition. The latter was a contest held sacred by the leading bodybuilding-industry magazine, *Muscle & Fitness*—which was also Weider-owned. It wasn't a huge market, not since the craze of the '80s had died down. But it was one that Vince coveted.

In the summer of 1990, Vince announced that his Titan Sports would be launching a magazine called *Bodybuilding Lifestyles*. He hired bodybuilding superstar Tom Platz to work in editorial for it. Vince spent $5,000 to secure a promotional booth for the magazine at the September 15 convention accompanying 1990's Mr. Olympia. The fee also bought a few minutes for Platz to speak to the crowd during the competition. Vince wouldn't be there.

The first big story of the weekend was the disqualification of 20 percent of the competitors for failing a drug test. The Weiders were taking the anti-steroid panic far more seriously than Vince was—they'd already stripped one competitor of a title after he'd tested positive, which was unimaginable in the WWF as of then. But the bodybuilders and those who profited off them were riled up and frustrated by these new restrictions.

When the appointed time came, Platz stepped up to the podium. He smiled.

"I have a very important announcement to make," Platz said. "We at Titan Sports and *Bodybuilding Lifestyles* magazine are pleased to announce the formation of the World Bodybuilding Federation. *And we are going to kick the IFBB's ass!*"

Reporter Irv Muchnick described what happened next:

The audience fell silent, and leggy models in slinky black evening gowns and *Bodybuilding Lifestyles* sashes emerged from the wings to distribute handbills promising "bodybuilding as it was meant to be"—a code phrase, some thought, for "no drug testing."

Vince McMahon had thoroughly upstaged the Weiders at their own event, and he still had one more trick up his sleeve. That evening, when the bodybuilding contestants returned to their rooms at the McCormick Center Hotel, they found WBF contract offers slipped under their doors.

"I'm not angry—you can quote me," Ben Weider told Muchnick after Vince's surprise attack. "I'm not even disappointed. But let's put it this way: It wasn't a very sophisticated or very honorable thing to do."

Around this time, Vince started working unusually hard to build his own body. "The WWF kingpin's fetish for pumping up is evident whenever he and his aides gather at one of their houses to screen [Ted] Turner's pay-per-view offerings," reported Muchnick. He quoted a staffer:

"During unimportant matches or interviews, Vince will go into another room with a pair of dumbbells. He'll come back all sweaty, with his shirt off and his chest and arms all pumped up. One of the guys, currying favor, will invariably say, 'Vince, you look better than your wrestlers!' and he'll beam."

The preceding decade and a half had been a turbulent one for Adnan Alkaissy. Wrestling had become a sensation in the Middle East, but the rising tide was a curse. "Eventually, I became too popular, and that was my undoing," Adnan wrote. "Saddam did not like anybody more popular than himself. Word got around that I was falling out of favor with him and that I was probably in danger of being assassinated." Adnan snuck out of his homeland, never to return.

He'd wrestled for the AWA throughout its terminal decline in the 1980s, and now found himself desperate for cash once again. In August of 1990, Adnan's onetime classmate unilaterally invaded Kuwait, sparking the first great international crisis of the post–Cold War era. The United States led a coalition of nations in bombing Iraq and threatening to do anything that was necessary to maintain order; they called it Operation Desert Shield. Adnan was following these developments avidly.

That's when Vince called.

Vince was facing a peril beyond that of the steroid clampdown, one of his own making. He had irreparably disrupted the balance of kayfabe in wrestling. No longer could a reasonable adult claim, however implausibly, that wrestling wasn't fixed. Gone was the creative ambiguity of not knowing. Vince's new tactic, for the most part, was to emphasize what remained of the kayfabe equation: audacious fantasy. As such, this was a transitional period, one of low stakes, ludicrous gimmicks, frustrated wrestlers, and collapsing popularity.

Vince had never worked with Adnan, but the wrestler's reputation preceded him. He would fit perfectly in Vince's new approach.

"[Vince] knew that I was Iraqi and he knew that I had worked with Saddam, so he had come up with a gimmick that would bring me back into the action," Adnan recalled. "I listened very intently. McMahon was a billionaire"—more like a multimillionaire—"and if he wanted you to perform for him, you did it."

The pitch was as simple as it was provocative. Sgt. Slaughter (Robert Remus), a former WWF wrestler with a patriotic drill-sergeant gimmick, would return to the company as a heel by swearing allegiance to Saddam—and Adnan would be Slaughter's Iraqi handler/manager. He'd appear in promos and at matches while Slaughter began a reign of terror. They'd call him "General Adnan."

"I agreed to do it," Adnan wrote.

The aging wrestler didn't look like he used to: most of his muscles had disappeared and his hangdog face was wrinkled beyond its years. He knew full well how the American public felt about Arabs, so he understood that he would hear more than his share of jeers and boos. Wrestlers call that kind of negative attention "heat"—and, for a heel from a marginalized community, it's quite the mixed blessing. "But I wanted to get back to work and I needed the money," Adnan wrote. "I was going to use Vince McMahon, and Vince McMahon was going to use me. To be honest, I really had no other options at that point."

On August 28, 1990, the day after that year's edition of the annual SummerSlam PPV, Adnan taped his first promos at a live show in Hershey, Pennsylvania. During a chat-show portion, Slaughter yelled that he would introduce his new master in the chain of command and brought out the General, clad in military fatigues and a head covering. Adnan, his mustache shaved to look like Hussein's, stood next to Slaughter with a strangely blank look on his face while the audience howled in hatred.

"This is pure garbage!" yelled Roddy Piper, who was on commentary that day. "*D'you know there's guys over there right now?*"

Adnan was given the microphone. His eyes suddenly lit up as he spoke in enthusiastic Iraqi-accented Arabic, the audience unaware of the meaning.

"In the name of God, the most beneficent, the most merciful," he crowed—a common Islamic invocation for prayers or significant events— "I seek refuge in God from the cursed Satan!" He then read a few lines from the Muslim *shahada*, or declaration of belief: "I bear witness that there is no God but God, and I bear witness that Muhammad, peace be upon him, is His servant and Messenger!"

"I am Adnan!" he concluded, still in the tongue of his ancestors. "May the peace and blessings of God be upon you!"

The crowd erupted in a crescendo of disgust.

"I always knew Sgt. Slaughter was no good," Vince told the crowd from the commentary booth. "But I never knew he would stoop to *these* depths."

As the tensions in the Gulf escalated over the next few months, Slaughter continued spouting anti-US sentiment in promos alongside Adnan. Adnan, for his part, would rant in Arabic about the greatness of both God and Saddam. In a surreal passing of the torch, the duo's first target was Nikolai Volkoff (Josip Peruzović), who had been a Soviet heel throughout the Cold War, but who was now a babyface representing the reborn Russian people.

When Adnan first published his memoir—cowritten by sportswriter and motivational speaker Ross Bernstein—in 2005, anti-Iraqi hysteria was at an obscene height in the United States. In the book, Adnan said his speeches alongside Slaughter were the exact opposite of how he felt.

"I was very against Iraq invading Kuwait; it was wrong," he wrote. "When the United States went over there to liberate Kuwait, I was all for it."

But when I tracked him down in 2021, he told a different version of the story. I asked if it had been uncomfortable for him to spout pro-Saddam rhetoric in the ring.

"No, it was not, really," Adnan replied. "I was very proud of it, which is a fact. There was no lie about it. . . .

"I like Saddam," he continued: "It's all legit. It's not a lie. Everything I said was true about back home."

I asked Adnan if Vince had been okay with him earnestly opposing the American military and backing its declared enemy.

"Vince was okay with it," the grappler replied. "He didn't have an objection about it."

That made perfect sense to Adnan. "Vince was a businessman," he says. "He knows how to get the thing over and he wants to make money, and that's the bottom line."

In his memoir, Adnan had recalled a close working relationship with the boss. "During our heyday, Vince used to call me all the time," he wrote. "It was fun to be in that position again, in a position of power. I found that power is like a drug; I craved it. I hadn't felt that powerful since my days of wrestling at Al-Shaab Stadium in Baghdad. . . .

"And Vince fed that feeling. He told me he had never seen anybody get more heat than me in all his years in the business," Adnan recalled.

"That was a pretty big compliment coming from him, because he is a very sharp guy and understands marketing better than just about everybody. He knew that the more heat a wrestler got, the more popular he was."

That equation, however, wasn't so simple anymore.

Perhaps, in the days of old kayfabe, the angle would have worked by allowing people to let themselves believe they were seeing actual treason and attain catharsis. But now, it just seemed like fiction in poor taste.

Business wasn't great. From 1984 to 1990, the WWF had been reliably increasing revenue every single year. But official company filings reveal that 1991 saw their first dip: a roughly 2.5 percent decrease in business transacted. TV ratings were in free fall. Though the folks who showed up to the shows were vigorous with their booing of Adnan and Slaughter, the total audience for the WWF's product was dwindling.

Vince had already booked the massive Los Angeles Memorial Coliseum for *WrestleMania VII*, teasing repeatedly on WWF programming that attendance would surely reach 100,000 and shatter the company record established at *WrestleMania III*. If Vince wanted to fulfill that promise, he'd have to rev things up a bit.

Slaughter and Adnan had been working as a mid-tier act, with Hogan and Warrior's story lines crowding them out. But as 1990 waned, it became increasingly clear that war was imminent in the Gulf. The time seemed ripe for a last-ditch appeal to national sentiment and rage. And so it was that Vince booked Slaughter in a rivalry against the championship-holding Ultimate Warrior, one that built over the course of December and January.

Vince had quickly come to regret his anointing of Warrior, who demanded VIP attention and routinely antagonized the other workers. Just as capriciously as Vince had decided to give Warrior the belt, he decided to take it away and give it back to Hogan. But he didn't give him the dignity of a rematch with his rival. He had something else in mind.

On January 12, the newly sworn-in congressman Rick Santorum—the recipient of Vince and Linda's first recorded campaign donations—voted to authorize the use of military force against Iraq, as did 249 other members of the House. On January 17, under cover of darkness, the US-led coalition invaded Iraq in what was known as Operation Desert Storm. Two days later, while American and Iraqi blood dripped into the sand, the Ultimate Warrior lost to Slaughter at the Royal Rumble in Miami.

Vince's plan had been to capitalize on the Gulf War by pivoting to a rivalry between Slaughter and Hogan, with Hogan bringing the belt back to the American people at *WrestleMania VII*. But history conspired against him: the Gulf War turned out to be a brief skirmish, all things considered. It was over by the end of February, and, having only lost 219 people in the war (to the Iraqis' 20,000-plus), America moved on.

However, it was too late to change the story line. With interest collapsing, Vince moved the event to the much-smaller Los Angeles Sports Arena (the official story was that there were security concerns about the initial location). The Hulkster and Slaughter were duly pitted against each other, though neither man was in good shape—Slaughter had accumulated a sizable gut and Hogan was hardly a lean spring chicken, either. They huffed and heaved around the ring for twenty minutes, looking like wounded dinosaurs. To add drama, Hogan covertly bladed in the middle, letting his face flood with plasma. Donald Trump was once again in the front row, and he looked delighted.

Near the end of the match, Hogan tore up an Iraqi flag, and, upon winning, proudly waved an American one. He posed and mugged for the camera while his theme song, a patriotic rocker called "Real American," blared on the speakers. After a few minutes of that, he grabbed Old Glory again; this time, he just used the Stars and Stripes to wipe the blood from his face.

Simultaneous to the Iraq angle, Vince was pushing his bodybuilding venture with increased vigor. The thirteen inaugural competitors of the WBF were featured on WWF programming as "BodyStars," with workout and interview segments littered throughout all three of the WWF's flagship shows: *WWF Challenge, WWF Superstars,* and *Prime Time Wrestling*.

It was all building up to June 15, 1991, the date of the inaugural WBF Championship, at which the BodyStars would show off and be judged. Trump would once again play host to Vince: the event would be held at the Trump Taj Mahal in Atlantic City, a massive, onion-domed structure both Brutalist and Orientalist in its design. The facility was not long for this world—it would declare bankruptcy a month later—but you'd never know it from the glitzy promos that Vince ran on WWF programming for his big night.

The event, when it finally came, featured lengthy videos of each competitor, many of whom had been forced to adopt nicknames and outlandish character traits: Tony Pearson became "The Jet Man," Johnnie Morant was dubbed "The Executioner" and walked through fog and flashing lights with a dual-bladed axe, and so on. There was a widespread rumor that the whole thing was fixed in favor of Vince's highest-paid prospect, Gary Strydom. After everyone else had flexed onstage, a voice saying "You've seen the rest, now get ready for the best!" blasted from the speakers and Strydom walked to the stage. Sure enough, by night's end, the judges awarded him the first-place trophy.

Just nine days after the inaugural WBF Championship, the federal government's steroid-distribution case against Dr. George Zahorian went to trial in Harrisburg, Pennsylvania. On the witness stand, Superstar Billy Graham claimed, as did a handful of other disgruntled wrestlers, that the WWF was a den of chemical iniquity, and that Zahorian was the pusher.

The WWF fought hard to keep Vince and Hogan from having to appear. But Piper? They were less willing to put the effort in. Rod Toombs was thus summoned to the stand on the morning after he sustained a head injury in the ring. He reportedly had a series of seizures on the plane to Harrisburg and, looking haggard, he told the jury he'd bought steroids from Zahorian. On June 27, the doctor was found guilty on twelve counts.

Bret Hart recounted how Vince called a meeting of his wrestlers the day the verdict came down. The boss made an announcement: "Everyone had to get off the juice," Bret wrote. Unlike the previous tests for drugs, which had been plagued by counterfeit urine, "it would be impossible to cheat because there would be two people watching you piss in a cup."

Although Vince and Hogan hadn't testified, their visibility meant they bore the brunt of media outrage. The *New York Times* ran stories on the trial proceedings that highlighted the WWF's locker-room culture of steroid use. *USA Today* ran a front-page story headlined "Hulk: Bulk from a Bottle?" To counter the media narrative, Vince placed a first-person op-ed piece in the *New York Times* on July 14.

"It's no fun picking up the paper in the morning to read about your company in the most unflattering terms," he wrote. "Yet as much as I resent the innuendo, unsubstantiated charges, and absence of objective reporting, I recognize that these aren't the issues. The only issue is, just what is the WWF and what do we stand for."

After a sentimental detour about how the company was built by his grandfather and father, Vince got to the essence of his philosophy: "Unlike my trailblazing family predecessors, I began to promote the WWF not as sport but as family-oriented sports entertainment." Emphasis on *family-oriented.* "Our performers became stars, our stars became superstars, our superstars became super heroes," he wrote. "We accepted the responsibility to set for ourselves and for our athletes the highest moral and ethical standards."

They would now be testing for steroids, he announced in the penultimate paragraph.

"Like my father and grandfather before me, I, too, am a proud man," he concluded. "I am determined to leave to the fourth generation McMahon, my son, a legacy of which he too can be proud."

Three days later, Vince was in the pages of the *New York Times* once again, this time as the subject of a short news item. "McMahon spoke at a news conference in New York yesterday to answer allegations that the federation is rife with steroid use," it read. "'I used a steroid that I got from Dr. Zahorian very briefly about three and a half or four years ago,' said McMahon, who is not a wrestler himself but does do some body building. He used the steroid only once, he said."

Just hours after that news conference, Hogan appeared on comedian Arsenio Hall's wildly popular, self-titled talk show. When Hogan had been a guest on the show back in 1989, it had gone quite well. This time was less of a success. To this day, rumors abound as to what Vince told Hogan to say on the air and whether the wrestler followed through properly.

"Basically, I'm upset, outraged, and mad, and all that other kinda stuff," Hogan told Hall in a calm, almost patronizing tone. "The papers printed these lies as fact, and it hurt me, it hurt my family. And, on top of that, I was different than a lot of the people [whose] names got thrown in the wringer. There's millions of kids that have believed in me and what I stand for. And, basically, they've put a dark cloud over everything that I believe in. . . .

"I'm not a steroid abuser," Hogan said, "and I do not use steroids."

Hogan hedged by telling a lengthy story about how he'd briefly used them in a medical capacity after an injury in 1983, then concluded, "That is the extent of Hulk Hogan's steroid use."

In the *Wrestling Observer,* Dave Meltzer assessed the damage. "Sponsors, particularly those aiming at kids, were in a panic, not over the hypocrisy, because anyone who understands the first thing about freakish physiques knew it was there from the start," he wrote. "Hypocrisy means nothing when it comes to making money. The panic was over exactly what Titan was having a nightmare over—not that it had a steroid problem, but that it had a PR problem that companies associated with Titan feared could be spread to them."

Columns ran in the *New York Times* and the *New York Post* denouncing Hogan and the WWF. Vince appeared on *Prime Time Wrestling* to deliver a submissive public service announcement: "It should come as no surprise to you that the WWF has one of the most comprehensive drug testing, education, and rehabilitation programs in all of sports," he said. "In short, the standards of excellence the athletes in the WWF live by will become the standard bearer for all professional sports for years to come. That's why, when you see this symbol"—he indicated the WWF logo— "you can be assured of drug-free sports entertainment that you and your entire family can be proud of."

The WWF's TV ratings were tanking at this point. Beyond any ethical concerns, the angles and stars simply weren't getting over anymore. Everyone was trying to get off steroids, but your body became addicted to them after consistent use, so withdrawal could be debilitating. Bret had an easier time of it than most, having never been as heavy a user. Indeed, his ease at transitioning into this scandal-induced lull in steroid use would prove to be a great advantage very soon. But most of the Boys were very publicly deflating.

Vince hoped to put some gas in the tank at that year's Summer-Slam PPV. It would feature the in-ring wedding of Randy Savage and Miss Elizabeth (a kayfabe event, as they'd already been legally married for seven years), as well as a "handicap" tag-team match where Hogan and Warrior would join forces to take on the threesome of Slaughter, Adnan, and the Iron Sheik. Sheik had been introduced to the sputtering story line as an Iraqi named Colonel Mustafa—no small degradation, given that Sheik was a proud son of Iran, a country that had recently fought a miserable war against Iraq. The tagline for the PPV was "A Match Made in Heaven, *A Match Made in Hell.*"

Warrior was in dire financial straits: his marriage had broken down and he was in the midst of a divorce, but he also wanted to buy an expensive house in New Mexico. He asked Vince for a $550,000 loan, to which

Vince agreed. Warrior would later speak of an "almost parental relationship that I had with Vince" and a "relationship that I had established with Linda where she's signing letters 'Mom.'" Even if those relationships had been relatively brief, they meant a lot to the man who had once been fatherless Jim Hellwig.

But now, he felt he was being mistreated. For one thing, he felt he deserved more money and more time off. But the real sticking point was an apology made under duress.

Warrior had allegedly refused to sign an autograph for a child who walked up to him at an airport. The child told his father, who happened to be the station manager of a TV channel that aired WWF programming. Warrior maintained that the incident never happened. Nevertheless, on July 9, 1991, Vince made Warrior record a personalized video apology to the child. It didn't acknowledge a specific offense, but nevertheless featured the wrestler showing contrition. Footage of the shoot survives—indeed, WWE allowed it to be used in a 2021 A&E Network documentary about Warrior—and it depicts a relationship on the edge.

"I understand that there comes times in everyone's life when they may regret certain things," Warrior says, following the script with his arms raised. "*Fuck!*" he yells, breaking character. "I didn't say nothin' to the goddamn kid!"

"I understand that!" Vince says, off camera.

"Well, no, you don't," Warrior counters, "because I'm fuckin' makin' a videotape to some *kid!*"

"It's a fucking work!" Vince yells—and it's slightly surreal to hear him say industry lingo aloud. "It's a *work*. That's all it is. It's a work. We're working here. That's it."

It took take after take, but Warrior eventually got through the whole surreal apology.

The next day, Warrior faxed a handwritten, spottily punctuated letter to Titan demanding to be paid the same fees as Hogan, as well as to be granted the full $550,000 of the loan, with strings no longer attached. "This will suffice as my *Wrestlemania VII* payoff," he added, "but let it be noted it is not fair."

Warrior wrote of being ordered to vacate the top spot in the WWF. "At first I was reluctant for what I believed were the right reasons—but once again I went with what I knew I could believe in—'Vince has never fucked me,'" he wrote. "I dealt with what you thought was best no matter what the cost to me, no matter the countless # of sleepless nights there were to come, no matter the # of times I had to knock on your door with questions I should never have had."

But the video apology was the final straw. "For the last 2½ years I should have never had the questions I did," he wrote. "To stand and make a videotaped apology for something I never did made me realize all we have is business."

Then, Warrior went in for the kill. He had an ultimatum. "I ask for these things Vince and the answers must come for the next event is upon you," the letter read. "You see it as business so whether I like it or not I must do the same. Whatever your decision I can and will live with it." In his elliptical way, Warrior was threatening to skip out on SummerSlam.

"Ultimate Warrior basically came to me and figuratively put a gun to my head," Vince would later say. "That's so unprofessional. You just don't do that."

Vince sent the wrestler a one-page memo on July 13, in which he appeared to acquiesce to Warrior's demands. "I regret the turmoil you've put yourself through and your agonizing over what you feel is fair compensation," it read. "I am resolved to work with you in the same honest and equitable way that I always have. Furthermore, I would like to express to you my deepest appreciation and admiration for you as a performer, as a member of the WWF family, as a man and as my friend." Warrior was satisfied. SummerSlam's main event would go on as planned on August 26.

But, as it turns out, Vince's letter was all kayfabe.

"I reluctantly agreed to Warrior's demand, knowing what I was going to do as soon as he came out of the ring," is how Vince later put it. "I could not *wait* to fire him."

A popular wrestler at Turner's operation, Sid Eudy, was looking for greener pastures and contacted Vince, who asked Eudy what he wanted. Eudy said he wanted Hogan's spot. Vince, no longer sure of Hogan or Warrior and enamored of Eudy's enormous size, signed him on.

SummerSlam was held at Madison Square Garden—the site of many changings-of-the-guard in the McMahon empire's history. Eudy—wrestling as "Sid Justice"—was the guest referee for the tag match of Warrior and Hogan versus Slaughter, Adnan, and Iron Sheik.

Near the end of the match, Warrior chased Adnan and the Sheik out of the main arena, a folding chair in his grip. Only Hogan and Slaughter were left in the ring. After Hogan pinned Slaughter, the crowd was expecting Warrior to run back out to celebrate the victory with his tag-team partner. But Warrior didn't reappear.

Instead, it was Eudy who came forward to clasp Hogan's hand and receive the applause. A new titan had been anointed.

Unbeknownst to the audience, after Warrior ran backstage, he had been confronted by Vince, who handed him a four-page letter. In broad strokes, Warrior was suspended for no less than ninety days (he was under contract until the next September). The humiliation, however, was in the details.

"Unfortunately, it now appears the fame that you have obtained through the efforts of Titan has gone to your head," the letter began. "Frankly, you have become impossible to work with, and you have completely forgotten your obligations to Titan and WWF fans, both ethically, professionally, and contractually."

It went on: "You have become a legend in your own mind; you are certainly entitled to your opinion. However, you are not entitled to vent your feelings by breaching and threatening to breach your contract. . . .

"Your behavior has become unreliable and erratic," Vince wrote, "which behavior is intolerable in the WWF."

Most of the rest of the text was written in legalese, but there was one little matter to be addressed in simpler English at the very end.

"Please be advised that I do not consider the purported modifications to your Contract dated July 13 and 22 to be valid or binding," Vince wrote, referring to the pre-SummerSlam agreement with which he'd pacified Warrior. "It is well established that contracts entered into under duress are voidable."

Adnan would later recall *SummerSlam '91* as his last great day in wrestling. "The crowd loved it," he wrote. "Again, the show brought in really big numbers, and McMahon was very happy."

PPV buy rates were actually down compared to the previous Summer-Slam, so the numbers weren't *that* big. But Adnan was a gentleman of the old school: he gauged success by the live experience, and MSG was, indeed, packed and excitable that night. Adnan had gone out to cheers; it mattered little that they were cheering at his defeat.

"With that, we were done," Adnan wrote. "That is how it is in this business: here today and gone tomorrow." Iraq was yesterday's news, and so was he. "I asked McMahon if I could continue with the company after that, perhaps working as an agent, but he said that there were no opportunities for me at that time.

"I was really pissed after that, because I went through a lot during that time and sacrificed a great deal for him," Adnan concluded. "I made him a lot of money and didn't feel like I was treated right when it was all said and done. But hey, it's a business, and we all knew that going in."

I had spent months trying to track down Adnan. When he finally returned my calls, it was the afternoon of January 7, 2021. I'll confess that the interview—our first of two—was not the best of my career. The US Capitol was still an active crime scene at that point, and I didn't quite know what to make of anything, much less the revelation that Adnan had actually been pro-Saddam during his big angle.

As he and I, two citizens of a country gone wrong, wrapped up our conversation, I asked him for final thoughts on the impresario who immortalized him as an object of hatred.

"I liked Vince very much," Adnan said. "He's a good person."

11

HEAT, ACT II
(1991–1992)

On a Sunday in March of 1992, Vince McMahon marched into a suite of law offices at 500 Fifth Avenue, a soaring prewar skyscraper just up the street from the New York Public Library. He was there for a meeting with a young man about whom he knew virtually nothing.

Vince arrived in the office of the Jacob D. Fuchsberg Law Firm, accompanied by Jerry McDevitt and Linda. When he reached the conference room where the meeting would take place, he saw the young man for the first time.

Tom Cole was just twenty-one—almost exactly Shane's age—with striking good looks. He had a mop of black hair, a square jaw, a gaze both confident and vulnerable. He was a big fellow, too: broad-shouldered and tall. He was somewhat infamous among his family and friends for his ability to smile and charm his way into anyone's heart.

But, for Vince, Tom represented a huge problem.

Tom Cole had been a ring boy. This was a long-standing role in the wrestling world: whenever a traveling promotion came to town, it would hire a few local kids—teenage boys, mostly. They would be put to work setting up and taking down the ring (a dangerous job that could end in broken fingers or crushed toes), running errands, and any number of other miscellaneous tasks. In the 1980s, when Tom Cole was recruited, the going rate for a ring boy was generally about eighty bucks, plus bragging rights and photos with the superstars.

At thirteen, Tom had fit the profile of most of the kids who became ring boys: a minor who didn't have a lot of adult supervision.

But at twenty-one, he was very different from other former ring boys: he was the first who had come forward with allegations of years of abuse, grooming, drugs, and sexual coercion within the ring boy program.

These accusations had the potential to tear down everything Vince had built. Especially since they weren't the only ones Vince was facing by then.

On December 3, 1991, before a show in San Antonio, Vince once again called his wrestlers to a meeting. With the FBI and the media scrutinizing the promotion, wrestlers would now be tested for all nonprescription drugs, including marijuana.

"My hands are tied," Bret remembers Vince saying. "I can't have any more scandals. I hate to do this to everybody, but I have to do it in order to protect the company."

The wrestlers all knew what this meant: one last epic party.

Bret's little brother, Owen, was in town that night. He'd wrestled for the WWF briefly a few years prior: Vince had stuck him with a gimmick where he wore a mask and cape and fought against evil as a superhero known as the Blue Blazer. Owen hated the gimmick almost as much as the crowds did, so he left to seek career advancement as a journeyman in Japan, Mexico, and Europe. Now Owen was back to try out again.

Bret had a big bag of Mexican weed some fans had given him the night before, at a show in El Paso. So he rolled his brother a joint. Owen didn't usually smoke, but Bret told him this was his last chance, so they lit up.

By the time the brothers made it to the venue, a strip club near the airport, they were both pretty high. The place was packed with wrestlers, all discussing the oncoming drug cutoff. Some of the guys—the ones who had gotten deepest into steroids—had a "panicked look in their eyes," Bret recalls to me. "It was like steroids are more important than their job."

Bret was feeling pretty mellow himself. It was a high-end club—"like, really good-looking girls"—and he was catching up with Owen, who had been wrestling the European circuit. Owen was telling him how big Bret was in Germany, which was nice to hear. But Bret's anxiety spiked when, around midnight, Vince strolled in.

This was extremely unusual. As a rule, Vince never hung out with his employees, and Bret was nervous the boss would notice that he and Owen were stoned. Then he realized that Vince was way more fucked up than they were.

"Shit-faced" was how Bret would describe him later; "slap-happy drunk." Vince's tie hung loosely around his neck as he made his way over to them,

Pat Patterson clutching at his arm and trying to walk him back out. But Vince shook Patterson off. Tonight, he was going to party with the Boys.

The boss's presence changed the mood. "When we realized Vince was drunker than any of us were, it was like, 'Okay, we don't have to worry about anything, because you can't reprimand us when you're in worse shape than we are,'" Bret recalls.

Vince grabbed a drink and settled in beside Davey Boy and Brutus Beefcake (Edward Leslie). Over in another corner, though, Bret could hear Hawk (Michael Hegstrand) and his tag-team partner Animal (Joseph Laurinaitis) joking about trying out their finishing moves on Vince. They *were* joking, that is, until Hogan told them, "You guys don't have the balls to do that. You're not gonna do it."

Well, Animal and Hawk couldn't let that stand. They had to impress Hogan. Suddenly they were marching over to Vince.

Bret recalls that Animal came up on Vince from behind him. "[He] goes between Vince's legs and picks Vince up like a bean bag, and Vince almost falls off his shoulders," he tells me.

This was the opening move of the Doomsday Device, Hawk and Animal's ballistic two-man finisher: Animal would lift the opponent onto his shoulders and Hawk would launch himself off the ring post to clothesline the unfortunate victim in midair. It's not something you want to try in a strip club.

"It was cement floor with carpet on it, so it's like, you can't do your finish on Vince in this bar," Bret says. "We're all skeptical, but we're all watching, everyone follows it like magnets, we gotta watch this happen."

Hawk cleared a stripper off one of the poles and climbed up on the dance platform. Holy shit, he really *was* going to do it.

"Hawk jumped off and gave [Vince] the most pansy, delicate clothesline," Bret says. "Vince sort of gently fell backwards." Beefcake and Hogan caught him and set him on his feet. There was a sigh of mixed disappointment and relief, and a round of polite clapping.

Bret rolled his eyes at Jim Neidhart. Neidhart yelled out, "The Hart Foundation would have had the balls to do it!"

Bret chimed in with "Damn right!" and turned back to keep talking to Owen. Then what he'd just said caught up with him. He looked back and Neidhart had Vince up in a fireman's carry, ready for the Hart Attack— a less aerial cousin of the Doomsday Device.

"I just remember Hulk Hogan looking at me like, *Have you got the balls to do it or are you gonna do it like Hawk?*" Bret says. "I remember I put the shot glass on the bar and I clotheslined Vince as hard as I could."

It was the first time Bret hit Vince. It would not be the last.

They hit the carpeted concrete floor hard. *What have I done?* Bret thought.

Bret and Vince lay together on the floor, both winded. Then Vince looked down at Bret. "You owe me a drink," he said.

"Whatever you want," Bret told him.

"Dewar's on ice."

They staggered to their feet. Bret ordered Vince the Dewar's. Vince drank it down.

"He got more and more drunk after that," Bret recalls. "A few minutes later everyone's doing their finish on Vince. I remember Davey Boy Smith and Beefcake running around the bar power-slamming Vince onto the carpet."

Everything was hilariously out of control. Vince was laughing, goofier than Bret had ever seen him.

Closing time came and went. The lights went on, but no one would leave. Finally the club owners called the police, and bemused law enforcement officers slowly herded a crowd of drunken wrestlers toward the exit. As they shuffled into the parking lot, there was suddenly a rumor, Bret recalls: "There's a party in Ric Flair's room, everyone's invited to Ric Flair's for a party."

The platinum-blond Flair, long a staple of the NWA, had jumped ship from Turner and joined the WWF a few months prior. He wasn't particularly popular with his coworkers, but he *was* staying at a ritzy suite in the Marriott Marquis.

Nobody in the club was fit to drive. No problem: the police were happy to escort them to the hotel. About thirty cars full of wrestlers, strippers, and hangers-on, flanked by police cruisers, arrived at the Marriott at about 3 a.m. The mob descended upon a young male desk clerk at the hotel, demanding to call Flair's room. No answer. They asked for a key. The flustered clerk said it was against hotel policy, but Vince cut him off.

"I'm Vince McMahon!" he yelled. "*Give it to me right now!*"

The clerk handed it over.

They went to Flair's room. He wasn't there, and it seemed to be double-locked from the inside. But Earl Hebner, a WWF referee, had been asleep on a rollaway and heard their knocking. "Earl opened the door and the party was on," Bret says.

Almost. There was nothing in the suite to drink—only a single bottle of vodka. Bret thought of the huge bag of weed back at his own hotel, handed his key to Owen, and told him to go get it.

Ten minutes later Owen was back, and the suite filled with pot smoke. Vince began losing clothes—he took off his jacket, then his shirt, then his pants. He got down to his tie and boxers; then he took off the tie. The social order was breaking down.

One by one, anyone who had to take a leak would go into the bedroom, stand on Ric Flair's bed, and pee on it. "It got to the point where you couldn't *not* pee on the bed; everybody peed on the bed," Bret says. "I think even Vince peed on it. Everyone was laughing, everyone was stupid drunk. I remember Vince was in his boxers and he was peeing in the planter—a plant was growing—and Vince was pissing in the planter and everybody was laughing and joking around."

Bret sounds wistful as he recounts all of this. "It was quite a fun night," he says. "I remember just a great sense of camaraderie. No one ever partied like this before."

Vince demanded more wrestling with the Boys. They indulged him, carefully. "We were pretty friendly and gentle with him," Bret says. "Playful. And I think Vince liked that, that we played around with him."

That is, until Vince knocked down Hercules Hernandez (Raymond Fernandez). "Hercules was pretty drunk and probably not the smartest guy in the world," Bret recalls. "He got really mad." Hernandez suplexed Vince and threw him backward into the air—almost to the ceiling. "Vince was out of control, he's in the air, upside down, in a dangerous, reckless way."

Vince landed on Earl Hebner's rollaway bed. *Oh my god*, Bret thought, *do you realize you're throwing the boss that writes your check every week?*

"I remember Vince looking at Herc and thinking he just locked that thought into his head," Bret says, "that the only thing he'll remember of this whole night is to fire that guy tomorrow."

And he did. "I never saw Herc again after that TV taping that week," Bret says.

This was a miniature version of what Vince would do on TV as Mr. McMahon in the years to come: act like a goofball and let the Boys take out the very real anger they'd developed toward him. It was a genius method of pressure release. It was a *carnevale*. But if one of them went too far, he would be gone.

At some point, the men all dispersed. After all, it was nearly dawn, and they had to drive to Austin for more TV tapings.

"It was just a really weird, almost dreamlike night that you wonder if it really happened," Bret says. "I never saw Vince let his hair down like that ever again."

As the memory of the revelry receded, sober reality set in.

Shults, the onetime Dr. D, gave an interview to a wrestling radio show a few days later and hinted at even bigger scandals buried in the WWF.

"Steroids is just the tip of the iceberg," Shults said.

Shults didn't elaborate. But within wrestling circles, ears perked up.

New York Post sports columnist Phil Mushnick had never been a wrestling fan, he says; he liked legitimate sports. His distaste was only reinforced by the cultural ubiquity of WWF wrestlers. That widespread name recognition proved to be an Achilles' heel for Vince, in this case.

"The *New York Times* ran a two-paragraph box during the Zahorian trial," Mushnick (no relation to fellow muckraker Irv Muchnick) recalls. He saw in the article that Hogan wouldn't have to testify. "I thought, *Wait a second*. This is the guy with the 'take your vitamins and say your prayers.' This is a role model. If this guy's pumped up on Dr. Zahorian's drugs, what do you mean? It should be injurious to his career."

In his regular column, Mushnick included a short note about his dismay that a children's icon was avoiding his just deserts. He left the office for the weekend.

"I got back into my office about three days later, and my answering machine was stuffed with messages from all over," he recalls. "Not just the country. Look, even from England, Germany. They all read essentially the same thing: '*You don't know the half of it.*'"

He published a column about the WWF, in the July 12, 1991, edition of the paper. Headlined "Bruno Rages About Roids," it was based on an interview with retired (W)WWF legend and Vince Senior favorite Bruno Sammartino. "I've made a good living from this business," Sammartino told Mushnick. "But I tell you, I'm ashamed of what it has become."

Tom Cole had been reading Mushnick's coverage while he was staying with his brother Lee in Utica. Little by little, he started to tell Lee what he'd been through: the sex, the drugs, the feet.

At thirteen, the year Tom had become a ring boy, he'd run away from his mother's Westchester home. Tom was always looking for more: more affection, more attention. He was an unusually beautiful boy—girls fawned over him.

It had been easy for Mel Phillips, a ring announcer and head of the ring crew, to spot him as a good prospect when they met at a local WWF show. And it had been easy for Tom to soak up the fatherly care Phillips offered him.

Tom had started out working shows whenever the WWF was in West-chester County. But soon he was working shows in Manhattan, too. Then Phillips had started taking Tom with him on a regional circuit of wrestling shows: Baltimore, Boston, Philadelphia, and so on.

"I'd go from New York to Philly, and he'd have young kids waiting for him, boys, at the shows," Tom would say in a 1999 interview published in a wrestling newsletter. "Mostly it was kids with a broken home with no father. Just a drunk mother, alcoholic, drug addict, whatever. That's pretty much the type of kid that Mel was geared toward."

Phillips would encourage Tom to invite his friends along.

"So Tom started taking his friends and bringing them to Mel," Lee, Tom's older brother, tells me. "But these guys were a little more street-smart than Tom. They said, 'Tom, this guy's creepy, I don't like him.' But Tom loved wrestling so much that he's like, 'Wow, I'm at these wrestling shows for nothing!'"

Sometimes, the friends would stick around long enough for Phillips to ask them for time alone.

"From there, it got weird," Lee says, "when he started playing with their feet and shit."

Years later, in a draft of a legal complaint, Tom's lawyer would claim that Phillips "would frequently caress plaintiff's feet and would rub them against [Phillips's] own genital area." Other ring boys would go on to say Phillips did similar things to them.

"The other guys would say, 'Tom, this guy ain't right, he's playing with my toes, and putting them up against his crotch and stuff,'" Lee says. "I guess Tom just thought he was willing to overlook that part as long as he didn't touch anything else."

Phillips's boss, the WWF staffer in charge of the ring boy program, was a man known as Terry Garvin. Garvin (born Terry Joyal) was a veteran wrestler from Quebec, a friend of Pat Patterson's, and, like Patterson, one of the first openly gay men in the squared circle. By the time Tom entered the WWF's orbit, Patterson had obtained an office job for Garvin that entailed overseeing Phillips and, with him, the entire ring boy operation.

In turn, Garvin's boss was Patterson, Vince's right-hand man. Tom said he had unwanted interactions with Patterson. "He'd look at you when he was talking to you, he'd look right at your crotch and he'd, like, lick his lips and shit," Tom said in that 1999 newsletter interview. "He'd make sexual gestures by looking at you like that. He'd put his hand on your ass and squeeze your ass and stuff like that."

According to Lee, once Tom turned sixteen, Garvin took an interest in him. During a car trip the two were taking from New York to Massachusetts, Garvin allegedly offered the teen drugs and alcohol, which Tom says he rejected. The draft legal complaint says Garvin made an "unwelcome homosexual solicitation" for Tom to "engage in immediate sexual activity with him," which Tom said he refused.

Whatever happened, Tom stopped getting ring boy work shortly afterward.

In 1990, Tom got a surprising call from Terry Garvin: the WWF wanted him back. Garvin allegedly offered nineteen-year-old Tom a warehouse job that Garvin said could lead to bigger things with the WWF. Tom eagerly accepted—he said he wanted to be a ring announcer, like Phillips. Garvin said they could discuss the matter at the Garvin family home. Tom went. They were alone.

Garvin allegedly asked if he could perform oral sex on Tom. Tom said no. Garvin dropped the matter. Garvin wouldn't drive Tom home, so Tom slept in Garvin's garage. The next day, Garvin drove the young man to the warehouse.

It was there, a few hours later, that Mel Phillips allegedly gave Tom some news: Garvin had changed his mind about the job. Tom was fired.

"There's laws against this," Tom recalled saying to Phillips. "You can't just do this shit to people. What am I going to do, man? I should fucking go to the paper. I should go to Vince McMahon or something."

He'd done nothing then. But now, the brothers decided they wanted to take Tom's story public.

In October of 1991, with no lawyer or publicist at his side, Lee got in touch with journalists he thought might be sympathetic, based on their critical coverage of the WWF. One was Jeff Savage of *The San Diego Union-Tribune*. One was Irv Muchnick, roving freelancer. And one, of course, was Phil Mushnick.

Lee spoke with Mushnick at length. "Phil said, 'You guys are in the position where you better just get a lawyer already,'" Lee recalls.

When I ask Mushnick if he told the men to find a lawyer, he says, "No. I remember just trying to tell them to be careful, that these are treacherous people."

The Coles, he recalls, struck him as "essentially grown kids. Vulnerable, vulnerable, vulnerable fans."

The Coles found an attorney through the Yellow Pages. They sought other ring boys to join them and found one named Chris Loss—he had a similar story of being recruited by Phillips at a young age and having his feet sexually fondled. They talked to reporters. They prepared a legal filing about Tom's experiences.

On February 26, 1992, the *Post* published a Mushnick column: "WWF to Face Suit Alleging Child Sex Abuse."

"According to several highly placed sources," Mushnick wrote, "a lawsuit will be filed soon alleging that male WWF administrative employees and executives sexually harassed and abused underage teen-age boys who were engaged as ring assistants in the mid- and late-1980s." These boys went unnamed in the piece.

Thus began six of the most turbulent weeks of Vince McMahon's life.

"Terry Garvin? All those stories are true," Dave Meltzer tells me. "The stories about Mel Phillips? True.

"I always found Tom Cole honest," he adds.

Like most people in the wrestling press, Meltzer had never heard of Tom Cole before Mushnick's story dropped. He'd been busy following leads on other scandals: in addition to the ongoing drugs and steroids meltdown, a wrestler named Barry Orton had just gone on a wrestling radio show to say that male-on-male sexual harassment was rampant under Vince and Patterson, and that Terry Garvin had once propositioned him (albeit before either of them were at the WWF). On top of that, a new announcer for the World Bodybuilding Federation (and, briefly, the WWF) named

Murray Hodgson had threatened a wrongful-termination suit against the WWF that alleged sexual harassment by Patterson.

At the time, Meltzer didn't think any of the accusations were going to amount to anything.

"Vince has gotten away with so much stuff," Meltzer says, "because, for the most part—except for five percent of the time—the sports people don't wanna discuss morality with Vince McMahon, and the entertainment people don't even wanna think he's part of their world, and politicians don't wanna be laughed at for looking at something that's fake."

Vince made defensive maneuvers: In response to the *Post* story, the WWF issued a statement saying it did not "tolerate illegal or improper behavior by any of our employees at any time" and that it would "take responsible action regarding any legitimate claims filed through lawful channels." And on Monday, March 2, Patterson, Garvin, and Phillips tendered their resignations.

Meltzer and Mushnick both promptly published stories that included comments from Vince.

Mushnick claims Vince called him. He scooped Meltzer's weekly newsletter cycle by printing a March 4 item: Patterson and Garvin had resigned "on the heels of a proliferation of reports that the WWF is headed for an enormously damaging sex and drugs scandal."

Vince "denied all of the charges against both Patterson and Garvin," Meltzer reported in the March 9 edition of the *Wrestling Observer*.

A few days went by without any major articles. But the industry was abuzz. "The *Post* story will soon be joined by other mainstream newspaper stories focused on the WWF in the coming weeks," warned a leading wrestling newsletter called *Pro Wrestling Torch* on March 5.

Trouble was brewing in another news medium, as well.

The Cole brothers' lives had been thrown into chaos. A producer for TV personality Geraldo Rivera, host of *Now It Can Be Told* and *The Geraldo Rivera Show*, caught wind of the Coles' conversations with other reporters and found Lee's home phone number. She called to ask if Tom would sit for an interview; Lee says she threatened to ambush him with cameras at his house unless he acquiesced. Tom and Lee went from Lee's home in Utica to New York City to film the interview.

"That's what started the whole journey, the insanity," Lee says, "because we decided to go down there."

After filming the interview with Tom—Lee was still staying out of the public eye—the producer suggested that the Coles hire a "big-time city lawyer," in Lee's recollection. Her recommendation led them to Alan Fuchsberg, the son of a prominent trial lawyer and judge.

Meanwhile, Vince had been running frantic defense. According to Mushnick, Vince made a "pour-his-heart-out phone call" to Mushnick. Apparently fearing that Mel Phillips would soon become part of the public scandal, Vince told him "that he had let Phillips go four years ago because Phillips' relationship with kids seemed peculiar and unnatural," Mushnick recalled. "McMahon said he rehired Phillips with the caveat that Phillips steer clear from kids."

"McMahon told me that it was his great regard for children, his own personal regard for children, that made him get rid of Mel Phillips," Mushnick would later say in a deposition. "Vince and Linda returned Phillips to the organization with the caveat that Mel steer clear of underaged boys, stop hanging around kids, and stop chasing after kids."

Vince allegedly said he'd brought Phillips back because the man "really missed the wrestling" and "really missed the scene," but that he was gone for good this time.

Vince would go on to sue Mushnick and the *Post* for defamation, but notably never disputed Mushnick's account of the call. Similarly, when reporter David Bixenspan contacted McDevitt during a reevaluation of the scandal, McDevitt "noted that Cole said in a deposition that he never saw Phillips masturbate, but did not address claims that Phillips rubbed boys' feet against his crotch. Nor did he address Mushnick's and Meltzer's claims that Vince McMahon told them he was aware of allegations against Phillips as early as 1988."

Meltzer claims he got a similar call from Vince around the same time. "He didn't say Terry Garvin and Mel Phillips were *guilty*, " Meltzer recalls. "He just goes, 'There was an innocent person here: Patterson.' He didn't say the others."

The morning of March 11 brought a *San Diego Union-Tribune* article by Jeff Savage, headlined "Sleaze No Illusion in World of Wrestling: Sex, Drug Abuse Seen in Industry of 'Heroes.'" It featured a long summary of the steroid scandal so far, as well as the Orton and Hodgson allegations. Savage waited until the very end of the feature to mention the ring boys— and to finally name them.

"Boys are getting propositioned and played with all the time," fellow accuser Chris Loss told Savage. "You sort of put up with it because you can make a lot of money."

"I know if I would've slept with those guys, I'd probably be rich right now," Tom said. "It was really sleazy."

As it turned out, the *Union-Tribune* had prepared a full week's worth of exposés about the WWF; the story for the next day, March 12, was about the psychological effects of steroids and so-called roid rage. That same day, the *Los Angeles Times* ran a story about the WWF's scandals, as did various newswires. That night, *Entertainment Tonight* gave Orton the floor to denounce the WWF. Later on in the night, on *The Tonight Show*, Johnny Carson compared WWF wrestlers to pop-music fraudsters Milli Vanilli. All in one day.

The next day, March 13, Fuchsberg faxed McDevitt a courtesy copy of the lawsuit text, a move that's not unusual, but certainly was not obligatory—and that gave the WWF a head start. Tom hadn't filed the complaint yet, but the text outlined Tom's allegations and his demand for more than $3.5 million in restitution.

That night, Vince appeared on talk show *Larry King Live*, which aired nightly on Ted Turner's CNN. Vince was in King's Washington, DC, studio, clad in a black suit and tie. His accusers were Sammartino, beamed in from a studio in Pittsburgh, and Orton, who called in by phone. Vince denied all wrongdoing; he even denied *knowledge* of any wrongdoing by others.

"All I know is what I read in the newspaper," he told King at the top of the segment. "We want to get to the bottom of all of this."

Sammartino and Orton did their best to attack Vince, but he was more nimble than they.

For example, Sammartino brought up Mel Phillips by name and said, "There have been people who have come forward who caught him with an 11-year-old boy having sex in a car."

"Did you actually see this incident in some sort of parking lot?" Vince asked, taking the show into his own hands as if it were *Tuesday Night Titans*. "Did you see that, Bruno?"

"Well," Sammartino said, "I was told about it right after it happened."

"You were *told* about it," Vince repeated, condescendingly.

"All right, that's hearsay," said Larry King, acting as referee; they moved on.

Vince also took the TV spot as an opportunity to call out his new-found foe: journalism and its practitioners.

"I think there are certain members of the media that I would suggest are something less than legitimate," he said midway through. "I'll mention one in particular: a fellow by the name of Mushnick who writes for the *New York Post*."

A caller to the show asked why Vince was being so defensive, and what he would do to prevent sexual misconduct at his business. He dodged the question, turning his fire toward the press again.

"The media has kept all of these accusers away from us," he said. "They don't want us to talk to them. They don't want us to get to the bottom of the story."

The segment ended with no clear victor, only muddied waters.

Minutes later, Lee got a call from Fuchsberg: Vince was ready to negotiate with Tom. They would have an in-person meeting in two days, on Sunday, March 15. It would prove to be a turning point in the lives of everyone present.

But Lee wasn't invited.

Fuchsberg and his sister, who was also working on the case, "decided to keep me out of the meeting," Lee says.

Lee agreed to stay in a motel room while the meeting happened. Lee told Fuchsberg to make an ultimatum. "I said, 'Alan, this is the offer: $750,000. If they don't pay, tell them no, and that we'll see them on TV,'" Lee recalls.

"That's what I told him," Lee says. "He didn't do that."

Sunday arrived, and so did Vince. He came to Fuchsberg's Fifth Avenue law office along with McDevitt and Linda. Tom and Alan sat opposite them at a table. It was the first time Tom and the McMahons had ever met in person.

Here is a reconstruction of what happened, according to the accounts of Tom, Lee, and Fuchsberg.

"I told [Vince] everything that happened to me," Tom would later recall. "He looked disgusted and upset about it."

"Well, you know, Tom, this is a terrible thing that happened to you," Vince said. "I want to make it right. This isn't the type of company that we run. These people have left the company."

Fuchsberg raised the possibility of a big-ticket settlement. "Well, that's a lot of money that we're talking about," Vince said.

"Listen, I'm not looking for money," Tom blurted out.

"It was probably the stupidest thing I ever said," Tom would later lament. "I believed what [Vince] was saying."

Fuchsberg "kept walking out of the room and leaving me in there for fifteen, twenty minutes at a time with Vince McMahon and his wife," Tom said. "He'd go on walks with [McDevitt] and leave me in the room. And McMahon would talk to me and say, 'It's terrible what happened to you and *ba-ba-ba*. We want you to come back and work for us,' and this and that. But what they really wanted was to find out any other kids' names and any other people who were involved."

Eventually, Fuchsberg and Vince started arguing. Vince's words grew frightening: "I'm like a rat," the boss said. "I'll go for the throat if I have to. I won't be backed into a corner."

Vince got up to leave, and Linda and McDevitt joined him.

Tom panicked.

"I loved wrestling," Tom would later say to justify what he did next. "I loved working for the business. It's what I wanted to do my whole life. There was never a better feeling than going into an arena or going to a wrestling show and meeting people and stuff like that. It felt so good inside. You were so happy to be there. It was the best feeling in the world."

"No, no, don't go!" Tom yelled to the departing McMahons. "I just want my job back!"

There was a stunned silence.

Fuchsberg left the room again. "I've told this story to people and they just don't get it," Lee says. "He left this kid, this twenty-one-year-old man who's a street kid without an education, alone with *Vince McMahon*."

"He was very shrewd," Tom would say of Vince, "and I was very young."

What did Vince tell Tom in that moment of intimacy?

"Mr. McMahon explained to Tom that he had a difficult childhood himself," is how Fuchsberg would describe it to a reporter shortly afterward.

Lee puts it more bluntly: "Vince McMahon started telling him, 'Tom, I was molested also when I was a kid.'"

"I want to start on a clean slate with you," Vince said. "I want to take care of everything. How would you feel about that?"

"Tom got a good feeling that Mr. McMahon really cared," Fuchsberg said. "He shook hands with Tom and offered him his job back."

"I thought that was the right thing to do," Tom would say. "I thought, *Let me give it a chance*. Maybe this guy *didn't* know anything that happened."

Fuchsberg was called back in. Tom agreed to accepting $55,000 in back pay and a job in the WWF's crew department. The $750,000 was never mentioned again. The lawsuit was dropped.

"I was in no league for Vince McMahon," Tom said. "The guy's methodical."

"After the negotiations," Lee says, "this is when everything got real ugly."

I first encountered Lee Cole in 2021, a few months after Tom killed himself.

Lee had tweeted the news of his brother's death, and it was through Twitter that I first got in touch with him. Once I'd gained his trust, over a series of phone and video calls, he laid out his account of what happened between the Coles and the McMahons.

By the time of Tom's suicide, Lee had given up on trying to expose wrestling's first family. But, according to Lee, his brother's final words to him—spoken over the phone mere minutes before his death—put him back on the case.

"If something ever happened to me, make sure that you keep going after these people," Tom allegedly told Lee just before he killed himself. "If something happens to me, Lee, one thing I know is that you will be able to hurt them bad."

But as of 1992, although Lee felt rage on his little brother's behalf, he was also acting out of self-interest.

The elder Cole had developed a criminal record. He had been convicted of robbery a few years prior (he tells me someone else committed the crime and he took the fall) and was serving probation for it. On top of that, there was a warrant out for his arrest on robbery charges from 1987. He had been living under a pseudonym for years. Money, he thought, could make at least some of his problems go away.

"At that time, it was about money with me," he tells me. "I'm not going to lie to you."

It's unclear how much Vince knew about Lee when he began his meeting with Tom. The elder brother was still an entirely hidden figure as far as the public was concerned. It appears that Fuchsberg, whatever his communications with McDevitt had been, hadn't mentioned Lee. "Vince, at this time, didn't know I was at the motel; he didn't know about me," Lee says.

But, while making post-negotiation conversation with Vince, Tom started talking about the origins of the now dead suit. "My older brother's at the motel; he's the one that put this together," Tom told Vince.

Vince replied with a proposal. "Well, I'm going to be going to the Phil Donahue show tomorrow," he said. "Why don't you bring your brother over and we can all meet?"

At the time, Phil Donahue was one of the kings of daytime talk-show TV, at what was arguably the height of that artform. Talk shows, like wrestling shows, were all about outlandish characters, rowdy audiences, and shifting levels of fiction. Were the guests telling the truth? Were they acting? Was the host in on it? None of that mattered so much as the thrill of the content. The topics were typically lurid and taboo, playing on libidinal biases and passions.

In other words, *Donahue* operated on the principles of kayfabe. Vince could work with that.

Tom came back to the motel room. Lee learned what had happened in the legal negotiation.

"I was really upset at Tom," Lee says. "But Tom came up and hugged me."

"I just want my job back, Lee," Tom told his brother. "That's all I want. I want to go back to work there."

"The way he said it, I felt so bad for him, I couldn't argue with him," Lee recalls. "That's what it comes down to."

Meanwhile, Vince and his team were concocting a plan with shocking swiftness.

He was slated to appear on *Donahue* alongside a panel of accusers and journalists: Orton, Sammartino, Hodgson, Meltzer, Billy Graham, former wrestler Tom Hankins, and wrestling talk-show host John Arezzi. The deck was stacked against Vince, so he brought an ace in the hole.

He would bring Tom to the studio audience. If anyone brought up the pedophilia charges, Vince would pull a classic daytime-talk move: he'd point to the audience and Tom would stand up and be expected to defend him.

On the morning of Monday, March 16, a limousine picked Tom up from the motel and took him to Fuchsberg's office to sign some paper-work before the show. Lee, meanwhile, walked to the NBC building in Midtown Manhattan. The temperature was freezing that morning as he waited outside.

"They showed up in two limousines," Lee recalls. From one of them, out stepped Vince and Tom; from the other, Linda and—to Lee's surprise—Miss Elizabeth.

"They brought the eye candy in," he says, "because they knew that they were dealing with Tom."

Vince walked up to Lee. It was the first time the two men had met. He was slightly overwhelmed by how imposing Vince was. "He had an aura about him," Lee recalls. "Nobody cared about Elizabeth. It was Vince McMahon that everybody was looking at."

Vince and Lee reached the elevator, but Tom and the women were close behind. "When they went to get in the elevator with us, Vince McMahon put out his hand and stopped them and closed the door," Lee says.

They reached the appointed floor. Lee was told to hang in a back room, away from the guests. Tom was told to go to the audience and sit with Elizabeth.

"They split us up," Lee says. "I shouldn't have allowed it."

Meanwhile, the other guests were in the green room. They didn't know Vince was going to be on. "This would be a situation that I was sure Vince wouldn't want to be any part of," Meltzer says.

Orton, who had been in contact with the Coles during the media circus, turned to Meltzer and said, "It's really weird: I haven't heard from Tom Cole all weekend. I think they might've paid him off. I'm not gonna bring the name up, and I don't think you should bring the name up either."

The susurrus of nervous anticipation rose in the cramped room. Then two figures appeared at the door. The room fell silent.

"Donahue brings McMahon in to say hello to everybody," Arezzi tells me. "That was the chilliest minute I've ever experienced. Bruno wanted to *kill* the guy. It was just the weirdest thing."

And then, just like that, Vince was ushered out. The guests were, too—separately.

The show began.

"The [World] Wrestling Federation: You know how you [say], 'Tee-hee, ha-ha, what a joke, ho-ho,'" Donahue said sarcastically in his introductory monologue. Nevertheless: "$1.7 billion in 1990. That's more revenue than has been generated by the NFL. So while you're laughing, somebody is whistling all the way to the bank."

The show was a crowded muddle of allegations. Hodgson and Hankins both claimed Pat Patterson had demanded sex in exchange for professional advancement. Orton told a tale of Garvin's licentiousness. Vince was given the opportunity to rebut the claims and focused mostly on Hodgson, deflecting by talking about how Hodgson had been fired due to incompetence and debating the specifics of his employment. Then it was on to a long discussion of steroid use. The Mel Phillips allegations came up—but nobody mentioned Tom by name.

It was tense television, but nothing too incriminating.

Donahue tried to sum and spice things up at the end. "Vince McMahon, here's the charge: You had to see this," he said, referring to all the misconduct they'd discussed. "Was the money so good, was the glamour so great, was the business exploding so wonderfully that you didn't have time to get into this kind of thing and you looked the other way and allowed it to happen?"

"I certainly didn't look the other way," Vince replied. "There's no reason for me to look the other way and risk everything that we have going for us."

"You didn't know any of this was going on, Mr. McMahon?"

"No, I did not."

An audience member had an outraged question for the various accusers who'd mentioned child molestation: How could they not have blown the whistle right away?

"You have to understand the wrestling business," Meltzer said.

Orton finished the thought: "By coming forward right now, I'm done, man," he said. "I'll never wrestle, never, ever again under any circumstances. I am done."

"You should have done something about it!" the audience member cried. "I don't care about your career!"

The next questioner said it was "a shame" that these panelists "are sitting there accusing Mr. McMahon, who so far has done nothing wrong."

Sammartino fielded that one: "You don't know what you're talking about, sonny," he said. "When you grow up, maybe you'll understand a little bit."

Shortly before cutting to commercial, there was another question: "Isn't wrestling fixed anyway?"

Donahue, to his credit, didn't make anyone answer that one. "That's a creative decision," the host said. "This is about crime."

Soon, the show was over. According to a later account by reporter Jeff Savage in *Penthouse*, Tom, who had gone wholly unutilized during the show, walked down to the front of the stage and confronted *Donahue* producer Ed Glavin.

"This show was bullshit," Tom said. "There's only one guy here who cares, and it's that guy right there."

Tom pointed at Vince.

The salacious headlines and TV spots about the WWF didn't stop. Mushnick pulled no punches. "Sex, Lies, and the WWF" read the *Post's* sports section front page on March 18. It was the headline for an extra-long, extra-outraged Mushnick column about the WWF's iniquity, and particularly about the end of the Cole suit that he had helped set in motion.

"Never will you encounter a human more cold-blooded, more devoid of honor and propriety than Vince McMahon, America's foremost TV babysitter," Mushnick wrote. "In your wildest, most twisted dreams, you won't meet up with the likes of McMahon, a miscreant so practiced in the art of deception, the half-truth and the bald-faced lie as to make the Artful Dodger appear clumsy."

It was here that Mushnick announced to the world that Tom Cole had been bought out. "Cole's attorney, Alan Fuchsberg, said yesterday that the deal is not a payoff, but rather an agreement, because Cole has returned to a job he once loved"—a distinction that Mushnick derided as "semantic obfuscation."

It was little wonder that Mushnick became Vince's bête noire, what with descriptions of Vince like these: "A George Steinbrenner or a Don King pale by comparison. So help us. Indeed, Hannibal Lecter is the only fictional character who comes close."

Coverage of the WWF's moral deficiencies continued apace. It was terrible timing for Vince: a new World Bodybuilding Federation TV show was slated to premiere on USA Network on April 4, and *WrestleMania VIII* was happening three days after that.

To make matters worse, on April 2, the WWF was served with a subpoena from the US Department of Justice. There would be a grand jury investigation of the company. The scope and focus of the investigation were mysteries.

But none of that was as personally bad for Vince as the shock of April 3.

That morning's *Post* brought another Mushnick column, in which he teased something big that was coming on that night's episode of Geraldo Rivera's *Now It Can Be Told*. Mushnick said he'd learned that "the show will air a tape of a woman, Rita Chatterton, who alleges that McMahon himself gave her a no-sex, no-job ultimatum while she served the WWF as a referee." He added that her lawyer said she'd passed a polygraph.

The show aired at 7 p.m. Eastern in New York. The lead segment, called "Wrestling's Ring of Vice," was hosted by Geraldo and his brother Craig. It alluded to child molestation, and Tom had, of course, filmed an interview for it—but the interview had been cut once the suit was dropped. As a result, the pedophilia charges were spectral. Hodgson and Orton spoke, the camera crew did stunts to try to enter Titan Towers and Pat Patterson's home. It was all prelude.

"Vince McMahon may not have been talking to us," Geraldo said at one point, clad in jeans and tie in a wrestling ring. "But plenty of other people were."

That's when they cut to Chatterton.

The first words of her clip were, "Next thing I know, Vince unzipped his pants." Dramatic synth music suddenly blared. The viewer was told there would be more after a commercial.

Sure enough, if you stuck around, you got to see a seated Chatterton uncomfortably recount the basics of her alleged 1986 rape. This was the first time Chatterton had ever gone public with her allegation. She wept into her fist as she gave her story.

She'd had a surreal few years. Chatterton had done a few more ref gigs for the WWF after the night of the alleged rape. However, she tells me her continued work with them was rare and at the behest of New York State, which still required certification for wrestling referees and had a deficit of them available. She says she never worked shows where Vince would be present.

Craig Rivera informed the viewer that Chatterton felt she couldn't speak up until now.

"I held off for a long time because of my parents," she told the camera. "Both of my parents were very ill. My mother died a year ago. My father died two weeks ago. Between not having to worry about my parents' health, and with other people coming forward? God, I just hope somebody listens."

There was, as one might expect, a flurry of ancillary media coverage of this new allegation—the first one to be focused solely on Vince, himself. The clouds were darkening over this year's WrestleMania.

That show was mediocre at best. Randy Savage beat Ric Flair for the WWF championship, Miss Elizabeth at his side—but, in reality, the couple were on the outs (possibly part of the reason she was willing to be Tom's date at *Donahue*). The big surprise of the night was the return of the Ultimate Warrior after his suspension: he ran in to save Hogan from a dastardly attack by Sid Justice in the main event.

The event was an end of an era. Warrior would soon be fired for trying to illegally import human growth hormone. It was Roddy Piper's last match for two years. The main event was teased as Hogan's retirement match; in reality, he was taking an indefinite hiatus to lower his now tarred profile.

Vince's reputation was as seemingly ruined as Hogan's was, and things only got worse on April 10, when Chatterton appeared on *The Geraldo Rivera Show*. It, like *Donahue*, was a daytime talk show, but a far less scrupulous one.

The topic that day was ostensibly sex scandals in the sporting world. Fellow guests included Hodgson and two women allegedly harassed by basketball player Dominique Wilkins and baseball player Jose Canseco. But equal weight was given to the other guests: a pseudonymous and shades-wearing woman who spoke lovingly of her affairs with hockey players; journalist E. Jean Carroll, who had written a magazine article in praise of sports-groupie culture; and, astoundingly, a woman known as Morganna the Kissing Bandit, who used to giddily run onto baseball fields and give semi-wanted kisses to the players.

"From baseball to boxing, hoops to hockey, the news on the sports pages has never been this hot," Geraldo said in his opening churn.

Then the camera cut to Chatterton, seated on the stage. "Meet Rita," Geraldo intoned. "Rita was allegedly forced to have sex with perhaps the most powerful man in the world of professional wrestling—and she'll tell us all about it."

Chatterton spoke of meeting Vince for the first time in his office. "I was told that I was going to be so big. My name would be a household item," she said. "His exact words were, 'How are you going to feel the first time you walk past a newsstand and see your face on the cover of *Time* magazine?' I mean, he just blew it up to be so unbelievable, but I knew it was possible because I was a novelty, I was the only female."

"There came a time when you and Vince McMahon were allegedly— I stress *allegedly* because he denies it—you were allegedly in a limousine," Geraldo said. "Tell us what happened."

And so it was that Chatterton gave the account of her alleged rape that was quoted earlier in this book.

"I want you to speak for yourself on the question of delay," Geraldo said.

"You people don't understand wrestling," Chatterton said. "No one talks. It's a complete *hush-hush* world."

She added that she did go to an attorney in 1986, but "I was told at that time that basically this was going to come down to my word against his, because I had no proof. I had to weigh that. At the time my mother was on oxygen twenty-four hours a day, my dad had a bad heart, and I didn't think either one of my parents could have been put through it. Especially at that time, where no one was opening up."

An audience member had a question for Chatterton. "Rita, what do you expect to get now?" he said. "It's been six years now, so what do you want? Did you just want to come on *Geraldo*?"

"What do I want?" Chatterton repeated. "I want people to understand what's really happening there. If you had a brother that went into wrestling—"

"If you did that seven years ago, you could have did that!" the audience member said. "You could have been the first!"

"You're right," Chatterton replied, sounding exhausted and embarrassed. "I could have done that seven years ago. You're absolutely right. Seven years ago, my mother was on oxygen twenty-four hours a day and my dad had a bad heart. After talking to the attorney . . ."

She trailed off. She shook her head. It was the last thing she was allowed to say on the show.

Rita Chatterton then disappeared from the public eye for almost thirty years.

★ ★ ★

The Ring Boy Scandal had ended before it could ever really begin.

According to Lee, not long after the *Donahue* broadcast, the Cole brothers were summoned to Titan Towers. Limousines picked them up. Linda and Miss Elizabeth were in one; Tom was told to ride with them. Vince was in the other; Lee was made his fellow passenger. Once they arrived, Tom went to Linda's office and Lee went to Vince's. Lee could tell what was going on.

"She came in as the mother, and we come from a broken family," Lee tells me. "Linda McMahon played the mother role with Tom. It was very obvious."

As Lee entered Vince's capacious and memorabilia-lined office, one object stuck out to him: "He had this hammer in a container up against the wall and it was from William F. Buckley," the legendary conservative columnist and founder of *National Review*. There was a message on the container—"To my dear friend, Vince McMahon"—along with Buckley's signature.

Vince asked questions to try to suss Lee out; Lee was evasive. Eventually, Vince proposed that the Coles stay at a nearby hotel so they could have another meeting the next day. In the meantime, how about dinner? Lee said sure.

They reconvened with Tom and Linda and went to the building's garage. "Linda had this beautiful Mercedes-Benz and Tom went with her," Lee says. "Vince had this sports car. Yellow. It was an old type of sports car, and I went with Vince."

As Vince drove, he made conversation about the crises he and his business were facing. He compared it to his period of bankruptcy in the late 1970s.

"I've lost it once before and got it back," Vince told Lee. "If I lose it this time, I'll get it back."

They arrived at an Italian restaurant. It was the dinner hour, but they were the only diners; the place had been cleared out. This was to be an incognito meeting. The McMahons made small talk about their kids, and asked the Coles about their lives. Afterward, Linda recommended that they have tea in the hotel lobby. Upon arriving, the Coles found a group of WWF wrestlers and managers there as a surprise.

"They were coming up and saying hi to us and introducing themselves,"

Lee says. Eventually, "Vince told us to go upstairs," Lee says. "He said, 'Room service is on us.' Bad mistake!" The Cole boys, raised with little, lived the high life that night. "That room service was beautiful," Lee says with a laugh. "We're a couple of guys who aren't used to living like these people lived, let's put it that way."

According to Lee, a meeting took place at Titan Towers the next day. A single limousine brought the young men back to the building. They entered a room; Vince, Linda, McDevitt, and some WWF execs were allegedly there. The conversation began, and Lee was astonished by what he heard.

Throughout the failed lawsuit process, Lee had been seeking other ex-ring boys who might want to come forward. He says there were many who were almost ready to talk, but had not yet done so. So Lee certainly didn't expect Vince to start mentioning the names of the young men Lee had been speaking with.

"They knew who they were and how to get to them before we even sat down in that meeting," Lee says.

"Do you have any other names of any kids?" Vince asked.

"Vince, I've got lots of stuff," was Lee's reply.

"And then Vince looked at me and sarcastically said, 'Oh, *you're* a smart one,'" Lee recalls. "I'll never forget that."

Lee says he puzzled over how the information could have leaked. Only the next day did he put it together. Lee had phone messages from many of the potential accusers on his answering machine. The machine had a feature whereby you could call it remotely and hear the messages. You just needed a code.

"Tom had my code," Lee says, "and Tom had given Linda my code."

"Everybody left a message," he adds, meaning the other victims. "So, at that point, they knew everybody I was talking to."

Tom signed papers releasing Patterson from all previous claims of misconduct, allowing Vince's right-hand man to be reinstated. Garvin and Phillips vanished from the public eye and died in 1998 and 2012, respectively.

Since the end of the Cole suit, no former ring boys have gone public with allegations of abuse. Bixenspan, the investigative reporter, found a man (whom he kept anonymous) who began a quiet suit in 1999 that claimed Phillips "rubbed Plaintiff's feet and toes against his crotch" and would "pull Plaintiff's toes apart until Plaintiff screamed." The suit appears to have been settled out of court.

Chris Loss, the other former ring boy in the failed Cole suit, also disappeared from the public eye. A former friend of his wrote a letter to the *Wrestling Observer* in March 2004, in which he said Loss had been "contacted by the WWF after his name got out. . . .

"He went up there for a visit, and came back to Niagara Falls a totally changed kid," the letter read. "He never said another word. He took a job at an AM radio station in Grand Island and never talked about the business to me, or anyone else."

Soon after the visits to Titan Towers, Lee was arrested for violating his probation. He is convinced Tom was tricked into telling the McMahons about it, and that they set in motion a complicated chain of events that led to his arrest. Lee tells a story that, whether or not it's true, is certainly indicative of the way Lee feels about Vince.

While out on bail, the story goes, he called the WWF. The call was forwarded to McDevitt.

"Jerry, you guys fucked up real bad," Lee said. "You had my brother throw me in jail."

"No, we didn't," McDevitt countered. "That's your brother."

"*Bullshit*, Jerry," Lee said. "I know exactly what happened. Now I'm coming for you guys, I just want to let you know that. I'm going to come really hard for you guys."

All of a sudden, he heard a familiar voice in the background on the line say, "Well, I'm sorry you feel that way, Lee."

Lee simply replied, "Fuck you, Vince."

"That's exactly what I said," Lee recalls. "And then I hung up the phone." Lee and Vince never spoke again.

Nor, for a long time, did the Cole brothers.

"I kicked Tom out; I told him he couldn't come back to the house," Lee says. "But Tom was trying to please them at that time. That's what it came down to. I have no hard feelings for what he was doing. These people were manipulating him. They're good at what they do. . . ."

"Vince McMahon," Lee tells me with grim confidence, "can get you to do anything."

12

HEAT, ACT III

(1992–1993)

T hey called me and told me he'd be coming in," Jim Weatherspoon re-calls. "And to have a forklift."

It was a winter morning and Weatherspoon, a funeral director at Powell Funeral Home, had just been told that he'd be receiving precious cargo. André the Giant needed to be cremated.

André Roussimoff's last days had been agony. He'd flown to France in a rush to see his ailing eighty-five-year-old father, and arrived just in time to see the elder man die. The blow of this loss only compounded André's worsening physical condition. Twelve days after his father's death, on January 27, 1993, André went to sleep at his hotel in Paris. At some point during the night, his heart gave out. He was forty-six years old.

André had specified that he wanted to be cremated and have his ashes scattered at the ranch he'd owned for about a decade and a half, in Ellerbe, North Carolina. He spent as much time there as he could, in his final years, raising Texas longhorns and eating at the local surf-and-turf joint.

But even in death, André's uncanny form posed problems for him.

The men who removed his stiffened corpse from the Paris hotel room found it necessary to break his arm in order to fit him through the door. There were no crematoria in France that could work with a body of that size. He was embalmed, then his entourage struggled to find a plane that could carry not only André's quarter-ton body, but also the three-hundred-pound box containing it.

When they finally found a flight and touched down at the Charlotte airport, no hearse—no pickup truck, even—was large enough to take the coffin. They had to use an enclosed box truck—like a moving truck—to transport the body to the only funeral home in south-central North

Carolina that could do the cremation: Powell, where Weatherspoon had worked for decades.

Powell is located in a remote part of the Tar Heel State. Specifically, it's located in Southern Pines.

Wrestling history is filled with eerie rhymes and coincidences, none stranger than the fact that André the Giant would be cremated within walking distance of the hospital where Vince McMahon had been born.

Weatherspoon, a lifelong Southern Pines resident born six years before Vince, had been good friends with Vince's stepbrother, Richard Lupton. Young Jim and Richard often played in the swampy woods behind the Lupton home; Vicki would call them in for supper at dusk.

"Back then, it was so simple," Weatherspoon says.

After the Luptons moved away, Weatherspoon didn't think much about them. He didn't watch wrestling, either. He didn't know who Vince McMahon was, let alone that Vince had once been his friend Richard's little brother Vinnie.

But Weatherspoon had known André.

He had been introduced to the wrestler years prior while helping promote an appearance the Giant made at the local motor speedway. After that, Weatherspoon would often run into André wolfing down "a pretty good plateful" at various Southern Pines restaurants—André was especially fond of a seafood-and-steak eatery called the Lob-Steer Inn.

"He was a gentle giant," Weatherspoon says, affection in his drawl.

Now, André was dead, and it would be Weatherspoon's responsibility to usher his body into its next form.

"I wouldn't say it was emotional," Weatherspoon says. "But it was trying."

While waiting for the body, he called the manufacturer of the crematory unit to see if it could burn a 520-pound body. "They said the machine was capable of it," he recalls. Still, he worried—would the body fit through the aperture into the furnace?

Weatherspoon did, in fact, borrow a forklift from a local building supply company. When the body arrived in its massive shipping container, they used the forklift to move André into the garage where the crematory oven was located.

Weatherspoon waited until the forklift operator left before he opened the box and saw André's placid face.

Usually, a cremation job takes one funeral home employee. André's took four. With great effort, the men moved André's body to a different wooden container, the one that would be burned with him. They usually used cardboard tubes to roll the deceased into the mouth of the furnace, but André would have flattened them. They substituted broom handles instead.

Weatherspoon activated the ignition.

A typical cremation takes about two hours. André's took seven. It remains the longest cremation Weatherspoon has ever experienced.

There was much grand ceremony over André and his ashes in the coming weeks. The WWF held ten-bell memorial salutes at their live shows. It was announced that André was the inaugural inductee into the WWF Hall of Fame. And a funeral service was held at André's ranch on a sunny February 24, attended by many of the top names in wrestling.

The ever-more-infamous Hulk Hogan gave a speech, selfishly rambling about how happy André was to get Hogan over in the main event of *WrestleMania III.*

Vince was there, too—less than an hour's drive from the place of his birth. He gave no eulogy.

Also in attendance was Rita Chatterton. André was one of the first wrestlers who had been kind to her, and she took his death as her signal to leave the industry. The day included an encounter with Vince, who, she recalls, walked up to her and introduced himself.

"Nice to meet you," Vince said.

"He knew *exactly* who I was," she adds. "I said, 'Nice to meet me?' I told him to go fuck himself and walked away."

After the funeral, Vince didn't stick around to visit anyone in his hometown. No trip down memory lane for him.

He knew André had hated him. "When his career was over, he had no value, y'know, to himself," Vince would tell a documentary crew decades later. "André more or less wanted to blame me and resented me a bit, because he knew the business was gonna go on without him."

When the interviewer asked Vince if he remembered his last conversation with André, the boss replied, "No, I don't."

"I have a facility to get rid of negatives very quickly," he added. "And if something hurts me, I get rid of it."

★ ★ ★

The World Bodybuilding Federation had gone out of business in July 1992, after a disastrously underwatched second championship pay-per-view. *Bodybuilding Lifestyles* magazine folded soon after.

In the late summer of '92, *Penthouse* had published a long feature on all the sex scandals in the WWF, sparing none of the details that more respectable publications had avoided. In November, Davey Boy Smith had been fired for using performance-enhancing drugs; that same month, the long-running WWF network-TV feature, *Saturday Night's Main Event*, ended its run.

Just after André's passing, former WWF wrestlers Kerry Von Erich (Kerry Adkisson) and Dino Bravo (Adolfo Bresciano) both died tragic and public deaths—suicide for the former, murder for the latter.

A wrestler named Kevin "Nailz" Wacholz had been furious with Vince over a financial dispute and, according to Bret Hart, "cornered Vince in his office and screamed at him for fifteen minutes" while Bret was just down the hall, then "knocked Vince over in his chair, choking him violently" until others pried him off. When police arrived, Wacholz told them that Vince had made a sexual pass at him. The two would be caught in inconclusive lawsuits for years.

Just days before he flew to North Carolina for André's funeral, Vince and Titan Sports filed their defamation lawsuit against Phil Mushnick for his *New York Post* coverage. Less than three weeks later, Vince and Linda sued Rita Chatterton, Geraldo Rivera, and others involved in Chatterton's segments.

Both suits would end inconclusively and with no fault assigned. But they set a template. Whereas before, Vince had tried to suck up to media outlets and get mainstream attention, he was now making angry skepticism about the media into official strategy.

"Mushnick's contribution to the stated goal of the *New York Post* to be the 'dirtiest and most mud-slinging paper' is a regular column he authors," the first suit read. "Mushnick does not provide the targets of his attacks any opportunity to comment upon the truthfulness or accuracy of his attacks, either before or after his articles are published."

The filing went on to say Mushnick "took steps to fabricate evidence to support his false and malicious statements," and, as such, "affiliated himself with Lee Cole, a convicted felon who had been a fugitive from justice."

Lee and Mushnick then "devised and implemented a calculated plan to induce an individual"—Tom Cole—"to 'stretch the truth' and claim that he had been sexually abused while a minor by a person formerly affiliated with the WWF."

The suit against Chatterton et al. was similarly vicious, arguing that Chatterton "was not a competent ring referee and posed a danger to herself in the ring" and alleging that Dr. D, David Shults, was in fact the hidden figure behind her. "Shults contacted Chatterton in order to induce her to make a false claim that McMahon had raped her while she was still affiliated with the WWF," the suit read. "Chatterton agreed with Shults to falsely accuse McMahon of raping her in 1986 in order that such charges could be made for the first time in the context of the filming and production of the *Now It Can Be Told* program."

As his suits made their way through the courts, Vince was promoting a new weekly WWF series, airing in prime time on USA Network and taped at the historic Manhattan Center in New York City. He called it *Monday Night Raw*—the "raw" part referring to the fact that the show was live. Outside of PPVs, the WWF had historically taped and edited most of its shows in advance. But with the hourlong *Raw*, the implication was that anything could happen.

Initially, *Raw* was a boost for Vince. Ratings were better than they had been for the show it replaced, *Prime Time Wrestling*. But the success was unsustainable.

The WWF's submission to Vince's creative whims was becoming a problem. His sense of humor and coolness were notoriously idiosyncratic, and he pushed characters like Yokozuna (ostensibly an evil sumo wrestler from Japan, he was, in fact, a Samoan named Agatupu Rodney Anoa'i), Irwin R. Schyster (a greedy Internal Revenue Service official played by Mike Rotunda), and Doink the Clown (Matt Borne in circus makeup). Vince hired a putdown-artist comedian named Rob Bartlett to act as one of his cohosts at the *Raw* commentators' table, only to find that they had no chemistry; by April, Bartlett was fired.

At the core of it all was . . . well, very little. That was the problem: the WWF had no grand figures to hold it together anymore. Hogan came back from hiatus—he'd used the time to star in a film called *Mr. Nanny*—but simply couldn't get back over with the public after everything he'd said and done. His schtick now just seemed sad.

Morale was low. Crowds were thin. Wrestlers were wilting.

And no one was more ticked off than the newest WWF champion.

A few months prior, on October 12, 1992, Bret Hart had been in Alberta, Canada, getting ready for a match, when Chief Jay Strongbow "pulled me aside to tell me that on Vince's direct orders I was to catch the very first flight the next morning to Saskatoon [TV tapings] and go straight to the building to see him."

Bret, like always, did as he was told. He arrived in Saskatoon, the city of his father's birth. Stu, in fact, was going to be there that night, standing in Bret's corner.

Bret was booked to have a match with the then-champion, Ric Flair. By then, Bret's devotion had been rewarded with two lesser belts, the Intercontinental title and the Tag Team title, at various times. But he had never held the WWF World Championship. This, despite the fact that he was probably the most popular wrestler in the company at the time, regularly drawing huge cheers—or "pops"—whenever he walked to the ring with his wailing-guitar instrumental theme music behind him and his trademark reflector shades on his face.

Bret entered the Saskatoon arena. "I patiently sat in a chair at the end of a long backstage hallway waiting to see Vince, who was having a closed-door meeting," the Hitman recalled. "After a few minutes the door opened and out came Flair, who turned around and shook Vince's hand in the doorway." Flair walked away. Vince waved Bret over.

"He shut the door behind us," Bret wrote. "I could detect neither good nor bad as I tried to read his face. He took his seat, tenting his fingers as he looked at me."

"You've been with me now for how many years?" Vince asked.

"Eight years," Bret replied.

Vince asked how many times Bret had missed a show; Bret said only once. Vince praised Bret for his dedication.

Then Vince said, "I've done everything I could think of—put the Tag belts on you, and the Intercontinental belt—and I finally reached the point where I don't know what else to do with you."

Bret felt a shock of anxiety. "I wondered if this cold-hearted son of a bitch was actually firing me the very same day that he was supposed to be flying my dad up to be in my corner!" he wrote. "I envisioned trying to explain all this to Stu. The blood going to my heart began to churn thick as mud."

Then, Vince's face cracked into a grin.

"So," the boss said, "that's why I've decided to put the World belt on you tonight!"

"Dead silence," Bret recalled. "I simply did not grasp what he'd just said."

"Hell, aren't you going to smile or something?" Vince asked, then laughed—"that famous Vince McMahon *yuk-yuk-yuk*," is how Bret put it.

"I promised him I wouldn't let him down," Bret wrote. "He said he wasn't worried about that. All I had to do was keep on being the best worker in the business, and he'd take care of the rest."

"Nothing's ever written in stone, but my plans are to keep the belt on you for at least a year," Vince said, in Bret's recollection. "From now on you'll fly only first class."

Bret and Flair had a humdinger of a title bout. Bret was executing his finisher, a submission hold dubbed the Sharpshooter, when his mind "flashed back to all those wrestling magazines I created as a kid; the times I made my own championship belts out of cardboard and broken bottle glass."

Flair submitted. Bret won. His time, it seemed, had come.

"God almighty, thank you for the greatest moment in my life!" Bret yelled in a post-match interview. "I'm proud to be the WWF World Champion!"

He had the belt. But something didn't feel right.

For reasons never explained to Bret, the match in which he "won" the belt wasn't actually aired on TV. His fans had to scratch their heads as they watched the next batch of WWF television programming and heard that their hero had been awarded the title, without them being able to witness it.

Previous champions had been granted the use of a limo every night in every town, along with a private dressing room "complete with fruit basket." Not for Bret, though—Vince said he had to cut costs.

And there were responsibilities that went along with the belt, even if it no longer came with the customary perks. Bret says Roddy Piper pulled him aside to explain that holding on to the championship meant continuing to cultivate the boss, "stressing how important it was for me to get close to Vince, to try to be his best friend."

Pat Patterson, too, advised Bret "that Vince liked to hear from his champion every day." Bret dutifully phoned Vince daily, "even though, to me, it just felt like brown-nosing."

He was slated to have a big match with Yokozuna at April 4, 1993's *WrestleMania IX*, not quite six months after winning the belt. The show of shows was being held at Caesars Palace in Las Vegas. It would be Bret's first WrestleMania as the champ, so he brought Stu and Helen to see him. In fact, Helen was going to have a family reunion with her four sisters there. The day before the show, Bret and his family spent some time together, celebrating his championship reign.

Then he got a call from Vince, summoning him to the boss's hotel suite.

Bret knocked on Vince's door, "and he answered it with that goofy grin." They sat down.

"This is what I want to do," Vince said. "I want you to drop the belt to Yoko tomorrow."

Yokozuna was being managed by veteran manager Mr. Fuji (Harry Masayoshi Fujiwara), who would interfere in the match. "I sat there dumbstruck as he went on to explain how Fuji would screw me by throwing salt in my face, blinding me," Bret wrote. "After Yoko was handed the belt, Hogan would rush to my aid and in some kind of roundabout way Hogan would end up winning the belt from Yoko right then and there!"

Hogan, of all people? After all that had happened? Well, no matter—Bret was a student of the Business. He knew what you say to a promoter who asks you to do the job.

"Like I was handing Vince my sword, I told him I appreciated everything he did for me and I'd do whatever he wanted," Bret wrote.

"Did you take the belt from me because I didn't do a good enough job?" the outgoing champ asked.

"Of course not!" came Vince's reply. "I'm just going in a different direction. It's still onwards and upwards for you. Nothing is going to change too much for you."

"I was totally crushed," Bret wrote.

Sure enough, the show came around the next day and Bret went through with the plan. Bret had his scripted loss, Hogan made his surprise entrance, and an impromptu match was declared.

"As scripted, with my face buried in the crook of my arm, I waved him to avenge my loss: 'Go get 'em, Hulk!'" Bret wrote. "I was really thinking,

*Go ahead, Hogan—take from me what I worked so hard to get. We'll see just
how long you last!"*

A few minutes later, Hogan came up to Bret. "Thank you, brother,"
the Hulkster said, in Bret's recollection. "I won't forget it. I'll be happy to
return the favor."

"I'm going to remember that, Terry," Bret replied.

What followed was a period for which we have dueling narratives:
Bret's, told in his autobiography, which was not approved by WWE; and
Hogan's, told in *his* first autobiography, which WWE published.

The only thing the two agree on is their mutual suspicion that Vince
was playing them off against each other. Where they diverge is on the
question of which wrestler was the bigger jerk.

Here's Bret's version: Eventually, Vince changed his mind yet again and
wanted Bret to beat Hogan and retake the belt—a suggestion Hogan vetoed,
because he felt Bret wasn't worthy. In this narrative, Bret confronted Hogan
backstage at a show. He reminded Hogan about his promise of reciprocity
at WrestleMania.

"As I understand it, now you don't want to even work with me, you won't
put me over and I'm not in your league," Bret said. Hogan was speechless,
so Bret continued: "Well, you're right. You're not in my league. On behalf
of myself, my family and most of the boys in the dressing room, you can go
fuck yourself." Bret eventually stormed off and wrestled his match.

After the show, Vince pulled Bret aside to "lecture me about how it was
unprofessional of me to tell Hogan off."

Vince had promised Bret that, even if he couldn't be champ, he could
be the winner of the first annual King of the Ring tournament. "Winning
the King of the Ring is great," Bret said, "but just doesn't pay the same as
being the World Champion, and you and I both know it!" In Bret's account, Vince had no comeback.

Then there's Hogan's version of events, in which the backstage confrontation between Bret and Hogan went differently. "You son of a bitch,
Vince McMahon told me you won't drop the belt to me," is how Hogan
recounts Bret's words. "He said you wouldn't drop the belt to me because
I'm not in your league and I couldn't lace your boots up."

Hogan said he'd done nothing of the sort. He suggested they confront
the boss together. They stormed his makeshift backstage office, shoulder
to shoulder.

Bret asked Vince, "Didn't you tell me that Hulk Hogan wouldn't drop the belt to me?"

"Bret," Vince replied, "that's just what you *thought* you heard."

"I had a feeling that Vince wasn't going straight up with Bret, and I think Bret felt the same way," Hogan wrote. "But Vince was the boss, so there was nothing Bret could do about it except fume a little."

Hogan was fuming, too. "To tell you the truth, I didn't care if Bret Hart got the belt or not," he wrote. "It just pissed me off that Vince had told me one thing and then told Bret another, because everybody thought it was my decision not to drop the belt to Bret. It made it look like I wasn't a team player."

Bret, too, claims there was a meeting between the three men. And although he disagrees about Vince's exact words (in Bret's version, Vince said, "I never, ever said it would be a title match"), he agrees with Hogan insofar as believing that Vince "coolly lied to my face. . . .

"I realized that there was some kind of head game going on between Vince and Hogan, and I was merely a pawn to be played with and discarded," Bret wrote. "When Hogan left the office, he had tears in his eyes. It would be a long time before I'd see him again."

Hogan's run in the World Wrestling Federation ended with a whimper. Vince was done with the horse he'd ridden to glory. He ordered Hogan to drop the belt at King of the Ring—to Yokozuna, no less. Hogan did as he was told.

It would be Hogan's final appearance in a Vince-owned PPV for nearly a decade. A contract dispute followed the event; Hogan did some nontelevised shows, then stopped wrestling altogether until his contract expired later in the year, gradually fading away from the scene.

For the rest of the summer of 1993, Yokozuna feuded with lantern-jawed former World Bodybuilding Federation BodyStar Lex Luger (Lawrence Pfohl). Luger had been introduced to WWF programming earlier in the year as "The Narcissist," a self-glorifying heel, but Vince abruptly decided to push him—not Bret—as the next Hogan.

He had Lex turn face by attacking Yokozuna during a Fourth of July match staged aboard the USS *Intrepid*, a decommissioned battleship, docked on the coast of Manhattan. Lex screamed, "What's wrong with America is bloodsucking leeches like *you!* An overstuffed, sushi-eating, rice-chomping wrestler we call a *champion!*" then body-slammed the six-hundred-pound Samoan.

Vince rebranded Lex in an ambitious publicity campaign, putting him into a red-white-and-blue bus dubbed the Lex Express and having him crisscross the country for promotional appearances "with much flag waving and hoopla," as Bret put it. "Vince couldn't have done more to get Lex over." But it wasn't working.

Meanwhile, in the actual wrestling matches, Bret was ordered to let Lex beat him over and over again, which worried Bret. "In pure sports, you win or lose based on ability," Bret wrote, "but in pro wrestling, even if you're the best, your credibility can be won and lost in no time at all with the stroke of a promoter's pen—if you don't stand up for yourself." He couldn't help thinking about what life might be like at Ted Turner's operation.

On August 13, 1993, Bret and Vince met at Madison Square Garden. "While I thanked him for my *WrestleMania IX* payout, I told him I felt frustrated with the direction I was going in," Bret recalled. He was ready to make a stink. But, "in Vince's usual evasive way, he switched trains on me."

Vince told Bret to forget about all that. There was a new plan. Vince and Bret were going to Memphis.

For a limited time only, and in only one television market, Bret would be turning heel for a few weeks.

More importantly, so would Vince.

13

HEAT, FINALE
(1993–1994)

The days of Vince acting as sole booker for his company were over. Although his ideas always took precedence, and although he retained veto power on all creative decisions, he had started relying on a booking brain trust. By the summer of 1993, it consisted of a French Canadian and two southern boys: Pat Patterson, Bruce Prichard, and Jerry Jarrett.

The reinstated Patterson had fought at Vince's side in the Territory War. So had Prichard, a Texan manager who used to perform on WWF TV as a rouged-up televangelist named Brother Love. But the newest member's arrival at the WWF had been recent and controversial.

Jarrett, born in Nashville in 1942, was a survivor. In 1977, he'd founded a breakaway promotion in Memphis and swiftly became lord of the region. He'd never let go since. He rebranded his territory as the United States Wrestling Association in 1989. Run by Jarrett, the USWA was a member of a near-extinct species: the regional wrestling promotion.

Memphis had long been one of the great wrestling cities. Venues were intimate, fans were rabid, and heroes were local—especially Jerry "The King" Lawler, a forty-three-year-old icon of the artform. Jarrett was the mastermind backstage, but Lawler was the star of the shows, acting as the last iconic American wrestler to never sell out to Vince or Turner.

For a time, anyway.

Jarrett had been close with Vince Senior and had always been cordial with Vince. During Vince's crises of early 1992, he struck up a direct relationship with Jarrett. "Vince became my Sunday telephone buddy," Jarrett would later say. "He would call me every Sunday, and we would talk—literally—for two hours." Vince would ask for advice on how to weather the storm, but he had an ulterior motive, says Jarrett: "Vince does nothing by accident."

As Jarrett tells it, one Sunday, Vince proposed a hypothetical: "If I had to go to jail," Vince supposedly said, "I have great people, but nobody knows how to find all the pieces of the wrestling business. Is there any way I can talk you into coming up here?" In other words: Jarrett would be the backup Vince.

"Of course, at first, I said no," Jarrett recalled. "But, four or five Sundays later, I said yes."

August of 1992 had brought the news that the USWA had a talent-sharing arrangement with the WWF. The advantages for Jarrett had been obvious: he would now get to bring popular WWF wrestlers and managers down to Memphis. Vince, meanwhile, in addition to exploiting Jarrett's booking talents, would get Lawler as a periodic commentator and wrestler. The King had bent the knee.

Memphis fans were, of course, furious. They had to be placated somehow. So WWF figures would come to town and crow about the superiority of the WWF, allowing Memphis diehards to vent their spleen at the evil empire. USWA was set up as the plucky underdog. Even if the visiting wrestlers were babyfaces *within* the WWF, they were ordered to be heels when they visited the USWA.

For the first time, Vince was capitalizing on hatred of his own product.

Jarrett commuted to Connecticut and started attending booking meetings with Vince, Prichard, and Patterson at Vince's mansion. The creative action no longer happened by the pool: "We would meet around his dining room table," Jarrett recalled. Vince would "go to a little market and get a ham sandwich." They'd chew the pork and envision the future.

Jarrett would later tell an interviewer that, in one such meeting, the group bemoaned their lack of compelling bad guys. Afterward, Jarrett and Vince were chatting when Vince said something antagonistic to Jarrett.

"Do you *try* to be a heel?" Jarrett asked Vince in response.

"What do you mean?" Vince said.

"You are just the most natural heel I've ever seen," Jarrett told Vince. "We're racking our brains trying to figure out who you can get as the heel for your company. You oughtta be your own talent!"

"Are you ribbing me, or are you serious?" Vince asked.

"I'm dead serious, Vince," Jarrett said. "You are a *natural*."

In a way, Vince had already been turned heel against his will. He was still presenting himself on TV as a morally upright announcer and commentator. However, the smarts in the crowd—the ones who followed wrestling news and felt Vince was the one responsible for all the bad decisions, corporate upheavals, and outrageous scandals plaguing the WWF—had started booing Vince when he appeared in the ring to announce something or do an interview. He was getting heat. But he wasn't harnessing it.

"I don't know how to do it," Vince said to Jarrett.

"Let's do it in Memphis," Jarrett said.

Jarrett laid out the plan: he'd hype up a rivalry between Lawler and Vince on USWA programming. Then, Vince would appear at a live show in Memphis. That way, he'd already be over as a heel by the time he arrived. If the turn didn't work, the WWF audience would hardly hear about it. But if it *did* get over, the possibilities from there were limitless.

Prichard, who can't stand Jarrett, tells a different story, albeit with similar motifs.

He says Vince had no plans to put Jarrett in charge of the company. And he says it was Vince, himself, who came up with the turn.

"Lawler had come in to do commentary with us, and Vince is a natural heel, man," Prichard would later say. In his account, Lawler and Vince were sitting at the commentary table, off the air, when the King told the boss, "Gosh, Vince, the most requests I get—the person most people in Memphis wanna see me knock out—is you."

"Hell, I'll take the shot for ya!" Vince told Lawler, in this version. "I'll go down there!"

Whatever the origin of the idea was, Vince and Jarrett decided to move forward with it.

"And," Prichard added, "it was easy for him."

Vince's Memphis story line was like one of those optical-illusion drawings that, depending on how your brain chooses to interpret it, looks either like a young woman or a crone. Or perhaps it was like gazing at yourself in a hall of mirrors: everything was reversed and reversed again, until you didn't know what you were looking at. All you knew was that it was as disorienting as it was unprecedented.

The story played out on both USWA *and* WWF programming, but with the moral polarities switching back and forth, depending on what you watched. Lawler may have been a hero in Memphis, but he was a whiny and pompous heel in the WWF. If you were one of the comparatively many people watching WWF programming, you saw Lawler engage in feuds with various of Vince's wrestlers, cheating and bragging all the way. If you were one of the local diehards watching USWA, you saw Lawler explain away whatever happened on the WWF as the actions of a southern boy who wanted to stand up for his birthplace.

Lawler's first foe was Bret Hart, who was booked to have a match with him at the end of August, at SummerSlam. On the 16th of that month, Bret and Owen Hart had a tag-team match in Memphis against Lawler and Jerry Jarrett's son, Jeff, which culminated in the Harts winning, albeit through the assistance of the USWA's resident heel referee, Paul Neighbors. Two days later, at a live WWF show in Massachusetts, the King publicly invited "the voice of the World Wrestling Federation, Mr. Vince McMahon," to have words with him.

This initial segment, which was only broadcast on USWA TV, was a delicate balancing act. It had to present Vince as a bad guy for the Memphis fans without baffling the live WWF crowd too much. As such, it was stilted and dull, but it did contain a surprise announcement: Vince would attend Lawler's next match, just to enjoy watching the King lose.

"Right in your own hometown of Memphis, you'll be exposed for the kind of king you truly are: a *Burger King!*" Vince said near the end.

"Well, I'll tell you this, Vince McMahon," Lawler replied. "Monday night, this Burger King is gonna give you a *Whopper!*"

"If that's the case, I assure you it will not be a *Happy Meal,*" Vince said, then walked away.

The segment was, in its way, a landmark: the first time Vince had ever presented himself as even vaguely evil on TV. But that's all the evil was, at that point: vague. It would soon sharpen.

Technically, the main event at Memphis's Mid-South Coliseum on August 23, 1993, was a visiting Lex Luger and Yokozuna in a nontitle match. But the *real* main event was Vince.

Lawler and Neighbors had entered the ring for a match against each other and were pacing around, ready to begin. That's when Vince stepped out from an entranceway, clad in an impeccable gray suit and red tie, Pat Patterson at his side. As soon as the crowd could see these interlopers, they started jeering.

Vince made his way to ringside. A USWA announcer walked up to him, holding two microphones—one for the cameras, one for the arena's speakers. "Ladies and gentlemen," the announcer said, "here's Mr. Vince McMahon!"

The boos intensified.

The announcer offered up the mics. Vince took them into his right hand; his left was in his pocket. He looked around at the crowd. He swayed back and forth a little bit, taking in the audience and their revulsion. He raised the mics to his mouth.

"Well," he said.

The word didn't sound remarkable. It was flat and bland; just another word. It almost sounded defeatist, when contrasted with the bitter enthusiasm of the Memphians. It sounded like he'd missed his line and missed his chance.

He paused for a millisecond. Then he tried again.

"Well, well, *well*," he said.

They were three musical notes in descending pitch. They were three syllables that oozed haughty contempt. It was one word, repeated three times, like an incantation to summon an ancient god. Today, you can only watch the moment on a grainy YouTube video. Even in that format, to watch is to witness a man transforming into what he was, perhaps, always meant to be.

He took another moment to inhale the crowd's hatred.

Then, his tone harsh and condescending: "It's no secret I don't *like* Jerry Lawler. And it's no secret I don't like anybody who *likes* Jerry Lawler, either."

Vince paused again, letting the crowd revile him, the way a crowd always wants to revile a heel.

He went on: "I'd like to introduce you to a man, standing on my right. His name is Pat Patterson, one of the all-time great wrestlers, and if you come close to me, you're gonna answer to Pat Patterson."

If the promo continued past that, the footage does not appear to have survived.

But the promo wasn't the end of the guest spot, of course. At one point during Lawler's match, Vince, still seated at ringside, stuck out his leg to trip a running Lawler. Lawler yelled at Vince. He later threw Vince into a ring post. Near the match's conclusion, Lawler verbally confronted Vince one more time.

Vince slowly, deliberately took off his suit jacket, revealing his red-silk vest. He reared back and threw a punch at the King.

Lawler sold it, dropping to his knees in faux-pain. The arena full of outraged Memphians—white, Black, children, seniors—screamed at the man who had reduced the territories down to their brittle rump. Vince was instantly over. Lawler went on to win the match, but the night's victor was the man in the suit.

"It was his first opportunity to be a heel," Lawler would later say. "And I think he fell in love with it."

For the next seven weeks, Memphis wrestling fans were treated to periodic video visitations from a wrestling character who had never been seen before. He didn't have his own special name yet—he still went by "Vince McMahon." But looking at that footage now, it's unmistakable: the character was already *Mr.* McMahon, wrestling's future evil emperor, fully formed and immediately recognizable on the first try.

He would be filmed against a velvet backdrop, clad in his tailored three-pieces, conjuring up serpentine disdain for the Memphis viewing public. In a bit of supreme irony, poor little Vinnie Lupton from Southern Pines had found his voice by playing a Northeastern rich prick.

"How could you have been so *rude?*" began the first of Vince's six pretaped promos. "That's southern hospitality? *How* could you have *been* so *rude?* I mean, come *on!* I'm simply introduced, and you people are booing! Why?"

He protested his innocence with heelish disingenuousness: "Jerry Lawler starts running around the ring as I'm sitting at ringside; starts running around the ring, trips over his own feet, points the finger at me, and blames me!" he said. "I had nothing to do with it!"

"I'm the voice of the World Wrestling Federation," Vince said in another promo. "Jerry Lawler is 'The King.' The king of what? That's what you have to ask yourself. Jerry Lawler, you know what you're the king of—you're the king of *nothing*."

In the fourth promo, Vince wore the USWA's championship belt around his waist; one of his WWF stars had won it in a match against Lawler. "And what are you gonna do about it, Jerry Lawler?" he said, a shit-feasting grin on his face. "Nothing. You're not gonna do one thing about it. I mean, Vince McMahon? Right here? With *this* in my *hands*, Jerry Lawler?"

In the promos, he held supreme control over his body and voice, often shifting gears abruptly, from laser-focused poise to explosions of mania. He'd threaten Lawler with upcoming in-ring beatdowns from his wrestlers, and the finest of the installments was the fifth, in which he talked up the visiting Macho Man Randy Savage.

"You really don't believe in the Tooth Fairy, now do you?" Vince said to the viewer. "I mean, you don't always believe what the *politicians* have to say, do you? Well, you certainly cannot believe what Jerry *Lawler* has to say all the time. Or, for that matter, *any* of the time."

He growled and snarled for delicious minutes, then hissed out his conclusion: "Even you Memphians know there are only three guarantees in life: Death . . . taxes . . . and *Randy Savage*."

Given the regional nature of the story line and the noise generated by the WWF's programming and controversies, Vince's heel turn barely made it to the wrestling newsletters. But as the promos continued to air, the written record gets more enthusiastic. By the end of the run, *Pro Wrestling Torch* was referring to "Vince McMahon's classic heel interviews" and Dave Meltzer noted in the *Wrestling Observer* that "McMahon's heel interviews are so eerie, they're incredible."

The final promo aired on October 9, in order to talk up Vince's next live appearance in the USWA, which happened on October 11. No footage of that appearance seems to have survived. But Vince may have been distracted during the show, as he had a problem on his hands: Lawler had spent much of the morning being questioned by the police.

The cops suspected that Lawler had committed statutory rape. Two underage girls in Kentucky, one thirteen and the other fourteen, reported that they'd had sex with Lawler repeatedly over the summer, while he had been touring with the WWF. One of them described Lawler coaxing them into the intercourse by letting them watch cartoons first.

Lawler said he knew the girls and "always thought they were friends of mine," but that they were sexually promiscuous and known to be liars. He denied the allegations and was allowed to go. Police interviewed him again on November 2; he repeated his rebuttals. On November 12, he was indicted by a grand jury on charges of rape, sodomy, and harassing a witness.

The story exploded across headlines in Tennessee, Kentucky, and the wrestling newsletters. Reporters revealed that there was a similar investigation about Lawler in Indiana. Lawler abruptly disappeared from the WWF and USWA.

The King would be back on the air within six months, after the girls declined to testify and the sex-crime charges were dropped. But by then Vince would have bigger troubles: on November 18, less than a week after Lawler's indictment, the Department of Justice charged Vincent Kennedy McMahon and Titan Sports with illegal distribution of steroids.

There are a handful of lingering, maddening mysteries in Vince McMahon's life. How did his parents meet? What was in his briefcase at Jimmy Snuka's police interview? Where did he get the money to buy the WWF?

And why did the US government decide to go after him?

The case the DOJ eventually brought was about steroids, but there is reason to suspect that they'd started out investigating something else.

In July of 1992, mere months after Tom Cole had gone public, a reporter for the *Miami Herald* had run a brief news item claiming that the WWF was "under investigation by the federal government on allegations of sexual abuse of minors and the illegal transportation of minors across state lines." According to FBI memos that were uncovered decades later, the feds even obtained a VHS tape that apparently showed Mel Phillips with an unnamed boy's foot in Phillips's "crotch area" for an "extended period of time."

However, it appears from the memos that the FBI concluded that, although Phillips "has a sexual preference for young adolescent boys which focuses around a strong foot fetish," when it came to the only hard evidence they had, the VHS tape, "too many alternative explanations could be offered" for what was seen.

They then aimed to ambush Phillips at his house and get him to turn state's witness against Vince, but he wasn't home when they arrived, and they seem to have dropped the matter after that.

Instead, they built a case around the steroid allegations.

There has been a great deal of mythmaking about Vince's eventual victory against the DOJ. In interviews, promos, and even an announcement of a scripted miniseries (still in development as of this writing), the boss has sought to depict himself as a scrappy underdog with genius lawyers. To be sure, the defense made some wise decisions. But they would have gotten nowhere if the prosecution hadn't made so many mistakes.

After nearly six months of fevered buildup in both the mainstream and wrestling press, Vince's trial ran from July 7 to July 22, 1994. On one side stood Assistant US Attorney Sean O'Shea; on the other side were Jerry McDevitt and a former federal prosecutor named Laura Brevetti. The vast majority of criminal cases that go to trial in the US, especially ones that result from an expensive federal investigation, end in guilty verdicts. But this one was something of a disaster for the DOJ.

For one thing, the case was tried in New York, as opposed to Connecticut, where all the corporate decisions were being made. That venue choice severely limited the number of alleged crimes the DOJ could pin on Vince and Titan. It seems they thought events at WWF shows at Long Island's Nassau Coliseum were their aces in the hole. The key thing that the prosecution needed to prove was that McMahon sent steroids directly to Hulk Hogan at the Coliseum on April 11 and October 18 of 1989.

However, as the defense easily pointed out, there had been no WWF shows at the Coliseum on either of those days.

The DOJ was supposed to get Vince's limo driver, Jim Stuart, to testify that he'd personally delivered the steroids for Vince. But he didn't show, and neither lawyers nor journalists ever tracked him down.

The DOJ prompted Dr. Zahorian to claim that he and Vince directly conspired to push steroids on the wrestlers. But the alleged conversation with Vince that Zahorian described sounded ludicrous to any wrestling insider: no one had needed Vince to directly *tell* them to do steroids, much less force them to do so. It was simply what was done back then.

It should not go without mention that Vince's legal team did allegedly have one quite effective idea.

Throughout the lead-up to the trial, Mushnick, Meltzer, and others who had been reporting on Vince were contacted by a man named Marty Bergman. He told them he was a producer at TV news show *60 Minutes*. He would ask for dirt on Vince, allegedly for a segment he was putting together.

Mushnick recalled Bergman calling him and saying, "Tell me about McMahon. What do you know that you haven't written that we can get into?"

Mushnick said whatever he knew, he put in his columns. But now he was suspicious. "I remember calling my wife's cousin, who's an entertainment lawyer," Mushnick recalled, "and I said, 'I heard from one of *60 Minutes*' producers today.' And he said, 'What's the name?'" Mushnick told him.

"Well, he's not a producer," the contact said. "That's his *brother*."

As it turned out, Bergman's brother was, indeed, a producer at the show, but Marty was just a freelance specialist in gathering information. Perhaps more importantly, he was the then-fiancé of Laura Brevetti, Vince's defense attorney.

A story co-bylined by Mushnick and reporter Jack Newfield in the *New York Post* after the trial identified Bergman's alleged tampering with witnesses, especially Vince's former secretary, Emily Feinberg—she had reportedly been grilled by Bergman, who then passed what he learned along to Brevetti. (WWE denies any tampering of witnesses.)

The trial began on July 7.

McDevitt and Brevetti's riskiest move was to not call any of their own witnesses. The idea behind such a bold choice is to send a message that you have nothing to hide. A prosecution team can't compel a defendant to testify against himself, so Vince never spoke at his own trial.

But the prosecution's most fatal error was that they had failed to account for wrestling's prime directive: *Protect the Business.*

One by one, the prosecution called wrestlers up to testify about the culture of steroids at the WWF. One by one, they admitted that steroids were rampant. Nailz even showed up to claim that Vince directly pressured him to do them. But he had been a terrible witness: Brevetti asked him if he "hated" Vince McMahon and Wacholz replied, "Yes," thus discrediting him as an objective observer. None of the other wrestlers said Vince had pressured them.

Even the resentful Ultimate Warrior didn't pin anything on Vince when he testified. Interviewed outside the courtroom, he said, "I think the whole thing is weak." A reporter asked him if he thought Vince was innocent. "I think he took professional wrestling to a level of success and he made a lot of enemies," Warrior replied.

Feinberg, the secretary, was a potentially devastating witness, as she knew a lot more about Vince than the defense would have liked her to know.

Feinberg and Vince had been close—indeed, she and Vince had an affair, as evidenced by the opening discussion between the attorneys and the judge on July 13, the day Feinberg testified.

"Now, was there any relationship between Emily Feinberg and Vincent McMahon besides employee/employer relationship?" the judge asked.

Both McDevitt and Brevetti replied, "Yes, your honor."

Brevetti added, "It is my present intention not to get into the affair that did occur."

"I direct all the lawyers to keep out of this case any affair that Ms. Feinberg had with the defendant McMahon," the judge ordered.

(I attempted at great length to track down Feinberg and eventually found a phone number for someone I am reasonably certain was her, so I texted it. The person who responded identified herself as Emily Feinberg, then when I asked whether she'd speak about Vince, she typed "Wrong person" and stopped responding.)

Feinberg was the woman the prosecution believed had executed a key steroid handoff. But the defense was surprisingly agile—perhaps due to the alleged advance research from Brevetti's fiancé.

"I remember watching Laura Brevetti cross-examining Emily Feinberg, and it's like she has ESP," Meltzer later said. "[Brevetti] knows every answer and she's got her comeback on every answer."

The most crucial witness was Hogan, who testified on July 14. Since his fizzle-out at the WWF, he'd signed a lucrative contract with Turner, and he certainly didn't lack for reasons to want to take Vince down. Clad in a suit and a black bandanna, Hogan spoke of how he'd lied on *The Arsenio Hall Show* and admitted to nonmedical steroid use. But Brevetti dropped the ball at a key moment.

It came when Brevetti cross-examined Hogan. "Isn't it a fact that you have no recollection of being in a room with Mr. McMahon, yourself and Dr. Zahorian, in person, having any conversation about steroids?" Brevetti asked the wrestler.

"No, not in a room," Hogan replied.

However, the prosecution didn't follow up to ask if they'd had a conversation in any context *other* than being in a room.

No matter what the prosecution said, Hogan wouldn't say Vince had done anything wrong.

"I knew what was on the line there," Hogan would say many years later by way of explanation. "And the problem was that, if they're going to put Vince McMahon in jail, they should've put the whole wrestling community in jail."

In other words, to destroy Vince McMahon would have been to destroy wrestling. And the Business must be protected at all costs.

On July 22, 1994, the courtroom was packed with fans, journalists, and those who simply wanted to see what it would be like if Vince's incredible, turbulent reign in the wrestling industry ended in spectacular defeat.

Vince was clad in a padded neck brace that his detractors had said was unnecessary and only used to garner sympathy, but which his team said was related to coincidental neck surgery. His face was solemn. By many accounts from friends and family, Vince was reasonably certain that, despite the prosecution's screwups, he was going to be convicted.

After long hours of deliberation, the jury finally delivered their verdict. Vince and Titan Sports were found not guilty.

As Meltzer put it in the next issue of the *Wrestling Observer*, "The courtroom exploded."

Vince jumped up and cheered for himself. He, Linda, and McDevitt joined in an impromptu group hug, immortalized by the court artist. The artist made sure to draw the audience clapping in joy and excitement.

Vince left the courtroom and delivered a prepared statement out front. "I left my fate in the hands of the jury and they responded nicely through all the insults the government threw at me," he said. "I didn't have a great deal of faith in the judicial system. But I had an overwhelming faith in humanity."

Later, Vince (still in the neck brace) and McDevitt did an exclusive interview on the evening news of New York's Fox affiliate, Channel Five, which also aired the WWF's syndicated programming.

"It's been two-and-a-half years that no American should endure," Vince said. "I was singled out unfairly."

For a moment, he sounded weak and defeated: "I had everything riding on this," he said. "I'd be less than candid to say I wasn't nervous. I was definitely very nervous."

Despite Hogan's refusal to take a shot at Vince, Vince said he still resented the grappler. "It feels bad when someone you worked with takes the stand and does not tell the whole truth and all of the truth," he said. "That hurt me very badly."

But by the end of the interview, Vince seemed to be in a state of unsettling serenity. He was sitting up straighter. His voice didn't have the usual corporate obsequiousness that he adopted in public statements. He smiled as he said, "Stay tuned, as we say in the World Wrestling Federation. And it could very well be that the *hunters* will soon be the *hunted*."

When the Brevetti/Bergman allegations came to light over a year later,

Vince even went so far as to deliver a pretaped promo on the New York City area airing of *WWF Superstars*. He identified himself merely as "Vince McMahon, of the World Wrestling Federation" and said he "always made it a point to refrain from personal commentary during WWF programming." But now, he had to speak.

He had to tell the world about Mushnick's "journalistic stalking." He had to defend Brevetti and Bergman, saying he "deeply" resented "any innuendo or accusation that my acquittal on the charges brought against me by the federal government was in any way tainted by any illegality."

Then, he went in for the kill.

"Now, most people—myself included—naïvely believe that government prosecutors and their investigators are the *good guys*," Vince said. "Unfortunately, I found this to not always hold true. I was constantly amazed at the utter lack of ethics of some of the *good guys* involved.

"I watched the *good guys* lie to the media, lie to the judge, lie to the jury," he continued. "And I saw the ultimate impact of the truth when the jury acquitted me and the World Wrestling Federation. . . .

"These same Keystone Kops who wasted taxpayer dollars," Vince said, "these same yellow journalists who had to eat crow for telling lies, are, once again, incestuously joining forces, trying to drum up support for their own personal agenda, trying to manufacture some reason to save face, attempting to perpetuate some theory of witness tampering.

"Gentlemen," he asked, "is that the *best* you can *do?*"

If you were a casual wrestling fan who didn't follow the news—and, to be sure, there were many of them—it was a baffling little segment. Why was the announcer telling you about his personal legal problems? What was this message, delivered with such grand revulsion? Who was this new Vince?

But if you were from Memphis, it all looked very familiar.

The first half of the 1990s was an era of danger for Vince. But it was also an era of radical reinvention.

He developed and refined a performance of sneering, entitled antagonism not just in his promos, but under the harsh gazes of wrestling fandom, the news media, and the criminal justice system.

Vincent Kennedy McMahon was thrust into an inferno.

Mr. McMahon was the part of him that did not burn to ash.

14

SUCK IT, ACT I
(1994–1996)

If Stone Cold Steve Austin was a rebel, it was because his boss allowed him to be one.

From 1996 to 2001, Austin was Vince's biggest star and most lucrative cash cow. He was lean, not steroidal or cut, but his hateful eyes and menacing gait made him seem like the kind of guy who would beat the shit out of you in a bar for no good reason. Middle fingers upraised, beer and obscenities spilling out of his mouth, he got over in mass culture like no wrestler had since Hogan's heyday. In a time of growing anticorporate sentiment, audiences were drawn to Austin's attitude of infinite scorn for Mr. McMahon and all forms of respectability. Indeed, WWE officially refers to the period in which Austin was on top as "The Attitude Era."

But all that rebellion was kayfabe. In reality, the man who had once been Steve Williams almost always followed Vince's orders—and Vince ordered him to act like he *hated* following orders.

Legions of viewers loved watching their blue-collar antihero stand up to the corporate suit in charge. Vince used the Austin character to co-opt his viewers' anger—at him, at their own bosses, at the whole American system—by satisfying two contradictory human impulses at once: the urge to defy and the urge to buy. If you wanted to stick it to the CEO, all you had to do was call the number on your screen to order the latest Stone Cold T-shirt.

By that time, Vince had revealed himself as the owner of the company, giving fans a target whenever they were unhappy with the WWF. The crowds would chant at him, "*Asshole, asshole, asshole,*" meaning it every time.

Even within the sycophantic culture of WWE, close observers will tell you that Mr. McMahon is only a slight exaggeration of the Vince they know. As Bruce Prichard once put it in a WWE-produced documentary, "Vince is crazy. He really is. That stuff is not far from what Vince would do, is what Mr. McMahon did."

But, surprisingly, Vince didn't see himself as the villain of the story he was acting out. He didn't even really see himself as *himself*.

"Mr. McMahon is a character that is, in no way in the world, like me," Vince would later say.

Instead, he—like the audience—identified with the antihero. "Stone Cold Steve Austin—that character is really Vince McMahon," Vince said. "I was the guy who bucked the system, so it's easy to relate to that."

The Austin-McMahon feud was thus a closed system, a snake eating its own tail. It was Vince vs. Vince, a man playing out a private war with himself in a very public setting. Perhaps it was even the return of the repressed: a story about an unhappy southern boy punishing a greedy Northeastern wrestling promoter.

Austin himself contributed greatly to the tale and the role he played in it. So did Vince's bookers. And there were many other angles and characters that made the WWF such a stunning success in the twentieth century's dying days. But ultimately, the Attitude Era was the story of one very powerful man convincing millions of people to watch him on live television as he worked out his issues.

"I'm the common man," Vince once said while describing this period of triumph. "I think one of the keys to WWE's success, quite frankly, is that I remain who I am."

Like Vince, Steve Austin was abandoned by his biological father at birth. Like Vince, Austin's stepfather was allegedly prone to beating his stepchildren. But, unlike Vince, Steve nevertheless adores the man who raised him in a town on the Gulf Coast, even going so far as to call his mother's husband his dad.

"My dad raised us right—firm, but fair," Austin wrote in his 2003 memoir.

"He could swing that belt and he'd bust your ass, but it was never child abuse."

Indeed, Austin says he and his siblings look back on this parental practice with great fondness. "I endorse the practice of cutting a switch," he wrote. "We always deserved it, it seemed. We love our dad very much, and know it was all to teach us something."

Young Steve started watching wrestling TV shows broadcast from Houston when he was a teen in the 1970s. "I didn't give a damn about the story lines," Austin wrote. "Bottom line, I just liked seeing those guys getting in the ring and wrestling each other, punching and kicking each other." He fantasized about growing up to wrestle as "The Western Fandango, Steve Williams"—"I didn't even know what a fandango was, but it sure sounded flashy."

Around 1988, while he was a college dropout working as a forklift operator, he saw an ad for a wrestling school on TV and decided to give it a try.

He still assumed wrestling was a legitimate sport. For a shockingly long time, no one disabused him of his illusions. Eventually, the young wrestler learned that a wrestling *match* is supposed to be cooperative, but that the wrestling *industry* is every man for himself. His first trainer, "Gentleman" Chris Adams, attempted to cheat him out of hundreds of dollars he was owed for his matches.

So Steve moved to USWA in Memphis, where they started calling him Steve Austin, after his city of birth. He persevered, subsisting on tuna fish and raw potatoes, until the spring of 1991, when he got a call to join the big leagues—not the WWF, but its main rival, the only other behemoth left standing.

Ted Turner had rebranded his wrestling operation under the same name that had once been used for Georgia Championship Wrestling's flagship TV show: the company was called World Championship Wrestling (WCW), and it was the number-two promotion and inheritor of the NWA mantle. WCW always prided itself on respecting veteran wrestlers and having more old-school technical wrestling than the ostentatious, youth-oriented WWF.

More importantly, it was backed by Turner's seemingly endless supply of money. "I knew that WCW would give me the chance to earn more than a few hundred dollars a month," Austin wrote. "A *lot* more."

During his otherwise disappointing four years with the Atlanta-based promotion, Austin made two highly consequential friends and one equally consequential enemy. Each of those three men was an innovator whom Vince McMahon would go on to shamelessly imitate.

The first friend was Paul Heyman, a large, loud, cunning man from Scarsdale who worked as a heel manager called Paul E. Dangerously. Heyman was "one of the best, world-class BSers I ever ran across," Austin wrote later. Austin was placed in Heyman's stable of baddies and their connection would prove important to both men later.

The second friend was a hard-partying Ohioan named Brian Pillman. He was slender for a wrestler, known for his ability to get airborne and execute spectacular maneuvers, but his most defining trait was his maniacal smile, like that of a man who's just snorted eight rails of pure cocaine. He and Austin were paired as a tag team of preening heels called the Hollywood Blonds, and they developed a bond that would continue until Pillman's untimely death just a few years later.

And then there was the enemy. Eric Bischoff—ten years younger than Vince, diminutive next to his wrestlers, a mat of dye-black hair on his head, typically seen grinning like an unscrupulous cat who caught a particularly juicy canary—was initially a WCW announcer. In 1994, he was promoted to the position of senior vice president, making him the de facto creative director of the promotion. Under the guidance of the puckish and confrontational Bischoff, WCW would launch *Monday Nitro*, a live flagship TV show that aired in competition with *Raw*.

Bischoff recruited Lex Luger, Vince's would-be star, to make a surprise appearance on the debut episode, announcing that he had defected to WCW. It was a shot across the bow even Vince hadn't seen coming; suddenly, WCW was cool and the WWF looked like idiots. The so-called Monday Night War had begun, with Bischoff as WCW's general, leading the charge.

But Bischoff didn't think much of Austin. The wrestler was developing as a good mid-card technical wrestler, but he didn't really have a gimmick. He'd just wrestle in jet-black trunks and boots. According to Austin, Bischoff didn't see potential in that (Bischoff claims Austin had a bad attitude and was injured too often), and in 1995, just before *Nitro* debuted, he dismissed Austin from WCW via phone call.

No sooner was Austin cut loose than he received a call from Heyman, who'd also been fired from WCW a few years before. Heyman had taken over a tiny promotion based out of Philadelphia called Eastern Championship Wrestling and transformed it into something revolutionary. He'd long been a fan of Japanese "deathmatch" wrestling, in which workers would perform in rings littered with barbed wire, thumb tacks, blunt objects, even open flames. He started imitating it with his wrestlers. The promotion gained a cult following among wrestling fans who were sick of the candy-coated nonsense in WWF and the conservatism of WCW. Heyman renamed the promotion Extreme Championship Wrestling. He wanted Austin on board.

However, at the time, Austin was suffering from an arm injury and couldn't wrestle. Heyman said that was no problem.

Heyman told Austin he wanted him to cut a promo.

"Sure," Austin said. "What do you want me to talk about?"

"Hell, anything," Heyman replied. "Whatever you want. What about getting fired? What about WCW? Talk about that. We'll just sit down, Steve, and talk about how you feel, for real."

Austin delivered a vicious, nearly eight-minute-long promo in September 1995, broadcast on ECW's weekly late-night cable show. It was delivered to the camera, with a cheap backdrop behind him, no audience to be found. It was an example of a new concept in wrestling: a "worked shoot," a moment in which it was made to appear that forbidden, non-kayfabe truth was being told. Delivered largely in the third person and aired in syndication, the promo was, in many ways, the birth of the character that Austin would go on to play so effectively in the WWF.

"Steve Austin is here to *wrestle*," Austin told the camera in a spiteful Texas drawl. "There's no Hogans here. There's no Flairs here . . . and there damn sure isn't an Eric Bischoff here. There's no one that can hold back Steve Austin now."

To be fair, Austin didn't do much wrestling—only two matches over the course of his tenure at ECW—but he kept appearing on ECW programming and doing worked shoots about the industry. It was catnip for the growing population of smarts and, though it had been Heyman's idea, Austin took to it with brutal grace.

One person who saw the promos was Jim Ross, by then a commentator and talent coordinator for the WWF. "I saw a side of Steve that I had not seen on TV before," Ross would later write. "It was as if he meant every word he said and, for the most part, at that time, he did."

Ross spoke to Vince and raised the possibility of hiring Austin. Vince was interested, but not because of the worked shoots, which he hadn't even seen yet. "Steve was hired by [the WWF] because he could wrestle," Ross wrote, "because he could work with anyone and have a good, solid match."

Austin was brought aboard, and had his first conversation with Vince. It was inauspicious, at best.

At the time, the WWF roster featured a wrestler-turned-manager named Ted DiBiase, "The Million Dollar Man," whose gimmick was that he was an abusive, wealthy jerk. Although DiBiase's cackling affect was different from the one Vince used in Memphis, some have suggested that the concept laid some seeds for the eventual Mr. McMahon turn. But, as of late 1995, DiBiase's popularity was on a downward trajectory and he needed a new in-ring protégé.

"Ted DiBiase is going to be your manager," Vince told Austin over the phone. "I want to bring you into [the WWF] as somebody called 'The Ringmaster'—you know, like the master of the ring."

That was as far as the concept went.

"I was thinking that it sounded like a damned circus act!" Austin wrote. But Austin was desperate for steady work. "So I said, 'Well, okay,' trying not to sound reluctant or apprehensive."

Then came the matter of his costuming. The WWF's official seam-stresses told him it had been decided that he'd wear green trunks. He hated the idea, but went along with it anyway.

He spoke to Vince about sprucing the look up a little. "What about a vest?" Austin said.

"Ah, you don't need a vest," was Vince's reply.

"Well, what about boots?"

"Ah, just wear your old boots."

Austin didn't like the idea that his outfit wouldn't match: "*I'm wearing old white boots with a black star on them and I got green trunks, because that's the color of money*," he wrote. "*What the hell?*"

Austin had already tapped into the wrestling zeitgeist. So had Ross, Heyman, Bischoff—even Pillman, who was doing much discussed worked shoots at WCW and had gained the official title "The Loose Cannon."

Pillman committed outlandish transgressions with a crazed look in his eyes. In his promos, he would talk trash with unusual vulgarity and in such a way as to reveal tantalizing backstage secrets. In a particularly fa-mous incident, he outed a wrestler as one of WCW's bookers; on another occasion, he so antagonized Bobby Heenan that Heenan blurted out an F-bomb on the air.

Vince was light-years behind all these men.

Though he kept his thoughts to himself, Austin was now deeply worried: "I'm thinking, *What the hell kind of plans do these guys have for me, man?*"

Vince did not yet see himself in Austin. His attentions were focused on his resident pretty boy.

The lithe Shawn Michaels (Michael Shawn Hickenbottom) had been a WWF performer starting in 1987. He'd first gained fame as one half of a tag team called The Rockers, but his sea-otter-like agility, ostentatious erotic charisma, and relatively minimal steroid use made him a rising star in the wake of Hogan's departure. Whether he was heel or face, he always played a self-obsessed sexpot, entering to the strains of a custom-written entrance song called "Sexy Boy." They called him "The Heartbreak Kid"— HBK, for short.

By the mid-1990s, he had fully gotten over with the promotion's remaining fans. More importantly, he'd gotten over with the boss.

"I did always think that Vince saw, with Shawn, what Vince wanted to be," says Dave Meltzer. "He wanted to be the ladies' man, he wanted to be the complete arrogant asshole who did all this stuff but could always get away with it because he was so good at what he did."

Shawn did, indeed, get away with a lot. For one thing, he was, at the time, an unrepentant and unreliable addict to any number of substances. He rarely failed to impress in the ring, however intoxicated he might have been, but he was living proof that the WWF's commitment to wrestler health was limited, at best.

"My life had spiraled so out of control—drinking too much, chasing women, doing drugs, popping pills—that I did not like who I really was," Shawn wrote in his second memoir. "A winner in the business, I had become a loser in life."

The two biggest stars in Vince's company, the icons of the immediate post-Hogan era, were Shawn and Bret. The two men faced off over and over again throughout the 1990s in matches that were regarded as masterworks. Their names will be forever intertwined. But, like so many great collaborations, the collaborators were never on the best of terms. Their personalities and in-ring personas couldn't have been more diametrically opposed: Bret with his deadly seriousness, Shawn with his endless desire to party.

What's more, in contrast to Bret's grim resignation to the injustices of the Business, Shawn would regularly berate Vince as soon as he was regarded as one of the top dogs.

"I would go off on Vince periodically and then call him back and say I was sorry, and that I had lost it," Shawn wrote. "He was always patient and forgiving. I think he put up with me because he really admired my desire to be good and, for lack of better words, my love for the business. Vince also knew that I would do just about anything for him."

To an extent, every top wrestler in the history of Vince's reign had a degree of leeway with Vince. Hogan, too, got away with being more defiant than his locker-room cohort, as long as his market value kept him safe. But Shawn did something no other wrestler in his position had done before or would do since. He initiated a successful, if informal, collective-bargaining agreement.

Shawn was close with four other WWF wrestlers: Diesel (Kevin Nash), Razor Ramon (Scott Hall), The 1-2-3 Kid (Sean Waltman), and Hunter Hearst Helmsley (Paul Levesque). They were some of the biggest attractions in the ailing WWF, and they knew it. So they did something unusual for wrestlers. They banded together for leverage against Vince while pursuing their interests. *Only* their interests—but that was still more solidarity than WWF wrestlers had ever shown each other. They started calling themselves "the Clique" (sometimes styled as "the Kliq") backstage.

They became the bane of the locker room, convincing Vince and his bookers to let them have influence on which wrestlers they got matched up with or who was going to get a push. Because the Clique members could easily defect to WCW en masse at any time, Vince couldn't screw with them as easily as he had others.

Vince also "appreciated that we were honest with him," Shawn wrote. "When he asked us a question, we gave him an honest answer. I think Vince respected us for that. Most people would tell him whatever they thought he wanted to hear. They were afraid of him. If he asked us about something and we thought it was bad, we told him."

It wasn't fair to the other wrestlers, but it was a vision of what those wrestlers could achieve, if they had that kind of solidarity on an industry-wide level. However, the Clique weren't interested in starting a union. By the time Austin arrived, they were just interested in holding on to their newfound power and safety. In fact, Shawn got so much backing from the front office that rumors started to swirl among wrestlers and smarts.

"There was always the, 'Oh, Vince and Shawn Michaels are having an affair, blah blah blah,' which I never bought for a second," Meltzer recalls. "'Why would you push Shawn Michaels on top?' Well, geez, he's better than everybody else!"

"The inmates were running the asylum, pretty much," is how Jake the Snake Roberts recalls the period. The Clique "were pretty much running the fucking show, man. Which I argued about. I said, 'That's the worst fucking idea you could do, is let these guys take over.' But, by strength in numbers, they pretty much forced Vince to do whatever they wanted. It was a fucking mess."

This was the environment that Steve Austin found himself in when he made his WWF debut on the January 8, 1996, edition of *Raw*, appearing at DiBiase's side as the nondescript Ringmaster. As he walked to the ring, clean-shaven and with a little buzz cut of blond hair, Vince hyped him up on commentary. But the praise was about his technical ability ("You talk about a *grappler*, you talk about a man that can mix it up in *any fashion at all!*" Vince crowed), not his attitude or philosophy.

In this first promo, Austin put his open palm up in front of the camera and said, "I want everybody out there in TV land to touch your screen and feel what it's like to be destined for *success!* Feel what it's like to be born a *champion*, man!"

The feed cut to the crowd. A few children were booing mildly, seemingly more out of boredom than antagonism. That was about as much response as the Ringmaster got, that first time.

However, Austin did one thing right: he didn't tick off the Clique. He got to wrestle Shawn in a series of well-regarded matches. "I was getting it done in the ring, but my gimmick was lame as hell," Austin wrote. "The Ringmaster had no upside."

One night, Austin watched a TV documentary about serial killer Richard "The Iceman" Kuklinski. "Man, I watched that show and it got my gears spinning, because I was a heel, and here was this cold-blooded guy who didn't give a damn about anybody," Austin wrote. "Not that I approved of what he did. It was just that cold, 'I don't have a conscience' attitude that attracted me."

He pitched the idea of becoming an Iceman-like psychopath. Vince was intrigued and had his creative team come up with a list of possible new ring names for Austin. In classic wrestling fashion, they were all just attempts to rip off "Iceman": "Temperature-based things like 'Fang McFrost,' 'Ivan the Terrible,' 'Ice Dagger,' names like that," Austin wrote. "The names were horrible. Our creative group did not 'feel' my new character idea."

At the time, Austin was married to Jeanie Clarke, an English former wrestling manager. So the story goes, she was pouring Austin a cup of tea while he was struggling to devise his moniker and had a revelation. Austin recounted the pivotal moment that followed:

> "Ah," she said, putting the tea down in front of me, "don't worry about it. Just go ahead and drink your tea before it gets stone-cold."
>
> Then she paused, with this light in her eyes, and said, "That's your new name: Stone Cold Steve Austin."
>
> I raised my eyes up from the cup of tea and said, "Yeah . . ."
>
> After I'd had a chance to think about it, I wondered if it might not be too long. "Stone Cold Steve Austin. That's four words," I said.
>
> But I liked it. It had a ring to it, those four words together.

Not yet having a direct line to Vince, Austin went to one of the boss's top lieutenants, ex-wrestler Jerry Brisco, and presented the idea. It was approved. On March 11, 1996, Austin walked to the ring on *Raw* as a new man.

However, "there was no big buildup or explanation or anything like that," he wrote. "There were no vignettes or interviews to provide some background on this cold-blooded guy."

"His peers here in the World Wrestling Federation dubbed him the Ringmaster; I would suggest to you, from the look on his face and his attitude, knowing him a bit better now, he's *stone cold*, if anything," Vince mused on the commentator's mic. "That, certainly, would describe his heart."

The audience had no context for the character. He wasn't getting a push.

"I still wasn't really going anywhere," Austin wrote. "I had to get this thing kick-started somehow."

★   ★   ★

As it turned out, another man's folly was Austin's gain.

In the spring, Kevin Nash and Scott Hall signed with WCW. Accounts differ: perhaps WWF management let them go because they were too much of a pain; perhaps the men just wanted WCW's higher performance fees, contracts that guaranteed you'd be paid a certain amount (as opposed to being subject to Vince's whims), and less rigorous work schedule. Whatever the case, Waltman was in rehab at the time, but the rest of the Clique wanted to express their love for one another at this time of transition.

At an untelevised show in Madison Square Garden on May 19, 1996, Nash and Hall had their final matches. The main event was between Shawn and Nash. When it concluded, the rest of the Clique walked to the ring. They all embraced as the fans cheered. However, this was a huge breach of traditional kayfabe etiquette: half of them were babyfaces and the other half were heels.

Kayfabe wasn't what it had once been, of course, and the smarts in the crowd already knew that these men were pals. Nevertheless, they were breaking character in the ring, and you simply don't do that in wrestling. Worked shoots were one thing—and the WWF wasn't even doing *those* yet—but this was a bridge too far. What became known as the Curtain Call was immediately controversial.

"Backstage, the agents and the boys were up in arms, and rightfully so: They thought Vince should have nipped such behavior in the bud," Bret wrote. "Vince had already left the Garden; when he found out what they had pulled, he was livid."

Vince reportedly fined all four men $2,500 each. He made the two who remained in the company, Shawn and Levesque, apologize to the rest of the locker room. Vince still couldn't or wouldn't punish Shawn too harshly, but Levesque was far less essential for the boss. Levesque had been booked to win the 1996 King of the Ring tournament the following month, which would have been a stepping-stone to bigger fame. Vince punished Levesque by taking away that shot.

Instead, he gave it to Austin. Accounts differ as to why.

The official WWE lore is that Austin worked up the courage to ask for an audience with Vince and asked if he could get a push.

"Any time you're putting your heart, liver, lungs and soul into a character and something doesn't go exactly as you perceive it to go, then naturally you have to raise it to an issue as high as you can and have a conversation with me about it," Vince would later say. "I know that Steve was putting everything he had into this character and felt strongly about it." In this version, Vince magnanimously agreed to give Austin a hand up.

Jake the Snake tells things differently.

At the time, Jake was forty-one years old, but he looked much older—years of intoxicants and travel had taken their toll. But he was set to be in the tournament, too: Vince had him booked in a babyface redemption story line about him quitting booze and drugs and finding Jesus—which was all kayfabe, as he hadn't yet gotten back on the wagon. In his promos, he would regularly quote the Bible, including the famed sixteenth verse of the third chapter of the Book of John: "For God so loved the world, that he gave his only begotten Son, that whosoever believeth in him should not perish, but have everlasting life."

At the same time, he was mentoring Austin behind the scenes.

"Steve, at the time, he was calling me every night and I was trying to help him learn how to get over," Jake tells me. It was appropriate, as Jake was Stone Cold *avant la lettre*. His gimmick in the 1980s had been that he was a badass loner: neither babyface nor heel, he was what they called a "tweener." Such figures were rare, even as of 1996. Within a few years, tweeners would be commonplace. Austin was the vanguard of that, but Jake may have been the grandfather of it all.

"I pitched Steve to be that superstar; nobody else did," Jake tells me. "I was the only fucking guy saying, 'This is your new guy.' Vince didn't think that he was going to be a superstar. He thought he was going to be the middle-of-the-card guy. I was like, 'No, no, no. If you let this guy go, he'll get it done in a big way.'"

Whatever the case, Vince needed something to amp up interest, and fast.

The WWF was bleeding cash. Annual business transacted had been around $123 million in 1993, then $89 million the next year, and $82 million the next. The year 1996 would be their worst-performing year, adjusted for inflation, since 1985.

Nitro had been swiftly catching up with *Raw* in the ratings. Earlier in the year, Vince had started running little pretaped skits in which he mocked Turner and the various personalities who had abandoned the WWF with vicious parody versions: "Billionaire Ted," "The Huckster," "The Nacho

Man," and so on. Rather than turning the tide, the skits just felt forced and petty.

By many accounts, the Monday Night War drove Vince to extremes of jealousy and confrontation. Vince loathed Bischoff and Turner and, in a rarity for Vince, came off not as imperious and threatening, but as insecure and loudmouthed.

Around the time of the Billionaire Ted skits, Vince and Bischoff engaged in a war of public statements about blading and bloodletting in wrestling. In an open letter to Turner issued on February 8, 1996, Vince (more than a little hypocritically) accused WCW of abusing the practice, in advance of one of WCW's shows.

"There have been numerous references on your rasslin' programming that this weekend's double-cage match will be so violent that one opponent will be 'bleeding to the point of no recognition,'" Vince wrote. "This encouraged practice of self-mutilation is disgusting. . . . Notwithstanding numerous unprecedented predatory practices against the WWF, if you continue to promote self-mutilation, I hope your stockholders hold you accountable for this unethically, gutturally, potentially unhealthy practice."

But Vince was on his back foot when May 27 brought a new shock.

The freshly defected Hall showed up on *Nitro*, but he did so in an unusual manner. Bischoff had him emerge from the crowd, dressed in civilian clothing, enter the ring, and take the microphone.

"You people, you know who I am," Hall said to the WCW fans in the arena and at home. "But you don't know why I'm here."

He delivered a short, cryptic promo that heavily implied he was still part of the WWF. He said he had a "challenge" for "Billionaire Ted, for the Nacho Man, and for anybody else in WCW: You wanna go to war? You want a war? You're gonna *get* one!"

As Meltzer noted in the next issue of the *Wrestling Observer*, "The crowd was somewhat stunned by all this, with some cheering and most not really reacting, out of shock."

In that brief moment, it seemed as though the impossible might happen. Was the war between WWF and WCW going to enter a stage where the two promotions' wrestlers competed against each other? Or was Hall some kind of saboteur, sent by Vince? Sure, most of wrestling was fake, but maybe *this* was real. Or at least, you *wanted* it to be.

It was the first great neokayfabe moment in American wrestling. And it hadn't been Vince's idea.

To add to the pile of embarrassments, on June 17, *Nitro* overtook *Raw* in the ratings competition. It did the same the next week, and the next, and stayed there. WCW was on top and would remain there, as it turned out, for eighty-three weeks.

Vince needed a miracle.

Austin had, by this point, shaved his head in imitation of Bruce Willis's character from the then-trendy *Pulp Fiction*, and he grew a goatee. His Stone Cold character, still developing into what it would become, was starting to get over with the crowds.

When the King of the Ring PPV came around on June 23, Austin entered to decently loud jeering. He got more heat as he wrestled with babyface Marc Mero in the tournament semifinal, then even more in the final, when he went up against Jake the Snake. The plan called for Stone Cold to be cruel to Jake, targeting Jake's "internal injuries" from earlier in the night by kicking him in the gut. He pinned Jake. The crowd booed.

As Austin walked up to announcer Michael Hayes and took to the microphone for a victory speech, it seemed like he was on his way to a successful career as an out-and-out heel, as per the plan.

"The first thing I want to be done is to get that piece o' crap outta my ring!" Austin yelled, pointing at Jake.

More booing from the audience.

"Don't just get him outta the ring, get him outta the WWF! Because I proved, son, without a shadow of a doubt, you ain't got what it *takes* anymore!"

Even more boos.

Austin later wrote that the next words out of his mouth "would never have happened or even come up if I was waiting for writers to tell me what to say. It all came from my heart."

"You sit there and you thump your Bible and you say your prayers, and it didn't get you *anywhere!*" Austin spat. "Talk about your psalms, talk about John 3:16. *Austin 3:16 says, 'I just whipped your ass!'*"

That's when something unexpected happened. The crowd started cheering.

"He *is* stone-cold," Vince said to the TV viewers from the announcer's table, sounding slightly confused by the reaction.

Austin continued his abuse of poor Jake the Snake: "All he's gotta do is go buy him a cheap bottle o' Thunderbird and try to get back some of that courage he had in his prime!" Austin yelled.

More cheers.

"All right, stop it," Vince said, ostensibly in the name of Jake's dignity, though Austin couldn't hear him.

"As the King of the Ring, I'm servin' notice to every one of the WWF Superstars: I don't give a damn *what* they are—they're all on the list!" Austin continued. "And that's Stone Cold's list! And I'm fixin' to start runnin' through *all* of 'em!"

The crowd was now showering Austin with affection.

"Steve Austin's time has come," the wrestler growled. "And when I get the shot, you're looking at the next WWF champion. And that's the *bottom line*, because *Stone Cold said so!*"

Though there were still a few boos, most of the audience erupted in enthusiasm.

Austin had gotten over. With the crowd, at least. The boss still needed convincing.

"Even after I did my 3:16 promo at King of the Ring and I introduced my new catchphrases, Vince still didn't listen to all my ideas," Austin wrote. "I was just a different breed of cat. I was trying to be a heel, but I was accepted universally as a babyface. This was new ground—for me too."

He kept taping promos, but when he was on pretaped episodes of WWF programs, his segments were often cut from the final broadcast. As Austin tells it, he worked up the courage to talk to Vince about the situation backstage.

"Man, what's going on?" Austin asked Vince. "It seems like every time I say something, y'all take it back to the shop and chop all my stuff out."

"We are concerned because, as a heel, we want the fans to *not* like you," Vince said.

"Man, if you take my personality away from me, I can't compete with anybody here," Austin countered. "But if you give me my personality, I can compete with anybody. I guarantee it."

"Okay," Vince said, and walked away.

After that, Vince "started letting me just go, and stopped editing a lot of my lines out of the show," Austin wrote. He would deliver promos of growing intensity, taking aim at anyone and everyone. He would quote verses from the "Book of Austin." The WWF produced and quickly sold out of T-shirts that simply read "Austin 3:16" in white block font on black cloth.

"A new star was born," Jim Ross would later write. "The 'merchandise king' had arrived, complete with his seemingly endless string of catchphrases that did nothing but make money for all involved."

Looking back on this period, Austin tried to explain how it all came together. He had paid his dues, he said—but that, alone, isn't what gets you to the top.

"I tell young wrestlers that they must always be thinking about their TV character, and wear down the WWE creative team with their ideas for that character," Austin wrote. "And, above all else, they have to develop a positive working relationship with Vince."

Even after Memphis, WWF programming had still never acknowledged that Vince was anything other than an announcer. But the time had come to confess. He saw fit to have himself finally outed. However, the outing wasn't done by Stone Cold Steve Austin. It wasn't even done by a wrestler.

And Vince was supposed to be a babyface.

WCW was eating the WWF's lunch in the ratings war, and the driving force had been the truth-warping angle that began with Scott Hall's bizarre arrival. Just a couple of weeks after Hall, Kevin Nash had shown up on *Nitro* and he, too, implied that he was there to take down the company, letting the viewers infer that he was still WWF-affiliated. On July 7, two weeks after the Austin 3:16 promo, WCW had its annual Bash at the Beach PPV. Hall and Nash teased that they would reveal another insurrectionist in their main-event tag-team match.

Bischoff is one of the most criticized men in the history of professional wrestling, but no one can argue that *Bash at the Beach '96* was anything less than tectonic. He did something no one had done since the days of Vince Senior: he booked Hulk Hogan as a heel.

Hogan had been languishing at WCW, but from the moment he attacked Hall and Nash's babyface opponents at the PPV, attentions perked up. "The first thing you gotta realize, brother, is this right here is the *future of wrestling!*" Hogan yelled with a rasp in a post-match interview. "You can call this the *new world order* of wrestling, brother!" Thus was born a new heel stable; Bischoff would dub them the New World Order, or nWo.

As dim as his star had become in recent years, Hogan had been every teenage wrestling fan's childhood hero; to have that hero come back as a heel was electrifying, and the move garnered TV and newspaper headlines around the world. The nWo story line borrowed generously from worked-shoot concepts first developed in Japan, but only a tiny sliver of Americans were aware of that. It seemed like Bischoff and WCW had figured out a new formula for bending reality.

It was infuriating. So Vince had the WWF make its first real attempt at a worked shoot.

Jim Ross—affectionately known to fans as "JR"—had more than his fair share of real-life grievances with Vince. Often regarded as the greatest wrestling play-by-play commentator of all time, Ross had been fired by Vince twice already since the man started working for him in 1993. The second time, Ross was dismissed just two weeks after suffering his first attack of Bell's palsy, a disease that continues to cause partial paralysis in half of his face.

As of the fall of 1996, the fan-favorite Ross had been back at the commentator's desk, in addition to doing talent relations, for a little over a year. That was when he was informed that he was going to do something no one had done before.

"I was to expose Vince as the owner of WWF, instead of the mere announcer that he had always played," Ross recalled in a memoir. "It was part of the plan Vince came up with to have me rip him for firing me after I got Bell's palsy."

And so it was that, on September 23, 1996, Ross entered the ring during *Raw* to deliver a worked shoot. "I'd rather not done it," Ross would later remark. Nevertheless, he'd been practicing the promo for hours and sold it with aplomb.

"There's something I've been waiting to say for a long, long time," Ross began, mic in hand. "And when I'm through telling you, many of you are going to question my loyalty to the World Wrestling Federation. So let's clear that up right now: I *have* no loyalty to the World Wrestling Federation! I've only got loyalty to Good Ol' JR."

The crowd let out a little confused cheer. They liked JR, but weren't they supposed to also like the WWF? What was the moral valence here?

Ross rattled off his real-life problems with Vince in his Oklahoma brogue. He spoke of his second firing: "Did you ever wonder where Ol' JR went to?" he asked. " 'Why isn't JR doing play-by-play anymore?' Let me tell you why. Because the egotistical owner of the World Wrestling Federation—and you know who I'm talking about, I'm talking about Vince McMahon—couldn't stand the *competition!*"

Now this . . . this was weird.

Was Ross really exposing Vince as the owner of the company? The crowd seemed to not know what to do, so they started booing. Were they booing Ross? Or were they booing Vince at Ross's mention of him? Did they even know? Where was this all going?

Ross shouted about getting fired after developing palsy. "You think I *like* that my left eye doesn't open all the way because I got sick?" Ross said. "Well, let me tell ya how warmhearted Mr. McMahon is. Mr. McMahon called me into his office on February the 11th, 1994, and he *fired* my ass!"

The crowd booed. That time, the booing was pretty clearly directed at Vince.

Ross said his role in talent recruitment had allowed him to seek vengeance: old guys were leaving for WCW, new guys like Austin were showing up to attack the roster and cast aside moral standards.

"You think all these guys comin' here was an accident? Absolutely not—I've been very busy," Ross said. "And right now, I wanna bring back one of your favorites. He's 'The Bad Guy,' Razor Ramon!"

The audience let out a little cheer, but it was tempered by confusion. Was Scott Hall really coming *back* to the WWF, after everything he'd done in WCW?

As the swaggering Latin percussion of Razor Ramon's theme music rang out, in walked Razor Ramon. But he wasn't being played by Scott Hall.

"Vince saw himself a little bit in [the Clique]; he understood where they were coming from," Ross wrote later. "He was one of those guys. And now . . . those guys were gone and fighting on the other team, and Vince once again wanted to say 'fuck you.'"

Vince had ordered two tall wrestlers who *vaguely* resembled Hall and Nash to dress up in Hall and Nash's old costuming patterns. Faux-Razor was Rick Bognar; his Diesel counterpart was played by Glenn Jacobs.

Vince owned trademarks to the character names, so he was fully within his legal rights to trot these impostors out. The point was not to fool the audience. It was to piss them off.

The confusing fictional concept was that Ross, angry with Vince, was taking his revenge and undermining the WWF by influencing hiring and firing practices, and that this whole impostor thing had been Ross's idea. You were supposed to boo Ross for the decisions Vince had *actually* been making.

As Ross would later write, "The point for Vince was: WWF owned 'Razor Ramon' and 'Diesel,' even if the guys who played them went elsewhere. It was part legal posturing, part entertainment, and part counter-programming."

The boss even made an appearance on *WWF LiveWire*, a low-rated weekly show that mimicked a news call-in program, on October 5, 1996. It was hosted by Hayes, a manager named Sunny (Tammy Lynn Sytch), and longtime industry factotum Jim Cornette. Early on, the episode featured a notable appearance by *WWF Magazine* writer Vince Russo, who performed and wrote as "Vic Venom," a paranoid parody of Meltzer-esque newsletter writers.

Vince was introduced on *LiveWire* as "the Chairman of the World Wrestling Federation"—his real, non-kayfabe title at the time. He said he was investigating Jim Ross over the Razor Ramon "incident" of a few days prior, but it was unclear what kind of power Ross was implied to have, if even the owner and/or chairman could be shown up by him like that. The whole thing didn't quite make sense, and not in a way where it was clear that anyone had any clue what they were doing.

Russo, who would soon become one of the most important individuals in the WWF, confronted Vince in a moment of neokayfabe: "You are sitting up there in your ivory tower, with all your cronies up there, afraid of what Vic Venom might say on television; afraid that Vic Venom might say the truth!" Russo whined in the tone of a needling reporter. "I have one question and one question only for you, and so does everybody else out there: How can this show be so *awful*, Mr. McMahon? Look at the production facilities! Look at the people you have working on the staff! How can this show be so *awful*?"

"I didn't think it *was*," Vince replied, with the particular smarm that he used as the voice-of-righteousness announcer.

"We're not being honest with the fans of the World Wrestling Federation, and I have a problem with that!" Russo said.

"It's an open forum," Vince said. "Anything can happen here in the World Wrestling Federation."

That's true, but just because something can happen doesn't mean anyone will like it.

Ross, in his memoir, recalled the Razor and Diesel fakeout angle with disdain: "The fans farted at it."

As the autumn of 1996 wore on, worked shoots started to become the order of the day across both WCW and WWF programming. All of a sudden, fans were tuning in not so much to see the wrestling as to see what strange truths might bubble to the surface.

Austin swiftly became the locus point for this pseudo-realism. He cut a promo in which he said the kayfabe president of the WWF, Gorilla Monsoon, was "just a puppet" and that Vince McMahon is the one "pulling all the strings." But mere acknowledgment of backstage politics was no longer enough to juice interest. So Vince and his team cribbed from one of the most popular TV programs of the day, the reality-TV sleaze-fest known as *Cops*.

On the November 4, 1996, episode of *Raw*—presented as live, but, in reality, taped on October 21—viewers saw things never before seen in wrestling. They were told at the beginning that Austin had threatened to show up at Pillman's home, and that the injured Pillman was holed up in his own house, afraid that Austin would come to get him and his wife Melanie. A camera crew was placed in a living room where the Pillmans waited anxiously.

Eventually, Austin burst through the door. Melanie shrieked and the crew scrambled in theatrical fear. Viewers saw a crazy-eyed Pillman lift up a pistol and aim it at Austin. Then, it was made to look like their satellite feed had cut out.

The three commentators that night were Vince, Jim Ross, and Jerry Lawler. There were still a bunch of matches that night, and, while the grapplers performed, the trio spoke solemnly to the viewers about their concern for the well-being of everyone in Pillman's house. They kept saying they were trying to get their feed back and learn if Pillman had shot anyone.

"It's a fine line, sometimes, between reality and what is portrayed, many times, in the World Wrestling Federation," Vince said as they waited. "Sometimes, in the World Wrestling Federation, individuals *can* get carried away. They almost can start *believing* in themselves."

Ross was still being pushed as a heel, and his tack was to criticize Vince for doing the entire home-invasion segment. "Well, I'll tell you something, Vince: You should feel pretty bad about this," he said. "You had to know that something like this was gonna happen. You had to know that this was gonna be good for television and good for ratings."

Ross continued with a statement that would prove tragically prophetic less than a year later: "And if anything bad happens to that poor Pillman family, it's gonna be on *your* shoulders, mister!"

"Now, this is no time for you to take some sort of 'popular stand,'" Vince said over the microphone, ignoring the match that was happening. "Don't give me that *crap!*" The wrestling was purely vestigial that night.

"Listen, guys, don't get into it!" Lawler yelled, playing peacemaker. "Let's call the match!"

"*That'd* be different!" Ross said.

"Don't . . . don't get smart," Vince replied. "Don't get wise."

Vince said he hoped the situation would be handled by the "appropriate authorities."

"That's *you!*" Ross crowed. "*You're* the head muckety-muck here!"

The satellite feed was "restored" near the episode's end, and the viewers saw more chaos, concluding with Pillman pointing the gun at Austin once again.

"That son of a bitch has got this coming!" Pillman yelled on the broadcast. "Get out of the fuckin' way!"

The last thing viewers saw was Melanie weeping in horror while Lawler yelled, "Grab the gun! Grab the gun! Somebody get the *gun!*"

And, once again, the feed cut out, and the episode ended before any resolution could be reached. Depending on how gullible you were, you were left wondering whether the Loose Cannon might have actually loosed his cannon and killed the WWF's fastest-rising star.

For adults, the segment was simply in poor taste. For children who were drawn to the tough-as-nails bad-assery of Austin, it was bone-chilling to think he might have died. Complaints lit up the USA Network phone lines. Vince was induced to issue a rare apology, albeit one delivered on the hardly watched *LiveWire*.

"We humbly apologize," Vince said. "The actions and the language were reprehensible and this will never, ever happen again in the WWF."

But, unbeknownst to the network execs, that statement was its own kind of kayfabe. Vince had no intention of toning things down. He had a sizzlingly popular new figure in the form of Austin, even if he still didn't entirely know what to do with him. The wrestler was still portrayed as a heel, but audiences just couldn't get enough of the previously unthinkable things he did.

Austin was becoming a new kind of babyface, one loved not for his inherent goodness, but for his perversely alluring amorality and hedonism. Some part of you longed to care as little about your fellow man as he did. Vince could work with this.

But if Vince had introduced a new kind of babyface, he would also have to reinvent the heel.

15

SUCK IT, ACT II

(1996–1997)

Bret Hart's contract with the WWF expired in the middle of 1996. It was very inconvenient timing for Vince.

Since 1983, no other promotion had threatened Vince's kingdom the way WCW did now. He'd been watching wrestlers slip through his fingers and leave to work for them, one by one. He still had Shawn Michaels, but Shawn's addictions were consuming him, making his promos slurred and his matches unsafe. He had Mark Calaway, a tall, intimidating, and reliable man who wrestled as the funereal Undertaker and had gained a substantial fan following.

But that was about it, as far as marquee names were concerned.

Except for Bret. And it was a foregone conclusion that Eric Bischoff would be reaching out to wrestling's hottest free agent.

In the waning days of June 1996, Vince invited Bret to his home in Greenwich; he wanted to convince him to sign a new contract, locking him into the WWF—one fewer thing to worry about.

But Bret had other plans.

He was a genuine star now, and he knew full well that gave him some measure of leverage over Vince. During his last contract negotiation, back in the early 1990s, Bret had used that leverage to advocate for his younger brother, Owen, who had been languishing in the WWF undercard and was thinking about getting out of the business entirely.

Back then, Bret had told Vince he'd sign the contract if Owen could work a brother-against-brother story line with him. Vince agreed, and Owen's career got a boost from the ensuing kayfabe feud.

Bret had also negotiated for the intellectual property rights to his ring name—if he ever left the company, he'd take the "Hitman" moniker with him.

"I was kind of shocked that they basically conceded and gave it to me," he tells me. "And I think they did because they just thought, 'He's the most important guy we got.'"

This time around, Bret had even more power, thanks to Bischoff's poaching campaign. And he knew his value—he could gauge how much he was worth by how many decibels the crowd reached when he walked into the ring.

So when Vince asked him to sign back up, he demurred. He was planning to take some time off, now that his contract was up, he told Vince. He didn't want to commit to another contract just yet; he was waiting for an offer he liked, with more money and a lighter schedule.

As Vince walked Bret to his limo, he made a remark that stuck with the wrestler for a long time: "You're much smarter than people give you credit for."

Within kayfabe, Bret's hiatus was explained as a soul-searching journey taken after losing the top championship. But by late July, he still hadn't signed a contract, and Vince was getting anxious. He'd started hearing rumors that Bret had already covertly signed with WCW and that he'd only find out through surprise, the way he had with the nWo and Luger. The boss flew a chartered jet from a TV taping in Yakima, Washington, to Calgary.

He put a contract in front of Bret and told him to name his price: "Whatever you want!" was Vince's phrase, in Bret's recollection.

But Bret only gave Vince a vague assurance that he'd come back in the fall. Vince left empty-handed.

Subsequently, Eric Bischoff made Bret an offer. On October 3, Bret called Vince, and Vince asked what the rival company's offer was.

Bret started to respond: "Three million dollars for a lighter schedule, 180 days a year—"

Vince cut him off: "I can't match it."

Bret said he wasn't asking to match it, just to know what Vince's counteroffer would be. "I'm in a position to make $9 million in just three years," he told Vince. "I don't want to leave, but I don't want to be stupid. I have to think about my family. What would you do? Saying no to this is like tearing up a lottery ticket."

All Vince could think to say in that moment was, "WCW would never know what to do with a Bret Hart."

★ ★ ★

On October 9, Vince flew to Calgary again to make Bret a new offer in person. The contract would be for the next twenty years of Bret's life, Vince said. He promised to pay Bret $10.5 million over that time: he'd wrestle for three years, be a senior adviser for seven, then take a decade of just being paid not to work with anyone else.

Such stability was unheard-of in the Business.

"I'll never give you a reason to ever want to leave," Vince said.

"I accepted the deal and we shook on it," Bret wrote in his memoir. "[Vince's] eyes glistened and he gave me that *yuk-yuk* smile as we agreed that all we had left to do was iron out some minor details."

The plan was for Vince and Bret to milk the situation for dramatic tension: Bret, who'd been absent for nearly seven months at that point, would appear on *Raw* later that month to announce whether he was staying with the WWF. Of course, the contract would already have been signed and the ink dry by that time, but they'd have him hem and haw for a while to rile up fans.

However, a week went by, and no contract arrived in Calgary.

Vince had a draft contract sent to Bret just three days before the taping. But when Bret had his lawyer look it over, "the draft bore no resemblance to the deal Vince and I had shook on," Bret would later write.

He called Vince, but couldn't get through. Finally, he reached Linda and told her that all bets were off unless they stuck to the deal he and Vince had agreed on.

Shortly thereafter, Vince's office called back: Oops, they'd sent him the wrong documents. Bret didn't buy it: as he tells it, this was the third time in his dealings with Vince that he'd been sent "the wrong documents."

But *Nitro* was still winning in ratings and it would be disastrous if Bret were to no-show at *Raw*. So the boss acquiesced, and sent Bret the "real" contract, for twenty years and $10.5 mil.

It also contained two concessions that made the contract even more unusual: (1) if Bret was injured and couldn't perform, he'd still be fully compensated for his wages; and (2) if he left the WWF for any reason, Bret would have creative control over how his character was ushered out in its final thirty days.

As Bret's friend, WWF exec Carl De Marco, put it to him at the time: "They can never, ever fuck you now."

★ ★ ★

Almost halfway through the October 21, 1996, *Raw*, the shrieking guitar notes of Bret's entrance music kicked in and he walked out in a T-shirt and jeans. He had signed the contract in front of Vince backstage an hour prior.

But in kayfabe, he was still undecided: "We are *live*, ladies and gentlemen!" Vince intoned from the announcer's table. "There's no telling what Bret Hart will say—or, for that matter, even *do!* Unbelievable personal pressures have been placed on Bret 'The Hitman' Hart: from his family, from his fans, from his friends! And *listen* to that reception!" The crowd roared in approval of their returning hero.

Bret stepped into the ring and Jim Ross asked him whether he would remain with the WWF. Bret monologued for a few minutes, saying he'd been approached by "a certain rival wrestling organization" with a "great offer" and that they'd "dealt with me with integrity, in nothing but an honorable fashion."

The camera cut to Vince at the announcer's table as Bret said, "I'm not greedy for money; I'm greedy for respect." Vince gritted his teeth and lowered his head, telegraphing faux-anxiety over what might happen.

"Nobody has any idea how much soul-searching I've done over this," Bret said.

"The WWF?" he added. "Well, I'll be with the WWF forever."

The crowd cheered and the camera immediately cut back to Vince, who theatrically wiped his brow in relief and said, "Whoa, all right!" He started clapping and repeated, "*All right!*"

Bret turned his promo toward his rivals. First, he said Shawn Michaels "will never ever be as tough as me, and he will never, ever be as smart as me."

"With all due respect, I'm not so certain I would concur with that," Vince murmured to the broadcast viewers—commentary neither the arena crowd nor Bret could hear.

Bret said Shawn was unworthy of his attentions, but that he *would* face another opponent: Steve Austin. They'd go up against each other at the 1996 Survivor Series, which would take place at Madison Square Garden. The crowd lost it.

"Steve Austin? Stone Cold?" Bret said. "We'll see who kicks whose *ass* at Madison Square Garden!"

The WWF was now making even the squeaky-clean Hitman use curse words. Things were changing.

When Bret entered at Madison Square Garden on November 17 for *Survivor Series '96*, the crowd cheered.

But when Austin entered, the crowd cheered just as much.

Austin was still being pushed as a heel. But he wasn't getting booed.

Bret, as per the plan, won the match. He did a victory lap around the ring. Vince reached out to shake the wrestler's hand. As Bret recalled, "Still wearing his headset, [Vince] smiled, and, with what I took to be the loving eyes of a father, he said, 'Unbelievable!'"

Only later, when Bret watched a recording of the match as televised, did he notice something: Vince and JR were "going to great lengths in their live commentary to subtly tear me down."

"Bret Hart can't *capitalize!*" Vince crowed at one point. "The *ring rust* here, apparent!"

"Bret's gotta realize: this is not 1991!" Ross said. "It's not even '94!"

Bret was ill at ease as he listened to the playback.

As he put it, "I got the first hint of what lay ahead for me."

Vince kept booking story lines in which Bret Hart's character got screwed.

Bret had a match against Sid Eudy that ended with Austin interfering and Bret losing. Bret participated in the Royal Rumble and was eliminated by a cheating Austin. After each of his losses, Vince would have the Hitman lament into the microphone about how he'd been mistreated. The boss hadn't made Bret into a heel, per se—but he was slowly making him look like a sore loser, a whiner, a prima donna. All classic heel traits.

Bret had never been the kind of wrestler who wanted to break kayfabe. He had been fine with the way things used to be. But, in his absence, the age of the worked shoot had begun, and Vince forced Bret to participate. Indeed, Vince made himself one of Bret's first targets.

Vince walked up to Bret before the January 20, 1997, edition of *Raw* and gave him unusual marching orders: he was to do a promo in which he railed against Vince for screwing him and then quit.

"It all seemed quite real, too real," Bret wrote, "but I did as Vince told me."

At the top of the show, Bret grabbed the microphone and stood in the ring, facing Vince, who was standing at ringside.

"I've been screwed by Shawn Michaels," Bret said. "I've been screwed by Stone Cold Steve Austin. I've been screwed by the World Wrestling Federation. And I've been screwed by *you!*"

Vince just stood there, looking disappointed, as Bret ran through a list of grievances. Finally, Bret screamed, "*I quit!,*" threw the microphone down, left the ring, hopped the guardrail, and exited through the confused audience, who were chanting, "*We want Bret! We want Bret!*"

Austin ran to the ring and took the mic while Bret walked away.

"Bret Hart, you can sit there and bellyache—you complain with the best of 'em, son!" spat the southern man, perhaps voicing his boss's own thoughts. "You sit there and talk about how Vince screwed ya, how everybody screwed ya, how I screwed ya. The bottom line is, son, when the going gets tough, the Harts get going—*back home!* Go on back to Canada, son!"

After the taping, Bret was summoned to Vince's office, where he was introduced to an exec from the USA Network, who was over the moon about the faux-realism Bret had brought to the complaints.

"The USA rep said it was the most exciting *Raw* they'd ever done," Bret recalled. "Vince gave me a proud slap on the back and said, 'It's all on account of him.'"

Bret's kayfabe resignation was reversed, of course. But his character wasn't going to go back to his customary role. On March 9, in a dressing room before a show in Springfield, Massachusetts, Vince asked him to formally turn heel.

"He enthusiastically went on to explain that he'd come up with a concept that had never been done before," Bret recalled, "and he was counting on me to pull it off."

Bret would become the hottest heel in the WWF, but only in the United States. He would constantly insult the US and its citizens, meaning he'd be jeered in the States, but cheered during the WWF's periodic visits to Canada and elsewhere.

"Everyone around the world loves to hate Americans," Vince said. "We come across like we're better than everyone else. This won't affect your merchandise sales because you'll be loved abroad for standing up to us Americans."

Bret had been a heel in the WWF before on some occasions, but he'd never used the cheap heat of attacking the USA. He thought it would alienate and confuse his fan base. Plus, his mom—an expat from the US—was a fierce American patriot; she'd hate it. Bret said he'd think it over.

The next morning, Vince's phone rang. It was Bret. "As long as it's done smartly and I have my hands on the controls of what I say and do, I'm in," he told Vince.

"You won't regret it," was Vince's reply.

At the March 16 *Raw* taping, Bret was booked to lose to Sid in a steel cage match, then do another worked shoot—even weirder than his previous ones.

"Vince had encouraged me to go berserk on camera and curse him out over the injustices I'd suffered, then shove him violently to the mat," Bret recalled. "He promised that they'd use the three-second delay to edit out my curse words."

Per the plan, after the match, Bret stuck around in the ring, looking dejected and furious. Vince walked up to him in his capacity as announcer.

"Bret Hart, you've gotta be terribly frustrated, extremely frustrated over what has just happened," Vince said.

Bret wasted no time. He took the mic, looked at Vince, then shoved him to the ground. Vince took the little bump—perhaps his first since his high school days—like a pro.

"Frustrated isn't the goddamn *word* for it!" Bret yelled. "This is *bullshit!*"

Vince stood up and walked out of the ring, looking like a disappointed dad trying to retain his dignity.

"You *screwed* me!" the wrestler yelled after him. "Everybody screws me and nobody does a goddamn thing about it! Nobody in the building cares! Nobody in the dressing room cares! So much goddamn injustice around here! I've had it up to *here!*"

He chased after Vince and kept screaming about how everyone was turning a blind eye to what was happening to him. While the camera closed in on Vince's disapproving face, Bret quoted his catchphrase: "Everyone in that goddamn dressing room knows that I'm *the best there is, the best there was, and the best there ever will be!* And if you don't like it, *tough shit!*"

Unbeknownst to Bret, Vince had lied: they weren't bleeping anything he said in the TV broadcast.

A video feed of Steve Austin began playing on the big projector screen, known as the Titantron, above the entrance. He and Bret were going to have a match at WrestleMania in a few days. In the story line of Bret's match with Sid, Austin had briefly appeared and interfered in such a way that could have been beneficial to Bret, but Bret had lost anyway. Austin, acting on Vince's instructions, ripped into the Hitman.

"All you wanna do, any time you go in the ring, is cry like a *baby!*" Austin yelled. "I tried to go out there and help ya, and you threw it all away, because you're a *loser!*"

WrestleMania 13 (the style of numbering for WrestleMania installments became more erratic as the years went on) came around on March 23 and Austin and Bret had a masterpiece of a match. Both men loved doing it. But the moral valences were still confused. Bret was acting petulant as he went up against the increasingly beloved Austin, but Bret hadn't quite turned on the *fans*, yet. He would get boos, but he'd also get cheers, and he'd still high-five his devotees as he entered and exited.

On March 24, at a live showing of *Raw* in Rockford, Illinois, it became clear that anyone who saluted the Red, White, and Blue was supposed to hate Bret. It was on that night that Bret cut an epic, twenty-minute live promo that had been carefully outlined by Vince. Bret was clad in a new black leather jacket adorned with a skull. There are many who regard what he said as the best heel-turn promo of all time.

"First of all, I wanna apologize," Bret said to a mix of cheers and jeers. He said he was sorry for his fans in Europe, Japan, the Middle East, South Africa, and Canada.

"And to you, my fans right here, across the United States of America . . ."

The camera cut to a confused-looking fan holding a sign that read, "I BELIEVE IN YOU BRET."

". . . to you, I apologize for *nothing.*"

The booing grew louder as Bret complained that, even though he had won the match with Austin, the fans had rooted for his opponent.

The camera closed in on Vince at the announce booth. He looked disgusted. Vince wasn't quite pushing himself as a babyface, but he hadn't let go of his vision of his character as an upright man who found arrogance offensive.

"The World Wrestling Federation needs a hero," Bret said. "They need a role model. They need somebody they can look up to, not somebody that's got earrings all over himself, and tattoos. Not somebody that poses for girlie magazines."

Shawn had recently posed as a centerfold in *Playgirl*.

"By the way," Bret continued, "I don't think it was a girlie magazine; I think it was a *gay* magazine!"

That line, like everything in the carefully planned rant, had been Vince's idea.

The whole thing occupied a strange zone of kayfabe: Bret kept talking about his matches as though they had been legitimate contests, but all the insults seemed so much more honest and vicious than anything Bret had ever said in the ring. And the camera, per Vince's orders, kept showing Vince's face while he listened intently to the promo he'd outlined for Bret.

"The poison is *spewing* from Bret Hart," Vince told the viewers.

"You'd rather cheer for heroes like Charles Manson and O. J. Simpson!" Bret told the Illinoisan crowd, who were now overwhelmingly booing him. "Nobody glorifies criminal conduct like the Americans do!"

Bret genuinely believed much of what he was saying. He was a man of the old school; he really did find it detestable that American fans were cheering for the evil deeds of Steve Austin.

That had been Vince's master stroke: he was simply unleashing and exacerbating the frustration Bret had bottled up for months.

"All you American wrestling fans, coast to coast, you don't respect me," Bret said. "So from here on in, the American wrestling fans, coast to coast, can *kiss my ass!*"

That's when Shawn Michaels walked in, per the plan. Vince had carefully scripted Shawn's response to Bret, too.

"I've tried and tried to take the high road," Shawn said. "I don't obsess like you do. I do this 'cause I *like* it. You do it because, in your mind, marked man, you really think all of this is *yours*."

"Boy Toy," Bret said, "I think you should go back to the dressing room; get the hell out of my face."

"How'd you know I was in that 'girlie' magazine?" Shawn taunted. "You couldn't help yourself, could you? You had to flip through the pages just a little bit!"

The crowd cheered.

Throughout the summer, Vince kept having Bret and Shawn do increasingly intense worked-shoot promos about each other. When Shawn took the microphone, he always attacked Bret as a sellout, a traitor.

"Bret Hart did not come back to the World Wrestling Federation for his fans," Shawn declaimed in one spot. "He came back for the almighty dollar!"

Shawn said Bret had taken time off the previous year not because he needed rest, but because he wanted to see if the WWF would be hurt without him.

"As a matter of fact, the World Wrestling Federation did the best business it has done in six years!" Shawn declared.

This was, of course, a lie—WCW had taken the top position in wrestling ratings almost immediately after Bret's departure and hadn't left it since. Nevertheless, Shawn turned to Vince, who had been interviewing him, and said, "You're the boss—am I right or wrong?"

Vince smiled and said, "You're right."

Vince got a call from a furious Bret. As Bret recalled, "Without a moment's hesitation, [Vince] told me that Shawn's behavior was inexcusable and that Shawn would be dealt with."

"Thinking back on it now, I am astonished that I believed him," Bret wrote. "I guess I just wanted to believe him."

Bret found out he needed knee surgery and went under the knife in Calgary on April 23. He was planning to return to WWF programming for promos and interviews, then, hopefully, wrestle again in the summer.

But the day after his surgery, Vince called and told him he needed him to show up at the next *Raw*, four days hence.

Bret said the doctor had told him to do nothing for a while. Vince was insistent.

Bret did as he was told and started making appearances. He would be on crutches or in a wheelchair, but it was still far earlier than medically recommended. Defying a doctor's orders because of a promoter's orders was nothing new for a wrestler. But, for Bret, hobbling around on his painful knee while listening to Shawn cut ever-more-intoxicated promos was becoming unbearable. In one of those promos, Shawn implied that Bret was having an affair with Sunny, the *LiveWire* cohost—an accusation that had often been thrown around in the locker room, but never on the air.

SUCK IT, ACT II

Vince had successfully backed the Hitman into an emotional corner. Bret truly hated Shawn at this point.

The two were slated to have a big match at a PPV eventually; so incensed was Bret by that point that, as he put it, "I wondered about beating the hell out of Shawn for real at the pay-per-view."

Vince called Bret to a sit-down before *Raw* on June 2. Instead of assuaging Bret's fears about Shawn's antics, Vince broke some bad news.

"He told me that the company was in financial peril and that he was only just hanging on: The next six months would either make him or break him," Bret recalled. "He told me he might have no other choice but to restructure my contract."

Vince told Bret he'd still get paid every dime—but perhaps only on the back end of the twenty-year span.

"I did call my lawyer to see what my options were if Vince tried to do that kind of a move," Bret wrote, "but, when it came right down to it, I didn't believe that he ever would."

A week later, just before the June 9 *Raw* started broadcasting, Bret and Shawn got into a verbal, then physical fight backstage.

Shawn marched to Vince's room, screamed at the top of his lungs that he was in an unsafe working environment, and stormed out, leaving the building.

Bret entered the room Shawn had just left and, as he put it, "Vince looked like a jilted lover whose boy toy had up and left him."

Nevertheless, Vince took responsibility. He said he'd get Shawn in line and told Bret to take the night off. Bret left the building and went back to his hotel to stew.

The show began.

Raw had been evolving at a rapid pace in the spring and summer of 1997. Bret and Shawn's all-too-real conflict was hardly the only attraction at that point—over the course of just a few short months, Vince and his creative team had built up buzz about an array of boundary-pushing story lines. If Bret had stuck around that night, he would have seen a perfect snapshot of a creative hotbed in transition.

The whole product was more aggressive, more *trans*gressive, than it ever had been. It had a new, longer name: *Raw Is War*. There was a live-action opening sequence for every episode, shot at great expense a few months prior, that depicted various wrestlers beating each other up in what was made to look like a war zone: burning barrels, bombed-out buildings, air-raid sirens, and lots of explosions. The music for that sequence had initially been the hit Marilyn Manson track "The Beautiful People"; now it was an original work called "Thorn in Your Eye," performed by a make-shift band of veteran rockers dubbed Slam Jam.

Vince was playing with fire in his choice of angles. He had booked a group of Black wrestlers as the Nation of Domination, a set of radicals in a white-nightmare vision of the Nation of Islam. He had a bunch of Puerto Rican wrestlers perform as a street gang called Los Boricuas. Yet another group, the Disciples of Apocalypse, featured white skinhead bikers. These three crews were booked against each other with regularity.

Sex was selling, too. The days of Wendi Richter's quasi-feminist gimmick were long gone. Women were almost never allowed to actually wrestle, but there was more than enough titillation for the teenage straight boys in the audience. Late in this episode, the camera lingered on a model-turned-manager named Sable (Rena Mero) for almost a full minute while an announcer read ad copy about the branded shirt she was wearing: "Well, here she is: a 'wild child' could be her label! We're talkin' about the sexy, hot, *hot*-lookin' Sable! And you wanted more of *Raw Is War*? Here's your opportunity: the *Raw Is War* T-shirt!"

Paul Heyman and two ECW wrestlers were there that night, too. Within kayfabe, ECW wrestler Rob Van Dam (Robert Szatkowski) was attempting to sign with the WWF; Heyman pretended that he was attempting to legally prevent the defection. It was all played to the hilt.

ECW was too small to ever pose a major threat to Vince; instead, at some point in 1996, Vince and Heyman decided to work together. Neither man has ever discussed the terms of the deal, but they staged occasional ECW-WWF crossovers, with wrestlers from one company visiting the other. Such crossovers elevated ECW's profile while stamping the WWF as hip. ECW also acted as a kind of feeder system for the WWF, with the best grapplers often getting a bump up to the big league. Call it collaboration or something more sinister; it grabbed eyeballs.

And of course, worked shoots were plentiful. In fact, worked shoots against Vince were becoming a trademark; something in him seemed to enjoy being cussed out by people whose grievances were real but who could never have voiced them without his permission.

For example, Paul Levesque dutifully ripped into Vince that night for demoting him after the Curtain Call incident: "I should've been the King of the Ring a year ago," he whined. "But because of *you* and *your politics*, I never got my shot, did I?"

Most of these worked shoots relied on shock value or confusion to juice interest. But there was one that relied on beauty. Mick Foley was a famed deathmatch wrestler who had worked for WCW and ECW in the past as an outlaw named Cactus Jack. With his unkempt brown hair, deliberately sloppy-looking outfits, and deep knowledge of what the average smart felt and wanted, he had become one of the great fan favorites of the era. Now he was wrestling for the WWF as Mankind, a madman in a *Texas Chainsaw Massacre*–style leather mask. Mankind would win matches by shoving his hand in his opponent's mouth for a submission maneuver known as the Mandible Claw.

In real life, Foley had wanted to hang on to his old outlaw gimmick, but Vince just hadn't found Cactus Jack interesting and demanded he become a psycho killer instead; Cactus Jack would linger on as just one voice in Foley's ostensibly shattered mind.

In a pretaped interview with Jim Ross that night, the rotund Foley feigned mental illness and spoke in a pained whine that occasionally burst into a terrifying shout.

"Why didn't Cactus Jack ever come to the WWF?" Ross asked.

"Because he . . . he wasn't welcome," Foley said. "Every time I put on the Mandible Claw, in my mind, that's Vince McMahon, and I'm saying, '*Why didn't you take me when I was good? Why didn't you take me when I was young?*'"

"Don't you believe that you, yourself, have caused and brought on all these problems?" Ross asked, sounding a lot like Vince when he talks about his wrestlers' health and well-being.

"Do I bring it onto *myself*?" Foley asked back. "All you've done to people is mislead them and let them think I'm having the time of my goddamn life when I'm in *pain!*"

And what of Bret and Shawn, a viewer might wonder? Their absence was explained away as the result of a locker-room fight. It made perfect sense for the story line, and not just because it was true.

Vince had already instituted a 1-900 number that fans could call in order to get worked-shoot gossip about what was happening backstage for the price of $1.49 per minute. And the WWF was also an early adopter of the internet—they were advertising their AOL presence that night, and they were well aware that news about Bret and Shawn's fight had already leaked out to the chatrooms.

They capitalized on it, in fact.

"Ladies and gentlemen, you want some big news? We've got some *huge* news!" Ross crowed on the broadcast. "Bret Hart, Shawn Michaels—they're making headlines all *over* the place! We'll tell you all about the latest *locker-room news* on the WWF Superstar Line!"

Just before the September 22 edition of *Raw* at Madison Square Garden, Vince called Bret to his office.

He told Bret he couldn't honor the twenty-year contract.

"He wasn't going to pay me my full salary because of problems he attributed to Ted Turner," Bret would recall. Calling Bret "the Cal Ripken of the WWF," Vince promised to pay him every dime promised to him . . . someday.

Vince told Bret to go pursue WCW again.

"He went on to say that if I left, I would actually be doing him a favor," Bret wrote, "because he was about to downsize into a northeastern US promotion." Vince said the stiff competition with WCW meant he was going to have to fire a large number of wrestlers. "He described me as the first guy in the lifeboat," Bret wrote.

As it would turn out, that proved to be an exaggeration. There was no mass layoff, nor did the WWF downsize.

But, at the time, Vince told Bret to keep it all a secret, because if Eric Bischoff found out Vince was in trouble, it would hurt Bret's chances. "Hurt my chances?" Bret wrote. "I was so stunned by how many promises he broke in one short conversation that I didn't know what to reply."

Vince said something else that Bret never forgot: "Nobody wants Bret Hart more than Vince McMahon."

That night, Vince did a landmark in-ring interview with Austin. Stone Cold had suffered a real-life neck injury that had forced him to stop doing matches. The WWF acknowledged the injury in kayfabe, but the story line was that Austin wanted to keep wrestling and the company was trying to stop him. In the interview that night, Vince tried to reason with Stone Cold: Would he *please* just follow orders and take some time off?

"Don't you know, people *care* in the World Wrestling Federation?" Vince said. "You've got to work within the *system*."

"I appreciate the fact that you and the World Wrestling Federation *care*," Austin replied. "And I also appreciate the fact that, hell, you can *kiss my ass!*"

And, with that, he kicked Vince in the stomach and performed his signature move, the Stone Cold Stunner, on the boss. The Stunner consists of kicking someone in the gut to make them bend over, then grabbing their neck, turning to face away from them, and abruptly sitting down, so as to make it look like you're practically snapping their spine.

The crowd went nuts over it.

The Austin-McMahon feud was born. The tone of the WWF barely resembled that of just a few years prior. Old-school wrestling, with its clearly defined heels and faces, was on the way out.

Despite any statements to the contrary, in Vince's calculations, Bret was no longer necessary.

On Sunday, October 5, Brian Pillman didn't show up for work at a PPV in St. Louis called *Badd Blood*. As it turned out, he had died in a hotel room in Minnesota, where he'd wrestled the previous night.

Vince learned of the death shortly before the show went on the air. But the show went on.

For the first three minutes of the PPV, it was as if nothing had changed: "Welcome, everyone, to a sold-out, jam-packed Kiel Center! Welcome, everyone, to *Badd Blood!*" Vince shouted at the top of the program. But eventually, the camera turned to the announcers' booth, where Vince's voice turned somber and he informed the viewers that Pillman had "passed away this afternoon."

Vince referenced the death throughout the broadcast, teasing the viewer with snippets of unconfirmed speculation: "Authorities expect no foul play was involved, in terms of the initial inspection," he said at one point. "Nonetheless, apparently they're concerned about a possibility of a drug overdose, be it prescription or recreational. Of course, that is a problem in *all* sport and *all* forms of entertainment."

The very next night, Vince opened *Raw* with a tribute to Pillman: he stood in the ring while a gaggle of wrestlers stood at the top of the entrance ramp. He read a statement and the ring bell sounded out ten times in tribute.

Then they started promoting an unusual interview.

Vince was slated to have a live chat, via satellite, with Melanie Pillman, Brian's widow, that night, just a day after she learned he was dead. The boss had the announcers hype it up all evening.

Pillman had trained with Stu Hart, and was like a brother to Bret. Bret was disgusted that Vince was using a real death as kayfabe hype, up to and including the interview with Melanie. But he was also furious about the material he had to work with in his own story line.

Vince had booked Bret to have a verbal confrontation with Shawn and his crew. "I want you to really shoot with 'em," were Vince's words to Bret beforehand.

Vince had recently added Shawn to the booking committee. His influence had been formalized. Shawn told Bret to throw in a homophobic slur or two when it went down.

Bret did as he was told.

"You're nothin' but a *homo!*" Bret told Shawn and his entourage during the show that night. "You may have barebacked your way to some kind of main event, one pay-per-view after another. But the fact is, I make more money than all three of you guys combined!"

After some back-and-forth, Shawn offered up a retort that became a catchphrase: "I've got two words for the Hitman, Bret Hart: *Suck it!*"

When Vince finally did the interview with Melanie that night, it made for some of the most uncomfortable television that the WWF had ever aired.

She sat on a couch in her home, looking completely dazed. The camera never left her face for the entire conversation.

"What can you tell us about what you have been told, as far as Brian's death is concerned?" Vince's disembodied voice asked.

"Well, um," she said, searching for the words and fighting back tears. "Apparently there was a problem with his heart, and apparently his heart was put under a lot of stress for some reason."

Vince said there was "speculation" that Brian had taken too much of a prescription, then asked, "If, in fact, that is proven to be the case—which it has yet to be—is there anything that you would wanna say to aspiring athletes who do get hurt and have to resort to prescribed medication, painkillers?"

"I think all athletes, to a degree, experience a reliance on pain medicine, and I knew it was just a matter of time before it happened to someone," Melanie said. "And, unfortunately, it was my husband. And I just want everyone to know that I hope it's a wake-up call for some of you."

"How are the children taking this news, and do they understand?" Vince asked.

"Well, our four-year-old doesn't understand," Melanie said, her tone anguished. "That's little Brian. He doesn't understand why daddy's not coming home." She explained that her stepdaughter, another child of Brian's, had lost her mother to suicide just two years prior. Melanie said that, upon hearing the news, the girl "just screamed for about fifteen minutes. And I don't know Vince, it's hard. It's just really hard. But I'm doin'—"

Vince cut her off. "Have you had any opportunity to think about what you, now, as a single parent, will do to support your five children?" he asked.

"Vince, I don't even really know what day it is," she said. "So I don't know what I'm gonna do."

"How would you like for Brian to be remembered by WWF fans and fans all over the world?"

Melanie said she'd like him to be remembered as a great father. Then she corrected herself.

"He also loved this business, Vince," Melanie said. "I guess you could say he lived for this business. And he died for this business. And I hope no one else has to die."

Bret did as Vince had suggested: he reached out to WCW, covertly. He and Bischoff closed a deal on November 1, eight days before *Survivor Series* '97. The PPV was booked to occur at Montreal's Molson Centre. All that week, Bret and Vince argued endlessly about how his main-event match with Shawn should go.

Bret, at that point, held the WWF championship. Vince told him over the phone that he wanted him to lose it to the Heartbreak Kid.

"He told me he can't have me showing up on the WCW TV show wearing his belt," Bret recounted.

It's true that there was a long tradition of belt-theft in wrestling. It had happened as recently as 1995, when the WWF's Alundra Blayze (Debrah Ann Miceli) went to WCW and dumped the WWF women's belt in a trash can on live TV. In 1991, Ric Flair took his NWA championship belt with him to the WWF, where Vince displayed it on air as the spoils of war. It was a rare but established way for a promotion to stick it to a rival after stealing away talent.

Bret said he would never do that.

Vince insisted that he had to be sure: Bret should lose the match and relinquish the belt right afterward.

"Fine," Bret said. "If you want me to drop the belt, I drop the belt. But not in Canada." Bret would prefer any kind of finish—even an inconclusive disqualification—over dropping the belt in his home country to a wrestler he hated. Plus, there *was* that clause in his contract about having creative control over the way his character went out. Even if Vince wouldn't honor the rest of the contract, Bret hoped that clause at least would stand.

"You told me I could leave any way I wanted," Bret reminded Vince, "and now you're throwing this at me?"

They hung up without coming to an agreement.

There was an independent documentary crew following Bret around at the time, and they recorded him immediately after that conversation.

"I've never said 'no' to Vince McMahon," Bret was recorded saying. "Ever."

For days, in person and over the phone, Vince pitched a wide array of potential Survivor Series finishes to Bret. One after another, Bret turned them down, per his contract.

One particularly convoluted proposal was a *faked* screwjob. According to Dave Meltzer's reporting, Vince at one point offered up the following: Bret would lose in some kind of controversial finish, then the wrestler would become enraged and expose the business's inner workings by (falsely) claiming that he'd been booked to win and was screwed by Vince. The next night on *Raw*, Vince and Bret could get into a worked-shoot argument in which Bret would punch Vince.

As Meltzer later wrote, "McMahon even suggested to hardway him (give him a hard punch that would either open him up or at least give him a noticeable black eye) to make it look legit."

Bret wouldn't budge.

There is no consensus on who came up with the initial idea to execute a *real* screwjob on Bret Hart.

It most likely wasn't Vince, whose trademark is latching on to others' biggest ideas and using them for his own ends.

Perhaps it was WWF exec Jerry Brisco. Bret would later claim he'd heard through the grapevine that Brisco was the one.

Maybe it was trash-talking, trend-following Vince Russo, newly installed as a booker and always looking for the next shocking thing to put on TV.

It could have been Jim Cornette, a fiercely traditionalist manager/promoter/historian who had also been made a lead booker.

One thing is for certain: Russo and Cornette hated each other.

"Vince Russo's never had any respect for professional wrestling," Cornette would later say. "He booked the wrestling program to pattern after Jerry Springer."

"The problem is he's still living in 1970," Russo would say of Cornette.

Such interpersonal conflict was fine by Vince. He liked it, in fact.

Cornette says he came up with the screwjob concept, inspired by a similar unscripted loss he knew about from 1931.

Russo insists it was all *his* idea, conceived purely through the creativity of desperation.

"I wish I didn't pitch the idea," Russo said. "It was one of the worst experiences in my life in the wrestling business."

Cornette is similarly regretful.

Brisco has outright denied coming up with the screwjob.

No one wants to be known as the person who came up with what Meltzer would go on to describe as "the single most famous finish of a pro wrestling match in the modern era."

According to both Dave Meltzer and Shawn Michaels, on November 8, the day before the PPV, Vince met with Pat Patterson and Shawn, among others, in a hotel room in Montreal to map out how the next day's match would go. (Patterson, who died in 2020, denied being there; indeed, he denied knowing anything about the screwjob prior to its execution.)

Shawn would put Bret into Bret's own signature submission hold, the Sharpshooter. Then, without warning Bret, Vince would run in and tell the referee, Earl Hebner (who would already be briefed on the situation), to call the match in Shawn's favor, despite Bret not submitting.

Bret would lose *and* look like a gullible fool.

The doc crew filmed Bret that same day. The footage shows a man still unclear on what the finish of the match would be. He seemed anxious.

"Really, what they would prefer to do to me tomorrow is to . . . The way I would liken it, is to actually rape me in the middle of the ring," Bret told the filmmakers, on camera. "And it'll be really tough for me to get through the next few weeks, if I even make it that far. I have no idea if I'll even make it that far. Because I won't let them rape me."

Bret says his and Vince's conversation at Montreal's Molson Centre before the PPV went as follows.

By then, word had leaked on the internet and in the newsletters that Bret had signed with WCW. The sold-out crowd was rabid with anticipation.

"What do you want to do?" Vince asked Bret, disingenuously. "You've got me by the balls."

Bret proposed, once again, that he retain the belt and forfeit it on *Raw* the next night. How about they have the big match end with other wrestlers running into the ring to disrupt it and end it in a disqualification? It was a common move; there was even wrestler lingo for it. They call it a "fuck finish."

Vince said that would work.

"I never, ever wanted to leave here with any kind of bad feeling," Bret told Vince. "But this week has been a bad week for me. I feel kinda betrayed, a little bit."

"Well, I do, too, a little bit," Vince said. "And, again, all we're talking about, really, is Ted Turner. That's what's coming between you and me. That's all. I can't tell you how appreciative I will always be for everything you've done."

They shook on the plan.

Bret met with Shawn backstage. Bret laid out the plan for the fuck finish.

"[Shawn] was visibly nervous," Bret recalled, "and said he wanted no problems with me, that he had no problems doing anything."

Vince wasn't on commentary that night, which was unusual for a PPV, but Bret didn't think anything of it. Indeed, during a long sequence in which camera crews followed Shawn and Bret individually as they walked from the bowels of the arena to the main hall, there was no commentary at all. In an eerie departure from the usual template, commentators Jim Ross and Jerry Lawler were silent under the noise of the fevered crowd.

Shawn could hardly be called a babyface by that point, and he often drew jeers. But there were many who loved to cheer on his sophomoric antics. Bret, too, still had his fan base, especially in English-speaking Canada. But this show was happening in Quebec, the francophone province that had just come close to seceding—uneasy territory for a Maple Leaf–flying patriot like Bret.

Collectively, the noise from the crowd wasn't cheering or booing. It was just chaos.

Bret and Shawn, per the plan, started tussling before the bell had even rung to formally begin the match. Vince and his lieutenants, Pat Patterson and Jerry Brisco, ran to the main hall to cajole Bret and Shawn into the ring to start the bout. They did. Vince lingered at ringside.

The two wrestlers put on a fantastic show, the kind of staged conflict that can only come in a collaboration between two men who, deep down, despise each other.

It went on for about twelve minutes.

Then, Shawn put Bret in the Sharpshooter.

It's a submission hold, meaning the person in the hold is supposed to telegraph awful pain until either some development breaks the hold or the person "submits" and thus loses the match. Typically, when someone is put in a submission hold, the referee gets near to them to listen for their submission.

The Sharpshooter is hard to describe in words, but it involves getting your opponent belly-down on the canvas, then straddling their body, twisting their legs, and leaning so the opponent's spine seemingly bends backward, against its natural curve.

Once Shawn had Bret in this humiliating position, Hebner, the referee, ran to the two men, ostensibly to listen for a submission.

Hebner waited for a few seconds.

Bret didn't break the hold, and he didn't tap out.

According to the rules, the match should have continued.

But Hebner signaled to the official bell-ringer, Mark Yeaton, and yelled, "Ring the bell!"—the universal signal of a match's conclusion.

Vince was next to Yeaton, who was paralyzed by stunned disbelief.

Vince shoved an elbow into Yeaton, hard.

"*Ring the fucking bell!*" Vince said.

Yeaton rang the bell.

The terrified Hebner ran as fast as he could out of the ring and up the ramp.

The orgasmic opening moans of Shawn's theme music, "Sexy Boy," started reverberating throughout the Molson Centre. The ring announcer said Shawn was the winner and new champion.

The camera closed in on Bret's face. He was on the canvas, panting. His sweat-drenched black locks hung around his face.

He broke into a little smile that seemed to say, *You son of a bitch.*

Everyone not already clued in to the plan tried to suss it all out. To the fans, it was clear that the match shouldn't have ended when it did. Someone had broken the rules. Someone had screwed Bret.

"What happened?" Jim Ross asked, sounding genuinely confused.

"*Bullshit, bullshit, bullshit,*" the crowd chanted.

Bret, his face now stone-grim, stood up. Vince was standing mere feet away from him, outside the ring.

Bret looked at Vince. He hocked up some saliva. He spat. He hit Vince directly in the face.

Shawn slid out of the ring, snatched up the precious belt, and ran away as trash and obscenities rained down.

"Wow, you talk about controversy," Ross said. "This crowd is *livid*."

Vince ran for the exit and locked himself in his makeshift office.

The broadcast ended.

Bret drew the letters "W-C-W" in the air. He walked to the announcer's booth, where Vince had sat for so many years as the voice of the WWF, and started smashing monitors, headsets, and other equipment.

Then he walked backstage.

Bret confronted Shawn, who said he'd known nothing about the screwjob in advance. Bret's then-wife, Julie, started telling off Levesque for allowing this to happen. The Undertaker banged on Vince's door and told the boss to talk to Bret.

Vince walked to Bret's dressing room and entered. Bret was in the shower. A wrestler named Rick Rude (Richard Rood) called out that Vince wanted to talk.

"Tell Vince to get the hell out of here before he gets hurt," Bret said. Vince wouldn't leave.

Bret walked out of the shower, sopping wet, naked before the man who had just screwed him.

As Bret picked up a towel, Vince simply said, "It's the first time I ever had to lie to one of my talent."

"Who are you kidding, you lying piece of shit?" Bret countered. "After fourteen years, you just couldn't let me leave with my head up?"

The men talked while Bret put on his underwear, pants, and shoes. He picked up his knee brace menacingly, then tossed it down.

Bret lunged. Vince didn't run. He threw his body against Bret's. They tied up, like wrestlers do.

Then Bret leaned back and threw an uppercut that hit Vince in the jaw, popping him off the ground—"Like a cork," as Bret put it.

Vince collapsed to the floor, unconscious. He would tell people he remembered little else about that night.

In another profession, someone might have called the police after a multimillionaire business owner was knocked out by one of his workers. But this was wrestling; it was all handled internally. Brisco jumped at Bret and the two struggled for a bit. Meanwhile, Shane McMahon helped drag his dazed father out of the room. Vince's entourage, satisfied, let Bret go.

Later that night, Bret wondered out loud to the documentary crew why any of this had happened.

"Maybe I was becoming too powerful," Bret said, "and now it's time for Vince McMahon, the promoter, to tear this guy down."

Then Bret offered another theory: "Maybe it's just something that he just wanted to prove to himself: that he can still do it."

He added: "I'll never know."

16

SUCK IT, ACT III
(1997–1999)

As the night of November 9 became the early morning of November 10, the wrestling world was deafened by the explosion of the so-called Montreal Screwjob.

"The mass audience reaction was one of confusion," one fan who'd watched that night wrote, almost two decades later. "Those few who were on the internet at the time thought 'VINCE YOU MOTHERFUCKER.'"

"Not long at all after the PPV ended," another fan recalled, "my inbox started blowing up with 'breaking news' and 'developing situation' emails." The subject lines promised juicy details: "What happened in the ring after Survivor Series went off air," "Hart knocks out Vince," "Half the locker room goes on strike," and so on.

"I was / still am a huge Bret Hart mark," that fan continued, "so by the time I was pretty sure it wasn't a work, I was pretty upset."

A Usenet email thread with the subject line "What the hell?" began with a user positing, "Ok either a) we have been worked like never before [or] b) vince doesn't trust bret at all."

"It['s] an angle," another user replied. "I see Bret on Raw tomorrow, complaining on how he was screwed and bashing the WWF."

"Bret got fucked," read another Usenet message, "and Vinnie gave us all a lube job, minus the lube."

These online denizens were among a new, growing cohort of wrestling fans, ones who identified not as marks or smarts, but rather as a hybrid: each one of them was a *smark*. To be one was to be deeply knowledgeable (or so you thought) about the realities of wrestling, but still capable of wild excitement about the artform and constantly trying to dig for the truth beneath wrestling's lies.

"Bret Hart Loses: Ambush or Angle?!?" read the headline of a notable

Usenet wrestling newsletter sent out soon after the Screwjob. "The truth is, we don't know yet. . . . To be honest, I can't recall ever awaiting an episode of RAW like I am awaiting tonight's. Maybe it's for the wrong reasons."

The wrestlers were Vince's first concern. Most of the locker room had threatened to boycott the *Raw* taping. By the time Vince arrived at Ottawa's Corel Centre, tempers had cooled enough for the Boys to listen to the boss's explanation for what had happened. Vince told them Bret had agreed to drop the belt in Montreal, but had reneged on that agreement on the day of the PPV. He said Bret had called himself a "Canadian national treasure" and was disrespecting the WWF, the Business, and the belt. Vince said he'd known he would face consequences from Bret, but that he'd taken the punch "for the Boys."

As Wade Keller of *Pro Wrestling Torch* reported soon afterward, "For those who needed a plausible explanation which they could cling to as a defense for not walking out on McMahon, McMahon provided it for them."

By then, writer Vince Russo's influence had pushed Vince toward a model that came to be known as "crash TV." Under this philosophy, WWF plots were barely mapped out in advance beyond some vague and malleable outlines. Instead, the team would focus on making the wildest, most eyeball-grabbing creative decisions on a week-to-week basis. And that week, the decision was to keep sticking it to Bret.

Shawn Michaels and his wrestling entourage, who had recently been dubbed D-Generation X, were the first attraction to enter. While the Canadian crowd showered them with boos, Shawn cut a slurred promo, poking his thumb in the eye of the man he'd beaten under such unfair circumstances.

"Now, for all you people that are chanting, 'We want Bret,' well, I got news for ya: You can sing it, but the fact of the matter is, the Heartbreak Kid, Shawn Michaels, beat Bret Hart in his home country, in his own finishing hold," Shawn said.

"I just beat a man who's a legend in his own mind last night and ran him out of the WWF," he added.

"It is this simple," Shawn continued. "Not Bret Hart, not Hulk Hogan, not Randy Savage, not *anybody* has the will—and it's that simple, the *will*—to be the best. And Shawn Michaels will out-will every one of them."

The next episode of *Raw* would be a pretaped one, filmed the very next day, November 11, in Ontario. It was in preparation for that episode that Vince made his fateful decision.

According to Vince Russo, a high-level meeting was called to discuss what to do about the new facts on the ground. "Everybody in the room wanted to bury it under the mat: 'Let's forget about it and move on.' 'Yeah—let's get back to rasslin'!' " Russo wrote. "I couldn't believe what I was hearing."

Russo spoke up and "basically said, 'What, are you guys nuts? This is all everybody is talking about—we've got to go with this.' "

Vince, in this telling, listened to Russo and took a long pause to think before saying, "I agree, we need to take advantage of this."

Whoever first had the idea, the boss went with it.

As Vince later put it, "We realized then we could put me in a venue where the public could express its anger."

When the pretaped *Raw* aired on November 17, viewers kept hearing commentator Jim Cornette tease an "investigative report on the truth behind the Bret Hart controversy." Finally, about twenty minutes into the show, they got to see Vince (bearing a black eye, though, notably, Bret said he had hit him in the jaw) make his case.

Vince's WWF heel turn didn't happen in the ring. It happened on a simple makeshift set: black backdrop, a small table, two chairs, and a cheap-looking cutout of Bret Hart in full Hitman garb hung up in the middle. Vince and Jim Ross recorded a worked-shoot interview there.

"Let's cut right to the chase," Ross said. "Did you or did you not screw Bret Hart?"

"Some would say I screwed Bret Hart," Vince replied, the camera zooming in on his dispassionate face. "I look at it from a different standpoint. I look at it from the standpoint of: the referee did not screw Bret Hart. Shawn Michaels certainly did not screw Bret Hart. Nor did Vince McMahon screw Bret Hart."

He paused for just a second.

"I truly believe that Bret Hart screwed Bret Hart," Vince said. "And he can look in the mirror and know that."

"What do you mean by that?" Ross asked.

"There's a time-honored tradition in the wrestling business, when someone is leaving, that they show the right amount of respect to the

WWF Superstars, in this case, who helped make you that superstar; you show the proper respect to the organization that helped you become who you are today," Vince said. "And Bret Hart didn't want to honor that tradition."

Ross asked if Vince had any sympathy for the Hitman.

"Sympathy? I have no sympathy for Bret, whatsoever; none," Vince replied. "Bret made a very, very selfish decision. Bret's gonna have to live with that for the rest of his life. *Bret screwed Bret*. I have no sympathy whatsoever for Bret."

D-Generation X was, at the time, comprised of Shawn, Levesque (now going by the ring-name Triple H), and Chyna (Joanie Laurer). On the November 24 *Raw*, Vince had them hit the ring for a promo at the top of the show.

"Bret Hart deserved better," Shawn said in a somber tone; then, he offered up a shocking claim: "God as my witness, Bret Hart and Shawn Michaels have finally had contact with each other without the knowledge of the media, without the knowledge of Vince McMahon, without the knowledge of the internet, without the knowledge of the underground dirtsheet writers."

Shawn said Bret was still under contract until the end of the month. He said Bret would, in fact, appear that night. The two of them would settle the dispute over the Survivor Series finish once and for all.

About half an hour later, D-X took to the ring again. "It's time to put it all aside and get the facts," Shawn declared. "Tonight, the controversy comes to an end! Ladies and gentlemen: Bret 'The Hitman' Hart!"

Bret's music hit the speakers. Many in the crowd started to howl with excitement.

It all sapped away when a little person wrestler—his name has gone unrecorded by wrestling history—walked out, clad in a Bret Hart Halloween mask and a tiny version of Bret's costume.

"I mean, we always knew Bret was short on *charisma*, short on *talent*, but this is *ridiculous!*" Triple H crowed.

Shawn taunted the faux Bret for a few minutes, even recreating the end of the Montreal Screwjob in miniature. Eventually, Triple H stuck a sign reading "WCW" on "Bret's" rear end and sent him back to the entrance.

"Don't cry, Hitman!" Triple H called after him. "It'll be all right!"

★ ★ ★

With the real Bret gone from WWF programming, Austin's stature and airtime only increased. Vince booked him to feud with another up-and-comer, third-generation wrestler Dwayne Johnson, then wrestling under the name Rocky Maivia or, simply, "The Rock." The two traded barbs and blows in November, culminating in a December 7 PPV match that featured Austin driving an "Austin 3:16"–branded pickup truck to the ring and attacking Johnson on the truck's hood.

The crowd loved it.

Vince opened the live December 8 *Raw* by walking alone down the entrance ramp. A thin smile was glued onto his face as the crowd booed him. It was their first chance to truly express their anger over what Vince had done to Bret.

"Ladies and gentlemen, there is no denying the popularity of Stone Cold Steve Austin," Vince said upon arriving in the ring. "However, I think you all will agree that Stone Cold, as of late, has been getting away with murder."

The crowd cheered.

"However, last night, Stone Cold Steve Austin went too far," Vince said. "Because last night, Stone Cold Steve Austin endangered the lives of you WWF fans by driving his pickup truck all the way into the arena, and all the way down to the ring! And then, furthermore, used that pickup truck as a *weapon* against his *opponent!*"

While Vince went on about all the rules Austin was breaking, the crowd started chanting, "*Austin, Austin, Austin!*" When the shattering-glass sound effect that kicks off the wrestler's music hit, they all went nuts.

Austin stomped to the ring. Vince bore an expression that conveyed a perfect balance of bravado and terror. Austin started chewing him out.

"I don't give a rat's ass who you are, personally," Austin said.

"Well, I'll tell you who I am," Vince said. "I'm the proud owner of the World Wrestling Federation. And, furthermore, Mr. Austin, I'm your— I'm your boss."

"That doesn't impress me one bit," Austin said. "And frankly, I don't give a damn."

Vince's voice rose to a shout as he said, "Well then, let me make it a little clearer for you, all right?" Vince said there would be "consequences" for Austin's actions.

"You talk about your consequences, all this and that, like you're some kind of big shot," Austin countered. "Stone Cold's got his own consequences."

Austin looked to the crowd and said, "If anybody wants to see Vince McMahon get his ass whipped, gimme a 'hell yeah!'"

The audience sounded like they were going to blow the roof off when they replied, "*Hell yeah!*"

Vince had booked another feud to begin that night, too. Shawn Michaels was going to take on Bret Hart's little brother Owen.

Owen Hart was a beloved presence in the WWF. He had a reputation for pulling elaborate ribs on his fellow workers, but that just made them love him more. A blond pate of hair rested above his Roman nose, his boyish smile, and his taut, compact body. He was pretty good at promos, but he excelled at the technical ring arts—Stu Hart had taught him well, and had treated him with rare gentleness. He was like the WWF's resident Golden Retriever, always eager to please and befriend.

The younger Hart had been part of the latest incarnation of the Hart Foundation, performing alongside Bret and other veterans of Stu Hart's dungeon.

When Bret got screwed, Owen refused to work the next couple of shows. According to Owen's wife, Martha, Owen asked Vince to be released from his WWF contract.

"Owen felt he simply could no longer work for a man he couldn't trust," Martha later wrote. "However, McMahon refused to let Owen out of his contract."

Owen had little choice but to go with his boss over his brother.

"McMahon's hard stand caused friction between Bret and Owen for a short time," Martha wrote. "Owen assured Bret he fully supported him regardless of whether he worked for McMahon or not and it wasn't long before their relationship resumed the status quo."

On that December 8 edition of *Raw*, at Vince's behest, Shawn Michaels delivered a scatological promo at Owen's expense.

"The Hart family, all of 'em together, are like one, big, huge, nasty, smelly, smokin', stinkin' *turd*," Shawn said. "So, D-Generation X thought we would do the fans of the World Wrestling Federation a favor and flush that big, huge turd called the Hart family down the commode, once and for all!"

The crowd booed—they were on Owen's side.

But they were also rapt.

"It all goes down," Shawn continued. "But one little, small, chunky, little *nugget* always seems to come back up to the surface."

"Owen Hart," he said, "you, my friend, are that small, little, stinky, stanky *nugget* that just refuses to get flushed down the hopper!"

The nickname "nugget" would stick to Owen for the rest of his short life.

On the next week's episode, Vince took to the ring and told Owen to come out and speak with him about the situation with D-X. Owen entered to massive cheers from the sympathetic crowd.

"Who do you think you are?" Vince asked Owen with a sneer.

"Who do I think *I* am?" Owen replied in his slightly raspy tenor, a mix of real and performative fury in his throat. "Who the hell do you think *you* are? You think I owe *you* a goddamn apology? I don't owe you a goddamn thing!"

Vince accused Owen of just wanting to get Shawn's WWF championship, the one title belt that had eluded him in his years with the company.

"How stupid *are* you?" Owen responded. "Is that what you think this is about? You think I give a damn about a worthless title? A piece of leather with tin on it? This is *real life*, Vince. This is *real life*. My life, my reputation, my respect, my dignity!"

The crowd began chanting Owen's first name over and over again.

"Has Owen Hart ever been more popular?" Jim Ross asked.

It was a good point: Owen had never enjoyed pops quite like this.

Vince had successfully closed a loop. He was channeling the public's rage over the Screwjob into enthusiasm for one of the characters on his weekly TV show.

He also wanted to make sure everyone knew that the nature of the show was changing.

Later in the episode, Jim Ross cryptically informed the viewers that they would now hear "some editorial comments from the owner of the World Wrestling Federation."

The camera cut to a gray backdrop. Vince sauntered into the frame from the right side, a look of impish glee in his eyes.

"It has been said that anything can happen here in the World Wrestling Federation," he intoned. "But now, more than ever, truer words have never been spoken. This is a conscious effort on our part to open the creative envelope, so to speak, in order to entertain you in a more *contemporary* manner. . . .

"Even though we call ourselves sports entertainment because of the athleticism involved, the key word in that phrase is *entertainment*," Vince said, adding that they "borrow" from "program niches" such as soap operas, sitcoms, daytime talk shows, and cartoons.

"We in the WWF think that you, the audience, are, quite frankly, tired of having your *intelligence* insulted," he said. "We also think that you're tired of the same old simplistic theory of 'good guys' versus 'bad guys.'"

He then took a dig at Hogan and, in a way, his own past self: "Surely, the era of the superhero who urged you to say your prayers and take your vitamins is definitely *passé*."

That was why, Vince said, they were now bringing "a far more innovative and contemporary creative campaign that is far more invigorating and extemporaneous than ever before."

He warned that *Raw* required "some degree of parental discretion," but that the WWF's other shows "need no such discretion."

"We are responsible television producers who work hard to bring you this outrageous, wacky, *wonderful* world known as the WWF," Vince said.

He thanked the TV networks that run the show "for allowing us to have the creative freedom. . . .

"But most especially," he said, "we would like to thank *you* for watching."

It was around this time that Vince reached out to one of the sporting world's best-known heels: former heavyweight boxing champion "Iron" Mike Tyson.

At the time, Tyson was simultaneously regarded as an all-time great of boxing and reviled as a convicted felon and force of destruction.

In other words, Tyson was the perfect celebrity for Vince's next grand plan.

Tyson had been released early from prison in 1995 after serving three years for the rape of eighteen-year-old Desiree Washington. On June 28, 1997, Tyson fought Evander Holyfield and, infamously, bit off part of Holyfield's right ear. Tyson was fined $3 million and pilloried in the media; the Nevada State Athletic Commission rescinded Tyson's license to box,

effectively blacklisting him from the sport. He followed this up with a devastating motorcycle crash under the influence.

Tyson had grown up as a huge fan of Vince Senior's programming—
he says he used to make WWWF championship belts out of canisters of
Pillsbury dough strung around his waist as a child. He idolized Bruno
Sammartino and Gorilla Monsoon and Billy Graham. As such, he was
delighted to hear from Vince.

In the final days of Vince's eventful year of 1997, the WWF closed a
deal with Tyson for the boxer to appear at *WrestleMania XIV* in March.
He would be paid roughly $3.5 million to do it.

The idea was that Vince, within kayfabe, would be drooling over the
prospect of a big Tyson appearance. He'd act like the deal hadn't been set
yet; then, Austin would get in Tyson's face, making it seem like the whole
thing was in jeopardy. People who liked Tyson would be on the edge of
their seat to see if the boxer would go through with it; people who hated
Tyson would cheer on Austin for confronting him.

Either way, Vince would be the winner.

One problem: wrestling was still regulated by the athletic commission
in Nevada, meaning Vince, if he wanted to stage shows in that state ever
again, had to play nice with the organization's head, a man named Marc
Ratner. Luckily, Ratner was a huge wrestling fan and was eager to take a
call from Vince.

Vince told Ratner he was thinking of having Tyson reenact the Holyfield ear bite.

"No, no," Ratner replied. It was way too soon for any of that.

All right, Vince said; how about having him act as guest referee in the
main event?

"That's probably okay," Ratner said. "I just hope it will be in good taste."

Rumors of the deal made it to the wrestling forums and newsletters,
but Vince mostly kept the arrangement under wraps until the last *Raw* of
the year, aired live on December 29.

"A huge story is developing," Jim Ross told the viewers more than an
hour into the broadcast. "Mike Tyson, the 'Baddest Man on the Planet,'
and the WWF—what's going on? We're gonna tell you right here tonight."

Around fifteen minutes later, the camera once again turned to Ross.
But this time, his headset was looped into the arena's stereo system, so the
crowd could hear him as he spoke.

"I can announce that the World Wrestling Federation, just today, has officially begun negotiations with the Baddest Man on the Planet, 'Iron' Mike Tyson, to participate this year at *WrestleMania XIV*, on March the 29th, in Boston," Ross said.

The crowd started booing the infamous boxer's name. Behind the commentator's table, a man from the audience could be seen giving aggressive thumbs-down motions.

That was all part of the plan.

The main event on *Raw* that night was a match between Shawn Michaels and Owen Hart. At the end, Triple H interfered and started attacking Owen with a metal crutch. Owen crumpled down in faux pain.

"D-Generation X, *assaulting* Owen Hart!" Ross screamed as the broadcast concluded. "Helmsley is *mauling* Owen Hart!"

The last thing you heard before the episode ended was Lawler crying out, "They're gonna *kill* him!"

The media bought the Tyson scheme. There were headlines around the country, all claiming that Tyson was "negotiating" or "in talks" with the WWF, despite the fact that everything was already set. Reporters speculated about whether Tyson would actually wrestle or do something else entirely. Mainstream journalists had no idea how to navigate wrestling in the burgeoning age of the worked shoot.

On January 12, Vince addressed the crowd via a video feed from backstage. Ross asked him if the negotiations had concluded yet. Vince said they were still underway, but that Tyson would be "an invited guest" at that Sunday's Royal Rumble.

The crowd booed. Vince swiveled his head around, as if he were trying to listen harder to the jeers.

"Yeah, they *love* you here, McMahon," Lawler said.

"There's no question about that!" Vince replied.

Throughout January 18's *Royal Rumble '98*, the camera would cut to Tyson in a VIP booth, high above the masses, sitting beside Vince. Vince's twenty-eight-year-old son, Shane, was there, too—a huge boxing fan, Shane had become Vince's liaison to Tyson's entourage. It was the first time Vince had allowed his son to have a significant role on the show.

Tyson clapped enthusiastically for Stone Cold during his match. Then, when Shawn was performing his main-event battle against the Undertaker, Tyson started doing the signature D-X move: a dual-hand chop toward one's groin area while yelling, "*Suck it!*"

It was a perfectly ambiguous gesture. Was Tyson honoring D-X by saluting them with their trademark gesture? Or, conversely, was he insulting D-X by inviting them to fellate him?

"I don't know if Mike likes Shawn Michaels or he doesn't," Jim Ross told the viewer while Tyson was crotch-chopping. "Well, I guess it doesn't really make any difference!"

Tyson appeared repeatedly on the next night's *Raw*. First came brief segments where WWF wrestlers—and their voluptuous female managers—were made to fawn over Tyson backstage. Then Vince went to the ring and introduced "a man who is simply the Baddest Man on the Planet; ladies and gentlemen, *Iron Mike Tyson!*"

Tyson walked down the entrance ramp in a black suit and a partially unbuttoned white dress shirt, accompanied by a mean-looking contingent of bodyguards. The crowd's response was a hearty mix of cheers and boos. That was fine for Vince.

"Mike," Vince said, "it is unquestionably an honor and a privilege to have you standing in a World Wrestling Federation ring."

"Well, it's just a pleasure for me to be here," Tyson said in his whispy tenor, sounding genuinely stoked. "I've been a fan. I've been following since I was eight, nine years old. I'm just happy to be here."

Vince said he had an announcement for everyone: "At WrestleMania, in this very ring, Iron Mike Tyson will—"

But before he could say whether Tyson would wrestle, Steve Austin's entrance music hit and the Texan marched down the ramp to the ring.

"Mr. Austin, why are you here?" Vince asked.

"Because I'm sick and tired of seeing Mike Tyson!" Austin said. "He comes in, he's shakin' everybody's hands, makin' friends with all the WWF Superstars, and it's made me so damn sick I been in the back, throwin' up!"

Tyson moved to shake Austin's hand.

"I ain't gonna shake your damn hand," Austin said, "because I ain't out here to make friends with ya."

He delivered his challenge: "I respect what ya done, Mike, but you're out here callin' yourself the Baddest Man on the Planet," Austin said. "Right now, you got your little beady eyes locked on the eyes of *the World's*

Toughest Son of a Bitch! I can beat you any day of the week, twice on Sunday!"

Tyson just smiled.

"I don't know how good your hearing is," Austin said, "but if you don't understand what I'm saying, I always got a bit of sign language, so here's *to* ya!"

He flipped Tyson two middle fingers.

Tyson shoved him.

Austin shoved back.

They started attacking each other and fell to the canvas, where the entourage and various WWF referees pretended they were trying to pry Austin away from the former heavyweight champ.

"It is *pandemonium* in the WWF!" Ross crowed.

Men pulled Austin out of the ring. Vince leaned over the top rope and screamed at Austin at the top of his lungs: "*You ruined it! You ruined it! You ruined it, dammit, you ruined it!*"

Austin flipped Vince off.

Tyson, Vince, and the bodyguards made their way backstage, where the viewer saw Tyson yelling for Stone Cold's head.

"Bring that coward out!" Tyson shouted.

"*Please,*" Vince said, hands up in a gesture of supplication.

Everyone was yelling. You couldn't make out what anyone was saying for a few seconds.

The last thing viewers saw on the broadcast was Tyson looking directly at the camera, as if he were addressing both Austin and the world, and simply yelling, "*Faggot!*"

For the next two months, Vince did everything he could to hype up Tyson's upcoming appearance at WrestleMania. The main event was going to be Shawn Michaels defending his title against Steve Austin. At the WWF's shows, Austin would cut promos about how much he hated Tyson. Shawn would talk shit about Tyson, too. But Vince continued to back Tyson, announcing the boxer would be a guest referee—"In effect," Vince said at a crowded news conference, "the *enforcer.*" Newspapers ran stories, the footage was gold on TV news, and buzz was overflowing.

For the first time since 1990, the WWF was actually *increasing* its revenue: the year 1997 had seen an abysmal take of roughly $82 million; by the end of 1998, it would reach $126 million.

Although WCW was still number one in the ratings, the WWF was catching up.

Vince's product was, at long last and at considerable moral expense, cool again.

In late February, Vince did his first extended interview with a real journalist since the Montreal Screwjob. It happened on Canada's *Off the Record with Michael Landsberg*.

"After fourteen years of service, less than a year after signing him to a twenty-year deal, you asked [Bret] to leave," Landsberg said. "Why?"

"A lot of reasons, actually," Vince replied. "Bret was breaking down, physically. Bret was getting to be a little bit of a pain in the ass, in terms of his attitude. He was disruptive in the locker room, to a certain extent. He wanted things his way."

More importantly, Vince said, Bret represented sports entertainment's past, and the past had to be left behind.

"We have to move on and we have to progress," Vince said. "We can't hold back. We can't keep things the way that they used to be for anybody."

Landsberg pressed him: Didn't Bret's contract allow the wrestler to have creative control over his exit? Hadn't Vince violated that clause?

"Umm . . ." Vince said before concluding, "No. I had asked Bret for any number of things, which he had refused."

He continued: "The worst thing that could have happened is Bret walking off before the event took place. Now, we'd have fans all over the world waiting to see this match and it wouldn't have happened. I didn't wanna take that risk."

Landsberg said Bret had told him he thought the match would end in a disqualification. "Is he lying when he says that?" the host asked.

"No, he's not lying about that," Vince said. "He thought, for sure, that it was gonna be a disqualification."

"So, when he says that you lied to him as he was heading into the ring . . ."

"He's right," Vince said.

Landsberg pointed out all the depravity that Vince was showing on his programming. "Is there anything that's out of bounds for you guys right now?" he asked.

"Well, sure," Vince said. "I mean, there are no guns or no knives. There are no rapes, there are no robberies." (In fact, the WWF had already depicted or would soon depict many of the above in its programming.)

Vince continued: "I think that we have to evolve. I think that's been one of the problems of two guys in their underwear wrestling around on a mat and a twenty-five-foot ring: it's awfully boring.

"So, when we hear some people squawking and whatever," Vince continued, "I think that's a good sign, because it says that we are going up to a certain edge, creatively."

In his final question, Landsberg said his—that is, Landsberg's—young children told him they had trouble distinguishing between fact and fiction in the contemporary WWF.

"Jeez, maybe you should talk with your kids," Vince said. "Maybe that aspect of reality—the fact that our cartoon characters are real people— maybe there becomes more confusion that way."

Vince then contradicted his statement of a few moments earlier: "I don't think there's any subject matter, by the way, that's off-bounds, that's off-limits," he said. "Because I think that people need to *know* there's racism in this world. There *are* some horrible males who beat up females. And why shouldn't *that* subject matter be broached?"

WrestleMania XIV was advertised as "The First X-Rated WrestleMania."

WrestleMania I had been a coming-out party for the version of the WWF that aspired to wholesome American greatness. *WrestleMania XIV* would do the same for Vince's unsettlingly irreverent new iteration.

Austin was his new Hogan, Shawn his new Piper, and Tyson acted as a sinister inversion of Mr. T.

In lieu of Liberace, Vince got Gennifer Flowers, who was then all over the tabloids with her claims of having had an affair with Bill Clinton, to make a cameo.

There was no Muhammad Ali this time, but disgraced baseball player Pete Rose was in attendance.

Nor was Gene Okerlund there to sing the "The Star-Spangled Banner"— but Vince had a group billed as "The D-Generation X Band" perform a thrashing, Rage Against the Machine–inspired medley of the national anthem and "America the Beautiful."

As the band concluded and the audience struggled to regain their sense of hearing, Jim Ross crowed, "Only in the USA, in the WWF, can there be this kind of *freedom of expression!*"

The screen then cut to an opening montage, first featuring clips of classic wrestlers of the past, then clips of the defiant new figures.

"Tonight," read the voice-over, "through sacrifice and pain, through breathtaking displays of athleticism that defy mortal boundaries, these men that *shun* tradition are destined to become *part* of it. . . .

"It's WrestleMania, the grandest of spectacles, the showcase of the immortals, a time to revel in the occasion," the voice-over concluded. "And somewhere, beyond the spotlights, the father of the World Wrestling Federation will revel in it, too."

That father's sons—Austin, Shawn, Rock, Undertaker, Triple H, Mick Foley, Owen Hart—were men who knew where their bread was buttered. They didn't put up fights the way Hogan, Warrior, or even Bret had.

The only women on the card that night were Sable, who had virtually no wrestling experience, and her foe, a brilliant and fully trained heel by the name of Luna Vachon (real first name Gertrude). Their rivalry had been based on the contrast between the statuesque Sable's conventional, platinum-blond good looks and the snarling Luna's side-shaven, horror-movie-inspired visage, which the commentators that night would describe as repulsive and unwomanly. They weren't even in a one-on-one match that night; it was a mixed-gender tag-team match, with their male partners doing most of the work.

The main event featured a kayfabe double-cross: Tyson started the match by crotch-chopping in the D-X mode. But, by the end, he'd shocked the crowd by siding with Austin and counting out Stone Cold's victory over the Heartbreak Kid, *one-two-three.*

"The Austin era has begun!" Jim Ross yelled.

Austin was now, for the first time, the WWF champion. He and Tyson walked up the ramp together, arms extended above their heads in triumph.

"I got a lot of criticism for appearing at WrestleMania," Tyson later wrote, "but it was really one of the highlights of my life."

Around this time, Vince started talking about himself.

He'd never been press-shy. But he'd rarely talked to reporters about his personal life or history. That changed in the early Attitude Era.

Throughout much of 1998, Nancy Jo Sales, a reporter from *New York* magazine, reported out a cover story on Vince and the WWF. She sat down with him at his capacious office in Stamford, where he munched on a PowerBar and told her about his youth.

"It's ironic that I now play an authority figure, although it's easy for me to," Vince told Sales. "I know all the right buttons to push because I've been there, on the flip side of it."

"Then," Sales wrote, "he started talking about his dad."

He told her about how he hadn't met his father until he was twelve: "It was one of those things," he said. "It just didn't happen for us."

He spoke of his early days in North Carolina—a first for him. He said he grew up rough, but made sure to add, "There are just no excuses for anything. I read about some guy who has excuses for his behavior because he comes from a broken home, or he was beaten, or was sexually abused, or got into the wrong crowd, or whatever the case may be—all of which have occurred in my lifetime—but there are no excuses."

Such admissions were unheard-of in all previous eras of Vince's life.

Not everyone found them convincing.

Around this same time, director Barry Blaustein was working on a documentary about the American wrestling industry called *Beyond the Mat*. Vince granted him unprecedented access to the inner workings of the company—and to Vince himself. They sat for a series of interviews. Vince told Blaustein stories similar to those he'd told Sales: his childhood, his hatred of his abusive stepfather, his longing for the love of his biological father. He teared up as he told Blaustein about being at his father's deathbed and finally hearing him say "I love you."

Blaustein was taken aback. The filmmaker turned to his cameraman and whispered, "I think this is an act. I think this is something he practiced on."

Blaustein had been in contact with Vince since 1995, and, after Vince debuted as a main character, Blaustein noticed changes in the man, changes that he'd seen in others who practice kayfabe.

"What happens to a lot of these guys is, they become their character," Blaustein tells me. "I saw him become Mr. McMahon."

To wit: There's a memorable scene that made it to the final film, in which Vince met with a new recruit named Darren Drozdov. The wrestler had an uncanny ability: he could vomit on command. Vince thought that was terrific.

While the cameras rolled, Drozdov sat across from Vince's desk and listened as Vince told him he wanted to build a character around the young man's unique talent. They'd call him "Puke."

"I've got one thing I want you to do for me, okay?" he said to Drozdov. He grabbed a small garbage bin from behind him and put it on the desk.

"Can you do *that*, huh?" Vince said. "You gonna get sick?"

Drozdov started heaving.

Vince launched into a parodic version of the voice he had once used as a commentator and announcer: "Oh my god, he's gonna . . . he's gonna . . . *he's gonna* . . . he's gonna . . . *heeeee's* gonna *puke! He's gonna puke! He's gonna puke! He's gonna pu—he's gonna puke!*"

Ultimately, Drozdov was only able to upchuck a little dribble, that time.

Vince cracked up into that *yuk-yuk* laugh Bret Hart used to hear.

"It was bizarre, because he was obviously performing for the camera," Blaustein says. "It had been an accelerated Vince."

But, Blaustein says, even when Vince is performing, "It's him. He's become him. He's become Mr. McMahon."

I ask what he means by that.

"All-powerful," Blaustein says. "Gets what he wants. What's good for him; that's all that matters."

With Sales, the *New York* magazine reporter, Vince made a concerted effort to distance himself from his character. It didn't quite work.

"This character that is on television . . . Oh, my God, some of the things I have said and have done," he said. "He's the most reprehensible individual on the planet. He's a horrible human being . . . uncaring, a powermonger, manipulative, *very* manipulative, always trying to get what I want and being very clever about it. Art imitating life and vice versa."

As Sales put it, "Vince's juggling of pronouns—*he* and *I*—seemed interesting."

Even as he was breaking his silence about his personal history, Vince was rewriting his future. He decided to put himself into actual wrestling matches—not just as a character, but as a combatant.

It started slow. On April 13, Vince took to the ring while Austin was there and, after some goading from Austin, agreed to wrestle for the WWF championship in the night's main event. Viewership skyrocketed as wrestling fans tuned in to find out whether Vince was so crazy that he'd actually risk grievous injury in the ring. Was this wealthy CEO going to put his mortal body on the line, just to get a pop?

"Who's gonna run this company if, if . . . ?" Jim Ross wondered aloud on the broadcast, acting like he didn't even want to say what could happen. "I just bought a house! I got a mortgage to pay off!"

Near the end of the episode, the camera followed Vince as he exited his dressing room and walked toward the arena-floor entrance. He was clad in what would become his wrestling uniform: a low-cut black tank top and black sweats.

It must have been a rush for him to finally show off his body.

He'd been working out mercilessly since Jerry Graham gave him his first weights in 1959, and he'd been on TV since the early 1970s, always looking strangely bulky in his suits. Writers who had described him as a broadcaster—or a defendant—would often point out his eerie size, so incongruous with his professional role. Now, it finally made sense to reveal what he'd made of himself.

"My Gosh, he's ripped; look at him!" Jerry Lawler told the viewers while Vince was shown getting ready backstage. Lawler sounded genuinely shocked at what he was seeing: "God, he looks *huge!*"

Vince walked through the entrance to the arena floor. His arms swung at his sides, his hands balled into fists. He had a look of ostentatiously grim determination on his fifty-two-year-old face. He strutted down the ramp, his weight shifting from side to side with every step, like a child's pantomime of a circus muscleman. Or like Baby Huey.

The crowd screamed out derision. In fact, it was on that night that the crowd in Philadelphia's CoreStates Center organically generated a chant that has been rained upon Vince ever since: "*Asshole, asshole, asshole . . .*"

He and Austin didn't actually do much in the ring; Vince mostly dodged Austin, and took a few easy bumps before Mick Foley, per the plan, entered the fray and broke up the match. Even without flashy moves, Vince had the audience riveted.

That night, for the first time since 1996, the WWF beat WCW in Monday-night ratings.

★ ★ ★

On the June 1 *Raw*, as Vince walked down the entrance ramp, the ring announcer referred to the boss by a new name: not as "Vince McMahon," but as "Mr. McMahon."

So did the commentators.

It was all they called him, in fact.

Throughout the broadcast, Jim Ross kept doing a bit where he implied that this name change was imposed by Vince, the character. Ross's character found that distasteful, but submitted himself to it. At one point, he started to say, "Vince," then cut himself off and dramatically said, "Or *Mr. McMahon*." Later, Ross said, "McMahon is making Austin defend the WWF title tonight" and Lawler cut him off to say, "That's *Mr.* McMahon to you!"

Of course, it actually *was* a name change imposed by Vince. Indeed, not too long in the future, it would be official policy for no one other than Austin or other members of the McMahon family to refer to Vince as "Vince McMahon" on TV. "Mr. McMahon" would come to be the trademarked name of the character, to distinguish him from the "real" Vince.

Once again, the man raised as Vinnie Lupton took on a new alias. This version of him, the one that survives in countless thousands of hours of television footage, had been drained of everything except an honorific of male authority and the name of the man who abandoned him.

Vince set out to replicate his success, booking himself in mini-matches throughout the rest of 1998. Through contrived circumstances, Mr. McMahon would wind up as Austin's tag-team partner, or as the guest referee in one of Austin's matches, or some other excuse for Austin to whale on him.

These Mr. McMahon story lines were deliberately repetitive, like a Punch and Judy show. Over and over again, the character would attempt to screw wrestlers—usually, but not always, Steve Austin—through sheer corporate power, then get a humiliating comeuppance before starting it all over again.

A year had passed since the Montreal Screwjob. That event had been, for him, a massive success. So he commemorated it by doing it again, this time in kayfabe.

In the main-event match at November 15's *Survivor Series '98*, the Rock—who had been established as Vince's loyal champion—locked Mick Foley in the Sharpshooter.

Right then, Mr. McMahon ordered the referee to ring the bell and declare Foley the loser, despite the fact that Foley hadn't submitted.

The crowd jeered.

The boss ran to the ring to deliver a promo.

"I know, I know," Mr. McMahon told the hollering crowd. "You're saying, 'I can't believe my eyes! I don't know what's going on!'"

His voice became sharper. "You know what? *Seeing is believing*," he said. "And you can believe this: you can believe that Vince McMahon didn't screw the people tonight."

He paused.

His voice became a hideous growl as he said, "*The people screwed the people.*"

Vince's capacity for self-humiliation was instrumental in making all this work. Austin always had to be the hero and Mr. McMahon the villain, and wrestling likes to degrade its villains. Austin would do things like spray Mr. McMahon down with a beer-spewing firehose, or pour cement into Mr. McMahon's prized convertible, or lunge at him from atop a still-humming Zamboni.

In one episode of *Raw*, after an attack by two wrestlers, Mr. McMahon was ostensibly injured so badly that he had to be taken to a hospital. The cameras depicted the boss in a hospital bed, attended to by a nurse. A doctor walked in and, wouldn't you know it, it turned out to be Steve Austin in disguise. Austin beat him, slamming an (empty) bedpan on Mr. McMahon's head. Finally, Austin bent McMahon over the bed and, as the heel supreme screamed in agony, Austin pretended to anally rape the owner of the company with an enema tube.

On the very day that the *New York* cover story was published, Vince did a sketch on *Raw* where Austin held him at gunpoint in the ring.

Mr. McMahon, kneeling in submission, demonstrated his theatrical fear by making himself cry.

"You think you're so damn cool," Austin said. "Look atcha now: you're pathetic, on your knees, crying in front of the world. You make me *sick*, Vince."

Mr. McMahon held his hands together and started mumbling in prayer.

"Now, what I want you to do is look up at that screen," Austin said.

The Titantron started to broadcast a live feed of Mr. McMahon's own face.

Mr. McMahon looked up. He saw what the viewers saw: his own tear-stained visage. He looked like a kabuki mask of weeping terror.

"Look up at the screen, Vince," Austin said. "Because your eyes are fixin' to pop out the front of your head."

Mr. McMahon screamed.

"If you want Vince's eyes to pop out the front of his head, gimme a hell yeah!" Austin said to the crowd.

"*Hell yeah!*" they cried, out for blood.

Austin took out a gun. He aimed it at Mr. McMahon's temple.

A dark stain appeared on Mr. McMahon's pant leg.

Austin pulled the trigger.

All that emerged from the barrel was a flag that read "BANG 3:16" in big letters.

"I think we got another T-shirt on the way," Austin said, lifting Mr. McMahon up and revealing his soiled dress pants. "And I think that T-shirt might just say, 'McMahon 3:16 Says I Just Pissed My Pants.'"

Just for good measure, Austin kicked Mr. McMahon in the gut and did the Stunner on him.

Vince had become the gravitational center of his own show. Everything revolved around Mr. McMahon. Of course, in reality, the company had revolved around one Mr. McMahon or another for nearly fifty years. It's just that now, one of them was being more open about it.

Or was he?

The magic of wrestling in the days of old kayfabe used to be that there was a sacred lie, and beneath that, there was the truth. The truth was never seen in the ring, but, on some level, it comforted wrestlers and fans to imagine that truth existed as a separate entity from their collective joyful fantasy.

However, by the dawn of 1999, wrestlers and audience alike lived in a world where the things they thought of as truth—the wrestlers' private lives, their wounds and tragedies—were fair game as fodder for the fantasy.

Vince's Punch and Judy show continued. In the titular battle royal at *Royal Rumble '99*, held in January, Mr. McMahon cheated his way to victory (he had his minions ambush Austin in a women's restroom) and was declared the winner of the Rumble. Although he didn't do any complicated wrestling maneuvers, he did take a steel chair to the head, which split open his forehead and necessitated stitches.

Then, on a February 14 PPV called *St. Valentine's Day Massacre*, the main event was a cage match between Austin and Mr. McMahon, with twenty-foot-high steel girders erected around the ring.

As Vince walked down the ramp, his new theme music played—an original song composed by an immensely talented in-house songwriter named Jim Johnston.

When Vince had tasked Johnston with coming up with the track, it was an unwelcome assignment. "I had been really upset with him about something at work," Johnston later recalled. "I found myself thinking: *You've got no chance against this guy!* He's got the power, the money, and, in terms of pro wrestling, he was pretty much the only game in town."

Johnston had been working on a menacing, downtempo funk-rock fusion track for a separate project, and it drifted back into his mind.

"I found myself singing, '*No chance, no chance*' over that groove," he recalled.

Thus, the lyrics that vocalist Chris Warren spat out in the recorded version, seemingly addressed to anyone who thought they could take Vince down—wrestlers, promoters, even the government:

No chance, that's what ya got
Up against a machine too strong
Pretty politicians buying souls for us are puppets
We'll find their place in line

The song was surprisingly slow, for a wrestling entrance theme. It didn't feel like the kind of track you'd listen to at the gym to get pumped up. It sounded more like the intimidations of an assassin, whispered into the ear of someone he's about to execute:

But tie a string around your finger now, boy
'Cause it's, it's just a matter of time
'Cause you've got no chance
No chance in hell

Vince didn't do much actual wrestling this time, either. He'd never mastered the fine points of the ring arts. But Mr. McMahon sure knew how to take a beating. Austin faux-pummeled him into oblivion inside the ring and up against the cage.

At one point, both combatants were climbing to the top of an outside wall of the cage, dangerously high above the commentators' area. They grabbed and punched at each other, slick with sweat. Finally, Austin pretended to slam Mr. McMahon's head into the cage, and Vince, telegraphing the impact of the faux blow, threw himself backward.

Per the plan, he fell.

He'd intended to tumble about twenty feet, directly onto the table that the Spanish-language announcers use during PPVs. The table was supposed to helpfully collapse and provide him with a cushion. Instead, he landed exactly on the table's hard outer edge, which didn't collapse quickly enough—that *hadn't* been part of the plan.

The audience saw the owner of a multimillion-dollar company, one of the longest-running personalities on television, crash spine-first into agony.

"*No! No! Mr. McMahon!*" shouted commentator Michael Cole. "*He may be dead!*"

Paramedics rushed to Vince's side and put him on a stretcher. They attached a neck brace, not unlike the one he'd worn at his steroid trial a few years prior. He squinted and left his mouth gaping.

"I don't think he knows where he is!" Cole said.

Vince definitely knew where he was. But he was in very real pain.

The announcer tried to say the match was over, but Austin took the mic. "That's bullshit," Austin said. "Is the son of a bitch still breathing?"

Vince could have improvised a way to avoid getting up again. He had badly wounded his tailbone, after all.

But no—he allowed himself to be grabbed from the stretcher and brought back to the ring (through the cage's door, this time).

While Stone Cold pummeled him, Vince covertly bladed his own forehead, causing blood to stream down his face.

"*The owner of this company is busted open!*" Jerry Lawler howled to the viewers.

After a substantial beatdown, Austin left Mr. McMahon lying prone in the ring and turned to leave the cage.

But Mr. McMahon rose to his knees.

As his own bitter plasma flooded into his wide-open mouth and squinted eyelids, Vince heaved his chest in a desperate attempt for breath. He tilted his torso slightly to the right. He bent his arms upward at the elbows. His hands were outstretched.

Without opening his eyes, Mr. McMahon pulled back all his fingers, save the middle ones.

"*Pure hatred*," Cole yelled, "*driving Mr. McMahon!*"

SUCK IT, FINALE

(1999)

Vince Senior had never wanted Vince in the Business. As of early 1999, Vince was of the opposite opinion when it came to his own children.

Shane was twenty-nine now; Stephanie was twenty-two. In turn, each had graduated from Boston University. Each had worked for their father during and after college. They have spoken of their affection for each other.

"I'm probably closer to Shane than anyone else," Stephanie once told a reporter. "My parents weren't around until later at night, so for the most part, Shane raised me. Shane and I communicated in a much more physical fashion. Suplexes and bodyslams were an everyday occurrence—not to forget my favorite, submission holds."

But if they were close as children, by the time they were adults, their personalities clashed.

"There'd be this antipathy," Brian Solomon, a former WWF/E employee and current wrestling historian who spent a lot of time around the McMahons at work, tells me. "Shane is a warmer guy. He's not gonna join MENSA anytime soon, but he's a warm, more salt-of-the-earth kind of guy. He's pushed to be more like his dad, but that's not his nature, in my experience."

As for Stephanie? "She is her dad's daughter," says Solomon. "She has that kind of coldness that he has, that you kind of need to have to succeed in the Business. She has that kind of quality. I've been alone with her, too, and talking to her, and getting that same sense I'd get around [Vince]."

The father and daughter had developed a closeness. "Stephanie always was the apple of his eye—the closest thing you would ever see to a soft spot would be her," Solomon says. "He will kiss her on the lips, and that sometimes weirds people out a little bit.

"The relationship with Shane is much, much more contentious," Solomon continues. "They really seemed to try to project this image of a lot more closeness than there really is."

But even if Shane and Vince weren't as close as subsequent kayfabe events would imply, the younger man fit perfectly into the story that Vince was telling on his programming.

A few months after Shane made his silent appearances on camera alongside Mike Tyson, Vince had begun to integrate Shane into the fiction of the WWF.

Shane had leapt into the fray in his dad's old position. Back on August 2, 1998, viewers had seen Mr. McMahon introduce a new ringside commentator: Shane Brandon McMahon.

But unlike Vince, Shane wouldn't be *just* an announcer. Everyone knew Mr. McMahon was his dad, and his real role was that of the smarmy, entitled, incompetent boss's son—the brash boy who could destroy the company if it fell into his hands. The character bore more than a little resemblance to the upstart Vince had once been.

Shane had been ostentatiously terrible on the mic when he'd debuted—screaming "*Wow!*" "*Oh yeah!*" and "*Did you see that?*" at the top of his lungs rather than identifying or describing anything that was happening in the ring. He'd sat at the announcer's table flanked by two busty models, grabbing at them throughout the episode.

Outside the ring, the WWF announced that Shane would be the director of "New Media" for the company. And in kayfabe, he was set up as coleader, along with his father, of a stable of wrestlers loyal to Mr. McMahon, known as the Corporation.

The other wrestlers were supposed to either hate or fear the boy who would be king.

On February 15, a day after his dad's cage match with Austin, Shane, too, climbed into the ring. He didn't have any more skills than his father, and hardly did any wrestling, but the story line had him cheat his way to winning the fourth-tier European Championship belt.

The gimmick worked. Fans found Shane's snotty promos irritating and did the "*asshole, asshole*" chant at him even harder than they did at Vince.

At the same time, Mr. McMahon's story line was taking a turn. That same *Raw* featured a sequence in which a penitent Mr. McMahon, limping, clad in a neck brace and bloodstained bandage, told Austin, "I stand before you tonight a broken man. I stand before you tonight a *humble* man. Austin . . ."

The crowd started chanting, "*Asshole, asshole . . .*"

Mr. McMahon turned to them, suddenly rageful, and said, "What do you want, *blood?*"

He wanted to bury the hatchet, he told the crowd. He just wanted Austin to apologize for hurting him.

"I'm sorry . . ." Austin replied with a dramatic pause, ". . . that I didn't beat your ass worse than I beat it!" Stone Cold turned to the crowd: "And if ya think Vince McMahon is *still* an asshole, gimme a hell yeah!" They howled their assent.

But this was a new era—an era in which an asshole could still be a hero. Austin was the prime example. Perhaps Mr. McMahon could be a hero, too.

Vince and his bookers decided that they wanted to put Mr. McMahon over as a babyface by pitting him against a villain even more dastardly and powerful than himself. They would, in fact, call this mysterious entity the Greater Power. The Greater Power would threaten Mr. McMahon, drumming up sympathy for him after his chastening loss to Austin. And this story line would also utilize the other of Vince's adult children—his daughter, Stephanie.

To act as the herald for the unseen Greater Power in the ring, they chose one of the most reliable and beloved workers on the roster, the Undertaker, Mark Calaway.

The Undertaker's gimmick was malleable: he could be a zombie, a demon, an outlaw biker, an actual undertaker, an honorable lone warrior, or, as he had been set up recently, an inhuman, death-metal personification of entropy and chaos.

Vince had a lot of affection for Calaway, and the affection was based on loyalty. While so many WWF wrestlers flew the coop for WCW in previous years, Undertaker—or "Taker," as fans call him—had stuck around. Nobody had a bad word to say about Calaway. He's long been referred to as "the locker-room leader."

Standing in the ring surrounded by his cult of wrestlers, the Ministry of Darkness, Taker addressed Mr. McMahon via the camera—staring through and past the viewer at his target.

"I own the key to your heart and your soul," Taker intoned cryptically. "While you were preoccupied with your petty obsessions, I have amassed an army. An army that will destroy you *and* your Corporation."

He dropped another hint: "Each soul that we take, we take in the name of a far *Greater Power* than even myself. And, in that power's name, in its grandest vision, in its grandest dream, and in my Ministry's destiny, *I will own the World Wrestling Federation.*"

The plan was to spend the next few weeks building up suspense about who the Greater Power really was. One problem: Vince and his bookers hadn't decided who it would be. Bruce Prichard and Vince Russo have both recalled that there was absolutely no plan for the resolution of the inadvertently four-month-long Greater Power angle as of its launch on that February 15, 1999, *Raw*.

They went down a long list of potential names: Mick Foley? A WCW hire? Shane? No one felt right.

They'd work on it.

By now, there could be fifteen-minute-long stretches of any given *Raw* where no wrestling whatsoever occurred, only promos and skits. What's more, with every passing week in the late winter and spring of 1999, those storytelling segments were increasingly taken up by operatic renditions of the boss's psychosexual nightmares.

At the end of the next week's *Raw*, Mr. McMahon did guest commentary during an "Inferno Match" between Undertaker and his kayfabe brother, Kane. The wildly unsafe gimmick of the match was that the ring was surrounded by open flames; the loser would be whoever had a body part catch fire first.

Mr. McMahon was depicted as excited about the prospect of his wrestlers—the villainous Taker, with his cryptic threats, in particular—being injured by the fire: "We're talking *careers* on the line," Mr. McMahon crowed, "and that's as it *should* be!"

Late in the match, Taker's manager, Paul Bearer (Bill Moody), brought a black box to Mr. McMahon. The owner opened it and saw a worn-out teddy bear inside. He turned his gaze back up; it looked as though all the blood had been drained from his body. He stood and wandered around at ringside, no longer paying attention to the match that had so thrilled him.

Eventually, Taker grabbed the bear and lit it on fire, causing Mr. McMahon to drop to his knees and scream out, "*No! No!*" while his face twisted in anguish.

This confusing and sinister pantomime would be explained in the weeks to come: it was Stephanie's childhood teddy bear. This was foreshadowing for Stephanie's debut as a plot device in her father's story.

She was cast in the role of the victim.

★ ★ ★

Stephanie was, at the time, not even a year out of college. In her junior year, her dad had asked her if she wanted to spend her life in the Business. "That struck me as being so odd, because I thought he knew," she would later say. "How could he not? But he didn't know until he asked me."

She said yes, that was what she wanted.

Stephanie interned at various departments of the WWF, including acting as an assistant to both Linda and Vince, at different times. "My internship with my father was the most challenging," she said. "Besides trying to learn everything at once and keeping a notepad on me at all times to jot down any fleeting thought that he said, I was even living with him at home, so I literally kept his schedule. The man does not sleep much."

She'd made a seconds-long cameo as a random WWF employee in 1998, right after she graduated. She was now working as an intern for her mother. According to Vince Russo, he came to Vince with an idea in early 1999: Why not include Stephanie in a more substantial way? A kidnapping would be the perfect way to drum up sympathy for the newly heroic Mr. McMahon.

Stephanie has never commented publicly on what it was like for her father to approach her and ask if she'd be willing to do the story line. It would be provocative, one of the most unsettling things that the WWF had ever aired. But Stephanie likes provocative.

"I think that fan participation is one of the greatest things about our show," she would later say. "To be able to elicit a reaction from all those people is pretty cool, no matter what they're calling me."

The March 29, 1999, episode of *Raw* was where Stephanie made her full-fledged debut. *WrestleMania XV* had aired the previous night— a relatively unremarkable installment, with the exception of one astounding moment in which the Undertaker and his Ministry appeared to tie a noose around a wrestler named the Big Boss Man (Ray Traylor Jr.) and hang him until he died. (He was, in reality, fine.) Such ideas, channeled through Taker, were giving the audience a taste of the darker portions of Vince's mind.

Along those lines, about twenty minutes into *Raw*, Taker and the Ministry ambushed Sable in the ring. Taker grabbed Sable by the throat and shoved her to her knees in front of him. He spoke into a microphone held by a lackey. "McMahon, I've got your precious little meal ticket," he said. "I want you to come out here right now before I snap her head right off her shoulders. And you *better* come *alone*."

The camera cut to a backstage area, where Mr. McMahon was sitting with Shane and Stephanie. The young woman was clad conservatively, almost girlishly, in a blue cardigan and dark slacks. No reason was given for Stephanie's unprecedented presence. When Mr. McMahon heard Taker's challenge, he resolved to go out there and save Sable, but told Shane to "stay with Stephanie and keep an eye on her. There's security out here, you'll be safe. Just stay *right here*."

Mr. McMahon entered the arena hall and began to berate Taker. Then he paused. His face slowly reshaped itself from fury to panic. "Stephanie!" he shouted, and ran backstage. Taker wore a little smile.

The boss reached the room he'd been in, only to find his daughter gone. "*Where is she?*" he kept shouting.

Shane kept responding, "I don't know! *I don't know!*"

"You saw what he did to Boss Man!" Mr. McMahon barked. "It was a damn *demonstration* last night! Who knows what he's gonna do to her?"

"I'm sorry, Dad; I'm sorry!" Shane whined.

Mr. McMahon began to cry.

A few minutes later, in another backstage segment, Mr. McMahon received a phone call.

"Vince, it *is* true, isn't it?" came the voice on the other end—it was Taker. "She really *is* sugar and spice and everything nice." Taker laughed. Mr. McMahon threw the phone to the ground.

The story line had wrestler Ken Shamrock (Ken Kilpatrick) volunteer to find Stephanie. Shamrock grabbed a member of the Ministry who was having a match and put him in a submission hold until he told Shamrock that Stephanie was in the basement of the arena.

The cameras followed Shamrock as he ran there and found a weeping Stephanie, kneeling amidst the pipes and concrete. Mascara was running out of her eyes. Apparently, Taker hadn't physically harmed her; this was just a warning.

Stephanie was returned to Mr. McMahon. The final backstage segment began with the young woman resting her head on her father's chest while he stroked her hair and kissed her head.

It would turn out to be far from the last time WWF viewers saw Stephanie McMahon violated.

★ ★ ★

For years, the Undertaker had worn a black trench coat during his walks to the ring. That article of clothing abruptly became a problem on April 20, 1999, when two high school students who had sometimes identified themselves as the "Trench Coat Mafia" walked into Columbine High School and murdered twelve students and a teacher.

The news media started to cast blame on violent pop culture. *USA Today* ran a story in which they juxtaposed Taker's trench coat with those of the killers. As a result, Taker didn't wear the coat at April 25's *Backlash '99* PPV. He did, however, kidnap Stephanie once again at the very end of the show.

The first thing viewers saw when they tuned into *Raw* on April 26 was a special message, in white font on black backdrop, written in response to Columbine.

"The WWF joins parents, teachers, and community leaders in recognizing the importance of banding together to meet the needs of troubled teens," it read in part. "Violence is never an answer."

The live program began. What viewers witnessed that night is almost never discussed by WWE, Undertaker, or anyone in the McMahon family.

Mr. McMahon was frantic all night over his missing daughter, wandering around the building trying to get answers. At one point, he got a call from Taker.

"If you so much as harm a hair on her head, so help me . . ." Mr. McMahon told him over the phone.

"Is that any way to talk to your daughter's *soul mate?*" Taker asked.

Mr. McMahon even went so far as to beg Austin for help. Austin refused. A terrified Mr. McMahon resolved to save Stephanie himself.

As if that weren't enough Freudian drama, the episode also featured an unrelated, pretaped skit introducing a new character, Beaver Cleavage.

Shown in black-and-white, with a saccharine melody playing, the skit was a crude parody of *Leave It to Beaver*, the classic midcentury television series about a rambunctious boy and his loving parents.

The WWF's Beaver was played by grown-up wrestler Charles Warrington, and he was seen here in the kind of clothing ensemble that boys were expected to wear in Vinnie Lupton's day: socks up to his calves, a nice jacket, a cute tie, a white button-down shirt. He sits at a kitchen table and pours himself a bowl of shredded wheat. He spits it out.

"This cereal *sucks!*" Beaver yells. "I can't eat this! It's *dry! Mom!*"

In walks his mother, Mrs. Cleavage (Marianna Komlos), a poised and busty blonde with a revealing blouse and a pearl necklace. She holds a tray with a giant carafe of milk.

"Is this what mother's little boy is looking for?" she asks. "Does mother's little hairy Beaver want some of *mother's* milk?"

Beaver looks to the camera and wordlessly grins at his good fortune, pumping his eyebrows up and down suggestively. End of skit.

Right after that, there was a match between wrestlers Jeff Jarrett and The Godfather (Charles Wright). The Godfather's gimmick was that he was a pimp. A Black man, he would walk the entrance ramp with a procession of female models, hired in whatever city the WWF was visiting that night; they were his "Ho Train." His slogan, which he'd prompt the eager audience to shout along with him, was *"Pimpin' ain't easy!"*

The Godfather was criticized by culture columnists as an over-the-top racist caricature even at the time, but the majority-white wrestling audience loved him anyway.

Jeff Jarrett, a gifted young wrestler, was in a team with Owen Hart at the time, and their manager was a woman named Debra Marshall, who was always referred to simply as "Debra." When she showed up in her short skirt, heels, and bra-revealing blazer, the crowd would often perk up and scream, *"We want puppies! We want puppies!"*—"puppies" being the term that Jerry Lawler used to describe breasts while verbally objectifying women for the viewer.

The stakes of the match: if Jarrett lost, Debra would have to join the Ho Train. Jarrett did lose, but, just as Debra was starting to get into the idea of doing whatever it is that these women do all day, Owen ran in and pulled her away.

The crowd booed him for robbing them of the puppies.

Over at the other end of the proverbial Madonna-whore spectrum that night was Stephanie, still in dire sexual peril at the hands of the Undertaker.

In the show's final ten minutes, the lights went down and ominous music played as a group of men carried a roughly eight-foot-tall crucifix—modified to look like the Undertaker's logo, but still a crucifix—down the ramp. The twenty-two-year-old daughter of the boss was tied to it at her hands and feet. She was wearing an all-black wedding dress and screaming in terror.

"Is Stephanie McMahon going to be *sacrificed* here?" Jim Ross asked aloud.

Jim Cornette was also on commentary that night and said, "JR, you know the sayin': 'The sins of the father.' But in this case, has even *Vince McMahon* ever, *ever* committed a sin that would justify this happening to an innocent young girl? And there's nobody to do anything about it!"

The rest of the Ministry of Darkness entered the ring to surround Stephanie as she wept and screamed, "*No! No! No!*"

"This is so sad," Ross said. "And so unnecessary."

"Before this ceremony begins," Undertaker said, "I must address the McMahon family: *I am not to blame for what is about to happen here.* Vince, this rests upon *your* shoulders."

The crowd was chanting for their superhero to end this spectacle— "*Austin, Austin, Austin . . .*"—but it just kept going. The Ministry enacted a Satanic wedding ceremony, with Paul Bearer as the officiant: "Will you, Stephanie Marie McMahon, accept the purity of evil and take the Lord of Darkness as your master and your spouse?" Bearer asked.

"*No! No!*" Stephanie screamed, her voice now hoarse.

Ken Shamrock ran in to save her, but was quickly dispatched.

Bearer turned to Taker: Would he "accept Stephanie Marie McMahon— her body, her mind, her soul, and even her *breath*—unto yourself and allow her to bear your offspring?"

"*I do,*" he replied.

Another wrestler ran in and was thrown out, further dispiriting the crowd.

"By the power vested in me by the Lord of Darkness," Bearer said, "I now pronounce you as the unholy *union* of darkness! You may now *kiss your bride!*"

Just then, Austin's music hit and he ran in to beat everyone up. He vanquished the forces of evil with his fists and released Stephanie from her bonds before she could be further violated.

"He didn't do it for the love of Vince McMahon!" Cornette crowed. "He just did it because it was right!"

Mr. McMahon ran in and embraced his only daughter with all his might. To Austin, he mouthed the words, "*Thank you.*"

The very next night, the WWF taped a pilot for a new series on UPN called *SmackDown*. The show began, naturally, with Mr. McMahon.

He entered with Stephanie on his arm and they went to the ring, where he admitted that he'd been ruthless in business, ungrateful to his collaborators, and neglectful of his family. The crowd did the *asshole* chant. "And you're right, I *have* been that," he said. "And hopefully, I can change."

Stephanie was beaming like a child.

He handed her the mic. She thanked Austin, then described her kayfabe ordeal with performative disgust.

She said, "I was taken against my *will*, stripped of my *clothes* . . ."

And here, she had to pause, because the crowd had started cheering.

Her expression went unchanged.

She resumed: ". . . and dressed in a black gown for an unholy *wedding!* And I have never felt so *powerless* and *violated* in all my life!"

The camera cut to Mr. McMahon, who was looking at his daughter with a solemn, inscrutable expression on his face.

"The Undertaker—he kept *touching* me!" Stephanie said with a frown. The crowd cheered again.

"And whispering in my ears that I was *his!*" she said. "And there was nothing I could do about it!"

She had a message for her would-be rapist: "I hope you *burn in hell!*"

Shane's theme music—"No Chance In Hell," the same as his father's—hit. He entered, flanked by the Corporation.

By now, in the story line, it had been established that Shane owned 50 percent of the company, with his father owning the other half. They were constantly jockeying for control.

Shane expressed disappointment in Mr. McMahon's new soft side. "All of a sudden, Vince McMahon is out here, apologizing for how you used to run business?" the younger man said. "What happened to the most ruthless tycoon in the history of the world? You all of a sudden grew a *conscience* overnight?"

"A *son*, talking to a *father* like *that!*" Jim Cornette said to the viewer.

"Now, you may leave—and take your precious little daughter with ya!" Shane barked. "This is *my* show!"

Later in that *SmackDown* pilot, Owen Hart taped an interview. By many accounts, Owen wanted to get out of wrestling. He had a beloved wife and two children in Calgary. He and the other Harts had been put through so much by the Business—and by Vince McMahon, in particular. He would tell the Boys he wanted to hang up the spurs and go home, just as soon as he could save enough money or find other work. Then again, they all said that from time to time.

Meanwhile, Vince had decided he wanted Owen to return to the gimmick he'd first used upon arriving in the WWF in 1988: the wholesome and enthusiastic superhero, complete with cape and mask, known as the Blue Blazer. Owen would pretend that he was having some kind of psychotic breakdown, which had resulted in him thinking he had actually *become* the character.

Owen protested; he'd never liked the gimmick, and it certainly didn't fit in the contemporary WWF. But Vince insisted. So the wrestler did as he was told.

On the *SmackDown* pilot, as commentator Kevin Kelly held the mic, Owen, in full Blazer getup, crowed that "the WWF needs a superhero like the Blue Blazer, one that can protect *good* from *evil!*" and urged "all my little Blue Blazers" to "take your vitamins, say your prayers, and drink your milk!"

Kelly asked why the WWF needed the Blue Blazer.

"The conditions here in the WWF have become *deplorable!*" Owen said. "There's too much *cleavage!*" He referenced another wrestler, Sean Morley, who performed as a male porn star named Val Venis. "And that Val . . . I can't even say his last name, but you know what it rhymes with! I can't even say it, but *he's* deplorable!"

Indeed, the Blazer told the viewer, "*Everything's* deplorable here in the WWF!"

On the next *Raw*, Shane cut a promo berating his father in the ring, while verbal abuse rained down on him from the crowd. Over the course of the *SmackDown* pilot, Shane had formed a new, merged version of the Corporation and the Ministry of Darkness. They called themselves the Corporate Ministry. He also got into a scuffle in which he hit Mr. McMahon. Now, on *Raw*, he boasted of that attack.

"It feels *good* to reach out there, to seize that power, to have destiny in my hands!" Shane said to the crowd. "How many of *you* would have the balls the size of grapefruits to slap your maker in the face? Not a single one!"

Mr. McMahon arrived to confront his son later in the episode, but he didn't come alone this time. He brought Linda.

Linda's appearance meant the entire McMahon quartet was now part of the story line. Everyone in Vince's nuclear family dwelled in kayfabe. Forevermore, it would be impossible to fully disentangle fact and fiction when it came to the McMahon clan.

"Shane, stop now before you go *too far*," the father told the son.

"Oh, no, no, I haven't *begun* to go far," Shane said. "I haven't begun to go far *enough*."

Jim Ross judged the young man for the viewers at home: "Wow, no respect at all for his own father. What kind of human being *is* he?"

"I think you're about to make a big mistake," Mr. McMahon said. "And I think you better think long and hard before you do. And you better get your stuff together, because your family is *not* standing behind you."

Shane started challenging his dad to a fight.

"How 'bout *me* and *you*?" he said. "Think of the box office, Vince! Y'know what? I've taken your company out from under you, I've taken everything, the only thing I wanna take right now is *your ass!*"

"The answer is no," Mr. McMahon said, not acknowledging the surprisingly sexual phrasing. "But if you won't listen to me, if you won't listen to your sister, Stephanie, then maybe, just maybe, your mother, Linda, you'll listen to her."

Linda took the mic and spoke, her voice quiet, halting, and distinctively North Carolinian—far from the cadences of the other McMahons in the ring.

"Shane, I'm begging you, son," Linda said. "In the name of our *family*—"

"*Shut your mouth, Mom!*" Shane shouted.

Mr. McMahon went to hit him.

The crowd chanted, "*Beat his ass! Beat his ass!*," but the older man held himself back. Shane prodded him further.

"Hey, Vince, you know what?" Shane said. "*I can have him do it again.* Who do you think was the mastermind behind the Undertaker abducting your little girl, Stephanie? It was me!"

Mr. McMahon now looked like he was going to combust.

"And Stephanie, who do you think picked out your *wedding* dress?" Shane said. "Wasn't it the *bomb?*"

This quasi-incestuous taunt sealed the deal: Mr. McMahon and Shane would duel in the ring. The match mostly consisted of Mr. McMahon taking bumps in faux agony, gripping his guts as though he were dying from the inside.

At one point, Shane put his shoe on his father's neck and yelled, "*You feel that? You feel that power?*"

He then arranged Mr. McMahon so the elder man's torso was propped up against one of the ring posts while he was ostensibly unconscious.

Shane walked to the opposite corner, then ran toward his dad and jumped up to execute a "bronco buster": a move where a wrestler shoves his legs between the ropes, puts his groin in his opponent's face, and bucks up and down, as if hitting the other guy's chest with his rear end.

Shane flew forward. His legs slid between the ropes. He humped his crotch up and down, centimeters from his father's mouth.

"*Yeah!*" the son yelled. "*Yeah! Yeah!*"

There was an audio clip that kept getting played in ads and teasers, enticing fans to buy May 23's *Over the Edge '99* PPV. It was the Undertaker saying, "You will be *sacrificed* to a power even *greater* than I."

The PPV and the following night's *Raw* were meant to be the climax of the Greater Power saga. The Undertaker would carry out his master's dark bidding at the PPV, then, on *Raw*, the master's identity would be revealed. But, as the date approached, Vince et al. still didn't have a satisfactory person to fill the role.

It had to be someone who could credibly want to arrange a young woman's sexual assault, then make her brother boast of his involvement in it. It had to be someone the audience would buy as the hidden hand behind everything bad that happened in the WWF. It had to be someone who was more powerful than death and the devil. It had to be someone who you would buy as Vince's cruelest enemy.

Ultimately, Vince and his bookers were pressed for time and, about a week before *Over the Edge*, made a choice that was both totally absurd and, in retrospect, wholly logical.

It had to be Mr. McMahon.

No other reveal would be as confounding, as nonsensical, as emotionally devastating for the fans. Rather than having been tormented by a foe, it would turn out that all this time Mr. McMahon was merely playing a victim—in order to manipulate the audience's emotions and expectations. It was a brilliant conceit because it had the benefit of being, in its own way, completely true.

The main event of *Over the Edge* was slated to be Austin defending his

WWF championship against the Undertaker, with, bizarrely enough, *two* guest referees: Shane and Mr. McMahon. Shane would arrange for his father to get beaten up before the match, perhaps even taken to the hospital, but then Mr. McMahon would make a triumphant return to help Austin.

All this would make it even more shocking when, the next night on *Raw*, the Greater Power would be revealed as Mr. McMahon himself.

However, there was an unexpected interruption that altered the specific course of events.

The WWF had a show called *Sunday Night Heat*, which was usually pretaped—unless it preceded a PPV, in which case both shows would air live. *Heat* was live in Kemper Arena in Kansas City, Missouri, that night, as a lead-in to *Over the Edge*.

The viewers cheered Mr. McMahon on as he chewed his son out early in the show. Shane might own half the company, he said—"That doesn't give you the right to be a *big shot*. That doesn't give you the right to throw your *weight* around; doesn't give you the right to *screw* with people's careers and *screw* with people's lives, Shane!"

Shane demanded that Vince have a match with a member of the Corporate Ministry, which, the commentators emphasized, would be "suicide" for the elder man.

"Michael Cole, you and I are fathers," said commentator Kevin Kelly. "I could never imagine my son, your son, doing that to us; having your own son send you to your *ultimate demise!* That's what Vince McMahon is facing right now."

Sure enough, Mr. McMahon had his match and was beaten to a pulp. The WWF did what wrestling promotions have often done, which was hire an ambulance full of EMTs to pretend to take the man in charge to the hospital. They pretaped a segment in which he was carried on a stretcher into the vehicle. It would be shown later.

The injury was fake, of course. No one was supposed to get hurt.

After *Heat* segued into the PPV portion of the evening, Owen Hart was slated to perform a risky and unusual stunt, even by wrestling standards.

There was a superhero-like WCW wrestler named Sting (in reality, Ultimate Warrior's old tag-team partner, Steve Borden) who was then famous for flying into the ring from the rafters in a harness, attached to a piece of equipment called a descender. The Blue Blazer had used the descender, too, in his capacity as a superhero—but only once, just a few weeks prior. This night, Owen was supposed to descend from the ceiling and land in the ring for his match against the Godfather.

Vince had hired a new descender technician who hadn't worked with the WWF before, and who had significantly less experience with the stunt than the technician who'd overseen similar entrances in the past.

As Owen climbed up to the catwalk, television viewers saw Michael Cole gravely interviewing Pat Patterson and Jerry Brisco backstage about Mr. McMahon's kayfabe injury.

"Jerry, Pat," Cole said, "from what we understand, WWF dot com is reporting that an ambulance is on its way to the arena to take Vince to a local medical center, and that this ankle injury suffered on *Heat* by Vince McMahon is much more serious than we first thought."

"As far as I'm concerned, his ankle is *broken*," Patterson said. "Jerry, I told you, he should've *never* went to that ring!"

Then it was on to a goofy little pre-edited montage of Owen running around in his Blazer outfit like a child on Halloween.

Owen was supposed to jump from his platform and zip down while the montage was wrapping up, so they could cut directly to him, mid-descent.

When the time came for the stunt, Vince was backstage, preparing for his return to the ring to save Austin at the end of the night. He didn't see what happened next.

Owen jumped from his platform. He began his descent. Then, a cable disengaged from his harness.

He fell.

After more than seventy feet of free fall, Owen hit the top rope chest-first, smashing many of his internal organs.

His body bounced backward, into the ring.

By the time he landed on the mat, he had lost consciousness.

The live feed was on a delay, and longtime director Kevin Dunn cut to a still graphic of Blazer and the Godfather before television viewers could see Owen fall. The live crowd in Kansas City were the only ones who saw it all happen, and they didn't know what they were looking at. Was that a dummy or something that had been thrown into the ring? Was it part of the show?

Someone told Jim Ross through his headset that they were going to cut to a pretaped interview. Ross, who didn't know if Owen was alive or dead, spoke to the viewers.

"Folks, let's take you now . . ."

He paused, almost imperceptibly.

". . . to the interview conducted earlier tonight, uh, with Kevin Kelly and, ah—and the Blue Blazer."

He paused again.

"And we got big problems out here."

Jerry Lawler, the other commentator for the night, ran to Owen in the ring, mere feet away. He saw the wrestler's face turn gray.

Television viewers watched Owen, as the Blue Blazer, give his pretaped interview. In the arena, the live audience saw Owen lying in the ring, surrounded by the EMTs who had been booked for Vince's fake injury.

When the interview footage ended, the broadcast cut back to Jim Ross's face, utterly pale. "Ladies and gentlemen, when you're doing live television, a lot of things can happen, and sometimes, they are not good," Ross said. "The Blue Blazer, as we know, is Owen Hart" and he "was gonna make a very spectacular, superhero-like entrance from the rafters, and something went terribly wrong here. . . .

"This is not your typical *wrestling story line*," Ross emphasized. "This is a *real situation*."

The EMTs were carrying Owen out of the ring on a stretcher. The crowd cheered him, as they would an athlete laid low by a broken limb. The ambulance that had been used as a set piece for Vince earlier in the night, which had been on its way to leave, was called back for real-life duty.

Where was Vince?

There are no public accounts of his exact actions immediately after Owen's fall, and the people present that night tend to say—truthfully or not—that it was so chaotic that they hardly remember the specific sequence of events.

But, at some point in those first minutes, Vince made a series of fateful decisions.

The wrestlers were to be told that Owen's fate was undetermined—which was technically true, as he wouldn't be declared dead until he reached the hospital.

The crowd in Kansas City was to be told nothing.

And the PPV would continue.

"And folks, again, there's so many things going on," Ross told the television viewers. "We will keep you updated on this situation."

He didn't even pause before he said, "And our mixed tag-team match, by the way, is coming up next."

Sure enough, Jeff Jarrett—one of Owen's closest friends—made his entrance alongside Debra in the ring to fight Val Venis and a woman named Nicole Bass. Eight minutes had elapsed on the broadcast since Owen's fall.

The crowd in Kansas City got back to cheering, presumably because they'd collectively decided to assume Owen would be fine.

That was the cynical result of this new form of worked-shoot kayfabe: the default assumption was that most things in wrestling were fake, even to an audience that had witnessed something as real as death.

Vince called Owen's wife, Martha, and told her that the wrestler had fallen and was hurt.

"Is this a serious call?" Martha asked.

"Yes, this is a very serious call," Vince replied.

"Is this *really* a serious call?" Martha said. "Or is this a part of your production?"

As Martha put it, Vince "seemed a bit stunned" as he replied, "No, it's not."

She asked if Owen was conscious. Vince said no. She asked for details of the fall. He kept saying, "I don't know."

Finally, he said, "Someone will call you soon," and hung up.

At about the same time, at the hospital, Owen was pronounced dead.

Someone at the hospital must have informed Vince. And Vince made another decision.

Around 8:40 p.m. Central time, Ross's voice became even more grave than it had been. He looked into the camera.

"I have the unfortunate responsibility to let everyone know that Owen Hart has died," he said to the TV viewers at home. "Owen Hart has tragically died from that accident here tonight."

A long pause. In the background, members of the still uninformed Kansas City crowd were hooting and cheering. Then, the broadcast cut to a teaser montage for the next fight.

In the final minutes of the main-event match with Austin and Taker, when the story line called for it to look like all was lost, Mr. McMahon made his triumphant "return" from the "medical facility" to which he'd been taken. He walked down the entrance ramp in his black tank top, looking like nothing would stop him from getting what he wanted.

"Vince McMahon, making . . . Well, it's a gutsy effort," Ross told the viewers. "You know he's hurtin' like hell."

"*Vince, Vince, Vince!*" the crowd chanted as the boss who brought them such entertainment entered the ring.

He rescued Austin, but then Shane, per the story line, turned the tables and cheated to help Taker get the pin.

Just before the broadcast cut out, you could see Vince standing there, in his capacity as a character, heaving his breath, trying to act. He was making a face of theatrical determination and distaste at Taker, who had been waving his newly won championship belt above his head.

Vince looked forward. Then, his face caught in shadow, he cast his head down.

The show was, at long last, over.

Vince hurried backstage, toweled himself off, and put on more professional clothing. Less than twenty minutes after pretending to lose out against the Lord of Darkness, Vince spoke at a hastily assembled news conference.

With a distraught expression, he confirmed the death and said they were looking into what happened.

"All of Owen's fans all over the world are saddened by this tragic loss," Vince said. "Right now, there are no answers."

A reporter asked why there wasn't another line connected as a backup.

"I'm not an expert in rigging," Vince replied, flush and sarcastic. "I guess you are."

The reporter pressed him, saying it seemed there were "no precautionary measures."

"First of all, I resent your *tone*," Vince replied, his face twisting in scorn.

"I resent the sarcasm," the reporter said.

"No, no, I resent your *tone*, lady, okay?" Vince said. "This is a tragic accident. This is a tragic accident. Don't try and put yourself in the *spotlight* here, okay?"

Immediately after Owen Hart's death became public knowledge, Vince saw a grim version of his longtime wish for outside validation fulfilled: one of his wrestling shows was a lead story around the world.

There were headlines and TV segments everywhere, announcing Owen's death and wondering how on earth Vince could have kept the show going after the accident, let alone after the thirty-four-year-old wrestler's death had been confirmed.

Before the next day's *Raw* in St. Louis's Kiel Center, Vince spoke to the press outside the venue.

"It was a tragic, tragic, horrible accident," he said, and vowed that the descender stunt would never be used again, "out of respect for Owen."

The show opened with a crowd of WWF wrestlers, referees, and leadership standing in solemn silence near the entrance ramp. Heels and faces were mostly intermingled. And yet, there was still a hint of kayfabe, as Vince, Linda, and Stephanie were arranged together in a line many feet away from the villainous Shane.

Everyone wore black armbands with white letters bearing Owen's initials.

The crowd started chanting, "*Owen, Owen, Owen!*"

As they chanted, the feed cut to a tight shot of Stephanie and Vince. The young woman had tears in her eyes.

The ring bell was struck ten times, then went silent.

The crowd applauded. The McMahons did, too.

The wrestlers didn't.

The program dissolved to a tribute montage. It showed Owen in his greatest moments, including one where he could be seen with Bret, while Vince read voice-over narration about how wonderful a man he was.

"With heavy heart and the deepest of sympathies for his family," Vince intoned, "we say goodbye."

They cut back to a live shot of Stephanie, crying even more. They cut to Vince, who looked as though he was attempting to hold back his own tears.

As the WWF cast slowly walked back through the entrance, Jim Ross told the viewers they were about to see "one of the most unique broadcasts ever, in the genre of sports entertainment, here, tonight." There would be "ten very unique matchups," but, more importantly, "you're going to be able to hear the candid and very, very *real* sentiments of many of Owen's fellow WWF Superstars. . . .

"This very special broadcast will continue," Ross said.

Over the course of the day, Vince and his crews had thrown together an unprecedented show in the history of wrestling. The Boys who had been scheduled to perform were given permission to opt out, should they choose. But everyone was encouraged to sit down in front of a camera and record little shoot interviews about Owen.

Some of the shoots were a nightmare to watch, especially for young viewers, as they featured dear friends of Owen, ostensible tough guys, breaking into jagged tears and saying they couldn't continue.

Mark Henry, who wrestled as "Sexual Chocolate," read an original poem; Paul Bearer recited lines from Laurence Binyon's World War I ode "For the Fallen."

Some of the segments were awkward because the speakers didn't know what to say, not having known Owen well.

Vince didn't do a tribute video, but Shane did. The scion told a story about hanging out with Bret and Owen, then said, "The McMahon, Hart families go back so many years and . . ." before trailing off and concluding, "Owen, you will be truly missed. Godspeed."

There were, indeed, matches, and the crowd in St. Louis had a great time during them, but no story lines were advanced and none of the wrestlers acted like they were particularly angry.

However, kayfabe wasn't entirely gone: no one walked out in their civilian clothes or broke character in the ring. It made the performances utterly surreal.

The Rock, when he entered, did his many well-known catchphrases for the hungry crowd. While still speaking in his character's slick, narcissistic, third-person cadences, he addressed the dead Owen, saying, "Dammit, you know the Rock loved you like no other; so it's with great pleasure that the Rock, along with the *millions* . . ."

Here, the crowd dutifully yelled out, "*AND MILLIONS!*"

". . . *and millions* of the Rock's fans dedicate the People's Elbow to you tonight"—that being the Rock's finisher.

Typically, when D-X member Road Dogg (Brian James) got to the ring, he would do an opening call-and-response portion. It would feature him saying, "Ladies and gentlemen, boys and girls, children of all ages, D-Generation X proudly brings to you . . ." at which point, the crowd would yell along with him as he reared back and said, ". . . the *tag*-team *cham*pions of the *wooooooorld!*" and recite his and his partner's names.

At the Owen tribute, Road Dogg took to the ring and did his opening patter, except, when he got to "proudly brings to you . . ." he said, in the same hollered intonations as his usual lines, ". . . y'know, sometimes I just *don't* under*stand* this *wooooooooorld!*"

In his tribute video, Owen's close friend Jeff Jarrett cried while looking away from the camera with aching eyes and said, "In this business, it's cold, it's callous, it's selfish, it's self-serving, it's unrealistic, it's a fantasy world. But Owen was *real.*"

The day after the Owen-tribute *Raw*, May 25, the WWF pretaped the next week's *Heat* and *Raw*. All the story lines resumed. All the sleaze, all the violence, all the kayfabe was back.

A few minutes into *Heat*, commentator Michael Cole told the viewer that the WWF and "everyone around the world" were saddened "with the tragic accident that cost Owen Hart his life last week. But, as Owen Hart would've wished, we are moving on."

Then it was back to the match. A wrestler named Meat (Shawn Stasiak), whose gimmick was that man-hating feminists manipulated him to do their bidding, was the heel.

Later in the evening, man-boy Beaver Cleavage made his in-ring debut, accompanied by an open-bloused Mrs. Cleavage.

There was a strange pretaped sequence that was made to look like it was candid-camera footage of two Black wrestlers in the bathroom, arguing over how stinky one of their shits was.

Mick Foley did a promo in which he joked about broad-shouldered female wrestler Chyna sexually assaulting him in the shower.

It's unclear whether the bookers were still intent on having Vince be the Greater Power by that point. The story line had been delayed due to Owen's death, so they had time for a last-minute search for other candidates. They may have been keeping their options open: the conclusion of the pretaped *Raw* featured Austin getting captured by the Corporate Ministry and being granted a glimpse of the robed and hooded Greater Power, but it was shot at an angle so the audience couldn't see the figure's face.

All they saw was Austin putting on a look of angry horror at the knowledge, like a man who's learned the darkest secret of the universe, then screaming, "*Son of a bitch!*"

★ ★ ★

Vince canceled four Canadian shows for May 27–29—the Harts are national heroes in Canada, so he likely knew his traveling show would get a poor reception up north—and spent the next few days in Connecticut.

At the Stamford offices, WWF staff kept plowing forward in their grief.

"Owen's death had affected me badly; I couldn't sleep, couldn't focus," Jim Ross would write later. "And every time I closed my eyes, I saw that horrifying scene replay over and over again. I knew I wasn't the only one; we were all trying to handle what was in front of us without looking back too much."

Ross said Vince was "quieter than usual—withdrawn. He went about his business but in a muted way."

On May 31, hundreds of members of the wrestling industry, Vince very much included, gathered in Calgary for Owen's funeral. Vince had his cameras film everything they could at the Hart compound during the day. He was going to air footage on *Raw* without Martha's permission.

When Martha spoke in the service, she wept, then made a prophecy.

"I am a very forgiving person, and I'm not bitter or angry," the widow said. "But there will be a day of reckoning."

The air outside Boston's Fleet Center was almost at the boiling point on June 7, 1999. The sold-out crowd gathered in the knowledge that they were about to witness a great unveiling.

That night, live on *Raw*, the Greater Power was—at long, *long* last—going to be revealed.

Online speculation about the character's identity was fevered. Who could possibly live up to the hype? There seemed to be no obvious pick, but that only fueled a deeper suspicion that whoever it was might be mind-blowing. Hadn't Vince been delivering them things they could never have imagined, live over the airwaves, week after week?

Backstage, Vince prepared for the show. Linda, Stephanie, and Shane were with him—they would all make appearances as part of the story. Shane would be revealed to have been in on the scheme all along; Linda and Stephanie would be reacting to the revelation that their own family members had been behind their suffering.

Stephanie would ask, "Dad, Shane? How could you be so cruel to me?"

"It's just *business*," Mr. McMahon would tell her. "*Love* doesn't have anything to do with it."

The hour of the show approached. The teeming crowd filed in. The McMahon family went over their lines. The wrestlers laced up their boots.

Perhaps Vince dwelled on the fact that precisely seventeen years and two days had passed since the day he shook his father's hand to begin his take-over of the company. Perhaps he thought about all that had changed since he ended his father's era. Perhaps he thought about all that had stayed the same.

Raw opened with a video montage about Steve Austin's war against the Greater Power, set to the apocalyptic strains of Carl Orff's adaptation of the Latin poem "O Fortuna." The stock-music choir sang:

Quod per sortem
sternit fortem
mecum omnes plangite!

"Since fate / strikes down the strong / all should weep with me!"

The time came. The Corporate Ministry walked down the entrance ramp and into the ring. The Undertaker spoke.

"For months on end, I prophesized of a power even greater than the Lord of Darkness," the behemoth said. "I assembled an army to prepare for his eventual arrival. And the Ministry and the Corporation laid the groundwork. So, nonbelievers . . ."

He paused.

". . . you must prepare for the *day of reckoning*—because it is at *hand*."

Taker gestured to the entrance. A recording of Gregorian chants began to play. Vince, his face obscured in a hooded, velvet robe of maroon hue, walked down the ramp. He walked alone.

He reached the ring and entered it. He stood there, surrounded by those who owed him fealty.

Then Shane entered—the audience could breathe a sigh of relief that *he* wasn't the Greater Power, at least. But, Shane said, he knew the man in question all too well.

"The Greater Power is omniscient," Shane said into the mic he held. "The Greater Power is cold and calculated, and a mastermind at *screwing* with people's minds."

Shane strolled toward the ring and continued to describe the mystery figure in the cloak.

"The Greater Power is also a master *planner*," the young man said. "The Greater Power is *methodical* in his methods—and a *master* in human psychology."

Shane had by now reached the ring steps. He climbed through the ropes, onto the canvas.

"The Greater Power knows what makes all of us tick, each and every one of us," Shane said. "He knows our fears, he knows our strengths, and our weaknesses—and exploits those fears, strengths, and weaknesses for the betterment of his Corporate Ministry and his own personal amusement."

But who *was* this Greater Power? Shane, now standing in the ring, said he'd tell everyone imminently. He just had one last thing to take care of.

"Vince, I want you to come down here, and I will bestow the honor upon you," Shane said. "I will give you that honor, to reveal the Greater Power to the entire world. Because Vince, *I can't wait to see your face.*"

Vince's pretaped visage appeared on the Titantron, as if it were a live feed to backstage.

"Shane, I say I'm close enough right where I stand, right here and now," the boss said. "I say the games are *over*, Shane. I say the evil, demonic SOB show his face to the world *now!*"

Without saying anything, Shane turned around and moved closer to the Greater Power, gingerly touching a finger to the edge of the hood.

Three seconds passed with no further motion. Only the faintest outline of a human face was visible. The crowd held its breath.

Then, the robed figure threw back the hood with his left hand and revealed himself to the world.

He was grinning like a skull, his eyes wide and aflame.

"*It's me, Austin!*" he screamed.

"*It was me, Austin!*

"*It was me all along, Austin!*"

The crowd began its chant: "*Asshole, asshole, asshole . . .*"

Mr. McMahon turned to face them.

"You all *bought* it!" he bellowed.

"You *all* bought it—hook, line, and *sinker! You all bought it!* Even my family—even my *immediate family*—bought it!"

He held aloft his left hand and eagerly pointed his finger at the crowd.

"Every damn *one* of you," he said, "were made *fools* of!"

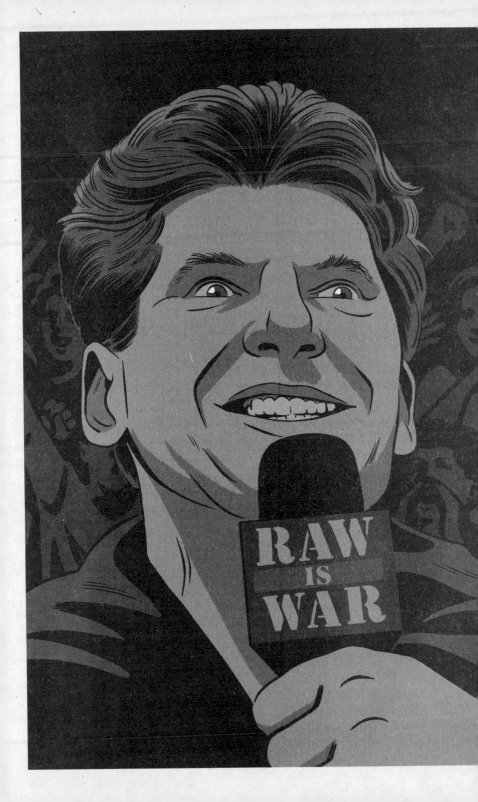

THE JOB

We have lived for a quarter of a century in the world Mr. McMahon made.

Not just wrestling fans—all of us.

WCW never regained the momentum it once had against the WWF. By the time of the Greater Power revelation, *Raw* had already returned to first place in the ratings battle with *Nitro*. WWF revenue nearly doubled, from $126 million in 1998 to an astounding $250 million in 1999. Vince continued to run roughshod over Ted Turner's wrestling operation. In early 2001, the WWF bought it outright, decisively ending the Monday Night War. Around the same time, ECW went bankrupt and Vince bought what remained of it, too.

In doing so, he essentially gained sole control of the professional wrestling industry in the US and Canada. There were a few comparatively tiny independent promotions that could sometimes drum up excitement among hardcore fans. But, for the next two decades, Vince would face no significant challenges to his sovereignty.

On August 23, 1999, Gallup released a poll which estimated that an astounding 20 percent of all Americans—roughly 55 *million* people, if the estimate is to be believed—identified as wrestling fans. Those fans were asked who their favorite wrestler was; number one with a bullet was Steve Austin, at 24 percent, and WCW's Hogan was a distant second, at 12 percent.

In a bid to become even more profitable and respectable, Vince and Linda made the WWF a publicly traded company on October 19, 1999. The two of them were the majority stockholders. By the closing bell that day, the long-married couple were worth more than one billion dollars.

In 2000, an environmentalist nonprofit called the World Wildlife Fund, founded in 1961, sued the WWF, demanding that it change its abbreviation. Per the terms of the settlement, the company changed its name in

2002 to WWE—ostensibly short for "World Wrestling Entertainment," but usually just referred to by its initials. After all, WWE doesn't promote wrestling, Vince always says. They make sports entertainment.

The name change was a minor setback for Vince. Overall, he had won. From 2001 onward, he alone set the agenda for what wrestling could be in America.

All major developments in the artform in that period were either made *by*, in mimicry *of*, or in rebellion *against* Vince. It was as if Major League Baseball only consisted of one team, led by one coach, who happened to also be the first baseman. Or perhaps it was more like a movie industry in which there was only one major studio, which only made movies made by one director, who always played a role in his own films.

And after the Greater Power revelation, that role was always the same one: he was always Mr. McMahon.

Vince never went back to his role as an announcer, nor did he assume a new character. He sometimes shaded into babyface territory, but it was never his resting state. People occasionally got permission to call him "Vince" on the show, but such instances were vanishingly rare. There have been periods when he has appeared on TV every week; in other periods, especially the past few years, he's been absent for long stretches at a time. But he always came back—and interest always spiked when he did. Forevermore, Vince would play the part of a greedy and ruthless businessman who cannot be trusted.

In all the ways that matter, he *became* Mr. McMahon.

Accusations of misconduct seemed to roll off his back. In 2006, a Florida tanning-salon employee accused him of sexually assaulting her. In response, Vince parodied the woman's accusations on WWE programming by having one of his female stars pretend to be a hysterical stalker who accuses an innocent man of assault. In real life, prosecutors declined to press charges, even though the local police said there was probable cause to do so.

On June 11, 2007, Mr. McMahon was ostensibly murdered. His limousine was blown up at the end of *Raw*. The pyrotechnics of the "killing" were extravagant, even by WWE standards; the company posted an official-looking story on their website claiming "initial reports indicate that Mr. McMahon is presumed dead"; and Vince stayed out of the public eye in the aftermath. The press didn't buy it, though Donald Trump allegedly did call WWE the morning after the explosion and asked, with earnest horror, "Did something happen to Vince?"

The story line was to take WWE even further into soap-opera territory, and one of Vince's bookers from the time has claimed there was serious discussion of incorporating Vince's older brother Rod into kayfabe. However, the story line never came to fruition. On June 24, 2007, just thirteen days after Vince faked his own death, a beloved and accomplished WWE wrestler named Chris Benoit murdered his wife and seven-year-old son and then killed himself.

Much was made of the autopsy, which revealed massive chronic traumatic encephalopathy (CTE) in his brain, likely due to all the abuse his skull had taken in the ring. Benoit's steroid abuse was also implicated in the tragedy.

There was outrage in the mainstream media the likes of which hadn't been seen since Owen Hart's death, and Vince and Linda were summoned to a congressional hearing on steroid abuse. It looked, for a moment, like Vince might actually be in trouble. But, ultimately, it blew over. No laws passed; no charges filed. The world moved on.

The one major change in the wake of Benoit's death was the general sanitization of the TV product. Soon after, everything was rated PG. That meant no more swearing, no more depictions of attempted rapes, no more self-induced bleeding, no more chair-shots to the skull, and so on. The moral gray areas sorted themselves once again into black-and-white. The top face was the clean-cut, positivity-obsessed, troop-respecting John Cena; his foes insulted his athletic ability as opposed to digging up his personal life.

The kid-friendly shift led to a slight uptick in safety for the workers, but it didn't mean they got real labor protections. They never unionized, and are still classified as independent contractors without employer-provided health insurance—a vision of the gig economy that would eventually take over the American workforce. And there is still no significant government oversight of WWE, no matter how many times Vince has found himself implicated in scandal.

Like the Fabulous Moolah—the late legend (she, too, died in 2007) whose approach to the Business prefigured all of this—Vince created and inhabited a public persona so dastardly and villainous that no truth or lie, no accusation or allegation could further tarnish him. He was already pitch-dark. Everything vanished into the sucking void of Mr. McMahon.

Even the Almighty couldn't escape. In 2006, Shawn Michaels was in the midst of a comeback after finding Christ and getting sober. He was back on WWE programming, doing a babyface angle, inspired by his real-life conversion. He'd talk honestly in the ring and in mainstream interviews about how much he loved God for turning his life around. He was doing shoot promos to praise Jesus.

Mr. McMahon, by that point, had become a remarkably deranged character; all his malevolent traits had been turned up to the maximum volume. As the all-powerful deity of the WWE, his story line had become a kind of Gnostic gospel, preaching the bad news: *God exists, and He hates you.*

So it only made sense, on some level, that Vince would book a story in which Shawn's newfound faith was ridiculed. Mr. McMahon began a feud in which he boasted that he was more powerful than the Christian God that Shawn so adored.

On TV, the heel started a new religion called "McMahonism." Linda, Shane, and Stephanie were all recurring players by now, and he did a sketch in which the family—himself included—all took to their knees and prayed. During one segment, Shawn told him, per the script, "You have finally gone *completely* insane."

That sentence-long sound bite was played ad infinitum in the lead-up to April 2006's *Backlash '06* PPV. It was there that WWE held the climax of the religion angle: a tag-team match that consisted of Mr. McMahon and Shane going up against Shawn Michaels and . . . God. Unable to appear in person, God was represented as a spotlight shining down from the rafters. At the end of the match, after a fair bit of cheating, Mr. McMahon pinned Shawn. The bell rang; the decision was final.

God lost.

The McMahons' influence spread. They had already dabbled in lobbying and influencing legislation; now they entered politics directly.

Near the end of the century, Vince and Linda began making significant political campaign contributions. Initially, they hedged their bets, giving to both Republicans (their first major donation of the 2000 election cycle was to the Connecticut Republican Federal Campaign Committee) and Democrats (Rahm Emanuel received cash from Linda throughout the ensuing decade).

Vince remained close with a man who, like him, thought of money first and consistent ideology second: Donald Trump. Trump made occasional appearances on WWE programming as an enthusiastic celebrity audience member, but his most memorable run came in 2007. Trump by then was a television veteran, having hosted his reality show *The Apprentice* for six seasons; for various reasons, it became financially advantageous for Trump and WWE to have a crossover.

They had a kayfabe feud in which Mr. McMahon and The Donald butted coiffeurs over who was the most badass rich guy. For months, they taunted each other, with Trump doing live appearances and pretaped promos in which he barraged Mr. McMahon with abuse. Each man chose a proxy wrestler and Vince booked them to fight in one of the marquee matches at *WrestleMania 23*. Whichever man saw his champion win would get to shave off his rival's precious hair. Steve Austin, of all people, would be the guest referee.

Trump and Vince were both ringside during the match, egging their wrestlers on and insulting one another; at one point, Trump did a running body check into Mr. McMahon, knocking the WWE owner over in spectacular fashion. Ever the master of making himself the joke, Vince booked himself to have his wrestler lose. Audiences from around the world watched as the future president of the United States took a razor to the head of one of his best friends. Trump was grinning the whole way through.

The McMahons also donated $4 million to the Donald J. Trump Foundation, Trump's fraudulent and pocket-lining faux charity, in 2007—the biggest donation it received that year. Indeed, Vince and Linda gave almost as much to that foundation as they did to their own Vince and Linda McMahon Family Foundation that year. In 2009, the McMahons donated zero dollars to their own foundation, but $1 million to Trump's. When reporters discovered these facts and requested explanations from WWE or Trump, they were given contradictory and confusing answers.

In 2017, at a time when President Trump was riling his base against the news media, a troll on Reddit modified a clip of Trump attacking Mr. McMahon at *WrestleMania 23*, placing a giant CNN logo over McMahon's head. Trump found it and tweeted it out. The incident became one of those long-forgotten scandals of the early Trump administration, but it raised quite a furor at the time.

Trump's homeland security adviser, Tom Bossert, was prompted to tell

ABC's *This Week* that the edited WWE clip wouldn't encourage violence against reporters: "No one would perceive that as a threat; I hope they don't."

But, Bossert added, "He's a genuine president expressing himself genuinely."

By the time of that scandal, the McMahons and the Trumps had become inextricable. Both families—previously heterodox in their donations—had made hard-right turns and found themselves in the Republican Party.

In 2008, Republican Connecticut governor M. Jodi Rell appointed Linda—by then a respected member of the Connecticut business community and a sought-after donor—to the state's board of education. In February of 2009, she was approved by the state's house of representatives by a vote of 96 to 45.

During Linda's brief tenure on the education board, Trump made a return appearance on WWE. Vince booked a story where Trump would execute a hostile takeover and buy *Raw* from Mr. McMahon. It only lasted two episodes, but one wonders about the alternate world where Trump had decided to simply take a full-time gig as a WWE heel: glorifying violence, playing to the lowest prejudices of his audience, and feasting on the adulation of the crowd.

By the time Trump was inducted into the WWE Hall of Fame a few years later, he had attempted to run for president and was contemplating doing it again. But he wasn't the only one in Vince's circle who had electoral aspirations.

In 2010 and 2012, Linda ran for the US Senate as a Republican, losing both times—but making connections and establishing herself as a widely respected "moderate," willing to fight for the GOP on the front lines of a "blue state." What's more, she demonstrated that she had trench-deep pockets, spending around $100 million on her own campaigns without breaking a sweat.

She became the GOP's money woman. In 2016, she donated $7 million to pro-Trump super PACs. Linda was among the most generous Republican donors in that world-changing election.

Throughout the campaign, Vince remained the closest thing Trump had to a real friend. Campaign adviser Sam Nunberg tells me there were only two people in the entire world whose calls Trump would take alone, rather than in front of an audience—and Vince was one of them. (The other was *The Apprentice* producer Mark Burnett.)

Upon his inauguration, Trump gladly announced Linda's nomination to his cabinet. She was confirmed as head of the Small Business Administration on Valentine's Day 2017. The votes for most Trump nominees had, predictably, been bitterly close, with everyone falling behind their respective party. The much beloved Linda, on the other hand, was confirmed by a vote of 81 to 19.

It was a perfect example of kayfabe morality. Linda had played the role of the kindly, moderate babyface; Trump had been the vicious, extremist heel. But they were working for the same promotion—the Republican Party. The differences between their politics are purely cosmetic.

Linda managed to run her whole term without a major scandal in the media, something almost unheard-of among Trump appointees. However, she developed a massive conflict of interest, one mostly overlooked by the press: Vince was in bed with the Kingdom of Saudi Arabia.

After Prince Mohammed bin Salman al-Saud (commonly referred to as MBS) seized power in June 2017, he set out to change his country's image abroad, as well as offer bread and circuses to his own subjects. Information about Saudi business dealings is always elusive—all the Saudi-focused journalists I spoke with asked to remain anonymous for fear of reprisals. Given what happens to journalists who critique MBS, I was happy to grant the anonymity.

At some point after MBS took control, he started making overtures to WWE about a partnership. On March 1, 2018, it was reported that Saudi sports minister Turki al-Sheikh signed a ten-year deal to produce WWE shows in Saudi Arabia. The shows began the same year as the deal; they continue to happen periodically, to this day. The deal is estimated to be worth well over $40 million per co-sponsored show. That money comprises a significant portion of WWE's operating budget.

It's no secret that MBS sought to curry favor with the Trump administration, and every expert I spoke with took it as a given that the WWE initiative was part of that. Access to Vince meant access to both a cabinet member and a president. Never before had a wrestling promoter been such a power broker; never before had one had a conflict of interest so large that it arguably constituted a national security risk.

Nevertheless, the Saudi connection was lost in the shuffle of all the Trump scandals. Linda stepped down in March 2019, to general applause from the business media and sharp hoots of acclaim from party leaders.

She immediately became head of the largest pro-Trump super PAC in the 2020 fray.

Vince also found major financial support from another controversial source: Rupert Murdoch's News Corp. In 2018, WWE signed a highly lucrative five-year deal with Fox to air *SmackDown* live on the network, having previously been on NBC. *Raw* is still on USA, its home for much of its existence, and the network clutches it with a death grip. The failing titans of conventional, nonstreaming television have been desperate for WWE in their recent years of declining viewership. Athletic content and reality shows are just about all that keeps TV afloat these days, and WWE is a perfect mix of the two—plus, it doesn't have an off-season (or a players union).

When COVID-19 hit, Vince was sent into a panic. He was starting a new football league—well, technically, his second, though the first had been an epic failure in its only season back in 2001. Both were called the XFL, and the second stab had a decent shot at making it, having had a successful first few games in early 2020. Then, after some fateful decisions by the WWE Hall of Famer in the Oval Office, the pandemic ran wild. There was no way to successfully run a nationwide football league in the face of lockdowns.

But even if football couldn't survive the coronavirus, wrestling could.

WWE has a training compound in Orlando, Florida. Linda coordinated a donation of $18.5 million for Republican ads in Florida. Coincidentally, that same week, Florida governor Ron DeSantis's office announced that WWE would be allowed to run shows—but without live crowds.

Those matches were eerily quiet, with wrestlers and a ref dancing around a ring in a small, empty venue, no bigger than a black-box theater. The audience-free wrestling was a fascinating dissection of the artform. As the workers grappled without applause or boos, you could hear their involuntary grunts and squeaks all the better. They had no crowd energy off which to feed, making it all the more admirable when they executed stunning maneuvers or compelling plot twists. That said, without the crowd, it wasn't exactly pro wrestling. The ebb and flow of audience enthusiasm is a crucial ingredient. The now infamous Silent WrestleMania of 2020 felt less like wrestling than a profoundly physical experiment in theater. Then again, hasn't wrestling *always* been a sibling of the theater?

After a few weeks of near silence, followed by a short period of using wrestlers to cheer like fans, Vince implemented a workaround. Using advanced audio technology, the company's programming started to feature computer-generated crowd responses that could weave seamlessly from cheering to jeering, depending on what Vince wanted.

Video screens were placed in the audience section of the small arena, and fans could watch and have their faces streamed to one of the screens, meaning the viewers at home could see and hear something that *felt* like a live audience, but really wasn't one.

The video streaming was manipulated—the fans' streams were recorded, and their faces could be used again at future shows. If Vince wanted a happy crowd, he could order one up. He was, once again, in total control.

By September 2021, America had chosen economic viability over COVID safety, and WWE was back to running shows with live audiences.

In fact, I went to a live episode of *SmackDown* that featured a twentieth-anniversary memorial of the 9/11 attacks. It was filmed at that long-standing outpost of McMahon power, New York City's Madison Square Garden. The arena hall was cavernous, the crowd was ethnically diverse, and everyone there was eager to get back to a sense of normalcy.

Before the show began, I wandered around MSG's halls, past the merchandise booths and concession stands, to ask contemporary WWE fans what they thought of Vince. The responses were steeped in respect.

"He's a businessman; he knows exactly what he's doing," said one attendee.

"He makes his own luck," said another, "and more often than not, he comes out on top."

I asked them all if they thought Vince had ever done anything bad.

"Some people might say he has a very ruthless approach, wiping out the competition," said one of them. "But for him to sustain the longevity he has, he has to be doing something right. There's only one Vince at the end of the day."

"I would say he's out of touch right now," said another. "Time to hang it up."

Not a single person mentioned Jimmy Snuka, Rita Chatterton, or Tom Cole. No one talked about the outrageous provocations or the criminal allegations. If they knew, they had forgotten. More likely, they had never been told in the first place.

We watched a waving flag on the Titantron while the national anthem rang out, but few seemed moved by any of it. Once the show began, there were a few scattered mentions of America's greatness, but nothing too heartfelt. Once, wrestling stirred the most deeply felt patriotism. Now, it merely breeds cynicism.

As I sat and watched the show that night, I thought about the fact that Vince had called his first MSG match almost exactly fifty years prior. Wrestling, which had once been an almost meditative experience of watching large men slowly shove and hold each other for twenty minutes at a time, was now a complete sensory overload. Massive LED screens surround the wrestlers' entranceway, displaying aggressively colorful animations while the performers preen. Original entrance songs for each wrestler are now de rigueur. The in-ring action moves at lightning speed. The artform has adapted, and Vince has been a massive part of that adaptation.

Vince wasn't performing that night, but, as was his wont, he was just behind the entranceway, watching and controlling the action with his monitors and headset. I couldn't see him, but I knew he was there, and I thought about one of wrestling's only constants: the completely disproportionate power that promoters hold over their industry.

Which brings us back to Trump. Wrestling has metastasized into the broader world, especially since the inauguration of the forty-fifth president. There's little difference between Trumpism and Vince's neokayfabe, each with their infinite and indistinguishable layers of irony and sincerity. Each philosophy approaches life with one goal: to remake reality in such a way as to defeat one's enemies and sate one's insecurities.

That's the magic of being a heel in this age of neokayfabe. You can project an image of parodic villainy in public to cover up any actual villainy you're committing in private.

In the late days of the Trump administration, I spoke to various DC staffers about wrestling. It wasn't a poll, merely a collection of conversations, but what I kept hearing was that, ever since Trump came to town, the athletic event of choice for water-cooler discussion was no longer baseball or basketball.

It was pro wrestling.

My theory is that has less to do with Trump, in and of himself, and more to do with the fact that those staffers were all male and under forty.

Wrestling shaped a whole generation of millennial men. If you were a thirteen-year-old boy in 1999, it was absolutely impossible to avoid wrestling. Although I was reluctant to start watching—I was more of a comics nerd, and all my bullies were big Steve Austin fans—once I was in, I was *in*. In fact, the earliest memory I have of my period of fandom was watching the Owen Hart memorial *Raw*, of all things. In spite, or perhaps because of that odd beginning, I remained a diehard for years.

I learned about earnest artifice, about the blurry line between good and evil in this world, about how people can change their moral valences on a dime. What's more, I learned how society wanted boys to be.

Even though I fell off on watching the artform, and even though I now identify as a woman, it had made an indelible mark on me—and *of* me.

I'm not alone in that. The generations who were children when the WWF's product seared itself into our brains in the 1980s and '90s are now ascending to positions of power. We are, in our ways, Vince's children, and we are about to inherit the earth.

What about Vince's other wayward children—the workers he used up, burned, or otherwise cast out?

Many of them, even those who had sworn they'd never work for Vince again, have found themselves returning to his never-ending show. What other options do they have? There's no pension plan. Hollywood has been an escape route for some, but only a lucky few. And charging for autographs at dismal conventions can only pay the rent so many months of the year.

Vince is always waiting, if you're ready to be seen in his embrace.

Hulk Hogan came back to WWE a little while after the collapse of WCW. He and Mr. McMahon had a match at the 2003 WrestleMania. The story line behind the match was that Mr. McMahon wanted all the credit for the Hulkamania phenomenon of the 1980s.

The lines Mr. McMahon said in the weeks leading up to the match were shocking in how heartfelt they sounded.

"I *created* Hulkamania!" the boss shouted at one point. "And, by God, at WrestleMania, I'm gonna *kill* it!"

"*You* did *not* create Hulkamania!" Hogan replied. "Hulkamania lives forever because of all *these* Hulkamaniacs!"

Of course, neither man created Hulkamania; that honor will always go to Verne Gagne. But as the story line deepened, it grew even more personal.

"I hate you because I created you and you turned your back on me! You walked *out* on me, Hogan!" Mr. McMahon said. "You testified against me before the *federal government* in the trial of my *life!*"

Hogan offered a threatening variation on the Demandments: "You better start trainin', you better start eatin' your vitamins, and you better start sayin' your *damn prayers*, McMahon!"

When the two stepped into the ring at WrestleMania, they put on what was arguably the most emotionally compelling match of either of their careers. Vince showed surprising physical prowess, and Hogan, though he'd never been much of an athlete and was far past his prime, put a tremendous amount of emotion into his performance.

"I don't like to use the word 'hatred' much," announcer Michael Cole said during the match, "but these men legitimately hate each other." In a way, it was true. But hating Vince has never been much of an obstacle to working with him.

Once he came back, Hogan never really left again. Even in 2021—years after Hogan had retired, become a reality star, launched a lawsuit that destroyed the consequential news website Gawker, and been caught on tape making that N-word-filled rant—you could see Hogan doing sit-down interviews in official WWE documentaries and attending *Raw*'s "WWE Legends Night."

Warrior, too, made an astounding reversal and came back into contact with WWE in 2013—just eight years after WWE had released a shockingly cruel DVD called *The Self-Destruction of the Ultimate Warrior*. That film had featured a wide array of wrestling luminaries—Vince very much included—talking shit about Warrior. The ex-wrestler had sued WWE, to no avail.

The aging Warrior was up the creek. He had little in the way of a livelihood other than signing autographs, writing spiteful blog posts, and doing his bigotry-filled speaking engagements.

But Vince decided it would be a sensation to bring Warrior back in some capacity. WWE reached out about Warrior returning to the fold, endorsing WWE, and—more importantly—getting royalties from new WWE merchandise that featured his likeness and brand. He said yes.

The company started filming a new in-house doc, *Ultimate Warrior: Al-*

ways Believe. It was to be as hagiographic as the previous one had been venomous. But by the time it was released, it had taken on tragic dimensions.

On April 5, 2014, Warrior was inducted into the Hall of Fame. The next night, he was trotted out at the thirtieth WrestleMania for a brief appearance alongside the rest of the class of inductees. The night after that, he appeared on *Raw* to deliver a promo. He entered the ring in civilian clothing, devoid of his trademark face paint. The crowd went nuts for him.

"As I thought about what I was gonna say this evening, it's been hard for me to find the words," he said, his voice sounding atypically soft and calm. But then, he reached into his jacket pocket and pulled out a little mask that WWE had been selling, which made it look (somewhat) like the wearer had the Warrior's face paint. He strapped it onto his face.

He spoke again. Suddenly, he had that familiar wild snarl. "Well then, *you* shut up, Warrior," he said in his old promo voice, "and let *me* do the talking." He had legally changed his name to Warrior. But this wasn't Warrior speaking. It was the *Ultimate* Warrior; an entirely separate entity, apparently.

"Every man's heart one day beats its final beat," he growled. "His lungs breathe their final breath. And if what that man did in his life makes the blood pulse through the body of others, and makes them *believe deeper* in something larger than *life*, then his essence, his *spirit*, will be immortalized by the storytellers, by the loyalty, by the memory of those who honor him and make the running the man did live forever."

He went on like that for a minute or so. He identified his fans as "the legend-makers of Ultimate Warrior"—it was up to them to keep his memory alive.

"I *am* Ultimate Warrior!" he screamed at the end, his voice hoarse. "You *are* the Ultimate Warrior fans! And the spirit of Ultimate Warrior will run *forever!*"

Less than twenty-four hours later, Warrior had a heart attack and died. He was fifty-four.

But perhaps most surprising of all the returns was that of Bret Hart.

In the immediate aftermath of Owen's death in 1999, Vince kept leaving voice mails for Bret, asking to talk.

Bret wasn't sure he wanted to talk to Vince. The two men hadn't spoken since the Montreal Screwjob, and Owen's death was still being investigated by the Missouri police. "I didn't want to be too friendly because I wasn't sure at that point that it was an accident," Bret tells me. "I didn't know if it was about revenge about what happened with me and Vince."

So Bret ignored Vince's calls for days. But shortly after Owen's body arrived home in Canada, Bret sent Vince a message through a mutual contact: he would meet with Vince in person on a park bench in Calgary, overlooking the Bow River.

It was an unseasonably cold, overcast day. "Vince wore a long heavy coat," Bret wrote when he told the story in his memoir. "He slapped me hard on the shoulders, hugged me, and told me how sorry he was."

He remembered Vince saying, "This is the worst thing to ever happen in the business, to the nicest guy who was ever in the business."

Bret told Vince that he hadn't liked Vince's decision to go on with the show after Owen died. Vince claimed that he and everyone else had been in shock, and hadn't known what else to do. Besides, the fans might have rioted if he'd shut the show down.

Bret wasn't buying it.

"I said that if Shane had been dropped from the ceiling, Vince would have stopped it fast," Bret recalled.

It never would have happened if he'd been there, he told Vince. He would have protected his brother.

Then, they had to talk about the reason Bret hadn't been there.

"There isn't a day that goes by that I don't regret what I did to you," Vince told Bret. "You need to come back and finish your career with me. I could put the belt back on you."

Vince paused, awaiting a response.

He got none.

"I could have a story line for you by tomorrow morning," Vince offered.

Bret said he couldn't imagine doing that.

Vince asked if there was anything he could do for Bret.

"When I still worked for him, we talked about doing a 'Best of Bret Hart' video collection, but that was more than unlikely after Montreal," Bret recalled. "I didn't have much of a history if Vince locked up everything I did in a warehouse somewhere."

So Bret said, "Well, it would mean a lot to me if I could have access to my video history and photos whenever I need them—"

Vince cut Bret off: "Anything you want."

"I don't want to lose my legacy," Bret told his old boss. "I don't want to be forgotten."

"You don't even need to ask," Vince said. "Anything you want."

"I found myself thanking him," Bret wrote, "and telling him how much this simple gesture meant to me, especially under the circumstances. If the police cleared Vince, then maybe I could forgive him."

They ended up spending two hours on the park bench together. They exchanged stories about Owen and even managed to laugh a little. They shook hands and headed back to their cars.

But a few months later, Bret saw Vince being interviewed on TSN's *Off the Record*, talking about their park bench meeting.

Vince told the interviewer that he'd met with Bret "only out of respect for Owen," but that Bret had barely mentioned his brother—"all he wanted to talk about was himself." He painted Bret as ghoulishly self-centered and intent only on rehashing their old grievances.

"It was like looking into the eyes of a skeleton," Vince said of Bret. "It seemed like he wasn't human."

"*That's pretty cold-blooded,*" Bret remembers thinking. "*Talking about me looking like a skeleton three days, five days after my brother died.*" By that time, members of the Hart family had filed a lawsuit against the WWF. It settled for $18 million in 2000; the WWF admitted to no wrongdoing.

Bret and Vince didn't speak again for years. Much of the footage of Bret's awe-inspiring work at the WWF would remain locked in the company vault. Even his later stint with WCW was beyond Bret's grasp: Vince had acquired the WCW archive when he purchased the promotion in 2001. Bret had sustained a massive in-ring injury in 2000 that had effectively ended his career.

Now, unable to wrestle, it was the *story* that mattered most to Bret: *his* story. And Vince had a monopoly on that story.

Every match Bret ever worked, every bump he took, every time the crowd roared for him in the WWF: few would ever see it all again without Vince's say-so.

"I didn't do all that work and have all those matches to just be forgotten," he tells me. "It was so important to me to not be erased."

To Bret, it was as if Vince was holding his past hostage. As the years went by, the company occasionally approached Bret to ask him to appear in one event or another—hinting that if he played along, they might find a way to release the footage of his work. Every time, Bret turned them down. Why should he bargain for access to something Vince had already promised to give him, back on that riverbank in 1999? At one point, a spokesperson told him Vince had no memory of the conversation.

Meanwhile, all anyone seemed to remember about Bret was the way his WWF career ended.

"Everywhere I went, it was always about the Screwjob. Every question, everything I did," he tells me. "'So what about Vince McMahon? What about the Screwjob? Did it really happen? Did you punch Vince McMahon? . . . Was it a work? Was it all pretend or was it a story line?'"

He'd always answer as honestly as he could, feeling himself tense up. He hated having to go over it, again and again, explaining what he did and defending his actions.

The worst part of it was that he had to admit Vince had played everything brilliantly. "When people would ask me all the time about the Screwjob, it was kind of obvious that Vince had come out much better than I did on it," he says.

The Screwjob had perfectly primed the audience for Mr. McMahon to become "the top heel in the industry," Bret says. "You couldn't have written it better. Like, you couldn't have given them a better concept or idea. It was new. It was fresh, and it was masterfully done."

So there Vince was, still riding high on the gimmick the Screwjob had launched. And here was Bret, his career over, his legacy obscured.

It was hard to swallow. But it was also hard to keep hating Vince.

When Bret tells me about his former boss, even as he lays out the many, many times Vince was cold or dismissive or manipulative or cruel, he keeps repeating that they could have gone further together. Bret thinks he could have ended his career as a booker, working with Vince to plot out incredible story lines. "I could have been his right-hand man," he says. He repeats it several times.

In 2002, Bret had a serious stroke that paralyzed half of his body. He was lying in his hospital bed, unsure of the extent to which he'd ever recover, when the phone rang.

"And it's Vince," he says, "lo and behold, it's Vince McMahon calling me, out of the blue, out of nowhere." The call caught him off guard. It was shocking to hear that voice, after three years.

"You're going to beat this thing," Vince told Bret on the phone. "You're one of the toughest, strongest guys I ever knew. You got the mind frame and you're going to get through this."

The pep talk meant a tremendous amount to the wrestler. "I ended up kind of softening a lot of my hate and anger toward him and really kind of appreciated what was once a very strong relationship," Bret says. "I kind of forgave a lot. I just felt a bit of a thread of what we had before the Screwjob happened."

Slowly, Bret recovered from his stroke. And in 2005, two years after the death of Stu Hart, Vince finally followed through and released a DVD called *The Best There Is, The Best There Was, and The Best There Ever Will Be*, which featured some of Bret's finest moments, along with a documentary. When it came out, WWE inducted Bret into the Hall of Fame, but Bret refused to participate in that year's WrestleMania. He still felt he should never appear in one of Vince's shows ever again.

However, in 2007, there came a night when Bret was all alone in his house in Hawai'i. He was going through a divorce, no work coming his way—his body had never come all the way back from the stroke, and he figured his time in wrestling was over for good.

WrestleMania was on. He decided to give it a watch. On the TV, Donald Trump—a man with no training or physical skill—was attacking Vince to the cheers of the crowd.

Hell, Bret thought. *I could do that.*

Bret called Kevin Dunn at WWE and said he might be willing to take Vince up on his standing offer to come back. Dunn, astonished, passed the word along. Vince was overjoyed and welcomed Bret back to the fold. In 2010, the Hitman made his world-stunning return to WWE programming as a character, doing low-impact pseudo-matches, taking bumps, and, most importantly, cutting promos about how he longed for vengeance against Mr. McMahon.

There was blowback. Bret says Martha, Owen's widow, was furious at him for selling out and going back to WWE after what had happened.

"I was like, 'You're still so bitter and angry,'" Bret recalls. "That's why I did what I did: it was so I wouldn't end up like that, [where] everything is about what 'they' did and how I'm going to get 'them' someday. . . .

"I just don't think Martha understands how my family *was* wrestling," he continues. "Everyone was so involved with wrestling. You couldn't just cut it out of your life. My brother Owen died, so I've got to forget every single thing I ever did in wrestling? I didn't want that."

Going back, he says, wasn't just about the money, or about letting go of his anger, or even about getting back in the ring. It was also about getting back into the story. "That was the biggest reason that I went back," he tells me. "I wanted to rewrite my ending."

And he did. "I don't get asked a lot of questions about the Screwjob anymore," Bret says. "My career hasn't been based solely on that moment. And I'm maybe the most popular today that I've ever been in my career. I think I'm recognized by a lot of the wrestlers in the industry and a lot of the fans as maybe the greatest wrestler of all time, or in the short list of the top ten or top five. . . .

"I'm always really glad for that," Bret says. "I could be still sitting in my house being miserable."

A few years later, Bret was diagnosed with prostate cancer.

On January 31, 2016, he was preparing to publicly announce his diagnosis.

"I was writing a statement to announce to the papers the next day that I was going in for prostate surgery," Bret says. "I had it written."

"And then," he says, "I just called Vince up."

He continues: "I remember thinking about it: *Why am I calling Vince McMahon, of all people?* But it was . . . it was just . . ."

The tired grappler trails off. He thinks for a second.

"I knew that Vince . . . that he should know," he says. "He's gonna talk about it; he would appreciate me letting him know I had cancer and that I was going in for surgery."

All surgery carries fatal risk. Bret had cheated death countless times, but, for all anyone knew, it could have been the Hitman's last night on earth.

He dialed the boss's number.

It went to voice mail. "And I said, 'I just want you to know that I'm going in for surgery in the morning and I've been diagnosed with prostate cancer,'" Bret says. "And I was obviously kinda scared, and worried about what was gonna happen.

"Vince called me literally three minutes later and gave me a very strong pep talk and told me I was gonna do fine. He even did a post on the WWE internet or whatever next day," Bret says.

"So I was glad I did it. I was glad I let him know that, for some reason, he was that father figure to me. That, maybe, he'd appreciate me letting him know what I'm dealing with."

Bret pauses. We've been talking about Vince McMahon for many hours. He only has one thing left to say about the man.

"I don't know how to explain my relationship with Vince," Bret says.

"But I do know that, if I'd never crossed paths with him, I wouldn't be the same man I am today."

On Wednesday, June 15, 2022, the *Wall Street Journal* reported that Vince was under investigation by the WWE board for millions of dollars in alleged hush payments to women with whom he'd had sexual relationships while they were working for the company.

The story was picked up by media outlets around the world. WWE announced the next day that Vince would step back as chairman and CEO, to be replaced by his daughter while the investigation continued, although Vince would retain control over creative decisions. For a little over twenty-four hours, it seemed like Vince might be in real trouble.

Then, WWE made another announcement: Mr. McMahon would be making an appearance on that Friday's live episode of *SmackDown*. Not Vince, but Mr. McMahon. The wrestling world wondered aloud online what would happen. Perhaps there would be some kind of prerecorded message addressing the situation. Perhaps he would be contrite. Perhaps he would say he'd changed.

When the show began, Mr. McMahon's theme music—still "No Chance in Hell"—started to play in the arena.

And then he stepped through the entranceway. He took a few steps and planted his feet. He threw his arms wide in a gesture of abundance and greeting. He smiled that *yuk-yuk* grin.

The crowd didn't know exactly what to make of Mr. McMahon. There were some boos, some cheers, and many befuddled looks. He walked to the ring. He took the microphone.

"It is a privilege, as always, to stand before you here tonight, the WWE Universe," he said. WWE's slogan as of then was "Then. Now. Forever. Together," and Mr. McMahon referenced it: "Those four words are 'then,' 'now,' 'forever,' and the most important word is 'together.'"

He smiled again. "Welcome to *SmackDown!*" he crowed, then tossed the microphone to the ground and walked out. That was it.

The TV ratings came in. Roughly 2,389,000 people had tuned in, making it the most watched *SmackDown* in years. Mr. McMahon made an appearance on the next episode of *Raw*, once again acting as if nothing was wrong. Ratings shot up 17 percent from the previous week.

It went on like that for nearly a month. The *Wall Street Journal* published more information about Vince's alleged misconduct, including forcing an unnamed female wrestler into oral sex and then demoting her. I published an article in *New York* magazine about Rita Chatterton's allegations—along with corroboration of them from a former WWF wrestler. But Mr. McMahon kept making appearances on TV, acknowledging none of it.

Then, without warning, on Friday, July 22, Vince announced his retirement. The word went out via his Twitter account and an official WWE statement. The wrestling world was stunned. Even the wrestlers and producers who had been preparing for that night's live *SmackDown* had been in the dark, forcing a last-minute creative panic. Stephanie was named the new co-CEO; the other CEO was WWE exec Nick Khan. Paul Levesque was made the new head of creative operations. The Vince McMahon era, it seemed, was over.

The following Monday, WWE made a filing with the SEC that shed light on why Vince stepped down. It stated that WWE would have to revise years' worth of prior filings because Vince had spent a previously unreported $14.6 million of his own money—reporters presumed it was the hush money—which "should have been recorded as expenses." More ominously, the filing then stated that WWE "has also received, and may receive in the future, regulatory, investigative and enforcement inquiries, subpoenas, or demands arising from, related to, or in connection with these matters."

But, as of this writing, it is still unwise to assume Vince will suffer much for these allegations of misconduct. He remains the single largest shareholder of the publicly traded WWE and controls about 80 percent of the shareholder votes. Even if the company is sold to another corporation, Vince stands to make a fortune.

The wrestling news outlets still write deferentially, sometimes even lovingly, about Vince. They point out that you have to take the good with the bad; that, whatever his sins, he gave a lot to the artform they so love. His legacy is secure in the industry he remade.

Mr. McMahon is an armor that virtue cannot destroy.

★　★　★

The sound of the ring.

The *thwap* of a body hitting the canvas, the squeal of the springs as they bounce; the creak of the elastic as someone is thrown into the ropes, the roar the workers emit as they execute their attacks; the smack of a hand slapping a chest, the hoots of the crowd in approval.

It's a warm, late-summer night in Taunton, Massachusetts. Inside a VFW hall, no more than a hundred people are packed to the walls. No one is masked; COVID is still thriving, but no one seems fearful of infection. They're rapt. They sit on the edge of their folding chairs, watching the wrestlers go at it.

It's a show put up by a microscopic indie promotion; the wrestlers are all moonlighters with day jobs. This form of wrestling has never posed a threat to Vince McMahon.

But it may outlive him.

Vince is now the last surviving member of his biological nuclear family. Vince Senior was only sixty-nine when he passed; Rod was seventy-seven when he died of COVID on January 20, 2021. Vicki lived to 101, and finally died in January 2022; Vince was not present at her funeral, though her friends told me they'd reconciled, and that he had made sure she wanted for nothing in her old age.

At seventy-seven, Vince is constantly dogged by rumors of poor health. His face is sunken and pale, his eyes are red, his voice is dry gravel. His muscular physique is withered. He can't outrun death forever. None of us can.

While I was watching that indie wrestling show in Taunton, seeing accountants and day laborers don tights for a night of gleeful, high-impact theater, I couldn't help but think about the staying power of the artform before me.

Storytellers have known the narrative power of unarmed physical struggle since *Gilgamesh*. In the millennia since, there have been countless apocalypses of one size or another, obliterating empires and entire ways of life. But wrestling endures.

So do stories. So do performers. So do audiences.

The world may end.

But the ring never dies.

AFTERWORD

was reluctant to write this afterword for the same two reasons I was initially reluctant to even write the book's coda more than a year prior.

First of all, I didn't want to undermine my own future readership potential with spoilers. I am planning a sequel that picks up mere seconds after the revelation of the Greater Power's identity, then follows through to Vince's final days, whenever those may be.

I had originally intended for *Ringmaster* to encompass Vince's life from birth to 2020 or so, and did research accordingly. I have a wealth of material about Vince's life and impact beyond 1999 (and, indeed, much from *before* 1999 that I haven't yet used), but when I sat down to write, I quickly learned that the man had *too much life* to fit into my strict contractual word count.

My publisher wisely concluded that readers who aren't already into wrestling would hesitate to buy a Robert Caro–sized brick about a wrestling promoter whose life's work is generally thought to be a niche interest. But I take much inspiration from Caro—I will never forget reading *The Power Broker* in Manhattan's Chinatown during my first post-college year—and hope readers who have tolerated his serial approach to Lyndon Johnson's life will tolerate mine vis-à-vis Vince McMahon.

The second reason I was tempted to simply end on a cliffhanger and eschew an epilogue was this: no matter what I write, it will immediately be out of date. Vince is a fast-moving target.

When I finalized the text for the first edition of *Ringmaster*, accuracy and due diligence demanded that I refer to him as the "former" chairman and CEO of WWE, for that was his status as of September 2022. When he'd initially stepped down, the *Washington Post* asked me to write an op-ed about the "end of the Vince McMahon era." I told them I'd only write it if I was allowed to say that era *wasn't* over, what with him still being WWE's principal shareholder and controlling the vast majority of shareholder votes. He could come back anytime he wanted.

And, sure enough, within a few months, Vince was back in the boardroom, making himself the *executive* chairman and purging those who he felt betrayed him. Stephanie McMahon left the company shortly after her father's return, citing a desire to be with her family, though there were surely other considerations at work. Right away, he started turning wheels for something unprecedented: he was going to sell the company.

Rumors swirled as to who the buyer might be. The speculation ended on April 3, 2023—quite literally days after the release of *Ringmaster*. In a joint press release, Ari Emanuel's titanic holding company, Endeavor, declared their intent to buy WWE and merge it with UFC, the central brand for (legitimate) mixed martial arts competition. Endeavor paid roughly 9.3 *billion* dollars to snag WWE. That was more than what Disney paid for the Marvel and Star Wars brands, combined.

And so, on September 12, the merger was finalized, and the company that had started life in 1957 as the Capitol Wrestling Corporation was, for the first time in its sixty-six-year history, not under the absolute control of a McMahon. Vince has to share his toys with Ari, or else.

The pair did a joint appearance on CNBC when the deal was first revealed, smiling and chuckling with each other while they were interviewed by an anchor (who, as it turns out, is repped by the agency that Emanuel owns). Given Emanuel's legendary temper, one shudders to think how a war between the two might play out. As of this writing, on November 14, 2023, such a war has yet to erupt.

Don't chalk that up to a newfound obedience on Vince's part. Instead, look to the situation in which he finds himself. That CNBC interview was the last time Vince has spoken to a journalist in months, and a rare instance of him even being seen in public. Since then, it has been revealed that Vince had to undergo a mysterious medical procedure. Perhaps more importantly, WWE announced that Vince is being investigated by the authorities in connection with alleged sexual misconduct. His phone was confiscated, but the full extent of the probe is not yet known.

Occasionally, paparazzi catch Vince out at a club or restaurant in New York City or elsewhere. He doesn't look like himself. He has a strange, Walt Disney–esque mustache and jet-black hair dye. He's deflated, no longer the muscleman he had worked so hard to be. He uses a cane. A source said she was at a restaurant in Manhattan where the proprietor politely told everyone they'd have to leave soon for a private party. The party turned out to consist solely of Vince and a young female companion. He shuffled in as my source skittered out. She says he looked like a man close to death.

But if there's one thing I've learned from researching and writing about the life of Vincent Kennedy McMahon, it's that you should never count him out. His mother lived to age 101. He's currently seventy-eight. One can imagine him pulling a Rupert Murdoch or Sumner Redstone and clinging on to some kind of power well into his nineties. I won't take a bet against his ability to beat back the reaper through sheer cussedness.

Even if Vince dies before the release of this paperback edition, that death will only be the beginning of lifetimes of posthumous research into his life. Many people I tried to speak to for this book told me they wouldn't go on the record because they feared one thing: Vince's retribution. When he's gone, perhaps lips will loosen.

But don't anticipate a sudden thaw from WWE. There will be no immediate release of incriminating documentation, no opening of the proverbial KGB archives. WWE will persist after Vince's death, for that is the nature of industry: humans create beasts that outlive them. It's all an effort to claim immortality.

Though one should always hesitate to grant the wishes of Vince McMahon, I think his *literary* immortality is a small price to pay for education and enrichment. I deeply hope that *Ringmaster* sparks journalistic and academic interest in Vince and professional wrestling. There need to be more people analyzing this transcendent art form and its hypercapitalist crimes. I have barely scratched the surface in the book you now hold.

It will be a generational process to dig up a more complete picture of this remarkable and terrifying man. I am a self-taught student of ancient history, and when I read the works of the world's earliest biographers, I see them writing about the minds, natures, and impacts of their amoral—often outright *immoral*—leaders. Plutarch and Suetonius wrote about men who thought themselves gods and about the consequences of their rule. There's a reason I plan to call *Ringmaster*'s sequel *God-Emperor McMahon*.

Until then, remember the ultimate lesson of this book: *choose your kayfabe wisely.*

ABRAHAM JOSEPHINE RIESMAN,
NOVEMBER 5, 2023

APPENDIX 1

"Wrestling Turned Me Cis, Then It Turned Me Trans"

This essay originally appeared on Polygon.com on March 29, 2023.

My bullies all loved pro wrestling.

It was the spring of 1999, we were thirteen-year-old kids at a public school in the Chicago suburbs, and, every day at recess, they would harass me. Though I long ago wiped my memory clean of any specific insults, the overall theme could be summed up as, *"Look at this faggot."*

I was a defective boy: I sang in the hallways, wore flared jeans, had platonic friendships with girls, and always leapt at the chance to play a woman in a class skit.

They were *real* boys: burly, cackling, anti-intellectual, and always ready to identify a homo.

I loved midcentury musical theater and weird British comic books.

They loved the World Wrestling Federation.

While they tormented me each day, the faces and slogans of their favorite wrestlers leered at me from their T-shirts: "Stone Cold" Steve Austin, The Rock, The Undertaker. There's a special little humiliation in being gay-bashed by someone wearing a jersey that—in the words of WWF squad D-Generation X—invites you to "SUCK IT."

I didn't exactly have a *political* objection to the WWF at that age. It was simply what the boys who hated me liked, and that was enough to repel me.

Then, something strange happened: my sole male friend, Brian, caught an episode of the WWF's weekly flagship show, *Raw Is War*, while channel-surfing. He was blown away by what he saw and immediately demanded that I watch it with him. I trusted Brian—he wasn't a bully. So I gave it a shot.

I fell in love.

I must have already known that "professional" wrestling was fixed, more of a scripted art form than a legitimate sporting competition. I absolutely didn't care. I was entranced by how these humans, these *men*, defied everyone who stepped into their path. They were my demographic's visions of ideal masculinity, and, suddenly, I wanted nothing more than to have their confidence.

I began watching WWF programs religiously, first with Brian, then with a small group of boys, most of whom I had never been close to prior to this. One kid's parents had a huge finished basement, and we'd gather there for the sacred viewing of pay-per-view events.

At one such event, I was surprised to find one of my bullies in attendance. By this time, school officials and our parents had stepped in to serve the two of us a kind of junior-high no-contact order, so I was prepared for the encounter to be awkward. But instead, we just did what we'd come to do: We watched and talked about wrestling. We were finally on the same side. We were the same thing: just fans. Just boys.

As the weeks and months wore on, this group became a tightly knit cohort—the first group of male friends I'd ever had. We watched the rampant homophobia, misogyny, racism, transphobia, and assorted other provocations, and we loved them. We learned that *this* was what it meant to be a man—to be safe, to be superior, to be powerful. The bullies had taught me that I had to be a man to be worth anything. Wrestling taught me that being a man was worth everything.

My fandom waned after a few rabid years. But, in early 2020, I began work on *Ringmaster*, a biography of longtime WWF owner Vince McMahon. To report it, I plunged back into McMahon's product, the visions of masculinity I'd consumed with such desperation as a kid—including McMahon's turn as the villain-protagonist that the crowd loved to hate and hated to love.

This time, though, I was an adult, and the toxicity was hard to ignore. In the last twenty years, even as the WWF's popularity has plateaued, the attitudes and devices it championed have spread into every aspect of our civic life. McMahon's close friend Donald Trump rehashed McMahon's hero/villain act on the national stage, while employing McMahon's wife in his cabinet, supported by a generation of voters who had accepted McMahon's version of masculinity. This time, I no longer wanted to be accepted by this nation of bullies. Rather, I wanted to defect, to secede.

But I also saw something I hadn't seen before. Wrestling is built around masculinity, but in its own way it is also transgressive—even *queer*. Men in wrestling wear bright colors. They intimately touch other men in public. When they're allied, they speak of each other in the warm terms of life partners; when they're at odds, they issue ambiguously sexual threats such as "I want your ass."

Most importantly, they show pain.

The essential, irreducible element of a wrestling match is the ability to show suffering—the very thing drummed out of every boy by high school, if not earlier. It's the heart of the art form. No matter how skilled a wrestler is technically, it doesn't count at all unless they can make the audience believe they're being hurt. Every wrestler has to spend a significant amount of every match showing nothing but raw, visceral agony. They have to show their secret face, the most vulnerable one of all.

Wrestling is an art form, one that turned out to have also planted seeds in my mind about how fun it is to dress up, show tenderness, be vulnerable, and do the things you're not supposed to.

A few days before I turned in the completed draft of my book, I told the world via Twitter that I'm not a man. I'm choosing to live as a trans woman. I go by "she" now. This is the conclusion I might have come to all those years ago if my bullies hadn't terrorized me out of it. Wrestling showed me how to be a man. But it also gave me a second message, one that had finally—*finally*—reached me. Wrestling taught me to be cis at thirteen, and then it taught me to be trans at thirty-six.

Vince McMahon, at age seventy-seven, still operates in an industry where machismo reigns. Last summer, he was confronted with a wave of sexual-misconduct allegations, including an accusation that he raped a female referee, and he made a surprising move: he stepped out of the spotlight. But it was a brief moment; McMahon hates looking like a loser. So he used his clout to restore himself as the head of the company and now rules it again with an iron, masculine fist.

But McMahon only has so much time left. Wrestling will outlast him. And when I think about the fans of wrestling who most *get* what makes it work, I think of all my queer and trans compatriots who watch and perform it. There has been an explosion in queer-oriented indie wrestling in recent years, driven by performers who can hear the art form's undertones. They make the implicit explicit, and it's a beautiful thing to behold.

I'm not sure what those individuals who bullied me are up to today. We were all kids driven by ideas about manhood that made us miserable. I am now unlearning them, and I hope their journeys have taken them that far as well.

To be a queer and trans wrestling fan is to invert and expand the industry that we all gawk at. Not everyone comes along on the ride. One of wrestling's virtues is how much it can bring disparate people together— which means there are still plenty of bullies who watch wrestling. But I've chosen to opt out of that demographic. I've seceded. I've shown the world my secret face. And I haven't looked back.

APPENDIX II

Author Interview

*The following conversation was recorded on February 10, 2023,
for the* Longform *podcast. It was conducted by Max Linsky.
The transcript has been edited and abridged for clarity and length.*

Before we go any further: You should know I am not a wrestling fan.
Good. You're the target demographic. The assumption was, if I do my job right, people who already like wrestling books will be interested in the book, but that has more to do with the topic than anything else. So my goal was to create something that would be appealing to total novices, total beginners, people who have no knowledge whatsoever of professional wrestling. So you are in exactly the right headspace for the book.

This is a weird question, but do you have any insight into people who are or aren't going to enjoy wrestling? Because from an intellectual standpoint, I find these concepts of kayfabe and "Is it real or fake?" intellectually fascinating, but my actual desire to engage with it as entertainment is almost at zero.
Oh, actually, that's a very common state for me. When it comes to comics . . . Not to jump ahead, but my first book was about Stan Lee. I reached a point with comics where it was really hard for me to enjoy it as an art form, but I've never stopped being interested in it as a product or as an industry. And that's sort of how I feel about wrestling to a certain extent. I have enormous respect for that art form—*enormous* respect. But even when I was a teenage wrestling diehard, I didn't have an ear for the *music* of a wrestling match, and I've never totally gotten it. I've been able to talk to enough people who do have that ear, who do have that perfect pitch, that I've been able to understand from a cognitive standpoint what makes a good match. But what's interesting to me are the *words*. I mean, I'm a writer, so that's going to be where I'm predisposed. But why do some

people get into it and some people don't? It's hard to say. One thing that I always like to point out is that there are two pathways into wrestling when you're young: there's "I was a kid who liked sports" and then there's the path I was on, which was "I'm a kid who likes musical theater."

I'll never forget the part of the book where all of the wrestlers, the people producing it, are convinced that everyone thinks it's real. But 99 to 100 percent of the people in there know it's not real. And yet, both sides believe that there is no future if there's any acknowledgment of both people knowing what the other one thinks.

I'll just hasten to say, I think the percentage is not 99 percent people. You will find all of these stories from the age of old kayfabe: there will be people where you think, *Wow, this was an intelligent person who is skeptical*, and they would say, "Yeah, I totally believed it was real. I completely believed it was all on the level." The point I was trying to make in that part of the book is not "everyone was in on it," just that there were a lot more people in on it than wrestling lore admits to. Wrestling lore is still kind of trapped in that kayfabe universe.

Well, and you also talk about how that kayfabe is not just in the ring. If you want to be a wrestling hanger-on and you're having a beer afterwards, everyone has to maintain the illusion in all areas. And that's something that I think really connects wrestling to politics. There are these forums where there is no dropping of character potentially for your entire life. You get buried in whoever you've become.

Yeah, absolutely. There was a period when you lived with kind of the old kayfabe system in wrestling *and* in politics, which was, there's a big, solid, flat, foundational lie, and the flat foundational lie is this: "What you're seeing is real." In politics, that was "This is democracy at work"; in wrestling, it was "This is a sport at work." And either you knew that that lie was a lie or you didn't, but it was tough and long-standing. However, we've entered into this world where you have, in politics, something that's existed in wrestling for the past three decades or so, which is what I perhaps over-ambitiously decided to call *neokayfabe*. And neokayfabe is a foundation that's much more like a bunch of slippery boulders. It's not a flat foundation.

The idea of neokayfabe is, you are *not* telling the person, "Hey, what you're seeing on this wrestling show is real." In fact, you're very emphatically saying, "Don't worry, it's all fake." But you also have to implicitly say, "This one aspect of the match is going to actually reflect what's *really* happening behind the scenes." Or "These two guys who are wrestling tonight, even though it's a fake wrestling match, they *actually* hate each other, so watch out—one of them *might* hurt the other!" So you end up with this manufactured truth behind the lie, and people have trouble combating that brain hack of saying, "What you're seeing is fake, but I'm going to let you in on the *real* secret about what's going on." When you introduce that sort of mental schema, you can manipulate people very easily; when what they're doing is not necessarily gauging the morality of what you're saying, but rather just going, *Is that real or not? Did that really happen? Or am I confused?* When you're feeling that conflict of *Could this insane thing be real? Or am I being deceived?*, you end up with a very impressionable brain. And that's unfortunately where we are in politics right now.

One of my best friends from high school is a film director. He's actually directing a Marvel movie right now, ironically, and we were flying on JetBlue together and we saw, I believe it was the first season of *Laguna Beach*, the reality show. It was amongst the first pieces of reality TV, and not reality TV in the sense of *The Real World*, but where people were getting into it and stuff was going on. And stuff did have that staged quality, but like you were saying, it seemed like it was a staged quality that was staging real relationships and scenarios.
Absolutely. Reality TV picked up what wrestling was putting down at least a decade earlier.

We kept talking about it in terms of the filmmaking. He was like, "Wow, they've got two cameras—that can't really be happening!" or whatever. But like you were saying, we couldn't get to a point of being clear about exactly what we thought was going on in *Laguna Beach*.
Exactly, exactly. You're sure that there's a level of unreality, but you're not sure that it's *all* fake. There's stuff there that seems plausible, or, sometimes, you go, *There's no way they could fake that.* And sometimes you're right. And a lot of times, it's somewhere in the middle. It's not as easily distinguished as saying, "*This* is fact and *this* is fiction," "*This* was scripted and *this* was improvised," whatever. You can't make those distinctions easily. And one of the things I hope comes out of the book, if it has any impact at

all, is to try and get us past this false binary between true and false. That's the trouble: we have a lot of people in power who got there by realizing that there's no actual incentive, in a political or financial sense, to distinguish between fact and fiction. It's not actually important if you're just trying to claw your way to the top for short-term gain—and sometimes even for very long-term gain. But that's me getting up on my high horse. I could talk about that all day.

You've written a book about Stan Lee, you've written a book now about Vince McMahon, and both of them and Trump are people whose lives don't fit into a neat, biopic, rise-and-fall kind of story. It's a lot of rises and a lot of falls and a lot of chaos. Now having done two of these, how do you think about structuring a book like that?

I wish I had some kind of systematic answer that I could bestow upon the world. But I mean, when it comes to the structure . . . [sigh] So much of it comes down to the aesthetics of what the table of contents looks like to me. That's going to sound so stupid. But once I've done all the research, I basically have a working document that is always in flux, and it's of the table of contents. For the first two books, the TOC was chronological. That periodization of going, *Okay, one chapter is talking about the story of this period* can be extremely useful—for me, at least—and the structure starts to just make itself known to me. That sounds so stupid and mystical. But I tend to draw more inspiration for structure from fiction than from nonfiction.

That was something I noticed: even though we're going linearly through time, there is a sense of theme in different sections of the book. The first section of the book is about fathers and sons and father-son relationships.

Nailed it. Yeah.

The second section of the book is about ruthless business tactics and how you build an empire, and also what becomes of you once you become singularly *focused* on building an empire.

And about *how* you build an empire in the twenty-first century, which is, you build it out of yourself: your brand, your own weird idiosyncrasies, anxieties, and complexities. That's what wins now, whether it's in the marketplace or in politics. What tends to win is people who did what Vince did before most people did, which is you take your libidinal urges, fears, and general preoccupations, and you put them into mass media in a well-crafted way—or at least a *provocatively* crafted way—and the sky's the limit. If you know your own id, or at least are really good at *expressing* your own id in ways that feel transgressive and feel like they're confusing as to whether they're real or fake, you can kinda get anywhere. We don't know how to deal with that level of uncanniness. Vince figured that out before a lot of other people did.

Hundreds of people are referred to in this book. Probably hundreds of *wrestlers*, alone, appear in that book. When you're tackling something of this scale, what's your strategy? How do you prioritize? How do you say, *This is the important thing to do right now*?
Oh, God. Here's the thing: I used to really struggle with that, and I still do on some level, but I've learned how to mitigate it. Basically, I have terrible ADHD, and the biggest manifestation of my ADHD is I am very often paralyzed by choice and by prioritization. It's very hard for me to not see everything that I have to do as top-priority, and therefore nothing becomes the priority. I've spent many years trying to-do lists and trying to order the lists like "I should do this first, and then that"—and I would never stick to them. It would always then frustrate me that I hadn't stuck to them. So what I've come to do is trust my gut on a given day about what I should pick, from amongst a general jumble of core topics that are urgent. I'm certainly guilty of occasionally going down paths that turn out to be busts. But I can usually generally tell: *Okay, this general topic area is something I should spend more time on, and I have some specific questions about that, and other things I just need to know the lay of the land for*—whatever.

I wake up in the morning—and I wish I could say that there is some journaling practice I do or whatever—but I basically drink my coffee, sit down at my computer and go, *What, just based on nothing, feels right as to what I should work on, among that grouping of things that are somewhat important to do or very important to do?* And I can't say it works insofar as I've done alternate-universe tests where I tried to write two books by doing a different method, but it did allow me to write those two books. It was a mix of prioritizing generally, and then just kinda being a leaf on the wind and going, *My gut is telling me that today I should research the Saudis*, or *My gut is telling me that today I should finally track down this wrestler*, or whatever. And I don't know, I wish I could say I had a better answer than just going with my gut, but that is very often what it comes down to.

How do you go about trying to get people to tell these stories that they're not supposed to be telling? These stories that really break some of the mystique of what was happening behind the scenes?

How do I do it? Sometimes I don't! [*Laughs.*] I only have the interviews that I got, as opposed to the many where people said, "No comment." I mean, very often the answer was either "There's no way I'm going to talk about Vince if I ever want to work in this town again," or "I'm broke, there's no way I'm going to talk to you unless you pay me." Approval from Vince or the WWE was out of the question, and I wasn't going to pay for interviews. So I ended up with a lot of people who wouldn't talk to me. But you just keep plucking away . . . *Plugging* away, rather. "Plucking," actually, is an interesting little Freudian slip, because sometimes it does feel like you're trying to pluck out all the Nos until you find that one Yes. I mostly had luck with the older generation of wrestlers, because if you were not starting in Vince McMahon's world, there's a much greater likelihood that you have independence of thought—and sometimes, even contractual independence, because you signed an older version of the contract and you're not bound to certain kinds of things. The core narrative of the book ends in 1999, and part of that was that Vince's life is just too eventful and I couldn't cram it all in there, but also, part of it was, I needed more time to pass. Because as time goes on, you're much more likely to get an answer at all and/or an honest answer from somebody who has been affected by the subject of your work.

The big thing is just being a decent human, not treating people like they're lab animals. People like being treated with dignity. If you can treat your interview subjects with dignity, you then become somebody who gets a good referral when you say, "Hey, is there any chance you could put me in touch with so-and-so who you mentioned?" And it's a lot better to get a referral than just to hear the name and cold-call as though you didn't have that relationship with the previous person. So, that's as good advice as I can give: just be a decent human. Your conversations with people should feel like they're having a conversation with another person as opposed to a question-asking robot. And that can take you very far, is what I have found in my little life.

What led you into writing? How did you end up here?
It's funny—I just found something in my grandfather's archives about this. My grandfather Robert A. Riesman Sr. had been an artillery officer in World War II. At the end of World War II, when he was an officer stationed in liberated Paris, he was writing letters home saying, "I don't want to come home and work for dad's company," which was an electrical equipment firm. "I want to stay here and be a foreign correspondent." And there's this letter where my great-uncle just writes to him and goes, "Don't be an idiot. You have to come home and run the company. You're the one dad's counting on." And lo and behold, he did. This was fascinating to me. I never knew my grandfather had any interest in being a writer. It makes total sense in retrospect. He was extremely gifted with words, both in the written form and in those delivered through speech. But I had no idea that being a journalist was something that he had really wanted to do. But my father also became a writer—this is later in my life, but he wrote a book, a biography of Big Bill Broonzy, who was a very influential blues musician who died in 1958. So maybe it's just something in my line: we have people who like the fun of words and the terror of words and all of that.

As for me personally, I just loved writing in class. I mean, it's as simple as that. You say, "When did you want to be a writer?" Well, unlike certain skills or trades where you have a very clear delineation of, "Okay, this is when I first picked that thing up," you're writing in a clean arc from the earliest days of your schooling, if not sooner. And it was always the thing I was best at, but also enjoyed the most, but I thought I was not going to be a writer. I thought I was going to be an actor. We had this very robust and wonderful theater scene at my high school in Oak Park, Illinois, and I really just adored the practice of being onstage. But then I got to college and I got sick of the social structures and expectations of being a theater kid. I was just not interested in a lot of the—if you'll forgive the pun—drama that was involved in that. Now, of course, the irony is I then was like, *Well, I'm going to go into journalism where there's none of that nonsense!* Which is, of course, ridiculous. But I didn't know that as of when I joined my college paper, which is the kind of thing you can just do back when you're in college, if you're lucky. It was an organic growth from there.

And what were your first professional experiences of trying to pitch stuff and write for editors and that kind of stuff?

I was at Harvard, writing for *The Harvard Crimson*. Writing for a college newspaper is something that I think everyone should have the opportunity to do. It's such a beautiful institution, the college newspaper—especially independent college newspapers. I really treasure the training I got at *The Crimson*. I went to college for all four years and got my degree, but most of what I learned was by working forty hours a week at *The Crimson*, first as a reporter, then as an editor, and then as one of the two heads of the arts section. And it was different back then because your pitches don't have to be as well formed. [*Laughs.*] And you can kind of just know somebody who is one of the editors and say, "Yo, wouldn't it be wild if I wrote an editorial about how this one popular band sucks now?" And there's a chance they might run that!

I learned a lot when I started dipping my toe into the *real*, professional journalism world, which initially was actually in public radio, as a reporting intern. I was an intern, but I was really a reporter—I was just unpaid. I was a full-time reporter for about a month and a half at WBAI, which is a very far-left radio station in downtown Manhattan. I stumbled into that, and that was fascinating because I would pitch stuff, but I didn't know anything about New York at that point, and it was very local, specific New York reporting. So I had to kind of sit at the feet of the masters of that organization, and it was very useful. I think the thing I eventually learned in the long arc of my career is this: If it *interests* you, and if you can start writing it, and if it somewhat makes sense, then follow that instinct. That's in opposition to what I did for a long time, which was trying to pitch what I thought the *editor* would find interesting. That just leads you to being a trend-chaser, and no editor wants that. The people in a position to hire you, they want to have their ears to the ground, hearing about the next development in whatever topic. And the only way they can find that stuff is if people who have niche interests in things that are currently narrow, but are going to be wider, come to them. In many ways, that's the secret of whatever level of success I've had: Just going, "Hey, here's this movie that nobody talks about, but that I love. Maybe if I write about it, we'll find that more people than just me love it." And sometimes that's not the case, but a lot of the time, that's how it works out. Because that's how we experience the world: very often in terms of, *No one's talking about this thing that matters to me*. And then, when that thing finally gets talked about, you get very enthusiastic. You're like, "Look, the thing I've been talking about in my head or with my friends is a phenomenon that happens to other people!" And then, all of a sudden, you've got a viral article on your hands.

Sometimes, I feel like the journalism and media world has gone a bit astray, because I'll talk to someone and they'll be like, "I want to write about climate." And I'm like, "Do you know a lot about climate?" "It's really important." I was like, "Yeah, I get that it's important, but you're not bringing anything to it."
You have to talk about the stuff that you have some understanding of. I think the *only* aspect of my weird little career that I can really translate to other people is this: *Don't disregard any of your interests or experiences*. Don't dismiss out of hand anything that's happened to you or that you have found interesting and gotten some level of even amateur expertise on. Because very often the stuff where you think, *Well, nobody cares about that* is actually the stuff that a lot of people care about. They just don't *know* other people care about it, or they'll be surprised and delighted to learn more.

You're transitioning right now, yes?
I am. Aren't we all? But yes, I came out as trans on the summer solstice of 2022. Not that you'd know it from my voice. I'm not changing a ton about myself in terms of my physical flesh, but I have been *en femme* since June of last year. I dress femme, I think femme, I am on Team Femme. But also Team Trans. I mean, that's one of the reasons why I haven't shaved my beard [*Editor's note: she has subsequently shaved her beard*] or done all that much in the way of changing my voice. I just feel like the playing field should be opened up to different expressions of gender. And I don't care if people see me as something in between. That's fine. I don't even really know. I mean, I could get into all kinds of gender theory about how I con-

sider myself. I don't want to bore everybody. But yes, I have been living a trans life of *trans*gression and hopefully *trans*cendence since last year.

I'm interested in how that interfaces with your life as a writer and putting together a book like this. What is it like to be having this personal transformation while you're also writing seven hundred to-do lists of wrestlers from the early 1990s that you need to email?

Well, it's funny, you got it a little backwards, because what happened was, I was three or four days away from having a completed first draft. And then Providence Pride happened here in Providence, Rhode Island, where I live. And I went and I had this very revelatory experience and realized I want to live as a lady. And then I finished the draft. And also that was the week that Vince McMahon first got hit with the allegations from the *Wall Street Journal* about sexual misconduct that led to his eventual stepping back. It was a crazy week, but all of those things felt tied up together. Maybe cause and effect are not so clearly delineated here, but it did feel like working on this book really disabused me of what remaining notions I had about the value of holding on to manhood. If people want to identify as men, that's fantastic. May you be a good man and try and dismantle the unjust system from within. But I'm defecting. I can't do anything with manhood, at least in the society in which I live. What I've decided to do is be diasporic, in a way. And part of that comes out of working on the book. I saw manhood in a new way through looking at Vince's trauma, and the way that trauma was then turned into traits that were trauma-inducing for other people. And part of my transition moment was having spent a couple of years in the head of one of the most macho men you'll ever meet, Vince McMahon, and kind of realizing, *Well, I don't really want to be a part of that.*

We used to have an app, the *Longform* app, and I was trying to create these catalogs, basically, of every *Longform* story a writer had written. And it makes you very tied to your name, right? Change your name, you just become a different person, and now you've got two pools. You just lost everything you wrote before you changed your name. And I don't think that just pertains to names. I think it pertains to identity as a whole. If I were to pick up the Stan Lee book, I think it would say "he" in the author bio.

Yeah, it said "he" back then. Absolutely.

And now I've got *Ringmaster* and it says "she," but they're both by the same person. It still—

It still says "Abraham Riesman." I know. Well, the cover of the *Ringmaster* hardback is kind of a funny story. I was approving the cover *right* when I was coming out as trans. I did not expect that timing to be happening the way it did, but it did, and I had already approved the cover, and then I was like, *I feel like I want to add some femininity to my name.* And I pretty quickly decided I wanted to be "Abraham Josephine Riesman," but I didn't want to mess with the graphic design of the cover. It felt like there was no room for the "Josephine." It needs to be what it is. So I figured, okay, on the inside flap, it'll say "Abraham Josephine Riesman." But I'm going to confuse people for a little bit. Maybe for the rest of my life—who knows? But I actually love my name. My birth name is not something I'm ashamed of. "Abraham" is something that I treasure, and that's why I use it still in the byline. I'm kind of ripping off two of my trans heroes—Charlie Jane Anders, the sci-fi writer, and Justin Vivian Bond, the performer—by doing the whole "boy name - girl name - last name" formulation.

As a format, as something to dig into, does the biography form work for you?

I've really dug it. My next project is a biography, or at least it's biographical in nature. I learned about writing a biography—a full biography of somebody who's already deceased, so you can tell their full story—with Stan Lee. Then, with Vince, what I learned—and a lot of this was a credit to my wonderful frontline editor, who is my spouse, S. I. Rosenbaum—is you can tell the story of Vince that you need to tell for this book without chronicling his entire lifespan. There is a story to be told, and that's the most important thing. So I think what I'm trying to do with this upcoming project, and hopefully future projects after that, is not necessarily try to think of myself as a *biographer*, as the entirety of it, but rather to use the framework of the chronology of a person's life as a way to talk about something bigger. I'm very proud of my Stan Lee book, *True Believer*, but I think if I could do it again, I would've thought bigger about some of the more global human implications of both this guy's life, and our understanding of human psychology when we see his life. I think I did that much better here—and, again, my editor S. I. Rosenbaum was very helpful with that. But I want to expand that.

I often think about the good biopics. A good biopic doesn't tell you the person's whole entire story. A good biopic picks its spots and goes, "This is the stuff that is important here. This is the stuff that's important there." And maybe you only have stuff that's in this one confined section of their life, but it tells you in microcosm what you need to know. So I'm hopefully going to keep using the biographical form. I like people much more than I like institutions. But I think people are often the gateway to an understanding of an institution or an era or a phenomenon or whatever. So yeah, I guess I'll try continuing with the biography format, but I want to use it to go into weird directions. And my dream at some point is I want to write about my aforementioned grandfather, to write my big fat Jewish book, which I don't think the world is ready for. Nor am I ready for it. At some point, I do want to be able to write a meditation on Jewish identity as I see it. But I have to earn my stripes before I can pull something like that off.

APPENDIX III

Notes on Vince McMahon's Families

Vincent Kennedy McMahon was born in Moore County, North Carolina, on August 24, 1945. His mother was Victoria Elizabeth Hanner (1920–2021). His stepfather was Leo Hubert Lupton Jr. (1917–1988). His father was Vincent James McMahon (1914–1984). Below is information on the lineages of these three notable individuals.

THE HANNERS

As the men of the Second Continental Congress ratified their Declaration of Independence in Philadelphia on July 4, 1776, twenty-four-year-old Robert Hanna could be found living four hundred miles to their southwest, in North Carolina's Guilford County. Just forty years prior, one couldn't have found a single white face among the oaks and maples of Guilford, as it was the domain of an indigenous tribe whose name has been Europeanized variously as Cheraw, Suali, Xuala, and Saraw. They had endured slaughter at the hands of both Europeans and fellow natives, and the year 1738 had brought with it a smallpox epidemic that more or less annihilated them, leaving the survivors with no option but to integrate into other tribes elsewhere. In the middle of the eighteenth century, white settlers had arrived and established scattered outposts; although they had grown, the land was still largely wild as of 1776. When the United States was founded, the Cheraw were a fading memory and the supremacy of the white man was firmly established.

Robert's family, Presbyterian descendants of Scotland's Clan Hanna, were settler landowners. Robert had been born in Pennsylvania, but his father, John, had received a grant for a seven-hundred-acre plot of land in Guilford, and the family lived there for decades afterward. Robert had already amassed enough of a fortune to buy portions of the plot from his father. That said, he and his wife of three years, Isabella Earwin, lived in the shadow of tragedy: their first child, a boy, born in 1774, had died after just 127 days of life. Within weeks of the death, they conceived again, and their next child, another son, was born about a year before his country was. They lived in relative comfort, but, unlike other wealthy members of the newly independent colonies, their wealth was not measured in the bodies of enslaved women and men. Not yet.

A war is fought; a war is won. The first federal census, that of 1790, finds Robert, Isabella, and their six children still living in Guilford. Robert was an established farmer by that time and was serving in the North Carolina House of Commons—a significant responsibility in a place that was figuring out how state government under the still fresh Constitution would function. One thing was certain about that government and that Constitution as of 1790: they allowed for chattel slavery. And, sure enough, in the following decade, Robert, with whatever justifications he chose to espouse, made his pact with the devil. The 1800 census lists him as the owner of eight Black people. Vince's ancestor's land had become a forced-labor camp.

Until Vince's rise to power, the most famous and wealthy scion of his mother's line was one of Robert's sons, John Henry Hanner (the spelling of last names was malleable back then), a prominent slaver born in 1777. For decades, he lived in comfort and local renown thanks to the unrewarded labor of a rotating cast of enslaved people on a 614-acre farm property—massive by local standards—in what is now Greensboro. He had some kind of nervous breakdown in 1831 and was mentally unwell until he died in 1850, just before that year's census could record that he was then holding ten people in captivity, including a sixty-five-year-old woman and a child who was an "idiot," the period term for people who had developmental or other disabilities.

The Civil War and its attendant universal de jure emancipation brought an end to the good times for Vince's matrilineal predecessors. John Henry's son Orpheus Smiley, grandson John George, and great-grandson Orpheus William lived their entire lives in the quiet obscurity of downward mobility: the first two men were property-owning farmers, but Orpheus William—Vince's grandfather—was an itinerant mechanic who rambled back and forth between North and South Carolina, barely making a living while working on automobiles (a relatively new technology as of then). The latter man's greatest accomplishment, perhaps, was getting married to Vince's maternal grandmother and middle-namesake, Victoria Kennedy.

Victoria is worthy of special attention, despite how little we know about her. In 2001, Vince was asked about who, in his youth, had made the biggest impact on him. "I don't know if there's any one person who has been profoundly influential," Vince replied. "But if I had to say, other than my dad, it would be my grandmother."

THE LUPTONS

Go to North Carolina's Craven or Carteret counties, on the southeastern coastline, and toss a stone into a crowd—you're liable to hit a Lupton. The progenitor of the line in America was an Englishman named Christopher Lupton, who arrived in New Amsterdam in 1654, a decade before it became New York. One of his great-grandsons, "Papa" Christopher Lupton, was a professional sailor who reportedly shipwrecked at Hog Island (in what is now Carteret County) around 1769 and, welcomed by the local white settlers, established a homestead there. He was fruitful, and multiplied: a 1980 Lupton family reunion in their informal capital city, New Bern, drew more than two hundred attendees.

There have been a great many Luptons of note: Rev. Dilworth Lupton was a famed Unitarian minister, John Thomas Lupton was an early investor in Coca-Cola, Christopher "Kit" Lupton was a beloved chief of police in New Bern, and so on. There are seven Lupton men who have had American towns named after them. No one will do so for the Lupton who became Vince's stepfather.

Kit's son was the first Leo Hubert Lupton, a carpenter and mechanic who moved often. At age twenty-two, he and his wife, Ernestine, were living in New Bern and welcomed what appears to have been their third child, the first boy, who bore the name of his father. Blue-eyed, brown-haired Leo Jr. faced troubles from early on: his knee was crushed by a truck at age three and he was told he might never walk again. Somehow, he overcame the injury, but received little fanfare for that achievement compared to his younger brother, yet another Christopher Lupton. Chris was part of the New Deal–era Civilian Conservation Corps, and was permanently maimed and nearly burned to death while fighting a massive New Jersey fire in 1936; he pulled through and received a medal from

President Franklin Roosevelt, as well as glowing coverage in local media. No one wrote news features about the hero's older brother.

THE McMAHONS

We do not know the birthdate of Elizabeth "Eliza" Dowling, Vince's paternal great-grandmother, but she was baptized on May 5, 1843, in Ireland's County Kilkenny. The whole of the island had been incorporated into the still new United Kingdom of Great Britain and Ireland in 1801, but the health and well-being of the Irish was hardly a priority for the London government, and when a crop blight hit in 1845, the population was largely left to fend for itself. Eliza was two, and *An Gorta Mór*—the Great Famine—had arrived. Kilkenny lost an estimated 20 to 30 percent of her population to death and immigration. The girl's first years came during one of her birthplace's many apocalypses.

In the summer of 1851, as the famine continued to emaciate their countrymen, the Dowlings escaped. The patriarch, Richard, likely came first, but the only available travel record is a ship manifest that says the rest of the clan arrived in the port of New York City aboard the SS *Constitution* on August 23, 1851. They did well for themselves, to say the least. By 1860, Richard was supporting his middle-class family as a shopkeeper, and he was privileged to own $800 in real estate and $300 in personal estate—significant sums, though not astronomical. However, the decade that followed was good to the Dowlings: by its end, Richard had bought, sold, and leased thousands of dollars in real estate in New York City's 12th Ward, which is today's Upper Manhattan. Eliza was, suddenly, heiress to a fortune.

Frustratingly, we know precious little about her husband, Vince's great-grandfather, Roderick McMahon. He was born to parents John and Mary sometime in the 1840s in County Galway, roughly 125 miles from Kilkenny. He seems to have arrived in New York around 1866, and within two years he and Eliza had met and wed. By 1870, twenty-five-year-old Roderick and his twenty-three-year-old bride were living on what is now West 126th Street, in Harlem. Significantly, Roderick held no real or personal estate as of then. He was not an independently wealthy man. He would soon become so, but largely by virtue of the woman he married.

The ensuing decade brought children: Catherine in 1870, Mary in 1872, Elizabeth Grace in 1874, Mary Loretta in 1875, another Catherine in 1877 (the first had died of diphtheria earlier that year), and Edward in 1880. Roderick worked a diverse set of jobs in that period: he was a hotel-keeper, dealt liquor, and worked in the oyster-harvesting trade, among other professions. But, more importantly, he was a landlord.

It appears that the once penniless Roderick got a significant cash infusion from his wildly successful father-in-law, and was soon in the real estate hustle. There are deeds that claim Roderick bought an astounding $8,700 worth of property between 1871 and 1881, and there are more deeds with unspecified—but likely enormous—sums after that. Surely, he was a cunning and skilled businessman. But without Eliza's love and largesse, he would probably have come to nothing.

By the time the couple had their seventh child, Roderick James, on May 26, 1882, the family was among the wealthiest in their neighborhood. Everyone called the new lad "Jess," and he was raised in comfort. When Jess was three, Eliza's father died and left most of his fortune to her, making them rich beyond the average Irish immigrant's wildest dreams.

But Jess, like Vince, grew up largely without a father: the elder Roderick died suddenly on October 30, 1888, at age forty-eight, when Jess wasn't yet seven years old. Eliza never remarried and raised the entire group from there on out as a single mother. Jess would go on to begin the family journey into professional wrestling, making his trajectory supremely important to Vince McMahon's story. And, just as the Hanners and Luptons were Vince's true shapers, we must remember Jess was a man formed and fueled almost entirely by his mother and the Dowlings.

Jess's familial wealth—as well as the increasing integration of Irish people into the construct of American whiteness—made it such that an array of career avenues were available to him. After obtaining a commercial diploma from Manhattan College in 1899, at age sixteen, Jess initially did unremarkable work in a series of industries: food, banking, haberdashery, even sewage inspection. But while he earned a wage elsewhere, his passion was sports. Within two years of graduation, the adolescent boy was managing the baseball team of his local athletic group, the Olympic Athletic Club (OAC). It doesn't seem that he aspired to be a ballplayer. He had bigger dreams.

Jess was, by all accounts, a boy genius at sports promotion. He and his brother Eddie were soon in control of the OAC, expanding it to incorporate new sporting events at a time when organized sports were coming into vogue across the city and country. They brought football to the OAC in 1901, while Jess was still just eighteen and Eddie only twenty, and their team did well for themselves in the sport, which was somehow more vicious then than it is now. (The McMahon family would return to football exactly one hundred years later, with the launch of the XFL, which aimed to recapture some of the bloody glory of young Jess's era.) The family's commitment to violence only escalated: by the end of 1905, Jess and Eddie had gotten into boxing.

Vince's grandfather was, like Vince, unafraid of controversy. If football was dangerous back in those days, boxing was practically a death sentence, and its legal status was one of the great points of contention in American public life. The state of New York had banned boxing in 1900 after public outcry over the moral degeneration that it supposedly enacted upon the populace. However, after a years-long stretch without boxing, a November 1905 ruling by a magistrate brought a miraculous loophole. Boxing could occur in a "private club," as long as only "members" would be allowed to view "exhibition" matches. Young Jess and Eddie established the OAC as one such club, staging its inaugural fight on December 16, 1905, at Harlem's Marion Hall, right at the famed intersection of Lexington and 125th. Two featherweights named Benny Yanger and Rube McCarthy fought to a draw. It was the first time a McMahon produced a piece of public combat.

The cops raided the OAC in February of 1908, then again in January of 1909, but the Brothers McMahon were crafty, and meticulously kept up the illusion that everyone who attended these matches was a "member"— far be it from them to sell off memberships like tickets, perish the *thought*. Even before the McMahon family touched pro wrestling, it was already adept at kayfabe. Nevertheless, a rival athletic club went overboard in publicly advertising a big fight in September, prompting powerful politicians to denounce boxing with renewed fervor. For months, terrified promoters like Jess and Eddie dared not put on any shows.

It wasn't all bad news: On November 1, in the midst of this excitement, Jess took the day off to marry a woman named Rose McGinn, a second-generation Irish American ice-dealer's daughter from what is now the Upper East Side. Exactly one week later, Jess and Eddie shocked the city when the OAC became the first club to stage a match since everyone went into hiding. The cops tried to storm the place while the "members" were filing in, but Jess locked the front door, shutting out everyone but the spectators who had already gotten in. The police had no legal authority to enter the club, so they stood guard outside and dispersed the crowd, thinking they had kept the lion's share of them outside and, thus, ruined the match. Little did they know that two hundred people had slipped in before they got there. The attendees got to watch a hell of a show, then slipped out the back door without trouble. The cops came again a week later; Jess pulled the same trick, to improbable success.

The OAC had opened up the floodgates, and other boxing clubs followed their example, leading the authorities to throw up their hands and get back to turning a blind eye. Less than a year later, Jess was a father and he and his brother were the official fight promoters for a significant Harlem casino. Still, like his grandson later would, Jess craved more.

His next moves were, in their way, brave ones. He had a lifelong fixation on baseball, and had accumulated a great deal of experience in running a team at the OAC, so it's not surprising that he opted to invest in the great American pastime. What's surprising is the people he wanted to boost and employ. For years, Jess had been a small-time investor in the Philadelphia Giants, a well-known member of the Negro Leagues of all-Black baseball teams. In 1911, riding high on his boxing success, he asked a former Giants star, Sol White, to put together a new team, and the resulting squad, the Lincoln Giants, was, as the *Brooklyn Daily Eagle* put it, "one of the strongest aggregations of colored ball players ever gotten together." Within two years, they'd won the national championship.

Jess deserves commendation for investing in Black athletes, to be sure. The contrast between his racial outlook and those of the people around whom Vince was raised in North Carolina is stark. One wonders what might have been if Vince had been allowed to meet his paternal grandfather, who died while Vince still knew only Hanners and Luptons. But before we give Jess awards for peacemaking between peoples, it is worth noting that, in 1913, the same year they won the title, a New York paper reported that the Lincoln Giants weren't being fully paid, with a bevy of legal complaints popping up from the disgruntled players. The club dissolved and lost its license in December.

Another example of this questionable racial legacy is worthy of note. Around this time, Jess established a relationship with the most intensely loved and hated boxer of the era, the Black and eternally over-the-top champion, Jack Johnson. In 1912, Jess and Eddie planned to stage a match between Johnson and Joe Jeannette, with a huge guaranteed payday for the former, but, in the face of public backlash over the idea of giving Johnson an opportunity to knock out a white man, Jess and Eddie caved and canceled it, much to Johnson's dismay. Jess went on in 1915 to promote a fight between Johnson and the white Jess Willard in Havana, Cuba, but Willard made history that day by beating the exhausted champ in the 26th round. Jess and Johnson's partnership withered away.

What's more, Jess and Eddie lost their license for the casino and another venue they'd been working. When boxing became legal again, Jess and Eddie were accused by the state athletic commission of failing to pay taxes or rent. They started another Black baseball team, the Lincoln Stars, but it swiftly went out of business. Even the OAC had to close due to renewed anti-boxing sentiment and the challenges of World War I. Just about the only good news Jess had in the mid-to-late 1910s was the birth of another son: Vincent James McMahon came into the world on July 6, 1914, twenty-two days before the outbreak of the Great War. He never got to know the woman to whom he owed his later success, his grandmother Eliza, who died when he was only two.

Vince Senior's youth was radically different from the one Vince would later have. Where Vince traversed the backwaters as his stepdad bounced from job to job, Vince Senior saw *his* father reverse his fortunes and go from strength to strength. In 1921, Jess got back into boxing with gigs booking matches for two Upper Manhattan venues; that same year, he established the first team of Black professional basketball players in history. The crowning achievement came in 1925, when, at age forty-three, Jess was appointed to be the matchmaker at the massive Madison Square Garden. In 1927, he put together a match at Yankee Stadium that drew an estimated eighty thousand spectators. Young Vince Senior was, like his father, a McMahon child who was lucky enough to be raised around success.

By 1929, Jess and his family were living in Rockaway, Queens, and fifteen-year-old Vince Senior was thriving at the pricey La Salle Military Academy on Long Island. His father was a power broker, and his young life was already under the microscope: an article about Jess in the *New York Evening Post* quoted a letter allegedly written by Vincent to his older brother from a summer camp in Massachusetts, where he wrote that he had "learned how to follow up a left-jab with a right-cross knockout punch" and made his brother swear not to tell their father, "for I want to surprise him one of these days." Fighting was now a family business. And the business was diversifying: in 1931, Jess made the historically consequential decision to promote his first professional wrestling match.

ACKNOWLEDGMENTS

When I pitched this book in the spring of 2020, I hadn't been a wrestling viewer in nearly two decades. That said, I had been a rabid fan in my teenage years, and had long been fascinated by Vince McMahon. The Greater Power revelation was one of my first distinct wrestling memories—Vince's grin after throwing the hood off was inscribed in my memory with a pen of fire. But I needed a lot of help to write this work into existence.

I began by studying the writing of longtime historians and journalists of the wrestling ecosystem. Shaun Assael and Mike Mooneyham's *Sex, Lies, and Headlocks* provided a crucial framework and introduction to Vince's life. Tim Hornbaker's remarkably detailed books on the history of the industry—especially *Capitol Revolution* and *Death of the Territories*—proved essential. Irv Muchnick's *Wrestling Babylon* almost made me weep with joy over the fact that a real journalist had done so much work to collect and analyze facts in periods when few journalists took wrestling seriously. Dave Meltzer, in addition to letting me interview him for hours on end, left a delicious trail of bread crumbs in the form of the *Wrestling Observer* archives. Same goes for old issues of *Pro Wrestling Torch*. The crew behind the Vice series *Dark Side of the Ring* created short documentaries that were profoundly enlightening. Brandon Thurston and his website, *Wrestlenomics*, were absolutely crucial for finding and interpreting the numbers behind the stories. Bret Hart, though not formally trained as a journalist, was another vital source of information, not only in our many hours of interviews, but in his astoundingly granular and diary-based memoir. Bill Hanstock's *We Promised You a Great Main Event* was an illuminating delight. I must also vigorously thank Brian Solomon, who provided me with an insider's perspective and, perhaps most important, provided me with an unpublished 2003 Vince McMahon interview he'd conducted that revealed a lot about Vince's early life and relationship with his father. And, last but *very* much not least, I must praise freelance journalist David Bixenspan: not only did he write countless essential articles about the grim underbellies of Vince and the wrestling industry, not only did he selflessly share a treasure trove of documents, but he also was kind enough to read a draft of the manuscript and leave suggestions that saved me from a great deal of embarrassment.

Although this is not an academic tome, I benefited a great deal from the work and words of many academics who have studied pro wrestling. Sharon Mazer, a pioneer and informal dean of the academic study of wrestling, was a constant support and guiding light. Eero Laine's analysis of kayfabe was vital. Benjamin Litherland was an essential resource, as well, and so was Sam Ford. I am deeply grateful to all of them.

I was also blessed to have a team of research assistants without whom this book would not have been possible. Kenny Herzog, veteran wrestling scribe, gave invaluable assistance in the early going, when I had few contacts and many gaps in my knowledge. Britina Cheng was my next superhero, applying her razor-sharp intellect to myriad research tasks that needed doing. When she obtained a full-time job as a fact-checker at *New York* magazine (they're lucky to have her), I enlisted the aid of the great Joshua Needelman, who was more than up to the task. When the time came for me to hire a fact-checker, Britina put me in touch with a genius named Rima Parikh, who did an astounding job and whose services I recommend to any nonfiction author looking to avoid humiliation. Rae Binstock, too, was a lifesaver: she built out the endnotes for the book, of which there are more than 1,800. I don't know how she did it. I must also offer metric tons of thanks to genealogist extraordinaire Meryl Schumaker, who helped me uncover and interpret secrets of the McMahon and Hanner families that I might never have found on my own. And I must offer deep gratitude to the incredible illustrator of this book, Madison Ketcham.

Ringmaster was entirely researched and written during the COVID-19 pandemic, meaning I did very little reporting that required me to leave my home. However, in the immediate aftermath of my vaccination, I rushed to North Carolina to find information about Vince's origins. I am eternally grateful to Susan Pockmire of the Moore County Historical Association and independent local researcher James V. Comer for providing guidance in my attempts to understand the area where Vince was born and initially raised. Vince's year in Weeksville was greatly illuminated with the help of Kate Rose Williams, who put me in touch with her mother, Angela Rose, who, in turn, put me in touch with Vince's earliest known friend, Shell Davis. In Craven County, I benefited greatly from the aid of Havelock mayor Will Lewis, as well as the librarians of both the Havelock Public Library and its sister library in New Bern.

Of course, none of this would have been possible without my literary agents, Ross Harris and David Patterson of the Stuart Krichevsky Literary Agency. Equally important was my editor at Atria, the wonderful Amar Deol. I'd also like to thank all the friends who helped along the way, including (but not limited to) Christine Brooks, Chandra Steele, David Lebowitz, Daniel Dockery, Ryan Foster, Roger Lussier, and Kristen S. Hé. And, above all, I must thank the journalist and editor S. I. Rosenbaum. It was in a conversation with her that the idea of a Vince McMahon biography was conceived (neither of us can remember who first brought it up). She was the first-round editor for the manuscript, and her thoughts about wrestling helped shape this book. I love her deeply, admire her even more, and look forward to our future collaborations.

NOTES

All quotations in this book that are described in the present tense are from interviews with the author, unless otherwise indicated.

Epigraph

vii **"It's still *real* to me, damn it!"**: Kane52630, "It's Still Real to Me Damn It," Know Your Meme, December 17, 2021, accessed August 2, 2022, https://know yourmeme.com/memes/it-s-still-real-to-me-damn-it.

Overture: SHOOT

1 **The COVID-19 pandemic has killed**: Cecelia Smith-Schoenwalder, "U.S. Coronavirus Death Toll Passes 30,000 as Trump Finalizes Reopening Guidelines," *U.S. News & World Report*, April 16, 2020, accessed June 29, 2022, https:// www.usnews.com/news/health-news/articles/2020-04-16/us-coronavirus -death-toll-passes-30-000-as-trump-finalizes-reopening-guidelines.

1 **"People have been starved for content"**: "Gov. Ron DeSantis Issues His Daily Briefing on the State's Response to the Coronavirus," Facebook Live, WPLG Local 10, April 2020, https://www.facebook.com/watch/live/?ref=external &v=2733598560201798.

1 **Five days prior, without announcing**: Jared Moskowitz, "Memorandum: Additions of Essential Services to the List Under EO 20-91," Florida Division of Emergency Management, April 9, 2020, https://www.flgov.com/wp-content /uploads/2020/04/Essential-Services-Additions-EO-20-91.pdf.

1 **the multibillion-dollar**: "World Wrestling Entertainment Enterprise Value Chart," *World Wrestling Entertainment Inc.*, YCharts, accessed June 29, 2022, https://ycharts.com/companies/WWE/enterprise_value.

2 **America First Action, was set to spend $18.5 million**: "America First Action PAC Announces $26.6M Investment in Battleground States," America First Action Super PAC, April 9, 2020, https://www.a1apac.org/news/america-first -action-pac-announces-26.6m-investment-in-battleground-states/.

3 **Jacob grabbed his brother Esau's heel**: Genesis 25:26.

3 **It emerged from the world of carnivals**: Scott Beekman, *Ringside: A History of Professional Wrestling in America* (Westport, CT: Praeger, 2006), ebook.

5 **reports emerged of well over $12 million in alleged hush-money payments**: Joe Palazzolo, Ted Mann, and Joe Flint, "WWE's Vince McMahon Agreed to Pay $12 Million in Hush Money to Four Women," *Wall Street Journal*, July 22, 2022, accessed August 2, 2022, https://www.wsj .com/articles/wwes-vince-mcmahon-agreed-to-pay-12-million-in-hush -money-to-four-women-11657289742.

5 **regulators launched investigations**: World Wrestling Entertainment, Inc., Form 8-K (filed July 25, 2022), from Investis, https://otp.tools.investis.com /clients/us/wwe/SEC/sec-show.aspx?Type=html&FilingId=15963103& Cik=0001091907, accessed August 2, 2022.

PART ONE: FACES

9 **"McMahon Junior is the modern-day Hitler"**: Ray Tennenbaum, "Sleeper Hold, Part 3," Ray Tennenbaum's text, accessed June 29, 2022, http://www .ray-field.com/content/article/sleeper-hold-part-3.

Chapter 1: FALL

11 **The Hanners arrived in the colony before**: Charles Elmer Rice, *A History of the Hanna Family: Being a Genealogy of the Descendants of Thomas Hanna and Elizabeth (Henderson) Hanna, Who Emigrated to America in 1763* (Damascus, OH: Pim & Sons Printer, 1905), page 12.

11 **John Henry Hanner, who, when he died in 1850**: "John Hanner," estate file, Superior Court, FHL DGS 7,641,392 (Guilford, NC), 1850.

11 **one of the area's larger forced-work camps**: Glenn Perkins (Curator of Community History, Greensboro History Museum), correspondence with author, September 18, 2020.

11 **Victoria Elizabeth Hanner was born in 1920**: Soumik Datta, "Vince McMahon Sends an Inspiring Message on His Mother's 100th Birthday," *Sportskeeda*, July 11, 2020, accessed June 29, 2022, https://www.sportskeeda. com/wwe/news-vince-mcmahon-sends-inspiring-message-mother-s-100th -birthday.

11 **Her mother was a farmer's daughter**: "1900 United States Federal Census," Jeffreys, Florence, South Carolina, digital image s.v. "Andrew McDonald Kennedy," Ancestry.com.

11 **her father an itinerant mechanic**: "1920 United States Federal Census," Florence, Florence, South Carolina, digital image s.v. "Orpheus William Hanner," Ancestry.com.

11 **Vicki appears to have been born in Florence, South Carolina**: "Victoria' Vicki' Hanner Askew," Sam Houston Memorial Funeral Home, January 2022, accessed June 29, 2022, https://www.shmfh.com/obituaries/VictoriaVicki -Askew/#!/Obituary.

11 **raised in Sanford, North Carolina**: "1930 United States Federal Census," Sanford, Lee, North Carolina, digital image s.v. "Victoria Elizabeth Hanner," Ancestry.com.

11 **a jaunt at Bob Jones College**: "Hanner-Patacca Vows Solemnized at Sanford," *Greensboro Daily News* (Greensboro, NC), December 14, 1941, section 3, page 10; "History of BJU," Bob Jones University, accessed June 29, 2022, https://www.bju.edu/about/history.php.

11 **a North Carolina birth index of 1939**: "North Carolina, U.S., Birth Indexes, 1800–2000," Mecklenburg County, North Carolina, digital image s.v. "Gloria Faye Hanner," Ancestry.com.

12 **On December 6, 1941**: "Hanner-Patacca Vows," *Greensboro Daily News.*

12 **Patacca was shipped up to New York City**: "Dennison Soldier Files for

Divorce," *The Daily Times* (New Philadelphia, OH), September 3, 1943, page 12.

12 **Vincent James McMahon was doing his own**: "Vincent James McMahon," military record, form 13164 (rev.02-02), National Archives and Records Administration, Freedom of Information Act.

12 **local newspaper item mentions**: "Lost—Wallet," *Wilmington Morning Star* (Wilmington, NC), June 30, 1942, page 9.

12 **Patacca had filed a vitriolic divorce petition**: "Louis G. Patacca v. Victoria Patacca," petition for divorce, Tuscarawas County, Ohio, August 18, 1943, pages 1–2.

12 **The military moved Vincent James McMahon**: "Vincent James McMahon," military record.

12 **Roderick James "Rod" McMahon, was born**: "Roderick James 'Rod' McMahon Obituary (1943 –2021)," Legacy.com, January 24, 2021, accessed August 2, 2022, https://www.legacy.com/us/obituaries/courier/name/roderick-mcmahon-obituary?id=7372979.

12 **they got married on September 4, 1944**: "Vincent James McMahon and Victoria Elizabeth Hanner," marriage license, no. 24270 (Horry County, SC), September 4, 1944.

12 **On August 18, 1945, three days after**: "Vincent James McMahon," military record.

12 **The couple's second son entered the world**: "Vincent Kennedy McMahon," birth certificate, BVS form 15-44 (NC), August 24, 1945.

12 **On September 16, young Vince was baptized**: Diana Wake, correspondence with Susan Pockmire, August 6, 2021.

13 **The Hanners were Presbyterians**: Rice, *A History of the Hanna Family*, page 124.

13 **the McMahons were Catholics**: Tim Hornbaker, *Capitol Revolution: The Rise of the McMahon Wrestling Empire* (Toronto: ECW Press, 2015), ebook.

13 **"You know, I'm not big on excuses"**: Kevin Cook, "Playboy Interview: Vince McMahon," *Playboy*, February, 2001, page 60.

14 **Leo Hubert Lupton Jr. was born**: "U.S. WWII Draft Cards Young Men, 1940–1947," The National Archives, Atlanta, Georgia, digital image s.v. "Leo Hubert Lupton," Ancestry.com.

14 **dropped out of high school after his freshman year**: "1940 United States Federal Census," Greensboro, Guilford, North Carolina, digital image s.v. "Leo Lupton," Ancestry.com.

14 **trained as an electrician**: "Electrical Contracting," *The Pilot* (Southern Pines, NC), March 2, 1951, page 11.

14 **married a girl named Peggy Lane**: "Lupton-Lane," *The Charlotte Observer* (Charlotte, NC), July 2, 1939, page 13.

14 **In May of 1940, Peggy gave birth**: "Richard Lane," birth announcement, *News & Observer* (Raleigh, NC), May 14, 1940, page 6.

14 **Leo had been convicted of abandoning his family**: "Sentenced for Abandonment," *News & Observer* (Raleigh, NC), June 8, 1941, page 7.

14 **a later newspaper item implies**: "Ernestine Taylor," birth announcement, *News & Observer* (Raleigh, NC), October 2, 1940, page 8.

14 **enlisting in the Navy for service**: "World War II Navy Muster Rolls,

1938–1949," National Archives, College Park, Maryland, digital image s.v. "Leo H. Lupton Junior," Ancestry.com.

14 **being on a boat that was present in Tokyo Bay**: "Idaho IV (Battleship No.42)," Naval History and Heritage Command, U.S. Navy, May 27, 2022, accessed August 2, 2022, https://www.history.navy.mil/research/histories/ship-histories /danfs/i/idaho-iv.html.

14 **his wife had a stillbirth**: "New York, New York, Extracted Death Index, 1862–1948," New York, New York, digital image s.v. "John Lupton," Ancestry.com.

14 **moved with them into his parents' house**: "Lupton-McMahon," marriage announcement, *News & Observer* (Raleigh, NC), April 27, 1947, page 28.

14 **Vicki's parents were also living in Mount Pleasant**: "Lupton-McMahon," marriage announcement, *News and Observer*.

14 **Vicki filed for divorce**: "McMahon," divorce report, no. 9622, vol. 15., BVS 4741 (Leon County, FL), March 18, 1947, page 204.

14 **Divorces were easy to obtain in Florida back then**: Kathleen Patton, Program Administrator, Vital Records Section, Bureau of Vital Statistics, Florida Department of Health, interview with author, August 13, 2021.

14 **the divorce was granted on March 18, 1947**: "McMahon," divorce report.

14 **on April 5, Vicki walked the aisle**: "Lupton-McMahon," marriage announcement, *News and Observer*.

14 **"He hit you with his tools, didn't he?"**: Cook, "Playboy Interview," page 60.

15 **Vince mused**: Emphasis added for clarity.

15 **Vince appeared on *The Howard Stern Show***: Howard Stern, "Interview with Vince McMahon," *Howard Stern Show*, March 22, 2001, accessed June 29, 2022, https://open.spotify.com/episode/0RYpaGb6oqJqlqTNJuew53.

15 **In the *Playboy* interview**: Cook, "Playboy Interview," page 60.

16 **Shortly after they got married**: "Announcing – Return of Coble Dairy Products," *The Pilot* (Southern Pines, NC), March 19, 1948, page 15.

16 **a childhood friend of Rod's**: James Fletcher, interview with author, June 17, 2021.

16 **Vince would later say he didn't know**: Vince McMahon, unpublished interview with Brian Solomon, September 18, 2003.

17 **a poor township with a population**: "Population of North Carolina, by Counties: April 1, 1950," U.S. Department of Commerce, Bureau of the Census, Washington, DC, August 14, 1950, page 4.

17 **West Southern Pines had briefly**: "West Southern Pines, N.C.," Southern Oral History Program, University of North Carolina Center for the Study of the American South, accessed June 29, 2022, https://sohp.org/digital-exhibits /west-southern-pines-n-c/.

17 **Southern Pines proper, on the other hand**: "State Press," *The Semi-Weekly Messenger* (Wilmington, NC), November 18, 1898, page 1.

17 **Vinnie's first house was right on the dividing line**: "Vincent Kennedy McMahon," birth certificate.

17 **Vicki volunteered with the town's Boy Scout troop**: "Unit Leaders of Moore Scout Program Honored at Annual Banquet Held Here," *The Pilot* (Southern Pines, NC), November 23, 1950, page 16.

17 **played tennis in local tournaments**: "Sandhills Tennis Association Plans Summer Activities," *The Pilot* (Southern Pines, NC), March 27, 1959, page 5.

17 **in August of 1953, she was in *On Stage America***: "'On Stage America' Uses Home Talent in Minstrel Show Thursday, Friday," *The Pilot* (Southern Pines, NC), August 7, 1959, page 5.

17 **In 1956, around when Vince was ten**: Weeksville High School, *Bow Wow* (Weeksville, NC), 1957, page 40, Ancestry.com.

17 **There was slightly more contact**: Shell Davis, interview with author, May 16, 2021.

17 **Vinnie attended the white one**: Weeksville High School, *Bow Wow*, page 40.

18 **"I was totally unruly"**: Cook, "Playboy Interview," page 60.

18 **"It's frustrating for a child to know"**: *Headliners & Legends with Matt Lauer*, "Vince McMahon," written by Jonathan Moser, starring Matt Lauer, Vince McMahon, Lou Albano, and Eric Bischoff, NBC, aired November 25, 2001.

18 **Leo moved his family once again**: Havelock High School, *The Rambler* (Havelock, NC), 1959, page 40, Ancestry.com.

18 ***The Epic of Gilgamesh*, the Sumerian**: Evan Andrews, "What Is the Oldest Known Piece of Literature?," History Channel, accessed June 29, 2022, https://www.history.com/news/what-is-the-oldest-known-piece-of-literature#:~:text=The%20Epic%20of%20Gilgamesh%20started,century%20B.C.%20by%20the%20Babylonians.

18 **gained the name "Israel" after a wrestling match**: Genesis 32:22–32.

18 **One possible translation of *Isra'el***: Walter A. Elwell, "Israel," *Bible Dictionaries*, Bible Study Tools, accessed June 29, 2022, https://www.biblestudytools.com/dictionary/israel/.

18 **The Greeks and Romans famously prized**: Beekman, *Ringside*, ebook.

18 **Wrestlers have been heroes in West Africa**: Jean-Baptiste Bat, "Initiation Wrestling in Togo," *The African* (Washington, DC), September 10, 2019, accessed June 29, 2022, https://myafricanmagazine.com/initiation-wrestling-in-togo/.

18 **Settlers wrestled in America's colonial days**: Bob Dellinger, "Wrestling in the USA," National Wrestling Hall of Fame, accessed August 2, 2022, https://nwhof.org/national-wrestling-hall-of-fame/pages/wrestling-in-the-usa.

18 **so did enslaved people**: Sergio Lussana, "To See Who Was Best on the Plantation: Enslaved Fighting Contests and Masculinity in the Antebellum Plantation South," *Journal of Southern History* 76, no. 4 (2010): 901–22. http://www.jstor.org/stable/27919283.

18 **George Washington wrestled**: "Athleticism," Mount Vernon Association, accessed June 29, 2022, https://www.mountvernon.org/george-washington/athleticism/.

18 **as did Abraham Lincoln**: Beekman, *Ringside*, ebook.

19 **Irish immigrants of the 1830s and '40s**: Ibid.

19 **The Civil War and its attendant conscription**: Ibid.

19 **Just two years after the peace at Appomattox**: Ibid.

19 **English immigrants brought another new style**: Ibid.

19 **this one from France but erroneously referred to**: Ibid.

19 **the post–Civil War growth of interest**: Ibid.

19 **what were then known as "hippodrome" bouts**: Ibid.

19 **This was when the term** *kayfabe* **emerged**: John Lister, "The clandestine jargon of professional wrestling," *Verbatim* 31, no. 1, https://web.archive.org /web/20081015060222/http://www.johnlisterwriting.com/verbatim.html.

19 **Possibly a garbled version of Pig Latin for "fake"**: Ibid.

20 **An oligarchy of promoters**: Hornbaker, *Capitol Revolution*, ebook.

20 **Promoters, having abandoned athletic legitimacy**: Beekman, *Ringside*, ebook.

20 **The nascent motion picture industry**: Ibid.

20 **Vince's grandfather—was born in 1882**: Roderick James "Jess" McMahon, death certificate, August 4, 1930, file no. 40076, Texas State Department of Health.

20 **His father, Roderick, died**: "Died," *New York Herald* (New York, NY), February 15, 1877, page 8.

20 **Eliza was the heiress**: 1870 U.S. census, New York County, New York, population schedule, New York City, first enumeration, ward 12, district 16, page 39 (penned), page 514 (stamped), dwelling 165, family 330, Richard Dowling; NARA microfilm M593, roll 990.

20 **her late husband had also made a small fortune**: New York County, New York, Surrogate's Court, Wills, vol. 412, page 140, Roderick McMahon; image s.v., Ancestry.com.

20 **Jess started promoting sports**: Hornbaker, *Capitol Revolution*, ebook.

20 **gained a college degree**: Ibid.

20 **married a woman named Rose McGinn**: "Mrs. McMahon, Kin of Promoter," *The Evening Star* (Washington, DC), February 28, 1958, page A-26.

20 **By July 6, 1914, when their second son**: "Florida Death Index, 1877–1998," Vincent J. McMahon, Ancestry.com.

20 **legends such as Jack Johnson**: Hornbaker, *Capitol Revolution*.

20 **became matchmaker at the legendary Madison Square Garden**: Hornbaker, *Capitol Revolution*.

20 **As of 1929, Jess, Rose, and their kids**: William Morris, "Around the Ring with William Morris," *New York Evening Post*, August 3, 1929, page 9.

21 **teenage Vincent was studying**: Ibid.

21 **A news item about Jess**: Ibid.

21 **in 1931, Jess, lured by a colleague**: Hornbaker, *Capitol Revolution*, ebook.

21 **setting up pro wrestling matches on Long Island**: Ibid.

21 **he was booking them throughout Kings County**: Ibid.

21 **expanded his operations to Washington, DC**: Ibid.

21 **sent his son Vincent to live in the nation's capital**: Ibid.

21 **hired as the general manager of DC's Turner's Arena**: Ibid.

21 **in 1952, he subleased the arena for himself**: Ibid.

21 **He got married again**: "Obituary: McMahon," *South Florida Sun Sentinel* (Fort Lauderdale, FL), January 19, 1998, page 12.

21 **On November 21, 1954, at age seventy-two**: "Pennsylvania, Death Certificates, 1906–1967," Pennsylvania Historic and Museum Commission, Harrisburg, Pennsylvania, "Roderick McMahan," image s.v., Ancestry.com.

21 **"He was always in a suit and tie"**: J. J. Dillon, interview with author, September 17, 2020.

21   **"You could be angry"**: Jesse Ventura, in special features of *Beyond the Mat: Unrated Director's Cut*, DVD, directed by Barry Blaustein (Burbank, CA: Universal Pictures Home Entertainment, 2004).

22   **some of the most popular programming**: Beekman, *Ringside*, ebook.

22   **renamed Turner's Arena as the Capitol Arena**: Tim Hornbaker, *National Wrestling Alliance: The Untold Story of the Monopoly That Strangled Professional Wrestling* (Toronto: ECW Press, 2007), ebook.

22   **broadcasting his shows through the DuMont network**: Hornbaker, *Capitol Revolution*, ebook.

22   **airing every Wednesday night**: Ibid.

22   **"We are getting reservation orders"**: Ibid.

22   **The first came in August of 1957**: Ibid.

22   **Roland Barthes's book *Mythologies***: Roland Barthes, *Mythologies*, trans. Annette Lavers (London: Paladin, 1972), ebook.

22   **"The virtue of all-in wrestling"**: Ibid.

Chapter 2: JUICE

23   **Vinnie was twelve**: Kevin Cook, "Playboy Interview: Vince McMahon," *Playboy*, February, 2001, page 62.

23   **where Vicki's parents had also settled**: "1958 New Bern City Directory," *The Mullin-Kille and Sun-Journal* (New Bern, NC), 1958, page 369.

23   **as Vince would later put it, Vicki's mom**: "Interview with Vince McMahon," *RAW Magazine*, March 2001.

23   **Vince Senior stepped in to become paterfamilias**: Carolyn Reardon, interview with author, September 25, 2021.

23   **Vince Senior lived near the Miedzinskis**: Ibid.

24   **Vince has sometimes told a version**: Cook, "Playboy Interview," page 62.

24   **"She was very interested"**: Vince McMahon, unpublished interview with Brian Solomon, September 18, 2003.

24   **"When I met my dad"**: Cook, "Playboy Interview," page 61.

24   **"I fell in love with him"**: Vince McMahon, "What I've Learned," *Esquire*, January 2005, accessed August 3, 2022, https://classic.esquire.com/article /2005/1/1/what-ive-learned-vince-mcmahon.

25   **"There was just an instant attraction"**: *Headliners & Legends with Matt Lauer*, "Vince McMahon," written by Jonathan Moser, starring Matt Lauer, Vince McMahon, Lou Albano, and Eric Bischoff, NBC, aired November 25, 2001.

25   **"I must have behaved myself"**: Cook, "Playboy Interview," page 61.

25   **six-foot-two, according to an official WWE encyclopedia**: Brian Shields, *WWE Encyclopedia: The Definitive Guide to World Wrestling Entertainment* (Indianapolis: DK/BradyGames, 2009), page 330.

25   **well over five million viewers tuning in**: Wayne Duggan, "WWE Goes Back to the 'Attitude Era' to Try and Freshen Up Sagging TV Ratings," *Yahoo! News*, June 27, 2019, accessed June 29, 2022, https://www.yahoo.com/now/wwe -goes-back-attitude-era-160354538.html.

26   **"I'm Stone Cold Steve Austin's character"**: *The Steve Austin Show*, "Vince McMahon," starring Steve Austin and Vince McMahon, *PodcastOne*, December 7, 2014.

26   **"You never change who you really are"**: Ibid.

26   **"When someone would, as a kid"**: Ibid.

27   **"He never said it"**: Cook, "Playboy Interview," page 64.

27   **"I loved it from the day I saw it"**: Cook, "Playboy Interview," page 63.

27   **"Oh, boy. It's 1959 and I'm looking up"**: Ibid.

28   **The dominant force in the industry**: Tim Hornbaker, *Capitol Revolution: The Rise of the McMahon Wrestling Empire* (Toronto: ECW Press, 2015), ebook.

28   **Capitol had an on-again, off-again**: Ibid.

28   **In 1959, a man named Bill Olivas**: David Bixenspan, "FBI Records Show Vince McMahon's Dad Caught on Tape Bragging About Threatening a Wrestler," *Deadspin*, March 27, 2017, accessed June 29, 2022, https://deadspin.com /fbi-records-show-vince-mcmahons-dad-caught-on-tape-brag-1793690848.

28   **Olivas complained**: Ibid.

28   **Vince Senior was accused**: Ibid.

28   **According to an FBI memo**: Ibid.

28   **upgraded to full member in 1960**: Hornbaker, *Capitol Revolution*.

28   **They had put a hidden microphone**: Bixenspan, "FBI Records Show . . ."

29   **"because if you do, you're hanging yourself"**: Ibid.

29   **They lived at one point in a trailer park**: Douglas Franks, childhood peer of Vince McMahon, interview with author, May 12, 2021.

29   **known locally as "Splinterville"**: Will Lewis, Mayor of Havelock, interview with author, May 19, 2021.

29   **Havelock High School was moderately sized**: Havelock High School, *The Rambler* (Havelock, NC), 1959.

29   **Teenie's presence at youth parties**: Jackie Trader, "Activity Ceases As Teenagers Burn Midnight Oil For Finals," *The Havelock Progress* (Havelock, NC), May 21, 1959, page unknown.

29   **the boys' high-scoring performances**: Ray Lanier, "Hawks, Seadogs Take Home Court wins," *The Havelock Progress* (Havelock, NC), December 23, 1959, page 6.

29   **"By the time I was 14"**: Cook, "Playboy Interview," page 60.

29   **"They'd pull up and there we were"**: Cook, "Playboy Interview," pages 60–61.

31   **"immediately saw these beautiful blue eyes"**: *Headliners & Legends*, "Vince McMahon."

31   **"I saw this statuesque"**: Ibid.

31   **"I had no idea what a family was"**: Joel Drucker, "King of the Ring," *Cigar Aficionado*, November/December 1999, https://www.cigaraficionado.com/article /king-of-the-ring-6149.

31   **one of the first in the state to integrate**: Darcy DeMille, "Spot Check Around South Shows Picture of School Integration," *Indianapolis Recorder*, September 12, 1959, accessed June 29, 2022, https://newspapers.library .in.gov/?a=d&d=INR19590912-01.1.3&e=————-en-20—1—txt-txIN————-.

31   **"I could go to a state-supported institution"**: *Headliners & Legends*, "Vince McMahon."

31   **"I had no reputation, so it was a new beginning"**: Drucker, "King of the Ring."

32 **there *was* a Vince McMahon**: Fishburne Military Academy, *Taps* (Waynesboro, VA), 1963, page 38.

32 **she sued him for divorce**: "Lupton," divorce report, no. SD-167 (Craven County, NC), June 3, 1963.

32 **they married about seven months after the divorce**: *Marriage Register, Craven County, N.C.*, 1963, page 3489, Ancestry.com.

32 **Leo absconded to Palm Beach, Florida**: "Florida Marriage Indexes, 1822–1875 and 1927–2001," Florida Department of Health, October, 1966, page 81, Ancestry.com.

32 **in October of 1966 he married**: Ibid.

32 **She was Vince's "cousin"**: Cook, "Playboy Interview," page 61.

32 **The next year, she and Leo had a child**: Kevin Lupton, interview with author, April 26, 2021.

32 **Leo died, twenty-two years later**: "Florida Death Index, 1877–1998," Ancestry.com.

32 **He fell behind on dues payments**: Hornbaker, *Capitol Revolution*, ebook.

33 **Late 1962 brought a dispute**: Ibid.

33 **a title match was held in Toronto**: Ibid.

33 **in January 1963 launched their own**: Ibid.

33 **The shows happened in the gym**: Gary Grier, interview with author, April 22, 2021.

33 **Vince wrestled under the moniker**: Alfonso Castillo, "Johnny Valiant coming to LI, looks back on his WWE career," *Newsday* (Long Island, NY), August 30, 2012, https://www.newsday.com/news/johnny-valiant-coming-to-li-looks -back-on-his-wwe-career-y99421.

34 **"I wasn't caught for some stuff"**: Cook, "Playboy Interview," page 61.

35 **the fracas was over "insubordination"**: Cook, "Playboy Interview," page 61.

35 **he said it was because there were rumors**: Drucker, "King of the Ring."

35 **because of a popular uprising**: Ibid.

35 **"The morning of graduation"**: Ibid.

35 **Vince graduated from Fishburne**: "McMahon's days at Fishburne: History," *The News Leader* (Staunton, VA), March 4, 2016, https://www.newsleader .com/story/news/local/history/2016/03/04/history-vince-mcmahon-fishburne -military-cadet-waynesboro-va/81314942/.

35 **began his college studies**: Beth Dawson, associate registrar for records and registration at East Carolina University, correspondence with author, April 20, 2021.

35 **He and Linda were wed in New Bern**: "Miss Edwards, Mr. McMahon Exchange Vows in New Bern," *News & Observer* (Raleigh, NC), August 7, 1966, page 67.

35 **She joined her husband as a student at ECU**: Ibid.

35 **they did on June 1, 1969**: Beth Dawson, correspondence with author, April 20, 2021.

35 **Vince "hated economics"**: Cook, "Playboy Interview," page 63.

35 **"Now, they figure this kid"**: Cook, "Playboy Interview," page 64.

36 **Shane Brandon McMahon, came into the world**: "Shane McMahon," IMDb, accessed August 2, 2022, https://www.imdb.com/name/nm0573075/.

36   **McMahon family unit was now based in Gaithersburg**: Ibid.

36   **an interviewer would point out**: Steve Kemper, "Vince McMahon," *Hartford Courant*, August 24, 1986.

36   **Rod, Vicki, and Harold had moved to a trailer park**: "Virginia, Marriage Records, 1936–2014," Hampton, Virginia, "Roderick James McMahon," November 3, 1967, Ancestry.com.

36   **then moved to Pembroke Pines, Florida**: Joan McIver, "In the Frisbee Nursery, Three Is a Happy Crowd," *Miami Herald*, September 11, 1986.

36   **Rod married and wound up in Texas**: "Roderick James 'Rod' McMahon, 1943–2021," *Courier of Montgomery County* (The Woodlands, TX), January 25, 2021.

36   **Teenie went to Virginia**: "U.S. Public Records Index, 1950–1993," "Ernestine L. Hanson," Ancestry.com.

36   **Richard became a Mormon and moved to Utah**: "Richard Lupton," *Daily Herald* (Provo, UT), December 9, 1995.

36   **He'd appeared on a 1957 yearbook page**: Weeksville High School, *Bow Wow* (Weeksville, NC), 1957, page 40, Ancestry.com.

Chapter 3: PLAY-BY-PLAY

38   **the National Wrestling Alliance's regime**: Tim Hornbaker, *National Wrestling Alliance: The Untold Story of the Monopoly That Strangled Professional Wrestling* (Toronto: ECW Press, 2007), ebook.

39   **welcomed back into the fold in 1971**: Tim Hornbaker, *Capitol Revolution: The Rise of the McMahon Wrestling Empire* (Toronto: ECW Press, 2015), ebook.

39   **there had been a glut and subsequent collapse**: Scott Beekman, *Ringside: A History of Professional Wrestling in America* (Westport, CT: Praeger, 2006), ebook.

39   **a man named Ray Morgan**: Hornbaker, *Capitol Revolution*, ebook.

39   **"Ray wanted a raise"**: *The Steve Austin Show*, "Vince McMahon," starring Steve Austin and Vince McMahon, *PodcastOne*, December 7, 2014.

40   **He'd been doing odd jobs**: Shaun Assael and Mike Mooneyham, *Sex, Lies, and Headlocks* (New York: Three Rivers Press, 2002), ebook.

40   **Linda had a paralegal position at a law firm**: Justin Barrasso, "Linda McMahon on her role with WWE and Women's Leadership," *Sports Illustrated*, June 20, 2016, accessed August 2, 2022, https://www.si.com/extra -mustard/2016/06/20/linda-vince-mcmahon-wwe-womens-leadership-live.

40   **By January 31, 1972**: "McMahon New Voice," *Herald-News* (Passaic, NJ), January 24, 1972, page 29.

40   **According to arbitration documents**: *Bruno Sammartino v. Capitol Wrestling Corporation and Vince McMahon*, no. 82-1979 (Western District PA), August 26, 1983.

40   **The typical portrayal**: *The Most Powerful Families in Wrestling*, featuring Bret Hart, Eddie Guerrero, Randy Orton, and Vince McMahon (2007, Stamford: WWE Home Video), film.

41   **Sometime later, Vince the younger told Dillon**: J. J. Dillon, interview with author, September 17, 2020.

41 **he even went so far as to name his memoir**: James J. Dillon, Scott Teal, and Philip Varriale, *Wrestlers Are Like Seagulls: From McMahon to McMahon* (Gallatin, TN: Crowbar Press, 2005), ebook.

41 **Vince also started acting as Vince Senior's emissary**: Assael and Mooneyham, *Sex, Lies, and Headlocks*, ebook.

41 **"If you don't make it, don't ever ask"**: Nancy Jo Sales, "Beyond Fake," *New York* magazine, October 26, 1998, page 44.

41 **their new home of West Hartford, Connecticut**: Brian Lockhart, "McMahons' Bankruptcy a Murky Chapter in Her Rags-to-Riches Tale," *CTPost*, October 1, 2010, accessed June 29, 2022, https://www.ctpost.com/local/article/McMahons-bankruptcy-a-murky-chapter-in-her-682114.php.

41 **Vince and four people who shared his accountant**: Ibid.

42 **"It was visions of sugarplums"**: Kevin Cook, "Playboy Interview: Vince McMahon," *Playboy*, February, 2001, page 64.

42 **In September 1973, they bought a Connecticut cement plant**: Daniel Altimari, "Cement Plant Deal Sheds Light On McMahon Bankruptcy," *Hartford Courant*, September 28, 2012, accessed August 2, 2022, https://www.courant.com/news/connecticut/hc-xpm-2012-09-28-hc-mcmahon-creditor-2012 0928-story.html.

42 **used to call upon wrestling promoters to help get turnout up**: Bob Arum, interview with author, September 25, 2020.

43 **The Montana-born Knievel was by then**: Leigh Montville, *Evel: The High-Flying Life of Evel Knievel: American Showman, Daredevil, and Legend* (New York: Anchor, 2011), ebook.

43 **Vince says he was the one who initially**: Ibid.

43 **customized white Cadillac**: Ibid.

43 **"You knew he was a different kind of cat"**: Ibid.

43 **"The only thing that surprised me"**: Ibid.

43 **Knievel was, by all accounts**: Ibid.

44 **Vince and Knievel were simultaneously speaking**: Ibid.

44 **on the weekend of May 25, 1974**: Ibid.

44 **"He hated the canyon jump"**: Ibid.

44 **set to be accompanied by a massive fair**: Ibid.

44 **the rocket prototype wasn't working**: Ibid.

45 **By the day of the jump, September 8, 1974**: Richard Severo, "Evel Knievel, 69, Daredevil on a Motorcycle, Dies," *New York Times*, December 1, 2007, accessed June 29, 2022, https://www.nytimes.com/2007/12/01/us/01knievel .html.

45 **estimated to have personally lost $250,000**: Assael and Mooneyham, *Sex, Lies, and Headlocks*, ebook.

46 **there wasn't even agreement**: Josh Gross, *Ali vs. Inoki: The Forgotten Fight That Inspired Mixed Martial Arts and Launched Sports Entertainment* (Dallas: BenBella Books, 2016), ebook.

46 **though he had long admired**: Denny Burkholder, "How Muhammad Ali's fascination with pro wrestling fueled his career, inspired MMA," *CBS Sports*, June 6, 2016, accessed August 2, 2022, https://www.cbssports.com/general

/news/how-muhammad-alis-fascination-with-pro-wrestling-fueled-his
-career-inspired-mma/.

46 **released a set of ostensible rules**: Gross, *Ali vs. Inoki*, ebook.

46 **much observed public appearances**: *Championship Wrestling*, "Gorilla Monsoon Goes Toe-to-Toe with Muhammad Ali," featuring Gorilla Monsoon and Muhammad Ali, WWF TV, aired June 1, 1976.

46 **Budokan sold out, and Vince Senior**: Andy Bull, "The forgotten story of . . . Muhammad Ali v Antonio Inoki," *The Guardian*, November 11, 2009, accessed August 2, 2022, https://www.theguardian.com/sport/blog/2009/nov/11/the-forgotten-story-of-ali-inoki.

46 **could even catch it on big screens in the United Kingdom**: Ibid.

46 **nearly everyone was on the same page**: Gross, *Ali vs. Inoki*, ebook.

46 **Vince says he was sent to Tokyo**: Ibid.

46 **In Vince's telling, he went to Ali's room**: Ibid.

46 **"I certainly remember Vince being there"**: Ibid.

47 **Vince later said he had updated his plan**: Ibid.

47 **"Even Ali wouldn't know"**: Ibid.

47 **"I don't know how my Dad found out"**: Ibid.

47 **Mike LeBell maintained that Vince**: Ibid.

47 **had just formed a joint company with Vince Senior**: Tim Hornbaker, *Death of the Territories: Expansion, Betrayal and the War That Changed Pro Wrestling Forever* (Toronto: ECW Press, 2018), ebook.

47 **"Vince McMahon, *Junior* didn't mean much"**: Gross, *Ali vs. Inoki*, ebook.

47 **he wasn't present at Budokan**: Andy Bull, "The forgotten story of . . ."

47 **Before the opening bell even finished**: Ibid.

47 **Inoki did get up and started a mix**: Ibid.

48 **On April 19, 1976**: Daniel Altimari, "Cement Plant Deal."

48 **they welcomed a daughter**: stephaniemcmahon, "My Birthday Wish," Instagram, September 24, 2020, accessed June 29, 2022, https://www.instagram.com/p/CFh4FhxJKY_/.

48 **she would go on to become:** "Stephanie McMahon," WWE.com, accessed August 2, 2022, https://www.wwe.com/superstars/stephanie-mcmahon.

48 **December 17, 1976, brought an ominous development**: Phil Rosenthal, "TBS Ted's Excellent Venture," *Orlando Sentinel*, January 5, 1992, accessed June 29, 2022, https://www.orlandosentinel.com/news/os-xpm-1992-01-05-9201031026-story.html.

49 **he'd started running monthly WWWF shows**: "WWWF on MSG Network: 25.10.1976," *Cagematch.net*, accessed August 2, 2022, https://www.cagematch.net/?id=1&nr=3910.

49 **the latter channel spun off:** "WWF Ring Results 1976," *The History of WWE*, September 14, 2019, accessed June 29, 2022, http://thehistoryofwwe.com/76.htmk.

49 **GCW and the WWWF had been grudgingly**: Hornbaker, *Death of the Territories*, ebook.

49 **tensions were suddenly ramping up**: Ibid.

50 **"Bobo, with a hard right hand"**: "Bobo Brazil vs Crusher Blackwell—MSG,"

WWE, YouTube, accessed June 29, 2022, https://www.youtube.com/watch?v=ouIIK5k7it8&ab_channel=WWE.

51 **Some reports say he was the one**: Assael and Mooneyham, *Sex, Lies, and Headlocks*, ebook.

51 **The couple hammered out a deal**: Ibid.

51 **they bought the local hockey team**: James P. Freeman, "A Mecca of Glaze & Haze: The Cape Cod Coliseum," *Cape Cod Life Magazine*, 2019 Annual, accessed June 29, 2022, https://capecodlife.com/a-mecca-of-glaze-haze-the-cape-cod-coliseum/4/.

51 **They called it Titan Sports**: Steve Marantz, "Troy, McMahon Pump Life into Struggling Club Scene," *Boston Globe*, May 30, 1982, page 29.

51 **decamped to South Yarmouth**: Hornbaker, *Death of the Territories*, ebook.

51 **bringing the Boston Bruins hockey team**: "Boston Bruins Plan First Cape Appearance," *The Register* (Cape Cod, MA), September 6, 1979.

51 **started booking year-round**: "Coliseum Plans Year-Round Shows," *The Register* (Cape Cod, MA), March 20, 1980.

51 **brought rock concerts back to the Coliseum**: Ernie Santosuosso, "Rock may return to Cape Coliseum," *The Boston Globe*, April 27, 1979, page 30.

51 **There was resistance from citizens and businesses**: Hollis Engley, "Few community problems follow J. Geils at Coliseum," *The Register* (South Yarmouth, MA), July 5, 1979, page 5.

52 **"There's not anything to say"**: "Coliseum Plans Year-Round Shows."

52 **Shane has said he started working**: "All in the Family," *RAW Magazine*, October 1999.

52 **"I ran straight for my father's arms"**: Ibid.

52 **"I'm a disciplinarian"**: Vince McMahon, "What I've Learned," *Esquire*, January 2005, https://classic.esquire.com/article/2005/1/1/what-ive-learned-vince-mcmahon.

52 **On January 27, they hit the town legislators**: "Coliseum Freed from Restrictions by Selectmen," *The Register* (Cape Cod, MA), February 5, 1981.

52 **"The hearing brought out"**: Ibid.

52 **The town fully ceded decision making**: Ibid.

53 **Turner's TBS was a hit**: Hornbaker, *Death of the Territories*, ebook.

53 **Jim Barnett leveraged GCW's national visibility**: Ibid.

53 **The year 1981 saw the AWA invade**: Ibid.

53 **Adding to the chaos was the retirement**: Ibid.

53 **Jerry Lawler had a much publicized**: Box Brown, *Is This Guy for Real?: The Unbelievable Andy Kaufman* (New York: First Second, 2018), ebook.

53 **"was making more money than it had"**: Nancy Jo Sales, "Beyond Fake," *New York* magazine, October 26, 1998, page 43.

53 **Vince would have to pay $1 million**: Hornbaker, *Death of the Territories*, ebook.

54 **He would later tell a reporter**: Sales, "Beyond Fake," page 43.

54 **On June 5, 1982, they signed the documents**: Hornbaker, *Capitol Revolution*, ebook.

54 **"I knew my dad wouldn't have really sold"**: *Headliners & Legends with Matt*

Lauer, "Vince McMahon," written by Jonathan Moser, starring Matt Lauer, Vince McMahon, Lou Albano, and Eric Bischoff, NBC, aired November 25, 2001.

Chapter 4: GET OVER, ACT I

55 **"Okay, get out your notebooks"**: Richard Meltzer, "The Last Wrestling Piece," *San Diego Reader*, May 30, 1985, accessed August 2, 2022, https://www.san diegoreader.com/news/1985/may/30/last-wrestling-piece.

55 **one of the first critics to probe rock music**: Richard Meltzer, *The Aesthetics of Rock* (New York: Da Capo, 1987); Jason Gross, "Interview with Richard Meltzer," *Perfect Sound Forever*, accessed June 29, 2022, https://www.furious .com/perfect/meltzer2.html.

57 **Back on June 5, 1982**: MSG Cablevision, "MSG June 5 1982," featuring Vince McMahon, aired June 5, 1982.

58 **"Until you have hunted man"**: Patricia Lopez Baden, "Ventura Defines Real Hunting as 'Hunting Man,'" *Star Tribune* (Minneapolis), April 5, 2001, page 23.

59 **she had for about thirty years**: "The Fabulous Moolah," *Dark Side of the Ring*, season 1, episode 6, Vice, May 15, 2019.

59 **a seven-foot-plus child of Bulgarian and Polish immigrants**: Bertrand Hébert and Pat Laprade, *The Eighth Wonder of the World: The True Story of André the Giant* (Toronto: ECW Press, 2020), ebook.

59 **It was Vince Senior who first started billing**: Ibid.

59 **three to five bottles of wine a day**: Dillon Mafit, "André the Giant's Amazing Feats of Drinking," *Thrillist*, February 6, 2017, accessed June 29, 2022, https:// www.thrillist.com/culture/andre-the-giant-drinking-records-and-facts.

59 **upward of a hundred beers in a single sitting**: Ibid.

60 **purchased a TV slot in the Buffalo market**: Tim Hornbaker, *Death of the Territories: Expansion, Betrayal and the War That Changed Pro Wrestling Forever* (Toronto: ECW Press, 2018), ebook.

60 **On August 9, the company triumphantly returned**: "1982," *The History of WWE*, accessed June 29, 2022, http://www.thehistoryofwwe.com/82.htm.

60 **"Even during the best of times"**: Keith Elliot Greenberg and Classy Freddie Blassie, *The Legends of Wrestling: "Classy" Freddie Blassie (Listen, You Pencil Neck Geeks)* (New York: Gallery Books, 2010), ebook.

60 **Their jointly owned Atlantic and Pacific Wrestling Corporation**: Tim Hornbaker, *Capitol Revolution: The Rise of the McMahon Wrestling Empire* (Toronto: ECW Press, 2015), ebook.

61 **LeBell was cash-strapped**: Hornbaker, *Death of the Territories*, ebook.

61 **At the syndicate's annual meeting**: Ibid.

61 **In August 1982, their show even got**: Ibid.

61 **GCW was racked by internal division**: Ibid.

61 **Barnett was a bespectacled nonwrestler**: Greg Oliver, "Jim Barnett was TV Innovator," *Slam!Wrestling*, September 19, 2004, accessed June 29, 2022, https://slamwrestling.net/index.php/2004/09/19/jim-barnett-was-tv-in novator.

61   **"Ole was a true curmudgeon"**: Gary Juster, interview with author, March 18, 2021.

61   **accused of running an informal brothel**: Mike Mooneyham, "'Thin Thirty' Details Scandals, Barnett," *The Wrestling Gospel, According to Mike Mooneyham*, September 30, 2007, accessed June 29, 2022, http://www.mikemooney ham.com/2007/09/30/thin-thirty-details-scandals-barnett.

61   **Barnett told the members**: Hornbaker, *Death of the Territories*.

62   **The promoters of the weakened West Texas**: Ibid.

62   **Southwest Championship Wrestling scored a show**: Ibid.

62   **New Year's Day 1983 brought**: Ibid.

62   **WWF had scored a slot on an Akron station**: Ibid.

62   **Barnett became an unlikely ally**: Ibid.

62   **March 5, when his WWF made its**: Ibid.

62   **The next day brought a show in L.A.**: Ibid.

62   **a show at the L.A. Sports Arena on April 23**: Ibid.

62   **a crowd of 5,500 people**: Ibid.

62   **"The biggest thrill in the world"**: "Interview with Vince McMahon," *RAW Magazine*, March 2001.

62   **tweeted out by Donald Trump**: Donald Trump, "The biggest thrill in the world," Twitter, October 18, 2012, accessed June 29, 2022, https://www.the trumparchive.com/?searchbox=%22%5C%22The+biggest+thrill+in+the+world %5C%22%22.

63   **Nancy Argentino was born and raised**: "Jimmy Snuka and the Death of Nancy Argentino," *Dark Side of the Ring*, season 2, episode 5, Vice, April 14, 2020.

63   **"My younger sister and I always say"**: Ibid.

63   **Argentino had been working as a dental assistant**: Ibid.

63   **the pair started dating**: Adam Clark and Kevin Amerman, "Jimmy 'Superfly' Snuka and the Mysterious Death of Nancy Argentino," *Morning Call* (Lehigh Valley, PA), June 18, 2013, accessed June 29, 2022, https://www.mcall.com /news/local/mc-jimmy-snuka-cold-case-20130608-story.html.

63   **his previous handler, Buddy Rogers**: *Dark Side of the Ring*, "Jimmy Snuka."

63   **On January 18, 1983**: David Bixenspan, "Who Failed Nancy Argentino?," *Mel Magazine*, 2020, accessed June 29, 2022, https://melmagazine.com/en-us /story/jimmy-snuka-girlfriend-nancy-argentino-death?utm_source =pocket_mylist.

63   **six feet tall and weighed**: Clark and Amerman, "Jimmy 'Superfly' Snuka."

63   **As local paper *The Morning Call* reported**: Ibid.

64   **According to another reinvestigation**: Bixenspan, "Who Failed Nancy Argentino?"

64   **"Vince McMahon tried to talk her out"**: Ibid.

64   **In April, the wrestler took a deal**: Ibid.

64   **Snuka donated $1,500**: Ibid.

64   **On Sunday, May 8, Argentino called**: *Dark Side of the Ring*, "Jimmy Snuka."

64   **What we know for sure**: Clark and Amerman, "Jimmy 'Superfly' Snuka."

64   **They found Argentino unconscious**: Ibid.

64   **"I had to basically drag things"**: Ibid.

64 **He claimed she had seemed fine**: Ibid.
64 **He told this version of the story**: Ibid.
65 **The coroner recommended a police interview**: *Dark Side of the Ring*, "Jimmy Snuka."
65 **Some cops took Snuka back to the hotel**: Ibid.
65 **"Vince says, 'Have you heard anything'"**: Ibid.
65 **Snuka changed his story**: Ibid.
65 **A wrestler who was trying to defend Snuka**: Ibid.
65 **But that was the story Snuka held on to**: Jon Chattman and Jimmy Snuka, *Superfly: The Jimmy Snuka Story* (Chicago: Triumph Books, 2012), ebook.
65 **So the WWF cooperated**: Clark and Amerman, "Jimmy 'Superfly' Snuka."
65 **Snuka was released without charges**: Ibid.
65 **Snuka returned to TV**: Ibid.
65 **"just out of my own selfish motivation"**: *Dark Side of the Ring*, "Jimmy Snuka."
66 **Louise Argentino, would later recall**: Ibid.
66 **"I believe that the case should be"**: Clark and Amerman, "Jimmy 'Superfly' Snuka."
66 **contains no information about what Vince said**: *Dark Side of the Ring*, "Jimmy Snuka."
66 **Robert Steinberg, later recalled**: Clark and Amerman, "Jimmy 'Superfly' Snuka."
66 **"Jimmy talked to me a lot about Vince"**: *Dark Side of the Ring*, "Jimmy Snuka."
66 **"He would sign papers"**: Ibid.
66 **At one point, I went with Vince**: Chattman and Snuka, *Superfly*, ebook.
67 **no charges were filed**: Ellie Kaufman, "Homicide charges dropped against ex-pro wrestler Jimmy 'Superfly' Snuka," CNN.com, January 5, 2017, accessed August 2, 2022, https://www.cnn.com/2017/01/04/health/jimmy-superfly-snuka-charges-dropped/index.html.
67 **filled to the brim with praise**: Chattman and Snuka, *Superfly*, ebook.
67 **new murder and involuntary manslaughter charges**: *Dark Side of the Ring*, "Jimmy Snuka."
67 **quietly remove him from their Hall of Fame**: Brandon Stroud, "'Superfly' Jimmy Snuka Has Been Removed From The WWE Hall Of Fame And Website," *Uproxx.com*, September 3, 2015, accessed August 2, 2022, https://uproxx.com/prowrestling/jimmy-snuka-removed-from-wwe-hall-of-fame/.
67 **found unfit to stand trial**: *Dark Side of the Ring*, "Jimmy Snuka."
67 **When Snuka died at age seventy-three**: Liam Stack, "Jimmy Snuka, Ex-Pro Wrestler Known as Superfly, Dies at 73," *New York Times*, January 15, 2017, accessed August 2, 2022, https://www.nytimes.com/2017/01/15/sports/jimmy-snuka-ex-pro-wrestler-known-as-superfly-dies-at-73.html.
67 **WWE aired a tender tribute**: WWE, "WWE Honors the Life of Superfly Jimmy Snuka," YouTube, 2017, accessed June 29, 2022, https://www.youtube.com/watch?v=TQaBEPDyhXw.
68 **Dozens of WWE wrestlers**: "The Rock, Roman Reigns and More WWE Stars Comment On The Passing Of Jimmy 'Superfly' Snuka," *IWNerd.com*, accessed August 2, 2022, https://www.iwnerd.com/rock-roman-reigns-wwe-stars-comment-passing-jimmy-superfly-snuka.

68   **"#RIPSuperfly one of the greatest"**: Ibid.

68   **moved to Greenwich, Connecticut**: Brian Lockhart, "McMahons' Bankruptcy a Murky Chapter in Her Rags-to-Riches Tale," *CTPost*, October 1, 2010, accessed June 29, 2022, https://www.ctpost.com/local/article/McMahons -bankruptcy-a-murky-chapter-in-her-682114.php.

68   **Cape Cod's *Barnstable Patriot* reported**: Kevin Naylor, "Coliseum Is Sold, Skaters Homeless," *Barnstable Patriot* (Barnstable, MA), May 17, 1984.

68   **At age thirteen, he graduated**: "All in the Family," *RAW Magazine*, October 1999.

69   **"I wanted to get a raise"**: Ibid.

69   **"When I was younger"**: Ibid.

69   **"There's no question about who runs"**: Deborah D. McAdams, "Queen of the Ring," *Broadcasting+Cable*, Future US Inc. January 07, 2001, accessed June 29, 2022, https://www.nexttv.com/news/queen-ring-95882.

69   **Vince Senior felt that his son needed**: Hornbaker, *Death of the Territories*, ebook.

69   **Vince just sent Scott down to Atlanta**: Greg Oliver, "George Scott: WWF's Biggest Booker," *SLAM! Wrestling*, November 15, 2001, accessed August 2, 2022, https://slamwrestling.net/index.php/2001/11/15/george-scott-wwfs-biggest -booker.

70   **"At first, when he took over"**: Pat Patterson and Bertrand Hebert, *Accepted: How the First Gay Superstar Changed WWE* (Toronto: ECW Press, 2016), ebook.

70   **"See, what a lot of people don't understand"**: "The Fabulous Moolah," *Dark Side of the Ring*, season 1, episode 6, Vice, May 15, 2019.

71   **in August of 1983, the NWA gathered**: Hornbaker, *Death of the Territories*, ebook.

71   **"If you want war, McMahon"**: Bret Hart, *Hitman: My Real Life in the Cartoon World of Wrestling* (London: Ebury Press, 2010), ebook.

71   **that very weekend saw the publication**: Sally Sommer, "Where the Good Guys (Almost) Always Win," *Parade*, August 21, 1983, page 4.

71   **WWF shows debuted in two new TV slots**: Hornbaker, *Death of the Territories*.

72   **the change was unannounced**: Ibid.

72   **enraging both fans and promoters**: Guy Evans, *Nitro: The Incredible Rise and Inevitable Collapse of Ted Turner's WCW* (Self-published, 2018), ebook.

72   **still a dues-paying member of the NWA board**: Hornbaker, *Death of the Territories*, ebook.

72   **or, for the most part, inside of it**: B. Brian Blair, WWF wrestler, interview with author, November 21, 2021.

72   **"My dad would get a phone call"**: Vince McMahon, unpublished interview with Brian Solomon, September 18, 2003.

72   **"My dad was on the outside now"**: Ibid.

72   **On August 31, Vince Senior sent a letter**: Hornbaker, *Death of the Territories*, ebook.

72   **invaded Northern California**: Ibid.

72 **"He just kind of lost his zest"**: Vince McMahon, unpublished interview with Brian Solomon, September 18, 2003.

72 **in November of 1983**: Carolyn Reardon, interview with author, December 28, 2021.

72 **"By the time they actually discovered it"**: Vince McMahon, unpublished interview with Brian Solomon, September 18, 2003.

73 **Terry Bollea was born about eight years**: Mark Dagostino and Hulk Hogan, *My Life Outside the Ring* (New York: Hodder & Stoughton, 2009), ebook.

73 **"The perception is that's where"**: Ibid.

73 **Bollea loved wrestling from a young age**: Ibid.

73 **"I can remember the first time"**: Michael Jan Friedman and Hulk Hogan, *Hollywood Hulk Hogan* (New York: Pocket Books, 2003), ebook.

73 **"I was the first white guy"**: Dagostino and Hogan, *My Life Outside the Ring*, ebook.

73 **Many years later, Bollea would be caught**: Sean Reuter, "Audio of Hulk Hogan's racist tirade released," CagesideSeats.com, April 14, 2016, accessed August 3, 2022, https://www.cagesideseats.com/2016/4/14/11432674/audio -of-hulk-hogans-racist-tirade-released.

73 **Bollea worked as a musician**: Dagostino and Hogan, *My Life Outside the Ring*, ebook.

73 **"a revelation that would change my life"**: Ibid.

74 **"After all this time, nobody'd ever smartened"**: Ibid.

74 **"I can see it's not a one-off thing"**: Ibid.

74 **He reached out to a local wrestling manager**: Ibid.

74 **recounted an anecdote about the inception**: Ibid.

74 **especially since his 2020 death**: Alex Traub, "Pat Patterson, a Wrestling Star Who Came Out, Dies at 79," *New York Times*, December 7, 2020, accessed June 29, 2022, https://www.nytimes.com/2020/12/07/obituaries/pat-patterson -dead.html.

74 **he was also an alleged sexual harasser**: For more allegations, see Chapter 12.

74 **"We got you in the car"**: Dagostino and Hogan, *My Life Outside the Ring*, ebook.

75 **He started managing a bar**: Ibid.

76 **Steroids were new to the general public**: NIDA, "What Is the History of Anabolic Steroid Use?," National Institute on Drug Abuse, April 12, 2021, accessed June 29, 2022, https://nida.nih.gov/publications/research-reports /steroids-other-appearance-performance-enhancing-drugs-apeds/what-history -anabolic-steroid-use.

76 **"There was no indication that this stuff"**: Dagostino and Hogan, *My Life Outside the Ring*, ebook.

76 **"But I was young and invincible"**: Ibid.

76 **He called up Billy Graham**: Ibid.

76 **Soon, he was wrestling for the promoter who ran Alabama**: Ibid.

76 **Bollea started wrestling as Terry Boulder**: Ibid.

76 **allegedly after promoter Jerry Jarrett pointed out**: Ibid.

76 **"I was eating everything in sight"**: Ibid.

76   **Bollea was making roughly $25 per match**: Ibid.

76   **decided to quit again in 1979**: Ibid.

76   **just before he could hang up the tights**: Ibid.

76   **He made an appealing offer**: Ibid.

77   **he ordered Bollea to change his ring name**: Ibid.

77   **despite having barely a drop of Irish blood**: IMDB, "Terry Gene Bollea," Geni.com, April 27, 2022, accessed June 29, 2022, https://www.geni.com /people/Hulk-Hogan/6000000004139570474#:~:text=Hulk%20Or%20 Terry%20Hogan,-Collection%3A&text=Hogan%20was%20born%20 Terry%20Gene,raised%20in%20Port%20Tampa%2C%20Florida.

77   **a surname that translated**: "Hogan Family History," Ancestry.com, accessed August 3, 2022, https://www.ancestry.com/name-origin?surname=hogan.

77   **made his debut on November 13, 1979**: WWE, "Hulk Hogan's WWE Debut," YouTube, 2014, https://www.youtube.com/watch?v=ZEYcnqiRcVM&t=4s &ab_channel=WWE.

77   **"As for McMahon's promise"**: Dagostino and Hogan, *My Life Outside the Ring*, ebook.

77   **six-foot-seven, 320-odd-pound Bollea**: "Hulk Hogan," WWE.com, accessed August 3, 2022, https://www.wwe.com/superstars/hulkhogan.

77   **Vince Senior saw fit to send Bollea**: "Hulk Hogan," *Puroresu Central*, accessed August 3, 2022, http://puroresucentral.com/hogan.html.

77   **Bollea received an urgent message**: Dagostino and Hogan, *My Life Outside the Ring*, ebook.

77   **"Stallone wanted me more"**: Ibid.

77   **went to work for Verne Gagne's AWA**: Dagostino and Hogan, *My Life Outside the Ring*, ebook.

78   *Rocky III* **premiered on May 28, 1982**: "Rocky III," IMDb, IMDb.com, May 28, 1982, accessed August 3, 2022, https://www.imdb.com/title/tt0084602/.

78   **"Hey, I know my dad fired you"**: Dagostino and Hogan, *My Life Outside the Ring*, ebook.

78   **In Bollea's telling**: Friedman and Hogan, *Hollywood Hulk Hogan*, ebook.

78   **"The idea," Bollea wrote**: Dagostino and Hogan, *My Life Outside the Ring*, ebook.

78   **"With all the fly-by-night promoters"**: Ibid.

78   **Around 4 a.m., they shook on a deal**: Ibid.

79   **Vince contacted Gagne to see if he might**: Shaun Assael and Mike Mooneyham, *Sex, Lies, and Headlocks* (New York: Three Rivers Press, 2002), ebook.

79   **Verne and his son, Greg, laid out a proposal**: Ibid.

79   **"And I'll never forget"**: *WWE: McMahon*, directed by Vince McMahon (2006, California: WWE Home Video).

79   **Vince had opened a back channel to KPLR**: Hornbaker, *Death of the Territories*, ebook; Albert Samaha, "St. Louis' Indelible Place in Professional Wrestling," *Riverfront Times*, January 24, 2012, accessed August 3, 2022, https:// www.riverfronttimes.com/news/st-louis-indelible-place-in-professional -wrestling-2590410.

79   **he'd pioneered a strategy**: Hornbaker, *Death of the Territories*, ebook.

79 **made a reel highlighting his hottest young star:** Ibid.

79 **On December 15, Gagne got a telegram:** Ibid.

79 **So the WWF stunned the world:** Ibid.

80 **staging a live show in St. Louis:** Ibid.

80 **Bollea made his triumphant return:** Friedman and Hogan, *Hollywood Hulk Hogan*, ebook.

80 **"After St. Louis and Minneapolis":** McMahon, unpublished interview with Solomon.

80 **The elder man suggested:** Ibid.

80 **Vince Senior threatened to publicly sever ties:** Ibid.

80 **On December 30, 1983, the WWF invaded:** Hornbaker, *Death of the Territories*, ebook.

80 **On New Year's Eve, Vince did a segment on a WWF TV broadcast:** "WWF ASW Victory Corner Vince McMahon DEC 31 83," Harry Monsoon, YouTube, October 8, 2021, accessed August 3, 2022, https://www.youtube.com/watch?v=g573J0zX8Xk.

80 **"I had never heard of him":** Peter Bonventre and Howard Cosell, *I Never Played the Game* (New York: Avon), 1986, pages 370–371.

81 **On January 23, 1984, only a year and a half:** "1984," *The History of WWE*, accessed June 29, 2022, http://www.thehistoryofwwe.com/84.htm.

81 **The arena had sold out:** Ibid.

81 **The lineup was star-studded:** Ibid.

82 **Vince Senior called a meeting in Allentown:** Friedman and Hogan, *Hollywood Hulk Hogan*, ebook.

82 **"You know, Terry, maybe Bob's got a point":** Ibid.

82 **"But Vince Jr. stopped me":** Ibid.

82 **"He pulled his dad aside for a long conversation":** Ibid.

82 **Vince once told a reporter about the final argument:** McMahon, unpublished interview with Solomon.

82 **"I can't be in business with you":** Ibid.

83 **"You know what?" the father said:** Ibid.

83 **After a match on that January night:** Ibid.

83 **in the locker room, announcer Gene Okerlund:** Ibid.

83 **Within the next four months:** "WWF MSG 1984 - The Iron Sheik Vs Hulk Hogan [WWF CHAMPIONSHIP]," WWE Archives, YouTube, accessed August 3, 2022, https://youtu.be/Kq0eK0NJ-_s.

83 **"We can bring in new talent":** Hornbaker, *Death of the Territories*, ebook.

84 **"In the cultural chain of late-century being":** Richard Meltzer, "The Last Wrestling Piece," *A Whore Just Like The Rest: The Music Writings of Richard Meltzer* (New York: Da Capo, 2000), page 477.

Chapter 5: GET OVER, ACT II

85 **"mark" is a term with roots:** Scott Beekman, *Ringside: A History of Professional Wrestling in America* (Westport, CT: Praeger, 2006), ebook.

85 **As early as 1905:** Ibid.

85 **Jack Pfefer infamously told a reporter:** David Shoemaker, "A Brief History

of Wrestling Fakery," *Grantland*, June 15, 2012, accessed June 29, 2022, https://grantland.com/features/john-cena-big-show-how-century-pretend-fighting-led-wwe-reality-era/.

86   **became a smart at age nine:** Dave Meltzer, interview with author, October 2, 2021.

86   **At ten, he briefly published** *The California Wrestling Report:* Ibid.

86   **estimated circulation of one hundred:** Ibid.

86   **started over with** *The International Wrestling Gazette:* Ibid.

86   **ended up with about 150:** Ibid.

87   **The age of consent in California:** Brian Palmer, "What's 'Unlawful Sexual Intercourse'?," Slate.com, September 28, 2009, accessed June 29, 2022, https://slate.com/news-and-politics/2009/09/the-explainer-s-roman-polanski-roundup.html.

87   **Today, Meltzer is known as the most prolific:** Jake Rossen, "In World of Wrestling, Trying to Keep It Real," *New York Times*, May 14, 2013, accessed June 29, 2022, https://www.nytimes.com/2013/05/15/sports/wrestling-reporter-dave-meltzer-tries-to-keep-it-real.html.

87   *Wrestling Observer Newsletter*, **began in 1982:** Ibid.

87   **It started as a side project:** Ibid.

87   **roughly five hundred subscribers:** Dave Meltzer, interview with author, October 2, 2021.

88   **The February 1984 issue went out:** Dave Meltzer, "No Prisoners," *Wrestling Observer*, February 1984, page 1.

88   **The issue's opening column:** Ibid.

88   **"The average fan, seeing Hogan as champion":** Ibid.

88   **"Once McMahon has the stars":** Ibid.

89   **"a real threat to the stability":** Letters, *Wrestling Observer*, March 1984.

89   **"Granted, they have several excellent":** Ibid.

89   **"the prototype that Orwell foresaw":** Ibid.

89   **a broadcast deal in Chicago:** Tim Hornbaker, *Death of the Territories: Expansion, Betrayal and the War That Changed Pro Wrestling Forever* (Toronto: ECW Press, 2018), ebook.

89   **the acquisition of the sizzling heel:** Ibid.

90   **a television-slot takeover in San Francisco:** Ibid.

90   **an invasion in Baltimore:** Ibid.

90   **a spot on Sacramento TV:** Ibid.

90   **In April, Vince caught wind:** Jim Wilson and Weldon T. Johnson, *Choke Hold: Pro Wrestling's Real Mayhem Outside the Ring* (Xlibris, 2003), ebook.

90   **tending to his sick mother in Wisconsin:** Shaun Assael and Mike Mooneyham, *Sex, Lies, and Headlocks* (New York: Three Rivers Press, 2002), ebook.

90   **sold a collective 67.5 percent of GCW:** Wilson and Johnson, *Choke Hold*, ebook.

90   **some accounts say the next day:** Ibid.

90   **Anderson says it was a couple of weeks:** TrueStrawberry8008, "Ole Anderson Talks About Meeting Vince and Linda for the First Time," Reddit, Novem-

ber 2021, accessed June 29, 2022, https://www.reddit.com/r/SquaredCircle /comments/qikqio/ole_anderson_talks_about_meeting_vince_and_linda/.

90 **Anderson would recall, years later:** Ibid.

90 **the two reached an agreement:** Assael and Mooneyham, *Sex, Lies, and Headlocks*, ebook.

90 **the first big ratings smash on USA Network:** Ibid.

90 **Koplovitz reached out to Vince:** Ibid.

90 **Sweglar proposed a talk show:** Ibid.

91 **in reality, he was just:** Greg Oliver, "Lord Al Hayes Dead at 76," *SLAM! Wrestling*, July 21, 2005, accessed August 3, 2022, https://slamwrestling.ne /index.php/2005/07/21/lord-al-hayes-dead-at-76.

91 **Take, for example, his first words:** *Tuesday Night Titans*, season 1, episode 1, "Cooking in the Wild Samoans' Kitchen," featuring Vince McMahon and Lord Alfred Hayes, USA Network, aired May 29, 1984.

92 **Born and raised in poverty:** John Cosper and David Shults, *Don't Call Me Fake: The Real Story of Dr. D David Schultz* (Seattle: Amazon Digital Services, 2019), page 2.

92 **he'd refuse to sign autographs:** Cosper and Shults, *Don't Call Me Fake*, page 15.

92 **Towering above the interviewer:** *Tuesday Night Titans*, "Cooking in the Wild Samoans' Kitchen."

93 **Lauper and her boyfriend/manager:** L. Jon Wertheim, *Glory Days: The Summer of 1984 and the 90 Days That Changed Sports and Culture Forever* (Boston: Mariner Books, 2021), ebook.

93 **He got the part in the video:** Ibid.

93 **Vince, Albano, Lauper, and Wolff concocted a story:** Ibid.

93 **"Remember: *I, Captain Lou Albano*":** *Tuesday Night Titans*, "Cooking in the Wild Samoans' Kitchen."

94 **Vince Senior had died two days earlier:** Associated Press, "Wrestling promotor [*sic*] Vince McMahon dies at 69," *The Journal News*, May 29, 1984, page 20.

94 **"I went to the hospital and I kissed him":** Kevin Cook, "Playboy Interview: Vince McMahon," *Playboy*, February, 2001, page 64.

94 **only discovered about six months prior:** Carolyn Reardon, interview with author, December 28, 2021.

94 **"He was always so proud of his hair":** Vince McMahon, unpublished interview with Brian Solomon, September 18, 2003.

94 **"he was a swimmer, so he had big legs":** Ibid.

94 **"His hair fell out, and all that":** Ibid.

94 **"It's certainly not the way that my kids":** Cook, "Playboy Interview," page 64.

94 **"That time in the hospital":** Ibid.

95 **"There was a very small wrestling contingent":** Assael and Mooneyham, *Sex, Lies, and Headlocks*, ebook.

Chapter 6: GET OVER, ACT III

96 **Growing up in Bossier City, Louisiana:** Mark Nulty, "Interview with Wendi Richter," *Shoot*, recorded 2005, accessed June 29, 2022, https://audioboom .com/posts/7916791-wendi-richter-shoot-interview-2005.

96 One day in the late 1970s: Ibid.

96 had long since drifted away: "The Fabulous Moolah," *Dark Side of the Ring*, season 1, episode 6, Vice, May 15, 2019.

96 Moolah had been brought up in the business: Ibid.

96 granted the championship in 1956: Richard Goldstein, "Mary Lillian Ellison, 84, the Fabulous Moolah, Is Dead," *New York Times*, November 6, 2007, accessed August 3, 2022, https://www.nytimes.com/2007/11/06/sports/06mo olah.html.

96 First with her husband, and then alone: "The Fabulous Moolah," *Dark Side of the Ring*.

97 "I thought to myself": Nulty, "Interview with Wendi Richter."

97 Richter walked up to the referee: Ibid.

97 Moolah laid out the deal: Ibid.

97 "Moolah never trained me": Ibid.

97 "You just practice throwing yourself": Ibid.

97 "You've always got to think": Ibid.

98 According to people who trained: "The Fabulous Moolah," *Dark Side of the Ring*.

98 "Y'know, hon, the nicer you are to him": Ibid.

98 When Victoria refused: Ibid.

98 "I love wrestling": Nulty, "Interview with Wendi Richter."

98 "She'd kick me in the chest": Ibid.

98 she and Wolff brought Vince into conversations: L. Jon Wertheim, *Glory Days: The Summer of 1984 and the 90 Days That Changed Sports and Culture Forever* (Boston: Mariner Books, 2021), ebook.

98 a pair of delightful WWF cameos: Jordan Zakarin, "How Cyndi Lauper Helped Raise the Popularity of the WWE," *Biography*, March 9, 2021, accessed June 29, 2022, https://www.biography.com/news/cyndi-lauper-wwe.

99 *Entertainment Tonight* and other outlets had reported: Ibid.

99 He bought a station slot in enemy territory: Tim Hornbaker, *Death of the Territories: Expansion, Betrayal and the War That Changed Pro Wrestling Forever* (Toronto: ECW Press, 2018), ebook.

99 He bought another in the Twin Cities: Ibid.

99 Okerlund said Vince "doesn't want to": Ibid.

99 WWF TV debuted in Portland: Ibid.

99 the WWF did a show in Oakland: Ibid.

99 emergency meeting of the NWA and AWA: Ibid.

99 eventually dubbed Pro Wrestling USA: Ibid.

99 temporary court order requested by Anderson: Ibid.

99 July 14, 1984, was a Saturday: Ibid.

99 the broadcast started in standard fashion: "NWA Georgia Wrestling 7/14/84 'Black Saturday,'" 4WrestlingFans, YouTube, accessed August 3, 2022, https://youtu.be/rPHcM4e5kLg.

99 "Hello, everybody, and welcome": Ibid.

100 The GCW takeover had finally gone through: Richard Zacks, "Cable networks grapple for wrestling show rights," *Electronic Media*, August 2, 1984, page 1.

100 **They called it Black Saturday**: Zach Linder, "Black Saturday: The unbelievable story of the original invasion," WWE.com, July 9, 2013, accessed August 3, 2022, https://www.wwe.com/classics/black-saturday.

100 **The rest of the broadcast**: "NWA Georgia Wrestling 7/14/84."

101 **A few days later, on July 23**: "The Brawl to End It All." IMDb, IMDb.com, accessed August 2, 2022, https://www.imdb.com/title/tt8648646.

101 **On MSG Network, you could see**: "The Brawl to End It All," featuring Wendi Richter, MSG Network, July 23, 1984.

101 **But if you tuned in to MTV**: "The Brawl to End It All," featuring Alan Hunter, MTV, July 23, 1984.

101 **the festivities in the locker room**: Ibid.

101 **In an interview decades later**: Nulty, "Interview with Wendi Richter."

101 **Moolah wasn't happy**: Ibid.

102 **Vince, at Richter's request, told her**: Ibid.

102 **"Moolah had been very jealous"**: "The Fabulous Moolah," *Dark Side of the Ring*.

102 **reportedly garnered the biggest viewership**: Kyle Anderson, "Captain Lou Albano, Mr. T and Hulk Hogan: 'The War to Settle the Score' on MTV," MTV, October 14, 2009, accessed June 29, 2022, https://www.mtv.com/news/2576905/captain-lou-albano-hulk-hogan.

102 **the hiring of the WWF's first female referee**: Rita Chatterton, interview with author, April 25, 2022.

102 **Ole Anderson formed a new company**: Hornbaker, *Death of the Territories*, ebook.

102 **Turner decided to give Anderson and CWG**: Ibid.

102 **Gagne and Charlotte-based promoter Jim Crockett Jr.**: Ibid.

102 **His and Linda's tax liens from the 1970s**: Brian Lockhart, "McMahons' Bankruptcy a Murky Chapter in Her Rags-to-Riches Tale," *CTPost*, October 1, 2010, accessed June 29, 2022, https://www.ctpost.com/local/article/McMahons-bankruptcy-a-murky-chapter-in-her-682114.php.

102 **bleeding money on the expansion**: Hornbaker, *Death of the Territories*.

102 **"They were on a trip, a vacation"**: Greg Oliver and Jon Waldman, eds., *SLAM! Wrestling: Shocking Stories from the Squared Circle* (Toronto: ECW Press, 2009), ebook.

103 **Crockett had concocted a so-called**: John Molinaro, "Starrcade Was the Original Super Card," *Slam!Wrestling*, December 17, 1999, accessed June 29, 2022, https://slamwrestling.net/index.php/1999/12/17/starrcade-the-original-super-card.

103 **someone suggested the name "Mania"**: Oliver and Waldman, eds., *SLAM! Wrestling*, ebook.

103 **immediately countered with "WrestleMania"**: Ibid.

103 **as Finkel, himself**: Caleb Smith, "'The Fink' Howard Finkel Shares His WrestleMania Memories," *SLAM!Wrestling*, April 2, 2014, accessed August 3, 2022, https://slamwrestling.net/index.php/2014/04/02/the-fink-howard-finkel-shares-his-wrestlemania-memories.

103 **Rex Jones, as Dave Meltzer has reported**: Dave Meltzer, "Editorial," *Wrestling Observer*, July 24, 2006.

103 **Vince had his heart set on a different name**: Greg Oliver, "Behind the Creation of WrestleMania," *SLAM!Wrestling*, March 6, 2001, accessed August 3, 2022, https://slamwrestling.net/index.php/2001/03/06/behind-the-creation-of-wrestlemania.

103 **Scott lobbied hard to reverse course**: Ibid.

103 **Journalist Ray Tennenbaum was reporting**: Ray Tennenbaum, "Sleeper Hold, Part 3," Ray Tennenbaum's text, accessed June 29, 2022, http://www.ray-field.com/content/article/sleeper-hold-part-3.

103 **eventually killed for unclear reasons**: Ray Tennenbaum, interview with author, September 8, 2021.

103 **"See, Crockett won't let Gagne"**: Tennenbaum, "Sleeper Hold, Part 3."

104 **"I don't watch myself on TV"**: *Real Sports with Bryant Gumbel*, "Deaths in Wrestling," HBO, June 24, 2003.

104 **As it turned out, he was right**: Liam Stack, "Roddy Piper, a Master Villain of Professional Wrestling, Dies at 61," *New York Times*, July 31, 2015, accessed August 3, 2022, https://www.nytimes.com/2015/08/01/sports/roddy-piper-one-of-the-most-hated-villains-in-professional-wrestling-dies-at-61.html.

104 **Vince snatched Toombs**: Hornbaker, *Death of the Territories*.

104 **Toombs started as a manager**: Jesse Gormley, "This Was How Much Roddy Piper Was Worth When He Died," Grunge.com, April 21, 2021, accessed August 3, 2022, https://www.grunge.com/389123/this-is-how-much-roddy-piper-was-worth-when-he-died.

104 **Toombs got a regular segment**: Tom Hawthorn, "Saskatoon native Rowdy Roddy Piper was among first WrestleMania stars," *Globe and Mail*, August 16, 2015, accessed August 3, 2022, https://www.theglobeandmail.com/news/saskatoon-native-rowdy-roddy-piper-was-among-first-wrestlemania-stars/article25981082.

105 **talk to Black wrestlers about soul food**: David Shoemaker, "A (Very) Concise History of Racism in Wrestling, 1980–Present," *Grantland*, November 6, 2013, accessed August 3, 2022, https://grantland.com/features/excerpt-david-shoemaker-new-book-concise-history-racism-wrestling.

105 **leered at his female guests**: "Roddy Piper visits Cyndi Lauper at studio (06-23-1984)," All Out of Bubblegum, YouTube, accessed August 3, 2022, https://youtu.be/uM4LW5-M3Vo.

105 **hit Jimmy Snuka on the head**: "Piper's Pit–Jimmy Snuka – 1984," Joey Cassata, YouTube, November 2, 2014, accessed August 3, 2022, https://youtu.be/GKXpSyjfIik.

105 **up to ninety days of hard-traveling work**: "Deaths in Wrestling," *Real Sports*.

105 **Speaking to the HBO reporter**: Ibid.

107 **"It followed you everywhere"**: *Biography: WWE Legends*, season 1, episode 2, "'Rowdy' Roddy Piper," directed by Joe Lavine, featuring Roderick Toombs and Vince McMahon, A&E, April 25, 2021.

107 **A date for the stunt was set**: Bruce Newman, "Who's Kidding Whom?," *Sports Illustrated*, April 29, 1985, accessed August 3, 2022, https://vault.si.com/vault/1985/04/29/whos-kidding-whom.

107 **The ABC news program 20/20**: "David Schultz [*sic*] and the Slap Heard

Round the World," *Dark Side of the Ring,* season 2, episode 7, Vice, April 28, 2020.

107   **Stossel had already been in touch**: Ibid.

107   **As Shults later recounted**: Ibid.

107   **"Why are you called 'Dr. D'?"**: "20/20 Expose on Pro Wrestling—1984," Free Is A Very Good Price, YouTube, accessed August 3, 2022, https://youtu .be/31hcFYBQaKU.

108   **Stossel was already talking about**: "David Schultz," *Dark Side of the Ring.*

108   **Vince told Shults he should get out**: Ibid.

108   **Wendi Richter arrived at the ring**: WWE, "Dick Clark Presents Cyndi Lauper with an Award in Madison Square Garden," YouTube, 2012, accessed June 29, 2022, https://www.youtube.com/watch?v=4jmgqSGtWxc0.

108   **had raised four million non-kayfabe dollars**: Lynne Ames, "The Captain vs. Multiple Sclerosis," *New York Times,* October 28, 1984, section 11WC, page 2.

109   **"Even though it was me that set this up"**: WWE, "Dick Clark Presents Cyndi Lauper with an Award in Madison Square Garden."

109   **According to a lawsuit filed years later**: *Damage Determination Report for United States Wrestling Association vs. Titan Sports Inc.*, trademark infringement, Ellis G. Godwin, November 19, 1992, page 3.

109   **By the end of 1985, income**: Ibid.

110   **attend the annual American International Toy Fair**: "Violent Toys Dominate Manufacturers' New Selections," *Daily Journal* (Vineland, NJ), February 12, 1985, page 8.

110   **"The toy industry has decided"**: Ibid.

110   **T first made an appearance**: "1985," *The History of WWE,* accessed June 29, 2022, http://www.thehistoryofwwe.com/85.htm.

110   **He'd been sent to Japan**: "David Schultz," *Dark Side of the Ring.*

110   **Vince ordered him to sign a statement**: Ibid.

110   **"I didn't think Mr. T should be"**: Ibid.

110   **Some say Shults made a beeline**: Ibid.

110   **Shults says he wanted to attack T**: Ibid.

110   **Shults was escorted out in handcuffs**: Ibid.

110   **a segment aired on February 16**: "1985," *The History of WWE.*

111   **cameos on each other's shows**: Ariel Teal Toombs and Colt Baird Toombs, *Rowdy: The Roddy Piper Story* (Toronto: Random House Canada, 2016), ebook.

111   **The branded name for the endeavor**: Newman, "Who's Kidding Whom?"

111   **The War to Settle the Score—a sequel**: WWF2WWEReleases, "MTV's War To Settle The Score Part 1 [WweReleases]," YouTube, August 31, 2012, accessed August 3, 2022.

111   **far more people watched it**: Newman, "Who's Kidding Whom?"

111   **Journalist Charles M. Young**: Rob Kemp and David Felton, "Charles M. Young, Rock Journalist Who Championed Punk, Dies at 63," *Rolling Stone,* August 19, 2014, accessed June 29, 2022, https://www.rollingstone.com /music/music-news/charles-m-young-rock-journalist-who-championed -punk-dies-at-63-178367/.

111 **he'd been put in charge of scripting**: WWF2WWEReleases, "MTV's War To Settle The Score Part 3 [WweReleases]," YouTube, August 31, 2012, accessed August 3, 2022, https://youtu.be/29O8BOWAUxQ.

111 **The hosts were Okerlund and VJ Alan Hunter**: WWF2WWEReleases, "MTV's War To Settle The Score Part 1."

112 **an inspiration for many a flashy pro wrestler**: Darren Paltrowitz, "3 ways in which Rock & Roll innovator Little Richard was tied to Professional Wrestling," *Sportskeeda*, July 23, 2022, accessed August 3, 2022, https://www.sportskeeda.com/wwe/3-ways-in-which-rock-roll-innovator-little-richard-was-tied-to-professional-wrestling.

112 **"Listen, I'm here because I'm really angry"**: WWF2WWEReleases, "MTV's War To Settle The Score Part 1."

113 **Of course, Steinem and Ferraro didn't go**: Newman, "Who's Kidding Whom?"

113 **Lauper, along with an MTV camera crew**: Ibid.

113 **Ferraro would later say**: Ibid.

113 **The most fascinating bit of the night**: WWF2WWEReleases, "MTV's War To Settle The Score Part 1."

114 **Finally, the broadcast dissolved**: WWF2WWEReleases, "MTV's War To Settle The Score Part 2 [WweReleases]," YouTube, August 31, 2012, accessed August 3, 2022, https://youtu.be/xKnH6_GG4rg.

114 **After seven minutes and forty seconds**: Ibid.

114 **Danny DeVito, who was working with Albano**: WWF2WWEReleases, "MTV's War To Settle The Score Part 3."

114 **Some two million people had watched**: Newman, "Who's Kidding Whom?"

114 **the unmistakable visage of Andy Warhol**: WWF2WWEReleases, "MTV's War To Settle The Score Part 3."

114 **He'd come to the show with some friends**: Peter Newman, friend of Andy Warhol, interview with author, October 26, 2021.

115 **Frank Tomeo, told a reporter**: Ray Tennenbaum, "Sleeper Hold, Part 1," Ray Tennenbaum's text, accessed June 29, 2022, http://www.ray-field.com/content/article/sleeper-hold-part-1.

115 **Tomeo's source was sportswriter Bert Randolph Sugar**: Ibid.

115 **Nielsen reported that four of the top ten**: Newman, "Who's Kidding Whom?"

115 *Tuesday Night Titans* **was, astoundingly**: Ibid.

115 **"It scarcely matters that wrestling's"**: Ibid.

116 **"You may not like professional wrestling"**: John Corry, "Critic's Notebook; Wrestling on TV a Kind of Virtuous Docudrama," *New York Times*, March 14, 1985, accessed June 29, 2022, https://www.nytimes.com/1985/03/14/arts/critic-s-notebook-wrestling-on-tv-a-kind-of-virtuous-docudrama.html.

116 **He was fed up with his ostensible broadcast partner**: Hornbaker, *Death of the Territories*, ebook.

116 **Turner gave a TBS show to Bill Watts**: Assael and Mooneyham, *Sex, Lies, and Headlocks*, ebook.

116 **reportedly went so far as to personally meet**: Ibid.

116 **Jim Barnett approached Jim Crockett Jr.**: Ibid.

116 **so he sold it for a song**: Ibid.

116 **public relations firm Bozell & Jacobs**: "The Marketing of March 31, 1985," *WrestlingMemorabilia*, March 28, 2013, accessed August 3, 2022, https://wrestlingmemorabilia.blogspot.com/2013/03/the-marketing-of-march-31-1985.html.

116 **stories in newspapers around the country**: *Wrestling '85* (Greensburg, PA), Volume 10, Issue 6, March/April 1985.

116 *NBC SportsWorld* **ran an episode**: Hornbaker, *Death of the Territories*, ebook.

117 **Vince and NBC exec Dick Ebersol**: *This Was the XFL*, directed by Charlie Ebersol (2017, ESPN).

117 **Hogan and Mr. T appeared on Richard Belzer's**: UPI, "Hulk Hogan Puts TV Show Host to Sleep," *South Florida Sun-Sentinel*, March 28, 1985, accessed August 3, 2022, https://www.sun-sentinel.com/news/fl-xpm-1985-03-28-8501120022-story.html.

117 **eventually sued the WWF for $5 million**: Barbara Goldberg, "Hulk Hogan settles lawsuit over 'chin lock,'" UPI, January 2, 1990, accessed August 3, 2022, https://www.upi.com/Archives/1990/01/02/Hulk-Hogan-settles-lawsuit-over-chin-lock/1835631256400.

117 **The next night, Mr. T walked onto the soundstage**: Don Giller, Letterman archivist, correspondence with author, January 1, 2022.

117 **Two nights later, a lucky break**: Howard Rosenberg, "Bod Couple Alive on Saturday Night," *Los Angeles Times*, April 1, 1985, accessed August 3, 2022, https://www.latimes.com/archives/la-xpm-1985-04-01-ca-28399-story.html.

117 **the company's official chronicles proclaim**: *The True Story of WrestleMania*, directed by Kevin Dunn (2011, New York, WWE).

117 **As one anonymous rival promoter put it**: Dan Bischoff, "The Wrestling Sensation Rocks the Nation," *Village Voice*, March 10, 1985, page 10.

117 **Vince and Linda moved their family**: Lockhart, "McMahons' Bankruptcy."

117 **They reportedly outfitted the house**: Assael and Mooneyham, *Sex, Lies, and Headlocks*, ebook.

118 **"The whole thing was done by a decorator"**: Ibid.

118 **Shane "had three or four friends"**: James J. Dillon, Scott Teal, and Philip Varriale, *Wrestlers Are Like Seagulls: From McMahon to McMahon* (Gallatin, TN: Crowbar Press, 2005), ebook.

118 **that same ex-employee remarked**: Ibid.

118 **"One time, I did kick a boy in the shin"**: "All in the Family," *RAW Magazine*, October 1999.

119 **The first thing you saw**: *WrestleMania I*, March 31, 1985, unofficial video reconstruction of original broadcast.

119 **Richter and Kai had always gotten along**: Nulty, "Interview with Wendi Richter."

119 **After about six minutes**: *WrestleMania I*, reconstruction.

120 **there had been disagreement**: Toombs and Toombs, *Rowdy*, ebook.

120 **"Roddy worried that if Mr. T pinned him"**: Ibid.

120 **Toombs had a remarkably good bargaining position**: Ibid.

120 **After Patterson slapped the canvas**: *WrestleMania I*, reconstruction.

120   **Dave Meltzer, in his write-up**: Dave Meltzer, editorial, *Wrestling Observer*, April 15, 1985.

121   **"Even though readers of this publication"**: Ibid.

121   **"has made it hard for me to enjoy"**: Ibid.

121   **The other, elder Meltzer, Richard, had watched**: Richard Meltzer, "The Last Wrestling Piece," *San Diego Reader*, May 30, 1985, accessed August 2, 2022, https://www.sandiegoreader.com/news/1985/may/30/last-wrestling-piece.

121   **At ALL times the *function***: Ibid.

122   **more times than Martin Luther King Jr. Day**: William E. Schmidt, "U.S. Countdown Starts for Dr. King's Holiday," *New York Times*, January 13, 1986, section A, page 10.

122   **Gladys Knight**: "WrestleMania IV celebrities," *WWE.com*, accessed August 3, 2022, https://www.wwe.com/shows/wrestlemania/4/celebrities.

122   **John Legend**: WWE, "John Legend sings 'America the Beautiful' at Wrestlemania XXIV," YouTube, February 23, 2015, accessed August 3, 2022, https://youtu.be/T27Nuu5H0UE.

122   **Ray Charles**: "Ray Charles sings 'America the Beautiful': WrestleMania II," WWE.com, accessed August 3, 2022, https://www.wwe.com/videos/playlists/america-the-beautiful-performances.

Chapter 7: GET OVER, FINALE

123   **He later told a story about it**: Brandon Stroud, "Jim Ross Once Overheard NWA Promoters Talking About Murdering Vince McMahon," *Uproxx*, August 16, 2019, https://uproxx.com/prowrestling/vince-mcmahon-nwa-murder-jim-ross-story.

123   **Vince's mansion on Hurlingham Drive**: Informational report, LexisNexis, Reed Elsevier Inc., created September 11, 2020.

123   **For two weeks after that show of shows**: "1985," *The History of WWE*, accessed June 29, 2022, http://www.thehistoryofwwe.com/85.htm.

123   **Poolside soon became a site for business**: Pat Patterson and Bertrand Hebert, *Accepted: How the First Gay Superstar Changed WWE* (Toronto: ECW Press, 2016), ebook.

123   **they'd started opening WWF shows**: Wrestling Reaper, "WWF Championship Wrestling (March 16, 1985)," YouTube, accessed August 3, 2022, https://youtu.be/ur_rciRzXqQ.

124   **He introduced a standard contract**: Tim Hornbaker, *Death of the Territories: Expansion, Betrayal and the War That Changed Pro Wrestling Forever* (Toronto: ECW Press, 2018), ebook.

124   **"Although Andre and Vince Junior"**: Dave Meltzer, editorial, *Wrestling Observer*, October 6, 1985.

124   **Vince, too, was still close with Juanita**: Carolyn Reardon, interview with author, December 28, 2021.

124   **adding stipulations to his agreements with venues**: Hornbaker, *Death of the Territories*, ebook.

124   **start trademarking his wrestlers' gimmick names**: Ibid.

125 **the creation of Saturday Night's Main Event**: "Saturday Night's Main Event," IMDb, IMDb.com, accessed August 2, 2022, https://www.imdb.com/title /tt0783198.

125 **The WWF filmed The Wrestling Classic**: Hornbaker, *Death of the Territories*, ebook.

125 **Vince took control of young Dave Meltzer's old haunt**: Ibid.

125 **He ended the AWA's exclusivity**: Ibid.

125 **When Bruce Newman's feature was published**: Bruce Newman, "Who's Kidding Whom?," *Sports Illustrated*, April 29, 1985, accessed August 3, 2022, https://vault.si.com/vault/1985/04/29/whos-kidding-whom.

125 **Hogan tries to help an honest politician**: *Hulk Hogan's Rock 'n' Wrestling*, "Ballot Box Boneheads," season 1, episode 8, October 5, 1985.

125 **Roddy Piper and Junkyard Dog have a car race**: *Hulk Hogan's Rock 'n' Wrestling*, "The Junkyard 500," season 1, episode 1, September 14, 1985.

125 **Iron Sheik teaches his nephew's baseball team**: *Hulk Hogan's Rock 'n' Wrestling*, "Cheaters Never Prosper," season 1, episode 5, September 21, 1985.

125 **I asked the creator of the show**: Jeffrey Scott, show creator, correspondence with author, December 12, 2020.

125 **Although Jimmy Snuka was no longer wrestling**: Kevin Conlon, "Jimmy Snuka – 'Superfly' of wrestling fame – charged in 1980s slaying," CNN.com, September 2, 2015, accessed August 3, 2022, https://www.cnn.com/2015/09/01 /us/jimmy-superfly-snuka-murder-charge.

126 **got paid a portion of the gate**: Chris Smith, "Breaking Down How WWE Contracts Work," Forbes.com, March 28, 2015, accessed August 3, 2022, https:// www.forbes.com/sites/chrissmith/2015/03/28/breaking-down-how-wwe -contracts-work/?sh=6a05a6516713.

126 **Richter said she would make**: Mark Nulty, "Interview with Wendi Richter," *Shoot*, recorded 2005, accessed June 29, 2022, https://audioboom.com /posts/7916791-wendi-richter-shoot-interview-2005.

126 **"He would pacify me"**: Ibid.

126 **the brisk, dry Manhattan afternoon**: "New York City, NY Weather History— November 25, 1985," Weather Underground, accessed June 29, 2022, https://www.wunderground.com/history/daily/us/ny/new-york-city/KLGA /date/1985-11-25.

126 **That night, she was scheduled**: David Shoemaker, "Wrestling's Greatest Shoots, Volume 4: Wendi Richter vs. The Spider, a.k.a. The Fabulous Moolah," July 29, 2013, accessed August 3, 2022, https://grantland.com/the-triangle /wrestlings-greatest-shoots-wendy-richter-vs-the-spider-a-k-a-the-fabulous -moolah.

127 **"I wasn't ugly, or yelled, or anything"**: Nulty, "Interview with Wendi Richter."

127 **"I'd wrestled the Spider Lady before"**: "The Fabulous Moolah," *Dark Side of the Ring*, season 1, episode 6, Vice, May 15, 2019.

127 **They started the match**: Ibid.

127 **"I knew it was Moolah"**: Nulty, "Interview with Wendi Richter."

127 **"Something that you easily kick out of"**: Ibid.

127 **"Whoa, was *that* close!"**: Fabulous One, "The Fabulous Spider, errr Moolah vs. Wendi Richter, 11-25-1985," YouTube, accessed August 3, 2022, https://youtu.be/JW36ll-hyT0.

128 **As Richter has sometimes told it**: *Dark Side of the Ring*, "The Fabulous Moolah."

128 **she has, at other times, implied**: Nulty, "Interview with Wendi Richter."

128 **Alone in the ring, Richter paced**: "The Fabulous Spider, errr Moolah," Fabulous One.

128 **"I was so angry that I just walked"**: Nulty, "Interview with Wendi Richter."

129 **years later, after another, more famous screwjob**: The so-called Montreal Screwjob of 1997 (see Chapter 15).

129 **Dave Meltzer didn't hear whispers**: Dave Meltzer, interview with author, January 3, 2020.

129 **Richter wrestled for other promotions**: Nulty, "Interview with Wendi Richter."

129 **"I make like three times in therapy"**: Ibid.

129 **Richter agreed to be inducted**: *WWE Hall of Fame*, season 10, episode 1, "Hall of Fame 2010," featuring Jerry Lawler, USA Network, March 27, 2010.

Chapter 8: HIGH SPOT

130 **He'd founded Stampede Wrestling**: Heath McCoy, *Pain and Passion: The History of Stampede Wrestling* (Toronto: ECW Press, 2005), page 2.

130 **whose sisters loved to "set him up"**: Bret Hart, interview with author, May 28, 2022.

130 **Bret was his parents' eighth child**: Bret Hart, *Hitman: My Real Life in the Cartoon World of Wrestling* (London: Ebury Press, 2010), ebook.

131 **Bret would descend into the Dungeon**: Ibid.

131 **Vince bought Stampede from Stu**: McCoy, *Pain and Passion*, pages 4–5.

131 **He met Vince for the first time**: Hart, *Hitman*, ebook.

131 **like no one so much as Big Boy**: Ibid.

131 **"I like my wrestlers to spend a lot of time"**: Ibid.

131 **a "human basketball"**: Ibid.

131 **"With Vince McMahon in the ascendant"**: Ibid.

131 **George Zahorian was the company's go-to**: Greg Oliver, "Steve Travis and the Dawn of the Drug Era," *SLAM!Wrestling*, November 1, 2007, accessed August 3, 2022, https://slamwrestling.net/index.php/2007/11/01/steve-travis-and-the-dawn-of-the-drug-era.

131 **"Vince was coked out of his mind"**: C. M. Burnham, "Interview with Matt Borne AKA Doink the Clown," Oklahoma Wrestling Fan's Resource Center, December 5, 2008, accessed June 29, 2022, http://www.oklafan.com/interviews/print/1861.

131 **Vince's chauffeur, Jim Stuart, later told**: Jeff Savage, "No-Holds-Barred," *Penthouse*, September 1992, page 172.

132 **"I can snort as much of that stuff"**: Shaun Assael and Mike Mooneyham, *Sex, Lies, and Headlocks* (New York: Three Rivers Press, 2002), ebook.

132 **"Steroids work," Vince would**: Vince McMahon, "What I've Learned," *Esquire*, January 2005, accessed August 3, 2022, https://classic.esquire.com/article/2005/1/1/what-ive-learned-vince-mcmahon.

132 **He worked out nearly every day**: Assael and Mooneyham, *Sex, Lies, and Headlocks*, ebook.

132 **"I find the gym to be a socially acceptable"**: Sean Hyson, "WWE Chief Vince McMahon is Still Making Gains," *Muscle & Fitness*, March 2016, accessed August 3, 2022, https://www.muscleandfitness.com/athletes-celebrities /interviews/wwe-chief-vince-mcmahon-still-making-gains.

132 **"even went so far as to hire an assistant"**: Assael and Mooneyham, *Sex, Lies, and Headlocks*, ebook.

132 **On June 30, 1986, Vince appeared**: "Transcript of 'Home Team Sportsbeat with Larry King,' June 30, 1986," *Wrestling '86* (1986).

132 **"The road really screwed up my sex life"**: *Beyond the Mat*, directed by Barry W. Blaustein (1999, Amarillo, TX: Universal Family and Home Entertainment, Imagine Entertainment, Lionsgate Films).

133 **"When Linda and I got married"**: Kevin Cook, "Playboy Interview: Vince McMahon," *Playboy*, February, 2001, page 67.

133 **Born Rita Filicoski and raised**: Rita Chatterton, interview with author, April 25, 2022.

133 **He was killed in a car crash**: "Crash in Stillwater Kills 2 Teen-agers," *Daily Gazette* (Schenectady, NY), March 5, 1979, page 27.

134 **the only one on the East Coast**: Paul Guernsey, "Taking Lumps at Wrestler School," *New York Times*, August 26, 1984, accessed June 29, 2022, https://www .nytimes.com/1984/08/26/nyregion/taking-lumps-at-wrestler-school.html.

134 **a WWF visit at the Orange County Fairgrounds**: Rita Chatterton, interview with author, April 25, 2022.

135 **"Rita?" the voice on the other line said**: Ibid.

135 **Chatterton made her TV debut**: *Tuesday Night Titans*, season 2, episode 7, "Salvatore Bellomo Returns to TNT to Teach More About Italian Culture," featuring the Iron Sheik, Nikolai Volkoff, "Classy" Freddie Blassie, "Dr. D" David Schultz [sic], and Salvatore Bellomo, USA Network, aired March 1, 1985.

136 **She even made an appearance**: Ibid.

137 **Vince's lawyers have denied the claim**: Charles R. Beeman, *McMahon and McMahon v. Rivera et al.*, declaration, no. 3:93 CV 468 (District of CT), page 1.

137 **"There was growing tension"**: Hart, *Hitman*, ebook.

138 **he had promised Stu**: McCoy, *Pain and Passion*, pages 5–6.

138 **Vince still hadn't paid Stu a dime**: Hart, *Hitman*, ebook.

138 **Vince eventually told Stu that he could reopen Stampede**: McCoy, *Pain and Passion*, page 9.

138 **There would be action in Los Angeles**: *WrestleMania 2*, starring Hulk Hogan, King Kong Bundy, Randy Savage (1986, Los Angeles: Coliseum Video, World Wrestling Federation).

138 **Fed up with the industry**: Steve Austin, November 5, 2016, *The Steve Austin Show EP.371: Jesse Ventura returns*, YouTube. https://youtu.be/EELZiVex BK8?si=lYZJAONJAQKnvJWh.

139 **Although it drew around 250,000 pay-per-view buys**: David Bixenspan, "I Fell Down a Historical PPV Buy Rate Rabbit Hole. Here's What I Found," *Babyface*

v. Heel, August 13, 2019, accessed June 29, 2022, https://babyfacevheel
.substack.com/p/i-fell-down-a-historical-ppv-buy.

139 **didn't fill all the seats in all the venues**: Tim Hornbaker, *Death of the Territories: Expansion, Betrayal and the War That Changed Pro Wrestling Forever*
(Toronto: ECW Press, 2018), ebook.

139 ***WrestleMania 2* turned a profit**: Ibid.

139 **Gagne began back-channel negotiations with Vince**: Ibid.

139 **an ambitious national tour called the Great American Bash**: Ibid.

139 **Crockett had filed a federal antitrust lawsuit**: Rob Walker, "Wrestling Promoter Suing Rival Over Bookings Here," *Times-Dispatch* (Richmond, VA),
December 3, 1985, page B-3.

140 **the WWF held a show in Charlotte**: Hornbaker, *Death of the Territories*,
ebook.

140 **Mike LeBell had sued Vince**: Ibid.

140 **Crockett's lawsuit eventually fizzled**: Ibid.

140 **the venue informed Verne Gagne**: Ibid.

140 **Crockett had invaded Gagne's territory**: Ibid.

140 **"Vince McMahon, Junior took our income"**: *WWE: McMahon*, directed by
Vince McMahon (2006, WWE Home Video).

140 **"I don't have much sympathy"**: Ibid.

140 **WWF tapings would be liberated**: Ibid.

140 **drawing eye-widening ratings**: "Saturday Night's Main Event TV Ratings,"
OSW Review, accessed June 29, 2022, http://oswreview.com/history/saturday
-night-s-main-event-tv-ratings/; Jessica Boggs, "Saturday Night Live Ratings
1975–2017," TVRG's Rating History, January 19, 2020, accessed June 29, 2022,
http://www.thetvratingsguide.com/2020/01/saturday-night-live-ratings
-1975-2017.html.

140 **placing in the top fifteen**: Assael and Mooneyham, *Sex, Lies, and Headlocks*,
ebook.

140 **Vince even opened a steakhouse**: "Vinnie's Ready to Rumble," *Triangle Business
Journal*, American City Business Journals, December 15, 1997, accessed June 29,
2022, https://www.bizjournals.com/triangle/stories/1997/12/15/story4.html.

141 **"When Vince took over from his father"**: Hornbaker, *Death of the Territories*, ebook.

141 **In 1986, the WWF earned**: *Damage Determination Report for United States
Wrestling Association vs. Titan Sports Inc.*, trademark infringement, Ellis G.
Godwin, November 19, 1992, page 3.

141 **Vince had taken George Scott off booking duties**: Hornbaker, *Death of the
Territories*, ebook.

141 **"It was terrible"**: Greg Oliver, "George Scott, WWF's Biggest Booker,"
Slam!Wrestling, November 15, 2001, accessed June 29, 2022, https://slam
wrestling.net/index.php/2001/11/15/george-scott-wwfs-biggest-booker.

141 **"Wrestling as it was went stage left"**: Ibid.

141 **partly to dull the pain from his acromegaly**: Bertrand Hébert and Pat
Laprade, *The Eighth Wonder of the World: The True Story of André the Giant*
(Toronto: ECW Press, 2020), ebook.

141   **In late 1986, he got the chance**: Ibid.
141   **As the gentle strongman Fezzik**: Ibid.
141   **The movie filmed in England and Ireland**: Ibid.
141   **He allegedly ran up a $40,000 bar tab**: Dillon Mafit, "André the Giant's Amazing Feats of Drinking," *Thrillist*, February 6, 2017, accessed June 29, 2022, https://www.thrillist.com/culture/andre-the-giant-drinking-records-and-facts.
142   **"They were turning him into a villain"**: Billy Crystal, live-streamed reunion of cast of *The Princess Bride*, September 13, 2020.
142   **In a climactic moment**: Wrestling Reaper, "WWF Superstars Of Wrestling (February 7, 1987)," YouTube, accessed June 29, 2022, https://youtu.be/TFQBKvNhB-g.
142   **"Wait, what's goin' on here?"**: Ibid.
143   **growl-shout the word *"Yes!"***: Waeggemann, "WWF Superstars of Wrestling 14 02 1987," YouTube, accessed June 29, 2022, https://youtu.be/GD—n0JTpWE.
143   **They both participated in a nonchampionship battle**: "Saturday Night's Main Event #10," ProWrestlingHistory.com, accessed August 3, 2022, http://www.prowrestlinghistory.com/supercards/usa/wwf/snme.html.
143   **should not have been wrestling**: Hébert and Laprade, *Eighth Wonder of the World*, ebook.
143   **"On that day, [André] had promised not to drink"**: Ibid.
143   **The weight of André's enormous bones**: Ibid.
143   **After about eleven minutes**: WWE, "Full Match—Hulk Hogan vs. André the Giant—WWE Championship Match: *WrestleMania III*," YouTube, 2021, accessed June 29, 2022, https://www.youtube.com/watch?v=rz8q5ZjboXY&ab_channel=WWE.
143   **seen live by an estimated 1 million to 1.5 million**: David Bixenspan, "Classic Wrestlenomics: Was WrestleMania III Even More Successful than We Believed?," *Babyface v. Heel*, December 28, 2021, accessed June 29, 2022, https://babyfacevheel.substack.com/p/wrestlemania-iii-ppv-buys-higher-than-believed?s=r.
144   **"I've got a big hole in my back muscle"**: Michael Jan Friedman and Hulk Hogan, *Hollywood Hulk Hogan* (New York: Pocket Books, 2003), ebook.
144   **"André told me with a sour look"**: Hart, *Hitman*, ebook.
144   **the WWF had released a novelty LP**: "The Wrestling Album," Discogs, accessed June 29, 2022, https://www.discogs.com/release/1649269-Various-The-Wrestling-Album.
144   **peaked on the Billboard charts**: Patrick Sauer, "The Wrestling Album: An Oral History," *Vice*, November 30, 2015, accessed June 29, 2022, https://www.vice.com/en/article/xyb88n/the-wrestling-album-an-oral-history.
144   **released a sequel album**: "Piledriver: The Wrestling Album II," Discogs, accessed June 29, 2022, https://www.discogs.com/release/3359097-Various-Piledriver-The-Wrestling-Album-II.
144   **He sang a track called "Stand Back"**: Jim Johnston and Vince McMahon, "Stand Back," Vinyl recording, *The Wrestling Album II: Piledriver*, Epic, 1987.
145   **Jim Crockett was set to hold**: Hornbaker, *Death of the Territories*, ebook.
145   **Vince responded by announcing**: Ibid.

145 **In the end, out of two hundred**: Ibid.

145 **Technically, this follow-up was billed**: Scott's Wrestling Collection, "WWF Slammy Awards 1987," YouTube, accessed June 29, 2022, https://youtu.be /Bh-J9sRHhyg.

146 **Vince performed "Stand Back" onstage**: Ibid.

146 **"There we were," the wrestler wrote**: Hart, *Hitman*, ebook.

146 **"To the best of my knowledge"**: Ibid.

PART TWO: TURNS

149 **"It's fun because some of it's true"**: Nancy Jo Sales, "Beyond Fake," *New York* magazine, October 26, 1998, page 43.

Chapter 9: PUSH

151 **started accepting their campaign dollars**: Santorum for Congress, "Report of Receipts and Disbursements," October 15, 1990, page 9.

151 **"I freely admit, as a boy"**: Rick Santorum, *It Takes a Family* (Wilmington, IL: ISI Books, 2005), ebook.

151 **He'd been chairman of his school's**: Michael Murray, "Santorum to visit Penn State," collegianonline, August 26, 2011, accessed June 29, 2022, https://web.archive.org/web/20130602071353/http://www.collegian.psu.edu /archive/2011/08/26/santorum_to_visit_penn_state.aspx.

151 **worked for a Republican lawmaker**: "Rick Santorum," Britannica.com, accessed August 3, 2022, https://www.britannica.com/biography/Rick-Santorum.

151 **joined the Pittsburgh firm Kirkpatrick & Lockhart**: David Freedlander, "The Return of the Native: Santorum Comes Home, But Do Pennsylvanians Still Pick Rick?", April 4, 2012, accessed August 3, 2022, https://observer .com/2012/04/the-return-of-the-native-santorum-comes-home-but-do -pennsylvanians-still-pick-rick.

151 **In January of 1987, Bret Hart's tag-team partner**: "Wrestler Acquitted on Assault Charge," *AP News*, April 17, 1987, accessed June 29, 2022, https://ap news.com/article/ba369004ebb8df045fb32e9894813f38.

151 **called Kirkpatrick & Lockhart lawyer Jerry McDevitt**: Tim Grant, "Ask Me About . . . Representing 'The Anvil' and the start of Wrestlemania," *Pittsburgh Post-Gazette*, January 17, 2022, accessed June 29, 2022, https://www .post-gazette.com/business/career-workplace/2022/01/17/Ask-Me-About -Jerry-McDevitt-Jerry-McDevitt-Vince-McMahon-and-the-WWE-Wrestle mania-Hulk-Hogan-Jim-The-Anvil-Neidhart/stories/202201160013.

151 **"I assume he probably regrets"**: Ibid.

152 **the McMahons' "family consigliere"**: Kathryn DeLong, "He's Who Vince McMahon Calls When the WWE Is Up Against the Ropes," *Pennsylvania Super Lawyers Magazine*, Super Lawyers, posted June 2008, updated June 10, 2009, accessed June 29, 2022, https://www.superlawyers.com/pennsylva nia/article/in-the-ring-with-jerry-mcdevitt/3ca50eb3-c56c-4470-9e51 -b51e9914263c.html.

152 **McDevitt got Neidhart released**: "Wrestler Acquitted on Assault Charge."

152   **defended him when the case**: Grant, "Ask Me About."

152   **Neidhart was acquitted on all charges**: "Wrestler Acquitted on Assault Charge."

152   **In the majority of the US**: Russell E. Eshleman Jr., "Pa. Sports Panel on the Ropes," *Philadelpia Inquirer*, November 22, 1987.

152   **The state commissions were mostly**: Irvin Muchnick, *Wrestling Babylon* (Toronto: ECW Press, 2007), page 42.

152   **an eager and longtime wrestling fan**: David Bixenspan, "The Boys Need Their Candies: The Trial of Vince McMahon and the WWF, Part 1," *Babyface vs. Heel*, July 5, 2019, accessed August 3, 2022, https://babyfacevheel .substack.com/p/the-boys-need-their-candy-the-trial.

152   **occasionally made on-camera appearances**: @allan_cheapshot, Twitter post, May 28, 2017, accessed August 3, 2022, https://twitter.com/allan_cheapshot /status/868970162707476480.

152   **On May 15, 1985, Republican state representative**: "Proceedings 1984," H-404, vol. 28, part 16, 5586-5932 (Connecticut General Assembly House).

152   **"We consider ourselves in the same"**: "Proceedings 1984," page 28.

152   **the bill quietly passed into law**: Debra (no last name given), Connecticut State Library reference librarian, correspondence with author, January 21, 2022.

153   **replicated their Connecticut victory in Delaware**: Muchnick, *Wrestling Babylon*, page 42.

153   **making progress in New Jersey**: Al Komjathy, New Jersey political staffer, interview with author, April 6, 2022.

153   **There, the state athletic commission**: Muchnick, *Wrestling Babylon*, page 55.

153   **"Pennsylvania was the most pernicious"**: Thomas Fitzgerald, "Conn. Race a Body Slam—with Pa. Ties," *Philadelphia Inquirer*, October 22, 2010, accessed August 3, 2022, https://www.inquirer.com/philly/news/homepage/20101022 _Conn__Senate_race_a_real_body_slam_-_with_ties_to_Pa_.html.

153   **He'd regularly treat leading lawmakers**: Ibid.

153   **After those shows were over**: Ibid.

153   **Santorum helped Linda prepare**: "Reputation Built on Impatience," *Pittsburgh Post-Gazette*, September 11, 1994, page 61.

153   **on June 11, 1987**: "Sunset Review," Ad Hoc Committee, State Athletic Commission, 03-01-025 (Pennsylvania House of Representatives).

153   **She was preceded by two executives**: Ibid.

153   **"the 'good old boy' system"**: Ibid.

154   **"Do you believe honestly"**: Ibid.

154   **"We provide quality, family entertainment"**: Ibid.

154   **"Does the Liquor Control Board"**: Ibid.

154   **Vince acted as the master of ceremonies**: "Vince McMahon," *Hartford Courant*, June 23, 1987, page 145.

154   **"agreed when it was suggested"**: Ibid.

154   **The previous month, the Iron Sheik**: "Two Professional Wrestlers Arrested On Drug Charges; Suspended," Associated Press, May 28, 1987, accessed August 3, 2022, https://apnews.com/article/eca94e958509fcd2842cc0a384056ae3.

155   **Vince had been livid**: Hart, *Hitman*, ebook.

155 **Duggan and the Sheik were summarily fired**: Ibid.

155 **legally known by the mononym**: Chad Venters, "The Name Change," *Warrior: The Man Behind the Icon*, accessed June 29, 2022, https://www.ultimatewarrior bio.com/name-change.

155 **Take, for example, one he did**: The Three Horsemen, "Ultimate Warrior: The Controversial UCONN Speech – April 5, 2005," accessed August 3, 2022, https://youtu.be/tttKYdCLjl8.

155 **the man's mother named him**: Chad Venters, "Early Years," *Warrior: The Man Behind the Icon*, accessed June 29, 2022, https://www.ultimatewarriorbio .com/early-years.

155 **He had first risen to prominence**: "Becoming Warrior," *Dark Side of the Ring*, season 3, episode 5, Vice, May 27, 2021.

156 **Arnold Schwarzenegger had first found fame**: "Arnold Schwarzenegger," Britannica.com, accessed August 3, 2022, https://www.britannica.com /biography/Arnold-Schwarzenegger.

156 **became an obsession**: Peter McGough, "The '80s Revolution: A Giant Leap for Bodybuilding," MuscularDevelopment.com, December 18, 2015, accessed August 3, 2022, https://musculardevelopment.com/news/the-mcgough-rep ort/14821-the-1980-s-revolution-a-giant-leap-for-bodybuilding.html.

156 **born and raised in poverty**: Chad Venters, "Early Years."

156 **Hellwig and a bodybuilding pal**: Chad Venters, "Before WWE," *Warrior: The Man Behind the Icon*, accessed June 29, 2022, https://www.ultimatewarrior bio.com/before-wwe.

157 **Hellwig worked stiff and was terrible**: *Dark Side of the Ring*, "Becoming Warrior."

157 **he'd taken to wearing angular**: Ibid.

157 **There was no real logic**: Ibid.

157 **"What kind of warrior is a Dingo Warrior?"**: *The Self-Destruction of the Ultimate Warrior*, directed by Kevin Dunn (2005, California: WWE Home Video).

157 **"For all you WWF fans out there"**: Davenport Sports Network, "On October 25, 1987 The Ultimate Warrior made his WWF television debut," Facebook video, October 25, 2021, accessed August 3, 2022, https://www .facebook.com/watch/?v=1088873091854533.

157 **"His energy, his mannerisms"**: "Becoming Warrior," *Dark Side of the Ring*.

157 **"To me, the man had no idea"**: Dunn, *The Self-Destruction of the Ultimate Warrior*.

157 **"I said, *Yeah, people who are on TV*"**: "Ultimate Warrior: The Controversial UCONN Speech."

158 **"Warrior kind of captured this rebellious"**: Dunn, *The Self-Destruction of the Ultimate Warrior*.

158 **"Liberals believe in a utopian society"**: "Ultimate Warrior: The Controversial UCONN Speech."

158 **As a kid growing up in Queens**: Ben Olson, "Sandpoint Man Was Grade Schoolmate of Donald Trump," *Sandpoint Reader* (Sandpoint, ID), August 19, 2016, accessed June 29, 2022, https://sandpointreader.com/sandpoint-man -grade-schoolmate-donald-trump/.

158   **"He would get an idea in his head"**: Ibid.

159   **Donald Trump and Vince McMahon appear to have first met**: Neil Vigdor, July 20, 2016, "Conn. Casts All 28 GOP Delegates for Trump," CTPost.com, https://www.ctpost.com/local/article/Conn-casts-all-28-GOP-delegates-for-Trump-8393743.php; Katiana Krawchenko, April 27, 2018, "From Stones Concert to the Cabinet: Linda McMahon on Her Long Friendship with Trump," CBS News, https://www.cbsnews.com/news/from-stones-concert-to-the-cabinet-linda-mcmahon-on-her-long-friendship-with-trump/. "GV Wire: Linda McMahon on WWE Life." YouTube, May 8, 2017. https://www.youtube.com/watch?v=NdsLxmjoeFA&t=107s&ab_channel=GVWire.

159   **According to WWE's official history**: *The True Story of WrestleMania*, directed by Kevin Dunn (2011, New York, WWE).

159   **"He said to me, 'Gee, I'd really love'"**: Ibid.

160   **"I will tell you, I have probably"**: Old School Wrestling TV, "Donald Trump Promo [1988-02-27]," YouTube, February 13, 2019, accessed August 3, 2022, https://youtu.be/fb6t1fmk8tE.

160   **"Well, why don't we create events"**: *The True Story of WrestleMania*.

160   **the weekend of March 26–27, 1988**: Ibid.

160   **"Everybody in the country wanted"**: Ibid.

160   **When the main program finally began**: *WrestleMania IV*, March 27, 1988, unofficial video reconstruction of original broadcast.

160   **In reality, the event was taking place**: Mark Lelinwalla, "Looking Back at Donald Trump's WWE Career," *Tech Times*, March 4, 2016, accessed June 29, 2022, https://www.techtimes.com/articles/138117/20160304/donald-trumps-history-wwe.htm.

160   **the show was something of a disaster**: Dave Meltzer, editorial, *Wrestling Observer*, April 4, 1988.

160   **"The Trump Plaza should have been called"**: Ibid.

161   **Attendance and PPV buy rates were down**: Ibid.

161   **"He went strictly to showbusiness"**: *The Self-Destruction of the Ultimate Warrior*.

161   **in less than a minute**: Ibid.

161   **the once unstoppable André the Giant**: Ibid.

161   **Warrior cut a promo in the fall of 1988**: Old School Wreslting TV, "The Ultimate Warrior Promo [1988-09-18]," YouTube, September 17, 2018, accessed August 3, 2022, https://youtu.be/V7BfuGVkBtw.

162   **"He would go off in almost a trance"**: *The Self-Destruction of the Ultimate Warrior*.

162   **Hemingway described the onset**: Ernest Hemingway, *The Sun Also Rises: The Hemingway Library Edition* (Scribner, 2014), ebook.

162   **Richard Belzer had sued Titan Sports**: Barbara Goldberg, "Hulk Hogan settles lawsuit over 'chin lock,'" UPI, January 2, 1990, accessed August 3, 2022, https://www.upi.com/Archives/1990/01/02/Hulk-Hogan-settles-lawsuit-over-chin-lock/1835631256400.

162   **Linda had said in sealed testimony**: Jim Wilson and Weldon T. Johnson, *Choke Hold: Pro Wrestling's Real Mayhem Outside the Ring* (Xlibris, 2003), ebook.

163   **The lawsuit was settled**: Goldberg, "Hulk Hogan settles lawsuit."

163   **in the spring of 1985**: Javier Ojst, "David Schultz and John Stossel – Slaps Heard 'Round the World!," ProWrestlingStories.com, accessed August 3, 2022, https://prowrestlingstories.com/pro-wrestling-stories/david-schultz-john-stossel.

163   **Vince gave sealed testimony for that one**: Wilson and Johnson, *Choke Hold*, ebook.

163   **"At a [WWF] show in Hershey"**: Muchnick, *Wrestling Babylon*, page 56.

163   **"Three months later, the vote"**: Ibid.

163   **"In other words, as usual"**: Ibid.

163   **the state charged a tax for TV sporting events**: Matty Karas, "Legislators Wrestling with the Question, Are They for Real?," *Asbury Park Press* (Asbury Park, NJ), March 2, 1989, page 42; *Titan Sports v. Athletic Control Bd.*, 11 N.J. Tax 259 (Tax 1990).

163   **Republican lobbyist and lawyer named John P. Sheridan Jr.**: Al Komjathy, interview with author, April 7, 2022.

164   **The lawmaker was a Democrat**: Ibid.

164   **In the spring of 1988**: Karas, "Legislators Wrestling with the Question."

164   **"an activity in which participants"**: Peter Kerr, "Now It Can Be Told: Those Pro Wrestlers Are Just Having Fun," *New York Times*, February 10, 1989, accessed June 29, 2022, https://www.nytimes.com/1989/02/10/nyregion/now-it-can-be-told-those-pro-wrestlers-are-just-having-fun.html.

164   **McManimon introduced the McMahons**: Komjathy, interview with author.

164   **The lobbyist Sheridan kept the charm offensive**: Ibid.

164   **Lawmakers debated and revised the bill**: Ibid.

164   **Finally, on February 10, 1989**: Kerr, "Now It Can Be Told."

164   **when the New Jersey bureau chief**: Peter Kerr, interview with author, April 20, 2022.

164   **37 to 1 in favor of deregulation**: Kerr, "Now It Can Be Told."

164   **the bill died in the state assembly**: Brett Pulley, "Trenton Deregulates Wrestling as (Gasp!) Nonsport," *New York Times*, March 18, 1997, accessed June 29, 2022, https://www.nytimes.com/1997/03/18/nyregion/trenton-deregulates-wrestling-as-gasp-nonsport.html.

165   **"Now It Can Be Told: Those Pro"**: Kerr, "Now It Can Be Told."

165   **"The promoters of professional wrestling"**: Ibid.

165   **"If this thing were real"**: Ibid.

165   **the *New York Post* ran its own**: Wilson and Johnson, *Choke Hold*, ebook.

165   **subsequently, TV news and other media outlets**: Ibid.

165   **reportedly told his wrestlers to cancel**: Ibid.

165   **"America, read my lips"**: Ibid.

165   **"I think the press is missing"**: Ibid.

166   **"See, I *told* you that kind of stuff"**: Ibid.

166   **"They've got a cartoon going there"**: Ira Berkow, "Even the Turkeys Were Purple," *New York Times*, February 23, 1989, accessed June 29, 2022, https://www.nytimes.com/1989/02/23/sports/sports-of-the-times-even-the-turkeys-were-purple.html.

166   **"I once asked Hulk Hogan"**: Ibid.

166   **"This Is the NWA"**: Wilson and Johnson, *Choke Hold*, ebook.

166   *WrestleMania V* was going to take place: Andrew Ravens, "Venue that hosted two WrestleMania events demolished," WrestlingNews.co, February 17, 2021, accessed August 3, 2022, https://wrestlingnews.co/wwe-news/watch-venue -that-hosted-two-wrestlemania-events-demolished.

166   "The Trump organization had done": Basil V. DeVito and Joseph Layden, *WrestleMania: The Official Insider's Story* (Austin, TX: Book People, 2001), page 50.

167   The two men had joined forces: Garrett Gonzalez, "Wrestlemania V: The Mega Powers Explode," *Bleacher Report*, March 8, 2009, accessed August 3, 2022, https://bleacherreport.com/articles/136017-wrestlemania-v-the-mega -powers-explode.

167   announcing on an episode of *Saturday Night's Main Event*: "1989," *The History of WWE*, accessed June 29, 2022, http://thehistoryofwwe.com/89.htm.

167   Sherri Russell, a wrestler who made her bones: "Sensational Sherri," WWE .com, accessed August 3, 2022, https://www.wwe.com/superstars/sensational -sherri.

167   But by the lead-up to the fifth WrestleMania: Ibid.

167   April 2, 1989's *WrestleMania V*: *WrestleMania V*, April 2, 1989, unofficial video reconstruction of original broadcast.

167   he had been fined $500,000": Muchnick, *Wrestling Babylon*, page 155.

167   "Can you give us some idea": *WrestleMania V*.

168   the "Three Demandments": Dollar Dave, "Drive, Determination, Demandments: Hulk Hogan (Part 1)," *Retroist*, April 1, 2014, accessed August 3, 2022, https://retroist.com/drive-determination-demandments-hulk-hogan-part-1.

168   "The thing about Vince is he": Mark Dagostino and Hulk Hogan, *My Life Outside the Ring* (New York: Hodder & Stoughton, 2009), ebook.

169   Hogan wrote that he had been approached: Michael Jan Friedman and Hulk Hogan, *Hollywood Hulk Hogan* (New York: Pocket Books, 2003), ebook.

169   "Originally, a writer had been hired": Ibid.

169   for either two: Dagostino and Hogan, *My Life Outside the Ring*, ebook.

169   or three days straight: Friedman and Hogan, *Hollywood Hulk Hogan*, ebook.

169   "wrote it from beginning": Dagostino and Hogan, *My Life Outside the Ring*, ebook.

169   Hogan would play wrestling champion: *No Holds Barred*, directed by Thomas J. Wright (1989, Topeka, KS: New Line Cinema, Shane Productions).

169   "We had to write the final fight": Friedman and Hogan, *Hollywood Hulk Hogan*, ebook.

169   "I was so tired that as soon as": Ibid.

169   "I told him to write as fast": Ibid.

169   "When we finished working our eighteen-hour": Ibid.

170   *No Holds Barred* was released: *No Holds Barred*.

170   Vince had named "Shane Productions": Ibid.

170   distributed by New Line: Ibid.

170   "The film is utterly lacking": Gene Siskel, "'Dead Poets Society' Is Refresher Course in Drama," *Chicago Tribune*, June 9, 1989, accessed June 29, 2022, https://web.archive.org/web/20140722111927/http://articles.chicagotribune

.com/1989-06-09/entertainment/8902080016_1_dead-poets-society-film
-star-trek.

170 **less than $5 million**: "No Holds Barred," *Box Office Mojo*, accessed August 3,
2022, https://www.boxofficemojo.com/title/tt0097987/?ref_=bo_se_r_1.

170 **sales dropped off a cliff**: Ibid.

170 **net loss for Vince**: Shaun Assael and Mike Mooneyham, *Sex, Lies, and Headlocks* (New York: Three Rivers Press, 2002), ebook.

170 **"It was the first time that Vince"**: Ibid.

170 **"Signs of strain between Emperor Vince"**: Hart, *Hitman*, ebook.

171 **"Vince would send little zingers"**: Ibid.

171 **At January's Royal Rumble**: WWE, "Hulk Hogan and Ultimate Warrior Go
Toe-to-Toe in the Royal Rumble Match: Royal Rumble 1990," YouTube, 2013,
https://www.youtube.com/watch?v=HSwf5guXOA4&ab_channel=WWE.

171 **A February 10 WWF TV broadcast**: Brian Bayless, "WWF Superstars of
Wrestling – February 10th, 1990," *Blog of Doom*, June 25, 2017, accessed
August 3, 2022, https://blogofdoom.com/index.php/2017/06/25/wwf-super
stars-of-wrestling-february-10th-1990.

171 **ended around Valentine's Day**: Hart, *Hitman*, ebook.

171 **"I didn't agree with him"**: Friedman and Hogan, *Hollywood Hulk Hogan*,
ebook.

171 **"Hogan agreed to do it"**: Hart, *Hitman*, ebook.

171 **"was still the WWF's biggest draw"**: Ibid.

172 **"most of us couldn't stand Warrior"**: Ibid.

172 *WrestleMania VI* **was held at SkyDome**: "WWF WrestleMania VI—'The
Ultimate Challenge,'" CageMatch, accessed June 29, 2022, https://www.cage
match.net/?id=1&nr=1764.

172 **attendance record**: Ibid.

172 **"Hulkamania is running wild"**: *WrestleMania VI*, April 1, 1990, unofficial
video reconstruction of original broadcast.

173 **"Hulk Hogan, *I must ask you*"**: Ibid.

173 **In 1990, the WWF took in the highest level**: *Damage Determination Report
for United States Wrestling Association vs. Titan Sports Inc.*, trademark infringement, Ellis G. Godwin, November 19, 1992, page 3.

173 **"It is the destiny of our age"**: Max Weber, *Charisma and Disenchantment:
The Vocation Lectures*, ed. Pal Reitter and Chad Wellmon (New York: New
York Review of Books, 2020).

Chapter 10: HEAT, ACT I

175 **"I first met Saddam Hussein"**: Adnan Alkaissy and Ross Bernstein, *The
Sheikh of Baghdad: Tales of Celebrity and Terror from Pro Wrestling's General
Adnan* (Chicago: Triumph Books, 2005), page 9.

175 **The boys lived in Adhamiya**: Alkaissy and Bernstein, *The Sheikh of Baghdad*, pages 4–5.

175 **"always had a book or newspaper"**: Ibid.

175 **"used to hang out after school"**: Ibid., pages 9–10.

175 **the friendship petered out**: Ibid., pages 11–12.

175   **earned the chance to study abroad**: Ibid., page 16.

175   **Early on in his US journey**: Ibid., page 18.

175   **Of course, he fell in love**: Mike Mooneyham, "The Sheikh of Baghdad," *The Wrestling Gospel According to Mike Mooneyham*, September 25, 2005, accessed June 29, 2022, https://web.archive.org/web/20170312031845/http://www.mikemooneyham.com/2005/09/25/the-sheikh-of-baghdad/.

175   **"It was really exciting to see"**: Ibid., page 29.

175   **moved back to Baghdad in 1969**: Ibid., page 55.

175   **ostensibly the humble deputy**: Ibid., pages 58–59.

175   **Adnan was summoned to an audience**: Ibid., pages 57–58.

176   **"He said that he really enjoyed"**: Ibid., pages 59–60.

176   **"Saddam thought this was all real"**: Ibid., page 87.

176   **Ba'athist Iraq's biggest celebrity**: Ibid., pages 60–80.

176   **So, in late 1970, Adnan approached**: Mooneyham, "The Sheikh of Baghdad."

176   **"the stadium was filled"**: Alkaissy and Bernstein, *The Sheikh of Baghdad*, pages 82–84.

176   **"Be victorious, Adnan"**: Ibid., pages 86–87.

176   **"I will put every bullet in there"**: Ibid., page 87.

176   **"also told me that Iraq was counting"**: Ibid.

176   **"I didn't know what Saddam might do"**: Ibid., page 88.

177   **"It was tough to do, but"**: Ibid.

177   **"The crowd went ballistic"**: Ibid.

177   **"was terrified and just lay down"**: Ibid.

177   **After that, Saddam started paying Adnan**: Ibid., pages 114–115.

177   **every visiting dignitary**: Ibid., page 117.

177   **"[Saddam] liked having me there"**: Ibid., page 119.

177   **It had been about a decade**: "Crack Epidemic," Britannica.com, accessed August 3, 2022, https://www.britannica.com/topic/crack-epidemic.

177   **five years since the word "crack"**: Jane Gross, "A New, Purified Form of Cocaine Causes Alarm as Abuse Increases," *New York Times*, November 29, 1985, accessed June 29, 2022, https://www.nytimes.com/1985/11/29/nyregion/a-new-purified-form-of-cocaine-causes-alarm-as-abuse-increases.html.

177   **In 1988, a sprinter was stripped**: James Montague, "Hero or Villain? Ben Johnson and the Dirtiest Race in History," CNN, July 23, 2012, accessed June 29, 2022, https://www.cnn.com/2012/07/23/sport/olympics-2012-ben-johnson-seoul-1988-dirtiest-race/index.html.

177   **By 1989, after a bipartisan act of Congress**: Ronald Reagan, "Remarks on Signing the Anti-Drug Abuse Act of 1988," Ronald Reagan Presidential Library & Museum, November 18, 1988, accessed August 3, 2022, https://www.reaganlibrary.gov/archives/speech/remarks-signing-anti-drug-abuse-act-1988.

177   **the full grip of a moral panic over drugs**: Michael Wines, "Poll Finds Public Favors Tougher Laws Against Drug Sale and Use," *New York Times*, August 15, 1989, accessed June 29, 2022, https://www.nytimes.com/1989/08/15/us/poll-finds-public-favors-tougher-laws-against-drug-sale-and-use.html.

177   **In 1990, the federal government published**: Associated Press, "Steroid Use by

Teen-Agers Cited," *New York Times*, September 8, 1990, accessed June 29, 2022, https://www.nytimes.com/1990/09/08/sports/steroid-use-by-teen-agers-cited .html.

177 **"Because of the insidious"**: Ibid.

178 **The Anabolic Steroids Control Act of 1990**: "Anabolic Steroids Control Act of 1990," U.S. Congress HR4658, October 5, 1990.

178 **In February 1990, an ailing**: Jim Wilson and Weldon T. Johnson, *Choke Hold: Pro Wrestling's Real Mayhem Outside the Ring* (Xlibris, 2003), ebook.

178 **an athletic coach from the University of Virginia**: Shaun Assael and Mike Mooneyham, *Sex, Lies, and Headlocks* (New York: Three Rivers Press, 2002), ebook.

178 **Through a series of whispered connections**: "The Steroid Trials," *Dark Side of the Ring*, season 3, episode 14, Vice, October 28, 2021.

178 **The bodybuilding industry was then**: Irvin Muchnick, *Wrestling Babylon* (Toronto: ECW Press, 2007), page 80.

178 **In the summer of 1990, Vince**: Ibid., page 78.

179 **Vince spent $5,000 to secure**: Ibid., page 80.

179 **the disqualification of 20 percent**: Ibid.

179 **"I have a very important announcement"**: Ibid., page 81.

179 **The audience fell silent, and leggy models**: Ibid.

179 **"I'm not angry—you can quote me"**: Ibid.

179 **"The WWF kingpin's fetish"**: Ibid., page 78.

180 **"During unimportant matches or interviews"**: Ibid.

180 **"Eventually, I became too popular"**: Alkaissy and Bernstein, *The Sheikh of Baghdad*, page 133.

180 **He'd wrestled for the AWA**: Mooneyham, "The Sheikh of Baghdad."

180 **In August of 1990, Adnan's onetime**: "This Day in History: Iraq Invades Kuwait," History.com, November 24, 2009, accessed August 3, 2022, https:// www.history.com/this-day-in-history/iraq-invades-kuwait.

180 **they called it Operation Desert Shield**: Eric Schmitt, "Confrontation in the Gulf; An Old Desert Hand Commands U.S. Forces," *New York Times*, August 13, 1990, accessed June 29, 2022, https://www.nytimes.com/1990/08/13 /world/confrontation-in-the-gulf-an-old-desert-hand-commands-us-forces .html.

180 **"[Vince] knew that I was Iraqi"**: Alkaissy and Bernstein, *The Sheikh of Baghdad*, pages 183–84.

181 **"I agreed to do it"**: Ibid.

181 **"But I wanted to get back to work"**: Ibid.

181 **On August 28, 1990, the day after**: "1990," *The History of WWE*, accessed June 29, 2022, http://thehistoryofwwe.com/90.htm.

181 **"This is pure garbage!"**: Wrestling with Paul, "WWF Wrestling September 1990," YouTube, accessed August 3, 2022, https://youtu.be/Q4kRFXqPf8o.

181 **"In the name of God, the most beneficent"**: Translation by an Iraqi friend who wishes to remain anonymous.

182 **"I was very against Iraq invading Kuwait"**: Alkaissy and Bernstein, *The Sheikh of Baghdad*, page 189.

182   **"During our heyday, Vince used to call me"**: Ibid., page 191.

182   **"And Vince fed that feeling"**: Ibid.

183   **From 1984 to 1990, the WWF:** *Damage Determination Report for United States Wrestling Association vs. Titan Sports Inc.*, trademark infringement, Ellis G. Godwin, November 19, 1992, page 3.

183   **1991 saw their first dip:** "Annual Statement of Proportion of Capital Stock," form 7, sec. 1703.07 ORC, H0001-1362 (1991); "Annual Statement of Proportion of Capital Stock," form 7, sec. 1703.07 ORC, H0083-1221 (1992).

183   **TV ratings were in free fall:** "TV Ratings 1991," *OSW Review*, accessed August 3, 2022, http://oswreview.com/history/tv-ratings-1991.

183   **Vince had already booked:** Arash Markazi, "How the L.A. Coliseum persuaded WWE to bring WrestleMania to Los Angeles," ESPN.com, March 29, 2018, accessed August 3, 2022, https://www.espn.com/wwe/story/_/id/229 56778/wwe-story-wwe-attempt-fill-la-coliseum-wrestlemania-vii.

183   **attendance would surely reach 100,000:** Ibid.

183   **On January 12, the newly sworn-in:** "Authorization for Use of Military Force Against Iraq Resolution," H.J. Res. 77 (102nd) January 12, 1991, accessed June 29, 2022, https://www.govtrack.us/congress/votes/102-1991/h9.

183   **On January 17, under cover of darkness:** "Operation DESERT STORM," U.S. Army Center of Military History, accessed June 29, 2022, https://history .army.mil/html/bookshelves/resmat/desert-storm/index.html.

183   **the Ultimate Warrior lost to Slaughter:** "1991," *The History of WWE*, accessed June 29, 2022, http://thehistoryofwwe.com/91.htm.

184   **It was over by the end of February:** "Operation DESERT STORM."

184   **having only lost 219 people:** "Iraqi Death Toll," *Frontline*, PBS, accessed June 29, 2022, https://www.pbs.org/wgbh/pages/frontline/gulf/appendix /death.html.

184   **Vince moved the event to the much-smaller:** Markazi, "How the L.A. Coliseum."

184   **They huffed and heaved:** *WrestleMania VII*, March 24, 1991, unofficial video reconstruction of original broadcast.

184   **The thirteen inaugural competitors:** David Bixenspan, "Body Blow: A history of the WBF," *Babyface vs. Heel*, March 10, 2022, accessed August 3, 2022, https://babyfacevheel.substack.com/p/body-blow-a-history-of-the-wbf-from.

184   **It was all building up to June 15, 1991:** Ibid.

184   **Trump would once again play host:** Javier Ojst, "World Bodybuilding Federation Fiasco – Where Did It Go Wrong?," ProWrestlingStories.com, accessed August 3, 2022, https://prowrestlingstories.com/pro-wrestling-stories /world-bodybuilding-federation.

184   **The facility was not long for this world:** Reuters, "Chapter 11 for Taj Mahal," *New York Times*, July 18, 1991, accessed June 29, 2022, https://www.nytimes .com/1991/07/18/business/chapter-11-for-taj-mahal.html.

184   **lengthy videos of each competitor:** "The Definitive History of the WBF," *Pro Wrestling Chronicle*, December 27, 2005, accessed August 3, 2022, https://web.archive.org/web/20051231112247/http://pwchronicle.blogspot .com/2005/12/history-definitive-history-of-wbf.html.

185   **There was a widespread rumor**: Ibid.

185   **Sure enough, by night's end**: Ibid.

185   **case against Dr. George Zahorian went to trial**: Associated Press, "Doctor Tied to Steroid Sales," *New York Times*, June 26, 1991, accessed June 29, 2022, https://www.nytimes.com/1991/06/26/sports/doctor-tied-to-steroid-sales .html.

185   **Superstar Billy Graham claimed**: Richard Demak, "Scorecard," *Sports Illustrated*, July 8, 1991, accessed June 29, 2022, https://vault.si.com/vault/1991/07 /08/scorecard.

185   **The WWF fought hard to keep**: Ibid.

185   **Rod Toombs was thus summoned**: Ariel Teal Toombs and Colt Baird Toombs, *Rowdy: The Roddy Piper Story* (Toronto: Random House Canada, 2016), ebook.

185   **On June 27, the doctor was found guilty**: "Doctor Sentenced to Prison for Selling Steroids to Wrestlers," *AP News*, December 27, 1991, accessed June 29, 2022, https://apnews.com/article/51120e417e48bbb4d78170352976949c.

185   **"Everyone had to get off the juice"**: Hart, *Hitman*, ebook.

185   **The *New York Times* ran stories**: Associated Press, "Trial Opens for Physician in Steroid Case," *New York Times*, June 25, 1991, accessed June 29, 2022, https://www.nytimes.com/1991/06/25/sports/wrestling-trial-opens-for -physician-in-steroid-case.html.

185   *USA Today* **ran a front-page story**: Assael and Mooneyham, *Sex, Lies, and Headlocks*, ebook.

185   **"It's no fun picking up the paper"**: Vince McMahon, "Backtalk; World Wrestling Federation Answers Body Slams," *New York Times*, July 14, 1991, accessed June 29, 2022, https://www.nytimes.com/1991/07/14/sports/backtalk -world-wrestling-federation-answers-body-slams.html.

186   **"McMahon spoke at a news conference"**: "Sports People: Pro Wrestling; Steroid Use Admitted," *New York Times*, July 17, 1991, accessed June 29, 2022, https://www.nytimes.com/1991/07/17/sports/sports-people-pro-wrestling -steroid-use-admitted.html.

186   **Hogan appeared on comedian Arsenio Hall's**: "Tonight on TV," *Los Angeles Times*, July 16, 1991, page 88.

186   **back in 1989, it had gone quite well**: Analog Indulgence, "Hulk Hogan | Interview | 1989 | The Arsenio Hall Show | No Holds Barred," YouTube, accessed August 3, 2022, https://youtu.be/x_ZIpyOIkWU.

186   **"Basically, I'm upset, outraged, and mad"**: Scott's Wrestling Collection, "Hulk Hogan on Arsenio Hall Show 1991," YouTube, accessed August 3, 2022, https://youtu.be/W-RggiPU2xQ.

186   **"Sponsors, particularly those aiming"**: Dave Meltzer, "Editorial," *Wrestling Observer*, July 22, 1991.

187   **in the *New York Times* and the *New York Post***: Wilson and Johnson, *Choke Hold*, ebook.

187   **"It should come as no surprise"**: UnclePKsWrestlingLuv, "Vince McMahon Says NO to anabolic steroids and drugs Public Service Anouncement [*sic*]," YouTube, accessed August 3, 2022, https://youtu.be/Y_auNFVxIDI.

187 **The WWF's TV ratings were tanking**: *OSW Review*, "TV Ratings 1991."

187 **It would feature the in-ring wedding**: "1991," *The History of WWE*, accessed June 29, 2022, http://www.thehistoryofwwe.com/91.htm.

187 **Sheik had been introduced**: Danny Djelosevic, "10 Things Fans Should Know About Iron Sheik," TheSportster.com, September 19, 2021, accessed August 3, 2022, https://www.thesportster.com/iron-sheik-wrestler-trivia-facts -wwe-champion.

187 **The tagline for the PPV**: *SummerSlam*, August 26, 1991, unofficial video reconstruction of original broadcast.

187 **Warrior was in dire financial straits**: Chad Venters, "The Year It All Changed," *Warrior: The Man Behind the Icon*, accessed June 29, 2022, https://www .ultimatewarriorbio.com/the-year-it-all-changed.

187 **He asked Vince for a $550,000 loan**: Ibid.

188 **"almost parental relationship"**: Ibid.

188 **Warrior had allegedly refused to sign**: Ibid.

188 **who happened to be the station manager**: Ibid.

188 **Warrior maintained that the incident**: Ibid.

188 **on July 9, Vince made Warrior record**: Ibid.

188 **WWE allowed it to be used**: *Biography: WWE Legends*, season 1, episode 6, "Ultimate Warrior," directed by Daniel Amigone, featuring Warrior and Vince McMahon, A&E, May 23, 2021.

188 **"I understand that there comes times"**: Ibid.

188 **The next day, Warrior faxed**: Venters, "The Year It All Changed."

188 **"At first I was reluctant for what I believed"**: Ibid.

189 **"Ultimate Warrior basically came to me"**: *The Self-Destruction of the Ultimate Warrior*, directed by Kevin Dunn (2005, California: WWE Home Video).

189 **Vince sent the wrestler a one-page memo**: David Bixenspan, "The Ultimate Reconciliation: An Inside Look at the Vince McMahon-Ultimate Warrior Relationship," *Babyface vs. Heel*, July 26, 2019, accessed August 3, 2022, https:// babyfacevheel.substack.com/p/the-ultimate-reconciliation-an-inside.

189 **"I reluctantly agreed to Warrior's demand"**: *The Self-Destruction of the Ultimate Warrior*.

189 **Sid Eudy, was looking for greener pastures**: Venters, "The Year It All Changed."

189 **SummerSlam was held at Madison Square Garden**: *The History of WWE*, "1991."

190 **Unbeknownst to the audience**: Bixenspan, "The Ultimate Reconciliation."

190 **"Unfortunately, it now appears the fame"**: Ibid.

190 **"You have become a legend"**: Ibid.

190 **"The crowd loved it"**: Alkaissy and Bernstein, *The Sheikh of Baghdad*, page 205.

190 **PPV buy rates were actually down**: "Home / WWE / Pay-Per-View Buyrates," 2X Zone, accessed June 29, 2022, http://www.2xzone.com/wwe/buyrates .shtml#.YovsHpNud24.

191 **"With that, we were done"**: Alkaissy and Bernstein, *The Sheikh of Baghdad*, page 205.

Chapter 11: HEAT, ACT II

192 **On a Sunday in March of 1992**: Lee Cole, interview with author, September 11, 2021.

192 **offices at 500 Fifth Avenue**: Alan Fuchsberg, correspondence with Bob Decker, March 18, 1992.

192 **a soaring prewar skyscraper**: "500 Fifth Avenue," Emporis, accessed June 29, 2022, https://www.emporis.com/buildings/114652/500-fifth-avenue-new-york-city-ny-usa.

192 **the going rate for a ring boy**: Cole v. WWF, Titan Sports, draft complaint, Supreme Court (NY), March 13, 1992.

193 **On December 3, 1991, before a show**: Bret Hart, Hitman: My Real Life in the Cartoon World of Wrestling (London: Ebury Press, 2010), ebook.

193 **wrestlers would now be tested**: Ibid.

193 **Bret had a big bag of Mexican weed**: Bret Hart, interview with author, March 6, 2022.

197 **"Steroids is just the tip of the iceberg"**: Jim Wilson and Weldon T. Johnson, Choke Hold: Pro Wrestling's Real Mayhem Outside the Ring (Xlibris, 2003), ebook.

197 **In his regular column, Mushnick**: Phil Mushnick, interview with author, February 26, 2021.

197 **He published a column about the WWF**: Phil Mushnick, "Bruno Rages About 'Roids," New York Post, July 13, 1991.

198 **At thirteen, the year Tom had become**: David Bixenspan, "WWE Cofounder Linda McMahon, Who Runs Trump's Biggest Super PAC, Once Hired a Suspected Child Molester on the Condition That He 'Stop Chasing After Kids.' He Didn't," Business Insider, October 29, 2020, accessed June 29, 2022, https://www.businessinsider.com/linda-mcmahon-once-employed-an-accused-child-molester-2020-10.

198 **Mel Phillips, a ring announcer and head**: Ibid.

198 **Tom had started out working shows**: Ibid.

198 **"I'd go from New York to Philly"**: Paul MacArthur and David Skolnick, "In Perspective: Tom Cole," Wrestling Perspective, vol. 10, no. 78, 1999.

198 **"would frequently caress plaintiff's"**: Cole v. WWF, Titan Sports.

198 **Other ring boys would go on**: Bixenspan, "WWE Cofounder Linda McMahon."

199 **Garvin (born Terry Joyal) was a veteran**: Ibid.

199 **"He'd look at you when he"**: MacArthur and Skolnick, "In Perspective."

199 **However, the draft legal complaint says**: Cole v. WWF, Titan Sports.

199 **Whatever happened, Tom stopped**: Ibid.; MacArthur and Skolnick, "In Perspective."

199 **In 1990, Tom got a surprising call**: Cole v. WWF, Titan Sports; MacArthur and Skolnick, "In Perspective."

199 **Garvin allegedly asked if he could**: Cole v. WWF, Titan Sports; MacArthur and Skolnick, "In Perspective."

199 **It was there, a few hours later**: MacArthur and Skolnick, "In Perspective."

199 **"There's laws against this"**: Ibid.

200 **In October of 1991, with no lawyer**: Lee Cole, interview with author, September 11, 2021.

200 **The Coles found an attorney**: Ibid.

200 **"According to several highly placed sources"**: Phil Mushnick, "WWF to Face Suit Alleging Child Sex Abuse," *New York Post*, February 26, 1992.

200 **gone on a wrestling radio show**: Wilson and Johnson, *Choke Hold*, ebook.

200 **On top of that, a new announcer**: Ibid.

201 **the WWF issued a statement saying**: Dave Meltzer, "Editorial," *Wrestling Observer*, March 9, 1992.

201 **And on Monday, March 2**: Ibid.

201 **printing a March 4 item**: Phil Mushnick, "Merv's Casino Deals from Bottom," *New York Post*, March 4, 1992.

201 **Vince "denied all of the charges"**: Dave Meltzer, "Editorial," *Wrestling Observer*, March 9, 1992.

201 **"The *Post* story will soon be joined"**: Wade Keller, "News & Analysis," *Pro Wrestling Torch*, no. 163, March 5, 1992.

201 **A producer for TV personality Geraldo Rivera**: Lee Cole, interview with author.

202 **Alan Fuchsberg, the son of a prominent trial lawyer**: Eric Pace, "Jacob D. Fuchsberg, 82, Dies; Lawyer and Appellate Judge," *New York Times*, August 28, 1995, accessed June 29, 2022, https://www.nytimes.com/1995/08/28/obit uaries/jacob-d-fuchsberg-82-dies-lawyer-and-appellate-judge.html.

202 **Vince made a "pour-his-heart-out phone call"**: Phil Mushnick, "Sex, Lies and the WWF," *New York Post*, March 18, 1992.

202 **Vince told him "that he had let Phillips go"**: Ibid.

202 **"McMahon told me that it was"**: Bixenspan, "WWE Cofounder Linda McMahon."

202 **Vince allegedly said he brought Phillip**: Ibid.

202 **Vince would go on to sue Mushnick**: *Titan Sports v. New York Post et al.*, no. 3:93CV345-TFGD (D. Conn., December 3, 1993).

202 **"noted that Cole said in a deposition"**: Bixenspan, "WWE Cofounder Linda McMahon."

202 **The morning of March 11**: Jeff Savage, "Sleaze No Illusion in World of Wrestling: Sex, Drug Abuse Seen in Industry of 'Heroes,'" *San Diego Union-Tribune*, March 11, 1992.

203 **"Boys are getting propositioned"**: Ibid.

203 **"I know if I would've slept"**: Ibid.

203 **the story for the next day, March 12**: "Search Results—'Wrestling Steroids,'" *San Diego Union-Tribune* Archives, accessed June 29, 2022, https://san diegouniontribune.newsbank.com/search?text=wrestling++steroids& content_added=&date_from=1992&date_to=1992&pub%5B%5D=SDUB& sort=old.

203 **the *Los Angeles Times* ran a story**: Wade Keller, "Titangate," *Pro Wrestling Torch*, no. 165, March 19, 1992.

203 **as did various newswires**: Ibid.

203 ***Entertainment Tonight* gave Orton the floor**: Ibid.

203   on *The Tonight Show*, **Johnny Carson**: Ibid.

203   **Fuchsberg faxed McDevitt a courtesy copy**: *Cole v. WWF, Titan Sports*.

203   **the text outlined Tom's allegations**: Ibid.

203   **Vince appeared on talk show**: *Larry King Live*, "Scandal in the Wrestling World," featuring Vince McMahon, Bruno Sammartino, and Barry Orton, CNN, Washington, DC, March 13, 1992.

204   **Minutes later, Lee got a call from Fuchsberg**: Lee Cole, interview with author.

204   **It was the first time Tom and the McMahons**: Jeff Savage, "No-Holds-Barred," *Penthouse*, September 1992.

204   **"I told [Vince] everything that happened"**: MacArthur and Skolnick, "In Perspective."

204   **"Well, you know, Tom, this is"**: Ibid.

205   **"Well, that's a lot of money"**: Ibid.

205   **"Listen, I'm not looking for money"**: Ibid.

205   **"It was probably the stupidest thing"**: Ibid.

205   **"kept walking out of the room"**: Ibid.

205   **"I'm like a rat"**: Ibid.

205   **"I loved wrestling," Tom would later say**: Ibid.

205   **"No, no, don't go!" Tom yelled**: Ibid.

205   **Fuchsberg left the room again**: Lee Cole, interview with author.

205   **"He was very shrewd"**: MacArthur and Skolnick, "In Perspective."

205   **"Mr. McMahon explained to Tom"**: Savage, "No-Holds-Barred."

205   **"I want to start on a clean slate"**: MacArthur and Skolnick, "In Perspective."

206   **"Tom got a good feeling"**: Savage, "No-Holds-Barred."

206   **"I thought that was the right thing"**: MacArthur and Skolnick, "In Perspective."

206   **Tom agreed to accepting $50,000**: Alan Fuchsberg, correspondence with Bob Decker, March 18, 1992. Other sources have said it was $55,000, but the only hard documentation I've seen is this letter, which says $50,000.

206   **"I was in no league for Vince McMahon"**: MacArthur and Skolnick, "In Perspective."

206   **Lee had tweeted the news**: Lee Cole, Twitter post, February 12, 2021, accessed August 3, 2022, https://twitter.com/leeroycole/status/1360406868187873280.

206   **"If something ever happened to me"**: Lee Cole, interview with author, September 12, 2021.

206   **The elder Cole had developed a criminal record**: Ibid.

207   **"My older brother's at the motel"**: Ibid.

207   **"Well, I'm going to be going"**: Ibid.

207   **Tom came back to the motel room**: Ibid.

207   **"I just want my job back, Lee"**: Ibid.

207   **On the morning of Monday, March 16**: Ibid.

208   **"It's really weird: I haven't heard"**: Dave Meltzer, interview with author, September 19, 2020.

208   **"The [World] Wrestling Federation: You know how"**: *Phil Donahue Show*, "Pro Wrestling Empire Hit with Teen Boy's Sex Scandal," featuring Barry Orton and Murray Hodgson, WLWD, March 16, 1992.

210   **According to a later account**: Savage, "No-Holds-Barred."

210 **"This show was bullshit"**: Ibid. *Penthouse* printed that Lee was the one who said this, but Lee assures me it was Tom, and that would make far more sense.

210 **"Sex, Lies, and the WWF"**: Phil Mushnick, "Sex, Lies, and the WWF," *New York Post*, March 18, 1992.

210 **"Never will you encounter"**: Ibid.

210 **a new World Bodybuilding Federation TV show**: Assael and Mooneyham, *Sex, Lies, and Headlocks*, ebook.

211 **That morning's *Post* brought another**: Wade Keller, "Former Female WWF Referee Says McMahon Equated Sex with Him with Job for Her," *Pro Wrestling Torch*, no. 168, April 9, 1992, page 3.

211 **The show aired at 7 p.m. Eastern**: "Friday Prime Time," *Public Opinion* (Chambersburg, PA), April 3, 1992, page 15.

211 **The lead segment, called**: *Now It Can Be Told*, "Wrestling's Ring of Vice," featuring Geraldo Rivera, ING, April 3, 1992.

211 **Chatterton had done a few more ref gigs**: Rita Chatterton, interview with author, April 25, 2022.

211 **"I held off for a long time"**: "Wrestling's Ring of Vice," *Now It Can Be Told*.

212 **a flurry of ancillary media coverage**: Keller, "Titangate."

212 **Randy Savage beat Ric Flair**: *WrestleMania VIII*, April 5, 1992, unofficial video reconstruction of original broadcast.

212 **the couple were on the outs**: Luke Norris, "The Tragic Deaths of 'Macho Man' Randy Savage and Miss Elizabeth," Sportscasting.com, June 20, 2020, accessed August 3, 2022, https://www.sportscasting.com/the-tragic-deaths-of -macho-man-randy-savage-and-miss-elizabeth.

212 **Warrior would soon be fired**: Chad Venters, "1992 WWF Return," *Warrior: The Man Behind the Icon*, accessed June 29, 2022, https://www.ultimatewarrior bio.com/1992-wwf-return.

212 **It was Roddy Piper's last match**: Ariel Teal Toombs and Colt Baird Toombs, *Rowdy: The Roddy Piper Story* (Toronto: Random House Canada, 2016), ebook.

212 **in reality, he was taking an indefinite hiatus**: Assael and Mooneyham, *Sex, Lies, and Headlocks*, ebook.

212 **Chatterton appeared on *The Geraldo Rivera Show***: Fair Use John Doe, "Geraldo 4/13/1992—'Sex Scandals of the Season' (with Rita Chatterton, Murray Hodgson, & others)," YouTube, accessed August 3, 2022, https://youtu.be /deVZ-zQIHNQ.

214 **According to Lee, not long after**: Lee Cole, interview with author.

214 **"I've lost it once before"**: Ibid.

214 **They arrived at an Italian restaurant**: Ibid.

215 **"Do you have any other names"**: Ibid.

215 **Tom signed papers releasing Patterson**: Oliver Lee Bateman, "Pat Patterson Was Simply Unreal," *The Ringer*, December 3, 2020, accessed August 3, 2022, https://www.theringer.com/2020/12/3/22150454/pat-patterson-obituary -wwf-wwe.

215 **Garvin and Phillips vanished from the public eye**: Bixenspan, "WWE Co-founder Linda McMahon."

215 **Bixenspan, the investigative reporter, found a man**: Ibid.

216 **"He went up there for a visit"**: Dave Meltzer, "Newsletter," *Wrestling Observer*, March 29, 2004.

216 **Lee was arrested for violating**: Lee Cole interview with author.

216 **"Jerry, you guys fucked up"**: Ibid.

Chapter 12: HEAT, ACT III

217 **André Roussimoff's last days had been agony**: Bertrand Hébert and Pat Laprade, *The Eighth Wonder of the World: The True Story of André the Giant* (Toronto: ECW Press, 2020), ebook.

217 **André had specified that he wanted**: Ibid.

217 **The men who removed his stiffened corpse**: Ibid.

218 **Weatherspoon, a lifelong Southern Pines resident**: Jim Weatherspoon, interview with author, March 4, 2022.

218 **He had been introduced to the wrestler**: Ibid.

219 **The WWF held ten-bell memorial salutes**: Hébert and Laprade, *The Eighth Wonder of the World*.

219 **the inaugural inductee**: Ibid.

219 **And a funeral service was held**: Ibid.

219 **Hulk Hogan gave a speech**: Ibid.

219 **Also in attendance was Rita Chatterton**: Rita Chatterton, interview with author, June 16, 2022.

219 **"Nice to meet you"**: Ibid.

219 **"When his career was over"**: *André the Giant*, directed by Jason Hehir (2018, Bill Simmons Media Group, HBO, WWE).

220 **The World Bodybuilding Federation had gone**: David Bixenspan, "Body Blow: A history of the WBF," *Babyface vs. Heel*, March 10, 2022, accessed August 3, 2022, https://babyfacevheel.substack.com/p/body-blow-a-history-of-the-wbf-from.

220 *Penthouse* **had published a long feature**: Jeff Savage, "No-Holds-Barred," *Penthouse*, September 1992.

220 **Ultimate Warrior and Davey Boy Smith**: Bret Hart, *Hitman: My Real Life in the Cartoon World of Wrestling* (London: Ebury Press, 2010), ebook.

220 **Saturday Night's Main Event, ended its run**: "Saturday Night Main Event – Nov. 8, 1992," WWE.com, accessed August 3, 2022, https://www.wwe.com/shows/snme/history/1985to1992/nov081992.

220 **both died tragic and public deaths**: "The Assassination of Dino Bravo," *Dark Side of the Ring*, season 2, episode 6, Vice, April 21, 2020; "The Last of the Von Erichs," *Dark Side of the Ring*, season 1, episode 4, Vice, May 1, 2019.

220 **"cornered Vince in his office"**: Hart, *Hitman*, ebook.

220 **The two would be caught in inconclusive**: David Bixenspan, "The Boys Need Their Candies: Bed of Nailz," *Babyface vs. Heel*, September 11, 2019, accessed August 3, 2022, https://babyfacevheel.substack.com/p/the-boys-need-their-candies-bed-of.

220 **Vince and Titan Sports filed**: *Titan Sports v. New York Post et al.*, no. 3:93 CV345-TFGD (D. Conn., December 3, 1993).

220 **Vince and Linda sued Rita Chatterton**: *McMahon et al. v. Rivera et al.*, no. 93-cv-468 (D. Conn., March 5, 1993).

220 **Both suits would end inconclusively**: Jim Wilson and Weldon T. Johnson, *Choke Hold: Pro Wrestling's Real Mayhem Outside the Ring* (Xlibris, 2003), ebook.

220 **"Mushnick's contribution to the stated goal**: *Titan Sports v. New York Post et al.*

220 **"took steps to fabricate evidence"**: Ibid.

221 **"was not a competent ring referee"**: *McMahon et al. v. Rivera et al.*

221 **"Shults contacted Chatterton"**: Ibid.

221 **Vince was promoting a new weekly WWF series**: Assael and Mooneyham, *Sex, Lies, and Headlocks*, ebook.

221 **Ratings were better than they had been**: "TV Ratings 1993," *OSW Review*, accessed August 3, 2022, http://oswreview.com/history/tv-ratings-1993.

221 **Vince hired a putdown-artist comedian**: Craig Wilson, "Whatever Happened to Rob Bartlett," *Ring the Damn Bell*, August 4, 2017, accessed August 3, 2022, https://ringthedamnbell.wordpress.com/2017/08/04/what -ever-happened-to-rob-bartlett.

221 **Hogan came back from hiatus**: Michael Jan Friedman and Hulk Hogan, *Hollywood Hulk Hogan* (New York: Pocket Books, 2003), ebook.

222 **on October 11, 1992**: Hart, *Hitman*, ebook.

222 **"pulled me aside to tell me"**: Ibid.

222 **"I patiently sat in a chair"**: Ibid.

223 **October 12, 1992, Bret and Flair**: WWE, "Ric Flair vs. Bret Hart (Part 2): October 12, 1992," YouTube, accessed August 3, 2022, https://youtu.be/tjrul3 NfGto.

223 **"flashed back to all those wrestling magazines"**: Hart, *Hitman*, ebook.

223 **"God almighty, thank you"**: cableguyxx9898xx, "Bret Hart First WWF Title Win Promo," YouTube, accessed August 3, 2022, https://youtu.be/OCPuwk HG_S8.

223 **Previous champions had been granted**: Hart, *Hitman*, ebook.

223 **Bret says Roddy Piper pulled him aside**: Ibid.

224 **Pat Patterson, too, advised Bret**: Ibid.

224 **April 4, 1993's *WrestleMania IX***: *WrestleMania IX*, IMDb.com, accessed August 3, 2022, https://www.imdb.com/title/tt0252102.

224 **being held at Caesars Palace**: Ibid.

224 **he brought Stu and Helen**: Hart, *Hitman*, ebook.

224 **Then he got a call from Vince**: Ibid.

224 **"and he answered it with that goofy grin"**: Ibid.

224 **"This is what I want to do"**: Ibid.

224 **"I sat there dumbstruck as he went on"**: Ibid.

224 **"Like I was handing Vince my sword"**: Ibid.

224 **Sure enough, the show came around**: Ibid.

224 **"As scripted, with my face buried"**: Ibid.

225 **"Thank you, brother"**: Ibid.

225 **Here's Bret's version**: Ibid.

225 **"Winning the King of the Ring is great"**: Ibid.
225 **Then there's Hogan's version of events**: Friedman and Hogan, *Hollywood Hulk Hogan*, ebook.
226 **"Didn't you tell me that Hulk Hogan"**: Ibid.
226 **"I had a feeling that Vince wasn't going"**: Ibid.
226 **"To tell you the truth, I didn't care"**: Ibid.
226 **"I never, ever said it would"**: Hart, *Hitman*, ebook.
226 **"I realized that there was some kind"**: Ibid.
226 **gradually fading away from the scene**: Assael and Mooneyham, *Sex, Lies, and Headlocks*, ebook.
226 **Luger had been introduced**: "1993," *The History of WWE*, accessed June 29, 2022, http://www.thehistoryofwwe.com/93.htm.
226 **He had Lex turn face by attacking Yokozuna**: "Yokozuna (Heavyweight Champion) Bodyslam Challenge HD—July 1993," YouTube, 2015, accessed June 29, 2022, https://www.youtube.com/watch?v=CbqlKGOlUDE.
226 **"What's wrong with America"**: Ibid.
227 **Vince rebranded Lex in an ambitious**: Assael and Mooneyham, *Sex, Lies, and Headlocks*, ebook.
227 **"with much flag waving and hoopla"**: Hart, *Hitman*, ebook.
227 **"In pure sports, you win or lose"**: Ibid.
227 **On August 13, 1993, Bret and Vince met**: Ibid.

Chapter 13: HEAT, FINALE

228 **By the summer of 1993, it consisted**: Martin James Dickinson, TheSportster .com, "The Jerry Jarrett Vs. Bruce Prichard Feud, Explained," June 22, 2022, accessed August 3, 2022, https://www.thesportster.com/the-jerry-jarrett-vs -bruce-prichard-feud-explained.
228 **Jarrett, born in Nashville in 1942**: IMDb, "Jerry Jarrett," accessed August 3, 2022, https://www.imdb.com/name/nm1243912.
228 **Memphis had long been one of the great**: *Memphis Heat: The True Story of Memphis Wrasslin'*, directed by Chad Schaffler, featuring Jerry Lawler, Jimmy Hart, and Jerry Jarrett (2011, Off the Top Rope Productions, Shangri-la).
228 **Jarrett had been close with Vince Senior**: Ryan Clark, "Jerry Jarrett Discusses Jerry Lawler Becoming 'The King,' Working with Vince McMahon, & More," *EWrestlingNews*, October 4, 2015, accessed June 29, 2022, https://www.e wrestlingnews.com/articles/jerry-jarrett-discusses-jerry-lawler-becoming -the-king-working-with-vince-mcmahon-more.
228 **"Vince became my Sunday telephone buddy"**: Ibid.
229 **"If I had to go to jail"**: Ibid.
229 **"Of course, at first, I said no"**: Ibid.
229 **August of 1992 brought the news**: Wade Keller, "Jarrett's USWA Strikes Work-ing Agreement with WWF," *Pro Wrestling Torch*, no. 188, August 20, 1992.
229 **Jarrett commuted to Connecticut**: Martin James Dickinson, "Who Would Have Ran WWE If Vince McMahon Was Arrested, Explained," TheSportster .com, April 20, 2022, accessed August 3, 2022, https://www.thesportster.com /who-would-have-ran-wwe-if-vince-mcmahon-was-arrested-explained.

229 **"We would meet around his dining room table"**: Matt Boone, "Jerry Jarrett Talks About His Involvement In Creation Of 'Mr. McMahon' Character," eWrestling.com, November 24, 2018, accessed August 3, 2022, https://ewrestling.com/article/jerry-jarrett-talks-about-his-involvement-creation-mr-mcmahon-character.

229 **Jarrett would tell an interviewer**: Jeffrey Harris, "Jerry Jarrett Discusses Pitching Vince McMahon Playing a Heel Character and Developing His Heel Debut in Memphis in 1993," *411Mania*, November 24, 2018, accessed June 29, 2022, https://411mania.com/wrestling/vince-mcmahon-jarrett-heel-pitch.

229 **"Do you *try* to be a heel?"**: Ibid.

230 **"I don't know how to do it"**: Ibid.

230 **He says Vince had no plans**: *Something to Wrestle with Bruce Prichard*, "Episode 103: #LoveToKnow," Cumulus Podcast Network, May 25, 2018.

230 **"Lawler had come in to do commentary"**: Ibid.

231 **On the 16th of that month**: Michael Chin, "That Time Bret Hart Turned Heel In 1993 . . . Only In Memphis," TheSportster.com, December 18, 2021, accessed August 3, 2022, https://www.thesportster.com/bret-hart-turned-heel-1993-memphis.

231 **at a live WWF show in Massachusetts**: popculturestu, "McMemphis: Chapter 3 – A Yankee in the King's Court," YouTube, accessed August 3, 2022, https://youtu.be/gXeWAhihvU4.

231 **"Right in your own hometown of Memphis"**: Ibid.

231 **Technically, the main event**: popculturestu, "McMemphis: Chapter 6 – The Heel Debut in Memphis," YouTube, accessed August 3, 2022, https://youtu.be/oGbVMMbi6nE.

231 **Lawler and Neighbors had entered**: Ibid.

233 **"It was his first opportunity to be a heel"**: Joseph Lee, "Jerry Lawler Says Mr. McMahon's First Appearance Was in Memphis," *411Mania*, June 10, 2018, accessed June 29, 2022, https://411mania.com/wrestling/jerry-lawler-says-mr-mcmahons-first-appearance-memphis.

233 **"How could you have been so *rude*?"**: popculturestu, "McMemphis: Chapter 7 – You Asked For It And You Got It," YouTube, accessed August 3, 2022, https://youtu.be/A3Fw7loEEfk.

233 **"I'm the voice of the World Wrestling Federation"**: popculturestu, "McMemphis: Chapter 13 – King of the Cheaters," YouTube, accessed August 3, 2022, https://youtu.be/_v-8vEwuOZo.

233 **In the fourth promo, Vince wore**: popculturestu, "McMemphis: Chapter 15 – Vince Wears the USWA Title," YouTube, accessed August 3, 2022, https://youtu.be/oI_1cW-1xZc.

234 **"You really don't believe"**: popculturestu, "McMemphis: Chapter 25 – Death, Taxes & Randy Savage," YouTube, accessed August 3, 2022, https://youtu.be/4I3mGNF1cLg.

234 **"Vince McMahon's classic heel interviews"**: Wade Keller, "Omni Draws 600, Boston Garden Sells Out," *Pro Wrestling Torch*, no. 247, October 9, 1993.

234 **"McMahon's heel interviews are so eerie"**: Dave Meltzer, "Editorial," *Wrestling Observer*, September 13, 1993.

234   **The final promo aired on October 9**: popculturestu, "McMemphis: Chapter 29 – The Final Interview 'Machovision'," YouTube, accessed August 3, 2022, https://youtu.be/AIJjWs_TXtQ.

234   **which happened on October 11**: "1993," *The History of WWE*, accessed June 29, 2022, http://www.thehistoryofwwe.com/93.htm.

234   **The cops suspected that Lawler**: David Bixenspan, "Jerry Lawler Wrote a Really Dumb Letter to Prosecutors in His 1993 Rape Case," *Deadspin*, February 13, 2018, accessed June 29, 2022, https://deadspin.com/jerry-lawler -wrote-a-really-dumb-letter-to-prosecutors-1822790447.

234   **one thirteen and the other fourteen**: Ibid.

234   **One of them described Lawler**: Ibid.

234   **"always thought they were friends of mine"**: Transcript, Louisville and Jefferson County Police interview with Jerry Lawler, October 11, 1993.

234   **was allowed to go**: Bixenspan, "Jerry Lawler Wrote."

234   **Police interviewed him again on November 2**: Transcript, Clark County Police interview with Jerry Lawler, November 2, 1993.

234   **November 12, he was indicted by a grand jury**: Cary B. Willis, "Pro wrestler Jerry Lawler charged with rape, sodomy of 13-year-old girl," *Courier-Journal* (Louisville, KY), November 13, 1993, page 7.

234   **Reporters revealed that there was a similar**: Ibid.

235   **The King would be back on the air**: "1994," *The History of WWE*, accessed June 29, 2022, http://www.thehistoryofwwe.com/94.htm.

235   **on November 18, less than a week**: David Bixenspan, "Vince McMahon's Defiant Paranoia Was Shaped By His Steroid Trial," *Deadspin*, July 26, 2019, accessed August 3, 2022, https://deadspin.com/vince-mcmahons-defiant -paranoia-was-shaped-by-his-stero-1836707000.

235   **In July of 1992, mere months**: Alex Marvez, "WWF under federal investigation," *Miami Herald*, July 15, 1992, page 33.

235   **According to FBI memos**: David Bixenspan, "FBI Memos Show Bureau Disregarding Video Tape of Mel Phillips Sexually Assaulting a Ring Boy," *Babyface vs. Heel*, October 27, 2021, accessed June 29, 2022, https://babyfacevheel .substack.com/p/wwe-ring-boys-fbi-mel-phillips-videotape.

235   **it appears from the memos that the FBI concluded**: Ibid.

235   **They then aimed to ambush Phillips**: Ibid.

235   **an announcement of a scripted miniseries**: Joe Otterson, "Vince McMahon Steroid Trial Scripted Series in the Works from WWE, Blumhouse Television," *Variety*, July 26, 2021, accessed June 29, 2022, https://variety .com/2021/tv/news/vince-mcmahon-steroid-trial-series-wwe-blumhouse -television-1235027046/.

236   **Vince's trial ran from July 7 to July 22, 1994**: Bixenspan, "Vince McMahon's Defiant Paranoia."

236   **The vast majority of criminal cases**: "Current and Recent Cases," United States Department of Justice, accessed August 3, 2022, https://www.justice .gov/civil/current-and-recent-cases.

236   **The key thing that the prosecution needed to prove**: "The Steroid Trials," *Dark Side of the Ring*, season 3, episode 14, Vice, October 28, 2021.

236 **there had been no WWF shows**: Ibid.

236 **The DOJ was supposed to get Vince's limo driver**: Ibid.

236 **The DOJ got Dr. Zahorian to claim**: Ibid.

236 **Throughout the lead-up to the trial**: William Bastone, "The Fixer: Journalist. Private Eye. Mole. Snitch. It's All in a Day's Work for Marty Bergman, the Zelig of New York's Information Highway," *Village Voice*, December 19, 1995.

236 **Mushnick recalled Bergman calling**: *Dark Side of the Ring*, "The Steroid Trials."

236 **"I remember calling my wife's cousin"**: Ibid.

237 **As it turned out, Bergman's brother**: Bastone, "The Fixer."

237 **he was the then-fiancé of Laura Brevetti**: Ibid.

237 **A story co-bylined by Mushnick**: Jack Newfield and Phil Mushnick, "Tampering Cloud Over Wrestling's Big Trial," *New York Post*, November 22, 1995, http://muchnick.net/nyposttext.pdf.

237 **WWE denies any tampering of witnesses**: *Dark Side of the Ring*, "The Steroid Trials."

237 **McDevitt and Brevetti's riskiest move**: Ibid.

237 **Nailz even showed up**: *United States of America v. Vincent K. McMahon, Jr. and Titan Sports, Inc., d/b/a World Wrestling Federation*, trial transcript, July 11, 1994, page 1166.

237 **Wacholz replied, "Yes"**: Ibid.

237 **"I think the whole thing is weak"**: *Dark Side of the Ring*, "The Steroid Trials."

237 **"Now, was there any relationship"**: *United States of America v. Vincent K. McMahon, Jr. and Titan Sports, Inc., d/b/a World Wrestling Federation*, trial transcript, July 13, 1994, page 1711.

238 **"I remember watching Laura Brevetti"**: *Dark Side of the Ring*, "The Steroid Trials."

238 **Hogan, who testified on July 14**: *United States of America v. Vincent K. McMahon, Jr. and Titan Sports, Inc., d/b/a World Wrestling Federation*, trial transcript, July 14, 1994.

238 **he'd signed a lucrative contract**: James Moffat, "Hulk Hogan: 5 Interesting Facts About His 1998 WCW Contract," *Bleacher Report*, October 28, 2015, accessed August 3, 2022, https://bleacherreport.com/articles/2583396-hulk-hogan-five-interesting-facts-about-his-1998-wcw-contract.

238 **Hogan spoke of how he'd lied**: *United States of America v. Vincent K. McMahon, Jr. and Titan Sports, Inc., d/b/a World Wrestling Federation*, trial transcript, July 14, 1994, page 1782.

238 **"Isn't it a fact that you"**: Ibid., page 1747.

238 **"I knew what was on the line there"**: *Dark Side of the Ring*, "The Steroid Trials."

238 **On July 22, 1994, the courtroom was packed**: Ibid.

239 **Vince was clad in a padded neck brace**: Ibid.

239 **Vince was reasonably certain**: Dickinson, "Who Would Have Ran WWE."

239 **Vince and Titan Sports were found not guilty**: "A Promoter Of Wrestling Is Acquitted," *New York Times*, July 23, 1994, section 1, page 25.

239 **"The courtroom exploded"**: Dave Meltzer, "McMahon, Titan: Not Guilty," *Wrestling Observer*, August 1, 1994.

239 **immortalized by the court artist**: *Dark Side of the Ring*, "The Steroid Trials."

239 **"I left my fate in the hands of the jury"**: Meltzer, "McMahon, Titan."

239 **did an exclusive interview on the evening news**: David Bixenspan, "Today in Wrestling History 7/22: Vince McMahon Talks Verdict, WWF Invasion PPV, Faarooq Debuts, More," *Wrestling Inc.*, July 22, 2015, accessed June 29, 2022, https://www.wrestlinginc.com/news/2015/07/today-in-wrestling-history -722-vince-mcmahon-talks-verdict-598582.

240 **Vince even went so far as to deliver a pretaped promo**: Lou Gregory, "Vince McMahon publicly addresses 'The Steroid Trial' (WWF 1995)," YouTube, accessed August 3, 2022, https://youtu.be/Ys6HLR7KtH8.

Chapter 14: SUCK IT, ACT I

241 **the WWE officially refers to the period**: "A special look at the Attitude Era," WWE.com, accessed August 3, 2022, https://www.wwe.com/inside/wwe featurepage/attitude-era#fid-25048305.

242 **"Vince is crazy. He really is"**: *Biography: WWE Legends*, season 1, episode 1, "'Stone Cold' Steve Austin," directed by Jacob Rogal, featuring Steve Austin, Jennifer Kirkpatrick, A&E, April 18, 2021.

242 **"Mr. McMahon is a character that is"**: Ibid.

242 **"Stone Cold Steve Austin—that character is really"**: *WWE Rivalries*, season 1, episodes 1 & 2, "Austin vs. McMahon," featuring Steve Austin and Vince McMahon, WWE, October 28, 2014.

242 **"I'm the common man"**: Sean Hyson, "WWE Chief Vince McMahon is Still Making Gains," *Muscle & Fitness*, March 2016, accessed August 3, 2022, https://www.muscleandfitness.com/athletes-celebrities/interviews/wwe -chief-vince-mcmahon-still-making-gains.

242 **Like Vince, Steve Austin was abandoned**: Steve Austin, Dennis Brent, and J. R. Ross, *The Stone Cold Truth* (New York: Pocket Books, 2003), page 22.

242 **raised him in a town on the Gulf Coast**: Ibid., page 23.

242 **"My dad raised us right—firm, but fair"**: Ibid.

242 **"I endorse the practice of cutting a switch"**: Ibid., page 34.

243 **"I didn't give a damn about the story lines"**: Ibid., page 52.

243 **"The Western Fandango"**: Ibid., page 53.

243 **Around 1988, while he was a college dropout**: Ibid., page 63.

243 **His first trainer, "Gentleman" Chris Adams**: Ibid., page 75.

243 **So Steve moved to USWA in Memphis**: Ibid., page 82.

243 **subsisting on tuna fish and raw potatoes**: Ibid., pages 85–87.

243 **he got a call to join the big leagues**: Ibid., pages 105–106.

243 **WCW always prided itself on respecting**: Guy Evans, *Nitro: The Incredible Rise and Inevitable Collapse of Ted Turner's WCW* (Self-published, 2018), ebook.

243 **"I knew that WCW would give"**: Austin, Brent, and Ross, *The Stone Cold Truth*, page 105.

243 **man from Scarsdale**: Thom Loverro, Tazz, Tommy Dreamer, and Paul Heyman, *The Rise and Fall of ECW* (New York: Pocket Books, 2006), ebook.

244 **"one of the best, world-class BSers"**: Austin, Brent, and Ross, *The Stone Cold Truth*, page 142.

244 **In 1994, he was promoted to the position**: Evans, *Nitro*, ebook.

244 **WCW would launch *Monday Nitro***: Ibid.

244 **Bischoff recruited Lex Luger**: Ibid.

244 **The so-called Monday Night War**: Ibid.

244 **According to Austin, Bischoff didn't see**: Austin, Brent, and Ross, *The Stone Cold Truth*, page 139.

244 **Bischoff claims Austin had a bad attitude**: Nithin Joseph, "WWE News: Eric Bischoff explains why he fired Steve Austin from WCW," *Sportskeeda*, July 22, 2022, accessed August 3, 2022, https://www.sportskeeda.com/wwe/wwe-news-eric-bischoff-explains-why-he-fired-steve-austin-from-wcw.

244 **just before *Nitro* debuted, he dismissed**: Austin, Brent, and Ross, *The Stone Cold Truth*, page 139.

244 **he received a call from Heyman**: Austin, Brent, and Ross, *The Stone Cold Truth*, page 142.

244 **Heyman had taken over a tiny promotion**: Loverro et al., *The Rise and Fall of ECW*, ebook.

245 **Heyman renamed the promotion**: Ibid.

245 **"I want you to do an in-ring interview"**: Austin, Brent, and Ross, *The Stone Cold Truth*, pages 142–43.

245 **nearly eight-minute-long promo in September 1995**: *Extreme Wrestling Championship*, "I'm gonna be the superstar that I always knew I could be!" promo, featuring Steve Austin, via CageMatch, aired October 10, 1995, accessed June 29, 2022, https://www.cagematch.net/?id=93&nr=39.

245 **"Steve Austin is here to *wrestle*"**: Lou Gregory, " 'Superstar' Steve Austin Promo (ECW 1995), YouTube, accessed August 3, 2022, https://youtu.be/xlN8-Su7RGs.

245 **Austin didn't do much wrestling**: "Search results—Steve Austin, also known as Stone Cold Steve Austin, Stunning Steve, Ringmaster, Steve Williams," *CageMatch*, accessed June 29, 2022, https://www.cagematch.net/?id=2&nr=635&page=4&search=ecw.

245 **"I saw a side of Steve"**: Austin, Brent, and Ross, *The Stone Cold Truth*, pages 147–48.

245 **Ross spoke to Vince and raised the possibility**: Ibid.

245 **"Steve was hired by"**: Ibid.

246 **"Ted DiBiase is going to be your manager"**: Austin, Brent, and Ross, *The Stone Cold Truth*, page 157.

246 **"I was thinking that it sounded"**: Ibid.

246 **The WWF's official seamstresses**: Ibid., pages 157–58.

246 **had gained the official title "The Loose Cannon"**: Evans, *Nitro*, ebook.

246 **he outed a wrestler as one of WCW's bookers**: Ibid.

246 **he so antagonized Bobby Heenan**: Michael Hamflett, "5 Times Foul-Mouthed Announcers Dropped The F-Bomb," *WhatCulture*, July 10, 2018, accessed August 3, 2022, https://whatculture.com/wwe/5-times-foul-mouthed-announcers-dropped-the-f-bomb.

247 **"I'm thinking, *What the hell*"**: Austin, Brent, and Ross, *The Stone Cold Truth*, page 158.

247 **had been a WWF performer starting in 1987**: Shawn Michaels and Aaron

Feigenbaum, *Heartbreak & Triumph: The Shawn Michaels Story* (London: Pocket Books, 2005), ebook.

247 **unrepentant and unreliable addict:** Shawn Michaels and David Thomas, *Wrestling for My Life: The Legend, the Reality, and the Faith of a WWE Superstar* (Grand Rapids, MI: Zondervan, 2014), ebook.

247 **"My life had spiraled so out of control":** Ibid.

248 **"I would go off on Vince periodically":** Michaels and Feigenbaum, *Heartbreak*, ebook.

248 **They banded together for leverage:** Ibid.

248 **"appreciated that we were honest with him":** Ibid.

249 **when he made his WWF debut:** LDorrProductions, "Steve Austin Debut as Million Dollar Champion on The Brother Love Show Raw January 8th 1996," YouTube, accessed June 29, 2022, https://youtu.be/fdObcAZAPd4.

249 **"I want everybody out there in TV land":** Ibid.

249 **"I was getting it done in the ring":** Austin, Brent, and Ross, *The Stone Cold Truth*, page 162.

249 **"Man, I watched that show":** Ibid., page 167.

250 **"Temperature-based things like":** Ibid.

250 **Austin recounted the pivotal moment:** Ibid.

250 **Austin went to one of the boss's top lieutenants:** Ibid., page 168.

250 **On March 11, 1996, Austin walked to the ring:** *Monday Night Raw*, season 4, episode 10, featuring Bret Hart and Shawn Michaels, WWE, aired March 11, 1996.

250 **"there was no big buildup or explanation":** Austin, Brent, and Ross, *The Stone Cold Truth*, page 168.

250 **"His peers here in the World Wrestling Federation":** *Monday Night Raw*, March 11, 1996.

250 **"I still wasn't really going anywhere":** Austin, Brent, and Ross, *The Stone Cold Truth*, page 168.

251 **In the spring, Kevin Nash and Scott Hall defected:** Wade Keller, "Diesel, Badd, Steiners Join Roster Shuffling," *Pro Wrestling Torch*, no. 379, March 16, 1996.

251 **perhaps WWF management let them go:** Andrew Thompson, "Post News Update: Molly Holly Discusses Her Trial Run as a WWE Producer," *Post Wrestling*, June 24, 2021, accessed June 29, 2022, https://www.postwrestling.com/2021/06/24/post-news-update-molly-holly-discusses-her-trial-run-as-a-wwe-producer/.

251 **perhaps the men just wanted the higher performance fees:** Liam Crowley, "Kevin Nash Says Bret Hart Incident Finally Led to Him Leaving WWE In 1996," *Wrestling Inc.*, July 25, 2021, accessed June 29, 2022, https://www.wrestlinginc.com/news/2021/07/kevin-nash-says-bret-hart-incident-finally-led-to-him-leaving-wwe-in-1996/.

251 **At an untelevised show in Madison Square Garden:** Wade Keller, "The Clique Break Character in MSG Finale," *Pro Wrestling Torch*, no. 389, May 25, 1996.

251 **"Backstage, the agents and the boys":** Bret Hart, *Hitman: My Real Life in the Cartoon World of Wrestling* (London: Ebury Press, 2010), ebook.

251 **Vince reportedly fined all four men $2,500:** Ibid.

251 **Levesque had been booked to win**: Jake Jeremy, "Triple H Talks Regrets in His Career, Not Winning the 1996 King of the Ring Due to Curtain Call Incident," *Wrestling News*, April 25, 2020, accessed June 29, 2022, https://wrestlingnews.co/wwe-news/triple-h-talks-regrets-in-his-career-not-winning-the-1996-king-of-the-ring-due-to-curtain-call-incident/.

251 **"Any time you're putting your heart"**: *WWE Rivalries*, "Austin vs. McMahon."

252 **Annual business transacted had been around $123 million**: "Titan Sports: Statement of Proportion of Capital Stock," lic. 762125, 1994 form 7 (Columbus, OH), April 5, 1994.

252 **$89 million the next year**: "Titan Sports: Statement of Proportion of Capital Stock," lic. 762125, 1995 form 7 (Columbus, OH), May 6, 1995.

252 **$82 million the next**: "Titan Sports: Statement of Proportion of Capital Stock," lic. 762125, 1996 form 7 (Columbus, OH), April 2, 1996.

252 **worst-performing year, adjusted for inflation**: "Titan Sports: Statement of Proportion of Capital Stock," lic. 762125, 1997 form 7 (Columbus, OH), December 30, 1997.

252 **little pretaped skits in which he mocked**: TheSourceWrestling, "WWF—01.01.1996—Raw—Billionaire Ted's Wrasslin' Warroom—Promo," YouTube, 2015, accessed June 29, 2022, https://www.youtube.com/watch?v=b2GWziOFeI&list=PLQmYwJ5Elb6eOHP3iVtqGgyMwjEHiAYXm&ab_channel=TheSourceWrestling.

253 **"There have been numerous references"**: Wade Keller, "WWF Teases a Michaels-Bret Confrontation," *Pro Wrestling Torch*, no. 468, November 29, 1997.

253 **"You people, you know who I am"**: WWE, "Scott Hall invades WCW: Nitro, May 27, 1996," YouTube, accessed August 3, 2022, https://youtu.be/_TcAfnVxEYo.

253 **"The crowd was somewhat stunned"**: Dave Meltzer, "Legendary Ray Stevens Passes Away at 60," *Wrestling Observer*, May 13, 1996.

254 **on June 17, *Nitro* overtook *Raw***: Rick Scaia, "RAW vs. Nitro: Year One," Online Onslaught, August 7, 2003, accessed June 29, 2022, https://web.archive.org/web/20080516125131/http://www.oowrestling.com/features/mnw-y1.shtml.

254 **for eighty-three weeks**: Ibid.

254 **in imitation of Bruce Willis's character**: Austin, Brent, and Ross, *The Stone Cold Truth*, page 173.

254 **When the King of the Ring PPV came around**: *King of the Ring '96*, June 23, 1996, unofficial video reconstruction of original broadcast.

254 **"The first thing I want to be done"**: Ibid.

254 **"would never have happened"**: Austin, Brent, and Ross, *The Stone Cold Truth*, page 173.

254 **"You sit there and you thump"**: Ibid.

255 **"Even after I did my 3:16 promo"**: Ibid.

255 **"Man, what's going on?"**: Austin, Brent, and Ross, *The Stone Cold Truth*, page 174.

255 **"started letting me just go"**: Ibid.

256 **The WWF produced and quickly sold out of**: Ibid., page 173.

256 **"A new star was born"**: Ibid., page 176.

256 **"I tell young wrestlers"**: Ibid., page 174.

256 **Kevin Nash had shown up on** *Nitro*: Evans, *Nitro*, ebook.

256 **On July 7, two weeks after**: Ibid.

256 **"The first thing you gotta realize"**: WWE, "Hulk Hogan Sides with The Outsiders: Bash at the Beach 1996," YouTube, 2020, accessed August 3, 2022, https://www.youtube.com/watch?v=sqTpZsZd5Xo.

257 **Vince had fired Ross twice already**: Jim Ross and Paul O'Brien, *Slobberknocker: My Life in Wrestling* (New York: Simon & Schuster, 2017), ebook.

257 **The fan-favorite Ross had been back**: Ibid.

257 **"I was to expose Vince as the owner"**: Ibid.

257 **"I'd rather not done it"**: Danny Hart, "'I'd Rather Not Done It'—Jim Ross Disliked Vince McMahon's WWE Storyline Idea for Him," *Sportskeeda*, November 20, 2021, accessed June 29, 2022, https://www.sportskeeda.com/wwe/news-wwe-news-jim-ross-disliked-vince-mcmahon-s-heel-turn-idea.

257 **"There's something I've been waiting to say"**: SlamZone, "Jim Ross SHOOTS on the WWF and Presents 'Razor Ramon' | RAW 9/27/96," YouTube, 2021, accessed June 29, 2022, https://www.youtube.com/watch?v=FFOcKTmfAes.

258 **"Vince saw himself a little bit"**: Ross and O'Brien, *Slobberknocker*, ebook.

258 **Vince had ordered two tall wrestlers**: "Fake Razor Ramon & Fake Diesel: The WWF'S Lowest Ebb," *Wrestling 20 Years Ago*, October 15, 2016, accessed June 29, 2022, https://www.wrestling20yrs.com/blog/fake-razor-ramon-fake-diesel-the-wwfs-lowest-ebb.

259 **"The point for Vince was"**: Ross and O'Brien, *Slobberknocker*, ebook.

259 **The boss even made an appearance**: Lee Gareth, "WWF LiveWire—October 5th 1996," YouTube, 2021, accessed June 29, 2022, https://youtu.be/2PE4hyhI8Go.

259 **"You are sitting up there in your ivory tower"**: Ibid.

260 **"The fans farted at it"**: Ross and O'Brien, *Slobberknocker*, ebook.

260 **On the November 4, 1996, episode of** *Raw*: "1996," *The History of WWE*.

261 **Complaints lit up the USA Network phone lines**: Shaun Assael and Mike Mooneyham, *Sex, Lies, and Headlocks* (New York: Three Rivers Press, 2002), ebook.

261 **"We humbly apologize"**: Ibid.

Chapter 15: SUCK IT, ACT II

263 **Bret Hart's contract with the WWF expired**: Bret Hart, *Hitman: My Real Life in the Cartoon World of Wrestling* (London: Ebury Press, 2010), ebook.

263 **Vince invited Bret to his home in Greenwich**: Hart, *Hitman*, ebook.

263 **During his last contract negotiation**: Bret Hart, interview with author, May 23, 2022.

264 **So when Vince asked him to sign back up**: Hart, *Hitman*, ebook.

264 **"You're much smarter than people"**: Ibid.

264 **Bret's hiatus was explained**: Barbara D. Phillips, "Our Critic Goes to the Mat," *Wall Street Journal*, December 14, 1998, accessed August 3, 2022, https://www.wsj.com/articles/SB913591842473934000.

264   **by late July, he still hadn't signed a contract**: Hart, *Hitman*, ebook.

264   **The boss flew a chartered jet**: Ibid.

264   **"Whatever you want!"**: Ibid.

264   **But Bret only gave Vince a vague assurance**: Ibid.

264   **Eric Bischoff made Bret an offer**: Ibid.

264   **On October 3, Bret called Vince**: Ibid.

264   **"Three million dollars for a lighter schedule"**: Ibid.

265   **On October 9, Vince flew to Calgary**: Ibid.

265   **The contract would be for the next twenty years**: Ibid.

265   **"I'll never give you a reason"**: Ibid.

265   **"I accepted the deal"**: Ibid.

265   **"the draft bore no resemblance to the deal"**: Ibid.

265   **Finally, he reached Linda**: Ibid.

265   **Vince's office called back**: Ibid.

265   **So the boss acquiesced**: Ibid.

265   **It also contained two concessions**: Ibid.

265   **"They can never, ever fuck you now"**: Ibid.

266   **Almost halfway through the October 21, 1996, *Raw***: Anthony Walker, "Raw 10-21-1996 [Full Episode]," *DailyMotion*, 2013, accessed June 29, 2022, https://www.dailymotion.com/video/x115wfb.

267   **When Bret entered at Madison Square Garden**: *Survivor Series 1996*, directed by Kevin Dunn, featuring Shawn Michaels, Sid Eudy, and Bret Hart (1996, Titan Sports).

267   **"Still wearing his headset"**: Hart, *Hitman*, ebook.

267   **"going to great lengths in their live commentary"**: Ibid.

267   **"Bret Hart can't *capitalize!*"**: Dunn, *Survivor Series 1996*.

267   **"I got the first hint of what lay ahead for me"**: Hart, *Hitman*, ebook.

267   **Bret had a match against Sid Eudy**: Brandon Stroud, "The Best and Worst of WWF Raw Is War 3/17/97: This Is Bullsh*t," *Uproxx*, November 7, 2016, accessed June 29, 2022, https://uproxx.com/prowrestling/best-and-worst-of-raw-march-17-1997/.

267   **Bret participated in the Royal Rumble**: John Canton, "WWE Royal Rumble 1997 Review," *TJR Wrestling*, January 5, 2022, accessed June 29, 2022, https://tjrwrestling.net/review/wwe-royal-rumble-1997-review/.

267   **Vince walked up to Bret**: Hart, *Hitman*, ebook.

267   **"It all seemed quite real, too real"**: Ibid.

268   **"I've been screwed by Shawn Michaels"**: *WWF Monday Night Raw*, USA Network, aired January 20, 1997.

268   **"The USA rep said it was the most exciting *Raw*"**: Shaun Assael and Mike Mooneyham, *Sex, Lies, and Headlocks* (New York: Three Rivers Press, 2002), ebook.

268   **"On March 9, in a dressing room"**: Hart, *Hitman*, ebook.

268   **"He enthusiastically went on to explain"**: Ibid.

268   **"Everyone around the world loves to hate Americans"**: Ibid.

269   **He thought it would alienate and confuse his fan base"**: Ibid.

269   **"As long as it's done smartly"**: Ibid.

269 **"Vince had encouraged me to go berserk"**: Ibid.

269 **after the match, Bret stuck around in the ring**: *WWF Monday Night Raw*, USA Network, aired March 17, 1997.

269 **They weren't bleeping anything**: Hart, *Hitman*, ebook.

270 **came around on March 23**: *WrestleMania 13*, March 23, 1997, unofficial video reconstruction of original broadcast.

270 **On March 24, at a live showing of *Raw***: *WWF Monday Night Raw*, USA Network, aired March 24, 1997.

271 **Shawn had recently posed as a centerfold in *Playgirl***: "The Heartbreak Kid," *Playgirl*, October, 1996.

271 **had been Vince's idea**: Hart, *Hitman*, ebook.

271 **he really did find it detestable**: *Hitman Hart: Wrestling with Shadows*, directed by Paul Jay, featuring Bret Hart, Owen Hart, and Brian Pillman (1998, Alberta, Canada: High Road Productions, National Film Board of Canada, TV Ontario).

272 **"Bret Hart did not come back"**: *WWF Monday Night Raw*, USA Network, aired April 7, 1997.

272 **"Without a moment's hesitation"**: Hart, *Hitman*, ebook.

272 **Bret found out he needed knee surgery**: Ibid.

272 **But the day after his surgery, Vince called**: Ibid.

272 **In one of those promos, Shawn implied**: *WWF Monday Night Raw*, USA Network, aired May 19, 1997.

273 **"I wondered about beating the hell"**: Hart, *Hitman*, ebook.

273 **Vince called Bret to a sit-down**: Ibid.

273 **"He told me that the company"**: Ibid.

273 **Bret and Shawn got into a verbal, then physical fight**: Ibid.

273 **Shawn marched to Vince's room**: Ibid.

273 **"Vince looked like a jilted lover"**: Ibid.

273 **He said he'd get Shawn in line**: Ibid.

274 **had initially been the hit Marilyn Manson track**: ThrowbackWrestling1, "WWF RAW IS WAR Intro 3/10/1997," YouTube, 2022, accessed June 29, 2022, https://www.youtube.com/watch?time_continue=6&v=bZlRy9QqD0M&feature=emb_title&ab_channel=ThrowbackWrestling1.

274 **now it was an original work**: "Full Metal (The Single)," Discogs, accessed June 29, 2022, https://www.discogs.com/release/875578-The-World-Wrestling-Federation-Superstars-Slam-Jam-Full-Metal-The-Single.

274 **Vince and Heyman decided to work together**: Thom Loverro, Tazz & Tommy Dreamer, and Paul Heyman, *The Rise and Fall of ECW* (New York: Pocket Books, 2006), ebook.

275 **Mick Foley was a famed deathmatch wrestler**: Mick Foley, *Have a Nice Day: A Tale of Blood and Sweatsocks* (New York: Regan Books, 1999), ebook.

275 **Foley had wanted to hang on to his old outlaw gimmick**: Ibid.

276 **Just before the September 22 edition of *Raw***: Hart, *Hitman*, ebook.

276 **"He wasn't going to pay me my full salary"**: Ibid.

276 **That night, Vince did a landmark in-ring interview**: *WWF Monday Night Raw*, USA Network, aired September 22, 1997.

277 **Brian Pillman didn't show up**: Dave Meltzer, "Editorial," *Wrestling Observer*, October 13, 1997.

277 **Vince learned of the death shortly**: Ibid.

277 **For the first three minutes of the PPV**: *WWF Badd Blood: In Your House*, pay-per-view broadcast, aired October 5, 1997.

278 **The very next night, Vince opened *Raw***: *WWF Monday Night Raw*, USA Network, aired October 10, 1997.

278 **Bret was disgusted that Vince was using a real death**: Hart, *Hitman*, ebook.

278 **"I want you to really shoot with 'em"**: Ibid.

278 **Vince had recently**: Ibid.

279 **He and Bischoff closed a deal**: Dave Meltzer, "The Montreal Screwjob," *Wrestling Observer*, November 17, 1997.

280 **"He told me he can't have me showing up"**: Hart, *Hitman*, ebook.

280 **when the WWF's Alundra Blayze**: Old-School-Wrestling-Clips, "Madusa (Alun-dra Blayze) Throws the WWF Women's Title in a Trash Can on WCW Nitro!," YouTube, 2021, accessed, https://www.youtube.com/watch?v=GrLwr BLV-lo&ab_channel=Old-School-Wrestling-Clips.

280 **In 1991, Ric Flair took his NWA championship belt**: WWE, "Bobby Heenan Brings Ric Flair to WWE: Prime Time Wrestling, September 9, 1991," You-Tube, 2013, accessed, https://www.youtube.com/watch?v=j8ggDRV5Rj4&ab _channel=WWE.

280 **"Fine," Bret said**: Hart, *Hitman*, ebook.

280 **"You told me I could leave any way I wanted"**: Ibid.

280 **"I've never said 'no' to Vince McMahon"**: Jay, *Hitman Hart*.

280 **Vince pitched a wide array of potential Survivor Series finishes**: Meltzer, "The Montreal Screwjob."

280 **According to Dave Meltzer's reporting**: Ibid.

281 **"McMahon even suggested"**: Meltzer, "The Montreal Screwjob."

281 **Bret would later claim he'd heard**: Hart, *Hitman*, ebook.

281 **"Vince Russo's never had any respect"**: "The Montreal Screwjob," *Dark Side of the Ring*, season 1, episode 2, Vice, April 17, 2019.

281 **"The problem is he's still living in 1970"**: Ibid.

281 **Cornette says he came up with the screwjob concept**: Ibid.

281 **Russo insists it was all *his* idea**: Ibid.

281 **"I wish I didn't pitch the idea"**: Ibid.

281 **Brisco has outright denied**: Matt Boone, "Gerald Brisco Gives Detailed Account Of Infamous WWE Montreal Screwjob As He Remembers It," eWrestling.com, February 6, 2021, accessed August 4, 2022, https://ewrestling.com/article /gerald-brisco-gives-detailed-account-infamous-wwe-montreal-screwjob-he -remembers-it.

281 **"the single most famous finish"**: Meltzer, "The Montreal Screwjob."

281 **both Dave Meltzer**: Ibid.

281 **and Shawn Michaels**: Shawn Michaels and Aaron Feigenbaum, *Heartbreak & Triumph: The Shawn Michaels Story* (London: Pocket Books, 2005), ebook.

282 **"Really, what they would prefer"**: Jay, *Hitman Hart*.

282 **"What do you want to do?"**: Hart, *Hitman*, ebook.

282   **"I never, ever wanted to leave here"**: Jay, *Hitman Hart.*
283   **"[Shawn] was visibly nervous"**: Hart, *Hitman,* ebook.
283   **Vince wasn't on commentary that night**: *WWF Survivor Series '97,* pay-per-view broadcast, November 9, 1997.
283   **uneasy territory for a Maple Leaf–flying patriot**: Famed Montreal wrestler and former member of the WWF roster Jacques Rougeau told me there were many French-Canadians in the crowd that night who felt no loyalty to Bret.
284   **the official bell-ringer, Mark Yeaton**: Meltzer, "The Montreal Screwjob."
284   **"Ring the fucking bell!"**: Ibid.
284   **locked himself in his makeshift office**: Ibid.
284   **Bret drew the letters "W-C-W" in the air**: Ibid.
284   **Bret confronted Shawn**: Jay, *Hitman Hart.*
284   **Bret's then-wife, Julie, started telling off Levesque**: Ibid.
285   **The Undertaker banged on Vince's door**: Meltzer, "The Montreal Screwjob."
285   **"Tell Vince to get the hell out of here"**: Hart, *Hitman,* ebook.
285   **Bret walked out of the shower, sopping wet**: Ibid.
285   **"It's the first time I ever had to lie"**: Ibid.
285   **"Who are you kidding"**: Ibid.
285   **Bret lunged**: Meltzer, "The Montreal Screwjob."
285   **"Like a cork," as Bret put it**: Hart, *Hitman,* ebook.
285   **Vince collapsed to the floor, unconscious**: Meltzer, "The Montreal Screwjob."
285   **Brisco jumped at Bret**: Hart, *Hitman,* ebook.
285   **Shane McMahon helped drag his dazed father**: Ibid.
285   **"Maybe I was becoming too powerful"**: Jay, *Hitman Hart.*

Chapter 16: SUCK IT, ACT III
286   **"The mass audience reaction"**: "The mass audience reaction was one of confusion," comment, Reddit, 2016, accessed August 4, 2022, https://www.reddit.com/r/SquaredCircle/comments/4yb5s7/did_anybody_here_witness_the_montreal_screwjob_in/.
286   **"Not long at all after the PPV ended"**: DrunkAndDisposable, "Not long at all after the PPV ended," comment, Reddit, 2016, accessed, https://www.reddit.com/r/SquaredCircle/comments/4yb5s7/comment/d6mhb6w/?utm_source=share&utm_medium=web2x&context=3.
286   **with the subject line "What the hell?"**: John Molea, "What the hell?," Usenet correspondence, November 9, 1997, accessed August 4, 2022, https://groups.google.com/g/rec.sport.pro-wrestling/c/KeGXl9XQJfc.
286   **"Bret got fucked"**: Tim Cossett, "Worst screw job ending ever?," November 9, 1997, accessed August 4, 2022, https://groups.google.com/g/rec.sport.pro-wrestling/c/QzxGJb3vABk.
286   **"Bret Hart Loses: Ambush or Angle?!?"**: Rick Scaia, "Bret Hart Loses: Ambush or Angle?!?," *The News from Dayton,* November 10, 1997, accessed August 4, 2022, https://rspw.org/nfd/nfd.971110.
287   **Most of the locker room had threatened**: Dave Meltzer, "The Montreal Screwjob," *Wrestling Observer,* November 17, 1997.

287 **Vince told them Bret had agreed**: Wade Keller, "McMahon Double-Crosses Bret in Title Match," *Pro Wrestling Torch*, no. 466, November 15, 1997.

287 **"For those who needed a plausible explanation"**: Ibid.

287 **came to be known as "crash TV"**: Two Man Power Trip, "Vince Russo On The Origin Of Crash TV In The Attitude Era," YouTube, accessed August 4, 2022, https://youtu.be/QeA79u98X_Y.

287 **While the Canadian crowd showered them**: *WWF Monday Night Raw*, USA Network, aired November 10, 1997.

287 **The next episode of *Raw* would be**: "1997," *The History of WWE*, accessed June 29, 2022, http://thehistoryofwwe.com/97.htm.

288 **"Everybody in the room wanted"**: Vince Russo, *Forgiven* (Toronto: ECW Press, 2005), ebook.

288 **"We realized then we could put me"**: Joel Drucker, "King of the Ring," *Cigar Aficionado*, November/December 1999, https://www.cigaraficionado.com/article/king-of-the-ring-6149.

288 **When the pretaped *Raw* aired on November 17**: *The History of WWE*, "1997."

288 **"Let's cut right to the chase"**: *WWF Monday Night Raw*, USA Network, aired November 17, 1997.

289 **"Bret Hart deserved better"**: *WWF Monday Night Raw*, USA Network, aired November 24, 1997.

290 **culminating in a December 7 PPV match**: *WWF D-Generation X: In Your House*, pay-per-view broadcast, aired December 7, 1997.

290 **Vince opened the live December 8 *Raw***: *WWF Monday Night Raw*, USA Network, aired December 8, 1997.

291 **Owen Hart was a beloved presence**: "The Final Days of Owen Hart," *Dark Side of the Ring*, season 2, episode 10, Vice, May 19, 2020.

291 **had treated him with rare gentleness**: Bret Hart, interview with author, May 22, 2022.

291 **Owen refused to work the next couple of shows**: Martha Hart and Eric Francis, *Broken Harts: The Life and Death of Owen Hart* (UK: M. Evans, 2004), ebook.

291 **"Owen felt he simply could no longer work"**: Ibid.

291 **"McMahon's hard stand caused friction"**: Ibid.

292 **On the next week's episode, Vince took to the ring**: *WWF Monday Night Raw*, USA Network, aired December 15, 1997.

293 **It was around this time that Vince reached out**: Mike Tyson and Larry Sloman, *Undisputed Truth* (London: Penguin, 2013), ebook.

293 **Tyson had been released early from prison**: Ibid.

293 **On June 28, 1997, Tyson fought Evander Holyfield**: Ibid.

293 **Tyson was fined $3 million**: Ibid.

293 **the Nevada State Athletic Commission rescinded**: Ibid.

294 **a devastating motorcycle crash**: Ibid.

294 **Tyson had grown up as a huge fan**: Ibid.

294 **the WWF closed a deal with Tyson**: Ibid.

294 **would be paid roughly $3.5 million**: Howard Ulman, "Tyson Has Role in Wrestlemania XIV," Associated Press, March 30, 1998, accessed August 4, 2022, https://apnews.com/article/880c40e1d88d8e26c17f0f787648437c.

294   **Luckily, Ratner was a huge wrestling fan**: Shaun Assael and Mike Mooney-ham, *Sex, Lies, and Headlocks* (New York: Three Rivers Press, 2002), ebook.

294   **Vince told Ratner he was thinking**: Ibid.

294   **"A huge story is developing"**: *WWF Monday Night Raw*, USA Network, aired December 15, 1997.

295   **On January 12, Vince addressed the crowd**: *WWF Monday Night Raw*, USA Network, aired January 12, 1998.

295   **Throughout January 18's *Royal Rumble '98***: *WWF Royal Rumble '98*, pay-per-view broadcast, January 18, 1997.

296   **Tyson appeared repeatedly on the next night's *Raw***: *WWF Monday Night Raw*, USA Network, aired January 19, 1998.

297   **"In effect," Vince said at a crowded news conference**: NostalgiaMania—Wrestling, "WWF LiveWire—WrestleMania 14 Press Conference (1998-03-07)," YouTube, September 2021, accessed June 29, 2022, https://www.youtube.com/watch?v=c8hxseFoI6M.

297   **the WWF was actually *increasing* its revenue**: "World Wrestling Federation Entertainment Inc.," 424B1 SEC 333-84327, accessed June 29, 2022, https://www.sec.gov/Archives/edgar/data/1091907/000095013099005812/0000950130-99-005812.txt.

298   **"After fourteen years of service"**: FirestormPurify, "Off the Record—Vince McMahon [02.24.98] FULL," YouTube, 2012, accessed June 29, 2022, https://www.youtube.com/watch?v=zXN7nDtAVX0&t=1s.

300   **"Only in the USA, in the WWF"**: *WrestleMania XIV*, pay-per-view broadcast, March 29, 1998.

300   **"I got a lot of criticism for appearing at WrestleMania"**: Tyson and Sloman, *Undisputed Truth*.

301   **Throughout much of 1998**: Nancy Jo Sales, "Beyond Fake," *New York* magazine, October 26, 1998.

301   **"It's ironic that I now play an authority figure"**: Ibid., page 43.

301   **a documentary about the American wrestling industry**: *Beyond the Mat*, directed by Barry W. Blaustein (1999, Amarillo, TX: Universal Family and Home Entertainment, Imagine Entertainment, Lionsgate Films).

301   **Vince told Blaustein stories similar to those**: Barry Blaustein, interview with author, October 23, 2020.

301   **The filmmaker turned to his cameraman**: Ibid.

301   **Blaustein had been in contact with Vince**: Ibid.

301   **There's a memorable scene that made it**: Blaustein, *Beyond the Mat*.

302   **"This character that is on television"**: Sales, "Beyond Fake," page 43.

303   **On April 13, Vince took to the ring**: *WWF Monday Night Raw*, USA Network, aired April 13, 1998.

303   **Viewership skyrocketed as wrestling fans**: "TV Ratings 1998," *OSW Review*, accessed August 4, 2022, http://oswreview.com/history/tv-ratings-1998.

303   **since Jerry Graham gave him his first weights**: Sales, "Beyond Fake," page 43.

303   **for the first time since 1996, the WWF beat WCW**: *OSW Review*, "TV Ratings 1998."

304 **On the June 1, *Raw*, as Vince walked**: *WWF Monday Night Raw*, USA Network, aired June 1, 1998.

304 **would wind up as Austin's tag-team partner**: *WWF Monday Night Raw*, USA Network, aired May 11, 1998.

304 **as the guest referee in one of Austin's matches**: *WWF Monday Night Raw*, USA Network, aired May 23, 1998.

304 **the main-event match at November 15's *Survivor Series '98***: *WWF Survivor Series '98*, pay-per-view broadcast, November 15, 1997.

305 **spray Mr. McMahon down with a beer-spewing firehose**: *WWE: Austin vs. McMahon—The Whole True Story*, directed by Kevin Dunn, featuring Steve Austin and Vince McMahon (2002, WWE).

305 **pour cement into Mr. McMahon's prized convertible**: Ibid.

305 **lunge at him from atop a still humming Zamboni**: Ibid.

305 **after an attack by two wrestlers**: *WWF Monday Night Raw*, USA Network, aired October 5, 1998.

305 **the *New York* cover story was published**: The cover date is October 26, but, having worked at *New York*, I can tell you that the printed dates were a week ahead of when they were actually released.

305 **Mr. McMahon, kneeling in submission**: *WWF Monday Night Raw*, USA Network, aired October 19, 1998.

306 **In the titular battle royal at *Royal Rumble '99***: *WWF Royal Rumble '99*, pay-per-view broadcast, January 24, 1999.

307 **split open his forehead and necessitated stitches**: Blaustein, *Beyond the Mat*.

307 **on a February 14 PPV called *St. Valentine's Day Massacre***: *WWF St. Valentine's Day Massacre*, pay-per-view broadcast, February 14, 1999.

307 **"I had been really upset with him"**: Thomas Hobbs, "An Interview with the Guy Behind WWE's Most Famous Wrestling Theme Songs," *Vice*, December 15, 2020, accessed June 29, 2022, https://www.vice.com/en/article/g5bjbm/jim-johnston-wwe-wrestling-theme-composer-interview-2020.

308 **The table was supposed to helpfully collapse**: Russo, *Forgiven*, ebook.

Chapter 17: SUCK IT, FINALE

310 **each had graduated from Boston University**: Boston University, correspondence with author, October 21, 2021.

310 **"I'm probably closer to Shane"**: This was from an issue of *RAW Magazine* that I've been unable to locate, but it was helpfully transcribed by an Angelfire user many years ago; "The RAW Interview: Growing Up McMahon," accessed August 4, 2022, https://www.angelfire.com/wrestling2/StephsThreeBs/stepharticle24.html.

311 **Back on August 2, 1998**: *WWF Sunday Night Heat*, USA Network, aired August 2, 1998.

311 **the WWF announced that Shane would be**: Dave Meltzer, "Editorial," *Wrestling Observer*, August 24, 1998.

311 **On February 15, a day after his dad's cage match**: *WWF Monday Night Raw*, USA Network, aired February 15, 1999.

312 **Vince and his bookers decided**: NOTE: the figure was also occasionally called the "Higher Power," but less often, and I wanted to keep the manuscript simple; William Windsor, "Bruce Prichard on Who Was Slated to Be 'The Higher Power' and Why It Was Nixed, Worst Gimmick, More," *Wrestling Inc.*, January 6, 2017, accessed June 29, 2022, https://www.wrestlinginc.com/news/2017/01/bruce-prichard-on-who-was-slated-to-be-the-higher-power-and-620965/.

312 **Vince had a lot of affection for Calaway**: Saunak Nag, "The Undertaker gives his honest thoughts on being inducted into the Hall of Fame by Vince McMahon," *Sportskeeda*, July 23, 2022, accessed August 4, 2022, https://www.sportskeeda.com/wwe/news-the-undertaker-says-relationship-vince-mc mahon-much-boss-employee.

312 **referred to as "the locker-room leader"**: Dakota Cohen, "JBL On The Undertaker Being A Locker Room Leader In WWE," *Wrestling Inc.*, December 12, 2021, accessed August 4, 2022, https://www.wrestlinginc.com/news/2021/12/jbl-on-the-undertaker-being-a-locker-room-leader-in-wwe.

313 **Bruce Prichard**: Marco Rovere, "Bruce Prichard Names Who Could Have Been Great Fit for WWE 'Higher Power' Angle," *Wrestling Inc.*, July 2, 2021, accessed June 29, 2022, https://www.wrestlinginc.com/news/2021/07/bruce-prichard-reveals-who-else-was-discussed-as-the-corporate-ministrys-higher-power/.

313 **Vince Russo**: Vince Russo, correspondence with author, March 23, 2022.

313 **At the end of the next week's *Raw***: *WWF Monday Night Raw*, USA Network, aired February 22, 1999.

314 **"That struck me as being so odd"**: "Growing Up McMahon."

314 **Stephanie interned at various departments**: Ibid.

314 **"My internship with my father"**: Ibid.

314 **She'd made a seconds-long cameo**: Ahmad Tv, "Stone Cold Looking for the Undertaker: Stephanie McMahon First Appearance Ahmad Tv," YouTube, 2019, accessed June 29, 2022, https://www.youtube.com/watch?v=ORt1m OOI3JM&ab_channel=AhmadTv.

314 **working as an intern for her mother**: "Growing Up McMahon."

314 **According to Vince Russo, he came to Vince**: Vince Russo, *Forgiven* (Toronto: ECW Press, 2005), ebook.

314 **"I think that fan participation"**: "Growing Up McMahon."

314 **The March 29, 1999, episode of *Raw***: *WWF Monday Night Raw*, USA Network, aired March 29, 1999.

314 **the Undertaker and his Ministry appeared to tie**: World Wrestling Entertainment, "WWE WrestlaMania 15: Undertaker vs Big Boss Man—Hell in a Cell Match," YouTube, March 2022, accessed June 29, 2022, https://www.youtube.com/watch?v=hN72He4zNZo&ab_channel=worldwrestling entertainment.

316 **April 20, 1999, when two high school students**: "Who Are the Trenchcoat Mafia?," *BBC News*, April 21, 1999, accessed June 29, 2022, http://news.bbc.co.uk/2/hi/americas/325054.stm.

316 ***USA Today* ran a story in which they juxtaposed**: Dave Meltzer, "Editorial," *Wrestling Observer*, May 3, 1999.

316   **The first thing viewers saw when they tuned into** *Raw*: *WWF Monday Night Raw*, USA Network, aired April 26, 1999.

317   **The Godfather was criticized by culture columnists**: Phil Mushnick, "Another Sacrificial Lamb Will Take His Place," *New York Post*, May 25, 1999, accessed June 29, 2022, https://nypost.com/1999/05/25/another-sacrificial-lamb-will-take-his-place/.

318   **The very next night, the WWF taped a pilot**: "1999," *The History of WWE*, accessed June 29, 2022, http://thehistoryofwwe.com/99.htm.

319   **He entered with Stephanie on his arm**: *WWF SmackDown*, UPN, aired April 29, 1999.

319   **Owen wanted to get out of wrestling**: Martha Hart and Eric Francis, *Broken Harts: The Life and Death of Owen Hart* (UK: M. Evans, 2004), ebook.

320   **Vince had decided he wanted Owen to return**: Ibid.

320   **Owen protested; he'd never liked the gimmick**: Ibid.

320   **On the next** *Raw*, **Shane cut a promo**: *WWF Monday Night Raw*, USA Network, aired May 3, 1999.

322   **about a week before** *Over the Edge*: Vince Russo, correspondence with author, March 23, 2022.

323   **The viewers cheered Mr. McMahon on**: *WWF Sunday Night Heat*, USA Network, aired May 23, 1999.

323   **The Blue Blazer had used the descender**: Hart and Francis, *Broken Harts*, ebook.

324   **That night, Owen was supposed to descend**: Ibid.

324   **Vince had hired a new descender technician**: Ibid.

324   **"Jerry, Pat," Cole said**: *WWF Over the Edge '99*, pay-per-view broadcast, aired May 23, 1999.

324   **Owen was supposed to jump from his platform**: Hart and Francis, *Broken Harts*, ebook.

324   **Vince was backstage, preparing for his return**: Bret Hart, *Hitman: My Real Life in the Cartoon World of Wrestling* (London: Ebury Press, 2010), ebook.

324   **Then, a cable disengaged from his harness**: Hart and Francis, *Broken Harts*, ebook.

324   **After more than seventy feet**: Ibid.

325   **ran to Owen in the ring**: Dinner with the King, "Jerry Lawler remembers Owen Hart – Episode 11," YouTube, May 23, 2017, accessed August 4, 2022, https://youtu.be/_iLLrzKZHhQ.

325   **The wrestlers were to be told**: Hart and Francis, *Broken Harts*, ebook.

325   **The crowd in Kansas City was to be told**: Ibid.

326   **Vince called Owen's wife, Martha**: Ibid.

327   **Less than twenty minutes after pretending**: Jason King and Matt Stearns, "Kemper Arena Crowd Sees Him Plunge into Ring," *Kansas City Star* (Kansas City, MO), May 24, 1999, page 29.

327   **"All of Owen's fans all over the world"**: Ibid.

328   **There were headlines and TV segments everywhere**: Dave Meltzer, "Editorial," *Wrestling Observer*, May 31, 1999.

328   **"It was a tragic, tragic, horrible accident"**: Jason King, "Veterans Say Risk Is

Part of Pro Wrestling's Allure," *Kansas City Star* (Kansas City, MO), May 25, 1999, page 79.

328 **The show opened with a crowd**: *WWF Monday Night Raw*, USA Network, aired May 24, 1999.

330 **May 25, the WWF pretaped the next week's**: *The History of WWE*, "1999."

330 **A few minutes into *Heat***: *WWF Sunday Night Heat*, USA Network, aired May 30, 1999.

331 **Vince canceled four Canadian shows**: Meltzer, *Wrestling Observer*, May 31, 1999.

331 **"Owen's death had affected me badly"**: Jim Ross and Paul O'Brien, *Under the Black Hat: My Life in the WWE and Beyond* (New York: Simon & Schuster, 2020), ebook.

331 **"quieter than usual—withdrawn"**: Ibid.

331 **On May 31, hundreds of members of the wrestling industry**: Wade Keller, "WWF-Harts Clash over Airing Funeral Footage," *Pro Wrestling Torch*, no. 552, June 12, 1999.

331 **"I am a very forgiving person"**: *Dark Side of the Ring*, "The Final Days of Owen Hart."

331 **almost at the boiling point**: "East Boston, MA Weather History—June 7, 1999," accessed June 29, 2022, https://www.wunderground.com/history/daily/us/ma/boston/KBOS/date/1999-6-7.

331 **Stephanie would ask, "Dad, Shane?"**: *WWF Monday Night Raw*, USA Network, aired June 7, 1999.

332 ***Raw* opened with a video montage**: Ibid.

332 ***Quod per sortem***: Charles Cave, "Carmina Burana Lyrics—Carl Orff," *Classical.net*, Schott Musik International, Mainz, Germany, accessed June 29, 2022, http://www.classical.net/music/comp.lst/works/orff-cb/carmlyr.php#track1/.

Coda: THE JOB

336 ***Raw* had already returned to first place**: Guy Evans, *Nitro: The Incredible Rise and Inevitable Collapse of Ted Turner's WCW* (Self-published, 2018), ebook.

336 **WWF revenue nearly doubled**: "World Wrestling Federation," SEC 333-84327.

336 **In early 2001, the WWF bought it**: Evans, *Nitro*, ebook.

336 **ECW went bankrupt and Vince bought**: Thom Loverro, Tazz & Tommy Dreamer, and Paul Heyman, *The Rise and Fall of ECW* (New York: Pocket Books, 2006), ebook,

336 **On August 23, 1999, Gallup released a poll**: Mark Gillespie, "Two out of Ten Americans Are Wrestling Fans, 'Stone Cold' Steve Austin Picked as Fan Favorite," Gallup, August 23, 1999, accessed June 29, 2022, https://news.gallup.com/poll/3637/two-ten-americans-wrestling-fans-stone-cold-steve-austin.aspx.

336 **Vince and Linda made the WWF a publicly traded company**: "Company Briefs," *New York Times*, September 23, 2000, accessed August 4, 2022, https://www.nytimes.com/2000/09/23/business/company-briefs-301833.html.

336 **than one billion dollars**: Evelyn Nussenbaum, "Martha Feasts on $612M Cut

from Her IPO—WWF'S McMahon Pockets $963.9M," *New York Post*, October 19, 1999, accessed August 4, 2022, https://nypost.com/1999/10/19/martha-feasts-on-612m-cut-from-her-ipo-wwfs-mcmahon-pockets-963-9m/.

336 **In 2000, an environmentalist nonprofit**: David Bixenspan, "Correcting the Record on Why the WWF Changed Its Name to WWE," *Forbes*, February 17, 2020, accessed August 4, 2022, https://www.forbes.com/sites/davidbixenspan/2020/02/17/wwe-wwf-name-change-true-story-ruthless-aggression-wwe-network-documentary/?sh=4adcf08425a6.

337 **In 2006, a Florida tanning-salon employee**: Ben Feuerherd, "She Said Vince McMahon Sexually Assaulted Her in a Tanning Booth. Police Found 'Probable Cause.' Prosecutors Shrugged," *Daily Beast*, January 26, 2018, accessed August 4, 2022, https://www.thedailybeast.com/she-said-vince-mcmahon-sexually-assaulted-her-in-a-tanning-booth-police-found-probable-cause-prosecutors-shrugged?ref=home.

337 **Vince parodied the woman's accusations**: David Bixenspan, "Witness: Vince McMahon Stared Down Groping Accuser For 45 Minutes From His Car," *Deadspin*, February 7, 2018, accessed August 4, 2022, https://deadspin.com/witness-vince-mcmahon-stared-down-groping-accuser-for-1822642014.

337 **prosecutors declined to press charges**: Ibid.

337 **On June 11, 2007, Mr. McMahon was ostensibly**: "Press Release—Who Blew Up WWE® Chairman Mr. McMahon?," Corporate WWE, June 12, 2007, accessed August 4, 2022, https://corporate.wwe.com/investors/news/press-releases/2007/12-06-2007.

337 **the company posted an official-looking story**: Ibid.

337 **Donald Trump allegedly did call WWE**: Gavin Evans, "Donald Trump Once Thought Vince McMahon Actually Died During a Staged Monday Night Raw Stunt," *Complex*, December 13, 2016, accessed August 4, 2022, https://www.complex.com/sports/2016/12/donald-trump-thought-vince-mcmahon-died-staged-monday-night-raw-stunt.

338 **one of Vince's bookers from the time has claimed**: Court Bauer, interview with author, January 8, 2021.

338 **Chris Benoit murdered his wife and seven-year-old son**: Brenda Goodman, "Wrestler Killed Wife and Son, Then Himself," *New York Times*, June 27, 2007, accessed August 4, 2022, https://www.nytimes.com/2007/06/27/us/27wrestler.html.

338 **revealed massive chronic traumatic encephalopathy implicated in the tragedy**: Irvin Muchnick, *Chris & Nancy: The True Story of the Benoit Murder-Suicide and Pro Wrestling's Cocktail of Death* (Toronto: ECW Press, 2021), ebook.

338 **Benoit's steroid abuse was also implicated**: Ibid.

338 **Vince and Linda were summoned**: "Linda McMahon Interview," Waxman Committee on Oversight and Government Reform, December 13, 2007; "Vince Kennedy McMahon Interview," Waxman Committee on Oversight and Government Reform, December 14, 2007.

338 **the general sanitization of the TV product**: Bill Hanstock, *We Promised You a Great Main Event: An Unauthorized WWE History* (New York: Harper, 2020), ebook.

338 **she, too, died in 2007**: Richard Goldstein, "Mary Lillian Ellison, 84, the Fabulous Moolah, Is Dead," *New York Times*, November 6, 2007, accessed August 3, 2022, https://www.nytimes.com/2007/11/06/sports/06moolah.html.

339 **Shawn Michaels was in the midst of a comeback**: Shawn Michaels and David Thomas, *Wrestling for My Life: The Legend, the Reality, and the Faith of a WWE Superstar* (Grand Rapids, MI: Zondervan, 2014), ebook.

339 **On TV, the heel started a new religion**: *WWE Monday Night Raw*, USA Network, aired April 17, 2006.

339 **"You have finally gone *completely* insane"**: *WWE Backlash '06*, pay-per-view broadcast, aired April 30, 2006.

339 **April 2006's *Backlash '06* PPV**: Ibid.

339 **Vince and Linda began making significant**: "Search results—Linda McMahon 2021–2022," Federal Election Commission, accessed August 4, 2022, https://www.fec.gov/data/receipts/individualcontributions/?contributor_name=linda+mcmahon&two_year_transaction_period=2022&min_date=01%2F01%2F2021&max_date=12%2F31%2F2022; "Search results—Vince McMahon," Federal Election Commission, accessed August 4, 2022, https://www.fec.gov/data/receipts/individualcontributions/?contributor_name=vince+mcmahon.

339 **to the Connecticut Republican Federal Campaign Committee**: Ibid.

339 **Rahm Emanuel received cash from Linda**: Ibid.

340 **it became financially advantageous**: Travis Waldron, "The Definitive History of That Time Donald Trump Took a Stone Cold Stunner," *Huffington Post*, February 14, 2017, accessed June 29, 2022, https://www.huffpost.com/archive/au/entry/donald-trump-wwe-wrestling_a_21715165.

340 **Trump and Vince were both ringside**: *WrestleMania 23*, pay-per-view broadcast, aired April 1, 2007.

340 **The McMahons also donated $4 million**: Dan Alexander, "Why Is WWE Listed as the Trump Foundation's Biggest Donor?," *Forbes*, April 20, 2017, accessed June 29, 2022, https://www.forbes.com/sites/danalexander/2017/04/20/why-is-wwe-listed-as-the-trump-foundations-biggest-donor/?sh=437b5245f900.

340 **as they did to their own Vince and Linda McMahon Family Foundation**: Ibid.

340 **In 2009, the McMahons donated**: Ibid.

340 **they were given contradictory and confusing**: Ibid.

340 **a troll on Reddit modified a clip of Trump**: David Nakamura, "Trump Appears to Promote Violence Against CNN with Tweet," *Washington Post*, July 2, 2017, accessed June 29, 2022, https://www.washingtonpost.com/news/post-politics/wp/2017/07/02/trump-appears-to-promote-violence-against-cnn-with-tweet/.

340 **Trump found it and tweeted it out**: Ibid.

341 **Trump's homeland security adviser, Tom Bossert**: Ibid.

341 **In 2008, Republican Connecticut governor**: Mark Pazniokas, "WWE Executive Is Rell's Pick," *Hartford Courant*, January 15, 2009, page A03.

341 **In February of 2009, she was approved**: Christine Stuart, "House Approves WWE Executive," *CT News Junkie*, February 25, 2009, accessed June 29, 2022, https://ctnewsjunkie.com/2009/02/25/house_approves_wwe_executive/.

341 **Vince booked a story where Trump**: Graham GSM Matthews, "Reliving the Time Donald Trump Sold WWE Raw Back to Vince McMahon," *Bleacher Report*, June 21, 2019, accessed June 29, 2022, https://bleacherreport.com/articles/2841552-reliving-the-time-donald-trump-sold-wwe-raw-back-to-vince-mcmahon.

341 **spending around $100 million**: Peter Applebome, "Personal Cost for 2 Senate Bids: $100 Million," *New York Times*, November 3, 2012, accessed June 29, 2022, https://www.nytimes.com/2012/11/03/nyregion/linda-e-mcmahon-has-spent-nearly-100-million-in-senate-races.html.

341 **In 2016, she donated $7 million**: Tal Kopan, "Donald Trump's SBA Nominee Gave $7M to Support Him," CNN, December 9, 2016, accessed June 29, 2022, https://www.cnn.com/2016/12/09/politics/linda-mcmahon-donald-trump-donations/index.html.

342 **confirmed by a vote of 81 to 19**: "PN48—Linda E. McMahon—Small Business Administration," 115th Congress (2017-2018), Congress.gov, accessed June 29, 2022, https://www.congress.gov/nomination/115th-congress/48.

342 **On March 1, 2018, it was reported**: Brandon Howard Thurston, "Trump's WWE Buddies Are Deeply in Bed with Saudi Regime," *Daily Beast*, October 13, 2018, accessed June 29, 2022, https://www.thedailybeast.com/trumps-wwe-buddies-are-deeply-in-bed-with-saudi-regime.

342 **well over $40 million per co-sponsored show**: Ibid.

342 **Linda stepped down in March 2019**: Andrew Restuccia, Eliana Johnson, Alex Isenstadt, and Daniel Lippman, "Linda McMahon to Leave Cabinet for Trump 2020 PAC," *Politico*, March 29, 2019, accessed June 29, 2022, https://www.politico.com/story/2019/03/29/linda-mcmahon-to-resign-as-head-of-small-business-administration-1243495.

343 **became head of the largest pro-Trump super PAC**: Ibid.

343 **In 2018, WWE signed a highly lucrative**: Ben Munson, "Fox Officially Signs 5-Year Deal for WWE's 'SmackDown Live,'" Fierce Video, June 26, 2018, accessed June 29, 2022, https://www.fiercevideo.com/video/fox-officially-signs-five-year-deal-for-wwe-s-smackdown-live.

343 **He was starting a new football league**: Kevin Seifert, "How the XFL came crashing down, and what its collapse means for the future of spring football," ESPN.com, August 3, 2020, accessed August 4, 2022, https://www.espn.com/xfl/story/_/id/29297846/how-xfl-came-crashing-its-collapse-means-future-spring-football.

343 **the first had been an epic failure**: *This Was the XFL*, directed by Charlie Ebersol (2017, ESPN).

343 **a successful first few games in early 2020**: Seifert, "How the XFL."

343 **There was no way to successfully run**: Ibid.

343 **Linda coordinated that donation of $18.5 million**: See notes for Chapter 1.

343 **Florida governor Ron DeSantis's office announced**: Ditto.

343 **The now infamous Silent WrestleMania of 2020**: *WrestleMania 36*, streaming broadcast, WWE Network, March 25–26, 2020.

344 **Using advanced audio technology**: Israel Lutete, "'Bayley Brought It to My Attention'—WWE Producer on Why the Company Started Piping in Fake

Crowd Noises," *Sportskeeda*, February 6, 2021, accessed June 29, 2022, https://www.sportskeeda.com/wwe/news-tyson-kidd-reason-wwe-started-fake-crowd-noises.

345 **Hogan came back to WWE:** *WrestleMania XIX*, pay-per-view broadcast, 30, 2003.

346 **"I *created* Hulkamania!":** Ibid.

347 **"I hate you because I created you":** Ibid.

347 **"You better start trainin'":** Ibid.

347 **When the two stepped into the ring:** Ibid.

347 **"I don't like to use the word 'hatred' much":** Ibid.

347 **Warrior, too, made an astounding reversal:** David Bixenspan, "The Ultimate Reconciliation: An Inside Look at the Vince McMahon-Ultimate Warrior Relationship," *Babyface vs. Heel*, July 26, 2019, accessed August 3, 2022, https://babyfacevheel.substack.com/p/the-ultimate-reconciliation-an-inside.

347 **cruel DVD called *The Self-Destruction of the Ultimate Warrior*:** *The Self-Destruction of the Ultimate Warrior*, directed by Kevin Dunn (2005, California: WWE Home Video).

347 **The ex-wrestler had sued WWE:** Bixenspan, "The Ultimate Reconciliation."

347 **WWE reached out about Warrior returning:** Ibid.

348 **On April 5, 2014, Warrior was inducted:** Ibid.

348 **trotted out at the thirtieth WrestleMania:** Ibid.

348 **he appeared on *Raw* to deliver a promo:** WWE, "2014 WWE Hall of Famer Ultimate Warrior speaks: Raw, April 7, 2014," YouTube, April 7, 2014, accessed August 4, 2022, https://youtu.be/xR08M6EUd0g.

348 **Warrior had a heart attack and died:** Bixenspan, "The Ultimate Reconciliation."

348 **Vince kept leaving voice mails for Bret:** Bret Hart, *Hitman: My Real Life in the Cartoon World of Wrestling* (London: Ebury Press, 2010), ebook.

348 **Owen's death was still being investigated:** Ibid.

349 **Bret sent Vince a message through a mutual contact:** Ibid.

349 **It was an unseasonably cold, overcast day:** Ibid.

349 **"Vince wore a long heavy coat":** Ibid.

349 **"This is the worst thing to ever":** Ibid.

349 **"I said that if Shane had been dropped":** Ibid.

349 **"There isn't a day that goes by":** Ibid.

349 **"When I still worked for him":** Ibid.

349 **"Well, it would mean a lot to me":** Ibid.

350 **Vince told the interviewer:** *Off the Record*, "Interview with Vince McMahon," featuring Michael Landsberg and Vince McMahon, TSN, July 27, 1999.

350 **"*That's pretty cold-blooded*":** Bret Hart, interview with author, May 23, 2022.

350 **members of the Hart family had filed a lawsuit:** Martha Hart and Eric Francis, *Broken Harts: The Life and Death of Owen Hart* (UK: M. Evans, 2004), ebook.

350 **It settled for $18 million in 2000:** "Record $18m Settlement for Wrestler's Family," *Missouri Lawyers Weekly*, November 27, 2000, accessed August 4, 2022, https://www.robbrobb.com/record-18-m-settlement-for-wrestlers-family.

350 **the company occasionally approached Bret**: Hart, *Hitman*, ebook.
351 **At one point, a spokesperson told him**: Hart, interview with author.
351 **In 2002, Bret had a serious stroke**: Hart, *Hitman*, ebook.
351 **But in 2007, there came a night**: Hart, interview with author.
352 **Bret called Kevin Dunn at WWE**: Ibid.
352 **In 2010, the Hitman made his world-stunning return**: "This day in WWE History: Bret Hart returns to the WWE," *Sportskeeda*, July 22, 2022, accessed August 4, 2022, https://www.sportskeeda.com/wrestling/this-day-in-wwe-history-bret-hart-returns-to-the-wwe.
353 **Bret was diagnosed with prostate cancer**: Tim Kenneally, "WWE Wrestler Bret Hart Reveals Prostate Cancer Diagnosis," February 1, 2016, accessed August 4, 2022, https://www.thewrap.com/wwe-wrestler-bret-hart-reveals-prostate-cancer-diagnosis.
354 **On Wednesday, June 15, 2022, the *Wall Street Journal***: Joe Palazzolo and Ted Mann, "WWE Board Probes Secret $3 Million Hush Pact by CEO Vince McMahon, Sources Say," *Wall Street Journal*, June 15, 2022, accessed August 4, 2022, https://www.wsj.com/articles/wwe-board-probes-secret-3-million-hush-pact-by-ceo-vince-mcmahon-sources-say-11655322722.
354 **WWE announced the next day that Vince would**: Michelle Chapman, "Vince McMahon will step down during WWE misconduct probe," Associated Press, June 12, 2022, accessed August 4, 2022, https://apnews.com/article/sports-vince-mcmahon-wrestling-28e22d3c652591f42d47ef0285564623.
354 **When the show began**: Joe Otterson, "Vince McMahon Makes Brief 'SmackDown Live' Appearance After Misconduct Allegations," *Variety*, June 17, 2022, accessed August 4, 2022, https://variety.com/2022/tv/news/vince-mcmahon-smackdown-live-wwe-1235297674.
355 **Roughly 2,389,000 people had tuned in**: Brandon Thurston, "Re-issued ratings and quarter-hours for WWE Smackdown and AEW Rampage, June 17," *Wrestlenomics*, June 23, 2022, accessed August 4, 2022, https://www.patreon.com/posts/re-issued-and-17-68165741.
355 **Ratings shot up 17 percent**: Brandon Thurston, "WWE Raw TV ratings for June 20," *Wrestlenomics,* June 21, 2022, accessed August 4, 2022, https://www.patreon.com/posts/wwe-raw-tv-for-68072145.
355 **The *Wall Street Journal* published more**: Joe Palazzolo, Ted Mann, and Joe Flint, "WWE's Vince McMahon Agreed to Pay $12 Million in Hush Money to Four Women," *Wall Street Journal*, July 22, 2022, accessed August 2, 2022, https://www.wsj.com/articles/wwes-vince-mcmahon-agreed-to-pay-12-million-in-hush-money-to-four-women-11657289742.
355 **I published an article in *New York* magazine**: Abraham Riesman, "She Was WWE's First Female Referee. She Says Vince McMahon Raped Her," NYMag.com, June 27, 2022, accessed August 4, 2022, https://nymag.com/intelligencer/2022/06/vince-mcmahon-accused-of-rape-by-first-female-wwe-referee.html.
355 **on Friday, July 22, Vince announced his retirement**: WWE, "Vince McMahon Retires," WWE.com, July 22, 2022, accessed August 4, 2022, https://corporate.wwe.com/news/company-news/2022/07-22-2022a.

355   **Even the wrestlers and producers**: Ross Berman, "Backstage News On 'Mass Confusion' Over Vince McMahon Retirement," July 22, 2022, accessed August 4, 2022, https://www.wrestlinginc.com/news/2022/07/backstage-news-on-mass-confusion-over-vince-mcmahon-retirement.

355   **Stephanie was named the new**: WWE, "WWE & Board of Directors Announce New Co-CEOs Stephanie McMahon and Nick Khan," WWE.com, July 25, 2022, accessed August 4, 2022, https://corporate.wwe.com/news/company-news/2022/07-25-2022.

355   **Paul Levesque was made the new head**: Sam Fels, "What's that thing about getting exactly what you want?," *Deadspin*, July 26, 2022, accessed August 4, 2022, https://deadspin.com/what-s-that-thing-about-getting-exactly-what-you-want-1849332235.

355   **The following Monday, WWE made a filing**: World Wrestling Entertainment, Inc., Form 8-K (filed July 25, 2022), from Investis, https://otp.tools.investis.com/clients/us/wwe/SEC/sec-show.aspx?Type=html&FilingId=15963103&Cik=0001091907, accessed August 2, 2022.

355   **Vince remains the single largest shareholder**: Lyle Kilbane, "Why Vince McMahon May Cling To Power," June 17, 2022, accessed August 4, 2022, https://tjrwrestling.net/news/why-vince-mcmahon-may-cling-to-power.

356   **Rod was seventy-seven when he died**: "Roderick James 'Rod' McMahon Obituary (1943 – 2021)," Legacy.com, January 24, 2021, accessed August 2, 2022, https://www.legacy.com/us/obituaries/courier/name/roderick-mcmahon-obituary?id=7372979.

356   **Vicki lived to 101**: "Victoria Hanner 'Vicki' Askew Obituary (1920 – 2022)," Legacy.com, January 22, 2022, accessed August 4, 2022, https://www.legacy.com/us/obituaries/courier/name/victoria-askew-obituary?id=32355976.

INDEX

Trump, Donald (*cont.*)
  WrestleMania 23 clip and, 340–341
  WrestleMania V and, 167–168
  at *WrestleMania VII*, 184
  wrestling and, 158–160
  on WWE programming, 340
Trump Plaza Hotel and Casino, 166
Trump Taj Mahal, Atlantic City, 184
Tuesday Night Titans (TNT), 90–94, 115, 117, 136
Tureaud, Laurence (Mr. T.), 109–110
  appearing on *Hot Properties* and *Saturday Night Live*, 117
  WrestleMania 2 and, 139
  WrestleMania I and, 120
Turner's Arena (Capitol Arena), 22
Turner, Ted, 166. *See also* TBS (Turner Broadcasting System)
  Bret Hart and, 276, 282
  dislike of Vince McMahon, 116
  GCW slot and, 90, 102
  Hulk Hogan and, 238
  Jim Barnett and, 61–62
  mocked on *Monday Night Raw*, 252–253
  satellite television and, 48–49
  World Championship Wrestling (WCW) and, 243
"tweener," 252
20/20 (television show), 107
Twisted Sister, 112
Tyson, "Iron" Mike, 293–297, 300

U

Ultimate Warrior (James Brian Hellwig)
  bodybuilding and, 155–156
  criticisms of, 157–158, 161
  DOJ steroid trial and, 237
  forced apology to child, 188–189
  Hulk Hogan and, 171–172
  at induction for the Hall of Fame, 348
  kayfabe and, 166
  loan from Vince, 187–188
  on moral relativity, 155
  name of, 157
  promo style, 161–162
  relationship with the McMahons, 187–188
  returning to WWE, 347–348
  Sgt. Slaughter rivalry with, 183
  SummerSlam and, 189–190
  Vince on, 158
  WrestleMania V and, 171, 172–173
  WrestleMania VIII and, 212
  wrestling in Memphis, 156–157
Ultimate Warrior: Always Believe (documentary), 347–348
Undertaker. *See* Calaway, Mark (Undertaker)

United States Wrestling Association (USWA), 228, 229, 230–232, 234, 243
USA Network, 49, 62, 90, 140, 210, 221, 343
USA Today, 185, 316
USS *Intrepid*, 226
USWA. *See* United States Wrestling Association (USWA)

V

Vachon, Luna (Gertrude), 300
Van Dam, Rob (Robert Szatkowski), 274
Ventura, Jesse "The Body," 58, 119, 165
Village Voice, The, 117
Vince and Linda McMahon Family Foundation, 340
Vinnie's steakhouse, 140
Virginia State Athletic Commission, 28

W

Wacholz, Kevin "Nailz," 220, 237
Wagner, "Gorgeous" George, 46
Wall Street Journal, 354, 355
Waltman, Sean (The 1-2-3 Kid), 248, 251
Warhol, Andy, 114–115
war on drugs, 177
Warren, Chris, 307
Warrington, Charles (Beaver Cleavage), 316–317, 330
Warrior. *See* Ultimate Warrior (James Brian Hellwig)
War to Settle the Score (MTV broadcast), 111–115
Washington, Desiree, 293
Washington, George, 18
Washington Monthly, 163
Watts, Bill, 116
WCW. *See* World Championship Wrestling (WCW)
Weatherspoon, Jim, 217, 218–219
Weber, Max, 173–174
Weeksville, North Carolina, 17
Weider, Ben, 178, 179
Weider, Joe, 178, 179
West Hartford, Connecticut, 41
West Texas territory, 62
Wide World of Sports, 49
Wilkins, Dominique, 212
Windham, Robert (Blackjack Mulligan), 59
Wisconsin, 140
Wolff, David, 93–94, 108
Women's World Championship, 96
women's wrestling
  The Fabulous Moolah (Lillian Ellison) and, 96–97
  forced prostitution in, 96, 98
  June 5, 1982 match, 58–59

ABOUT THE AUTHOR

Abraham Josephine Riesman is a freelance writer whose work has appeared in *New York* magazine, the *Washington Post*, the *Wall Street Journal*, the *New Republic*, and many other outlets. Riesman is the author of *True Believer: The Rise and Fall of Stan Lee*. Learn more about her at abrahamriesman.com.